MW00624589

EZEKIEL

THE NIV
APPLICATION
COMMENTARY

From biblical text . . . to contemporary life

EZEKIEL

THE NIV APPLICATION COMMENTARY

From biblical text . . . to contemporary life

IAIN M. DUGUID

ZONDERVAN®

GRAND RAPIDS, MICHIGAN 49530 USA

ZONDERVAN.COM/
AUTHOR**TRACKER**

We want to hear from you. Please send your comments about this book to us in care of zreview@zondervan.com. Thank you.

ZONDERVAN®

The NIV Application Commentary: Ezekiel
Copyright © 1999 by Iain M. Duguid

Requests for information should be addressed to:

Zondervan, *Grand Rapids, Michigan 49530*

Library of Congress Cataloging-in-Publication Data

Duguid, Iain M. 1960–
    Ezekiel / Iain M. Duguid.
        p. cm. — (NIV application commentary)
    Includes bibliographical references and indexes.
    ISBN-10: 0–310–21047–X (hardcover)
    ISBN-13: 978-0-310-21047-4 (hardcover)
    1. Bible. O.T. Ezekiel — Commentaries. I. Title. II. Series.
BS 1545.3.D84 1999
224'.4077 — dc21   99–30790

This edition printed on acid-free paper.

Printed in the United States of America

---

06 07 08 09 10 11 12 • 15 14 13 12 11 10 9 8

Contents

7
Series Introduction

11
General Editor's Preface

13
Author's Preface

15
Abbreviations

17
Introduction

40
Outline

42
Select Bibliography

45
Text and Commentary on Ezekiel

553
Scripture Index

563
Subject Index

565
Author Index

The NIV Application Commentary Series

When complete, the NIV Application Commentary
will include the following volumes:

Old Testament Volumes

Genesis, John H. Walton

Exodus, Peter Enns

Leviticus/Numbers, Roy Gane

Deuteronomy, Daniel I. Block

Joshua, Robert L. Hubbard Jr.

Judges/Ruth, K. Lawson Younger

1-2 Samuel, Bill T. Arnold

1-2 Kings, Gus Konkel

1-2 Chronicles, Andrew E. Hill

Ezra/Nehemiah, Douglas J. Green

Esther, Karen H. Jobes

Job, Dennis R. Magary

Psalms Volume 1, Gerald H. Wilson

Psalms Volume 2, Jamie A. Grant

Proverbs, Paul Koptak

Ecclesiastes/Song of Songs, Iain Provan

Isaiah, John N. Oswalt

Jeremiah/Lamentations, J. Andrew Dearman

Ezekiel, Iain M. Duguid

Daniel, Tremper Longman III

Hosea/Amos/Micah, Gary V. Smith

Jonah/Nahum/Habakkuk/Zephaniah,
    James Bruckner

Joel/Obadiah/Malachi, David W. Baker

Haggai/Zechariah, Mark J. Boda

New Testament Volumes

Matthew, Michael J. Wilkins

Mark, David E. Garland

Luke, Darrell L. Bock

John, Gary M. Burge

Acts, Ajith Fernando

Romans, Douglas J. Moo

1 Corinthians, Craig Blomberg

2 Corinthians, Scott Hafemann

Galatians, Scot McKnight

Ephesians, Klyne Snodgrass

Philippians, Frank Thielman

Colossians/Philemon, David E. Garland

1-2 Thessalonians, Michael W. Holmes

1-2 Timothy/Titus, Walter L. Liefeld

Hebrews, George H. Guthrie

James, David P. Nystrom

1 Peter, Scot McKnight

2 Peter/Jude, Douglas J. Moo

Letters of John, Gary M. Burge

Revelation, Craig S. Keener

To see which titles are available,
visit our web site at http://www.zondervan.com

NIV Application Commentary
Series Introduction

THE NIV APPLICATION COMMENTARY SERIES is unique. Most commentaries help us make the journey from our world back to the world of the Bible. They enable us to cross the barriers of time, culture, language, and geography that separate us from the biblical world. Yet they only offer a one-way ticket to the past and assume that we can somehow make the return journey on our own. Once they have explained the *original meaning* of a book or passage, these commentaries give us little or no help in exploring its *contemporary significance*. The information they offer is valuable, but the job is only half done.

Recently, a few commentaries have included some contemporary application as *one* of their goals. Yet that application is often sketchy or moralistic, and some volumes sound more like printed sermons than commentaries.

The primary goal of the NIV Application Commentary Series is to help you with the difficult but vital task of bringing an ancient message into a modern context. The series not only focuses on application as a finished product but also helps you think through the *process* of moving from the original meaning of a passage to its contemporary significance. These are commentaries, not popular expositions. They are works of reference, not devotional literature.

The format of the series is designed to achieve the goals of the series. Each passage is treated in three sections: *Original Meaning*, *Bridging Contexts*, and *Contemporary Significance*.

 THIS SECTION HELPS you understand the meaning of the biblical text in its original context. All of the elements of traditional exegesis—in concise form—are discussed here. These include the historical, literary, and cultural context of the passage. The authors discuss matters related to grammar and syntax and the meaning of biblical words. They also seek to explore the main ideas of the passage and how the biblical author develops those ideas.

After reading this section, you will understand the problems, questions, and concerns of the *original audience* and how the biblical author addressed those issues. This understanding is foundational to any legitimate application of the text today.

Bridging Contexts

THIS SECTION BUILDS a bridge between the world of the Bible and the world of today, between the original context and the contemporary context, by focusing on both the timely and timeless aspects of the text.

God's word is *timely*. The authors of Scripture spoke to specific situations, problems, and questions. The author of Joshua encouraged the faith of his original readers by narrating the destruction of Jericho, a seemingly impregnable city, at the hands of an angry warrior God (Josh. 6). Paul warned the Galatians about the consequences of circumcision and the dangers of trying to be justified by law (Gal. 5:2–5). The author of Hebrews tried to convince his readers that Christ is superior to Moses, the Aaronic priests, and the Old Testament sacrifices. John urged his readers to "test the spirits" of those who taught a form of incipient Gnosticism (1 John 4:1–6). In each of these cases, the timely nature of Scripture enables us to hear God's Word in situations that were *concrete* rather than abstract.

Yet the timely nature of Scripture also creates problems. Our situations, difficulties, and questions are not always directly related to those faced by the people in the Bible. Therefore, God's word to them does not always seem relevant to us. For example, when was the last time someone urged you to be circumcised, claiming that it was a necessary part of justification? How many people today care whether Christ is superior to the Aaronic priests? And how can a "test" designed to expose incipient Gnosticism be of any value in a modern culture?

Fortunately, Scripture is not only timely but *timeless*. Just as God spoke to the original audience, so he still speaks to us through the pages of Scripture. Because we share a common humanity with the people of the Bible, we discover a *universal dimension* in the problems they faced and the solutions God gave them. The timeless nature of Scripture enables it to speak with power in every time and in every culture.

Those who fail to recognize that Scripture is both timely and timeless run into a host of problems. For example, those who are intimidated by timely books such as Hebrews, Galatians, or Deuteronomy might avoid reading them because they seem meaningless today. At the other extreme, those who are convinced of the timeless nature of Scripture, but who fail to discern its timely element, may "wax eloquent" about the Melchizedekian priesthood to a sleeping congregation, or worse still, try to apply the holy wars of the Old Testament in a physical way to God's enemies today.

The purpose of this section, therefore, is to help you discern what is timeless in the timely pages of the Bible—and what is not. For example, how do the holy wars of the Old Testament relate to the spiritual warfare of the New? If Paul's primary concern is not circumcision (as he tells us in Gal. 5:6), what *is* he concerned about? If discussions about the Aaronic priesthood or Melchizedek seem irrelevant today, what is of abiding value in these passages? If people try to "test the spirits" today with a test designed for a specific first-century heresy, what other biblical test might be more appropriate?

Yet this section does not merely uncover that which is timeless in a passage but also helps you to see *how* it is uncovered. The authors of the commentaries seek to take what is implicit in the text and make it explicit, to take a process that normally is intuitive and explain it in a logical, orderly fashion. How do we know that circumcision is not Paul's primary concern? What clues in the text or its context help us realize that Paul's real concern is at a deeper level?

Of course, those passages in which the historical distance between us and the original readers is greatest require a longer treatment. Conversely, those passages in which the historical distance is smaller or seemingly nonexistent require less attention.

One final clarification. Because this section prepares the way for discussing the contemporary significance of the passage, there is not always a sharp distinction or a clear break between this section and the one that follows. Yet when both sections are read together, you should have a strong sense of moving from the world of the Bible to the world of today.

THIS SECTION ALLOWS the biblical message to speak with as much power today as it did when it was first written. How can you apply what you learned about Jerusalem, Ephesus, or Corinth to our present-day needs in Chicago, Los Angeles, or London? How can you take a message originally spoken in Greek, Hebrew, and Aramaic and communicate it clearly in our own language? How can you take the eternal truths originally spoken in a different time and culture and apply them to the similar-yet-different needs of our culture?

In order to achieve these goals, this section gives you help in several key areas.

(1) It helps you identify contemporary situations, problems, or questions that are truly comparable to those faced by the original audience. Because contemporary situations are seldom identical to those faced by the original audience, you must seek situations that are analogous if your applications are to be relevant.

(2) This section explores a variety of contexts in which the passage might be applied today. You will look at personal applications, but you will

also be encouraged to think beyond private concerns to the society and culture at large.

(3) This section will alert you to any problems or difficulties you might encounter in seeking to apply the passage. And if there are several legitimate ways to apply a passage (areas in which Christians disagree), the author will bring these to your attention and help you think through the issues involved.

In seeking to achieve these goals, the contributors to this series attempt to avoid two extremes. They avoid making such specific applications that the commentary might quickly become dated. They also avoid discussing the significance of the passage in such a general way that it fails to engage contemporary life and culture.

Above all, contributors to this series have made a diligent effort not to sound moralistic or preachy. The NIV Application Commentary Series does not seek to provide ready-made sermon materials but rather tools, ideas, and insights that will help you communicate God's Word with power. If we help you to achieve that goal, then we have fulfilled the purpose for this series.

The Editors

General Editor's Preface

SOME THINK THAT EZEKIEL is difficult to interpret because of its visions. By their nature, those people say, such books are not meant to communicate truth in a literal manner. These truths do not lend themselves to scientific language. They are heavy with a surplus of meaning that goes beyond the scientific.

True, Ezekiel does have visions. True, Ezekiel is difficult to interpret. As Iain Duguid points out in his introduction to this excellent commentary, at one time or another the church fathers have called the book difficult, early rabbis considered it dangerous, and most of us have despaired of figuring out what God's message is in its pages.

However, as Professor Duguid also points out, Ezekiel's difficulty emerges not only from the visions, but also from the fact that Ezekiel was written over a number of years that spanned a chaotic, confusing time. Ezekiel spoke to people at three different phases of a crisis situation: when they were about to be overrun by a desperately cruel foreign political power, when they were overrun and deported to an alien land, and when their restoration to their lost land was in view. Each phase elicited a distinct message from the prophet.

As any parent knows, the content and tone of messages delivered before disaster strikes and those delivered afterward can be very different. When my now twenty-two-year-old son, David, was ten years old, I presented him, as a birthday present, a Swiss Army knife. Along with the knife I made a speech: "You are a responsible young man now," I intoned, "capable of handling a valuable tool that at its worst can also be used as a weapon. I fully expect you, however, never to misuse it in that way."

Two days later I arrived home from work to a house filled with the heavy, anxious air of crisis. David had threatened the seven-year-old boy next door with his Swiss Army knife. I found David in his room and made another speech: "You have misused your trust. You must apologize—and you must give me back the knife." Several days later, I made a third speech: "I love you still and always will. I believe you can handle a Swiss Army knife in the way it was meant to be used. Together we will discover the time and place for you to be a knife owner again."

Three very different speeches about the same subject: the first ritualistic, the second moralistic, the third pastoral. The first aimed at celebration of life, the second at rule-keeping and correction, the third at restoration. I did not change in my understanding of what a Swiss Army knife was and how it was to be used. But the circumstances of David's and my relationship and life did change. Thus, the speeches changed accordingly.

How should we understand the changing and sometimes irreconcilable passages of Ezekiel? Many hermeneutical principles come to bear. But one of them must be an awareness of the historical circumstances of Ezekiel's time, as Professor Duguid commends. Once that background is in place, some coherence begins to emerge.

Even with all this help, however, a key ingredient is still missing. Where does the story come from, the story that holds all the changing pieces together? It doesn't come from the Assyrians. It doesn't come from the Egyptians. It doesn't come from the Babylonians. It doesn't even come from the changing fortunes of Judah, Israel, or Jerusalem. To fully understand Ezekiel we must fast forward six hundred years to the life of Jesus of Nazareth. There we discover a story so inspiring, so unifying, so redemptive that the difficulties, dangers, and despairs of life begin to take on a slightly unreal cast, like the horrors of a bad movie.

In their place what becomes increasingly, overwhelmingly real is the fact of our restoration in the hands of a loving God. The last act of our lives, the third speech, is so filled with God's love that everything else takes on additional meaning. In our darkest hours, the cupped hands of God are there to catch us. The Lord is in control. Thanks be to God!

Terry C. Muck

Author's Preface

THE ART OF WRITING COMMENTARIES, like that of creating movies, is far easier to criticize than to execute. Unlike the task of writing a doctoral dissertation or a scholarly monograph, which merely demands that you write exhaustively on a topic of limited scope, a commentary demands that you write something interesting, stimulating, and relatively brief on every portion of your assigned book. A commentary series like the NIV Application Commentary series demands reflection not only on the ancient setting of the prophet but also its address to contemporary readers. Such a task could not be completed without the involvement of a host of people, each of whom in his or her own way has helped to shape the commentator or his book.

In preparing the Original Meaning sections, I have been reminded over and over of the substantial debt I owe to those who were my teachers in the study of the Old Testament. While I was a student at Westminster Seminary in Philadelphia, I had the enormous privilege of learning at the feet of Ray Dillard, Bruce Waltke, and Tremper Longman III, while Hugh Williamson guided my doctoral research on the book of Ezekiel at Cambridge. In the Bridging Contexts and Contemporary Significance sections, I hope that the influence of those from whom I learned how to preach is evident. The impact of the teaching of Edmund Clowney, alongside whom I now teach at Westminster Seminary in California, has been incalculable, as has the instruction and example of Tim Keller, now pastor of Redeemer Presbyterian Church in Manhattan, New York. The manuscript versions of my work have been read carefully and commented on by Robert L. Hubbard Jr. and Terry Muck, both of whom have contributed greatly to the final product. In addition, the editing skills of Jack Kuhatschek and Verlyn Verbrugge have been much appreciated. My student, Shaun Nolan, prepared the diagrams in electronic form for me. The faults of the commentary, however, remain my responsibility

Writing a book of this size can be a trying task not only for the commentator but also for his family. I therefore want to thank my wife, Barb, for her unfailing love and enthusiastic support. With perceptive insight, she always asks the question that penetrates to the heart of the issue, often before it has occurred to me. Like her favorite author, John Newton, she also reminds me daily to keep my eyes focused on the grace of God extended to us as sinners. In addition, thanks are due to my children, Jamie, Sam, Hannah, Robbie, and Rosie, who allowed me to devote some days to working on this commentary when we could otherwise have been playing on the beach. I pray that each of you may, as you grow up, come to be passionately devoted to Ezekiel's God and mine, the God whose wrath and mercy met at the cross and there accomplished our salvation. To Him be all the glory!

Abbreviations

AB	Anchor Bible
ABD	*Anchor Bible Dictionary*. D. N. Freedman et al., eds. 6 vols. New York: Doubleday, 1992.
AnBib	Analecta biblica
ANET	*Ancient Near Eastern Texts Relating to the Old Testament*. J. B. Pritchard, ed., 2d ed. Princeton: Princeton Univ. Press, 1955.
BASOR	*Bulletin of the American Schools of Oriental Research*
BBR	*Bulletin for Biblical Research*
BDB	F. Brown, S. R. Driver, and C. A. Briggs, *A Hebrew and English Lexicon of the Old Testament*. Oxford: Clarendon, 1959 reprint.
BETL	Bibliotheca ephemeridum theologicarum lovaniensium
BHS	*Biblia hebraica stuttgartensia*
Bib	*Biblica*
BibSac	*Bibliotheca Sacra*
BWANT	Beiträge zur Wissenschaft vom Alten und Neuen Testament
BZAW	Beihefte zur Zeitschrift für die alttestamentliche Wissenschaft
CBQ	*Catholic Biblical Quarterly*
ConBOT	Coniectania biblica, Old Testament
CurTM	*Currents in Theology and Mission*
DBI	*Dictionary of Biblical Imagery*. L. Ryken, J. C. Wilhoit, and T. Longman III, eds. Downer's Grove, Ill.: InterVarsity, 1998.
EvQ	*Evangelical Quarterly*
FOTL	The Forms of Old Testament Literature
GTJ	*Grace Theological Journal*
HSM	Harvard Semitic Monographs
HUCA	*Hebrew Union College Annual*
ICC	International Critical Commentary
Int	*Interpretation*
ITC	International Theological Commentary
JANESCU	*Journal of the Ancient Near Eastern Society of Columbia University*
JAOS	*Journal of the American Oriental Society*
JBL	*Journal of Biblical Literature*
JETS	*Journal of the Evangelical Theological Society*
JPS	Jewish Publication Society
JSOT	*Journal for the Study of the Old Testament*

Abbreviations

JSOTS	*Journal for the Study of the Old Testament* Supplement Series
JSS	*Journal of Semitic Studies*
LXX	Septuagint
MT	Masoretic Text
NCB	New Century Bible
NICOT	New International Commentary on the Old Testament
NIV	New International Version
NIVAC	NIV Application Commentary Series
NJPS	New Jewish Publication Society Version
NLT	New Living Translation
NTS	*New Testament Studies*
OTL	Old Testament Library
PTR	*Princeton Theological Review*
RB	*Revue biblique*
RSV	Revised Standard Version
SBLDS	Society of Biblical Literature Dissertation Series
SBLMS	Society of Biblical Literature Monograph Series
SBT	Studies in Biblical Theology
ScrHier	Scripta hierosolymitana
SOTSMS	Society for Old Testament Study Monograph Series
TDOT	*Theological Dictionary of the Old Testament.* G. Botterweck and H. Ringgren, eds. Tr. D. Green et al. Grand Rapids: Eerdmans, 1974–.
THAT	*Theologisches Handwörterbuch zum Alten Testament.* E. Jenni and C. Westermann, eds. 2 vols. Munich: Kaiser, 1971–1976.
TbZ	*Theologische Literaturzeitung*
TNTC	Tyndale New Testament Commentaries
TOTC	Tyndale Old Testament Commentaries
TynBul	*Tyndale Bulletin*
UF	*Ugarit-Forschungen*
VT	*Vetus Testamentum*
WBC	Word Biblical Commentary
WTJ	*Westminster Theological Journal*
ZAW	*Zeitschrift für die alttestamentliche Wissenschaft*
ZDPV	*Zeitschrift des deutschen Palästina-Vereins*

Introduction

Why Read Ezekiel?

IF YOU WERE to ask your Christian friends to name their favorite book of the Bible, the book of Ezekiel would not spring to most people's minds. There are exceptions, of course. My fourteen-year-old niece is a big fan of the book, especially of the opening vision. But she is surely in the minority. In fact, I suspect that few of you picked up this commentary out of love for the book of Ezekiel. Most of you are probably reading this commentary out of curiosity, or desperation, or a mixture of both. You are seeking help in making some kind of sense out of this Old Testament book.

The book of Ezekiel is a certainly a difficult book to understand. That is hardly a new observation. The church father Jerome remarked:

> As for Isaiah, Jeremiah, Ezekiel and Daniel, who can fully understand or adequately explain them? . . . The beginning and ending of Ezekiel, the third of the four, are involved in so great obscurity that like the commencement of Genesis they are not studied by the Hebrews until they are thirty years old.[1]

Before Jerome, the rabbis had themselves struggled with the book of Ezekiel. For them the chief problems lay, as Jerome noted, in the beginning and ending of the book. Study of the obscurities of the opening chariot vision, which became a mystical pursuit in some circles, was thought to be not only difficult but even potentially dangerous. The rabbis recorded the cautionary tale of a child who picked up a copy of the book of Ezekiel at his teacher's home and apprehended the true meaning of the extremely obscure and much-debated Hebrew word ḥašmal, the substance of which the divine figure appears to be comprised (Ezek. 1:27). Instantly, fire came out from the ḥašmal and incinerated him.[2] Herein lay part of the reason for restricting study of the book in Jewish circles to those of more mature years.

At the other end of the book, the rabbis also had a problem with Ezekiel's temple vision. Here the difficulty lay in harmonizing the regulations of Ezekiel with those prescribed by Moses in the Pentateuch. That the problems

---

1. Jerome, *Ep. ad Paulinam*, 8.
2. *b. Ḥag.* 13a.

of harmonization remained unresolved by them was certainly not for want of effort on their part. One of their number, Hananiah ben Hezekiah, is said to have hidden himself away in his attic and burned three hundred barrels of oil in his lamp in his search for a reconciliation between the different laws. Thanks to the success of his labors, the book of Ezekiel as a whole was saved from being excluded from the canon.[3] Unfortunately, however, the fruits of his work have not been preserved for us. Should they ever turn up, they will undoubtedly make fascinating reading. Bereft of his wisdom, other rabbis gave in to the counsel of despair, something many readers of Ezekiel can sympathize with. At those moments, they simply referred their pupils to a higher authority: Elijah would explain it all when he came.[4]

Notwithstanding the very real difficulties that exist, I do not think that we need to despair of understanding this book. Elijah has come (Mark 9:12–13); the Holy Spirit has been poured out on the church, and it is the Spirit's task to guide us into all truth (John 16:13). The book of Ezekiel is part of God's Word, part of the truth that the Holy Spirit is assigned to open up to us. It is part of what Paul was thinking about when he said that "all Scripture is God-breathed and is useful for teaching, rebuking, correcting and training in righteousness" (2 Tim. 3:16). Therefore, at least in principle, the book of Ezekiel is both comprehensible and profitable to the man or woman whose eyes have been opened by the Holy Spirit.

As we proceed through this commentary, our goal will not be to study the book as an exercise in ancient history or literature but rather to seek what the Spirit has to teach us from the biblical text, where he will rebuke us, how he will correct us, and how he will train us in righteousness. Such a study will be full of relevance for contemporary Christians, for at its heart the whole of Scripture is a testimony about Jesus Christ (John 5:39). As we proceed, therefore, we will be continually looking to see how in particular ways Ezekiel points us forward to Christ.

Historical Background

THE BOOK OF EZEKIEL was composed for a particular moment in time. Unlike the Book of Mormon, the Bible is not an abstract revelation that descended to the prophet on tablets of gold from heaven. What is more, unlike some of the other prophetic books within the Bible whose historical setting is hard to date with certainty, Ezekiel provides us with precise dates that enable us to determine accurately where in the history of God's people his writings

---

3. *b. Šabb.* 13b.
4. *b. Menaḥ.* 45a.

belong. It is a prophecy given to a particular person in a particular situation at a particular juncture in redemptive history. Ezekiel was by the Kebar River in Babylonia in the fifth year of the exile of King Jehoiachin when the visions began (1:2–3). In order to understand the book, we must explore the theological significance of that location (see comments on Ezek. 1:1–3). But for now we need to sketch in the historical background. How did a company of God's people end up in such an apparently God-forsaken location?

Part of the answer is contained in the movements of "secular" history of that day. In the preceding centuries, the neo-Assyrians, whose capital city was Nineveh, had dominated the Near East.[5] The limits of their empire had ebbed and flowed, reaching as far as Egypt. In their forays to the west, they imposed tribute on Jehu and the northern kingdom of Israel in 841 B.C. A century later, under Tiglath-Pileser III and his son Shalmaneser V, the Assyrians made inroads into the territory of the northern kingdom, finally absorbing it in 722 B.C. The Israelite population was exiled to various parts of the Assyrian empire, and they were replaced with other people groups (2 Kings 17). Within twenty years, the Assyrians swept up to the very gates of Jerusalem itself under Sennacherib, shutting up the would-be rebel King Hezekiah "like a bird in a cage."[6] Hezekiah's bacon was saved (if one may be permitted to use such a non-kosher idiom) only by the direct intervention of the angel of the Lord, who put to death 185,000 of the Assyrian army (2 Kings 19:35).

At the same time, the powerful Chaldean ruler Merodach-Baladan was causing trouble for Sennacherib closer to home. He sought to encourage Hezekiah's rebellious ways by sending envoys, whom Hezekiah treated to a royal display of his wealth and weaponry (2 Kings 20:13). Obviously, Hezekiah had swiftly forgotten that it was neither his wealth nor his weaponry that had rescued him when the Assyrians had come calling earlier. He probably viewed the Babylonians as a potentially useful political and military ally against their mutual foe. But such dependence on human allies, whether in the shape of the might of Egypt or of Babylon, was always reprehensible in a Judean monarch. He ruled his kingdom as a man under authority, as the vassal of King Yahweh. He was therefore not free to make and break military and political alliances based on his own reading of political necessities. This is a theme we will see emerge again in Ezekiel.

---

5. On the history of the Assyrian empire, see William C. Gwaltney Jr., "Assyrians," in *Peoples of the Old Testament World*, ed. A. J. Hoerth, G. L. Mattingly, and E. M. Yamauchi (Grand Rapids: Baker, 1994), 77–106.

6. James B. Pritchard, ed., *Ancient Near Eastern Texts*, 2d ed. (Princeton: Princeton Univ. Press, 1955), 288.

Therefore, God sent his ambassador in Jerusalem in the shape of the prophet Isaiah. His task was to confront Hezekiah with his sin (2 Kings 20:14–18). If Hezekiah was so enthusiastic about Babylon, then he should know that at some unspecified time in the future those same Babylonians would come back and strip his palace of everything of value. The Babylonians would carry off into exile his own flesh and blood, so that they might become eunuchs in the house of the Babylonian king. It is a marker of the political and military pressure brought to bear on a small nation like Judah in such times of political uncertainty that Hezekiah regarded this oracle as *good* news, since it seemed to indicate that his own life, at least, would be lived out in peace (20:19).

Indeed, these were trying times for most small nations in the ancient Near East. Though Sennacherib crushed the Babylonian monarch in 689 B.C. and tore down the sacred city of Babylon, dragging off her patron deity Marduk, the power of the Assyrians was already on the wane. By 625 B.C., the Babylonians had freed themselves from the Assyrian yoke again, this time under the generalship of Nabopolassar. Ten years later, in 616 B.C., he marched into Assyrian territory and began to capture city after city. Even the astonishing switch in loyalties of the Egyptians, Assyria's traditional enemy, who came to the aid of their former foes, was insufficient to stem the tide. Nineveh fell in 612 B.C.; and after the decisive battle at Carchemish in 605 B.C. the Assyrio-Egyptian alliance was destroyed. Shortly thereafter, Nabopolassar died and his place was taken by his son, who is well-known to readers of the Bible by the name Nebuchadnezzar.

Although not directly involved in these events, Judah had already been caught in the crossfire. Good King Josiah, the last good king of Judah, who had led prominent reforms in public worship, went out to try to intercept the Egyptian forces marching to the aid of Assyria in 609 B.C. The motivation behind this action is not entirely clear, unless he thought to reestablish Judah as the dominant force in the Levant, something not seen since the time of David and Solomon. Whatever his reasoning, he was tragically killed in battle against the Egyptians at Megiddo.

With his death, the brief Judean experiment with orthodoxy came to an abrupt end. He was succeeded by his son Jehoahaz, whose three-month reign followed in the wicked ways of grandfather Amon rather than in the righteous ways of father Josiah. After three months the Egyptians intervened, carrying Jehoahaz off into exile in Egypt and placing his elder brother, Eliakim, on the throne (2 Kings 23:34). As an act demonstrating covenant lordship, Pharaoh Neco renamed him Jehoiakim ("the Lord raises up"), an ironically orthodox name for yet another bad king, especially for one who had been installed on the throne by a foreign superpower.

Around 605 B.C., the Babylonians came knocking. The Egyptians were driven out of Palestine and Jehoiakim wisely switched sides, swearing allegiance to the Babylonians. Hostages were taken to Babylon from the nobility, including Daniel and his three friends. But Jehoiakim had no intention of keeping his commitments to the Babylonians, which, to be fair, probably included crushing tribute requirements. He rebelled against them in 598 B.C., no doubt crying "No taxation without representation."

This was all noble and heroic, but in the light of his pattern of wickedness in the eyes of the Lord, only one outcome was possible. The Babylonians returned and crushed his revolt; in the process, Jehoiakim died, either executed by the Babylonians[7] or assassinated by the Judeans in hopes of winning clemency from the Babylonians.[8] In his place, the Judeans installed his son Jehoiachin on the throne. Jehoiachin turned out to be no better than his father, either in the eyes of God or of Nebuchadnezzar. Instead of submitting to Babylon, as Jeremiah advised, he looked to Egypt for help (the perennial alternative in the Old Testament to trusting in the Lord), and within three months he was dragged off to exile in Babylon along with many of the temple treasures and more of the leading citizens. Ezekiel was one of those taken into exile in this wave.

After Jehoiachin's exile, Nebuchadnezzar placed Jehoiachin's uncle Mattaniah on the throne and renamed him Zedekiah (2 Kings 24:17). Once again, one wonders who thought up the name "The Lord is righteous" for this particular individual! It probably wasn't Nebuchadnezzar himself, nor Zedekiah, whose personal righteousness is regarded as highly problematic not only by the book of Kings but also by both Ezekiel and Jeremiah.

Zedekiah, whose personal hold on the throne appears to have been sufficiently tenuous that he did not always know or control what his officials were doing, voted for revolt in 589 B.C. Doubtless his confidence was bolstered by the promise of help from Tyre and Ammon and high hopes of Egyptian aid. It was a fatal mistake. Nebuchadnezzar came loaded for bear. Gradually the lights went out across Judah, as one fortified city after another was pummeled into submission. Jerusalem itself came under a siege that lasted for over a year. Finally, the walls were breached, and although Zedekiah fled, he was captured and brought to Riblah. There Nebuchadnezzar made him watch while his sons were put to death, before gouging out Zedekiah's eyes and taking him away to Babylon.

The city of Jerusalem was then torn down and burned, with most of the remaining inhabitants of the land being carried off into exile. Only the poorest

---

7. Daniel I. Block, *Ezekiel 1–24* (NICOT; Grand Rapids: Eerdmans, 1997), 3.

8. John Bright, *A History of Israel*, 3d ed. (Philadelphia: Westminster, 1981), 327.

of the poor remained, struggling without skills or resources to scratch out a living from the land. If you imagine the kind of doomsday scenario painted in movies like *The War of the Worlds* or *Terminator*, in which society as we know it has been reduced to rubble and ash and a few shell-shocked human beings remain, desperately trying to keep themselves alive among the ruins, then you won't be too far off the mark of what life must have been like for those who remained in Judah. Just substitute the fearsome Babylonians for the Martians or the Cyborgs and you get the picture.

The years leading up to that ultimate cataclysm form the background to the prophecies in the book of Ezekiel, which span a twenty-year period before and after Jerusalem's destruction. You cannot understand this book unless you see it as the response to *Holocaust Now!*, warning God's rebellious people of the oncoming juggernaut—and then scraping up the pieces of what remained off the highway. The book itself is fundamentally arranged about the central event of the fall of Jerusalem, or more precisely, around the event of the arrival among the exiles of the news of the fall of Jerusalem (anticipated in Ezek. 24:27; realized in 33:21–22). This forms the turning point in the experience of both the prophet and God's people in exile. The prophecy, which begins by clearly depicting the end of the road for God's rebellious people (Ezek. 1–24), closes by showing that the end of the road is not the end of the story (Ezek. 34–48). Even his people's sinfulness and rebellion cannot ultimately prevail against God's electing grace.

In the providence of God, the Babylonians and the Assyrians had very different policies of exile. The Assyrians adopted the policy of divide and conquer; they would take large numbers of people from one area of their empire and resettle them in small groups in different parts of the empire.[9] By breaking up old ties and alliances, they hoped to render the defeated peoples disorganized and disoriented, unable to mount any effective revolt. Their policy therefore represented a shuffling of the people groups around the margins of their empire, in what you might call a "melting pot" policy of imperial rule. The aim was that people would lose their original ethnic identity and become simply "Assyrians."

The Babylonians, on the other hand, followed a less assimilationist "tossed salad" model of empire. They took the leaders and skilled workers from the subjugated nations and brought them from the margins of the empire to the center, to Babylonia itself. There they treated them reasonably well and allowed them to settle in ethnic groups and to advance within the Babylon-

---

9. *ANET*, 283, 288. On the Assyrian deportations, see Bustenai Oded, *Mass Deportations and Deportees in the Neo-Assyrian Empire* (Wiesbaden: L. Reichert, 1979), and K. Lawson Younger Jr., "The Deportations of the Israelites," *JBL* 117 (1998): 201–27.

ian system. The goal, from a Babylonian perspective, was to incorporate these diverse people groups in the service of the empire by bringing their various talents and gifts into the center, while allowing them to retain their own ethnic identities. In addition, the margins of the empire were thereby left impoverished and leaderless and therefore less likely to rebel against the power of the center.[10]

The results, from the perspective of Israel and Judah, were the different fates of the northern and southern kingdoms in exile. The northern kingdom of Israel was dispersed and effectively destroyed. Individual believers presumably remained, keeping hope alive among the Diaspora of a future reunion of the twelve tribes (as we will see in Ezekiel), but as a political entity, the northern kingdom was finished. Their land was occupied by a half-breed mixture of different ethnic groups, who had little more than a superstitious interest in the God of their land. Judah, on the other hand, remained largely denuded of population after the debacle of 586 B.C., allowing the possibility of a genuine return from exile on the part of those who had kept the faith. It was one of these groups of exiles living by the Kebar River in Babylonia, which included both faithful and not so faithful, to whom Ezekiel was commissioned to prophesy.

Authorship and Date

WHO WROTE THE BOOK that bears Ezekiel's name? There are, and have been for some time, four schools of thought on the subject. (1) Some scholars have taken the radical view that very little of the book can be traced back to the prophet himself. This view became temporarily fashionable following the publication in 1924 of Gustav Hölscher's book, *Hesekiel: Der Dichter und das Buch*.[11] Hölscher ascribed to Ezekiel a mere 144 verses out of the canonical 1,273, on the basis that all of the authentic oracles of the prophet were poetic or elevated prose. Although few scholars actually found Hölscher's method of separating out genuine Ezekiel texts from later accretions convincing, his successors have continued in attempting to distill out a small base layer from the later dross by a variety of means.

The criteria employed by these scholars have frequently included the requirements that the original oracles be terse and strictly uniform in style. Each oracle is allowed only to have one opening and closing formula. Texts that pick up and develop ideas from earlier in the book are held to be "clearly" secondary; only oracles expressing ideas that can be paralleled from elsewhere

---

10. Bright, *History of Israel*, 344–45.
11. BZAW 39; Giessen: Töpelmann, 1924).

in preexilic prophecy are allowed to stand as original.[12] Once the various texts have been detached from their immediate surroundings, continuities of thought or style are then used to link these separate texts into a number of different "layers" or "strata." Since the layers of text separated out by these methods do not come with signatures, the scholars often then make elaborate attempts to determine the social and historical contexts that gave birth to the different layers, and sometimes warnings are issued that even the "earliest" layer cannot naively be assumed to stem from the "historical prophet."[13]

This last observation is indeed true, though in an entirely different sense from that usually intended. It can be shown, for example, that Ezekiel 22:25–29 is based on Zephaniah 3:3–4.[14] The distinctive language of Zephaniah has been picked up and adopted, though not without changes that make the style distinctly that of Ezekiel. It is possible for us to unfold and identify these changes, but only because we have the base text of Zephaniah with which to compare it. If we did not have the text of Zephaniah, we would not be able to reconstruct it from Ezekiel's version. What is more, even if we were able to do so, our hypothetically "reconstructed" text would not be what originally belonged in Ezekiel 22. It is the present "reworked" text that is the original in this case.

This practical example suggests that in the absence of such points of comparison, the whole scholarly enterprise of reconstructing "original" texts is fraught with fundamental methodological questions. It is like cleaning "accretions" from the ceiling of the Sistine chapel and crying "Aha" once you reach the bare plaster. In the process, it is not merely centuries of dirt that have been removed but the work of Michelangelo as well! The text as it stands is our only sure datum.

(2) In a different direction, Hölscher's work encouraged a few scholars to argue that the entire book of Ezekiel was a pseudepigraphic work dating from much later than the Babylonian exile. C. C. Torrey, for example, argued that the book is a unity that belonged to the period around 230 B.C. For a while in the 1930s and 1940s, these two opinions captured a significant percentage of scholarly critical opinion.

(3) But gradually the pendulum swung back to a more moderate critical position, which argues that the vast majority of the book comes from the prophet himself and his immediate disciples, and that it was essentially com-

---

12. For an evaluation of these yardsticks of originality, see Moshe Greenberg, "What Are Valid Criteria for Determining Inauthentic Matter in Ezekiel?" in *Ezekiel and His Book: Textual and Literary Criticism and Their Interrelation*, ed. J. Lust (BETL 74; Leuven: Leuven Univ. Press, 1986), 123–35.

13. So Jörg Garscha, *Studien zum Ezechielbuch* (Bern: Herbert Lang, 1974), 15.

14. See my *Ezekiel and the Leaders of Israel*, 72–74.

plete by the end of the exilic period. The outstanding figure supporting this position has been Walther Zimmerli, whose massive German commentary, with its English translation, remains the reference point of critical scholarship on Ezekiel, even though it is now thirty years old. These scholars make some use of the criteria of authenticity described above to detect significant editorial additions and changes, and thus diversity of authorship within the book; however, in contrast to the radical scholars, they date most of those changes relatively close to the lifetime of the prophet himself.

(4) In recent academic work, there has been something of a resurgence of support for a more conservative position regarding the relationship of the prophet and the book. The excellent commentaries by Daniel Block in the New International Commentary on the Old Testament series and by Moshe Greenberg in the Anchor Bible series acknowledge in principle the possibility that there may have been editorial additions and revisions made by the disciples of the prophet. Indeed, Ezekiel 1:2–3 seems to be a fairly routine example of just such an editorial comment, locating the work of the prophet in space and time for those who did not hear him or know him firsthand. Yet both commentaries work in practice from the initial assumption that the present contents of the book essentially come to us from the hand of the prophet himself, an assumption that their own work helps to support. As Greenberg puts it:

> the persuasion grows on one … that a coherent world of vision is emerging, contemporary with the sixth-century prophet and decisively shaped by him, if not the very words of Ezekiel himself.[15]

Their position still remains a minority opinion in scholarly circles, compared to the moderate critical position argued by the disciples of Zimmerli. Nonetheless, it is the firm conviction of this writer that they are fundamentally accurate in their assessment. When the text is allowed to speak for itself, it conveys a coherent and consistent worldview that addresses the situation of those exiled from Judah in the sixth century B.C. There seems, therefore, little good reason to assign significant portions of it to late and clumsy redactors. What is more, if the editing process is neither late nor clumsy, why must we assign it to anyone other than the prophet himself?[16] It is simpler to accept the testimony of the book itself than to multiply unnecessarily complex theories of authorship.

---

15. Moshe Greenberg, *Ezekiel 1–20* (AB; Garden City, N.Y.: Doubleday, 1983), 27. For an example of Greenberg's critique of traditional critical approaches to the book, see "Note on Criteria of Authenticity: The Sidon Oracle As an Example," *Ezekiel 21–37* (AB; New York: Doubleday, 1997), 597–99.

16. See Block, *Ezekiel 1–24*, 22.

Ultimately, however, the authority of the text does not lie in our ability to demonstrate that it comes to us directly from the mouth of the prophet. Nor does it lie in the assessment of the book by an authoritative body of human beings, whether a council of academics or a council of the church, that it is worthy of a place in the canon. In the final analysis, as the Reformers insisted, Scripture is self-authenticating. Though there may be supporting witnesses, such as the testimony of God's people down through the ages or the testimony of those who have studied the book in depth, for us to be convinced of its divine origin and authority over us requires a work of the Holy Spirit in our hearts. Only this internal illumination will enable us to recognize the book and receive it for what it really is: nothing less than the word of the Sovereign Lord.[17]

Interpreting Ezekiel

WITHIN THE HISTORY of the church, probably the most popular method of interpreting Ezekiel has been the allegorical method. Thus the church father Gregory the Great, in his homily on Ezekiel 40:6–8, identified the East Gate of the temple as Jesus, the steps leading up to the gate as the merits of the virtues that lead to salvation, and the threshold of the gate as the ancestors of Jesus. The chamber inside the gate has length, which symbolizes long-suffering in expectation, and breadth, which symbolizes amplitude of charity.[18] A millennium later, the Puritan William Greenhill's commentary on Ezekiel 40:16 finds significance in the windows of the visionary temple as denoting the spiritual light and joy that should be in the church of Christ. According to him, the fact that there are windows also in the "little chambers" means that even the least churches and the least saints shall not be without light and joy, teaching and comfort.[19] In this kind of allegorical approach, the interpretation does not flow out of an understanding of the text in its original context; rather, it fastens on certain details in the text and applies them directly to our present context.

This method of interpretation is undoubtedly motivated by pastoral concerns. These preachers desired to help their people benefit from *all* of Scripture. After all, is not all Scripture inspired by God and profitable in the life

---

17. See *The Westminster Confession of Faith*, I.4 and I.5. See John Murray, "The Attestation of Scripture," in P. Woolley, ed., *The Infallible Word*, 3d ed. (Philadelphia: Presbyterian and Reformed, 1967), 1–54.

18. *The Homilies of Gregory the Great on the Book of the Prophet Ezekiel*, trans. T. Gray (Etna, Calif.: Center for Traditionalist Orthodox Studies, 1990), 179–85.

19. William Greenhill, *An Exposition of Ezekiel* (Edinburgh: Banner of Truth, 1994 reprint), 780.

of the believer (2 Tim. 3:16)? Indeed, although unfashionable in the contemporary world, not everyone would agree that such an approach to difficult texts is problematic. Charles Spurgeon, that prince of Victorian preachers, defended the practice of allegorizing—or as he called it, "spiritualizing"—on the grounds of its pragmatic value. According to him, provided that it is done within certain limits,

> a great deal of real good may be done by occasionally taking forgotten, quaint, remarkable, out of the way texts; I feel persuaded that if we appeal to a jury of practical, successful preachers, who are not theorizers, but men actually in the field, we shall have a majority in our favour. It may be that the learned rabbis of our generation are too sublime and celestial to condescend to men of low estate; but we who have no high culture, or profound learning, or enchanting elegance to boast of, have deemed it wise to use the very method the grandees have proscribed; for we find it one of the best ways of keeping out of the rut of dull formality and it yields a sort of salt with which to give flavour to unpalatable truth.[20]

On the grounds of gospel success, Spurgeon therefore defends (to cite just one example) a sermon preached on the text: "The owl, the night hawk and the cuckoo" (Lev. 11:16). If you wonder how it might be possible to get a profitable sermon out of that verse, his explanation is well worth reading! He would have been quite happy to "spiritualize" Ezekiel's visionary temple in the same way as William Greenhill did.[21]

It is interesting, however, to note the tone of Spurgeon's defense. Insisting that you should always preach the "plain, literal sense" of the text is, according to him, an elitist proposal. It is the kind of idea forwarded by the "learned rabbis," those who esteem "high culture" and "profound learning." Of course, he is right. What I mean by that is that it is a difficult task to expound what he describes as the "plain, literal sense" of the text (i.e., the meaning of the text within its original context) week after week. To do so requires a significant amount of hard work and depth of biblical knowledge. This is particularly true in the case of a book like Ezekiel, whose surface meaning seems at first sight singularly uninviting. It is not surprising that so many ordinary preachers and Bible study teachers shy away from such an approach to Ezekiel, feeling unprepared to tackle its numerous complexities. On the other

---

20. Spurgeon, *Lectures to My Students* (Grand Rapids: Zondervan, 1972 reprint), 97.

21. As Spurgeon does in his sermon on Ezekiel 47:5, "Waters to Swim in," published in *The Metropolitan Tabernacle Pulpit: Sermons Preached and Revised in 1872*, vol. 18 (Pasadena, Tex.: Pilgrim, 1971 reprint), 313–24. By no means all of his sermons on the book of Ezekiel are allegorical, however.

hand, it is relatively easy to preach the simple gospel week by week and merely vary the text from which you preach it.

Those who by the grace of God are "learned rabbis," whether as a result of formal academic study or self-directed reading, should not despise such simple proclamation of the gospel. In the history of the church, many have been brought into God's kingdom and nourished on the central truths of the gospel in that way. What God has chosen to use, let us not be overly hard on. As we have already noted, this kind of allegorical interpretation stemmed from a firm conviction of the inspiration and usefulness of every portion of God's Word; thus, rather than not expound part of the Word because its plain sense was not understood, these preachers proclaimed what they knew to be true from elsewhere in the Bible.

Yet we should also recognize that such allegorical interpretation has many dangers. Spurgeon himself was aware of some of them: The exposition given may strain common sense, as in the case of the preacher who discoursed on the Trinity from the three baskets on the head of Pharaoh's baker. Allegorical interpretation may also be used as a means of impressing your audience with what a clever person you are. In some cases, it may lead to undervaluing or forgetting the factual and historical nature of the texts on which you are preaching. But one of the biggest drawbacks of allegorical interpretation, even at its best, is that it does not train your listeners to interpret the Scriptures for themselves. Even when done well, it almost inevitably leaves the people impressed by the teacher's personal ability and "spirituality" rather than being equipped to feed themselves from the Word. The congregation comes out of church saying, "I would never in a million years have seen that truth there," instead of, "How obvious it is! How could I have missed what the passage was clearly saying?"

Jim Elliot, one of the five missionaries who were killed in 1957 while attempting to reach the Auca Indians of Ecuador with the gospel, was an intensely—dauntingly—spiritual young man. Yet he once wrote this entry in his journal:

> Meditation yesterday on the curtains and boards [of the tabernacle] seemed fruitless.... Somehow the study of the tabernacle seems fruitless. I can see no plausible interpretation method. My brethren who are older and much more experienced have been able to draw much from it in type. Lord, I need to have my spirit refreshed with some new thought from Thy Word. Open my eyes and let me behold some of those "wondrous things" contained in Thy Law.[22]

---

22. *The Journals of Jim Elliot* (Old Tappan, N.J.: Revell, 1978), 39–40.

Growing up in Brethren circles on a diet of allegorical preaching, Elliot felt that only a direct infusion of divine insight could enable him to understand such a difficult text. As a result, he berated himself for being unable to pull a spiritual rabbit out of the exegetical hat in the way his favorite preachers always seemed able to do. The true fault lay more with his favorite preachers than with him, however. The purpose of this commentary is to enable you to understand more fully what the text is about in its original context. In that way, understanding its true meaning, there need be no resort to allegorical interpretation to derive spiritual food from this portion of God's Word.

On the other hand, it is necessary to point out that what we mean by "understanding the text in its original context" does not imply what is sometimes termed in contemporary discussion *literal interpretation*. This latter approach means, according to Charles Ryrie, "interpretation which gives to every word the same meaning it would have in normal usage, whether employed in writing, speaking or thinking."[23] To put it like this begs the question of what "normal" usage is in the prophets, as Ryrie is himself aware. Ryrie's response to that potential objection is that his approach does not deny the possibility of figurative or symbolic speech. However, it insists that "prophecies are to be *normally* interpreted . . . as any other utterances are interpreted."[24] The key point to observe is that for him, the genre of prophecy is fundamentally one of normal or plain speech. He supports his case by citing the fulfillment of Micah 5:2, which prophesies that the Christ will be born in Bethlehem. Indeed, Jesus was literally born in Bethlehem, not just in some analagous small town in Judah.

But does the Bible itself support Ryrie's claim? Certainly *some* Old Testament prophecies were fulfilled literally in the New Testament. Some of those Old Testament prophecies were equally clearly understood in a literal manner prior to their fulfillment. Thus, Herod could be advised by the chief priests and teachers of the law where to go looking for the Christ child on the basis of Micah 5:2 (Matt. 2:4–5). However, other prophecies from the Old Testament were fulfilled in a way that would have been completely unexpected to preceding generations, even though they too were fulfilled in a literal way. What first-century B.C. prophecy conference would have been clearly predicting the birth of Messiah from a virgin on the basis of Isaiah 7:14? Or his crucifixion on the basis of Psalm 22? Or his physical resurrection on the basis of Psalm 16? These texts are clearly viewed by the New Testament as messianic prophecies that were literally fulfilled, yet they were only seen to be such with the benefit of 20–20 hindsight after their fulfillment in Christ, not before.

---

23. *Dispensationalism Today* (Chicago: Moody, 1986), 86.
24. Ibid., 87.

Still other Old Testament prophecies are transformationally fulfilled; that is, their New Testament fulfillment is clearly related to the Old Testament promise, but it is not exactly literal. Thus Isaiah 40:3 speaks of the coming of a messenger whose message is: "In the desert prepare the way for the LORD; make straight in the wilderness a highway for our God." The New Testament sees that promise fulfilled in the coming of John the Baptizer, who is, to quote Luke, "a voice of one calling in the desert, 'Prepare the way for the Lord, make straight paths for him'" (Luke 3:4). In other words, in the New Testament, the "desert" is no longer part of the message as it was in Isaiah's proclamation, but has become the location of the messenger.

This transformational fulfillment is repeatedly found in the New Testament, perhaps in classic form in what John does in Revelation 22 with Ezekiel's temple vision of chapters 40–48. We will examine that connection in much greater detail further on in the commentary, but for now suffice it to say that the New Jerusalem is not a literal fulfillment of Ezekiel's temple, nor is the latter a millennial preparation for it. The book of Revelation shows us the temple of Ezekiel viewed through the lens of our redemption accomplished in Christ.

Nor is this merely an exegetical observation of what the New Testament does in practice in a few cases with Old Testament prophetic texts. It is in principle what the Old Testament itself tells us to do with prophetic texts. The classic Old Testament text on the nature of prophetic visions is Numbers 12:6–8, where the Lord says:

> When a prophet of the LORD is among you,
>> I reveal myself to him in visions,
>> I speak to him in dreams.
> But this is not true of my servant Moses;
>> he is faithful in all my house.
> With him I speak face to face,
>> clearly and not in riddles;
>> he sees the form of the LORD.

The point of this text is a distinct contrast between the revelation by Moses (i.e., the Torah or Pentateuch) and that by means of the (true) prophets. The latter is characterized as being indirect—by vision (*marʾâ*) and dream (*ḥᵃlôm*). In stark contrast, the revelation by Moses is characterized by four expressions that emphasize its directness. (1) It is "face to face," or more precisely, "mouth to mouth," a unique phrase that focuses on the verbal nature of that revelation. (2) It is "plain" or "clear" (*marʾeh*), not by means of dreams or visions. (3) It is "not in riddles" (*ḥîdōt*), unlike prophets such as Ezekiel, who were explicitly commanded by God to speak riddles (Ezek.

17:2).The revelation by Moses is transparent and self-explanatory in comparison to the obscurities that attend the words of the prophets. (4) Finally, the revelation by Moses is superior in directness to that by the prophets because Moses saw "the form of the LORD," a reference to his encounter with God on Mount Sinai, which was so transformational that it made his face shine.[25]

The entire burden of this text, then, is that the Old Testament should not be read in a uniform manner. Moses (the Pentateuch) should be read in a straightforward way, according to "literal interpretation." When reading the prophets, on the other hand, we should *expect* to find nonliteral forms, dreams, visions, and riddles, which are not intended to be interpreted literally but rather will be unfolded in the light of the clearer revelation of God.

But what prevents us from sliding into the morass of subjectivism in interpreting the prophets, of which Ryrie warns? Does this approach not inevitably lead to speculative allegorizing that wrenches out of the texts spiritually uplifting messages that they were never intended to bear? The answer is to recall the words of Jesus on the Emmaus road. When Jesus caught up with those two despondent disciples, who were leaving Jerusalem unaware of the resurrection, he took them back on a tour of the Old Testament Scriptures. He exposed their woefully inadequate knowledge and exegesis, saying (Luke 24:25–27):

> "How foolish you are, and how slow of heart to believe all that the prophets have spoken! Did not the Christ have to suffer these things and then enter his glory?" And beginning with Moses and all the Prophets, he explained to them what was said in all the Scriptures concerning himself.

In other words, Jesus gave these two followers a classic redemptive-historical sermon, unfolding the Old Testament and showing them how it is fulfilled in him. The point is that according to Jesus, we should expect the message of all of the prophets to be Jesus Christ! The disciples' response was not to be amazed at his cleverness in uncovering references to himself in such a wide range of sources! Rather, they were astonished at their dullness in not having perceived before what these familiar books were about.[26] Nor was that simply his message on one particular occasion. Luke 24:44–47 gives us the substance of Jesus' teaching to all the disciples in the climactic forty-day postresurrection period:

---

25. Edward J. Young, *My Servants the Prophets* (Grand Rapids: Eerdmans, 1952), 46–54.
26. See Edmund P. Clowney, *Preaching and Biblical Theology* (Nutley, N.J.: Presbyterian and Reformed, 1975), 76.

"This is what I told you while I was still with you: Everything must be fulfilled that is written about me in the Law of Moses, the Prophets and the Psalms."

Then he opened their minds so they could understand the Scriptures. He told them, "This is what is written: The Christ will suffer and rise from the dead on the third day, and repentance and forgiveness of sins will be preached in his name to all nations, beginning at Jerusalem."

This is Jesus' master class in Old Testament interpretation. Note the comprehensiveness of the language he uses: "Everything must be fulfilled that is written about me in the Law of Moses, the Prophets and the Psalms." These three terms make up the three comprehensive divisions of the Old Testament, what Luke later designates "the Scriptures." In other words, the focus of Jesus' teaching was not a few "messianic" texts but rather the entire Old Testament.[27] According to him, the whole Old Testament Scriptures are a message about him. More specifically, the central focus of the entire Old Testament is his sufferings, his resurrection, and the proclamation of the gospel to all nations.

Nor was the teaching of Jesus lost on his disciples. In Acts 3:18, preaching in front of the temple, Peter described the crucifixion of Jesus in these words: "This is how God fulfilled what he had foretold through all the prophets, saying that his Christ would suffer." The apostle went on to speak of Jesus' second coming from heaven as being something God "promised long ago through his holy prophets.... Indeed, all the prophets from Samuel on, as many as have spoken, have foretold these days" (3:21, 24). Once again, notice the assertion that the central message of the prophets is Jesus' suffering and the glories that would subsequently flow from that event.

Peter explicitly formulates that principle in 1 Peter 1:10–12:

Concerning this salvation, the prophets, who spoke of the grace that was to come to you, searched intently and with the greatest care, trying to find out the time and circumstances to which the Spirit of Christ in them was pointing when he predicted the sufferings of Christ and the glories that would follow. It was revealed to them that they were not serving themselves but you, when they spoke of the things

---

27. Edmund P. Clowney, "Preaching Christ From All the Scriptures," in S.T. Logan, ed., *The Preacher and Preaching* (Phillipsburg, N.J.: Presbyterian and Reformed, 1986), 164. See also Bryan Chapell, *Christ-Centered Preaching: Redeeming the Expository Sermon* (Grand Rapids: Baker, 1994), 272; Sidney Greidanus, *The Modern Preacher and the Ancient Text: Interpreting and Preaching Biblical Literature* (Grand Rapids: Eerdmans, 1988), 118–20.

that have now been told you by those who have preached the gospel to you by the Holy Spirit sent from heaven. Even angels long to look into these things.

So too did Paul, who testified before King Agrippa (Acts 26:22–23):

I am saying nothing beyond what the prophets and Moses said would happen—that the Christ would suffer and, as the first to rise from the dead, would proclaim light to his own people and to the Gentiles.

This was Paul's exegetical method that he put into practice in Thessalonica, where on three consecutive Sabbaths, he reasoned with the Jews "from the Scriptures, explaining and proving that the Christ had to suffer and rise from the dead" (Acts 17:2–3).

To sum up, then, the message of the prophets in general, and Ezekiel in particular, is not simply instruction addressed to their own day and age. Still less is it a manual to help you interpret current events in the Middle East and work out the countdown to Armageddon. The message of the prophets is Jesus, and specifically "the sufferings of Christ and the glories that would follow." Thus, when you interpret Ezekiel correctly, without allegory, you will find that his message is not primarily morality, or social action, or eschatology. His central message is Jesus.

To be sure, understanding this gospel will lead to a new morality in the life of believers; it will motivate and empower them for meeting the needs of a lost world and engage their passion for the eschatological vision to be realized in fullness with the return of Christ. But the heart of Ezekiel is a witness to Christ, which centers in on his suffering and glory, his death and resurrection. The goal of this commentary is to show how this Christ-centered approach opens up the heart of the message of the ancient prophet for the contemporary believer.

Some of my readers are likely to be concerned at this point that I am selling short the ethical imperatives of the prophets in general and of Ezekiel in particular. I appreciate their concern, and I will respond with two simple points.

(1) The gospel (the good news about Jesus' death and resurrection) is not merely the power by which dead sinners are raised to new life, it is also the power by which God's people are transformed. The gospel is not merely the starting point from which we move on to ethics; it is the heartbeat of our lives as Christians. That is why Paul could say in 1 Corinthians 2:2: "I resolved to know nothing while I was with you except Jesus Christ and him crucified." Presumably, Paul is not saying that he only preached evangelistic sermons while ignoring the task of discipleship. Rather, he means that every sermon

he preached had a focus on the cross of Christ, whose implications he then drew out for every area of life.[28] To put it simply, he never preached Ephesians 4–6 (the ethical imperatives) without Ephesians 1–3 (the gospel indicative). Our sanctification flows out of our justification.

(2) This is important in our contemporary context because relatively few believers are short of ethical knowledge. There may be exceptions to the general rule, and there are certainly some areas where ethical instruction is sorely needed by the church. But in my own experience most Christians know a great deal about how they ought to live. Their problem is that they don't live up to what they know.[29] The gap is not in their knowledge but in their obedience.

How do we address this gap? Ethical sermons and Bible studies, no matter how accurately biblical their content, tend simply to add to the burden of guilt felt by the average Christian. Such teaching yields little by way of results. The gospel, on the other hand, has the power to change lives at a deep level, as men and women come to see both the depth of their sin (and therefore that their feelings of guilt were actually far too shallow) and at the same time the glorious good news that Jesus is their substitute, who has taken upon himself the punishment their sin deserved and has lived the perfect life in their place. Freed from their guilt, freed from their fear of failure, freed from their love of reputation, these people are now equipped to change.[30]

Finally, this approach requires a different orientation to preaching (and, I would argue, Bible study) than is common in our churches. Typically, we have drawn a sharp division between "worship" (the first part of our service) and "preaching." Often, the latter has degenerated into "instruction" with the sole measure of its efficacy, "How much have people learned?" To aid the communication of information, we put diagrams on overhead projectors and issue handouts. Yet biblical preaching is much more than instruction: The preaching and hearing of God's Word is itself worship in its most profound sense.[31] Its goal is doxological, that is, that men and women might be brought to see in a new way the glory of God and to bow their hearts in adoration and praise. Such preaching will certainly change lives, but it will be con-

---

28. Chapell, *Christ-Centered Preaching*, 272.

29. See John Newton, "On the Inefficacy of Knowledge," in *The Works of John Newton* (Carlisle, Pa.: Banner of Truth, 1985 reprint), 1:245–53.

30. On the power of the gospel to change lives, see C. John Miller, *Outgrowing the Ingrown Church* (Grand Rapids: Zondervan, 1986), 120–34. Similarly, Richard F. Lovelace, *Dynamics of Spiritual Life: An Evangelical Theology of Renewal* (Downer's Grove, Ill.: InterVarsity, 1979), 95–144.

31. See Hughes Oliphant Old, *The Reading and Preaching of the Scriptures in the Worship of the Christian Church.* Volume 1: *The Biblical Period* (Grand Rapids: Eerdmans, 1998), 189.

cerned even more fundamentally that God should be glorified. Like the apostle Paul, we pray (Eph. 3:20–21):

> Now to him who is able to do immeasurably more than all we ask or imagine, according to his power that is at work within us, to him be glory in the church and in Christ Jesus throughout all generations, for ever and ever! Amen.

Central Themes of the Book of Ezekiel

THE TASK THAT was assigned to Ezekiel was to prophesy to the exiles of Judah, who had been carried away into captivity in distant Babylonia. It was an audience close to despair, asking why this disaster had come on them and where God was in the middle of their personal holocaust. Their assessment of their own condition was: "Our bones are dried up and our hope is gone; we are cut off" (Ezek. 37:11). What use was a God who seemed unable or unwilling to protect his own land? What use was a God who allowed his own temple in Jerusalem to be defiled? What use was a God who allowed his own people to be carried away from the land he had promised to the patriarchs? Even if he were to intervene now on behalf of his land, how would that help those who were far away in exile? These were the questions with which the exiles struggled.

The answers to these questions permeate the book. The first and overarching theme of the entire prophecy is *the sovereignty and glory of God*. Ezekiel's opening vision is a vision of the glory of God, in all of his power and majesty (Ezek. 1). This visible glory was the mark of God's presence in the midst of his people in former times, which had first filled the tabernacle and subsequently fell on Solomon's temple at its dedication (2 Chron. 7:1–2). God had chosen the temple in Jerusalem to be his dwelling place. But now, amazingly, this same glory of God is seen by Ezekiel by the Kebar River, that is, in the midst of the exiles! The glorious and majestic sovereign God has gone into exile with his people (Ezek. 11:16).

Ezekiel 8–11 explains in visionary form why this shift has happened. The temple in Jerusalem has been utterly polluted by the abominations of the people (Ezek. 8). God's response to this defilement is twofold: He first decrees the destruction of the city and the temple (Ezek. 9), and then his glory departs from the temple to the east. He leaves slowly, haltingly, as if sorrowing over the scene, and moves towards those already in exile (Ezek. 10–11). The point of the vision is that God has not been evicted from his home by a superior force, impotent in the face of the Babylonian horde. Rather, because of the sin of his people he deliberately abandons the city of Jerusalem and its temple, decreeing their destruction. The Babylonians are merely a tool to do his will (Ezek. 21).

God's control over the entire situation is such that he can even determine the outcome of the Babylonian king's efforts to consult *his* gods through examining the liver of an animal (Ezek. 21:21)! As Proverbs 16:33 puts it: "The lot is cast into the lap, but its every decision is from the LORD." For wicked Jerusalem that is bad news, because it means that the punishment already decreed by God will surely come about and nothing can avert it (Ezek. 21:8–17). But for those already in exile, this same sovereignty represents hope. If it is indeed God who has scattered them among the nations, then he may also gather them back to himself and to their land again (11:17). He who voluntarily withdraws his glory from the defiled temple in chapter 11 is able to choose to return to a renewed and cleansed temple in chapter 43. God's sovereignty guarantees both the destruction of the sinner and the salvation of those who hope in him.

The second main theme in the book of Ezekiel could not contrast more strongly with the first: *the utter sinfulness of humans.* Yet the two themes are interrelated: To become aware of the glory of God is to receive a heightened awareness of the awfulness of sin, as Isaiah had earlier discovered (Isa. 6:5). All of the prophets preached against the sin and idolatry of their own day, but perhaps none was quite as comprehensive or as sweeping in their indictments as Ezekiel. For him, the sin of God's people stretched back throughout their entire history. Jerusalem had acted like a prostitute from the day of its birth (Ezek. 23:3) and was actually worse than Sodom (16:46–48)! Even from earliest times, from the day when God had called Israel out of Egypt and brought them into the desert, they had rebelled against him (ch. 20).

In addition to stretching back through time, the sin of God's people also stretched throughout society. It affected kings, priests, bureaucrats, prophets, the elite families of Jerusalem, elders, women—in short, every layer of society (see esp. Ezek. 22). It included sins against God (idolatry, neglecting the Sabbath, despising God's holy things; 22:7–12), as well as crimes against their fellow men and women (slander, violence, sexual impurity, bribery, extortion, oppression of the weak; 22:7–12). In order to make his point abundantly clear, Ezekiel deliberately adopts the most shocking language possible. Parts of Ezekiel 16 and 23 have been deemed by many scarcely suitable to be read aloud in church, and an ancient audience would have found its bluntness no less offensive.

The message is crystal clear, however: Sin cannot be swept under the carpet. It cannot be prettified, excused, or ignored. It is ugly, dirty, and offensive and cannot coexist with the presence of a holy God. When Jeremiah complained of those prophets and priests who dressed the wound of the people as though it were not serious, who said "Peace, peace" when there was no peace (Jer. 8:10–11), he was certainly not thinking of his younger contemporary, Ezekiel.

The third theme of the book grows out of the first two: *the inescapable coming of judgment*. That judgment will come first of all on Judah and Jerusalem. Jerusalem will be made a ruin and a reproach among the nations. Its destruction will be almost total and its people will be scattered to the four winds (Ezek. 5). It is literally the end of the road for Judah (chs. 7, 12, 15, 17, 21). They are the meat in the cooking pot, about to be cooked not simply medium-rare or even extremely well-done, but until they are turned into a charred heap of ashes (ch. 24). What is more, this holocaust is not the result of blind fate or the expansionist ambitions of arrogant world rulers. Rather, it is the outpouring of the wrath of a holy God on a land full of bloodshed and a city full of injustice (9:9).

Nor is there any mediator who will be able to turn away God's wrath from his people. Even if Noah, Daniel, and Job were miraculously present, between them they would have only enough righteousness to save themselves, not the people of the land (Ezek. 14:12–20). There is no prophet to stand in the gap on behalf of the people and thus prevent their destruction (22:30). Ezekiel himself is prevented from interceding for the people or remonstrating with them. He is struck dumb, only able to speak to declare the word of the Lord to them (3:26–27).

Judgment begins in God's program at the center, with his sanctuary (Ezek. 9:6). But it does not end there. Just as God's sovereignty extends to the ends of the earth, so also does his judgment. Thus, after the extensive section on Israel's sin and punishment, we find a section of prophecies against the other nations (chs. 25–32). They too have sinned in their pride and mocking of Judah's fallen state, and judgment will fall on them as well.

We might call these last two themes the bad news according to Ezekiel. It is bad news indeed, but it is a reality that had to be faced nonetheless. Judah was now going into exile, and her people needed to acknowledge that the cause of this situation was their own sin, not their fathers' sin or their brothers' sin. This is the point of Ezekiel 18, a point repeated in chapter 33 at the beginning of the section on the future hope. Until Judah acknowledges the rightness of God's action, she cannot receive forgiveness.

Yet there are signs from the opening pages of the book that God's judgment will be tempered by mercy. Ezekiel's vision of God includes a throne surrounded by a rainbow (Ezek. 1:28), the covenant sign that judgment against sin will never obliterate the remnant of God's true people (see Gen. 9:13–15). This theme is reiterated in many ways: a few hairs tucked away (Ezek. 5:3), a promise to spare some (6:8), the marking of the faithful (9:4), and so on. Yet it is no coincidence that Judah must first come face-to-face with the reality and ugliness of its sin in chapters 1–24 before it can receive the promise of a new future in chapters 33–48.

The turning point of the entire book comes with the coming of news of the fall of Jerusalem, an event anticipated at the end of Ezekiel 24, which then actually occurs in 33:21–22. Now the prophet's dumbness is removed, and the good news of restoration dominates. Now the positive side even of the oracles of judgment against the foreign nations can be seen: It is a mark that at least part of God's covenant with Abraham is still in force, that "whoever curses you I will curse" (Gen. 12:3). Is it not then true that the part of the covenant that promised ultimate blessing to Abraham's descendants is also intact?

The exploration of that possibility provides the central theme for the remainder of the book, which deals with *the return of the King and the restoration of the people to their land and a state of blessing.* The heart of Ezekiel's vision of the renewed temple is the return of the divine glory to the Most Holy Place (Ezek. 43:1–5). Once it has returned, the East Gate of the temple is closed forever. God will never again depart from his people as he did earlier. In order to assure this continuous presence for blessing, God promises to act to transform the people, starting from the top down. Their leadership is first on his agenda. A multiplicity of bad shepherds will be replaced by one good shepherd, a new David, by whom God will restore justice for all (Ezek. 34). He will unite in himself all of God's people, from the former northern and southern kingdoms (37:15–28). The priesthood will also be purified, with only those who remained faithful permitted access to the inner part of the sanctuary (44:6–16). Laws will be established that prevent the possibility of any return to the nation's former sins (e.g., 46:16–18). The old structures of the society that transgressed are completely swept away.

But sin does not reside simply in the structures of society; it pervades the hearts and minds of men and women. What the people need is nothing less than a new heart and a new spirit—a heart that will be willing and a spirit that will be obedient. That is what God promises to give them (Ezek. 37:1–14). What is promised is nothing short of a new creation, a radically changed world that will rise out of the ashes of the old. Even the very land in which they live will be transformed from a harsh, barren wilderness to a fruitful paradise (36:11, 35). Even though the enemies of God may still seek to stir up trouble against his people, they will never again come as an act of God's judgment and prevail against them. From henceforth, God will fight on behalf of his people, not against them (Ezek. 38–39). Judah is promised a return to Eden, but it is now an Eden that is populated with purified Adams and that has a high fence around the forbidden tree.

These, then, are the themes we find in the book of Ezekiel: God's glory and sovereignty, human sinfulness, the certainty of judgment, and the promise of mercy and hope for the future. From a New Testament perspective, the picture presented of the future still has an air of "not yet" about it. The most prominent feature of the new temple is not free access to God, but massive gatehouses designed to keep sinners from defiling it. There is a cleansing stream flowing from the temple (Ezek. 47), yet there is still a need for regular atonement sacrifices offered by the prince on behalf of his people (45:17). There is salvation for the Promised Land (Ezek. 48), and even for the alien and stranger in their midst, but not yet for the whole world. In all of this, there is still room for a greater revelation of hope.

This greater revelation of hope is revealed in Christ, to whom Ezekiel points us forward. The Glory of God, which Ezekiel saw coming to the temple, arrived in the person of Jesus, of whom John testifies: "We have seen his glory, the glory of the One and Only, who came from the Father" (John 1:14). Just as the Glory of God departed from Jerusalem and went to be with his people in exile, so Jesus left his Father's side to identify with sinful humanity, suffering "outside the camp" on behalf of his people (Heb. 13:12–13). The mediator who could not be found to turn aside judgment from Judah is now found in Jesus, the mediator of the new covenant, who offered his own blood for the sins of his people (9:11–15). Jesus is the Good Shepherd promised by Ezekiel, who will restore justice for his sheep (John 10:11). All who are in him are completely new creatures, filled with the Spirit of God (2 Cor. 5:17; Eph. 5:18).

But the salvation revealed in Jesus is far greater even than that which was revealed to Ezekiel. The reality is far better than the anticipation. It turns out that the prophet's wildest dreams were simply not wild enough! In Christ, we have boldness to approach the throne of grace (Heb. 4:16; 10:19). The city toward which we press needs no temple (Rev. 21:22), for the final sacrifice has been offered once and for all by Christ (Heb. 10:10). In it will be not only the full number of the tribes of Israel but a great multitude of all nations, tribes, peoples, and languages (Rev. 7:5–9).

Truly, the gospel is present in the book of Ezekiel for those with eyes to see it. It may not be with the full measure of revelation found in the New Testament—indeed it could not be—yet Ezekiel, too, deserves his place among those who "predicted the sufferings of Christ and the glories that would follow" (1 Peter 1:11).

Outline

I. Ezekiel's Call and Commissioning (1:1–3:27)
   A. Preface: The Prophet's Social and Physical Location
      (1:1–3)
   B. The Vision of the Divine Throne-Chariot (1:4–28)
   C. The Prophet's Call (2:1–3:15)
   D. Commissioned as a Watchman (3:16–27)
II. Oracles of Doom (4:1–24:27)
   A. Prophecies Against Jerusalem and Her Land (4:1–7:27)
      1. Sign-Act #1: The Besieged Brick (4:1–3)
      2. Sign-Act #2: The Prone Prophet (4:4–8)
      3. Sign-Act #3: The Siege Diet (4:9–17)
      4. Sign-Act #4: The Shaved Head (5:1–4)
      5. Interpretation of the Sign-Acts (5:5–17)
      6. Judgment on the Mountains of Israel (6:1–14)
      7. The End Is Nigh (7:1–27)
   B. The Vision of the Temple (8:1–11:25)
      1. Four Scenes of Abomination (8:1–18)
      2. The Visionary Destruction of Jerusalem (9:1–11)
      3. The Departure of the Divine Throne-Chariot From
         the Temple (10:1–22)
      4. Judgment on Israel's Leaders (11:1–15)
      5. Hope for the Exiles (11:16–25)
   C. Further Oracles of Judgment (12:1–24:27)
      1. A Sign-Act of Preparing For Exile (12:1–20)
      2. Prophecy Will No Longer Be Delayed (12:21–28)
      3. False Prophets and Prophetesses Will No Longer
         Be Tolerated (13:1–23)
      4. Internal Idolatry Condemned (14:1–11)
      5. Divine Judgment Unavoidable (14:12–23)
      6. The Parable of the Worthless Vine (15:1–8)
      7. The Parable of the Unfaithful Wife (16:1–63)
      8. The Parable of the Vine and Two Eagles (17:1–24)
      9. The Proverb of Sour Grapes Answered (18:1–32)
      10. The Parable of the Two Lion Cubs (19:1–9)
      11. The Parable of the Uprooted Vine (19:10–14)
      12. Israel's History of Rebellion (20:1–44)

13. The Song of the Sword (20:45–21:32)
14. The Indictment of Jerusalem (22:1–31)
15. The Parable of the Two Adulterous Sisters (23:1–49)
16. The Parable of the Cooking Pot (24:1–14)
17. The Death of Ezekiel's Wife; The End of Jerusalem Is Nigh (24:15–27)

III. **Oracles Against the Nations (25:1–32:32)**
   A. An Oracle Against Ammon (25:1–7)
   B. An Oracle Against Moab (25:8–11)
   C. An Oracle Against Edom (25:12–14)
   D. An Oracle Against Philistia (25:15–17)
   E. An Oracle Against Tyre and Her Ruler (26:1–28:19)
   F. An Oracle Against Sidon (28:20–23)
   G. Judgment for the Nations Means Salvation for Israel (28:24–26)
   H. An Oracle Against Egypt and Her Ruler (29:1–32:32)

IV. **Oracles of Good News (33:1–48:35)**
   A. The Turning Point (33:1–33)
      1. The Prophet's Commission and the Call to Repentance (33:1–20)
      2. The News of Jerusalem's Fall Received (33:21–22)
      3. Challenge to Those Remaining in the Land and to Those in Exile (33:23–33)
   B. Oracles of Restoration (34:1–37:28)
      1. A New Shepherd (34:1–31)
      2. A Renewed Land (35:1–36:15)
      3. A Renewed Covenant (36:16–38)
      4. A Renewed People (37:1–14)
      5. A Renewed Unity (37:15–28)
   C. The New Order Put to the Final Test (38:1–39:29)
      1. The Raising Up and Defeat of Gog (38:1–23)
      2. The Final Disposal of Gog (39:1–29)
   D. The Renewed Temple (40:1–48:35)
      1. The Formation of the Sacred Space (40:1–42:20)
      2. The Filling of the Sacred Space (43:1–46:24)
      3. The Sacred Life-Giving River (47:1–12)
      4. The Redivision of the Renewed Land and City (47:13–48:35)

Select Bibliography

Commentaries

Allen, Leslie C. *Ezekiel 1–19*. WBC 28. Dallas, Tex.: Word, 1994.

———. *Ezekiel 20–48*. WBC 29. Dallas, Tex.: Word, 1990.

Blenkinsopp, Joseph. *Ezekiel*. Interpretation. Louisville: John Knox, 1990.

Block, Daniel I. *Ezekiel 1–24*. NICOT. Grand Rapids: Eerdmans, 1997.

———. *Ezekiel 25–48*. NICOT. Grand Rapids: Eerdmans, 1998.

Calvin, John. *Ezekiel I*. Trans. D. Foxgrover and D. Martin. Grand Rapids: Eerdmans, 1994.

———. *Ezekiel II*. Trans. T. Myers. Grand Rapids: Baker, 1989.

Clements, Ronald E. *Ezekiel*. Louisville: Westminster/John Knox, 1996.

Cooke, George A. *Ezekiel*. ICC. Edinburgh: T. & T. Clark, 1936.

Craigie, Peter C. *Ezekiel*. Daily Study Bible. Philadelphia: Westminster, 1983.

Eichrodt, Walther. *Ezekiel*. Trans. C. Quin. OTL. London: SCM, 1970.

Ellison, Henry L. *Ezekiel: The Man and His Message*. London: Paternoster, 1956.

Fairbairn, Patrick. *An Exposition of Ezekiel*. Grand Rapids: Sovereign Grace, 1971 reprint.

Feinberg, Charles L. *The Prophecy of Ezekiel*. Chicago: Moody, 1969.

Greenberg, Moshe. *Ezekiel 1–20*. AB. Garden City, N.Y.: Doubleday, 1983.

———. *Ezekiel 21–37*. AB. New York: Doubleday, 1997.

Greenhill, William. *An Exposition of Ezekiel*. Edinburgh: Banner of Truth, 1994 reprint.

Hals, Ronald M. *Ezekiel*. FOTL 19. Grand Rapids: Eerdmans, 1989.

Hengstenberg, Ernst W. *The Prophecies of Ezekiel Elucidated*. Trans. A. C. & J. G. Murphy. Edinburgh: T. & T. Clark, 1874.

Keil, Carl F. *Ezekiel*. Trans. J. Martin. 2 volumes. Grand Rapids: Eerdmans, 1988 reprint.

Lind, Millard. *Ezekiel*. Believer's Church Bible Commentary. Scottdale, Pa.: Herald, 1996.

Skinner, John. *The Book of Ezekiel*. The Expositor's Bible. New York: Armstrong & Son, 1895.

Stuart, Douglas. *Ezekiel*. Dallas, Tex.: Word, 1988.

Taylor, John B. *Ezekiel*. TOTC. Downer's Grove, Ill.: InterVarsity, 1969.

Thomas, Derek. *God Strengthens: Ezekiel Simply Explained*. Welwyn Commentary. Darlington: Evangelical Press, 1993.

Vawter, Bruce, and Leslie J. Hoppe. *Ezekiel*. ITC. Grand Rapids: Eerdmans, 1991.

Wevers, John W. *Ezekiel*. NCB. Grand Rapids: Eerdmans, 1982.

Zimmerli, Walther, *Ezekiel*. Trans. R. E. Clements. 2 volumes. Hermeneia. Philadelphia: Fortress, 1979.

Other Monographs on Ezekiel

Boadt, Lawrence. *Ezekiel's Oracles Against Egypt: A Literary and Philological Study of Ezekiel 29–32*. Biblica et Orientalia 37. Rome: Biblical Institute, 1980.

Carley, Keith. *Ezekiel Among the Prophets*. SBT 31. London: SCM, 1975.

Davis, Ellen F. *Swallowing the Scroll: Textuality and the Dynamics of Discourse in Ezekiel's Prophecy*. JSOTS 78. Sheffield: Almond, 1989.

Duguid, Iain M. *Ezekiel and the Leaders of Israel*. Leiden: E. J. Brill, 1994.

Ebach, Jürgen H. *Kritik und Utopie: Untersuchungen zum Verhältnis vom Volk und Herrscher im Verfassungsentwurf des Ezechiel (Kap. 40–48)*. Ph.D. diss. Hamburg: Univ. of Hamburg, 1972.

Friebel, Kelvin G. *Jeremiah's and Ezekiel's Sign-Acts: Their Meaning and Function As Nonverbal Communication and Rhetoric*. Ph.D. diss. Madison: Univ. of Wisconsin, 1989.

Galambush, Julie. *Jerusalem in the Book of Ezekiel: The City As Yahweh's Wife*. SBLDS 130. Atlanta: Scholars, 1992.

Joyce, Paul. *Divine Initiative and Human Response in Ezekiel*. JSOTS 51. Sheffield: JSOT Press, 1989.

Krüger, Thomas. *Geschichtskonzepte im Ezechielbuch*. BZAW 180. Berlin: de Gruyter, 1989.

Levenson, Jon D. *Theology of the Program of Restoration of Ezekiel 40–48*. HSM 10. Missoula, Mont.: Scholars, 1976.

Lust, J., ed. *Ezekiel and His Book: Textual and Literary Criticism and Their Interrelation*. BETL 74. Leuven: Leuven Univ. Press, 1986.

Matties, Gordon H. *Ezekiel 18 and the Rhetoric of Moral Discourse*. SBLDS 126. Atlanta: Scholars, 1990.

Renz, Thomas. *The Rhetorical Function of the Book of Ezekiel*. Ph.D. diss. Cheltenham and Gloucester College/Univ. of Bristol, 1997.

Reventlow, Henning G. *Wächter über Israel: Ezechiel und seine Tradition*. BZAW 82. Berlin: Töpelmann, 1962.

Sedlmeier, Franz. *Studien zu Komposition und Theologie von Ezechiel 20*. Stuttgarter Biblische Beiträge 21. Stuttgart: Verlag Katholisches Bibelwerk, 1990.

Stevenson, Kalinda R. *The Vision of Transformation: The Territorial Rhetoric of Ezekiel 40–48*. SBLDS 154. Atlanta: Scholars, 1996.

Tuell, Steven S. *The Law of the Temple in Ezekiel 40–48*. HSM 49. Atlanta: Scholars, 1992.

Willmes, Bernd. *Die sogenannte Hirtenallegorie Ezekiel 34: Studien zum Bild des Hirten im AT*. Beiträge zur biblischen Exegese und Theologie 19. Frankfurt: Peter Lang, 1984.

Ezekiel 1:1–3

I N THE THIRTIETH YEAR, in the fourth month on the fifth day, while I was among the exiles by the Kebar River, the heavens were opened and I saw visions of God.

²On the fifth of the month—it was the fifth year of the exile of King Jehoiachin—³the word of the LORD came to Ezekiel the priest, the son of Buzi, by the Kebar River in the land of the Babylonians. There the hand of the LORD was upon him.

THE OPENING THREE VERSES of Ezekiel serve to locate the prophet's ministry in time and space. Verse 1 tells us that the prophet received his call on the fifth day of the fourth month in the thirtieth year, among the exiles beside the Kebar River. This verse may originally have stood simply as the heading for the opening vision, addressed to people familiar with the prophet and his situation. At a later date, when the prophecies were addressed to a wider (Judean?) audience, it became necessary to clarify the details of verse 1. It was at this point that the next two verses were added, either by the prophet or someone else. This addition equates the "thirtieth year" of verse 1 with the fifth year of the exile of King Jehoiachin (593 B.C.), specifies the "I" of verse 1 as "Ezekiel son of Buzi the priest" (see NIV text note), and identifies the Kebar River, where the exiles lived, as being "in the land of the Babylonians."

The original meaning of the "thirtieth year" in verse 1 has been much discussed from the time of the rabbis onward. The text gives us no indication from what datum the thirtieth year is counted. Three major possibilities have emerged.

(1) It is the thirtieth year since a specific event. This method of dating is well attested in the Old Testament (see, e.g., 2 Chron. 23:1, where "the seventh year" is the seventh year since the usurpation of the throne by Athaliah). Elsewhere in Ezekiel, the dates have as their consistent baseline the exile of King Jehoiachin (as in Ezek. 1:2), while Amos dates his prophecy with reference to an earthquake (Amos 1:1).

On the basis of the other dates in Ezekiel, some have thus seen the "thirtieth year" as the "thirtieth year of King Jehoiachin's exile," which would make verse 1 refer to the date of the final prophecy of the whole book.[1] Other commentators from ancient times have sought an event thirty years previous to 593 B.C. that might serve as a suitable datum point. The identification of Josiah's reform (ca. 621 B.C.) as that "point zero" goes back to the Targum and was held by Jerome,[2] while David Kimḥi favored the idea of the thirtieth year since the last year of Jubilee.[3]

(2) It is the thirtieth year in the reign of a specific king. This is the most common dating method in the Old Testament, used not only of the kings of Israel and Judah but also of a foreign king in Nehemiah 1:1 and 2:1. Indeed, the references in Nehemiah are of particular interest since the first simply speaks of "the twentieth year," which is not more specifically defined until the next chapter, where it becomes clear that the "twentieth year" in question is that of King Artaxerxes. Some have therefore argued that the dating in Ezekiel 1:1 is based on "Babylonian time," beginning with the accession of Nabopolassar in 625 B.C.[4]

(3) It is the thirtieth year of the prophet's life. This view goes back to Origen and has found several contemporary supporters.[5] One would normally expect an additional phrase in the Hebrew to indicate it as his age; yet there is a parallel at Genesis 8:13, where the "six hundred and first year" is that of Noah, as 7:11 makes clear. This date would have been significant for Ezekiel, for at that age he would have taken up his priestly ministry in the Jerusalem temple, had it still been standing.

There is no simple solution to this problem (self-evidently, since otherwise it would not continue to be discussed!). Some reference point that was presumably transparently clear to the original audience is no longer available to us. More significant, whoever added the additional notes of verses 2–3 chose not to highlight the "thirtieth year" but rather offer the date from Jehoiachin's exile. It is thus perhaps best to leave the question open and not base our exegesis on inevitably speculative reasoning. What is clear and underlined in the present form of the text is that the opening vision of the

---

1. Douglas Stuart, *Ezekiel* (Dallas, Tex.: Word, 1988), 29; A. D. York, "Ezekiel 1: Inaugural and Restoration Visions?" *VT* 27 (1977): 82–98.

2. See George A. Cooke, *Ezekiel* (ICC; Edinburgh: T. & T. Clark, 1936), 7. In the seventeenth century, this view was advocated by William Greenhill, *An Exposition of Ezekiel* (Edinburgh: Banner of Truth, 1994 reprint), 9.

3. So also John Calvin, *Ezekiel I,* trans. D. Foxgrover and D. Martin (Grand Rapids: Eerdmans, 1994), 14.

4. For this view, see Claus von Orelli, *Das Buch Ezechiel und die zwölf kleinen Propheten,* 2d ed. (Munich: Beek, 1896).

5. J. E. Miller, "The 'Thirtieth Year' of Ezekiel 1.1," *RB* 99 (1992): 499–503; Margaret S. Odell, "You Are What You Eat: Ezekiel and the Scroll," *JBL* 117 (1998): 229–48; Leslie C. Allen, *Ezekiel 1–19* (WBC 28; Dallas, Tex.: Word, 1994), 21; Joseph Blenkinsopp, *Ezekiel* (Interpretation; Louisville: John Knox, 1990), 16; Block, *Ezekiel 1–24,* 82.

prophet Ezekiel is placed in the fifth year of Jehoiachin's exile, that is, 593 B.C., while the prophet lived among the exiles of Babylonia. Historically and socially, therefore, Ezekiel's message was addressed to those in exile.

There in exile, Ezekiel was confronted by a dramatic spectacle: The heavens were opened and he saw "visions of God" (*mar'ôt 'elōhîm*, 1:1). The prophet was taken behind the scenes, as it were, and given a different, divine perspective on the events unfolding around him. The phrase "visions of God" or "divine visions"[6] encompasses not only the opening vision of the divine throne-chariot, but all of the visions that play such an important part in Ezekiel's message.

Although Ezekiel, like other Old Testament prophets, hears the word of the Lord, for him the visual aspect of God's revelation has a particularly prominent place. Thus the book is in important ways structured around the vision of God's throne-chariot prepared for action in chapter 1, that of the abominations that cause the glory to depart from the Jerusalem temple in chapters 8–11, the vision of the renewal of the dry bones in chapter 37, and the vision of the new temple in chapters 40–48. God is dramatically at work even in the apparently hopeless situation of the exiles, a work that the prophet is invited to "show and tell" to those around him.

Bridging Contexts

GOD'S WORD FOR the exiles. One common mistake in interpreting the prophets (and perhaps esp. Ezekiel) is to get bogged down in the minor details and thus attempt to overinterpret the text. For instance, some commentators build extensively on the "thirtieth year" of verse 1, speaking of that as the time when the prophet would have expected to enter priestly service had he been at home in Jerusalem. Yet the presence of Ezekiel 1:2–3 already serves to play down the importance of the exact identity of the thirtieth year. If verse 1 is the original heading of (part of) the prophecy for the original audience, verses 2–3 are the heading for the wider audience, that is, for *us!* They address those who do not know what the thirtieth year is, need to be informed which prophet is speaking, and cannot be expected to know that the Kebar River is in Babylonia unless that fact is made clear.

The basic point, then, of the introductory verses is that *God's word comes to the exiles.* Now it may seem self-evident to contemporary readers that God can address us and we can come to him wherever we are. The prophet's original

---

6. On *'elōhîm* as an appellative ("divinity") in this phrase rather than a proper noun, see Block, *Ezekiel 1–24*, 85.

hearers, however, had a different understanding of their relationship to the place where they lived. If we are to understand Ezekiel's message, we must seek to understand what it meant to the people of his day to be in exile. It was not merely that they happened to be living somewhere other than they would have preferred to be; rather, their entire world had caved in upon them. In the same way that contemporary Jewish theology can be described as "Theology after Auschwitz," because every understanding of God and the world has to take into account the experience of the Holocaust, so also this part of Old Testament theology must be designated the "Theology of Exile," because of the radical impact of that earlier holocaust. Tamara Eskenazi expresses it thus:

> Exile. It is not simply being homeless. Rather, it is knowing that you do have a home, but that your home has been taken over by enemies.
> Exile. It is not being without roots. On the contrary, it is having deep roots which have now been plucked up, and there you are, with roots dangling, writhing in pain, exposed to a cold and jeering world, longing to be restored to native and nurturing soil. Exile is knowing precisely where you belong, but knowing that you can't go back, not yet.[7]

Weeping and dreaming. What do you do in exile? The first thing that you do is sit down and weep. As the psalmist put it in Psalm 137:1–4:

> By the rivers of Babylon we sat and wept
>   when we remembered Zion.
> There on the poplars
>   we hung our harps,
> for there our captors asked us for songs,
>   our tormentors demanded songs of joy;
>   they said, "Sing us one of the songs of Zion!"
> How can we sing the songs of the LORD
>   while in a foreign land?

In exile, life cannot be "business as usual." How can there be joy in exile? How can there be joy when the memory is still filled with the demolition of all that is precious: Jerusalem's stones torn down, her infants slaughtered (Ps. 137:7–8)? In view of God's apparent rejection of his people, who can but pour out tears unceasingly (Lam. 2:18; 3:49)? Joy is gone and dancing turned to mourning (Lam. 5:15).

This mourning is not simply grief at the random sorrows of life, the "slings and darts of outrageous fortune," to use Shakespeare's phrase. Rather, in the

---

7. "Exile and Dreams of Return," *CurrTM* 18 (1990): 192.

midst of the pain, there is a recognition of the cause of that pain. Judah's calamity is a consequence of her own sin (Lam. 3:42; 4:13). Paradoxically, though, in the midst of that recognition is also the beginning of hope. If tragedy is not a random event but the result of God's sovereignty, then there may be hope of a new beginning.[8] The one who has bruised can also bind up; the one who has rejected his people can restore them to himself (Lam. 5:21). God's covenant love, his *ḥesed*, is the basis for hope in the midst of tears.

Just as Moses appealed to the covenant with Abraham, Isaac, and Jacob so that God would not destroy his people utterly after the incident with the golden calf (Ex. 32:13), so also in the Exile, God's commitment to the covenant brought hope. Added to this self-commitment was the basic character of God as gracious and compassionate, again as he had revealed himself originally to Moses (Ex. 34:6). Because of those facts, the possibility of forgiveness and restoration was real. Thus the book of Lamentations closes: "Restore us to yourself, O LORD, that we may return; renew our days as of old unless you have utterly rejected us and are angry with us beyond measure" (Lam. 5:21–22).

Such a restoration could not be claimed presumptuously, however. The temptation, even in exile, was to hang on to glib hopes rather than truly to mourn and repent. Thus Jeremiah wrote to the exiles furiously denouncing those who promised a quick end to their troubles (Jer. 29:15–23). Such prophets found a ready audience for their words, but Jeremiah criticized them for failing to listen to God's words through the prophets, words that spoke of the sword, famine, and plague (29:17–19). Until the dregs of the bitter cup of exile had been drained, there could be no talk of a new future. For the foreseeable future—for seventy years, which in most cases was far more than their life expectancy, their future lay in Babylon. Only after the cup of wrath had been drained would a new future be possible for Israel; only after the sin had been paid for would it be possible to speak tenderly to Jerusalem and proclaim her comfort (Isa. 40:1–2).

In the meantime, alongside weeping, there was also room for dreaming.[9] According to Psalm 126:1, "When the LORD brought back the captives to Zion, we were like men who dreamed." The dreaming actually started a long time before the captives began to return. When everything has been torn down to the foundations, when nothing remains of the structures of the past, but when at the same time there is confidence that the nation will rise again, phoenix-like, from the ashes, visionary dreams can flourish. There can be dreams of a future that will preserve the best of the past while avoiding the worst.

---

8. Ibid., 197.
9. Ibid., 198.

Ezekiel's task. This context of weeping and dreaming describes well Ezekiel's task. On the one hand, he speaks clearly and unequivocally of judgment and destruction. During the early years of his ministry, he spoke of more judgment yet to come. In 589 B.C., in spite of the warnings of Ezekiel and Jeremiah, Zedekiah rebelled against the Babylonians, hoping to break free with Egypt's help. It was a disastrous error of judgment; in the aftermath, the temple itself was destroyed and Jerusalem razed to the ground (see 2 Kings 25). The people needed to know that the events of the fall of Jerusalem and its temple were no mere accidents of fate but were the result of the people's sin. Those responsible had to be called to account.

Yet while he was called to tear down the ruins of the past, at the same time Ezekiel was called to portray also a message of hope for the future. Though the judgment was from God, so also was the possibility of restoration. In the opening portion of the book the emphasis is on tearing down: The ruins must first of all be cleared, yet hope for the future is not completely lacking. Likewise, in the latter portion of the book, though the emphasis is on hope and dreams of the future, there is also room for a return to criticism and weeping for the past.

There is thus both continuity and discontinuity in Ezekiel's presentation of the Exile. On the one hand, things can never again be as they once were. Because of the idolatry of the past, God's judgment has come upon his people with devastating effect. The glory has departed, not just symbolically but really from Israel. God has turned his face away, abandoning his people, leading to their certain death. Had that been all there was to the history of redemption, no one could have faulted God.

But amazingly in the midst of that sentence of death comes God's re-creative word of life. *God speaks to these people where they are, in exile!* God tears the heavens open and invites his chosen prophet to see his glory, the grounds of both judgment and hope. There will be, after the Exile, life from the dead—not because of any claim Israel may have but simply because of the mercy of God. In the meantime, Israel in exile is not forgotten or abandoned by God but is to live in the light of that promise, with hope. Though they live after the coming of night before even the first rays of dawn, yet in the light of who God is and his free promise to his people, they can live in expectant hope.

Contemporary Significance

LEARNING TO LIVE **in exile.** It seems to me that the social location of the book of Ezekiel in the Exile is one of the reasons for its contemporary neglect. The image of the Christian life as exile is not a common one in our days. We don't think of ourselves as exiles, and so we neglect the literature of the Exile, not simply in favor of the New Testament, but of the literature of the Exodus and of the periods of conquest and monarchy. We even prefer the writings of the return to Judah to those of the Exile; Moses and Joshua, David and Nehemiah are our mentors, not Ezekiel. Why is that? Perhaps it is because in our culture we prefer heroes and idolize success; our models are strong, "can-do" types, people who seem able to take on the world with one hand tied behind their backs. The primary paradigm we have adopted is that of the victorious Christian life.

How then do we live with the reality of life in a very different world, where victories are frequently hard to come by and right living does not always lead to success? How can we speak an encouraging word to those barely able to keep their heads above water, to those who are not living the victorious Christian life but for whom it is an achievement simply to live the surviving Christian life? What does God have to say to those of us who frequently find ourselves, like the prodigal, far away from where we should be, suffering the deserved consequences of our actions? The answer is to balance the biblical models of exodus and conquest with the equally biblical models of wilderness and exile.

In fact, the biblical image of life in exile has actually never been more timely than it is today, for we live in a time in which people are experiencing a growing sense of alienation from the world around them. Fewer and fewer people find themselves "at home" where they live. On the one hand, in our generation millions across the globe have been forced to flee their homes through migration and ethnic cleansing, through persecution and war, as well as through economic migration in search of job opportunities.[10] On the other hand, even safe and affluent communities in the West have turned relocation—and dislocation—into a way of life.[11] Sometimes our email addresses seem to be the only "constant" in a rapidly changing world. In such a world, the pressing question for many is, "Where do I belong?" What address can we give that describes where our hearts are? Some of us can identify a geographical area as "home," the part of the world where we would live if we could, where our language is spoken and our faces fit. But for many, home is not where we live. We live geographically uprooted lives.

Even among those who have not experienced such a physical uprooting, there are many who endure their own personal, internal experiences of "exile." The comfortable veneer of life is easily scraped away, perhaps with the loss

---

10. These causes of the sense of exile, while perhaps new to some of us, have been familiar to our brothers and sisters in the African-American and Hispanic-American community for generations. See Jean-Pierre Ruiz, "Exile History and Hope: A Hispanic Reading of Ezekiel 20," *The Bible Today* 35 (1997): 106–13.

11. See Ursula Pfafflin, "Displacement and the Yearning for Holding Environments: Visions in Feminist Pastoral Psychology and Theology," *Journal of Pastoral Care* 49 (1995): 391.

of a job and the comfortable lifestyle that went with it, or with the death of a loved one. There are times when the props in which we trusted are knocked away and we are left winded and gasping, not knowing which way is up or where to turn. Our entire personal world has caved in upon us in an experience that will forever shape who we are.

The tendency is at such times to feel isolated and alone in feeling this way. However, it is a far more common experience than we think. Paul Simon gave expression to the sense of alienation and disorientation of an entire generation of young Americans when he wrote:

> I don't know a soul who's not been battered;
> I don't have a friend who feels at ease;
> I don't know a dream that's not been shattered or driven to its knees.[12]

The universality of the sense of exile ("so far away from home") that Paul Simon is describing is conveyed in the title he gave to this lyric: "An American Tune." It describes the experience of all those who have metaphorically sailed off on the Mayflower into the American dream. Nor is that a uniquely American experience. Almost all of us in the modern world know what it is to live with battered souls and shattered dreams.

In those times of personal tragedy and uprootedness, our first response is to mourn and weep, and rightly so. We turn to the psalms of lament and pour our tears out before God. But we are not to weep forever. There comes a time when we need to move on and hear the challenge of God's Word as well as its comfort. Where it is our sin that has brought us into this situation, we are to confess it to God and acknowledge our own responsibility. Even where the pain we are suffering is not caused by our sin, we need to hear his words of discipline, as he reminds us that, as Christians, we can never be "at home" in this world. As the writer to the Hebrews puts it, "Here we do not have an enduring city, but we are looking for the city that is to come" (Heb. 13:14). The Christian life is, in a profound sense, always one of exile in a strange land, far from home.

Ancient believers understood this. The writer of the early second-century *Epistle of Mathetus to Diognetus* reminded his friend:

> As citizens, Christians share all things with others, and yet endure all things as foreigners. Every foreign land is to them as their native country and every land of their birth as a land of strangers. . . . They pass their days on earth, but they are citizens of heaven. They obey the prescribed laws, and at the same time surpass the laws by their lives.[13]

---

12. "An American Tune," words and music by Paul Simon; © 1973 Paul Simon (BMI).
13. Cited by Miroslav Volf in "Allegiance and Rebellion," *The Christian Century* 114 (1997): 633.

Why then do we moderns persist in seeking to live as though it were not so? We put down roots as though we were here on this earth to stay forever, and we pursue the trinkets of time while ignoring the essentials of eternity. Truly, we need to learn how to live in exile.

Our true home. But living in exile is not simply a matter of gritting our teeth and getting on with it in the manner of the Stoics; we are not called to accept that life stinks, so that all we can do is make the best of a bad job. As exiles, we are not homeless and hopeless. We do have a home—it is just not here. Though we cannot go home yet and though we feel the pain of not being home, we can still *dream* of home. As an "exile" in the United States, I have plastered the walls of my office with reminders of home: I have a map of Britain on my wall, a calendar with views of Scotland, a Scottish flag to fly on days of national significance. I read a British newspaper daily via the Internet to keep up with current events. So also, as citizens of heaven, our lives should be filled with tokens of our true home. As Paul puts it in Colossians 3:1–2: "Since, then, you have been raised with Christ, set your hearts on things above, where Christ is seated at the right hand of God. Set your minds on things above, not on earthly things."

Why do we love to read the Scriptures daily? Because they speak to us of home. Why do we live differently from those around us? Because we remember that we are soon going home (1 Peter 4:1–7). Why are we willing to suffer and even die for our faith? Because we are sure of what we hope for and certain that to be with God, even through pain, is better by far than to be comfortable without him (Heb. 11:1–2, 13–16).

But we do not simply dream about heaven, our true home; we do what we can to establish an enclave of heaven where we live. In exile, the Sabbath and the synagogue became key institutions for the Jewish community as the means by which they maintained their distinctiveness. So too for us, if we appreciate what it means to be living in exile, our Sundays will become precious and distinctive as opportunities to experience in the company of other believers a foretaste of heaven. In fact, how you use Sunday says a lot about what you really believe about heaven. If you think that heaven is a successful career and a large house, you'll use Sunday to put in extra time at work. If you think heaven is eternally doing nothing, you'll snooze Sunday away on the sofa. If you think heaven is shopping till you drop, Sunday will find you at the local mall. But if you think that heaven is to "glorify God and enjoy him forever," how are you going to spend Sunday? By glorifying him and enjoying him now! To those who look forward to spending eternity praising God among his people, spending one day in seven in like manner is surely no hardship; rather, it is an antidote to the harsh reality of life in exile.

Equally, the experience of exile should lead us to value all the more the counterculture of the new community of the saints. The exiles focused their lives around the synagogue: It was the heart of their social lives as well as their spiritual lives. In a similar way, the infant church formed an alternative community from their earliest days, eating and spending time in one another's company as well as worshiping together (Acts 2:42–47). This is the natural response of exiles to life in an alien land and will act as an accurate measure of just how much we as Christians are truly citizens of heaven first and citizens of our earthly country second. If we truly believe that those we worship with week by week are our brothers and sisters with whom we will gladly spend eternity, then it will be entirely natural for them to be our closest friends and companions here and now.

All this is possible because to us too, in our contemporary exile, God speaks and reveals himself. Whereas in the past he spoke to the exiles through the prophet, now in these last days he has spoken to us by his Son, Jesus (Heb. 1:1–2). In the coming of Jesus, God has definitively drawn aside the curtain and revealed his heavenly purpose to all of his people—that in all things God is working for the good of those who love him, so that in Christ we may ultimately be more than conquerors (Rom. 8:28, 37). To be sure, as we look around us, we do not yet see everything in subjection to Jesus (Heb. 2:8). That is part of the experience of living in exile. But by faith, we do see Jesus, crowned with glory and honor at the right hand of the Father, and believe that our present suffering is part of God's perfect plan to mold us into the image of the one who suffered first for us (2:9–10).

Ezekiel 1:4-28

I LOOKED, AND I SAW a windstorm coming out of the north—an immense cloud with flashing lightning and surrounded by brilliant light. The center of the fire looked like glowing metal, ⁵and in the fire was what looked like four living creatures. In appearance their form was that of a man, ⁶but each of them had four faces and four wings. ⁷Their legs were straight; their feet were like those of a calf and gleamed like burnished bronze. ⁸Under their wings on their four sides they had the hands of a man. All four of them had faces and wings, ⁹and their wings touched one another. Each one went straight ahead; they did not turn as they moved.

¹⁰Their faces looked like this: Each of the four had the face of a man, and on the right side each had the face of a lion, and on the left the face of an ox; each also had the face of an eagle. ¹¹Such were their faces. Their wings were spread out upward; each had two wings, one touching the wing of another creature on either side, and two wings covering its body. ¹²Each one went straight ahead. Wherever the spirit would go, they would go, without turning as they went. ¹³The appearance of the living creatures was like burning coals of fire or like torches. Fire moved back and forth among the creatures; it was bright, and lightning flashed out of it. ¹⁴The creatures sped back and forth like flashes of lightning.

¹⁵As I looked at the living creatures, I saw a wheel on the ground beside each creature with its four faces. ¹⁶This was the appearance and structure of the wheels: They sparkled like chrysolite, and all four looked alike. Each appeared to be made like a wheel intersecting a wheel. ¹⁷As they moved, they would go in any one of the four directions the creatures faced; the wheels did not turn about as the creatures went. ¹⁸Their rims were high and awesome, and all four rims were full of eyes all around.

¹⁹When the living creatures moved, the wheels beside them moved; and when the living creatures rose from the ground, the wheels also rose. ²⁰Wherever the spirit would go, they would go, and the wheels would rise along with them, because the spirit of the living creatures was in the wheels.

²¹When the creatures moved, they also moved; when the creatures stood still, they also stood still; and when the creatures rose from the ground, the wheels rose along with them, because the spirit of the living creatures was in the wheels.

²²Spread out above the heads of the living creatures was what looked like an expanse, sparkling like ice, and awesome. ²³Under the expanse their wings were stretched out one toward the other, and each had two wings covering its body. ²⁴When the creatures moved, I heard the sound of their wings, like the roar of rushing waters, like the voice of the Almighty, like the tumult of an army. When they stood still, they lowered their wings.

²⁵Then there came a voice from above the expanse over their heads as they stood with lowered wings. ²⁶Above the expanse over their heads was what looked like a throne of sapphire, and high above on the throne was a figure like that of a man. ²⁷I saw that from what appeared to be his waist up he looked like glowing metal, as if full of fire, and that from there down he looked like fire; and brilliant light surrounded him. ²⁸Like the appearance of a rainbow in the clouds on a rainy day, so was the radiance around him.

This was the appearance of the likeness of the glory of the LORD. When I saw it, I fell facedown, and I heard the voice of one speaking.

FOR EZEKIEL AMONG the exiles by the Kebar River, God's word became sight. "The heavens were opened and I saw visions of God" (1:1). Ezekiel saw in his vision an astonishing revelation of God's glory. Now there was nothing particularly new in a prophet seeing God's glory. Isaiah had seen it in a vision of the Lord in the Jerusalem temple, high and exalted on the throne (Isa. 6). Moses himself, the archetypal prophet (Num. 12:6–8; Deut. 18:15, 18), saw God's glory on Mount Sinai— a vision so glorious that it made his face shine (Ex. 33:18–23). God's glory is the visible manifestation of his presence among his people. Thus, at the dedication of Solomon's temple, the Lord demonstrated his approval of the building by filling the structure with his glory-cloud (1 Kings 8:10–11). What is new in Ezekiel, however, is the exact form that the manifestation of God's glory takes, as a comparison with Isaiah's vision makes clear.

Isaiah's vision was stately and essentially static, as befits a vision in the temple, the symbol of God's permanent resting place in the midst of his settled people.[1] To be sure, there was sin to be atoned for, yet atonement was accomplished by a simple touch from the coals on the heavenly altar (Isa. 6:6–7). Though there was a message of judgment for the prophet to give to a stubborn people, a judgment that would continue until the cities lay ruined and the land deserted (6:11), there was no sense of that destruction reaching to Mount Zion and bringing down the temple itself.

Indeed, the events of Isaiah's own lifetime seem to have contributed to the comfortable idea that no matter what else happened, Zion was secure. The Lion of Judah would roar from Zion (Amos 1:2), but he would not abandon it. Thus, when the Assyrian king Sennacherib swept across the ancient Near East like a flood in 701 B.C., even though he reached the gates of Jerusalem, God intervened to deliver his people by means of a dramatic plague (Isa. 36–37). Lamentations 4:12 sums up the theological conclusion drawn from these events: "The kings of the earth did not believe, nor did any of the world's people, that enemies and foes could enter the gates of Jerusalem."

In the context of this popular Zion theology, it is easy to see the difficulty that Ezekiel's earlier contemporary Jeremiah faced. He was called to oppose the complacency of those who kept repeating, "The temple of the LORD, the temple of the LORD, the temple of the LORD" (Jer. 7:4). His prophecies of judgment against Jerusalem were interpreted as high treason because they struck at the heart of this belief (Jer. 26:11).[2] The temple itself had become viewed as an amulet, a lucky charm to ward off evil. In response, Jeremiah simply pointed to the lessons of history. In the past, in the days of Samuel's youth, Israel had placed the same kind of faith in the ark of the covenant, the *symbol* of God's presence, instead of in the *reality* of God's presence. The result had been the destruction of Shiloh and the "exile" of the ark (Jer. 7:12–15; cf. 1 Sam. 4, esp. v. 22, which reads lit., "Glory has gone into exile from Israel, for the ark of God has been captured").

It was this same false perception of safety that Ezekiel's vision challenged. Two kinds of imagery dominate the opening vision of Ezekiel: images of motion and images of judgment. In contrast to Isaiah's static temple imagery, Ezekiel's vision is filled with movement.[3] Whereas Isaiah saw the Lord seated

---

1. Notice the significance of "rest" as a precondition for building the temple in Deut. 12:10; 2 Sam. 7:1; 1 Chron. 22:9. See Roddy L. Braun, *1 Chronicles* (WBC 14; Waco, Tex.: Word, 1986), 224–25.

2. Ronald E. Clements, *Isaiah and the Deliverance of Jerusalem* (JSOTS 13; Sheffield: JSOT Press, 1980), 98. Clements points to this belief as a significant factor in the "confident, but ill-founded way in which the kings of Judah reacted to the constraints of outside political pressure . . . and . . . were guilty of the most crass and reckless political misjudgments."

3. See Iain Duguid, "Ezekiel," *Dictionary of Biblical Imagery*, ed. Leland Ryken, James C. Wilhoit, and Tremper Longman III (Downer's Grove, Ill.: InterVarsity, 1998), 256–57.

in the temple, Ezekiel's vision opens with the Lord in the midst of a motion-filled "windstorm" (*rûaḥ seʿārâ*, Ezek. 1:4) in the land of the exiles. God is not dead or sleeping, nor is he restricted to the temple; on the contrary, he is living and active and on the move. The Lion of Judah is restless. In general, such a depiction of the Lord's coming to intervene in the lives of his people would be a positive development. However, in this case God's activity does not bode well for the temple or for Jerusalem. It is only a short step from Ezekiel 1, where the glory of God is in motion, to Ezekiel 10, where the glory abandons the temple, leaving it defenseless against the Babylonian invaders.[4]

Movement dominates Ezekiel's description of the approach of a mighty windstorm. The windstorm itself is in motion, while the living creatures it contains not only have legs but wings as well. Torches are moving back and forth between the creatures (Ezek. 1:13), while alongside the creatures are various wheels, with each "wheel intersecting a wheel" (1:16).[5] All of these wheels move together and stop together under the control of "the spirit of the living creatures" (*rûaḥ haḥayyâ*, 1:20). Everywhere the prophet looks, he sees bustling activity.

What is more, the activity has ominous import. Ezekiel's vision, however bizarre it may seem to us, draws on a number of traditional ancient Near Eastern elements. The imagery of the Lord riding on the storm, surrounded by fire and lightning, was a common way of describing the coming of the divine warrior (see Ps. 18:9–14; Nah. 1:3). The wheels of Ezekiel's vision represent a chariot, another typical aspect of the divine warrior image.[6] Frequently, the image of God as a warrior was adopted by the prophets to speak of the Lord's coming to deliver his people. In this instance, however, it is significant that the windstorm is coming "out of the north" (1:4), the traditional source of Judah's foes.[7] The divine warrior is here approaching to wage war against his own people, not to deliver them. The covenant-breaking people can find no comfort in the imminent personal arrival of their God.

The Lord's throne-chariot is supported by living creatures, which are instantly recognizable as cherubim from their role as throne-bearers (cf. Ps. 18:10) and indeed are explicitly identified as such in Ezekiel 10:1. These extraordinary winged creatures have nothing to do with the rosy-cheeked, naked infants of popular mythology. They have four faces each—that of a man, a lion (the highest wild animal), an ox (the highest domestic animal),

---

4. Robert R. Wilson, "Prophecy in Crisis: The Call of Ezekiel," *Int* 38 (1984): 125.

5. These wheels intersect with one another at right angles to enable the chariot to move in any direction without turning (so v. 17). See John W. Wevers, *Ezekiel* (NCB; Grand Rapids: Eerdmans, 1982), 46.

6. See "Chariot," *DBI*, 139.

7. Allen, *Ezekiel 1–19*, 25.

and an eagle (the highest bird)—symbolizing the fact that they embody within themselves all of the highest attributes of living creation.[8] Thus they are appropriately called "living creatures."

As well as being God's throne-bearers, the cherubim are the guardians of God's holiness, God's heavenly bodyguard. The threatening nature of their presence comes from their role as enforcers of divine judgment. Thus, when the man and the woman were thrown out of the Garden of Eden, cherubim were appointed to bar the way back into God's presence, preventing any intrusion of the profane into the realm of God's holiness (Gen. 3:24).

In fact, in many respects the events of Genesis form the backdrop for Ezekiel's vision. The mighty windstorm recalls not only creation, where the Spirit (*rûaḥ*) of God was hovering over the waters (Gen. 1:2), but also the Flood, where God sent a wind (*rûaḥ*) to dry up the floodwaters (8:1). The connection with these two pivotal events of protohistory is underlined as the chapter unfolds. We read about the living creatures (*ḥayyôt*; cf. Gen. 1:24, 28) and an awesome "expanse" (*rāqîaᶜ*, Ezek. 1:25) over the cherubim, like that of Genesis 1:6. The aura of God's radiance is compared to a rainbow in the clouds on a rainy day (Ezek. 1:28), which evokes Genesis 9:13–16.[9] These references set the tone of Ezekiel as an account of creation-uncreation-recreation, similar to that of the early chapters of Genesis. They invite the first readers of the book to compare their own experience of exile with Adam and Eve's banishment from the Garden of Eden and with Noah's endurance of the Flood.

While the emphasis of Ezekiel 1 is almost exclusively on the gathering clouds that threaten rain, yet the mention of the rainbow (v. 28) allows the possibility of a ray of hope even in the midst of the gloom. That hope does not deny the possibility of judgment, any more than the rainbow denies the possibility of rain. Indeed, without the rain there could be no rainbow! What the rainbow asserts is the faithfulness of God even in the midst of overwhelming judgment. It is a sign of God's self-commitment to his promise. God's judgment must fall on his rebellious people, yet because of commitment to his covenant he will not wipe them out. In the darkness of exile, God's covenant faithfulness, his *ḥesed*, was Israel's only hope. Thus the writer of Lamentations, without in the least diminishing the nature of the calamity that

---

8. This was recognized already by the rabbis, who explained: "Four kinds of proud beings were created in the world: the proudest of all—man; of birds—the eagle; of domestic animals—the bull; of wild animals—the lion; and all of them are stationed beneath the chariot of the Holy One" (*Exod. Rab.* 23.13). See Moshe Greenberg, "Ezekiel's Vision: Literary and Iconographic Aspects," in *History, Historiography and Interpretation: Studies in Biblical and Cuneiform Literature*, ed. H. Tadmor and M. Weinfeld (Jerusalem: Magnes, 1983), 165.

9. The idea of God's setting his bow in the clouds is unique to these two passages.

had befallen his people, could say: "Because of the LORD's great love (*ḥasdê-yahweh*) we are not consumed, for his compassions never fail. They are new every morning; great is your faithfulness" (Lam. 3:22–23).

But where can one flee from this impending judgment of God? The message of the vision is that flight is useless. The throne-chariot can proceed as easily to any of the four points of the compass, without even having to turn, symbolizing God's omnipresence (Ezek. 1:12, 17). The wheels are covered with eyes, symbolizing the omniscience of God. As the prophet Jonah had earlier discovered, when God stirs the storm there is literally no place to run and nowhere to hide. In the face of such an awesome, ominous appearing of God, it is small wonder that Ezekiel fell on his face (1:28). The certain, unavoidable judgment of God is a terrifying spectacle to behold.

Bridging Contexts

CALL NARRATIVE. Ezekiel's prophecy opens with a typical "call narrative," outlining the details of his commissioning to be a prophet (Ezek. 1:1–3:15; cf., e.g., Jer. 1). The prophetic call narrative was an important part of every prophecy. On the one hand, it served to give legitimacy to the prophet's words, for he spoke not on his own account but as an ambassador sent by the Great King, the Lord himself. In it, the prophet gave details of how he had been singled out for the prophetic office. On the other hand, the call narrative often introduced the themes that the prophecy would encompass in greater detail, just as the overture to a symphony introduces in brief form the musical motifs that will form the basis for the work to follow.

Thus, Ezekiel's vision begins the process of communicating God's judgment to Israel. Again, as with the introductory verses of Ezekiel's prophecy, it is easy to get drowned in the details. It is possible to get caught up in the complexities of creatures with legs and faces and wings, of coals and torches and lightning, of wheels within wheels. Such overattention to details can easily lead to allegorical interpretation, in which meaning is read into the text rather than out from the text.[10] Rather, we must see how Ezekiel's vision of movement and impending divine judgment has a challenge for our day.

---

10. For example, William Greenhill adduces from the text that "each one went straight ahead; they did not turn as they moved" (v. 9), the application that Christians ought to mind their own business and not meddle in the affairs of others (*Ezekiel*, 39). Similarly, Gregory the Great identified the four faces of the living creatures with the four Evangelists (*Homilies on the Book of Ezekiel*, 4.1). In this, he may have been influenced by the earlier identification of the four (separate) living creatures of Rev. 4 with the gospel writers by Irenaeus (*Adv. Haer.* 3.11.8) and Victorinus (*Comm. in Apoc.* 4.3–4). In each case, the application is arbitrary rather than growing out of an understanding of the text in its original context.

The challenge for our day. (1) God is not tied to the old ways of doing things. Just as Ezekiel's contemporaries put their trust in the temple rather than in the God of the temple, so also in our day there are many who place their faith in the gifts of God rather than in the Giver. The complacency of such people, then and now, needs to be challenged. The true and living God is not a tame God. He cannot be comfortably manipulated into a box and made to do our bidding. If he were, he would hardly be worthy of following. God's radical freedom to be God, bound only by his own self-revelation, means that his ways can never be reduced to a pat formula or a trite slogan. If his people abandon him, he may abandon them and fight against them. A lady reputedly asked Abraham Lincoln during the dark days of the Civil War if he was confident that God was on their side. "Madam," he is said to have replied, "I am less concerned whether God is on our side than whether we are on his side." No matter what our past history, we cannot assume God is on our side unless we are constantly and faithfully on his side.

(2) To those tempted to place their hope in fallible earthly institutions, a warning note of judgment needs to be sounded. God's presence in the midst of his people is not always good news, for he is a holy God who will judge evil. He is still the divine warrior, who comes to establish justice without favoritism or partiality. That is bad news indeed to those who are counting on a comfortable continuance of the status quo. But, paradoxically, at the same time God's coming in judgment is still viewed as *good news* in the Bible. He comes not merely to punish the wicked but to establish his kingdom, news that is good indeed to those whose hope is firmly placed in him. No matter how black the gathering clouds may be, those who trust in the Lord will live in the light of his covenant faithfulness.

This same note of the danger of impending judgment on the complacent is struck in the New Testament analogue of Ezekiel's opening vision—that of the apostle John on Patmos (Rev. 1:10–20). The allusions to Ezekiel 1 in Revelation 1 include the terrifying images of blazing fire and glowing bronze, a human figure surrounded by radiance, and the noise of rushing waters.[11] Like Ezekiel, John falls down at the feet of the glorious revelation of God (1:17). He is then commissioned with a message for the seven

---

11. Other images from Ezek. 1 appear in the vision of the heavenly throne room in Rev. 4: a throne on a surface like crystal, four living creatures covered with eyes, and partaking of the likeness of a lion, an eagle, an ox, and a human being. Yet along with the similarities there are also differences. The "expanse" (*rāqîaʿ*) becomes a "sea of glass," the living creatures now each have the likeness of one kind of animal instead of each having the faces of all four, and now they have six wings (like Isaiah's seraphim) instead of four. The eyes have moved from the wheels (which have disappeared) onto the living creatures themselves.

churches of Asia Minor, which combines judgment to come on the unrepentant with hope for those who persevere.

God is not merely a distant observer of our struggle, for he walks in the midst of the seven lampstands (Rev. 2:1). What is more, he is no respecter of tradition when it becomes merely the dead heritage of the past. He will remove the lampstand from the midst of those who have forsaken their first love. Only living and active faith will overcome all the trials that face people and enter into life (see Rev. 2:5–7). But those who are seeking to serve the Lord in the midst of many trials can take comfort from the powerful presence of the Lord in their midst. God knows their deeds (2:2; 3:1, 8, 15), their hard work and perseverance (2:2, 19), their afflictions and poverty, the slanders ranged against them (2:9), and the unique problems of where they live (2:13). Nothing escapes his observation—and now he is ready to act!

THE REALITY OF JUDGMENT. The message of judgment is indeed never popular to proclaim. Some contemporary churches have completely removed any mention of sin and its consequences from their messages, on the grounds that it turns people away. One pastor recently described the goal of his church's "seeker services" in the following terms: "In a non-threatening atmosphere, the 'seekers' share a delightful, thought-provoking hour in which they are introduced to the person of Jesus Christ."[12] It is doubtful that Ezekiel would have described his encounter with the living God as "a delightful, thought-provoking hour"; the reality of God's presence created, on the contrary, a threatening atmosphere. It is never comfortable for sinners to stand in the presence of an angry God. But in exile, when all that has meaning and value is torn away, people do not seek entertainment but reality; what they require is not so much to have their thoughts provoked as to have their hard questions answered. Perhaps this is one reason why we find the book of Ezekiel so hard to grasp today in our Western culture, with our delusions of adequacy. We are more used to reading the Bible as a kind of self-help manual, which provides ten top tips for cultivating the roses in our spiritual garden.

But the world through which we walk is not a safe place. It is a wilderness walk, in which every turn of the road brings into view new challenges and dangers. It is a world where things break down and fall apart, even for the best of people. It is a world marred by sin—your own sins and the sins of others. Without a recognition of sin and the curse that lies on our world

---

12. "The Seeker Service at Fair Haven," *Reformed Worship* 23 (1992): 10.

because of sin (Gen. 3:16–19), the brokenness of life does not make any sense. You are left with the dilemma that either God is good but not powerful enough to avert life's disasters, or that God is not good. The Bible shows us a third possibility: God is both good and all-powerful, but because of human sin the world is under God's curse.

That does not mean that *all* bad things happen because of our individual sins. Jesus rejected that solution in John 9:3 when he asserted of the man born blind, "Neither this man nor his parents sinned . . . but this happened so that the work of God might be displayed in his life." But it does mean that we have to reckon with a God who is just and holy as well as loving and compassionate, who judges in wrath as well as graciously forgives.

This is the God with whom Israel has to deal, and his character has not changed over the intervening centuries. God continues to act in judgment on sin as well as to bring justice to the oppressed, even though only in a partial way in our present era. But into the situation of pain and anguish, of dislocation and alienation, even as it is revealed to be (in this case) the direct judgment of God's wrath, comes the trumpet sound of Ezekiel's prophecy: You are not alone. Surrounded by clouds that will bring a deluge on God's rebellious people, the rainbow still shines. God continues to reveal himself to his people in the exile that they merited for themselves. Indeed, in the situations of pain and anguish, the sound of his voice is often most clearly heard. We will not always like what he has to say, of course. His Word confronts us with our sin as well as comforts us with his grace. But the truly astonishing thing is that in spite of our sin, he still speaks to us and through us. There is no other word for that but grace.

The challenge to the church. But God's challenging Word comes not only to individuals but also to societies. The cities of Europe are filled with the great cathedrals and churches of past centuries, many of which are now empty. Some have been turned into mosques, others into restaurants or carpet showrooms, the symbols of a post-Christian society. Invariably, the way to such a post-Christian society lies through a contentment with the externals of religion, a society in which it is enough to have the form of godliness, while denying its power (2 Tim. 3:5). The church in Ephesus was warned that it had lost its first love and unless there was repentance, the church itself would cease to exist (Rev. 2:5). Coldness, if left untouched, leads to hardness and then deadness.

Yet this perilous condition may be present even while the externals are all in place; orthodox theology and activism in good works may continue long after love has grown cold (Rev. 2:2–4). Within a generation a similar fate could easily befall the churches of our cities. Only constant repentance and ever-renewed trust in the living God ensures continued life and usefulness for a church. We should therefore pray continually for the Spirit's life-giving power to be at work within our churches, lest our churches likewise become mere monuments to God's powerful work in the past.

There is no magic formula for measuring and maintaining the life of a church. The classic "marks of the church" formulated by the Reformers—the pure preaching of the Word and right celebration of the sacraments—certainly focus our attention on important issues, but they are both too broad and too narrow. They are *too narrow* insofar as they would refuse the name "church" to many gatherings of our true brothers and sisters in Christ. After all, those who practice paedo-baptism and those who practice adult baptism cannot both be celebrating the sacrament rightly, yet there are many bodies of true believers on both sides of the argument. And these marks are *too broad* since they dignify with the term *church* some institutions that may have a form of external orthodoxy, yet lack genuine life. Love of doctrine is not enough, not even the love of true doctrine.

The one clear mark of true discipleship that the Lord himself instituted is love for one another (John 13:35). This trait, though perhaps hard to define quantitatively, yet is surely possible to recognize when experienced. It is the external evidence of the internal reality of eternal life, or, to put it another way, it is the primary fruit of remaining in living connection with Jesus (15:9–17). Of course, where that living connection is present, the other aspects of the fruit of the Spirit's work in our hearts will not be lacking either (Gal. 5:22–26).

It is not merely a challenge to the complacent to remember that God is not tied to the past. It is good news for his people. God is living and active and constantly doing new things. Should the existing structures of the church grow moribund and useless, he can and does raise up for himself new organizations and denominations to achieve his purposes. The coldness and deadness of the eighteenth-century Church of England may have seemed unpromising soil for a potent movement of God's Spirit, yet God caused George Whitefield and John Wesley to spring out of it as powerful witnesses to the truth of his Word. The encouragement and challenge to our contemporary churches is that the living God will achieve his purposes—with or without us!

Given that truth, Christians need to adopt a balance between progressivism and traditionalism. On the one hand, not everything that is new is of God. Christians need to be discerning in their evaluation of movements and trends within the church, measuring all things against the yardstick of the Scriptures. On the other hand, neither is everything new automatically suspect. Our understanding of the Scriptures and how they are to be applied to our present times is constantly growing as new challenges drive us back to reread old passages and reevaluate the traditions we have received from our forefathers in the faith.

Like Abraham Lincoln, we need to be constantly posing ourselves the question in every situation, "Am I on the Lord's side?" As we do so, may the Spirit convict us of our sins and point us afresh to Christ, the divine warrior who bore the full weight of God's wrath for us, so that we may experience the full light of his presence without being consumed.

Ezekiel 2:1–3:15

H E SAID TO ME, "Son of man, stand up on your feet and I will speak to you." ²As he spoke, the Spirit came into me and raised me to my feet, and I heard him speaking to me.

³He said: "Son of man, I am sending you to the Israelites, to a rebellious nation that has rebelled against me; they and their fathers have been in revolt against me to this very day. ⁴The people to whom I am sending you are obstinate and stubborn. Say to them, 'This is what the Sovereign LORD says.' ⁵And whether they listen or fail to listen—for they are a rebellious house—they will know that a prophet has been among them. ⁶And you, son of man, do not be afraid of them or their words. Do not be afraid, though briers and thorns are all around you and you live among scorpions. Do not be afraid of what they say or terrified by them, though they are a rebellious house. ⁷You must speak my words to them, whether they listen or fail to listen, for they are rebellious. ⁸But you, son of man, listen to what I say to you. Do not rebel like that rebellious house; open your mouth and eat what I give you."

⁹Then I looked, and I saw a hand stretched out to me. In it was a scroll, ¹⁰which he unrolled before me. On both sides of it were written words of lament and mourning and woe.

3:1And he said to me, "Son of man, eat what is before you, eat this scroll; then go and speak to the house of Israel." ²So I opened my mouth, and he gave me the scroll to eat.

³Then he said to me, "Son of man, eat this scroll I am giving you and fill your stomach with it." So I ate it, and it tasted as sweet as honey in my mouth.

⁴He then said to me: "Son of man, go now to the house of Israel and speak my words to them. ⁵You are not being sent to a people of obscure speech and difficult language, but to the house of Israel—⁶not to many peoples of obscure speech and difficult language, whose words you cannot understand. Surely if I had sent you to them, they would have listened to you. ⁷But the house of Israel is not willing to listen to you because they are not willing to listen to me, for the whole house of Israel is hardened and obstinate. ⁸But I will make you as unyielding and hardened as they are. ⁹I will make your forehead like the hard-

est stone, harder than flint. Do not be afraid of them or terrified by them, though they are a rebellious house."

¹⁰And he said to me, "Son of man, listen carefully and take to heart all the words I speak to you. ¹¹Go now to your countrymen in exile and speak to them. Say to them, 'This is what the Sovereign LORD says,' whether they listen or fail to listen."

¹²Then the Spirit lifted me up, and I heard behind me a loud rumbling sound—May the glory of the LORD be praised in his dwelling place!—¹³the sound of the wings of the living creatures brushing against each other and the sound of the wheels beside them, a loud rumbling sound. ¹⁴The Spirit then lifted me up and took me away, and I went in bitterness and in the anger of my spirit, with the strong hand of the LORD upon me. ¹⁵I came to the exiles who lived at Tel Abib near the Kebar River. And there, where they were living, I sat among them for seven days—overwhelmed.

THROUGHOUT HISTORY, mystics have sought to experience visions of God. They have often gone to great lengths in their pursuit of this ultimate experience, subjecting their bodies to innumerable hardships in order to attain to a great spiritual "high." They have traveled to the ends of the earth and undergone fastings, lack of sleep, isolation, self-denial, and self-flagellation in search of contact with the Divine. In contrast, God comes to Ezekiel entirely unsought and reveals himself to the prophet not for the sake of giving him the quiet time to end all quiet times but rather to commission him for a task and to entrust to him a message. The message that Ezekiel is to proclaim is not his own, but God's; for that reason, only God can empower him and authorize him to deliver it. On the most basic level, therefore, the call vision and commissioning serve to authenticate Ezekiel's ministry, both to himself and to his audience.

But in addition to that general authentication, the manner of the prophet's calling also speaks to his hearers of the task to which the prophet has been called. In Ezekiel's case, that task will not be an easy one. He has not been sent to the Gentiles, with whom the only problem in communicating his message would have been linguistic (Ezek. 3:4—6). Had he been sent to them, they would surely have listened, even though their speech was obscure and their language difficult (lit., "a people deep of lip and heavy of tongue," 3:5). Being a Wycliffe Bible translator would have been a straightforward assignment in comparison to what Ezekiel has been called to do.

Instead, Ezekiel is being sent to the Israelites, who are a "rebellious nation" (*gôyim hammôrᵉdîm;* Ezek. 2:3).[1] Notice how the traditional language of election has been reversed here, so that the Gentiles have become *ᶜam* (a "people") while Israel has become *gôyim* ("nations"). The chosen nation has become, appropriate to their own action, unchosen. The depth of Israel's alienation from God further emerges in 3:11, where Ezekiel is sent to "your countrymen in exile." God is not willing to call them "my people," a sure sign of disaster to come.[2] Nor is this state a temporary aberration on the part of this present generation but rather a continuation of a long history of disobedience. They are simply the "sons of Israel" (*bᵉnê yiśrāʔēl,* 2:3), a term that brings out the hereditary nature of their rebelliousness: They are true children to their rebellious parents (2:3—4).[3]

The essence of the people's transgression lies in their rebellion, that is, their refusal to recognize God's sovereignty over them.[4] In that attitude they have hardened themselves, externally and internally, becoming "obstinate" and "stubborn" (Ezek. 2:4). Though language will not be a barrier, they will not listen to Ezekiel because they are not willing to listen to the One who sent him (3:7). If responsiveness is to be the measure of success, Ezekiel's mission is declared a failure before it even begins. But Ezekiel's mission will be judged by another standard, for even though the people will not listen to his words, yet "they will know that a prophet has been among them" (2:5). That is, when the predicted disasters befall Israel, they will recognize that God had previously warned them of what was about to happen.

The prophet himself is to provide an alternative model of behavior. Unlike Israel he is to listen to what the Lord says to him and not to rebel as they do (Ezek. 2:8). Throughout the vision, Ezekiel is the very picture of compliant obedience to the Word of God. When he comes face-to-face with the glory of God, he falls face down in humble submission (1:28); he is not obstinate in God's presence. When God speaks, he listens; when he is commanded to stand, he rises to his feet (2:1—2). However, this obedience comes not because of some special measure of holiness intrinsic to Ezekiel but because of an infu-

---

1. This identification of Israel with the paradigm of rebellion, the "nations" (*gôyim;* e.g., Ps. 2:1), probably explains the unexpected plural here.

2. Compare with the opening chapter of Hosea, where Israel has become "Not my people" (*lōʔ-ᶜammî,* Hos. 1:9). Similarly, in Ex. 32:7—14, after the sin with the golden calf, God sends Moses back to "your people, whom you brought up out of Egypt" (v. 7, reflecting Israel's self-identification in v. 1); the resolution to the crisis is not reached until the Lord relents and does not bring the threatened disaster upon "his people" (v. 14).

3. Moshe Greenberg, *Ezekiel 1—20* (AB; Garden City, N.Y.: Doubleday, 1983), 62.

4. "'The primary sense of *mārad* is refuse allegiance to, rise up against, a sovereign'; its antonym is *ᶜābad* 'serve, be subject to'" (Greenberg, *Ezekiel 1—20,* 63).

sion of divine Spirit (*rûaḥ;* 2:2). The entry of the Spirit not only raises him to his feet but enables him to hear God's speech (2:2). God not only hands the scroll to Ezekiel, he causes him to eat it (3:2). He is the One who will strengthen Ezekiel to make him as tough as his opponents.[5] When the vision and commissioning are over, the Spirit lifts Ezekiel up and deposits him among the exiles again, where he sits motionless. Without God's power, Ezekiel literally can do nothing.

This depiction of Ezekiel as the model of Spirit-infused submission suggests that there is more than one dimension to the Lord's characteristic address to Ezekiel as *ben-ʾādām,* usually translated "son of man." This expression occurs over ninety times in Ezekiel, compared to a mere fourteen times in the rest of the Old Testament. As has often been recognized, this form of address sharply distinguishes Ezekiel from the Sovereign God and the divine beings of chapter 1; *ben-ʾādām* marks him out as a mere mortal.[6]

But this expression may perhaps also mark him out from all of his contemporaries. They are the "sons of Israel" (*bᵉnê yiśrāʾēl,* 2:3), the true descendants of the one whose nature was to strive with God (Gen. 32:28); Ezekiel, on the other hand, is literally designated "the son of Adam." Just as the first Adam received the breath of life from God (Gen. 2:7), so Ezekiel as "son of Adam" receives an infusion of divine Spirit (*rûaḥ*), which raises him, as it were, to renewed "life" by enabling him to obey. This unusual form of address may thus be an aspect of the creation theme we saw in chapter 1. This re-creation theme emerges more clearly in the related passage in Ezekiel 37, where the coming of the Spirit (*rûaḥ*) into the skeletons brings new life to the dry bones, but what happens later for the community happens first of all here to the prophet.[7] Ezekiel himself is to be the founding member of a new community, empowered by the infusion of the divine Spirit to a life of radical obedience.[8]

Like the first Adam, Ezekiel faces a test of obedience that revolves around the idea of eating, though in his case he is to eat whatever the Lord commands him to (Ezek. 2:8) rather than to abstain from eating what the Lord

---

5. There is a play on the prophet's name here, for Ezekiel means "God strengthens." See John B. Taylor, *Ezekiel* (TOTC; Downer's Grove, Ill.: InterVarsity, 1969), 66.

6. Thus John Skinner would translate *ben-ʾādām* simply by "member of the human race," arguing that "it expresses the infinite contrast between the heavenly and the earthly, between the glorious Being who speaks from the throne and the frail creature who needs to be supernaturally strengthened before he can stand upright in the attitude of service" (*The Book of Ezekiel* [The Expositor's Bible; New York: Armstrong & Son, 1895], 44).

7. "What the entire people should achieve is to be realized in the one son of man who is their representative" (Walther Eichrodt, *Ezekiel,* trans. C. Quin [OTL; London: SCM, 1970], 64). For the connection between Ezek. 37 and Gen. 2:7, see Blenkinsopp, *Ezekiel,* 173.

8. Compare Ezek. 36:26–27.

prohibits.[9] In another reversal of the original sin, what Ezekiel is given to eat is anything but "good for food and pleasing to the eye, and also desirable for gaining wisdom" (Gen. 3:6); rather, it is a scroll covered on both sides with words of lament and mourning and woe (Ezek. 2:10). But though its appearance is unattractive, to the obedient eater it tasted "as sweet as honey" (3:3). Ezekiel's obedient consumption of the scroll is his only activity in an otherwise completely passive vision. By it, he is equipped as God's messenger to go and speak the unpalatable truth to his fellow exiles.

Yet the vision ends on what appears at first sight to be a discordant note in 3:14–15. The prophet who has been called, empowered, and equipped is found sitting down, overwhelmed, filled with feelings of anger. These verses underline, however, the dual nature of the prophet's task. On the one hand, he remains under "the strong hand of the LORD" and therefore begins to feel the feelings that the Lord has toward the people—feelings of wrath and anger (3:14).[10] On the other hand, he sits among the exiles, living where they live, and thus sees the effects of God's wrath from the other side: the forthcoming overwhelming devastation of his people (3:15).[11]

Ezekiel's proclamation is not delivered from the safety and comfort of an ivory tower but flows out of personal experience of the suffering of his people. Indeed, it may not be too strong to say that he has already ingested their suffering, in the form of the scroll covered with words of lament, mourning, and woe, just as in the temple ritual the priests would ingest the sin offering and thus absolve the guilt of the people.[12] But in the absence of the temple, there is no sacrifice to take away the guilt of the people, only a scroll that records it. In the meantime, these feelings of wrath and desolation must remain inside the prophet until the Lord opens his lips and gives him the words to say (3:16).

Bridging Contexts

THE SPIRIT IN the old and new eras. In what ways is our task as messengers of the gospel similar to and different from that assigned to Ezekiel? In some ways, as New Testament Christians we live in a different era. The role of the Holy Spirit in particular changes radically from the Old Testament period to that of the New. In the Old Testament the

---

9. This may be the reason why the metaphor of Jer. 15:16 has become a concrete experience for Ezekiel.

10. Ernst W. Hengstenberg, *The Prophecies of Ezekiel Elucidated,* trans. A. C. & J. G. Murphy (Edinburgh: T. & T. Clark, 1874), 37.

11. The Hebrew word translated "overwhelmed" (*mašmîm*) comes from the root *šāmam*, which occurs frequently throughout Ezekiel in the sense of "devastate, ravage, make desolate."

12. Odell, "Ezekiel and the Scroll," 244.

Spirit is given to specific people to accomplish specific tasks, especially the ability to speak God's word to his people.[13] The hope and expectation of a universal outpouring of the Spirit was there throughout the Old Testament, but it remained something for the future (Joel 2:28—29). In the New Testament era, however, the promise is fulfilled. The Spirit has been poured out on all of God's people, young and old, male and female, influential and insignificant alike, commissioning and equipping them for the prophetic task (see Acts 2). Thus, we now live in the age of "the prophethood of all believers."

In the book of Acts, a prominent theme is the fact that the coming of the Holy Spirit gives believers power to witness about Jesus Christ. As was the case for the prophet Ezekiel, the major impediment in that task is not merely linguistic (though the Holy Spirit deals with that problem as well in Acts 2:4!). It is the fact that we are trying to communicate the gospel to people who are "dead in . . . transgressions and sins" (Eph. 2:1). What people need is not simply new information but new life. The essence of human sin continues to be rebellion against God's sovereignty, a state in which people desire to suppress the truth about God (Rom. 1:18).

Whereas Ezekiel was called to bring this message to Israel, God's chosen people, we bring the message to the Gentiles as well. They too, though once "far away," now have access to the Father by the same Spirit that Israel does, as Paul reminds us in Ephesians 2:17—18. The process of bringing that gospel to the nations is often a painful one, however. God continues to use as his messengers not the strong but the weak, placing his treasure in clay pots to show that strength really belongs to him (2 Cor. 4:7). Like Ezekiel, we need to fall on our faces in God's presence, recognizing that we have no strength, no gifts, nothing that we can contribute to the task, and pleading with him to fill us with his Spirit so that we can be faithful servants. Like Ezekiel, we must be willing to die to ourselves and to our desires and comfort to be useful to God. As Paul puts it in 2 Corinthians 4:5, hitting both themes of weakness and self-denial: "We do not preach ourselves, but Jesus Christ as Lord, and ourselves as your servants for Jesus' sake."

The Son of Man. That ministry is ours because in the meantime the final "Son of Man" has come, Jesus Christ himself. He is The Human One in fullness, just as Ezekiel was a "mere human" in contrast to the exalted title used for God, "Sovereign LORD." But Jesus is also the heavenly Christ, the "one like a son of man"—picking up on the majestic imagery of Daniel 7, an exalted, regal figure (see Rev. 1:13). These two aspects seem at first sight incongruous,

---

13. William J. Dumbrell, "Spirit and Kingdom of God in the Old Testament," *Reformed Theological Review* 33 (1974): 1—10.

even contradictory. Yet that is why it was such a perfect title for Jesus to adopt for his incongruous mission.[14] In his earthly ministry, it is the "mere humanity" aspect that is prominent. In Eugene Peterson's words, "this Son of Man has dinner with a prostitute, stops off for lunch with a tax-collector, wastes time blessing children when there were Roman legions to be chased from the land, heals unimportant losers and ignores high-achieving Pharisees and influential Sadducees."[15] Ultimately, he hangs pierced and bleeding on a cross. He dies, the most human and radically undivine of acts.

But his majesty, while veiled, is still present in his earthly ministry. He teaches as one with authority, he speaks of possessing a kingdom. Both aspects are present because Jesus is son of man and Son of Man, very man and very God, taking on our humanity and combining it with undiminished deity. For the first disciples the lesson necessarily focused on his humanity because they had to learn that salvation comes not through the advent of a triumphal heavenly figure bearing a sword, blasting his opponents with fire from heaven, as James and John thought (Luke 9:54). Rather, it came through the advent of a baby in a manger, who grew up to bear a crown of thorns and a cross. The "son of man" had come not (as you might expect from Dan. 7) to be served but to serve and give his life as a ransom for many (Mark 10:45).

But for the hearers of the book of Revelation, the lesson is reversed. The return of our Lord will not be the same as his first advent. Christ is not eternally suffering on the cross, but will return (as the Son of Man!) in glory on the clouds, bearing a sword to blast his opponents with fire from heaven. James and John were not entirely wrong, they just had their advents confused; they mixed up the son of man and the Son of Man. The answer to both is "the son of man"—first in his state of humiliation and second in his state of exaltation; as the ancient liturgy puts it: "Christ has died, Christ is risen, Christ will come again."

The human Christ of the crucifix, the son of man in his state of humiliation, is not all there is. According to Revelation 1, even now in his state of exaltation, the heavenly, exalted, glorious Christ rules and reigns. But he reigns in the middle of the seven golden lampstands, which are later identified as the seven churches. It may seem a strange location for the Glorious One, in the midst of seven small, undistinguished churches, tarnished by sin and weakness. Yet where else should we expect to see the One whose nursery was a cowshed and whose coronation ceremony took place on a cross? He is there in the midst of real, ordinary communities of faith—not idealized, sanitized versions—and he is there dressed in priestly garb, with kingly

---

14. See Bruce Chilton, "The Son of Man—Who Was He?" *Bible Review* 12 (1996): 34–46.
15. *Reversed Thunder* (San Francisco: Harper & Row, 1988), 30.

accouterments and the power of the prophetic word. He is there as prophet, priest, and king, on behalf of his people.

Jesus is also the Second Adam, who by his obedience undoes the effects of the first Adam's fall (Rom. 5:19; 1 Cor. 15:44–49). He is the one on whom the Spirit rested in fullness of power and through whom the Spirit is poured out on the church, to create the new community of his people. Jesus does not need to swallow the Word of God; he is himself the Word of God, the manifestation of the divine glory (John 1:14). He is the One who came to earth to preach good news to the poor (Luke 4:18); he is also the One who will return to earth to tread the winepress of the fury of the wrath of God Almighty (Rev. 19:15).

The imagery of scroll-swallowing reappears in Revelation 10, where the apostle John is told to eat a scroll that will turn his stomach sour, though, as with Ezekiel, it had been sweet in his mouth. The ingested Word of God will provide him with the material to prophesy about many peoples, nations, languages, and kings (10:11); however, bearing such testimony is frequently a bittersweet experience, as the fate of the two witnesses in Revelation 11 indicates. To some, the message of the gospel is the aroma of life, sweeter than honey, while to others it is the aroma of death, to be opposed and destroyed (2 Cor. 2:16).

CONTEMPORARY EVANGELISM. What do the models of Jesus and Ezekiel tell us about our efforts in evangelism and missions? In the first place, surely they challenge the common notion in the church that "bigger is always better." There is a lot of pressure from many quarters in our times to measure success in terms of numbers. Whether it is evangelistic crusades that speak of thousands of "decisions for Christ" or popular books that suggest that adopting certain methodologies will inevitably bring church growth, the "bigger is better" philosophy reigns in much of the contemporary church.

In support of this doctrine, the biblical image of the harvest is pressed into service. It is asserted on the one hand that the faithful Christian will inevitably be the fruitful Christian, seeing many people brought to Christ, and on the other hand that fruitfulness should determine strategy, so that the maximum number of harvesters are sent to where the fruit is ripe. On this approach, the primary goal of missions and evangelism is to see the world come to Christ.

The call of Ezekiel (and of some of the other prophets) should challenge this simplistic assumption. He is specifically called and sent to a people who have been unresponsive in the past and will be unresponsive in the future. Not only that, but God tells the prophet that if he had sent him to the Gentiles, a far greater response to his preaching would have occurred. The faithfulness of this man's ministry cannot be measured in numerical terms. The primary goal of his ministry is not to see people converted but to bring glory to God by preaching (and modeling) the message he has been given. As John Calvin put it: "When God wishes to move us to obey him, he does not always promise us a happy outcome to our labor; but sometimes he wants to test our obedience to the point that he will have us be content with his command, even if people ridicule our efforts."[16]

That is not to say that we should adopt a kind of reverse psychology, whereby we assert that we must certainly be faithful if no one is being reached by our message! We must labor to the utmost of our ability to remove any stumbling block that stands in the way of communicating the gospel, becoming "all things to all men so that by all possible means [we] might save some" (1 Cor. 9:22). Yet we do so recognizing that a work of the Holy Spirit is necessary in the hearts of men and women if they are to become Christians, a work that is the sovereign prerogative of God to impart. At times, God opens the hearts of men and women to himself through the most unlikely of messengers, such as Jonah's concise and not exactly heartfelt preaching to the Ninevites (Jonah 3:4), while at other times the eloquent pleading of God's messengers falls on deaf ears.

This truth should be both a comfort and a challenge to us in our evangelism. On the one hand, sharing the gospel is far easier than we think. God is not limited by the weakness of my efforts; he can, if he chooses, save in spite of my incompetence. As one person put it, passing on the good news is simply a matter of one beggar telling another where to find bread. That should motivate us to witness boldly for Christ wherever we go. On the other hand, however, sharing the gospel is far harder than we think. Even the most brilliant performance on my part may still fail to convince my hearers, not because they are dense but because they are still "dead in . . . transgressions and sins" (Eph. 2:1). That should motivate us to pray far more passionately than we do for those around us—and around the world—who are not Christians.

The missionary task of the church. This perspective should also challenge much of our thinking on the missionary task of the church. Were those pioneer missionaries who died within days or weeks of arriving on the mission field wasting their lives, because they saw no one converted? Are those who today labor for many years in the difficult areas of the Middle East or Japan, while seeing only a handful of converts, operating in the wrong place? If the

---

16. *Ezekiel I,* 61.

primary goal of missions is to see the world converted, then the answer to both questions is yes. But if the primary goal of missions is the same as the goal set before Ezekiel—faithfulness to the task to which one has been called, no matter what the consequences, so that God may be glorified—then the answer is different. In biblical perspective, reaching the world is only the secondary goal of missions, behind the primary goal of bringing glory to God through faithful obedience.[17]

We are, after all, followers of the Son of Man, who came to his own and his own did not receive him (John 1:11). Yet to all those who did receive him, and to all those who will receive him through our proclamation, he gives the right to become children of God (1:12). In this obedient mission, he brings glory to the Father's name (12:27–29).

In order to carry through such a ministry where there is little success in the eyes of the world, a strong sense of calling is essential. Why should we preach the gospel to those who stubbornly refuse to hear? Because God has called and sent us, and he has the right as our Sovereign King to use us as he sees fit. He is not only the One who calls us to the task and strengthens us for it; ultimately he alone is the One whom we are seeking to please. Thus, in Isaiah 49, when the Servant of the Lord struggled with the idea, "I have labored to no purpose; I have spent my strength in vain and for nothing," his reply to himself was, "Yet what is due me is in the LORD's hand, and my reward is with my God" (49:4). The Puritan William Greenhill comments:

> Sometimes God gives large encouragement, promises, hope, success, providing for our infirmities; at other times a bare commission and command must suffice to do that which would make one's heart ache: it is his prerogative to send whom he will, and upon what service he will.[18]

The role of the Spirit. Moreover, to fulfill that service we must be people of the Spirit and people of the book. Ezekiel could not even stand up without the Spirit's empowerment, yet we frequently feel able to preach sermons, counsel the struggling, comfort the dying, and equip the saints for ministry in our own strength—or at least we act as if we do. When we neglect to pray in order to get out and do, we are proclaiming a practical theology of self-reliance, whatever our theological formulations may be. It is striking that seminaries typically have few courses teaching future ministers of the gospel about prayer compared to those instructing them how to preach or how to witness. Is it any wonder, then, that we frequently turn out pastors who have

---

17. John Piper, *Let the Nations Be Glad! The Supremacy of God in Missions* (Grand Rapids: Baker, 1993), 14–15.

18. *Exposition of Ezekiel*, 79.

not learned how to wait patiently upon the Lord and to seek his Spirit's power?

Such pastors, in turn, naturally preach more sermons to their congregations on the importance of witnessing than they do on the centrality of prayer. The result is that our churches are frequently intensely busy places, but the busyness is ours, not Christ's. Christians need to remember that they are founding members of the new Spirit-filled community—or, more precisely, that Christ, the new Adam, is the founding member into whose community the Spirit builds us. This means that our greatest need is not for us to be more active but for the Spirit to be more active in and through us.

Yet that Spirit does not come to draw attention to himself. The Spirit's work is always to bring Christ to bear on a person's life (cf. John 16:15). That is why Christians are always people of the book. They are those who have ingested the Word of God in its written form, from which comes their message for the world. That is why our pastors, like the first apostles, need to be freed up from other responsibilities, such as waiting on tables (and serving on committees?), so that they can devote themselves to the ministry of the Word and to prayer (Acts 6). The world may listen—or it may not. It is the Spirit's prerogative to open and close the doors to the hearts of men and women. But wherever they go, God's people are witnesses to the truth about God, revealed in his Word and declared in the power of the Spirit.

Ezekiel 3:16–27

AT THE END of seven days the word of the LORD came to me: [17]"Son of man, I have made you a watchman for the house of Israel; so hear the word I speak and give them warning from me. [18]When I say to a wicked man, 'You will surely die,' and you do not warn him or speak out to dissuade him from his evil ways in order to save his life, that wicked man will die for his sin, and I will hold you accountable for his blood. [19]But if you do warn the wicked man and he does not turn from his wickedness or from his evil ways, he will die for his sin; but you will have saved yourself.

[20]"Again, when a righteous man turns from his righteousness and does evil, and I put a stumbling block before him, he will die. Since you did not warn him, he will die for his sin. The righteous things he did will not be remembered, and I will hold you accountable for his blood. [21]But if you do warn the righteous man not to sin and he does not sin, he will surely live because he took warning, and you will have saved yourself."

[22]The hand of the LORD was upon me there, and he said to me, "Get up and go out to the plain, and there I will speak to you." [23]So I got up and went out to the plain. And the glory of the LORD was standing there, like the glory I had seen by the Kebar River, and I fell facedown.

[24]Then the Spirit came into me and raised me to my feet. He spoke to me and said: "Go, shut yourself inside your house. [25]And you, son of man, they will tie with ropes; you will be bound so that you cannot go out among the people. [26]I will make your tongue stick to the roof of your mouth so that you will be silent and unable to rebuke them, though they are a rebellious house. [27]But when I speak to you, I will open your mouth and you shall say to them, 'This is what the Sovereign LORD says.' Whoever will listen let him listen, and whoever will refuse let him refuse; for they are a rebellious house."

Original Meaning

AT THE END of Ezekiel's seven-day waiting period (3:16), the prophet receives a further communication from God. His prophetic commissioning continues in two sections. The first outlines his responsibility as a "watchman for the house of Israel" (3:17–21), while the second unfolds further the limitations that his calling will place on him as he becomes, literally, the mouthpiece of God (3:24–27). The intervening reprise of the vision of chapter 1 in 3:22–23 ties these two sections together with the opening call vision, a link underlined by the common themes of "the hand of the LORD" (3:22; cf. 3:14), the appearance of "the glory of the LORD" (3:23; cf. 1:28), and the Spirit's setting Ezekiel on his feet.[1]

The idea of the prophet as a "watchman" is a familiar one in the Old Testament (see Isa. 56:10; Jer. 6:17; Hos. 9:8). A watchman was someone appointed as a lookout to provide the people with advance warning of the coming of an enemy so that they could run to shelter (Ezek. 33:2–3). It was the Old Testament equivalent of the Second World War's "Air Raid Warden," the person who sounded the alarm as bombers approached so that the people could flee to the safety of the shelters. In this case, the "enemy" of whom the people have to beware is none other than God himself!

By giving Ezekiel the revelation of chapter 1, where as we saw, the Lord is depicted as the divine warrior coming from the north to judge his people, Ezekiel has been shown the reality of judgment to come. That vision was not given to him for his own personal edification but in order to share it with others. His mission is a matter of life or death. To those who heed his warning of judgment, it will be a message of life; to those who refuse him, it will be a message of death. In either case, his responsibility is the same: to sound the warning note clearly so that he discharges his own obligation. Otherwise, he too will share in the judgment.

The focus of the present passage is not so much on the change that may be wrought in individuals who hear his message, but on the responsibility laid on Ezekiel to preach to all, regardless of their response. The situations proposed ("When I say to a wicked man 'You will surely die . . .'"; "When a righteous man turns from his righteousness and does evil. . .") are purely hypothetical: Ezekiel is not thereby commissioned to the pastoral care of individual souls.[2] Rather, the two classes of people, the "wicked" and the "righteous," are all-encompassing. Just as a watchman has to shout his message of danger to everyone in the city, so also Ezekiel must address his message of judgment to all, whether righteous or wicked, and whether they listen or fail

---

1. Odell, "Ezekiel and the Scroll," 231.

2. So Gerhard von Rad, *Old Testament Theology*, 2 vols. (New York: Harper, 1962, 1965), 2:231.

to listen (cf. Ezek. 2:7).[3] Thus, 3:17–21 does not expand the scope of Ezekiel's ministry beyond what is already required of him in 2:7, where the Lord told him: "You must speak my words to them, whether they listen or fail to listen, for they are rebellious." What it does is set before him clearly the consequences of any failure to fulfill his responsibilities.

For each class of hearers, righteous or wicked, there are the same two potential outcomes to Ezekiel's preaching: Either they hear and respond and live, or they ignore Ezekiel's message and perish. Those who respond faithfully to his proclamation will "live," a term describing not merely physical life but rather the fullness of relationship with the Sovereign Lord that flows from obedience.[4] Death, on the other hand, means estrangement from both God and the covenant community. To be cut off from God's people is to be "dead," even while physically still alive, for one is separated from the source of life. Indeed, cut off from the Promised Land and the temple, many of the exiles presumed themselves to be effectively "dead" (cf. 37:12).

However, in the message given to Ezekiel the wicked are not closed out from life by their present status; there is still time to hear the word of the prophet and turn and live. Similarly, the righteous cannot presume on their status. They too must listen to the word of the prophet in order to live. In other words, what marks the righteous out from the wicked, what marks out those who "live" from those who "die," is the fact that they listen to the word of the Lord through the prophet and respond to it. The wicked are wicked precisely because they do not change their ways in response to the prophetic message, whereas the righteous heed the warning and receive life.

Here again, as in chapter 2, Ezekiel himself is the model of what he prophesies. For whether he himself lives or dies depends on his "righteousness"—his faithfulness to the commission he has received. If he obeys the word of the Lord to him and proclaims his warning, then he will live. If he disobeys and fails to give a warning, then the blood of those whom he failed to warn will be required at his hand—in other words, he too will die.[5] Ezekiel's commission is thus an equivalent test for this "son of Adam" to the tree of the knowledge of good and evil for the first Adam (Gen. 2:17). Having swallowed the scroll—for unlike the first Adam, Ezekiel *is* commanded to eat—Ezekiel is able to speak God's word, which distinguishes between good and evil. If he is faithful in his submissive obedience, he will himself live and will bring the possibility of life to those who hear and obey the message that comes through him. But if he fails, he and his hearers "will surely die" (Ezek. 3:18; cf. Gen. 2:17).

---

3. Greenberg, *Ezekiel 1–20*, 95.

4. On the concepts of "life" and "death," see Walther Zimmerli, "'Leben' und 'Tod' im Buche des Propheten Ezechiel," *ThZ* 13 (1957): 494–508.

5. Compare 2 Sam. 4:11–13. See Greenberg, *Ezekiel 1–20*, 85.

The depth of the prophet's self-emptying becomes apparent in 3:24–27. Once again, he is confronted with a vision of God's glory, similar to what he saw before, in response to which he falls to the ground. When he is placed on his feet by an infusion of the divine Spirit, Ezekiel is ordered to remain confined to his house and told that he will be dumb (3:24–26). The completeness of his captivity is underlined by the three different pronouns used in verses 24–26. The prophet is told, "Go, shut *yourself* inside your house. And you, son of man, *they* will tie with ropes. . . . *I* will make your tongue stick to the roof of your mouth."[6] Had his isolation been self-inflicted, he could have ended it when he chose; had it been inflicted by others, he could perhaps have escaped. But since it is placed on him by himself, by others, and by God, there is no escape.

The nature of the prophet's isolation will be twofold: He is to be confined to his house and he will lose his power of free speech. He is God's prisoner, a situation vividly depicted by the ropes that bind him.[7] Even his tongue is God's prisoner, bound to the roof of his mouth, except when God frees it to speak his oracles.[8] His dumbness is not total; he is still able to warn of the danger to come, as he has been commissioned to do in 3:17–21. But his speech is totally restricted to the reproduction of God's words of judgment—the words of lament, warning, and woe inscribed on the scroll he has swallowed.[9]

This restriction on the prophet's speech will make him unable to function as a mediator (ʾîš môkîaḥ, 3:26; NIV, "to rebuke"; lit., "an arbitrating man") for the house of Israel.[10] He may not intercede for the people, nor may he seek the Lord on the people's behalf. The time for appeals for mercy is past; the appeals process is exhausted. The prophet's role, at least up until the fall of

---

6. Nicholas Tromp, "The Paradox of Ezekiel's Prophetic Mission: Towards a Semiotic Approach of Ezekiel 3,22–27," in *Ezekiel and His Book: Textual and Literary Criticism and Their Interrelation*, ed. J. Lust (BETL 74; Leuven: Leuven Univ. Press, 1986), 209.

7. Derek Thomas, *God Strengthens: Ezekiel Simply Explained* (Welwyn Commentary Series; Darlington: Evangelical Press, 1993), 40.

8. Commentators have disagreed over whether the dumbness allows intermittent speech at the divine command (so Greenberg, *Ezekiel 1–20*, 102) or is total until its lifting at the fall of Jerusalem, foretold in 24:27 (so Walther Zimmerli, *Ezekiel*, trans. R. E. Clements, 2 vols. [Hermeneia; Philadelphia: Fortress, 1979], 1:160). At issue is the question of whether the "when I speak to you" of 3:27 has a repetitive sense ("whenever") or a momentary sense ("at the time when"). In favor of Greenberg's view is the parallel construction in 3:18, which undeniably has an iterative sense.

9. Ellen F. Davis comments: "Ezekiel must fall 'silent' and let the scroll which he has swallowed speak through him" (*Swallowing the Scroll: Textuality and the Dynamics of Discourse in Ezekiel's Prophecy* [JSOTS 78; Sheffield: Almond, 1989], 52).

10. For the evidence for the *môkîaḥ* as an arbitrator or mediator between the two parties involved in a legal case, see Robert R. Wilson, "An Interpretation of Ezekiel's Dumbness," *VT* 22 (1972): 99–101. So also Block, *Ezekiel 1–24*, 157.

Jerusalem, is restricted to the delivery of the divine sentence of judgment: "This is what the Sovereign LORD says." Whoever has ears to hear, let them hear those words (3:27).

Bridging Contexts

WE ARE USED to thinking of the offices of priest and prophet in the neat and tidy categories of systematic theology. Thus, Louis Berkhof is expressing a widely held view when he states: "The prophet was appointed to be God's representative with the people, to be His messenger and to interpret His will. . . . The priest, on the other hand, was man's representative with God."[11]

In our society, when we think of a "prophetic figure," we think of a wild-eyed man, delivering a message from God in thundering tones regardless of how it is received. In fact, both offices normally had a two-way function. The priest, just as much as the prophet, was the interpreter and teacher of God's will, while the prophet, just as much as the priest, was the representative of the people, interceding with God on their behalf.[12] Because Ezekiel's ministry fits our preconceptions of what a prophetic ministry "ought" to look like, we may fail to see how unusually restricted he is in his prophetic calling. Further, just as not everyone is called to be a prophet, so not every prophet is called to exercise his ministry in the way Ezekiel did. That means that we will have to be careful in universalizing the principles of Ezekiel's calling.

On the other hand, the very strangeness of Ezekiel's behavior tends to make it difficult for us to bridge the gap. Not a few people have sought, if not to tie Ezekiel up with ropes, at least to place a straightjacket on him, arguing that he suffered from dangerous psychoses. Placed on the psychiatrist's couch, Ezekiel is then analyzed and diagnosed as having suffered extreme problems in his relationship with his mother, probably in addition to serious childhood sexual abuse.[13] To those without a relationship with the living God, the idea of someone giving oneself over completely to become God's slave will inevitably seem nonsensical or abhorrent, the sign of certain mental disorder.

Yet though Ezekiel's obedience required of him harder and stranger tasks than those who preceded him, his basic orientation was simply that expressed by the prophet Isaiah: "Here am I. Send me!" (Isa. 6:8). Similarly, the apostle Paul persisted in his calling to ministry to the Gentiles in spite of the catalog

---

11. *Systematic Theology*, 4th ed. (Grand Rapids: Eerdmans, 1941), 361.

12. See, for instance, Gen. 20:7, where it is the fact that Abraham is a prophet that qualifies him to intercede on Abimelech's behalf.

13. David Halperin, *Seeking Ezekiel: Text and Psychology* (State College, Pa.: Pennsylvania State Univ., Press, 1993).

of hardships he faced (2 Cor. 6:4–10) and the settled conviction from the Holy Spirit that this would always be the way of ministry for him (Acts 20:23). Though his life was dogged by "a thorn in [my] flesh" (2 Cor. 12:7), he had the confidence to pour out his life in the service of God, assured that no matter what happened to him, the gospel was not chained (2 Tim. 2:9). Such total self-sacrifice in the cause of the gospel is undoubtedly rare in our day and age and might well be considered a sign of mental imbalance by psychoanalysts, but we are all the poorer for its absence.

But why is the prophet thus constrained? On the one hand, his bonds bind him even more closely to the exiles, for whom "bondage" was a typical image of their fate (Isa. 49:9; 61:1).[14] On the other hand, it serves as a real restriction on his proclamation. He may not go where he wishes to go or speak what he wishes to speak. There is no room in his life for any spirit of independence or for any involvement with lesser tasks. He is entirely shut up to his fate as God's mouthpiece, proclaiming as a watchman the warning of impending judgment, but unable in any way to avert it.

OUR CALLING. Recently, as my wife and I were driving along the highway, we saw a hand-made road-side sign that read, "Repent, the end is nigh!" Our first thought was to wonder if there was some unseen road hazard ahead into which we were about to run! Perhaps around the corner the road simply ran off the edge of a cliff! That slogan has been so overused as the butt of jokes that it is hard, even for us as Christians, to take its message seriously. It seems old-fashioned and out of date. Nowadays, we are far more likely to say to people whom we wish to reach for Christ: "God loves you and has a wonderful plan for your life," or, "Do you know for sure that you are going to heaven when you die?" We like to focus on the "good news" aspect of the gospel.

Yet Ezekiel's calling, at least during the first part of his ministry, is to be the bringer of bad news, the news of impending judgment. The people need to know that God's patience with them is running out and the ax is about to fall. So great is God's determination to judge their sin that Ezekiel is not even allowed to act as mediator between God and Israel, seeking to bring the two parties together. Though it may have seemed for generations that God's mercy and his love towards Israel was such that he would never judge them, now that the sentence has been pronounced it will fall so swiftly and terribly that it may seem as if God will never again be merciful. Ezekiel would cer-

---

14. Odell, "Ezekiel and the Scroll," 245.

tainly have agreed with the writer to the Hebrews when he wrote, "It is a dreadful thing to fall into the hands of the living God" (Heb. 10:31). In order that the people may know that this is not just a random event but the bringing of the covenant curses on his rebellious people, God calls Ezekiel to be his prophet and to act as watchman for the people.

We said above that not all are called to fulfill the distinctive kind of prophetic ministry to which Ezekiel was called; yet as Christians, we too have a calling from God. According to Paul, we share in the work of reconciliation that God is doing in the world: "We are therefore Christ's ambassadors, as though God were making his appeal through us" (2 Cor. 5:20). We are God's messengers, just as the Old Testament prophets were, taking God's Word to the world. The Spirit of God that inspired the prophets now indwells us; only instead of swallowing a scroll, as Ezekiel did, we imbibe a book, the Bible, through whose pages God continues to speak to his people and to the world. This is the message we have been given to communicate and to which we are confined. Though we may be creative in the way we communicate the message, we are not free to be creative in the content of the message that we are to deliver.

God's message to the world. God's message to the world contains both good news and bad news. Naturally, we prefer to tell people good news. After all, which job would you prefer: to be the one who goes around telling people they have won millions in the lottery, or the bailiff who goes around telling the bankrupt person he is here to take away one's possessions?

The first challenge that this passage presents to you and me, then, is to present a balanced picture of who God is and who we are in relation to God. We must tell people that by nature, we are in rebellion against God and objects of his wrath (Eph. 2:3); we are darkened in our minds, separated from the life of God and hardened in our hearts (4:18), sinners deserving eternal death (Rom. 6:23). Indeed, the bad news of the Bible is far worse than the average person believes. Forget the problems of global warming and the world economy; left to ourselves we face the certainty of eternal judgment. The bailiff is at the door, waiting to strip God's rebellious subjects of even the few possessions they have and drive the unrepentant out into outer darkness.

But the good news of the gospel is also far better than the average person believes. Some churches have spent so much time proclaiming hellfire and damnation that they never got around to the positive message of the gospel. God loved the world so much that he stepped into the midst of our rebellion to bring about reconciliation. By his great love and rich mercy, he has intervened on our behalf in Jesus Christ, transferring us out of the family of the evil one and into the family of God. Jesus went to the cross to make our bad news his, and the good news concerning him ours. Through his death he not only paid off the debts that would have forced our bankruptcy, but he also endowed us with all spiritual riches through his perfect life. The gospel is thus both good news and bad news for the world, and we are called to proclaim both clearly.

We are also called to bring the news to everyone, without distinction. Ezekiel was not to seek out a congenial audience of the righteous, who might be expected to give his message a fair hearing. He was to proclaim it to righteous and wicked alike and to let God sort them out. The watchman must proclaim his message to everyone, without distinction. Like the sower in the parable of the soils (Matt. 13:1–23), Ezekiel was to scatter his seed all over the field.

Here too there is a challenge to you and me. We tend to sort our friends and family into "likely prospects" and "hard cases," focusing our efforts on those who we think are most likely to listen. But who are you to say that one person is more likely to listen than another? The Bible is full of "hard cases" who have come to faith in Christ, like the apostle Paul, formerly the great persecutor of the church. Equally, it records the cases of those who are "not far from the kingdom," like the rich young ruler (Matt. 19:16–22), who turn and walk away. Thus, our calling as watchmen is not to engage in endless soil analysis so that we can deliver the gospel with pinpoint accuracy to those who we think are ready to receive it. Rather, we are to be faithful shouters of the Word, proclaiming the good news and bad news faithfully into the lives of all those around us.

Suggestions for ministry in our day. To my mind this is one of the advantages of what may be considered the rather old-fashioned practice of taking the gospel from door-to-door in the neighborhood of the church. Almost no other form of witnessing enables you to meet such a complete cross section of the community who live next door to you. Not everyone, of course, will appreciate your efforts: To those being saved the gospel is the aroma of life, while to those who are perishing it is the stench of death (2 Cor. 2:15–16). The four kinds of soil that receive the seed in the parable of the sower display the differences of their nature by their responses. The result of the sower's sowing is not that the whole field bursts into fruitfulness, but that the good soil bears fruit. As with Ezekiel, some will hear your message gladly and turn and live; others will fail to hear your message and consequently will die. But at least they will never be able to claim that no one loved them enough to tell them about Jesus.

For the preacher, this kind of door-to-door witness has the added advantage of bringing you face-to-face with real people and their real objections to the gospel. In consequence, if you are willing to listen to what these men and women tell you of their struggles, you will not be so likely to waste your sermons answering objections with which no one wrestles. Instead, you will have a store of real-life questions to answer from the Scriptures in a way that rings true to people in the pew, who are frequently far more in tune with their non-Christian neighbors than their pastors are.

The perseverance of the saints. Moreover, the good soil continues to bear fruit. The distinction between the righteous and wicked, between good soil and bad soil, is not a matter of past history but of inward response to the Word. It doesn't make any difference whether you have lived a notorious life of sin or have been a pillar of the Sunday school all your days; what counts to God is your response to his Word. Do you receive the gospel, turning away from your sins and trusting in what Jesus has done for you on the cross as your only hope in life and death? Do you accept fully the bad news, that you are indeed a sinner, by nature a rebel against God, deserving of eternal judgment? Do you delight in God's righteousness and holiness, which is too pure to coexist with sin? Do you see the good news of the gospel not only as a good idea in general, but personally good news for you? Is your present trust not in any goodness of your own, but solely in the righteous life and atoning death of Jesus as your substitute? That is the key test of whether you are a Christian.

Nor can we make premature assessments of where others stand. It is possible for the seemingly righteous to fall and the defiantly wicked to repent, just as it is possible for the seed that sprang up quickly to wither through the absence of depth of soil or being choked by thorns. In high school, I helped lead a Christian club with two other young men, both of whom seemed at the time far more committed in their love for the Lord than I. One of them is now a pillar in his church, still passionately devoted to following the Lord; the other has not, to my knowledge, darkened the door of a church in years. To be righteous in the Old Testament means to be in right relationship with God; this is not something that can be stored up for a rainy day, but must be a constantly renewed reality.[15] Thus the biblical doctrine of the perseverance of the saints is not a kind of cosmic ski lift, which once you are seated carries you all the way to your destination without effort. Rather, it is the truth that those who are indeed saints will actually persevere.

God's preservation of the saints. The reverse side of that doctrine is its partner, the preservation of the saints. This encourages believers that what counts in our persevering is not our weak grip on our heavenly Father, but his strong grasp on us. This twofold combination of human responsibility and divine assurance is brought out clearly in 2 Timothy 2:19. There Paul, having mentioned the apostasy of Hymenaeus and Philetus, concludes: "God's

---

15. Maurice E. Andrew, *Responsibility and Restoration: The Course of the Book of Ezekiel* (Dunedin: Univ. of Otago Press, 1985), 26.

solid foundation stands firm, sealed with this inscription: 'The Lord knows those who are his,' and, 'Everyone who confesses the name of the Lord must turn away from wickedness.'" So the saints are those who persevere to the end, but they do so because of God's preservation.

This is good news for the weak sinners that we are. As I write this, I am shortly to go to a church where I will meet with an elder, a man I love and respect, who has abandoned his family and gone off with another woman. He knows that what he has done is wrong, but does not seem to know whether it can be put right. The good news of the preservation of the saints is that even those who have made shipwreck of their faith can be rescued and brought safely home to their heavenly Father. The Lord knows those who are his, and even in their attempts to flee from him, they cannot escape his loving embrace. I hope to be able to tell this man that those whom God loves, he will not let go.

But to be such a channel of God's good and bad news is often a costly, self-denying business. If you say to God, "Here am I, send me," frequently he will! Sometimes, God sends his children to be his witnesses in uncomfortable situations—whether halfway around the world, to preach to villagers in Irian Jaya, or round the corner, to speak God's word in the jungles of corporate America. Such total yieldedness to God will often be regarded as certifiably foolish, or perhaps even worse, by a world that does not know God, especially when there seems little fruit to show for the sacrifice. But who is really the one being unwise? Jim Elliot, who met his death at the hands of the Auca Indians with whom he had planned to share the gospel, once wrote in his journal: "He is no fool who gives up what he cannot keep to gain that which he cannot lose."[16]

Our example in all of this is the self-sacrifice of Jesus Christ. Was Ezekiel confined to his house? Jesus was "despised and rejected by men, a man of sorrows, and familiar with suffering" (Isa. 53:3). Was Ezekiel made dumb? Jesus was "led like a lamb to the slaughter, and as a sheep before her shearers is silent, so he did not open his mouth" (Isa. 53:7). Was Ezekiel bound with ropes? Jesus was nailed to the cross and suffered there not for any transgressions of his own but for ours. The shackles of death designed for our wrists were placed on his. Thus has the greater "Son of Man" fulfilled the ministry of the earlier "son of man," giving us the good news of the gospel, which is the antidote to the bad news of our natural state. What price, then, can be too great for us to play our part in the great work of the triune God, bringing to himself a harvest of men and women from every tribe, nation, and language group, that they too might receive eternal life in Christ Jesus?

---

16. *The Journals of Jim Elliot* (Old Tappan, N.J.: Revell, 1978), 174.

Ezekiel 4

❧

NOW, SON OF MAN, take a clay tablet, put it in front of you and draw the city of Jerusalem on it. ²Then lay siege to it: Erect siege works against it, build a ramp up to it, set up camps against it and put battering rams around it. ³Then take an iron pan, place it as an iron wall between you and the city and turn your face toward it. It will be under siege, and you shall besiege it. This will be a sign to the house of Israel.

⁴"Then lie on your left side and put the sin of the house of Israel upon yourself. You are to bear their sin for the number of days you lie on your side. ⁵I have assigned you the same number of days as the years of their sin. So for 390 days you will bear the sin of the house of Israel.

⁶"After you have finished this, lie down again, this time on your right side, and bear the sin of the house of Judah. I have assigned you 40 days, a day for each year. ⁷Turn your face toward the siege of Jerusalem and with bared arm prophesy against her. ⁸I will tie you up with ropes so that you cannot turn from one side to the other until you have finished the days of your siege.

⁹"Take wheat and barley, beans and lentils, millet and spelt; put them in a storage jar and use them to make bread for yourself. You are to eat it during the 390 days you lie on your side. ¹⁰Weigh out twenty shekels of food to eat each day and eat it at set times. ¹¹Also measure out a sixth of a hin of water and drink it at set times. ¹²Eat the food as you would a barley cake; bake it in the sight of the people, using human excrement for fuel." ¹³The LORD said, "In this way the people of Israel will eat defiled food among the nations where I will drive them."

¹⁴Then I said, "Not so, Sovereign LORD! I have never defiled myself. From my youth until now I have never eaten anything found dead or torn by wild animals. No unclean meat has ever entered my mouth."

¹⁵"Very well," he said, "I will let you bake your bread over cow manure instead of human excrement."

¹⁶He then said to me: "Son of man, I will cut off the supply of food in Jerusalem. The people will eat rationed food in anxiety and drink rationed water in despair, ¹⁷for food and water will be scarce. They will be appalled at the sight of each other and will waste away because of their sin.

IN EZEKIEL 1–3, we saw how the prophet was called and commissioned to bring a message to his people. There were hints throughout that the message, when it came, would not be good news. The Lord appeared in the form of the divine warrior, ready to deliver judgment, and he came from the north, like Israel's traditional enemies. In the face of this impending danger, Ezekiel was appointed as a watchman, to cry out a warning of the wrath to come. But just how bad is the bad news? The full extent of the bad news begins to become clear in the first message Ezekiel is given to deliver to the exiles (chs. 4–5), which is made up of a series of related symbolic actions, or "sign-acts," along with their explanation.

The first of Ezekiel's sign-acts symbolizes the siege of the city of Jerusalem and the reason for it. He is to take a clay brick (perhaps the size of one or two sheets of standard 8-1/2" x 11" paper),[1] and draw on it a map or picture of Jerusalem. Having created this visual model, he was to "lay siege to it" (4:1–2). The extent of the depiction of the siege with its accompanying siege works, ramps, army camps, and battering rams seems to have a deliberate element of overkill in it; clearly this was no halfhearted effort but the extension of the entire might of the Babylonian army to crush errant Jerusalem.

Yet something more is at work in the onslaught than Babylonian imperialism. In Ezekiel's depiction, the invisible aggressor who stands behind the Babylonians becomes visible. Acting the part of the Lord, Ezekiel is to set up a large iron plate between himself and the city (4:3), symbolizing the cutting off of relationships between God and his people. There is now no channel by which the people can communicate with God, even if they wanted to do so.[2]

In the previous chapter, the prophet had been told that he would not be able to act as an intercessor for the people; the appeals process had been exhausted. This is now visually depicted. The prophet is told to "turn [his] face toward" Jerusalem (4:3), adopting an implacable attitude toward it. The iron wall and Ezekiel's expression communicate God's abandonment of the city (cf. chs. 8–11), and the dual agency of destruction (human and divine) emerges in 4:3: "It will be under siege, and you shall besiege it." The catastrophe will not simply be an event of human history ("It will be under siege") but specifically the result of direct divine action ("You [i.e., the prophet, representing the Lord] shall besiege it"). By his pantomime, Ezekiel is to make the invisible aggressor visible.

---

1. According to Kurt Galling, ancient Near Eastern bricks had dimensions ranging from 6" to 13-1/2" wide and 10" to 24" long ("Ziegel," *Biblisches Reallexikon*, ed. K. Galling, 2d ed. [Tübingen: J.C.B. Mohr, 1977], 364).

2. Compare the comments on Ezekiel's dumbness above.

At this point the sign changes to a new, though related figure, in which the prophet shifts into the role of siege victim. This sign-act is more complex than the previous one, not so much in terms of the act described, which is straightforward enough,[3] but of interpretation. The prophet is instructed to lie first on his left side for 390 days, "bear[ing] the sin [*tiśśāʾ-ʾet-ʿăwōnām*] of the house of Israel," then to lie on his right side for forty days, "bear[ing] the sin of the house of Judah" (4:4–6). While in a prone position, he is to continue to prophesy against Jerusalem (4:7), and he is to subsist on siege rations (4:9–17). The latter is a near-starvation diet, a mere eight ounces per day of an unpalatable mixture of grains and legumes, along with two-thirds quart of water (4:9–11). According to Moshe Greenberg, the strange mixture symbolizes a situation where the scarcity was such that no one kind of grain was plentiful enough on its own to make a whole loaf. He also records an interesting experiment carried out in the third century A.D. that apparently demonstrated that even a dog would not eat Ezekiel's bread![4]

Not only were the rations small and unappetizing, Ezekiel was further instructed (at first) to prepare them by baking them over human excrement, a way that would have rendered him ceremonially unclean—representing the unclean food that the Israelites would eat in exile. This would be particularly abhorrent to a priest like Ezekiel. However, in response to Ezekiel's protest, the Lord permitted the prophet to substitute animal dung as the fuel.

What are we to make of this strange activity? There are several interconnected exegetical difficulties here. (1) Who is intended by "the house of Israel" and the "house of Judah"? In the context of the remainder of the Old Testament, one thinks immediately of the northern and southern kingdoms of Israel and Judah, which split apart during the reign of Rehoboam.[5] Is that their meaning here? (2) What does it mean for the prophet to "bear their sin" (*nāśāʾ ʿăwōnām*)? This can mean either "bear their guilt"—as the priests were said to "bear the iniquity" of Israel and thus atone for them (cf. Ex. 28:38; Lev. 10:17)—or it can mean "undergo punishment" (as in Num. 14:33, where Israel must "suffer for [their] unfaithfulness" [lit., "bear your punishment"]

---

3. At least to understand, though not to perform! For this reason, many older interpreters viewed it as a purely visionary action that was never actually performed (e.g., Calvin, *Ezekiel 1*, 116; Skinner, *Ezekiel*, 65; Patrick Fairbairn, *An Exposition of Ezekiel* [Grand Rapids: Sovereign Grace, 1971 reprint], 25). More recent commentators, stressing the public nature of sign-acts, tend to play down the difficulty by imagining the prophet as performing it on a part-time basis (e.g., Taylor, *Ezekiel*, 81; Allen, *Ezekiel 1–19*, 67; Kelvin G. Friebel, *Jeremiah's and Ezekiel's Sign-Acts: Their Meaning and Function As Nonverbal Communication and Rhetoric* [Ph.D. diss.; Madison: Univ. of Wisconsin, 1989], 546).

4. *Ezekiel 1–20*, 106.

5. This is perhaps what explains the reading of 190 years instead of 390 years found in the LXX. See Zimmerli, *Ezekiel*, 1:167.

for forty years). (3) Finally, what is the significance of the time periods, 390 days and forty days respectively, which are said to represent periods of years?

In answer to the first question, though Ezekiel can speak of the northern and southern kingdoms in terms of "Israel" and "Judah" (see, e.g., Ezek. 37), this is not his normal practice. Moreover, if we adopt this approach, we run into insuperable difficulties when we attempt to interpret the time periods.[6] Rather, for Ezekiel the "house of Israel" is the whole covenant people of God, and their sins are centered in the Jerusalem temple, the heart of the southern kingdom. Their 390-year history of sin, pictured by the prophet's 390-day prostration on his left side, stretches back in time to around the construction of the first temple.[7] Likewise, the "house of Judah" appears here to be a designation for the community of the exiles in Ezekiel.[8]

When we combine this approach with the dual significance of the phrase "bear their sin," the following interpretation emerges: Ezekiel is to lie on his left side for 390 days, representing 390 years, bearing the guilt of the entire covenant community of Israel. The iniquity of the community is placed on him (4:4). During this period he symbolizes Israel's long history of accumulated sin, which culminates in the siege and fall of Jerusalem, concretely depicted by eating siege rations throughout the 390 days (4:9). Then during the period of forty days, he represents the punishment of the Exile, which he depicts in terms of the symbolic figure of forty years.[9] Just as Israel's ancestors in the desert were a lost generation, spending forty years in the desert for their sin (Num. 14:34), so the exilic generation is condemned to a similar fate for the nation's long history of sin.[10]

It is clear that Ezekiel's "bearing sin" for the people has no substitutionary purpose. The siege and destruction of Jerusalem are not averted by his sufferings. Thus, throughout his period of prostration he is to continue prophesying against Jerusalem with bared forearm and set face (Ezek. 4:7). The purpose of his action is to illustrate the accumulation of the people's sin rather than to be effective in removing that sin. In this respect, his action is comparable to the whole Old Testament sacrificial system, which, according to the writer to the Hebrews, could not effectively remove sin (Heb. 10:1–11), but rather served as "an illustration for the present time" (9:9). By this means, Ezekiel is to communicate graphically to the people the weight of the accumulated burden of their history of sin as the cause for the impending con-

---

6. For an example, see Greenberg, *Ezekiel 1–20*, 105.

7. The exact dates are variously rendered, depending on whether you start from the exile of 598 B.C. or that of 586 B.C.; however, the import is clear.

8. Cf. Ezek. 25:3; see Allen, *Ezekiel 1–19*, 68.

9. Compare the same period predicted for the exile of the Egyptians in Ezek. 29:12–13.

10. Compare the similar ideas expressed in Ezek. 20:35–36.

flagration of Jerusalem and the exile of the people in a land not their own. The punishment for that sin is coming upon them with full force, no matter what the optimistic false prophets may be saying (Jer. 6:14; 8:11).

But, as with the opening vision, at the end of the judgment a glimmer of hope surfaces. Though the tunnel may be long and dark, there is a tiny light at its end. For the total number of days of the sign-act is 430, a number that parallels Israel's years of sojourn in Egypt (Ex. 12:40). Judgment must come, a judgment that effectively wipes out the entire present generation, just as the desert generation was wiped out. Yet by depicting the total period of sin and judgment in terms of a renewed Egyptian bondage, the prophet invites the hope, even the certainty, that at the end of the appointed time of punishment there will be a new exodus and a new entry into the land.[11] Forty years may be a long time— a lifetime—for Ezekiel's hearers. But God's abandonment of his people is not forever. The rainbow continues to shine through the gathering gloom.

Ezekiel's diet during this period has a twofold aspect: As indicated above, the rations are small and poor quality, symbolizing the siege diet of the people of Jerusalem. Moreover, Ezekiel is instructed to cook them in a ceremonially unclean way, symbolizing the defiled food that the Israelites will eat in exile (Ezek. 4:13). By this means, the twofold message of judgment is proclaimed on all Israel, both those who remain in Jerusalem and those who are in exile. Yet another aspect emerges, however, as the prophet protests the divine decree in verse 14. Ezekiel asserts that he has never consumed anything defiled, and the decree is promptly emended by the Lord to allow the prophet to maintain his ceremonial purity. Ezekiel thus stands as a picture of a righteous remnant: Though he is in exile, living among the nations just as the people of Israel will do, he nonetheless has managed to maintain his purity. Though the majority of the people may eat defiled food, through the grace of God and their commitment to him others will not.

Bridging Contexts

SIGN-ACTS OF the prophets. One of the great difficulties for the contemporary reader of Ezekiel is the outlandish nature of his behavior. We are uncomfortable with extreme commitments to religious beliefs, identifying those as typical of the "cults." If one of our relatives were to behave similarly to Ezekiel under the influence of his or her religious beliefs, we would probably seek some means of "deprogramming" that person. The recent mass suicide of about thirty members of the "Heaven's Gate" cult, who believed that there was an alien space ship concealed behind the

---

11. Stuart, *Ezekiel*, 58.

Hale-Bopp comet waiting to take them up to "the next level," illustrates the presence of such cults within our society. But the problem with the Heaven's Gate cult was not, as many seem to suppose, the irrationality of their belief that there is something more to existence than this life. Rather, the problem was that what they believed was not true.

Of course, we should not make the mistake of thinking that Ezekiel's behavior was considered normal in his society either. By their standards too, his behavior was distinctly odd. But, unlike us, they would not have found it hard to believe that someone should be so taken up by the message he had received from God that it became the sole determining reality in his life. "Sign-acts" were a regular part of the way prophets went about their business.

Many of the prophets were instructed by God to perform dramatic actions to accompany their verbal messages. These ranged in content from simple sermon illustrations, such as when Jeremiah publicly smashed a clay jar to depict the coming destruction of Jerusalem (Jer. 19:1–13), to more complex acted-out parables, such as when the unnamed man of God pretended to be a soldier who had abused his trust by failing to guard a prisoner committed to his care (1 Kings 20:35–43).

It has been pointed out that there are basically two possible motivations for such actions: the belief that they have an influence on future events through the process of "sympathetic magic,"[12] and the desire to provide a dramatic visual aid to increase the impact of the message.[13] These are, of course, not mutually exclusive motivations. However, since the words of the true prophet were nothing less than the word of the Lord and thus certain of coming true (Deut. 18:22), it is not clear how symbolic actions could have been perceived as having any greater power on events than the prophet's word.

Moreover, the essentially public nature of the symbolic acts of the prophets (whether that public was the general populace or a select group of disciples),[14] along with the importance attached to an interpretation of the sign-act, suggest that the second motivation was more significant. "Sympathetic magic" would do its work *ex opere operato*, regardless of the presence or

---

12. The process by which significant actions in the present can create the future by "pre-enacting" it. An example would be the voodoo practice of sticking pins into a model of a person in the belief that thereby real hurt will be caused to the person concerned.

13. For the former see von Rad, *Old Testament Theology*, 2:96–97; Zimmerli, *Ezekiel*, 1:156; for the latter, Bernhard Lang, "Street Theater, Raising the Dead, and the Zoroastrian Connection in Ezekiel's Prophecy," in *Ezekiel and His Book*, 305.

14. W. David Stacey has objected that many of the prophetic sign-acts took place in private; for instance, Ezekiel's eating of the scroll (*Prophetic Drama in the Old Testament* [London: Epworth, 1990], 265). However, the public recounting of the sign-act performed in private immediately makes it a public act.

absence of an audience, but communication only takes place where an audience is present. Word and action support one another to create effective communication. As Leslie Allen comments: "If actions speak louder than words, here they were a megaphone for the prophetic words."[15]

The language of "visual aid" is altogether too weak, however. Ezekiel's sign-acts are not diagrams on overhead projector slides with which he helps the slow-witted capture a difficult theological idea. They are "affective aids," aimed not at people's eyes but at their hearts and wills, the seat of their "affections."[16] They are designed not merely to help people *see* the truth, but to *feel* the truth. In the same way as the sacraments are not merely visual aids to the gospel but are "signs and seals of the covenant of grace,"[17] so also the sign-acts are given not so much to clarify the message of the prophet as to drive it home to the people's hearts.

Ezekiel's communication style. Why, though, should the presence of sign-acts be "particularly characteristic of Ezekiel"?[18] Why, out of all the prophets, should he have been required to act out his message so frequently? Perhaps it is due to the especially difficult communication task that faced this prophet. Up until the fall of Jerusalem, he had to preach a message of that city's destruction to a people who believed it inviolable; after its fall, he had to communicate a vision of hope to a people tempted to despair. To a people well supplied with prophets telling them what they wanted to hear, Ezekiel had to say what God wanted them to hear, a task likened to being surrounded by briers and thorns and sitting on scorpions (2:6).

To get his message across, Ezekiel adopted some extreme measures at the Lord's command, including the performance of an unusually large number of sign-acts, which not only reinforced the content of his message but also underlined the extent of his self-commitment to the message.[19] One might think of similarities to the Civil Rights movement in the 1960s in the United States. Speeches were all very well, but dramatic actions such as boycotting the buses or breaking the rules against eating at "all-white" lunch counters had more impact on the unconverted. They were much harder to ignore.

Ezekiel's communication style was as unique as his situation. He had swallowed the word of God, and now that message "took flesh" before the eyes of the exiles in the visible form of the acted-out scene of judgment on

---

15. *Ezekiel 1–19*, 66.

16. For this use of "affections," see Jonathan Edwards, *A Treatise on the Religious Affections* (Carlisle, Pa.: Banner of Truth, 1986 reprint), 25.

17. Westminster Confession of Faith, 27.1

18. So Zimmerli, *Ezekiel*, 1:28.

19. See Lang's comments on the ability of sign-acts to gain a hearing for a potentially unpopular message ("Street Theater," 301).

Jerusalem. No one could doubt his commitment to communicate that message, even though it would fall on deaf ears. The form of communication was ideal for a potentially hostile audience: a graphic, "in-your-face" message that would not easily be forgotten.

VISUAL AIDS FOR the contemporary church. How do we communicate the message of God's wrath to a lost and dying world, a message that sinners would much rather suppress than hear? How, in our day and age, do we "make the invisible aggressor visible," as Ezekiel was called to do? In the past, people used vivid word pictures. Older preachers worked to portray in technicolor vocabulary and dramatic word pictures the pains of hell and the horror of sinners swept away unheedingly into the awful void. Thus, George Whitefield once depicted the sinner as being like an aged and blind beggar. This old man was being led by a little dog on a leash and was feeling his way along by tapping the ground in front of him with a cane. Gradually and unwittingly, he approached a yawning chasm; as he got nearer it, he first lost the dog's leash, then dropped his cane, and as he stepped forward to retrieve it his foot found only empty air. At that point in the depiction, we are told that Lord Chesterfield leapt to his feet shouting out, "He's gone! He's gone!"[20] In this case, the message had been effectively communicated.

But word pictures have their limitations in an increasingly visual age. The impact of television and video technology has transformed our time from a "word-centered" to an "image-centered" society.[21] In such a visual age, many churches are experimenting with the use of drama and other visual aids in their worship services in a desire to communicate to modern people. Frequently, the prophetic sign-acts are cited as biblical justification for this approach. Is this a justified comparison?

Certainly, there are points of contact. Well-executed drama has an affective function, touching emotions not easily reached by words while stimulating and holding interest.[22] It communicates to an indifferent audience more powerfully than words alone, which is why drama is particularly valued by "seeker-sensitive churches." Yet we should not fail to see the differences between the prophetic sign-acts and contemporary dramas. The prophetic sign-acts were more than mere visual aids or attention-getting

---

20. Arnold Dallimore, *The Life of George Whitefield* (Westchester, Ill.: Cornerstone, 1980), 2:388.

21. Neil Postman, *Amusing Ourselves to Death* (New York: Viking Penguin, 1985), 8.

22. H. David Schuringa, *Hearing the Word in a Visual Age* (Ph.D. diss., Kampen, 1995), 220–32.

devices. They were delivered with divine authority and thus functioned as the divine word made visible and sure. In Ezekiel's case, the message took over the messenger in a life-dominating way.

The ultimate sign-act. The real significance of the prophetic sign-acts emerges when we ask the question, "How did *God* communicate his wrath and his love to a lost and dying world?" He did so through the ultimate prophetic sign-act of the Incarnation, whereby the Word became flesh and dwelt among us, not to act out a ten-minute dramatic sketch but to live in our midst for thirty-three years. God did not merely put on human costume, he became a human being. The culmination of Jesus' earthly ministry was the profound sign-act of the cross, where God's wrath and mercy met. There that wrath was visibly depicted as the Sinless One was abandoned by God the Father. Just as Jerusalem was once abandoned by God because of her sins, so also Jesus was abandoned by God because of his people's sins. Jesus was not playacting when he cried out, "My God, my God, why have you forsaken me?" (Matt. 27:46).

Unlike Ezekiel, however, Jesus was genuinely doing away with the accumulated guilt of his people as their substitute, which meant enduring the turning away of the Father's face. No wonder the sky grew dark and the earth shook! There on the cross was also depicted the love of God, whose passion for sinners was such that he would rather die than let them go. In the words we know so well that we frequently forget their awesome profundity, "God so loved the world, that he gave his only begotten Son, that whosoever believeth in him should not perish, but have everlasting life" (John 3:16, KJV).

The cross is an "in-your-face" message of God's love and his wrath, his justice and his grace. That is why the message of the crucified Christ is a stumbling block and foolishness to many (1 Cor. 1:23). It refuses to trivialize sin, insisting that only the death of the Son of God was sufficient to atone for it. It refuses to compromise with our cozy delusions of adequacy, whereby we fondly imagine that our best efforts will be enough to satisfy the demands of God's holy law. It refuses to flatter our religious pride that demands a complicated scheme of salvation that allows us to earn our way to heaven.

Moreover, in the sacraments we perform dramatic reenactments of God's once-and-for-all sign-act. We are baptized into his death, visibly passing through the waters—a sign that assures us that if by faith we are crucified with Christ and if his death was for our sin, then we will certainly also be raised with him. We receive the broken bread, just as his body was broken for us, and the poured out wine, just as his blood was poured out for us, which remind and assure us that the efficacious sacrifice was made for us personally.[23] In liturgical

---

23. Dan G. McCartney, *Why Does It Have to Hurt? The Meaning of Christian Suffering* (Phillipsburg, N.J.: Presbyterian and Reformed, 1998), 60.

churches, this personal aspect of the Lord's Supper is underlined by the repetition of the sentence, "The body of Christ broken for you; the blood of Christ shed for you." These sacraments are given not simply to feed our senses, as if the preached word by itself were insufficient; rather, they are given to minister to our affections, to drive home to our hearts the reality of our salvation in Christ, the message that has been preached to us.

In but not of the world. But the cross is not simply something that has been borne for us, it is also something that we are called on to bear (Matt. 10:38). God's "wonderful plan for your life" may easily involve suffering or even martyrdom for the sake of Jesus. Like Ezekiel, we are to be totally taken up by the message with which we have been entrusted. Many people will find our behavior odd in consequence, as we seek to remain pure in a world that is not our home. We are called to be "Puritans" in the best sense of the word, living in a compromised world as those whose lives are uncompromisingly committed to obedience to God's Word and "perfecting holiness out of reverence for God" (2 Cor. 7:1). Our very lives are letters to the world from Christ, inscribed by his Spirit (3:3).

At the same time as our lives may be too pure for the taste of those outside the kingdom, we are not to be so separate from sinners in our desire for holiness that we fail to share the gospel with them. In the New Testament, the apostle Peter had a similar vision to Ezekiel's, in which he too was commanded to eat unclean food (Acts 10:13). His response echoed that of Ezekiel: "Surely not, Lord! . . . I have never eaten anything impure or unclean" (10:14). But unlike Ezekiel, he is instructed not to call impure that which God has made clean (10:15). This vision, so important to the book of Acts that it is related three times,[24] forms the theological basis for the mission to the Gentiles. The old laws of cleanliness, with their emphasis on separation from that which was unclean, had now been transformed on the basis of the new revelation in Jesus. As a result, the doors of the kingdom are now thrown open to "unclean sinners" and Gentiles alike, through faith in Christ.

In obedience to this vision, we are not to build walls to keep the prostitute and the drug addict out of our churches, nor are we to treat those who come into the kingdom with a checkered sexual or marital history as second-class citizens. These too, if they have washed their robes in the blood of the Lamb, are declared by God as clean (cf. 1 Cor. 6:11). Like Jesus and Ezekiel, we are called to lives of identified purity, living in the world but not of it, loving every one of our neighbors even while living radically different lives from them.

---

24. Twice in full (Acts 10:10–16; 11:5–10) and once in summary 15:7–9 (I. Howard Marshall, *Acts* [TNTC; Grand Rapids: Eerdmans, 1980], 181).

Ezekiel 5

N OW, SON OF MAN, take a sharp sword and use it as a barber's razor to shave your head and your beard. Then take a set of scales and divide up the hair. ²When the days of your siege come to an end, burn a third of the hair with fire inside the city. Take a third and strike it with the sword all around the city. And scatter a third to the wind. For I will pursue them with drawn sword. ³But take a few strands of hair and tuck them away in the folds of your garment. ⁴Again, take a few of these and throw them into the fire and burn them up. A fire will spread from there to the whole house of Israel.

⁵"This is what the Sovereign LORD says: This is Jerusalem, which I have set in the center of the nations, with countries all around her. ⁶Yet in her wickedness she has rebelled against my laws and decrees more than the nations and countries around her. She has rejected my laws and has not followed my decrees.

⁷"Therefore this is what the Sovereign LORD says: You have been more unruly than the nations around you and have not followed my decrees or kept my laws. You have not even conformed to the standards of the nations around you.

⁸"Therefore this is what the Sovereign LORD says: I myself am against you, Jerusalem, and I will inflict punishment on you in the sight of the nations. ⁹Because of all your detestable idols, I will do to you what I have never done before and will never do again. ¹⁰Therefore in your midst fathers will eat their children, and children will eat their fathers. I will inflict punishment on you and will scatter all your survivors to the winds. ¹¹Therefore as surely as I live, declares the Sovereign LORD, because you have defiled my sanctuary with all your vile images and detestable practices, I myself will withdraw my favor; I will not look on you with pity or spare you. ¹²A third of your people will die of the plague or perish by famine inside you; a third will fall by the sword outside your walls; and a third I will scatter to the winds and pursue with drawn sword.

¹³"Then my anger will cease and my wrath against them will subside, and I will be avenged. And when I have spent my

wrath upon them, they will know that I the LORD have spoken in my zeal.

¹⁴"I will make you a ruin and a reproach among the nations around you, in the sight of all who pass by. ¹⁵You will be a reproach and a taunt, a warning and an object of horror to the nations around you when I inflict punishment on you in anger and in wrath and with stinging rebuke. I the LORD have spoken. ¹⁶When I shoot at you with my deadly and destructive arrows of famine, I will shoot to destroy you. I will bring more and more famine upon you and cut off your supply of food. ¹⁷I will send famine and wild beasts against you, and they will leave you childless. Plague and bloodshed will sweep through you, and I will bring the sword against you. I the LORD have spoken."

THE IMAGE OF RELENTLESS judgment that we saw in Ezekiel 4 reemerges at the beginning of chapter 5. Here Ezekiel is called upon to shave his head and his beard, a sign of humiliation (cf. 2 Sam. 10:4). The instrument of this humiliation is described as both a "sharp sword" and a "barber's razor" (*ta'ar haggallābîm*). The first term serves to link this image with what precedes and what follows, underlining the military nature of the coming disaster, while the latter term shows that what God calls Ezekiel to do is to act out in concrete form the imagery of Isaiah 7:20. In that passage, the prophet spoke of the Lord hiring a razor (*ta'ar*) from beyond the river (i.e., from the region on the east of the Euphrates) to shave the head, beard, and feet of Israel. Here Ezekiel records the arrival of the razor to do its work on the prophet, representing the people.

The prophet's hair itself becomes the medium for the last sign-act of the prophet in this sequence. Using a set of scales, he is to divide it carefully into three parts, representing the different fates that will meet the inhabitants of Jerusalem (Ezek. 5:2–4). God's judgment is not delivered in a haphazard fashion but is meticulously measured.[1] Some of the hair is to be burned with fire, symbolizing those who die in the city; some he is to strike with the sword all around the city, symbolizing those who die outside the city; the remainder he is to scatter to the winds, symbolizing those in exile. A few of this last group he is to gather up and store in the apparent safety of a fold of his garment, which acted like a pocket. But even there they are not free from

---

1. Block, *Ezekiel 1–24*, 193.

danger, for he is to take some of those hairs from their refuge and throw them back into the fire.

The interpretation of these last two signs is given in Ezekiel 5:5–17. The thoroughness of the devastation needs little clarification; that much was clear from the original sign. However, the reason for the devastation becomes clearer: Israel has transgressed her covenant relationship with God. The language Ezekiel adopts in these verses is not his own creation but is largely borrowed from Leviticus 26, a chapter that lays out the blessings and curses attached to the covenant.[2] There covenant obedience is defined in terms of submission to the Lord alone, specifically through the avoidance of idolatry and respect for the Lord's sanctuary (Lev. 26:1–2). This matches the nature of the charge made against Israel in Ezekiel 5: They have committed idolatry and thus defiled the sanctuary (Ezek. 5:9, 11). More generally, they have not followed the Lord's decrees or kept his laws (5:6; cf. Lev. 26:14–15).

As a result, the curses of Leviticus 26 will be operative in their midst. The Lord's face will be set against them (Lev. 26:17).[3] The result will be plagues of wild animals (Lev. 26:22; Ezek. 5:17), the sword and pestilence (Lev. 26:25; Ezek. 5:17), famine through a cutting off of the food supply (Lev. 26:26; Ezek. 5:16),[4] eating of one's own children (Lev. 26:29; Ezek. 5:10), being scattered among the nations, and being pursued by the sword (Lev. 26:33; Ezek. 5:12). This threatened exile will be a consequence of the iniquities of that generation and their fathers (Lev. 26:39; cf. Ezek. 4:5).

Even the Jerusalem-centered focus of the judgment reflects on an aspect of Israel's covenant relationship with her Lord, this time related to the Lord's covenant with David. When the Lord established that covenant, Jerusalem became, in his eyes, "the center of the nations" (Ezek. 5:5). When he chose Mount Zion as the site for the temple, that city was designated the dwelling place for his name (Deut. 12:11). Thereby, the Lord staked his name particularly on the land of Canaan, on the people of Israel, whom he had established there, and on the Davidic house.[5] But the Lord's immediate presence,

---

2. Henning G. Reventlow, *Wächter über Israel: Ezechiel und seine Tradition* (BZAW 82; Berlin: Töpelmann, 1962), 25–26.

3. It is tempting to read Ezekiel's iron pan against the background of Lev. 26:19, which speaks of the heavens becoming like iron to the covenant breakers. Though in the original context in Leviticus the iron heavens are joined to earth of brass, suggesting that drought is the curse intended, Ezekiel may have taken up the imagery and reapplied it in concrete form, much as he does with Isaiah's hired razor, to symbolize the closing of the lines of communication between humankind and God.

4. In both cases lit., "breaking the staff of bread." For an explanation of this phrase in terms of the practice of carrying ring-shaped loaves on a pole, see H. Schult, "Marginalie zum 'Stab des Brotes,'" *ZDPV* 87 (1971): 206–8.

5. Ronald E. Clements, *God and Temple* (Philadelphia: Fortress, 1965), 49–50.

the crowning blessing of the covenant relationship, is no blessing to a rebellious people but rather a curse. For the Lord who is there is no longer with them but against them.[6]

This covenant context is important because it demonstrates that the judgment that will befall Jerusalem is neither arbitrary nor unfair. The judgments coming on that city are not random afflictions thought up on the spur of the moment, as if God has lost his temper; they are the execution of the curses on the covenant breakers. Indeed, Israel has not merely failed to live up to God's standards; they have not even lived up to the standards of the nations around them (5:7). Instead of being a light to the nations, they have led the nations further into the darkness. For this reason, God must act to judge. As in Deuteronomy 13:9, where Israelites were forbidden to show compassion toward even their nearest and dearest or to spare them if they were attempting to lead others into apostasy, so the Lord will not show pity or spare his beloved but rebellious people (Ezek. 5:11).

The focus of each of the sign-acts is on the gloom rather than the rainbow, the tunnel rather than the light. Yet each contains within it, hidden away yet nonetheless present, the possibility of hope. The final sign-act is no different, for recalling the covenant curses of Leviticus 26 should also lead to remembering the promise of 26:44–45:

> Yet in spite of this, when they are in the land of their enemies, I will not reject them or abhor them so as to destroy them completely, breaking my covenant with them. I am the LORD their God. But for their sake I will remember the covenant with their ancestors whom I brought out of Egypt in the sight of the nations to be their God. I am the LORD.

Both Leviticus 26 and Ezekiel 5 hold out the hope that the Lord's anger will reach an end before Israel will. Yes, God's anger and wrath must be poured out on Israel so that they may know the Lord as a jealous God (Ezek. 5:13; cf. Ex. 20:5), a God who will not share the devotion of his people with another. For now, they will be a ruin and reproach in the sight of the nations (Ezek. 5:14). But God's anger will cease and his wrath will subside once it has been fully vented (5:13), for the Lord is merciful and gracious as well as jealous (Ex. 34:6, 14). To put it more precisely, God has covenanted himself to his people and has made a commitment he will not break, even though his people are unfaithful (Lev. 26:44). The purpose of this present chastisement, therefore, is not to destroy them utterly and forever but in order that the Lord may once again amaze the nations by accomplishing a new exodus of his people.

---

6. Block, *Ezekiel 1–24*, 217.

Bridging Contexts

THE SUZERAINTY TREATY. The idea of the relationship between God and his people as a covenant is central to the Old Testament, and it is a key idea underlying Ezekiel 5. As already indicated, the judgments coming on Jerusalem are not random afflictions but curses attached to the covenant between Israel and her God. In the ancient Near East there were different kinds of covenants, but one of the forms most commonly compared with biblical covenants is the suzerainty treaty, known from Hittite sources.[7]

This type of treaty was a kind of diplomatic surrender document, whereby a great king (the suzerain) agreed to enter into a relationship with a lesser king (the vassal). In return for the protection and benefits of a good relationship with the suzerain, the vassal king agreed to submit to the suzerain, to serve him alone, and to pay tribute to him. A vassal could only have one suzerain, though a suzerain might have many vassals, who would have obligations to respect the rights of the other vassals as well as the suzerain. At the end of these treaty documents, there were attached blessings and curses, which invoked the power of the only higher authority in international politics, the gods. In the absence of any appeal to a United Nations, the gods formed the ultimate sanction and were called upon to deliver blessings if the vassal king was faithful and curses if he broke the terms of the covenant.

Like these Hittite treaty documents, the Lord's covenant established with Israel on Mount Sinai concluded with blessings and curses (Lev. 26). If the people were faithful in obeying the stipulations of the covenant, they would experience material blessings in their land of peace and prosperity, culminating in the crowning blessing of the Lord's dwelling in their midst (26:11). But if they were disobedient to the terms and conditions of the covenant, serving other gods and rejecting their true suzerain, then they and their land would experience curses, culminating in the crowning curse of exile from God's land (26:33–39).

Ezekiel's point in picking up the language of Leviticus 26 is that because of Israel's unfaithfulness in her relationship to the Lord, pursuing other gods and serving them instead of the true God, all of the curses of the covenant are now falling on her. God's jealousy, power, and faithfulness to his Word are good news as long as Israel is faithful to him; but when she turns away, she cannot expect him not to act. Sure, certain, devastating judgment will fall on the unfaithful city and people.

Christ and the covenant(s). In the New Testament period, the covenant relationship made with Israel on Mount Sinai, as well as the earlier covenants made with Adam, Noah, and Abraham, find their consummation

---

7. For a brief analysis of the Hittite treaty form, see Delbert R. Hillers, *Covenant: The History of a Biblical Idea* (Baltimore: Johns Hopkins, 1969), 27–39.

in Christ.[8] He is the One who fulfills the conditions of the covenant for us, enabling us as his people to experience every blessing in him (Eph. 1:3). He is the One who took upon himself the curse that we deserved as covenant breakers, so that we might be redeemed by his blood (1:7). He is the One in whom the nations can find their inclusion into the one new people of God, the new Israel, the new temple in which God dwells by his Spirit (2:19–22).

For this reason, blessing and curse in the New Testament take on a different complexion from the Old Testament. The blessing we pronounce on God's people is that they may experience God's grace and favor in Jesus Christ through the ministry of the Holy Spirit: "May the grace of the Lord Jesus Christ, and the love of God, and the fellowship of the Holy Spirit be with you all" (2 Cor. 13:14). This blessing of life in God's presence is for all who keep the words given in God's book (Rev. 22:7).[9] However, there still remains a place for curse in the New Testament, specifically on those who attempt to pervert the gospel, either by proclaiming a different gospel (Gal. 1:8–9) or by tampering with the true gospel (Rev. 22:19).

If that is true, what then is our relationship, as New Testament believers, to the concepts of blessing and curse? We should note that the New Testament blessings and curses are spiritual, pertaining to life in God's presence or death separated from God. The Old Testament shadows, whereby the blessings and curses were associated with material prosperity or disadvantage in the land of promise, have passed away; the reality is found in Christ. For us, then, blessing is not a new Cadillac and a house on the golf course, but to be united with Christ in his death and resurrection. The curse that we have avoided is not poverty and a dull life but eternal separation from the One who makes life worth living. Praise God, then, from whom all spiritual blessings flow!

GOD, SIN, AND JUSTICE. If you have ever talked to people about God and the world, then I am sure that someone somewhere will have brought this up to you as an objection: "Where is this good God you talk about in a world gone mad? If he were really half as good as you say and half as powerful as you say, then evil would be instantly eliminated. Where is this God of justice? Why are there so many pointless wars and so much suffering in this world? Why doesn't God step in and do something?"

---

8. O. Palmer Robertson, *The Christ of the Covenants* (Phillipsburg, N.J.: Presbyterian and Reformed, 1980), 271–300.

9. Though the original reference is only to the book of Revelation, it forms a fitting conclusion to the New Testament and the Bible as a whole. See Meredith G. Kline, *The Structure of Biblical Authority*, 2d ed. (Grand Rapids: Eerdmans, 1975), 37.

Ezekiel's message to the Israelites is that God is about to step in and do something. He is about to act against unrighteousness and injustice. But that is not good news for Ezekiel's contemporaries, because he is coming as their judge. It is as if in an old Western movie the beleaguered cowboys hear the bugle call that sounds to announce the arrival of the Seventh Cavalry—only to find that this time the cavalry are fighting on the side of the dispossessed Indians. Our basic problem in longing for justice is that we ourselves are sinners. For such as ourselves, the coming of the judge brings with it a problem: "Who can endure the day of his coming?" (Mal. 3:2).

Is there then no hope? Are we all doomed? The early chapters of Ezekiel certainly give a more negative outlook than we are accustomed to. We must not undercut the prophet's message by focusing exclusively on the glimmers of light and ignoring the tunnel. The prophet would have people understand the depth of their sin—greater transgression than that of the nations around them, who did not know God (Ezek. 5:7)—and the extent of the wrath of God against sin, especially the sin of idolatry. When the Bible says that God is of purer eyes than to look upon evil (Hab. 1:13), what that means is that his face is set against sinful men and women. In other words, we all are under his judgment—or, to use Pauline language, we are all "by nature objects of wrath" (Eph. 2:3). Thus, left to ourselves, we have nothing to hope for on the last day except judgment and eternal separation from God. Because of our sin, we all sit on death row.

This fact is true not merely because of our own sin, which is bad enough, but also because of our history of sin. Indeed, humankind has a history of sin that stretches back not merely 390 years, as symbolized in Ezekiel 4, but back to the beginning of time and the sin of the first couple in the garden. Our problem is not simply that we have broken the covenant made at Mount Sinai and defiled the temple, making the place where God has chosen to dwell with his people unfit for divine habitation. Rather, in Adam we have all broken the original covenant relationship between God and humanity and made the world unfit for divine habitation. We were intended to be vassal rulers under God, ordering the world in submission to the Great King, serving him and him alone.[10] Instead, we rebelled against him, pursuing the idolatries of our hearts and bringing down on ourselves the sentence of death. Thus, for us as sinners, encounter with the living God can never be "a delightful and thought-provoking hour," but rather an awesome and terrifying encounter (cf. Heb. 12:21).

The flicker of hope and its fulfillment in Jesus Christ. Yet if we must not overplay the flickering candle of hope in Ezekiel 4–5, we must also not

10. Meredith G. Kline, *Kingdom Prologue* (priv. publ., 1991), 28.

ignore it altogether. Even on death row, God has his people. If Ezekiel himself is a model of the righteous remnant, undefiled in the land of exile, if there may be some preserved through the judgment, even if only a small fraction, if there is the possibility of a renewed exodus on the other side of the renewed Egyptian bondage, then there is hope. But how can that be? Justice must be done and the covenant curses must fall. If the wages of sin are indeed death, how can we survive payday?

Ezekiel does not yet begin to answer the question how. But by pointing his listeners back to Leviticus 26 and the covenant nature of the forthcoming destruction, he is already inviting them to consider the grounds of hope implicit within the covenant itself, the faithfulness of the One who established the covenant, God himself. God has purposed in establishing the covenant in the first place to win for himself a people, and he will not allow that purpose to be thwarted, not even by the sins of those whom he has chosen. As Malachi 3:6 puts the equation: "I the LORD do not change. So you, O descendants of Jacob, are not destroyed."

But still how can this be? Even though God is faithful and loving, he is also just. He is a holy God, of purer eyes than to look upon evil. So how can he forgive the guilty and still be just? Ezekiel does not give us a very clear answer to that question. He leaves it open. He knows that it is true, for God has revealed it to him, but he doesn't know how it can be true. But we who live this side of Christmas have a much clearer understanding. How can God be just and still forgive the guilty? How can the fire pass over us and not completely burn us alive? It is only because it has already passed over Jesus and poured its heat out on him.

The judgment that was to fall on Jerusalem for her sins was truly horrendous, so awful that few, a bare remnant of a remnant, would live to tell the tale. Yet it was nothing compared to the wrath of God that was poured out on his beloved Son on the cross for the sins of his people. The sword of God's wrath descended on Jesus; the fire of God's wrath burned him. He became an object of reproach to those passing by, who taunted him, "Come down from the cross, if you are the Son of God" (Matt. 27:39–40). But the result was that the wrath of God was exhausted on him; he has been avenged on sin, his wrath is spent (Ezek. 5:13).

As a consequence, there is now no condemnation for us who are in Christ Jesus (Rom. 8:1). As Paul puts it in 1 Thessalonians 5:9–10: "For God did not appoint us to suffer wrath but to receive salvation through our Lord Jesus Christ. He died for us so that, whether we are awake or asleep, we may live together with him." The wrath of God came on him once and for all, so that it might not now or in the future have to fall on us, his people.

Ezekiel 6

THE WORD OF THE LORD came to me: [2]"Son of man, set your face against the mountains of Israel; prophesy against them [3]and say: 'O mountains of Israel, hear the word of the Sovereign LORD. This is what the Sovereign LORD says to the mountains and hills, to the ravines and valleys: I am about to bring a sword against you, and I will destroy your high places. [4]Your altars will be demolished and your incense altars will be smashed; and I will slay your people in front of your idols. [5]I will lay the dead bodies of the Israelites in front of their idols, and I will scatter your bones around your altars. [6]Wherever you live, the towns will be laid waste and the high places demolished, so that your altars will be laid waste and devastated, your idols smashed and ruined, your incense altars broken down, and what you have made wiped out. [7]Your people will fall slain among you, and you will know that I am the LORD.

[8]"'But I will spare some, for some of you will escape the sword when you are scattered among the lands and nations. [9]Then in the nations where they have been carried captive, those who escape will remember me—how I have been grieved by their adulterous hearts, which have turned away from me, and by their eyes, which have lusted after their idols. They will loathe themselves for the evil they have done and for all their detestable practices. [10]And they will know that I am the LORD; I did not threaten in vain to bring this calamity on them.

[11]"'This is what the Sovereign LORD says: Strike your hands together and stamp your feet and cry out "Alas!" because of all the wicked and detestable practices of the house of Israel, for they will fall by the sword, famine and plague. [12]He that is far away will die of the plague, and he that is near will fall by the sword, and he that survives and is spared will die of famine. So will I spend my wrath upon them. [13]And they will know that I am the LORD, when their people lie slain among their idols around their altars, on every high hill and on all the mountaintops, under every spreading tree and every leafy oak—places where they offered fragrant incense to all their

idols. ¹⁴And I will stretch out my hand against them and make the land a desolate waste from the desert to Diblah—wherever they live. Then they will know that I am the LORD.'"

LIKE THE EVER-WIDENING circle of ripples that come from dropping a stone into still water, Ezekiel 6 builds on the previous judgment oracle and expands it.[1] Whereas before the prophet addressed the city of Jerusalem, the political and religious center of the land, now he is told to set his face against the mountains of all Israel. The geographical boundaries of judgment have been widened.[2] The focus on judgment is clear from the structure as well as the content. The chapter divides into two parts, verses 2–10 and 11–14, each of which begins with a hostile gesture on the part of the prophet ("set your face," v. 2; "strike your hands together and stamp your feet," v. 11) and concludes with the recognition formula ("they will know that I am the LORD"). The Lord's wrath has been aroused and he will not be ignored.

There is more at stake in Ezekiel's choice of the expression "the mountains of Israel" for the central region of Israel than a mere nostalgia for the lost mountain grandeur of their homeland among the exiles living in the flat terrain of Babylon.[3] While the borders of Israel expanded and contracted at different times in Israel's history, the hill country was always Israel par excellence. It was the Lord's "home turf," as the Arameans recognized (1 Kings 20:28), though they were also to discover that he could win fixtures "on the road" just as easily![4] Moreover, Ezekiel's preference for phrases combined with the patronym "Israel" ("mountains of Israel" [*bārê yiśrāʾēl*], "land of Israel" [*ʾadmat yiśrāʾēl*]) emphasizes the fact that this land will always be Israel. Even though the people may be in exile and another nation rule the territory, they can never own it, for these are in a special way "my [the LORD's] mountains" (Isa. 14:25; 65:9; Ezek. 38:21), which he has irrevocably given to his people Israel.

Yet it is precisely into that home turf that idolatry has penetrated. Ezekiel 6 expands the accusation of the previous chapter with clearer accusations of

---

1. Note the explicit connection between Ezek. 5:17, "I will bring the sword against you," and 6:3, "I am about to bring a sword against you" (Thomas Renz, *The Rhetorical Function of the Book of Ezekiel* [Ph.D. diss., Cheltenham and Gloucester College/Univ. of Bristol, 1997], 52).

2. See Lawrence Boadt, "Rhetorical Strategies in Ezekiel's Oracles of Judgment," in *Ezekiel and His Book*, 188.

3. So Allen, *Ezekiel 1–19*, 86.

4. Cf. Isa. 14:25; 65:9. See Zimmerli, *Ezekiel*, 1:185.

the nature of Israel's offenses. For the hill country is also the location of "high places" (*bāmôt*, 6:3). These are "high places" not necessarily in the sense of geographical elevation, for they can be located in a valley as easily as on a hilltop (Jer. 7:31; 32:35), but in the sense of a raised stone platform on which an altar and other cultic objects are constructed.[5] Alongside the altars for animal sacrifice are frequently buildings for the associated festivities (*hammānîm*),[6] which may also have housed idols (*gillûlîm*).

Prior to the building of the Jerusalem temple, the people were permitted to use the high places as locations for offering sacrifices to the Lord (1 Kings 3:2). Once that structure was completed, however, the worship of Israel was to be centralized in Jerusalem (Deut. 12). But in practice old habits died hard, especially when the old ways offered more convenient locations and more flexible rules. These local high places became the entry points for Canaanite religious ideas and images, whether the figures of Baal and Asherah or the practices that went along with Canaanite fertility religions.[7] For that reason, the repeated failure of the reigning monarch to suppress the high places in both the northern and southern kingdoms is a major concern in the book of Kings; only Hezekiah and Josiah attempted to destroy them. Syncretism was at some times actually officially encouraged, while at other times the authorities simply turned a blind eye to it.

But Israel's rulers were not free agents in their choice of worship location; they were vassal kings under the rule of God. Though the vassal kings might ignore the breach of covenant that this false worship involved, with the people serving other gods instead of the one true God, the Great King would no longer tolerate it. Once more, as in Ezekiel 5, an echo of Leviticus 26 is unmistakable, as the covenant curses fall on the rebellious people.[8] Leviticus 26:30 threatens: "I will destroy your high places [*bāmōtêkem*], cut

---

5. Patrick H. Vaughn, *The Meaning of 'bāmâ' in the Old Testament: A Study of Etymological, Textual and Archaeological Evidence* (SOTSMS 3; London: Cambridge Univ. Press, 1974), 29–55.

6. Most English translations render this word as "incense altars." However, evidence from an Aramaic temple foundation inscription that equates *ḥmn'* with *naos* suggests that they should rather be understood as sanctuaries of some kind. See H. J. W. Drijvers, "Aramaic *ḥmn'* and Hebrew *ḥmn*: Their Meaning and Root," *JSS* 33 (1988): 174; Block, *Ezekiel 1–24*, 225–26.

7. See 2 Kings 23:4–7. Those ministering at the high places of Josiah's day apparently included Yahwistic priests (*kōhᵃnîm*; 23:9) as well as pagan priests (*kᵉmārîm*; 23:5), so there was evidently syncretism as well as outright pagan idolatry. Recent archaeological discoveries from the eighth century B.C. also support the picture of syncretistic worship. On these, see William G. Dever, "Asherah, Consort of Yahweh? New Evidence From Kuntillet ʿAjrûd," *BASOR* 255 (1984): 21–37, and Ziony Zevit, "The Khirbet el-Qôm Inscription Mentioning a Goddess," *BASOR* 255 (1984): 39–47.

8. Allen, *Ezekiel 1–19*, 87.

down your incense altars [*ḥammānêkem*] and pile your dead bodies [*pigrêkem*] on the lifeless forms of your idols [*gillûlêkem*]." Similarly in Ezekiel 6:3–5 the Lord says: "I will destroy your high places [*bāmōtêkem*] ... and your incense altars [*ḥammānêkem*].... I will lay the dead bodies of the Israelites [*pigrê bᵉnê yis-rāʾēl*] in front of their idols [*gillûlêhem*]."

It was not uncommon in the ancient world to defile altars by burning corpses on them, putting the profane in the place of the holy (1 Kings 13:2; 2 Kings 23:16). Here, however, the corpses are not burned on the altar but scattered around the altar so that they surround (*sābab*) it. This acts as a macabre parody of the ritual dances around (*sābab*) the altar, which served to sanctify it as a sacred place (Ps. 26:6; 118:27).[9] The effect is nonetheless the same: The places of idolatry will be rendered unfit, and the idolaters themselves will be put to death (cf. Deut. 13:9). God will do what successive generations of kings failed to do and put an end to this abomination.

When God acts decisively in this way, the result will be that Israel "will know that I am the LORD" (Ezek. 6:7). This so-called "recognition formula" is characteristic of Ezekiel and occurs no fewer than four times in this chapter (6:7, 10, 13, 14).[10] It stresses the fact that the knowledge of the Lord comes about not through self-examination and navel-gazing but rather as a direct result of God's actions in history.[11] A remnant will survive the coming judgment, who will look back from exile and recognize that the Lord is the God who acts in history and that the fate suffered by his people is no more than just. There in exile they will become aware of their sinful state and God's righteous judgment. His words, whether those brought by Ezekiel or the covenant curses of Leviticus 26 or both, are not empty threats (Ezek. 6:10). They will know that the Lord is there and is not silent, to quote Francis Schaeffer's memorable phrase.[12]

This raises the question, however, as to what kind of knowledge of God they will attain in exile. Is it the forced knowledge of the rule of God in the world such as the Egyptians received, when after plague upon plague, they

---

9. See W. O. E. Oesterley, *The Sacred Dance: A Study in Comparative Folklore* (Cambridge: Cambridge. Univ. Press, 1923), 88; Robert Burrelli, "Dance and Related Expressions of Worship" (unpub. Th.M. thesis; Dallas: Dallas Theological Seminary), 16. A similar ritual seems to have developed as part of the later Lulab Festival at the Feast of Tabernacles (*m. Sukka* 4:5).

10. Again, an element of heightening from the previous chapter, where it occurs only once (Ezek. 5:13).

11. See Walther Zimmerli, "The Recognition of God According to the Book of Ezekiel," in *I Am Yahweh*, ed. W. Brueggemann, trans. D. Stuart (Atlanta: John Knox, 1982), 29–98.

12. Cf. the title of one of his books, *He Is There and He Is Not Silent* (London: Hodder and Stoughton, 1972).

saw their horses and chariots drowned in the Sea of Reeds? The purpose of that power encounter was so that "the Egyptians will know that I am the LORD" (Ex. 14:4, 18), yet the knowledge they received is the knowledge of despair, not hope. Or is it the knowledge of God that comes to the repentant, whose attachment to sin is broken through discipline?

Both possibilities seem present in this passage. "To remember" in the Old Testament is never simply the recalling to mind of the past, but includes the idea of a present action that flows from that recollection.[13] Remembering the Lord seems to be universally positive in the Old Testament and elsewhere can clearly be used to describe repentance (e.g., Jonah 2:7). The content of what the people will remember about the Lord is his grief at their adulterous actions,[14] and the result flowing from that remembrance will be self-loathing at their evil ways (Ezek. 6:9). This seems to imply the possibility on the part of at least some of the exiles of a repentant return to the Lord. This provides a model to Ezekiel's exilic audience, "overhearing" his words directed to the distant mountains: Even now they can act the part of the righteous remnant by remembering the God who acts and repenting of their sin and the sins of their fellow countrymen in going after dead idols who cannot save (Isa. 44:6–20). As much as their sin of idolatry delighted them in the past, now it will become an object of horror in their eyes.

However, in keeping with the focus on the dark side in these chapters, Ezekiel does not end his oracle on this happy thought. Instead, he returns to the theme of judgment on the house of Israel because of their abominations (Ezek. 6:11–14). The threefold judgment of sword, famine, and plague is once again unleashed on the land (v. 11). This fearsome trio is familiar from Leviticus 26 and Ezekiel 5, and they are three of the four "horsemen of the Apocalypse" in Revelation 6. The comprehensiveness of their activity is underlined in Ezekiel 6:12: Normally the two categories of "he that is far away" and "he that is near" comprehensively include everyone (e.g., Isa. 57:19), but here a third category is added: "he that survives and is spared." Even those seemingly fortunate ones who fall into this last category and escape immediate destruction will be subject to death, just as some of the hairs that Ezekiel preserved in Ezekiel 5:3 were later taken out again and thrown into the fire. Then,

---

13. See Zimmerli, *Ezekiel*, 1:189.

14. The Hebrew of v. 9 is difficult; various suggestions have been made to emend the text to read, "I have broken their adulterous heart and eyes," rather than the MT, "I have been broken [by?] their adulterous heart and eyes" (see Allen, *Ezekiel 1–19*, 83). Perhaps the difficulty has been caused by an attempt to link this verse with the destruction of vv. 4, 6, so that the Lord is in effect saying, "I have been broken [*nišbartî* = grieved] by the judgment necessary to break their adultery in which their altars will be broken [*nišb'rû*; v. 6]"; as we would put it, "This is hurting me as much as it is hurting you."

when the people are slain around their idolatrous altars and the entire land from south to north[15] is turned into a desolate waste, the knowledge of the Lord will be established.

This twofold ending to the two oracles seems to envisage two opposite possibilities: repentance and return to the Lord (Ezek. 6:8–10), or the total devastation of the land and the wiping out of the entire people (6:11–14). Both are indeed possible endings to Israel's story; in either event, the Lord's justice will be seen and known. Both are likewise possible endings to the story for each individual in Ezekiel's audience: They can remember the Lord and find hope, or they can simply continue on their present course and be utterly destroyed. By including both endings, Ezekiel invites his hearers to ponder their own condition. By choosing to end with the picture of total destruction, however, he underlines the dark future for the land of Israel: total desolation from one end to the other.

ATTITUDE TOWARD OTHER religions. To a contemporary pluralistic society, Ezekiel's words of judgment seem unduly harsh. Indeed, even that statement may be too mild. For Ezekiel's favorite word for idols, *gillûlîm*, appears to be deliberately offensive, artificially formed out of the words for "to roll" (*gālal*) and "detestable objects" (*šiqqûṣîm*).[16] This imagery of round, rolling objects that defile evokes the idea of excrement and amounts to calling the idols "sheep droppings," only in rather less polite terminology.[17]

Such is not the typical language of interfaith dialog in our culture. We are used to seeing the practice of different religions and the operation of cults of one kind or another all around us, and are typically tolerant of their practices, provided they will be tolerant of ours. We do not normally expect judgment to fall on our nation as a result of the proliferation of differing religious viewpoints and practices. In the light of Ezekiel's words, is this a mistake? Ought we instead, as Christians, be working to ensure that the true worship of God alone is legally enforced in our land?

---

15. Reading "Riblah" for MT "Diblah"—the consonants "r" and "d" were easily confused in Hebrew. Riblah is a city in the Syrian territory of Hamath, north of Israel. It is not the normal northern boundary of Israel, which was at Lebo Hamath (Ezek. 47:16; 48:1); it was perhaps chosen because of its associations with the exiling of Jehoahaz after Josiah's defeat and death (2 Kings 23:33), which made it a suitable place of judgment (Cooke, *Ezekiel*, 73).

16. Daniel Bodi, "Les *gillûlîm* chez Ézéchiel et dans l'Ancien Testament, et les différentes pratiques cultuelles associées à ce terme," *RB* 100 (1993): 481–510.

17. Block uses graphic terminology in *Ezekiel 1–24*, 226.

To do so would, I think, be to misunderstand the special position that Israel held as a nation in the Old Testament. She was uniquely God's chosen nation, called at Mount Sinai into a special covenant relationship with God. Part of that special relationship was a commitment on the part of Israel to be separate from the nations, belonging to the Lord alone. He would be their God and they would be his people, as the repeated covenant refrain goes. That special relationship was not in effect in the same way prior to Sinai, with the result that the patriarchs lived with a quite different attitude towards the religious beliefs of the surrounding nations. As Gordon Wenham characterizes it:

> Though the patriarchs are faithful followers of their God, they generally enjoy good relations with men of other faiths. There is an air of ecumenical bonhomie about the patriarchal religion which contrasts with the sectarian exclusiveness of the Mosaic age and later prophetic demands.[18]

Nor does the relationship between God and his people carry over in the same way in the New Testament era of redemptive history. Thus, while Paul is distressed by the rampant idolatry of the Athenians (Acts 17:16), he addresses the assembled Areopagites in relatively complimentary terms, saying, "I see that in every way you are very religious" (17:22). He does not threaten the immediate judgment of God on their nation for their idolatry, though he urges them in no uncertain terms to abandon their futile idols and turn to the true and living God (17:30–31). The reason for Paul's different approach from Ezekiel is that Athens as a city-state was not in covenant with God and therefore not subject to the blessings and curses of the Sinai covenant.

Modern nation-states are likewise no longer in a covenant relationship with the Lord.[19] Instead, it is the church that is the covenanted people of God. For this reason, Paul's harshest language is reserved for those who claim to be Christians but actually are preaching a false gospel. With such people there can be no polite dialog; for them, Paul is willing to envisage eternal

---

18. Gordon J. Wenham, "The Religion of the Patriarchs," in *Essays on the Patriarchal Narratives*, ed. A. R. Millard and D. J. Wiseman (Leicester: InterVarsity, 1980), 184.

19. The tendency to view one's country as an elect nation (or worse, *the* elect nation) is an unfortunate tendency within Puritan thought in general (see Leland Ryken, *Worldly Saints: The Puritans As They Really Were* [Grand Rapids: Zondervan, 1986], 198). The sense of unique destiny was amplified in the American context by the circumstances behind the founding of the New England colonies, such that they viewed themselves as "a city set upon an hill . . . a people in covenant with God." From there, the idea of "manifest destiny" spread more widely into the American consciousness, along with other (more positive) aspects of Puritan thought. The notion of national covenants with God is also found in certain strands of British, and especially Scottish, theological thought, particularly among those strongly influenced by the Puritans.

condemnation (Gal. 1:8; cf. also the strong language of 5:12). They are no better than "dogs" (Phil. 3:2; Rev. 22:15), a term whose strong emotive content is not easily conveyed in our context.[20] Jude is similarly scathing in his verbal assault on false teachers (Jude 8–16). Therefore, our application of this passage should be in terms of the faithfulness (or otherwise) of *the church* rather than the state. We should explore the dominant idolatries that readily invade the church and are advocated and encouraged by some within the church itself, and be ready to condemn them in the strongest possible terms.

Contemporary idolatry. What kind of idolatries is Ezekiel addressing, however, and how do they relate to the contemporary situation? The idolatries of the high places, with their representations of Baal and Asherah and altars for offering sacrifices, seem distant and foreign. Bowing down to stone and wood seems a mark of ancient credulity to us. Yet if you analyze the appeal of Baal and Asherah, it is possible to see that their hold continues down to the present, even though their form has changed. Baal was the storm god, the chief god of the pantheon, the god of power and fertility, who if appeased could deliver victory in battle, and in peacetime the rain so vital to cultivation in Canaan. Asherah, his consort, was the goddess of fertility, perhaps better known to us in her Greek form as Aphrodite. By worshiping these gods, the Israelites sought to impose order on the chaos of the world around them and to invoke the aid of a higher power on their behalf. The idols promised power and security.

In addition, the sexual practices of ritual prostitution that were probably associated with the fertility cult needed little theological justification. To put it in the contemporary vernacular, Baal and Asherah were in effect the patron saints of sex and guns and rock 'n' roll, promising to deliver a potent mixture of satisfaction to the desires for power, success, and pleasure. This promise remains as attractive to people of the contemporary world as it was to those of ancient times, as any quick review of the recent offerings from Hollywood will demonstrate. However, the security and satisfaction that these sources offer is both illegitimate and ephemeral. God alone deserves the worship that these idols demand from us, and he alone is able to deliver the lasting satisfaction that we seek. Though our hearts restlessly wander from one idol to another, they will never find rest until they submit to the one true and living God.

But could Israel ultimately have been totally destroyed by God, no matter what their sin? God had set his name on her, allying his reputation inti-

---

20. "Son of a bitch" retains the canine reference but has perhaps become too commonplace an insult in general society. However, if you translate it into the context of the pulpit, its shocking force is perhaps still present.

mately with her fate. This consideration had saved Israel before in the time of Moses when they worshiped the golden calf (Ex. 32:9–14). This remains a powerful and valid argument down into New Testament times, where Paul regards as unthinkable the possibility that God has rejected his own people (Rom. 11:1). But the ultimate certainty that God will be faithful to his covenant promises to redeem his people must never be transposed into a complacent attitude toward the threats he makes concerning those who break the covenant. Though God will preserve for himself a remnant for the sake of his name, yet he may equally definitively judge those who continue to rebel against him, be they Abraham's children or not, for our God combines in himself both kindness and severity (11:22).

A MATTER OF life and death. How many times have you heard people say, "It doesn't matter what you believe as long as you are sincere"? That is not an idea Ezekiel would have endorsed. According to him, judgment was coming on Israel, a judgment that was nothing less than the outpouring of God's wrath from heaven, which would level everything in its path. It was not coming because the Israelites had mistreated one another (although, as we will see, they had). Nor was judgment coming because they had taken advantage of the poor or been unfaithful to their wives, or even because they had robbed each other and filled the land with violence, but essentially because they held to a false religion. For them, what they believed would literally be a matter of life and death.

If what you believe is indeed a matter of life and death, then it is not nearly enough to be sincere. It is intensely important to be right. When you jump out of an airplane, you are not content merely to believe sincerely that your parachute is strapped on correctly. Rather, you will check and double-check that it is really so, because you understand all too clearly the consequences of getting it wrong. Indeed, the lengths to which people go to check the correctness of their beliefs in a particular matter is an accurate marker of how important they believe the matter to be. The people who say, "It doesn't matter what you believe about God as long as you are sincere," are those to whom it doesn't matter what you believe about God. But if, in fact, there is a God who designed the whole cosmic and human story with a purpose, so that the chief end of humanity is indeed to glorify this God and enjoy him forever, then what you believe becomes a matter of supreme and decisive importance.[21]

---

21. Lesslie Newbigin, *The Gospel in a Pluralist Society* (Grand Rapids: Eerdmans, 1989), 15–16.

It matters intensely to God what his people believe about him. He entered a covenant with Israel at Mount Sinai, where he declared himself a passionate God, whose name is Jealous, who would not share his people's affections with another (Ex. 34:14). His faithfulness to his covenant commitment meant a curse descending inexorably on those who broke the covenant and went after other gods, just as surely as it would mean blessing for those who faithfully sought after him (Lev. 26). Ezekiel's warning is that the time is at hand for God's jealousy to overflow into action as he judges his rebellious people.

A renewed people. But that outpouring of God's wrath can never be the end of the story. Though God is faithful to his covenant commitment to bring judgment on the rebels, he is also faithful to his deeper purpose to establish a renewed people, a restored remnant. That is small comfort to the people of Judah, who live in the path of the oncoming storm. To them, the gestures of Ezekiel bespeak God's settled attitude: God is determinedly against them and will not relent. But to the exiles, who overhear the conversation, there is a ray of hope. They are already in the situation described in 6:9 and can identify with the remnant by remembering their own sin and recognizing God's righteous judgment.

Today, we too live in a world full of idolatry. In our situation, the idols are not of wood and stone, but they are nonetheless real. Each of us has "personal centers," areas of our lives in which we seek to find our identity and significance. These centers come in a variety of shapes and forms, ranging from pleasure and work to spouse and family. Even church can function as an idol, the place from which we seek approval and affirmation.[22] Our "high place" may be the office, where we sacrifice our relationships to win the blessing of the god "career." It may be the family room, where we consecrate our "prime time" to the god of entertainment, or the kitchen and laundry room, where we devote ourselves to ensuring that our children have all of their physical and material needs met perfectly.

We measure our value and success by the extent to which these gods smile on us and consider ourselves of little value when they frown. In that respect, nothing has changed between ancient Israel and us. Like the rich

---

22. Stephen Covey lists a number of possible "personal centers" that can be helpful both in diagnosing personal idolatries and in helping unchurched people understand the concept of idolatry (*The Seven Habits of Highly Effective People* [New York: Simon & Schuster, 1989], 118–25). Covey's answer to these "personal centers" is a life that is "principle centered," and he goes on to advise on how to write a mission statement that will clarify one's own principles. From a Christian perspective, this may well end up merely replacing one "ineffective" idolatry with a more "effective" one, that of "principles." Any center other than the true and living God, who has revealed himself in the Scriptures, is idolatry. Of course, assisting people to manufacture effective idolatries sells books.

young ruler who came to Jesus and asked him, "What good thing must I do to get eternal life?" (Matt. 19:16), something other than God is driving our lives. How ashamed we will be to stand before the Maker of the universe and realize how much of our thinking has been controlled by and centered on things that are not gods, to which we attributed godlike significance! Of how many will it be revealed that they spent their lives mucking about in the sandpit of life, living for insipid pleasures and weak fancies instead of launching out in dependence on the only true God? Truly, we will all have much of which to be ashamed. As C. S. Lewis put it:

> Indeed, if we consider the unblushing promises of reward and the staggering nature of the rewards promised in the Gospels, it would seem that the Lord finds our desires, not too strong, but too weak. We are half-hearted creatures, fooling about with drink and sex and ambition when infinite joy is offered us, like an ignorant child who wants to go on making mud pies in a slum because he cannot understand what is meant by the offer of a holiday at the sea. We are far too easily pleased.[23]

Not all of us will face the kind of judgment Ezekiel prophesied over Israel during our lifetimes, however. Many, like the rich young ruler, appear to prosper in their idolatry. But those whose idols are blessing them, in whose lives there is apparently no difficulty and disappointment, are more to be pitied than to be envied, for the judgments of God often serve as a wake-up call to our deaf ears. As Calvin comments: "The scourges of God are more useful to us, because when God indulges us, we abuse his clemency and flatter ourselves and so grow hardened in sin."[24]

Two possible outcomes. Yet the judgments of God in this life do not work automatically. Two outcomes are possible, just as they were for Ezekiel's hearers. We may be moved by the pain of the situation to remember God's grace, and therefore to be disgusted over our sin and turn from it. Our eyes may be opened from our self-deceptive stupor to see the hatefulness of what we have given ourselves over to, so that we thrust it away from us as eagerly as we would a poisonous spider or a scorpion. Or we may continue unmoved, perhaps even further hardened in our sin, inexorably hastening towards final destruction. It is a sobering fact that those who fail to listen to God speaking to them become increasingly unable to hear God speak to them. But in either event, whether in the final destruction of those who continue to be rebellious against him or in the final salvation of those whom he brings to himself, God's justice is vindicated.

---

23. *The Weight of Glory and Other Addresses* (Grand Rapids: Eerdmans, 1965), 1–2.
24. *Ezekiel I*, 156.

Ezekiel 7

THE WORD OF THE LORD came to me: ²"Son of man, this is what the Sovereign LORD says to the land of Israel:
The end! The end has come upon the four corners of the land. ³The end is now upon you and I will unleash my anger against you. I will judge you according to your conduct and repay you for all your detestable practices. ⁴I will not look on you with pity or spare you; I will surely repay you for your conduct and the detestable practices among you. Then you will know that I am the LORD.

⁵"This is what the Sovereign LORD says: Disaster! An unheard-of disaster is coming. ⁶The end has come! The end has come! It has roused itself against you. It has come! ⁷Doom has come upon you—you who dwell in the land. The time has come, the day is near; there is panic, not joy, upon the mountains. ⁸I am about to pour out my wrath on you and spend my anger against you; I will judge you according to your conduct and repay you for all your detestable practices. ⁹I will not look on you with pity or spare you; I will repay you in accordance with your conduct and the detestable practices among you. Then you will know that it is I the LORD who strikes the blow.

¹⁰"The day is here! It has come! Doom has burst forth, the rod has budded, arrogance has blossomed! ¹¹Violence has grown into a rod to punish wickedness; none of the people will be left, none of that crowd—no wealth, nothing of value. ¹²The time has come, the day has arrived. Let not the buyer rejoice nor the seller grieve, for wrath is upon the whole crowd. ¹³The seller will not recover the land he has sold as long as both of them live, for the vision concerning the whole crowd will not be reversed. Because of their sins, not one of them will preserve his life. ¹⁴Though they blow the trumpet and get everything ready, no one will go into battle, for my wrath is upon the whole crowd.

¹⁵"Outside is the sword, inside are plague and famine; those in the country will die by the sword, and those in the city will be devoured by famine and plague. ¹⁶All who survive and escape will be in the mountains, moaning like doves of the valleys, each because of his sins. ¹⁷Every hand will go

limp, and every knee will become as weak as water. [18]They will put on sackcloth and be clothed with terror. Their faces will be covered with shame and their heads will be shaved. [19]They will throw their silver into the streets, and their gold will be an unclean thing. Their silver and gold will not be able to save them in the day of the LORD's wrath. They will not satisfy their hunger or fill their stomachs with it, for it has made them stumble into sin. [20]They were proud of their beautiful jewelry and used it to make their detestable idols and vile images. Therefore I will turn these into an unclean thing for them. [21]I will hand it all over as plunder to foreigners and as loot to the wicked of the earth, and they will defile it. [22]I will turn my face away from them, and they will desecrate my treasured place; robbers will enter it and desecrate it.

[23]"Prepare chains, because the land is full of bloodshed and the city is full of violence. [24]I will bring the most wicked of the nations to take possession of their houses; I will put an end to the pride of the mighty, and their sanctuaries will be desecrated. [25]When terror comes, they will seek peace, but there will be none. [26]Calamity upon calamity will come, and rumor upon rumor. They will try to get a vision from the prophet; the teaching of the law by the priest will be lost, as will the counsel of the elders. [27]The king will mourn, the prince will be clothed with despair, and the hands of the people of the land will tremble. I will deal with them according to their conduct, and by their own standards I will judge them. Then they will know that I am the LORD."

MANY PEOPLE THINK of the message of the prophets as, "Repent, the end is near." Ezekiel's message in this chapter, however, is: "It's too late to repent; the end has come." Just as in the days of Noah's Flood (Gen. 6), the sins of the people have reached such a pitch that it is time to wipe the land clean of them.

There is a twofold expansion in Ezekiel 7 in the scope of the judgment from that described in his previous messages. (1) It is once more expanded geographically. Just as Ezekiel began with the city of Jerusalem in Ezekiel 5 and moved on to the heartland of Judah, the mountains of Israel, in Ezekiel 6, so now he widens his scope of attention to include judgment on the whole "land of Israel" (7:2). Indeed, judgment has come upon the "four corners of the land [world]." The global language may be applied to a judgment that affects "only" Judah since, as Greenberg puts it, "from the prophet's viewpoint, the doom of his people is tantamount to the end of the world."[1]

The phrase "land of Israel" (*ʾadmat-yiśrāʾēl*) is unique to Ezekiel. *ʾadāmâ* ("land," "ground") has a substantial semantic overlap with *ʾereṣ* ("land," "earth"), and in some contexts the former term may be chosen simply to provide a contrast with the latter. Thus in 11:17 the "land of Israel" (*ʾadmat-yiśrāʾēl*) contrasts with "the lands where you have been scattered." Yet the physical and agricultural overtones that *ʾadāmâ* contains may still be present, especially on the lips of an exile, denoting the land of promise as a place intended for fruitfulness and blessing (see, e.g., its repeated use in the covenant blessings of Deut. 28). However, as Ezekiel 7 unfolds, it emerges that what has been growing in this fertile soil has been something other than what God intended.

(2) Ezekiel insists repeatedly that doom is not merely imminent but has actually arrived. Whereas the previous oracle spoke of a certain judgment to come at an unspecified time in the future, here we see a certain judgment now present. Thus verses 3 and 8 in Hebrew both start with the word "now," while verse 7 announces (lit.): "The time has come, the day has arrived." Further, in this chapter for the first time there is not even a glimmer of the light at the end of the tunnel, no mention of a possible remnant. The focus is entirely on the darkness of the descending gloom that is now falling over the land.

The language that Ezekiel adopts is influenced heavily by the traditional language of the Day of the Lord. This "Day" was frequently longed for during times of difficulty as the day when the Lord would come to judge the nations; however, the prophets had pointed out that it was also the time when God would judge his own people Israel (cf. Amos 5:18–20). The outcome of that Day of Judgment was likely to be far from positive. Thus Amos was shown a vision of ripe summer fruit (*qāyiṣ*, Amos 8:1), a vision that leads into an oracle of Israel's end (*qēṣ*, 8:2). Likewise, in Genesis 6:13, God had told Noah that he was about to bring an end (*qēṣ*) to all people, and the result was the Flood. So here, when Ezekiel speaks repeatedly of the coming of an end (*qēṣ*) on the people, what Judah is being threatened with is nothing less than complete and immediate annihilation.[2] What Amos had foreseen concerning the northern kingdom is now happening in parallel fashion to the southern kingdom.

Ezekiel 7 opens with a brief oracle that summarizes the themes of the chapter (vv. 1–4). The prophesied end is coming on the whole land of Israel

---

1. *Ezekiel 1–20*, 161. For that reason, this translation is to be preferred to that of the NIV: "four corners of the land."

2. Zimmerli, *Ezekiel*, 1:204.

(v. 2), and it is coming now (v. 3). That devastating event is nothing less than the personal "sending" (*šālaḥ*) of the Lord's anger against them, just as earlier he had threatened to "send" his arrows of famine against them (5:16). But the Lord's action in destroying them is neither arbitrary nor unfair; it is simply judging them according to their conduct and repaying them for all their detestable practices. Measure for measure, they will receive what they deserve for their abominations (7:3), without favoritism or pity, resulting in an understanding of the Lord's power and holiness.

The second oracle (7:5–9) picks up from the first oracle the theme of the personal nature of divine judgment on the people's sin. All of the first person verbs from the first oracle expressing the outpouring of the Lord's wrath recur, along with a significantly modified version of the recognition formula, "Then you will know that it is I the LORD who strikes the blow" (7:9). No longer does the Lord reveal himself to his people as "the LORD, who heals you," as he did during the wanderings in the desert (Ex. 15:26); rather, he has now become "the LORD who strikes."

The third oracle (Ezek. 7:10–27) unfolds the theme of the comprehensiveness of judgment from the first oracle. It begins with a brief introduction (vv. 10–11), which draws out the organic connection between Judah's sin and her punishment. This was already prepared for by the agricultural background of the language of the "end" (*qēṣ*); the "end" is the time for harvesting ripe fruit. Now the sin of Judah has reached full ripeness and it is time for the harvest of God's judgment. According to verses 10–11, Israel's "doom[?][3] has burst forth, the rod has budded, arrogance has blossomed! Violence has grown into a rod to punish wickedness." Alongside Israel's blossoming pride and violence, however, the rod of God's judgment has been growing, namely, Babylon. It will mete out punishment corresponding to the crime until there is nothing left. The people who filled the city with violence (7:23) will themselves be attacked by violent men (7:22; NIV "robbers"); the wicked will be turned over to "the wicked of the earth" (7:21); the arrogant will be humbled (7:24).

Suitably to its theme of comprehensive judgment, the oracle is itself massive and wide-ranging, consisting of two parallel cycles of judgment scenes that move from the general to the particular.[4] These may be broken down as follows:

---

3. This translation of *ṣ^epîrâ* is widely accepted by commentators; however, it is only "a guess based on the context" (Greenberg, *Ezekiel 1–20*, 148). Block prefers the translation, "The leash has gone forth," seeing *ṣ^epîrâ* as a reference to the chains in which Judah will be led into captivity (*Ezekiel 1–24*, 252, 254).

4. Greenberg, *Ezekiel 1–20*, 158.

A: the futility of commercial transactions (vv. 12–13)
  B: the announcement and arrival of war and devastation (vv. 14–16)
    C: universal ineffectiveness, terror, and mourning (vv. 17–18)
A': the futility of gold and silver (vv. 19–20)
  B': dispossession, looting, and desecration (vv. 21–24)
    C': ineffectiveness, terror, and mourning by all classes (vv. 25–27)

When the threatened judgment falls, commercial transactions will lose their meaning; there will be no such thing as a good deal or a bad deal, whether for the buyer or the seller (Ezek. 7:12). The use of the traditional pairings of opposites ("buyer/seller," "rejoice/grieve") underlines once more the comprehensiveness of the disaster, while the following verse underlines the lasting nature of the disaster: "The seller will not recover the land he has sold as long as both of them live" (7:13). Even gold and silver will be worthless, able neither to save their owners nor to satisfy them (7:19). Indeed, these precious metals will be worse than worthless; they will not simply be regarded as trash, to be carelessly disposed of, but as something ritually unclean, contaminated in itself and with the power to contaminate anyone whom it touches (7:19). The reason for that loathing is because gold and silver furnished the materials for the people's idolatry (7:20), "for it has made them stumble into sin" (v. 19); it was the iniquity that caused their downfall.[5]

The nature of the disaster is the focus of the next section in the cycle: Though preparations are made for war, no battle will be joined, for God's wrath is on all her masses (*hᵃmônāh*, Ezek. 7:14; NIV "crowd").[6] Judah will be given over into the hand of her enemies, and all her possessions will be handed over as plunder (7:22). This is a reversal of the normal themes of holy war, whereby no battle would be necessary for the Israelites because the Lord would fight on their behalf, giving their enemies into their hand as plunder (cf. 2 Chron. 20). Now, however, the Lord will turn away his face (Ezek. 7:22), allowing the wicked of the earth to pollute the land and even to desecrate "my treasured place" (*sᵉpûnî*; v. 22).

That change of attitude toward Judah meant that even the temple, where David had earlier expressed confidence that God would hide him (*sāpan*; Ps. 27:5), is no longer a safe place. It would be defiled along with their other (pagan) sanctuaries (Ezek. 7:24). Since Israel failed to distinguish between true and false places of worship and did not destroy the high places, now God's judgment will be similarly nondiscriminatory, destroying not only the pagan sanctuaries but his own temple.

---

5. Block, *Ezekiel 1–24*, 146.
6. This word often has military connotations (BDB, 242c).

In the face of this disaster, no coherent policy will be formulated or implemented. All hands will hang passively by their sides. Paralyzing fear will result in loss of control of bodily functions (Ezek. 7:17).[7] The people will put on a show of mourning by means of their clothes and their shaven heads (7:18), yet no mercy or forgiveness will be found there, as God already announced (7:4). The people will seek peace and not find it (7:25), whether they seek it through the channel of religious leadership or political leadership. There will be no effective guidance through the religious leadership, whether the prophet (from whom a vision might be sought), the priest (from whom Torah, or instruction from the priestly law, might be sought), or the elders (from whom wisdom and counsel might be expected). Nor will there be effective leadership in the political realm. Not a "king" or a "prince" or any of the "people of the land"[8] will act decisively to save the day (7:27).[9] Rather, they too will be judged "by their own standards."

Bridging Contexts

A DAY OF RECKONING. The immediacy and comprehensiveness of the judgment of which Ezekiel speaks may, at first sight, seem to distance his situation from ours. We live in a world where immediate, comprehensive justice is not poured out on nations that transgress God's laws. However, judgment delayed is not justice denied. The fact remains that there will be a day of reckoning for all sin and for all sinners, when comprehensive justice will be done. Thus the writer to the Hebrews tells us: "Man is destined to die once, and after that to face judgment" (Heb. 9:27), while Jude writes: "The Lord is coming with thousands upon thousands of his holy ones to judge everyone, and to convict all the ungodly" (Jude 14–15). Though this judgment may not be immediate, it will surely be comprehensive and also entirely fair: The just desserts ("wages,"

---

7. The Hebrew reads lit., "Every knee will go (or flow) water," which the NIV, along with most other English versions, renders as "every knee will become as weak as water." However, most modern commentators understand "water" as urine in this context, a view that goes back to the LXX. The intended referent is not loss of strength but rather loss of bladder control. For the ancient Near Eastern comparative evidence, see Greenberg, *Ezekiel 1–20*, 152.

8. The phrase ʿam hāʾāreṣ can either cover a rather general group of people or, as here, a specific political grouping closely linked to the Davidic monarchy. See Shemaryahu Talmon, "The Judean hāʾāreṣ in Historical Perspective," in *King, Cult and Calendar in Ancient Israel: Collected Studies* (Jerusalem: Magnes, 1986), 68–78.

9. The balance between these two triads suggests that there is no reason to collapse the two references to king (melek) and prince (nāśîʾ) into a single person. Although Ezekiel frequently uses nāśîʾ to refer to the reigning monarch, that preference is not absolute. For a defense of the present text, see Duguid, *Ezekiel and the Leaders of Israel*, 21.

---

in Paul's terminology) of a life of rebellion against God is eternal death, exclusion from the presence of the one who is himself Life (Rom. 6:23). Those wages will have to be collected, sooner or later.

Notwithstanding that final judgment, there are also situations here on earth where our sins catch up with us. In Romans 1, Paul speaks of sinners who have "received in themselves the due penalty for their perversion" (Rom. 1:27). Because the world is God's world, to sin is to act in violation of the basic structure of the universe and thus to call down on oneself the consequences of one's action. Because of God's mercy and common grace, we do not immediately receive the full consequences of all of our actions; otherwise each of our lives would be short and pain-filled. Yet God's mercy is not to be presumed upon and his judgments are not to be ignored.

If we presume on God's mercy, we assume that "of course God will forgive me; it is his job."[10] To the contrary, Ezekiel asserts that sometimes God reaches the point where he will not look on us with pity or spare us, but instead will repay us for our sins (Ezek. 7:4). Instead, the kindness of God is intended to bring us to repentance while there is yet time (Rom. 2:4). Nor are we to ignore his judgments on us, for they too can have the gracious effect of breaking our stubborn attachment to our sins. Yet to remain stubborn and unrepentant in the face of all of God's patience is nothing less than "storing up wrath against yourself for the day of God's wrath, when his righteous judgment will be revealed" (Rom. 2:5).

The agents of justice. It is not hard to envisage the perfect meting out of judgment on the last day by the Judge of all the earth, the One "to whom all hearts are open, all desires known and from whom no secrets are hid."[11] The agents of God's justice here on earth, however, are often less than just themselves. In fact, in Ezekiel's situation the agents of divine wrath are themselves termed "the wicked of the earth" (Ezek. 7:21). But how can justice be done by the wicked? And how can God use the wicked to achieve his purposes without becoming tainted by them? There is an element of mystery here, as Calvin freely admits: "God works through them in such a way that he nevertheless has nothing in common with them. They are borne along by a depraved disposition, but God has a wonderful plan, incomprehensible to us, according to which he impels the wicked here and there—without becoming involved in their guilt."[12]

God is able to write straight with a crooked pencil and to achieve his perfect ends through the use of less than perfect instruments, without him-

---

10. The quotation is attributed to the nineteenth-century German author, Heinrich Heine.

11. The language is that of *The Book of Common Prayer*, "Collect for Communion."

12. *Ezekiel I*, 188.

self being tainted or hampered by their imperfection. Indeed, it must necessarily be so if God is to do anything through the agency of human beings in this world, since "all have sinned and fall short of the glory of God" (Rom. 3:23). The statement that "in all things God works for the good of those who love him" (8:28) applies just as much to the wicked persecutions of the Roman emperor Nero and the genocides of the contemporary world as it does to the "impersonal" forces of nature. That is why it is not simply famine and danger that cannot separate us from the love of God but even persecution and the sword (8:35).

What is more, God's power is demonstrated not merely in restraining such outbreaks of wickedness, but even in harnessing them. Do we find that surprising? Perhaps the fact that we are astonished that God can achieve his purposes through someone like Nero or Hitler, while at the same time being unsurprised at God's achieving anything through us, shows how shallow an understanding we really have of the depths of our own sin and defilement. In truth, it is really no more of a miracle that God accomplishes his purposes through the sin-tainted acts of Pol Pot or Stalin than that he does so through your sin-tainted acts or mine.

THE ISSUE OF BLAME. Passing the buck for sin is an intrinsic part of present-day human nature. As the contemporary saying goes, "It's not whether you win or lose, but how you place the blame."

Whenever something goes wrong, we seek to find someone else who is responsible. When we sin, we seek to pass the buck for our sin by saying, "It wasn't my fault; it's just the way that I was made"; or, "It's my parent's fault, or my family's fault, or my environment's fault." Interestingly, animals never do this. My dog can, and frequently does, do wrong. When you find him with his head in the garbage (again!), he can look as guilty as can be. He knows that he should not do it. But he never points the paw at someone else and says, "It was all his fault. He made me do it." Only humans do that.

This is, of course, not merely a modern condition; it goes back all the way to the Fall. When God confronted the first man and woman with their sin, immediately the excuses began to flow (Gen. 3:12–13). The man said: "The woman you put here with me—she gave me some fruit from the tree, and I ate it." In the Hebrew, the word order is revealing: Adam starts off blaming God ("The woman *you* gave to be with me"), then he moves on to the woman (the feminine pronoun is emphatic, "*she* gave it to me"); only with the last word of the sentence do we get to anything close to a confession ("and I ate," which is a single word in Hebrew).

Then God turns to the woman: "What is this you have done?" She, in turn, starts her list (lit., "The serpent, he deceived me"), and then with the final word of the sentence the single word confession ("and I ate"). God's judgment, however, falls on them all—in spite of their excuses—for all have sinned. So it is with contemporary men and women. All of our excuses will not save us from the judgment to come because that judgment is truly comprehensive: *All* will stand before God to give an account of their lives.

Appearing before the judgment seat. The reality and certainty of the coming Day of Judgment is what exposes the futility of all the idolatries to which we give ourselves. Is your idol your career? Do you really expect your position in the company to impress anyone on that day? Is your idol your possessions? Your Cadillac and your mansion in Beverly Hills will not be with you on that day. Is your idol your children? Will they be able to gain you preferential treatment on that day? Is your idol your church? There will be no "fast track" for those who have belonged to the "correct" denomination on that day, or for those who have filled respected positions such as pastors, elders, and deacons. Gold and silver will be of no value either, nor will connections—all the things in which we have trusted will turn to dust. On that day, the separation between the sheep and the goats will simply be based on the presence or absence of a living relationship with the Living God, through Jesus Christ.

But if that is the end of all things, why do we live in the meantime as if the present reality is what is really important? Why do we strive so hard to accumulate possessions that will not last and to gain influence and power that will not ultimately benefit us? The reason is that we have given ourselves over to our various idolatries and have forgotten our inescapable accountability to the one true God. Even believers will have to give an account for their actions, as the apostle Paul reminds us: "For we must all appear before the judgment seat of Christ, that each one may receive what is due him for the things done while in the body, whether good or bad" (2 Cor. 5:10). We need to learn to see the end from the beginning, to envisage the future vividly here and now and to let that vision dominate our lives.

Living in the light of the future. Have you never wondered why the Bible gives us such vivid depictions of heaven and hell? Do you ever sit down and imagine yourself joining in the praise and worship with a full heart of thanksgiving for what Jesus Christ has done for you? Do you imagine yourself hearing the Lord saying to you, "Well done, good and faithful servant" (Matt. 25:21)? Do you see yourself walking down the streets of gold, meeting and sharing fellowship with loved ones who have gone before and with the great Christians of the past?

And do you also hold before your eyes the awesome reality of the eternal damnation of the lost? Part of our problem is that this world seems very real and solid, and the other world shady and unreal. Thus, we think to ourselves, "Yes, I would like the Lord to return . . . but not before I get married, or before I finish this project at work, or before I go on this trip." But of course, it is really the other way about. It is heaven that is real and solid and substantial, while this world is shadowy and unsubstantial.

In his book *The Great Divorce*,[13] C. S. Lewis pictures a group from hell on a day trip to heaven. One of the things they find bothersome is that everything there is far more real than they are. Even the grass is more substantial than they are and so it does not bend under their weight, making it painful for them to walk. In just the same way, the things that are so real and substantial to us in this world are unreal and unsubstantial when compared to the world to come.

Have you ever had a powerful experience of God's presence and closeness, perhaps in prayer or in a worship service? That is nothing compared to the presence of God that we will experience in glory. Or have you experienced the frustration of a single night without sleep, even in a comfortable bed, or weeks and months of unrelenting pain? That is nothing when set beside the fearsome reality of eternal separation from God, eternal torment, and frustration. As you replay over and over in your mind the videotape of the scriptural presentation of eternity, it becomes more real and substantial in your thinking. For Christians, that should mean a growing longing for that day; for those that are not Christians, repeated exposure to the truth of eternity should mean a growing (and appropriate) fear of the prospect. For that reason, heaven and hell should feature prominently in the preaching of our churches.[14]

It is striking that those for whom the present world holds least attraction are most passionate in their desire for the new world. Those experiencing persecution for their faith die witnessing to their expectation of immediately being present with the Lord. Those whose bodies are worn out or broken down look with eagerness to being free of their shackles, even as they may fear the pain of the process or lament leaving the ones they love. I have preached on the Beatitudes several times in different churches but never with such power as when I spoke to a congregation traumatized by the

---

13. New York: MacMillan, 1946.

14. For an extended example of how this can be done, see Thomas Boston's classic *Human Nature in Its Fourfold State* (Edinburgh: Banner of Truth, 1964 reprint). This book describes the original situation of the human race in the state of innocence before the Fall, the post-Fall situation apart from Christ, the Christian's present situation in this world, and finally a description of one's final state in heaven or hell. The material originated as sermons that were preached to a rural community in eighteenth-century Scotland and therefore represents a pastorally motivated rather than a doctrinally motivated presentation.

recent discovery of a recurrence of breast cancer in the wife of a beloved elder. In that pain, the proclamation of the reality and nearness of heaven became infinitely precious to those who were there.

Experiencing God's grace in the here and now. Some, however, will experience greater consequences here and now for their sin, just as the generation of Ezekiel's day found the ax of God's judgment descending on them. Pride, while it may precede a fall, is rarely fatal. Sexual immorality, on the other hand, may lead to contracting AIDS, with all of its deadly consequences. That does not mean that sexual immorality is a worse sin than pride, or that all those who have AIDS are under God's wrath. The present judgments of God (those times when we do receive in this life the consequences of our sin) and the present mercies of God (all those times when we do not receive the consequences of our sin) are both intended to lead us to repentance. If God were never gracious to us, we would have little reason to expect forgiveness from him; but if God never judged sin, we would be likely to consider it a matter of little importance to him. The balance in the world is intended to reinforce the biblical teaching that God is a God of holiness and mercy, of justice and grace.

What specifically do the present judgments of God achieve in our lives? In the first place, as mentioned above, they act as a demonstration of his justice and a restraining influence on the spread of sin. When someone abandons a spouse and children and runs off with someone else, and then lives to regret the pain he or she has caused to all concerned, that may deter others from committing the same sin. But in addition, when the judgment of God falls upon us in the present, it exposes the nature of all the false hiding places to which we run.

Judah was warned they would find no hiding place in their wealth, for the whole commercial endeavor would be undermined (Ezek. 7:12, 19). They had turned their wealth into idolatry—in their case literally, by constructing idols out of their silver and gold. But in the day of distress, it would be evident that their idols could do nothing for them. If God does not intervene, they may never discover how empty of lasting value their lives are. But if God causes them to lose the objects of their idolatry, it becomes clear that the blessings their idol offered were empty, unable to fill the yawning void in the soul. As a precursor of the final judgment, a present judgment may become the means for turning a life around. The pain of the lives we have shattered, including our own, may cause us to be humbled and return to our heavenly Father.

Or it may not. There are plenty of people whose idol has been shattered by God's intervention, yet they have not turned to God. Their wealth may be gone, yet they cling to the hope that someday it will return. Their health may be broken, yet they may simply become embittered and despairing.

Their long-term friendships may be destroyed, yet rather than listen to the appeals of those friends they turn in on themselves. There is nothing automatic about repentance. Only under the sovereign grace of God do his judgments produce the fruit of changed lives.

We must, therefore, take God's grace seriously while it is offered to us. It is possible for a society to reach a point of hardness where God removes his witnesses from it, leaving it to its fate. The countries of Asia Minor, where many of the first churches were established, have been in many cases virtually without a gospel witness for centuries. We cannot presume that our case as a nation will be different. Nor can we as individuals assume that the offer of the gospel will be forever open to us. Even if our lives are spared, yet it is possible to become hardened to the gospel to such a point that there is no return. We become so inured in our pride that we are deaf to the only good news that can save us. God's only word to us is then imminent and comprehensive doom.

Ezekiel 8–9

I N THE SIXTH YEAR, in the sixth month on the fifth day, while
I was sitting in my house and the elders of Judah were sitting before me, the hand of the Sovereign LORD came
upon me there. ²I looked, and I saw a figure like that of a man.
From what appeared to be his waist down he was like fire, and
from there up his appearance was as bright as glowing metal.
³He stretched out what looked like a hand and took me by the
hair of my head. The Spirit lifted me up between earth and
heaven and in visions of God he took me to Jerusalem, to the
entrance to the north gate of the inner court, where the idol
that provokes to jealousy stood. ⁴And there before me was the
glory of the God of Israel, as in the vision I had seen in the
plain.

⁵Then he said to me, "Son of man, look toward the north."
So I looked, and in the entrance north of the gate of the altar I
saw this idol of jealousy.

⁶And he said to me, "Son of man, do you see what they are
doing—the utterly detestable things the house of Israel is
doing here, things that will drive me far from my sanctuary?
But you will see things that are even more detestable."

⁷Then he brought me to the entrance to the court. I
looked, and I saw a hole in the wall. ⁸He said to me, "Son of
man, now dig into the wall." So I dug into the wall and saw a
doorway there.

⁹And he said to me, "Go in and see the wicked and
detestable things they are doing here." ¹⁰So I went in and
looked, and I saw portrayed all over the walls all kinds of
crawling things and detestable animals and all the idols of the
house of Israel. ¹¹In front of them stood seventy elders of the
house of Israel, and Jaazaniah son of Shaphan was standing
among them. Each had a censer in his hand, and a fragrant
cloud of incense was rising.

¹²He said to me, "Son of man, have you seen what the
elders of the house of Israel are doing in the darkness, each at
the shrine of his own idol? They say, 'The LORD does not see
us; the LORD has forsaken the land.'" ¹³Again, he said, "You
will see them doing things that are even more detestable."

¹⁴Then he brought me to the entrance to the north gate of the house of the LORD, and I saw women sitting there, mourning for Tammuz. ¹⁵He said to me, "Do you see this, son of man? You will see things that are even more detestable than this."

¹⁶He then brought me into the inner court of the house of the LORD, and there at the entrance to the temple, between the portico and the altar, were about twenty-five men. With their backs toward the temple of the LORD and their faces toward the east, they were bowing down to the sun in the east.

¹⁷He said to me, "Have you seen this, son of man? Is it a trivial matter for the house of Judah to do the detestable things they are doing here? Must they also fill the land with violence and continually provoke me to anger? Look at them putting the branch to their nose! ¹⁸Therefore I will deal with them in anger; I will not look on them with pity or spare them. Although they shout in my ears, I will not listen to them."

⁹:¹Then I heard him call out in a loud voice, "Bring the guards of the city here, each with a weapon in his hand." ²And I saw six men coming from the direction of the upper gate, which faces north, each with a deadly weapon in his hand. With them was a man clothed in linen who had a writing kit at his side. They came in and stood beside the bronze altar.

³Now the glory of the God of Israel went up from above the cherubim, where it had been, and moved to the threshold of the temple. Then the LORD called to the man clothed in linen who had the writing kit at his side ⁴and said to him, "Go throughout the city of Jerusalem and put a mark on the foreheads of those who grieve and lament over all the detestable things that are done in it."

⁵As I listened, he said to the others, "Follow him through the city and kill, without showing pity or compassion. ⁶Slaughter old men, young men and maidens, women and children, but do not touch anyone who has the mark. Begin at my sanctuary." So they began with the elders who were in front of the temple.

⁷Then he said to them, "Defile the temple and fill the courts with the slain. Go!" So they went out and began killing throughout the city. ⁸While they were killing and I was left alone, I fell facedown, crying out, "Ah, Sovereign LORD! Are you going to destroy the entire remnant of Israel in this outpouring of your wrath on Jerusalem?"

⁹He answered me, "The sin of the house of Israel and Judah is exceedingly great; the land is full of bloodshed and the city is full of injustice. They say, 'The LORD has forsaken the land; the LORD does not see.' ¹⁰So I will not look on them with pity or spare them, but I will bring down on their own heads what they have done."

¹¹Then the man in linen with the writing kit at his side brought back word, saying, "I have done as you commanded."

THE VISION OF Ezekiel 8–11 is a unified whole, as readily becomes apparent when 8:1–3 is compared with 11:24–25. Nevertheless, for the sake of simplicity, we will divide it up into two parts: chapters 8–9 and 10–11.

The vision opens with a date: the fifth day of the sixth month of the sixth year (of Jehoiachin's exile); in our reckoning, that would be September 18, 592 B.C. In other words, some fourteen months have passed since the opening vision of the book. The intervening time has been largely spent in performing the sign-acts of Ezekiel 4; depending on the interpretation of the 390 plus 40 days, Ezekiel has either just completed that period or is close to completion of that period.[1]

However, although the date formula serves to mark chapters 8–11 off from what precedes, the close connection with chapter 7 is maintained. Ezekiel 8 unfolds and details the accusation of "detestable idols and vile images" made in 7:20, while the theme of "the land ... full of bloodshed and the city ... full of injustice" (9:9) echoes the charge of 7:23. The divine response to this state of affairs is: "I will not look on them with pity or spare them, but I will bring down on their own heads what they have done" (9:10; cf. 7:4). In the same way, the divine destruction of chapter 9 corresponds to that threatened in chapter 7. Thus, it would not be inappropriate to say that Ezekiel 8–9 depicts in visionary form what Ezekiel 7 stated in oracular style.

Nevertheless, there are also differences. The vision of Ezekiel 8–11 is intended for a specific audience, "the elders of Judah," who have gathered at Ezekiel's house. Though the purpose of their visit is not recorded, they were presumably seeking a favorable oracle, perhaps one proclaiming an early

---

1. The period is understood as completed by including the 40 days within the 390 or assuming an intercalatory month (Taylor, *Ezekiel*, 80); however, there seems no objection to the vision taking place within the period of the sign-act (Greenberg, *Ezekiel 1–20*, 166).

end to the Exile.[2] Second Kings 6:32 describes the elders of Samaria sitting with Elisha and receiving an encouraging word from the Lord (see 7:1), while Ezekiel 14:1 and 20:1 record similar visits by the elders to Ezekiel.[3] What the elders receive from the prophet is no word of comfort but rather a categorical denunciation of their sins and the sins of the community they represent. They are not simply the audience to whom the vision is related, but also one of the chief targets of the vision.[4]

As the vision opens, Ezekiel sees a glowing figure in human form, corresponding to what he had seen in 1:27. Once more he is transported by the agency of the Spirit and shown a vision of the glory of God (ch. 10); the context of the vision, however, is no longer the situation of the exiles but the defiled city of Jerusalem. The prophet is shown four scenes of increasing abomination, with the offense to God being greater as the scenes in which they take place move nearer to the center of the temple.

(1) His tour begins with a vision of an "idol of jealousy" at the north gate of the city (8:3–6).[5] This seems to have been an idol in the shape of a human being, perhaps the Canaanite goddess Asherah, whose location at the outer north gate suggests that she was intended to guard the city from attack. As we saw in Ezekiel 1, the north was the traditional direction from which Jerusalem's enemies approached. If so, then the goddess is powerless to prevent the sack of the city by the Lord's appointed destroyers in Ezekiel 9. The focus of the attention here, however, is the effect that this image has on the Lord. It "provokes [him] to jealousy" (8:3; cf. Deut. 32:16); God will not share Israel's worship, which rightfully belongs to him, with other gods, and he has proof of her infidelity.

---

2. According to Jer. 28, in the fourth year of Zedekiah's reign the prophet Hananiah had declared that within two years the Babylonian yoke would be broken, while the captives and the temple treasures would be returned. If this oracle was known among the exiles, the fact that the clock was running down to zero on this prophecy may have prompted some expectation of imminent help.

3. In 14:1; 20:1 they are called "the elders of Israel," not "the elders of Judah." But the two expressions are in many cases virtually synonymous in Ezekiel. Notice, for instance, how the charges in Ezek. 8 implicate both the house of Israel (8:6, 10–12) and the house of Judah (8:17). Indeed, the summary statement of 9:9 indicts "the house of Israel and Judah." See Walther Zimmerli, "Israel im Buche Ezechiel," *VT* 8 (1958): 82.

4. Halperin, *Seeking Ezekiel*, 58.

5. The NIV translation "to the entrance to the north gate of the inner court" is based on the MT. The phrase lit. translates: "to the entrance of the gate, the inner one, facing to the north." The word "inner one" is a feminine adjective that hangs oddly beside the masculine word "gate" (note that the participle "facing" is masculine); "inner one" is not attested by the LXX, and it disturbs the general flow of the chapter from outer parts inward (as in chs. 40–43) and should therefore be omitted. See Zimmerli, *Ezekiel*, 1:217.

(2) However, abominable though this idolatry is, worse is yet to come. Next, Ezekiel is shown seventy elders of the house of Israel, leaders among the lay community, offering incense to idols in a secret chamber (8:7–13). What was done in public at a distance from the temple is also being done in private at the entrance of the temple courtyard. The elders are portrayed as standing before a wall of carved animal figures, each offering clouds of incense from a burner (8:11).[6]

In contrast to the Canaanite origin of the Asherah idol, the practice of offering incense to animal figures may well have an Egyptian provenance.[7] The motivation was probably apotropaic, that is, to ward off dangers from demonic forces.[8] Their actions provide a shocking contrast to the seventy "elders of Israel" in the Pentateuch, Israel's leaders in the desert period, who received the unique privilege of seeing God (Ex. 24:1–11) and were endowed with the same Spirit as Moses (Num. 11:16–30). Here these "non-Spirit-filled" elders find justification for their conduct in the belief that the Lord does *not* see (Ezek. 8:12). One of their number is named as Jaazaniah, who is designated the son of Shaphan—and thus equally shockingly associated with a family that was prominent in the reforms of Josiah's days (2 Kings 22:3–14).[9]

The identity of these secret transgressors as "elders of the house of Israel" is repeated for emphasis in the next verse (Ezek. 8:12), along with their own self-justification for their idolatrous acts: "The LORD does not see us; the LORD has forsaken the land." In the light of what they saw as God's abandonment of them, they felt justified in pursuing other deities who might help out. The Lord's response to this statement will emerge in 9:9; however, for the present it is sufficient to point to the vision itself as contradicting their belief. The Lord does indeed see, as the repeated refrain "Son of man, do you see ...?" underlines (8:6, 12, 15, 17).[10] Far from the Lord's having abandoned the land, it is they who have driven the Lord away (8:6). Far from their incense-burning being an effective means of warding off dangers, it is one of the causes of God's impending judgment on them. Ironically, it is their vision that is clouded, not the Lord's.

(3) Worse still is the sight of women weeping for Tammuz at the north gate of the temple itself (8:14–15). With each new scene we approach closer

---

6. The only other place in the Old Testament where an "incense burner" (*miqteret*) is found is in 2 Chron. 26:19, where Uzziah is similarly convicted of cultic irregularities.

7. Martin Schmidt, *Prophet und Tempel* (Zurich: Evangelischer Verlag, 1948), 139.

8. Block, *Ezekiel 1–24*, 293.

9. Schmidt, *Prophet und Tempel*, 139. This family was also closely associated with Jeremiah (Jer. 26:24; 29:3; 39:14); cf. Burke O. Long, "Social Dimensions of Prophetic Conflict," *Semeia* 21 (1982): 46.

10. Compare the opening vision, which described the wheels of the divine chariot as "full of eyes" (1:18).

to the heart of Israel's worship. Weeping for Tammuz was a Babylonian ritual, marking the death and descent into the underworld of the god Dumuzi, whose mythological course of death and "resurrection" (or more accurately, "return") was thought to be parallel to the annual rhythm of nature. The cultic act of mourning was believed to counteract the loss of power of new life, thus hastening the return of fertility.[11] Lamentation for the dead had been substituted for the worship of the living God.[12]

(4) The final and supreme act of idolatry takes place within the inner court of the temple itself, where Ezekiel sees twenty-five men turning their backs on the temple proper and prostrating themselves to the east, in worship of the sun (8:16).[13] This is the ultimate abomination: Instead of bowing down to worship the Lord and seeking his face, they turn their backs on God and worship the created order.

In four brief scenes, then, Ezekiel has been shown the comprehensive nature of the sins of Jerusalem. Their sin extends from outside the city gate to the inner courtyard of the temple itself. It involves both men and women, even the seventy elders, symbolic of the leadership of the whole people. It includes idolatry imported from all sorts of surrounding nations (Canaan, Egypt, and Babylon) and involving all kinds of gods (male and female human figures, animal figures, and stellar bodies). This is a unified, universalized religion, the ultimate multifaith worship service. From the Lord's perspective, however, the picture is one of abomination piled on abomination.

The combination of such a mass of idolatry with their sins against humanity (summarized in 8:17 under the general title "violence") is an explosive mixture. They have continually provoked the Lord to anger and will now receive their just desserts. Even as the ax is poised to fall, their last gesture is one of defiant idolatry, "putting the branch to their nose" (8:17).[14] They will receive what they deserve as the Lord deals with them in his wrath, neither pitying nor sparing. He will be deaf to their loudest cries for help.

What is more, the Lord will do some shouting of his own, and unlike their ineffectual cries, his voice will make things happen (Ezek. 9:1).[15] He summons six "guards," each of whom appears armed with a club. These guards

---

11. Thorkild Jacobsen, "Toward the Image of Tammuz," in *Toward the Image of Tammuz and Other Essays,* ed. W. L. Moran (Cambridge, Mass.: Harvard Univ. Press, 1970), 100.

12. Block, *Ezekiel 1–24,* 296.

13. These men are not here further identified; however, Ezek. 9:6 makes it clear that they too are elders. On this, see Duguid, *Ezekiel and the Leaders of Israel,* 70.

14. This obscure Hebrew phrase has inspired vast amounts of literature attempting to clarify it. In general it has been understood either as an insulting gesture or action of some kind, or as a final act of idolatry. See Block, *Ezekiel 1–24,* 299.

15. "He called in my hearing with a loud voice" (lit.) in Ezek. 9:1 closely parallels "[Though] they call in my hearing with a loud voice" (lit.) in 8:18.

would normally have had the responsibility of standing at the gates, protecting the realm of the sacred from profane intrusion.[16] Here they appear together with a priestly figure dressed in linen, armed only with a writing kit.

These figures are normally interpreted as angelic beings because of their superhuman role in the vision and the symbolic nature of their total number (seven). However, it is worth noting that if 9:1–2 existed as a fragment, without the surrounding context, we would naturally understand it as speaking of normal human figures obeying the summons of the king. This helps us to remember the dual nature of these figures. On the one hand, in the vision they are the angelic servants of the Most High, wreaking his judgments on the earth; on the other hand, those same judgments are carried out in history through human agency, so the six destroyers may equally aptly be seen to represent the Babylonian invaders. If this much is true, is it not also true that the seventh figure, the priestly writer, acts in some sense as Ezekiel's own *alter ego*? He obediently passes among the people prior to the judgment, distinguishing the righteous from the wicked, marking out those who sigh and cry[17] over the detestable things done in Jerusalem (9:4).

Hard on his heels come the agents of destruction, who themselves take on the attitude of God toward the people (9:5): They are to strike (cf. 7:9) without pity or compassion (cf. 8:18). Their destructive work is a kind of reenactment of the first Passover, only with Judah instead of Egypt as the scene of the devastation. Just as the Lord passed through (*ʿābar*, Ex. 12:23) Egypt, handing over those without a protective mark to the destroyer (*mašḥît*, Ex. 12:23), so also the six are to "pass through" (*ʿābar*) the city, "slaughtering to destruction" (*tahargû lᵉmašḥît*) anyone who does not bear the mark. All those without the mark are to be slain—young and old, male and female (9:5–6).[18] The categories listed demonstrate that even the defenseless, the frail, and the innocent are condemned to destruction.[19]

The slaughter is to begin at the temple with the chief idolaters: the twenty-five elders who were worshiping the sun (9:6; cf. 8:16). Unlike in the case of Queen Athaliah, who was dragged out of the temple complex before being executed so that it would not be defiled by her blood (2 Kings 11:15–

---

16. So in 44:11 the Levites are assigned the duty of serving as guards ("having charge of" is the same word trans. "guards" in 9:1) at the gates of the new temple. See Rodney K. Duke, "Punishment or Restoration: Another Look at the Levites of Ezekiel 44.6–16," *JSOT* 40 (1988): 65.

17. The assonance of the Hebrew *hanneᵉnāḥîm wᵉhanneᵉnāqîm* is lost in the NIV: "those who grieve and lament." Block translates "groan and moan" (*Ezekiel 1–24*, 307).

18. This total annihilation recalls the "holy war" associated with the occupation of the Promised Land (cf. Josh. 6:21).

19. Block, *Ezekiel 1–24*, 308.

16), now the killing takes place within the temple itself (Ezek. 9:7). It is already so contaminated by their idolatry that God himself has no compunction about defiling it further (9:7; cf. 7:22: "They will desecrate my treasured place").

In the midst of the carnage, Ezekiel is left alone (9:8) before the Lord. He begins to fear that he may really be all alone—a remnant of one—and he cries out "Ah, Sovereign LORD! Are you going to destroy the entire remnant of Israel in this outpouring of your wrath on Jerusalem?" The Lord's answer to the prophet's question appears to be yes. He points to the depth of the abominations and sin of the house of Israel and Judah. The land is full of bloodshed and the city full of injustice. The attitude of the elders is summed up in this phrase: "The LORD has forsaken the land; the LORD does not see" (9:9). Therefore, they can expect no pity or compassion, but just retribution for their actions, which is the final proof that he has indeed seen everything that has transpired.

Yet at this critical juncture, precisely when it appears that all hope is gone, suddenly the priestly figure with the writing kit reappears, saying, "I have done as you commanded" (9:11). His appearance also answers Ezekiel's question concerning the remnant, for he stands mute testimony to the Lord's purpose to save those who sigh and mourn over the abominations of Jerusalem. We are not told how many he has marked—indeed, we are not even told that he has marked any—yet his presence acts to mitigate slightly the awful severity of the judgment, just as the rainbow of 1:28 tempers slightly the coming windstorm of God's wrath. As at the time of the Exodus, there is shelter from God's destruction for those who are willing to take refuge in the appointed sign. But on this occasion, it seems that those being saved will indeed be few.

Bridging Contexts

ROTTEN TO THE CORE. When interpreting these chapters, it is essential to remember that what is recorded here is a vision. That does not mean that the events recounted here are *unrelated* to reality: For instance, the destruction of Jerusalem that Ezekiel witnessed was the foreshadowing of the very real destruction of that city by the Babylonians in 586 B.C. But it does mean that they are not *directly* related to historical events. The six armed guards represent the Babylonian forces,[20] but they are not the same as them. This distinction means that we should not assume

---

20. Thus it is not coincidental that they appear at the north gate, the direction from which both divine and human enemies come in Ezekiel.

that the view Ezekiel received of Jerusalem would have been that open to any-one touring the temple precincts in 592 B.C.; rather, it is a stylized repre-sentation of reality intended to make a particular point.[21]

That particular point is not hard to find: The core of Israel's being is rot-ten with idolatry. The people as a whole had abandoned the true God and instead gone after every possible alternative god. Even when the worship took place in the temple precincts (under the title of Yahwism?), the true God was not being worshiped. The incompatibility of the alien religions with the true religion is nowhere clearer than in the case of the twenty-five sun-worshipers, who turn their backs on the temple building proper (and thus on the Lord) to carry out their devotions (8:16). If the bastion of true religion has thus been infected, then there must be no true worship left anywhere in Israel.

Yet in the midst of this comprehensive catalog of idolatry, we should not miss the essentially lay and democratic nature of the cults described.[22] There are no priestly or royal figures leading the worship; instead, the leading fig-ures are repeatedly identified as "elders." It is thus the mass of the laity, rep-resented by the elders, who are identified as primarily responsible for the idolatrous abominations that fill the land.[23] This observation, of course, grows in significance when it is remembered that Ezekiel's audience is com-posed of "the elders of Judah" (8:1). There is no one else on whom to lay the blame for Jerusalem's destruction.

The Lord as a God of judgment. The result of comprehensive idolatry is apparently comprehensive slaughter. The practice of holy war, whereby all the inhabitants of a town were to be slaughtered, was commanded by God when Israel occupied the Promised Land. On that occasion, Israel filled the place of the armed angelic beings, acting as agents of God's righteous judgment. They functioned as the human equivalent of the burning sulfur from heaven that destroyed Sodom and Gomorrah and all its residents, young and old. The Canaanites were not to be destroyed because they were in the way of progress, innocent bystanders mown down by the juggernaut of God's gentrification of their neighborhood. They were judged because their sin reached full measure, as Abraham had been informed (Gen. 15:16). Now, however, Israel has become exactly like the Canaanites they replaced; their sin has reached full measure, and God's judgment will descend likewise on them.

---

21. On the whole question of the veracity of Ezekiel's vision, see Duguid, *Ezekiel and the Leaders of Israel,* 65–68.

22. Bruce Vawter and Leslie J. Hoppe, *Ezekiel* (ITC; Grand Rapids: Eerdmans, 1991), 66. Compare in this regard Moshe Greenberg's conception of "private" cults (i.e., those admin-istered without benefit of clergy) in "Prolegomenon," *Pseudo-Ezekiel and the Original Prophecy by C. C. Torrey and Critical Articles* (New York: Ktav, 1970), xxxiii, n. 47.

23. See my *Ezekiel and the Leaders of Israel.*

This is an aspect of God's character that we do not often think about. We like to think of God as "the LORD, the LORD, the compassionate and gracious God, slow to anger, abounding in love and faithfulness, maintaining love to thousands, and forgiving wickedness, rebellion and sin" (Ex. 34:6–7). Yet he goes on to reveal himself also as the One who "does not leave the guilty unpunished; he punishes the children and their children for the sin of the fathers to the third and fourth generation." As one writer comments about the fate of Sodom and Gomorrah: "The Lord waits long to be gracious, as if he knew not how to smite. He smites at last as if he knew not how to pity."[24] When judgment fell on Canaan, it was swift, inexorable, completely lacking in pity. Now the "new Canaanites," Israel will experience the same inexorable wrath of God.

Such a concept of judgment is not palatable to modern minds. But we may not realize that it was no more palatable to ancient "civilized" thought either. The ancient heretic Marcion drew a radical distinction between the wrath-filled God of the Old Testament and the purely loving God and Father of our Lord Jesus Christ, revealed in the New Testament. In response, Tertullian pointed out what an emasculated, inconsistent figure Marcion's god was. This supposed deity:

> plainly judges evil by not willing it, and condemns it by prohibiting it; while on the other hand, he acquits it by not avenging it, and lets it go free by not punishing it. What a prevaricator of truth is such a god! What a dissembler to his own decision! Afraid to condemn what he really condemns, afraid to hate what he does not love, permitting that to be done which he does not allow, choosing to indicate what he dislikes rather than deeply examine it![25]

Such an attitude of speaking forcefully against evil, while all the time being unwilling to act against it, is considered utterly reprehensible in world leaders. Yet Marcion's modern followers, who shy away from the idea of God's wrath against sin, have a picture of God that makes him appear not unlike Neville Chamberlain, returning from Munich waving a piece of paper proclaiming, "Peace in our time!" unwilling to confront the growing power of Hitler with actions. In Niebuhr's classic description of liberal theology, they picture "a God without wrath, who brought men without sin into a kingdom without judgment, through the ministrations of a Christ without a cross."[26]

Holy war stands as the clearest possible declaration of God's commitment to the purity and holiness of his people, totally separate from possibly

---

24. Robert S. Candlish, *Studies in Genesis* (Grand Rapids: Kregel, 1979 reprint), 327.
25. Tertullian, *Against Marcion*, 1.27.
26. H. Richard Niebuhr, *The Kingdom of God in America* (New York: Harper, 1959), 193.

defiling influences. God's holiness remains implacably opposed to sin. In the present, we are therefore enrolled as his people in a no-holds-barred contest with the forces of the evil one (Eph. 6:10–18), while in the future there will yet come a day when God's wrath will be poured out comprehensively on the wicked (Rom. 2:5).

Vengeance belongs to the Lord. At the same time, there is a danger with being too comfortable proclaiming the wrath of God. In those periods of history where the church has been entirely comfortable with divine judgment, people have sometimes been quick to call it down on their opponents or set themselves up as the agents of divine vengeance. Jesus had to rebuke James and John for wishing to initiate eschatological vengeance (fire from heaven) on a village that would not receive Jesus (Luke 9:54). In our present situation in redemptive history, we are not to slaughter our enemies but to win them over with inexplicable deeds of tolerance and kindness (Matt. 5:39–42; Rom. 12:17–21). Now is the time for the preaching of the gospel to all nations, the bringing in of those who are outside into the covenant community.

What gives urgency to our task is the knowledge that there is a sure and certain Day of Judgment coming. Perhaps it may be a morning like this, when people are out taking their kids to school and doing the shopping. They may be planning weekend trips to Disneyland and the lake, looking forward to weddings and family gatherings, busy with the chatter of what they did yesterday and what they plan to do tomorrow. On just such a day the heavenly shout will be heard, just as Ezekiel heard it in his vision, and the time of judgment will begin. Those spared in that judgment will be only those who, like Ezekiel's remnant, sigh and mourn over the abominations that surround them and whose foreheads have been marked out with the name of the Lamb and of his Father (Rev. 14:1). For the rest, there will be nothing to expect but eternal fire. The destruction of the idolaters of Jerusalem stands for us as an awful warning of God's wrath to come.

CONTEMPORARY IDOLATRIES. In all good soap operas—and most bad ones as well—the plot revolves around the various idolatries of the characters. Now I have to confess at this point that I am not a regular watcher of soap operas, so I cannot really speak from firsthand experience. But while doing some academic research on the subject I came across this summary of the characters in *Melrose Place*:

> Sydney has been a hooker, an exotic dancer, and a drug addict. Jo harpooned Reed, the father of her child, then Kimberly kidnapped the kid, forcing Jo to go to the authorities, who put the child up for adop-

tion so that neither one would have it. Matt was framed for the murder of his lover; Jake pushed his half-brother off a building; Alison became an alcoholic; went into recovery, then fell off the wagon again, before temporarily going blind in the 1995 explosion (courtesy of Kimberly) that blew the apartment complex to bits.[27]

Just an everyday tale of ordinary folk, isn't it? It tells the story of the usual selection of lust, love, murder, mayhem, and addictive behaviors. Well, perhaps it is not exactly everyday, but what makes these soap operas so fascinating to people is the fact that these characters have no restraints on the expression of their idolatries. Why do they fall into bed with one another so easily? It is because their feelings of lust have become an idolatry, an idolatry that says that nothing in the world is of comparable significance to meeting the demands of these feelings right now. God's law, which forbids immorality and adultery, is considered by them a matter of relatively insignificant weight.

Why do they murder one another at the drop of a hat? It is because their feelings of jealousy and anger have become an idolatry that says, "Feed me or I will make your life miserable!" Why do they lie and cheat and steal? It is because their covetous hearts have fastened onto an idol that they must have, regardless of the consequences. These are idolaters who live out the full scope of their idolatries. Face it, without idolatry every soap opera would be reduced to the most basic, not to say boring, story lines.

In Ezekiel 8, the prophet depicted abominations of *Melrose Place* proportions. In this chapter, he sees four visions of idolatrous groups operating within the Jerusalem temple itself, turning it from the Lord's place into Marduk's Place . . . and Asherah's Place and the home of every idolatry under the sun. To those involved in these idolatrous practices, he gives the warning that the result of comprehensive idolatry will be comprehensive slaughter, which he describes in visionary form in Ezekiel 9.

The dangers of practical polytheism. We too face an abundance of idols all around us in our multicultural age. Frequently, people speak of ours as being an age of pluralism, as if that somehow makes our time distinct from the past. This is palpable nonsense, for at many times in the past, not least during the New Testament era and the time of the Exile, God's people have found themselves placed in a melting pot of world religions. The options available in the "marketplace of religions" have often been just as diverse in previous centuries as they are at present.

In the face of such diversity, several responses are possible. Some take a smorgasbord approach and "mix and match" elements from a variety of

---

27. Rob Owen, *Gen X TV: The Brady Bunch to Melrose Place* (Syracuse: Syracuse Univ. Press, 1997), 101.

religions according to their own taste.[28] Such a "practical polytheism" may well be popular with the man or woman in the street, for it demands only what you wish to give and offers whatever you wish to ask. It makes no unwanted ethical demands, though it can take an ascetic form if that is your preference. The reward it offers can be an ethereal nirvana or materialistic success or a combination of both, depending on your taste.[29] In short, the hallmark of any pluralistic age is that idolatry comes in all shapes and sizes and encourages us to attend regularly the church or religious institution of our choice.

In contrast, the Bible urges us that the "choice" facing us is not between equally valid methods of expressing our spirituality but between truth and falsehood, between worshiping the God who created us or bowing down to abominations that are not gods at all. The essence of idolatry is not so much denying the reality of God but the relevance of God. Thus the saying of the elders of the house of Israel was, "The LORD does not see us; the LORD has forsaken the land" (8:12). They did not deny the existence of God but simply asserted his irrelevance. This perhaps sheds some light on the repeated finding in the polls that an overwhelming proportion of Americans believe in God's existence and in the Bible as his Word, yet never go to church or read the Bible. They are practical polytheists, who have created a religion to fit their own preferences.

Sometimes such practical polytheism even invades the church. There are those who support the idea of "multifaith" services, on the grounds that we are really all worshiping the same God, only under different labels. Ezekiel's vision, on the other hand, would categorically condemn such an approach. All of the worship that he sees, no matter what its source or how exalted and noble its liturgy, is a matter of turning one's back on the Lord, of foul abominations for which the judgment of God is coming on his people.

Nor is that simply a matter of Old Testament narrow-mindedness on Ezekiel's part. The apostle Paul is equally insistent on the incompatibility of Christianity and other religions. He urges the Corinthian Christians to flee from idolatry (1 Cor. 10:14). They are not to participate in pagan sacrifices alongside their Christian profession, for as he says: "You cannot drink the cup of the Lord and the cup of demons too; you cannot have a part in both the Lord's table and the table of demons. Are we trying to arouse the Lord's jealousy? Are we

---

28. See, for example, the account of such eclectic blends of religious elements among students given by Diane Winston in "Campuses Are a Bellwether for Society's Religious Revival," *The Chronicle of Higher Education* (January 16, 1998), A60.

29. One young lady, Sheila Larson, has explicitly dubbed her own brand of customized faith "Sheilaism." Others have followed the same course more implicitly. For a description of "Sheilaism," see Robert N. Bellah et al., *Habits of the Heart: Individualism and Commitment in American Life* (New York: Harper & Row, 1986), 221, 235.

stronger than he?" (1 Cor. 10:21–22). For Paul, just as much as for Ezekiel, participation in idolatry will rouse the Lord's jealousy, a thing greatly to be feared.

Baptism as an identifying mark. This radical distinction between the community of God's people and the rest of the world is the reason why we are baptized. Baptism, similar to circumcision in the old covenant, functions as a mark placed on an individual, identifying him or her as belonging to the covenant community.[30] It is a sign that they are under the authority of the covenant overlord, God himself. This aspect of baptism as marking one out from the world and under the authority of Christ is frequently not understood today. William Willimon tells of an experience he had after participating in a panel discussion on "Homosexuality and the Church." After the discussion, a young man came up to him saying that he was "a baptized Episcopalian" and "none of you have a right to tell me who I am. I define myself." Willimon's response to this person was to point out that if his first declaration were true ("I am a baptized Episcopalian"), his second declaration ("none of you have a right to tell me who I am") was necessarily false. In baptizing the young man, the church had staked a clear claim to tell him who he was.[31]

As those who have been baptized, we do not have the right to "choose for ourselves" whom we will serve or how we will serve. We are members of Christ's army, men and women under authority, who have been given our marching orders in the Scriptures. We must march in step with our commander or face the consequences. Within the church there is no room for compromise. Our devotion and loyalty must be uniquely committed to the Lord. Within our

---

30. In the early church, baptism often involved the actual marking of the child with the sign of the cross on the forehead, which was seen as an exact parallel to the marking with a *tāw* that Ezekiel envisaged in 9:4, since *tāw* in the ancient script took the shape of a cross (Origen, *Selecta in Ezechielem*, 13.800d; Tertullian, *Against Marcion*, 3.22; Jerome, *Commentary on Ezekiel*, 9:4–6). The Reformers were unconvinced by this (correct) observation (see Calvin, *Ezekiel I*, 218), and their Puritan followers argued strenuously against the "noxious ceremony" of signing the cross, seeing it as a superstitious, man-made ritual. The *Directory of Public Worship* produced by the Westminster Assembly therefore requires baptism to be "by pouring or sprinkling of water on the face of the child, without adding any other ceremony." However, though the ceremony itself may be unwarranted, the intent of those who defended the ceremony was in line with the biblical concept of baptism, as the words of the *Book of Common Prayer* make clear: "We receive this child into the congregation of Christ's flock and do sign him with the sign of the cross, in token that hereafter he shall not be ashamed to confess the faith of Christ crucified, and manfully to fight under his banner, against sin, the world and the devil, and to continue Christ's faithful soldier and servant unto his life's end." The sign of the cross was not a magic amulet ensuring salvation, but a draft notice, enlisting the baptized into Christ's army. Having received "the king's shilling," as it were, one must now fight for Christ or face the consequences of being a draft-dodger.

31. *Peculiar Speech: Preaching to the Baptized* (Grand Rapids: Eerdmans, 1992), 7. See esp. the quote from the *Book of Common Prayer* in the previous note.

hearts we must be aware of our own idolatries and root them out remorselessly through the repeated application of the Truth, God's Word. Moreover, we need to practice in our churches the kind of challenging preaching and biblical church discipline that confronts people's comfortable idolatries with the truth of God's wrath and the danger of being deceived into thinking that such idolatry can safely coexist with a Christian profession of faith. As Richard Lovelace puts it:

> We may need to challenge more, and comfort less, in our evangelism and discipleship. We need to make it harder for people to retain assurance of salvation when they move into serious sin. . . . We need to tell some persons who think they have gotten saved to get lost. The Puritans were biblically realistic about this; we have become sloppy and sentimental in promoting assurance under any circumstances.[32]

A proper attitude toward idolatry outside the church. Yet that does not mean that we must adopt a belligerent attitude to members of other religions. As we have already noted, Paul's attitude among the philosophers of Mars Hill in Athens, recorded in Acts 17, was different both from that of Ezekiel's vision and his own attitude toward the Corinthians. Surrounded by the temples of false religion, far from calling down fire and brimstone on them, he instead addressed them respectfully as people who were very religious (Acts 17:22). His attitude to idolatry *outside* the church was thus radically different to idolatry *inside* the church. To the pagans he spoke with great politeness, seeking to present the gospel to them in a winsome manner. But to those who sought to bring pagan practices from the outside into the church, he had no tolerance.

Similarly, we should be polite and respectful in our dealings with people who are not Christians. Whether they come to your door attempting to share their faith with you or you encounter them in your regular course of life, your motto should be 1 Peter 3:15–16: "Always be prepared to give an answer to everyone who asks you to give the reason for the hope that you have. But do this with gentleness and respect, keeping a clear conscience, so that those who speak maliciously against your good behavior in Christ may be ashamed of their slander." Yet as we answer them with politeness and gentleness, we must be under no illusions that they are simply seeking God by a different route, far less that "it doesn't matter what you believe as long as you are sincere." On the contrary, we are to remember with Peter that there is a judgment coming that begins "with the family of God; and if it begins with us, what will the outcome be for those who do not obey the gospel of God?" (1 Peter 4:17).

---

32. "Evangelicalism: Recovering a Tradition of Spiritual Depth," *The Reformed Journal* (September 1990): 25.

Ezekiel 10–11

ILOOKED, AND I SAW the likeness of a throne of sapphire above the expanse that was over the heads of the cherubim. ²The LORD said to the man clothed in linen, "Go in among the wheels beneath the cherubim. Fill your hands with burning coals from among the cherubim and scatter them over the city." And as I watched, he went in.

³Now the cherubim were standing on the south side of the temple when the man went in, and a cloud filled the inner court. ⁴Then the glory of the LORD rose from above the cherubim and moved to the threshold of the temple. The cloud filled the temple, and the court was full of the radiance of the glory of the LORD. ⁵The sound of the wings of the cherubim could be heard as far away as the outer court, like the voice of God Almighty when he speaks.

⁶When the LORD commanded the man in linen, "Take fire from among the wheels, from among the cherubim," the man went in and stood beside a wheel. ⁷Then one of the cherubim reached out his hand to the fire that was among them. He took up some of it and put it into the hands of the man in linen, who took it and went out. ⁸(Under the wings of the cherubim could be seen what looked like the hands of a man.)

⁹I looked, and I saw beside the cherubim four wheels, one beside each of the cherubim; the wheels sparkled like chrysolite. ¹⁰As for their appearance, the four of them looked alike; each was like a wheel intersecting a wheel. ¹¹As they moved, they would go in any one of the four directions the cherubim faced; the wheels did not turn about as the cherubim went. The cherubim went in whatever direction the head faced, without turning as they went. ¹²Their entire bodies, including their backs, their hands and their wings, were completely full of eyes, as were their four wheels. ¹³I heard the wheels being called "the whirling wheels." ¹⁴Each of the cherubim had four faces: One face was that of a cherub, the second the face of a man, the third the face of a lion, and the fourth the face of an eagle.

¹⁵Then the cherubim rose upward. These were the living creatures I had seen by the Kebar River. ¹⁶When the cherubim

moved, the wheels beside them moved; and when the cherubim spread their wings to rise from the ground, the wheels did not leave their side. ¹⁷When the cherubim stood still, they also stood still; and when the cherubim rose, they rose with them, because the spirit of the living creatures was in them.

¹⁸Then the glory of the LORD departed from over the threshold of the temple and stopped above the cherubim. ¹⁹While I watched, the cherubim spread their wings and rose from the ground, and as they went, the wheels went with them. They stopped at the entrance to the east gate of the LORD's house, and the glory of the God of Israel was above them.

²⁰These were the living creatures I had seen beneath the God of Israel by the Kebar River, and I realized that they were cherubim. ²¹Each had four faces and four wings, and under their wings was what looked like the hands of a man. ²²Their faces had the same appearance as those I had seen by the Kebar River. Each one went straight ahead.

¹¹:¹Then the Spirit lifted me up and brought me to the gate of the house of the LORD that faces east. There at the entrance to the gate were twenty-five men, and I saw among them Jaazaniah son of Azzur and Pelatiah son of Benaiah, leaders of the people. ²The LORD said to me, "Son of man, these are the men who are plotting evil and giving wicked advice in this city. ³They say, 'Will it not soon be time to build houses? This city is a cooking pot, and we are the meat.' ⁴Therefore prophesy against them; prophesy, son of man."

⁵Then the Spirit of the LORD came upon me, and he told me to say: "This is what the LORD says: That is what you are saying, O house of Israel, but I know what is going through your mind. ⁶You have killed many people in this city and filled its streets with the dead.

⁷"Therefore this is what the Sovereign LORD says: The bodies you have thrown there are the meat and this city is the pot, but I will drive you out of it. ⁸You fear the sword, and the sword is what I will bring against you, declares the Sovereign LORD. ⁹I will drive you out of the city and hand you over to foreigners and inflict punishment on you. ¹⁰You will fall by the sword, and I will execute judgment on you at the borders of Israel. Then you will know that I am the LORD. ¹¹This city will not be a pot for you, nor will you be the meat in it; I will exe-

cute judgment on you at the borders of Israel. ¹²And you will
know that I am the LORD, for you have not followed my
decrees or kept my laws but have conformed to the standards
of the nations around you."

¹³Now as I was prophesying, Pelatiah son of Benaiah died.
Then I fell facedown and cried out in a loud voice, "Ah, Sovereign LORD! Will you completely destroy the remnant of
Israel?"

¹⁴The word of the LORD came to me: ¹⁵"Son of man, your
brothers—your brothers who are your blood relatives and the
whole house of Israel—are those of whom the people of
Jerusalem have said, 'They are far away from the LORD; this
land was given to us as our possession.'

¹⁶"Therefore say: 'This is what the Sovereign LORD says:
Although I sent them far away among the nations and scattered them among the countries, yet for a little while I have
been a sanctuary for them in the countries where they have
gone.'

¹⁷"Therefore say: 'This is what the Sovereign LORD says: I
will gather you from the nations and bring you back from the
countries where you have been scattered, and I will give you
back the land of Israel again.'

¹⁸"They will return to it and remove all its vile images and
detestable idols. ¹⁹I will give them an undivided heart and put
a new spirit in them; I will remove from them their heart of
stone and give them a heart of flesh. ²⁰Then they will follow
my decrees and be careful to keep my laws. They will be my
people, and I will be their God. ²¹But as for those whose
hearts are devoted to their vile images and detestable idols, I
will bring down on their own heads what they have done,
declares the Sovereign LORD."

²²Then the cherubim, with the wheels beside them, spread
their wings, and the glory of the God of Israel was above
them. ²³The glory of the LORD went up from within the city
and stopped above the mountain east of it. ²⁴The Spirit lifted
me up and brought me to the exiles in Babylonia in the vision
given by the Spirit of God.

Then the vision I had seen went up from me, ²⁵and I told
the exiles everything the LORD had shown me.

Original Meaning

WHILE FOR THE purposes of simplicity we have treated Ezekiel 8–9 separately from Ezekiel 10–11, it must not be forgotten that they belong together as a single vision. In fact, there is a structure underlying the whole sequence of these four chapters, which may be analyzed as follows:

A: Introduction to the vision, including reference to divine glory (8:1–4)

  B: Four visions of cultic abominations, along with accusations of social wrongdoing, centering on the elders (8:5–18)

  C: A vision of divine judgment on account of cultic abominations and social wrongdoing, beginning with the elders (9:1–10:7)

  D: The prophet intercedes with God to preserve a remnant (9:8)

  E: The departure of the divine glory from the temple and city (10:8–22)

  B′: Accusation of social wrongdoing, centering on the leaders of the people (11:1–6)

  C′: A message of divine judgment on the leaders, followed by a vision of divine judgment on Pelatiah, one of the "leaders of the people" (*śārê hāʿām;* 11:7–13)

  D′: The prophet intercedes with God to preserve a remnant (11:13)

  E′: The promise of the divine presence with the exiles as a temporary "sanctuary" and the eventual return of the exiles (11:14–21)

A′: Conclusion of the vision, including reference to the divine glory (11:22–25)

The structure of the vision makes its fundamental message clear: It is about the location of the presence of God. If God were still present in his temple in Jerusalem, then the confidence of those who remain in the land would perhaps be justified. But what this temple vision shows conclusively is that because of the sins of the inhabitants of Judah, both in terms of their responsibilities toward God and of their responsibilities toward their fellow human beings, the glory has departed from Judah and gone to dwell with those living in exile. The first have become the last and the last have become first.

Chapter 10 opens with a continuation of the judgment scene of Ezekiel 9. There we saw the city being overrun by divinely appointed executioners, scattering dead bodies in their wake as if starring in a cosmic *Rambo* movie. Now, on top of that destruction of life, follows the destruction of property. The seventh angel returns to the fray. This is a priestly figure, who in Ezekiel 9 is the sole mediator of life in the midst of the cataclysm, marking out for salvation those who sigh and mourn over the abominations of the city. This time, however, his action is not intended for salvation but for destruction. At the Lord's command, he takes burning coals from beneath the heavenly throne in order to burn the city to the ground (10:2). Like the city of Sodom, who Ezekiel calls Jerusalem's "sister" in 16:46, Jerusalem will be burned up by fire from on high.

Ezekiel is here simply giving us a glimpse behind the scenes at the cosmic realities that underlie history. When the physical Jerusalem fell to Nebuchadnezzar and was razed to the ground in 586 B.C., the Babylonians were nothing more than the human instruments in the hands of an angry God. In the ancient Near East, it was a commonplace that a city could not be captured unless its gods were either defeated or had abandoned it to its fate.[1] Thus the Cyrus Cylinder, which records the victory of the Persians over Babylon in 539 B.C., tells how Marduk was angry at the cultic and social sins of the Babylonian king and therefore departed from the city, leading to its destruction and the annihilation of its population.[2] Similarly here, the Lord's wrath at the sins of the people leads to his departure from his chosen city and its consequent destruction.

After the priestly figure departs to carry out the Lord's bidding, there follows a renewed description of the divine chariot with its supernatural attendants. The lengths to which the prophet goes to describe the vision of the divine glory may seem redundant to us, but they serve to underline its status as the central feature of the whole temple vision. What Ezekiel sees is exactly the same vision as he saw in chapter 1 (in Babylonia!), but here in the temple context, certain features snap into sharper focus. In the building filled with representations of cherubim, it becomes clear to the prophet that the "living creatures" he saw in chapter 1 are themselves cherubim.[3]

On top of the cherubim, the prophet sees a throne, at first empty (10:1). The divine chariot is drawn up on the south side of the temple (10:3), as far away as possible from the abominations on the northern side of the city. Then Ezekiel sees a cloud filling the inner court and the glory of God on the move once more, just as it had been in the days of the desert wanderings (cf. Ex. 40:34—37). It departs slowly, haltingly, as if reluctant to leave.[4] First it

---

1. On divine abandonment, see Daniel I. Block, *The Gods of the Nations* (Jackson, Miss.: Evangelical Theological Society, 1988), 125—61.

2. Allen, *Ezekiel 1—19*, 155.

3. This may explain why the problems of gender confusion with regard to these creatures in chapter 1 are resolved in chapter 10: They are due to the tension between the grammatical gender of the living creatures (feminine) and the reality they represent, the cherubim (masculine). See Greenberg, *Ezekiel 1—20*, 199.

4. Greenberg, *Ezekiel 1—20*, 191.

passes from the earthly cherubim in the Most Holy Place to the threshold of the temple (10:4), then from the threshold of the temple to the divine chariot over the (real) cherubim (10:18). From there the glory moves to the east gate of the temple courtyard (10:19), where there is a pause during which the prophet receives a further oracle and vision. Finally the glory moves on to the Mount of Olives, east of Jerusalem, outside the city limits. The city itself is now effectively doomed, cut off from divine aid from its true protector, waiting for the ax to fall. The Lord has abandoned the city to the empty hope offered by the idols for which the people abandoned him.

Not everyone within the city of Jerusalem has the same perspective, however. At the entrance to the east gate, Ezekiel sees a group of men whose number (twenty-five, 11:1) and whose function (giving advice, v. 2) suggest them to be elders.[5] Included in their number are two "leaders of the people" (śārê hā‘ām), who are named as Jaazaniah ben Azzur (not the same as Jaazaniah ben Shaphan in 8:11) and Pelatiah. The "leaders" (śārîm) were a small council of high officials of the king, who wielded considerable power in Judah.[6] During the reign of Zedekiah, they apparently extended their powers in the face of his weakness and were even able to act independently of the king to some degree (see Jer. 38:25).[7]

In the vision, Ezekiel is told that these leaders have been "plotting evil and giving wicked advice in this city" (Ezek. 11:2). In opposition to the prophetic word of forthcoming judgment on Jerusalem, they have apparently been arrogantly asserting the security of their position. The exact meaning of the terse expression in 11:3a (lit., "not near building houses") has been much debated. The NIV, along with most translations and commentators, takes the "near" in a temporal sense, construing the phrase as a question: "Will it not soon be time to build houses?"[8] However, a better sense is obtained if "near" is taken in a spatial sense, so that the inhabitants of Judah are referring to themselves as those who are "near," in contrast to the exiles as those who are "far away" (cf. 11:15).[9] The phrase then becomes, "It is not for the one who

5. See my *Ezekiel and the Leaders of Israel*, 114.

6. See J. P. M. van der Ploeg, "Chefs du peuple d'Israel et leurs titres," *RB* 57 (1950): 42; Udo Rüterswörden, *Die Beamten der israelitischen Königszeit: Eine Studie zu śr und vergleichbaren Begriffen* (BWANT 117; Stuttgart: Kohlhammer, 1985), 64.

7. Thomas Overholt, *The Threat of Falsehood: A Study in the Theology of the Book of Jeremiah* (SBT 16; London: SCM, 1970), 32.

8. So also Wevers, *Ezekiel*, 77. The RSV translates similarly, but as a statement rather than a question.

9. The spatial pairing "near" and "far off/away" is a standard one in Hebrew and is also found in Ezekiel 6:12 and 22:5, though without the same overtones of "inhabitant of the land/exile." In his commentary, Zimmerli notes that the nearest parallel to the unique

is near to build houses," with an obvious reference to the letter that Jeremiah sent the exiles urging them to "build houses" (Jer. 29:5). As Fairbairn paraphrases it: "Those who are far off in the land of exile may, if they please, take the prophet's advice and set about building houses for themselves; that does not concern us."[10]

This understanding seems to fit better with the second half of their statement: "This city is a cooking pot, and we are the meat" (Ezek. 11:3b). This may be interpreted as a statement of the relative value of those who remain in Jerusalem and the exiles (the best part, the "meat," is put in the cooking pot while the undesired portion, the offal, is thrown into the fire).[11] Alternatively, it may speak of the relative safety of the Jerusalemites (the cooking pot, while not a safe place to be, is at least better than being in the fire—as is implied in our proverb "Out of the frying pan, into the fire),[12] or it may imply both.[13] In either case, a contrast is implied between those who remain in Jerusalem and the exiles, a contrast that favors the inhabitants of the city.

To pick up the further quotation of their thoughts in 11:15, on the Jerusalemites' view, "They [the exiles] are[14] far away from the LORD; this land was given to us as our possession." On the grounds that "possession is nine-tenths of the law," they regard the de facto situation as an expression of God's favor on them and displeasure with those in exile. They think of themselves as the true remnant while those in exile are under God's judgment.

In the oracle that follows, the Lord rejects their claim. Because of the violent crimes committed by these leaders, by which they have filled the city with corpses, the city will provide no protection for them (11:7). The sword that they fear will come on them and they will fall by it (11:8, 10). The land will not be their possession; rather, the Lord will bring them out of the city to judge them at the very edge of the land, at the "borders of Israel" (11:10–11).

In this prophecy there is not simply reference to the actual events of history, whereby many of the leading citizens were put to death by Nebuchadnezzar at Riblah (2 Kings 25:21), but more fundamentally there is a challenge to the Jerusalemites' claim to possess the land. The language is carefully chosen to depict their fate as a kind of anti-exodus. The Lord will

---

Hebrew form used here occurs in the "far off" in Ps. 10:1, though he himself did not adopt a spatial understanding of "near" here (*Ezekiel*, 1:258).

10. *Ezekiel*, 54.

11. Allen, *Ezekiel 1–19*, 160; Greenberg, *Ezekiel 1–20*, 187.

12. Wevers, *Ezekiel*, 77.

13. Eichrodt, *Ezekiel*, 167; Cooke, *Ezekiel*, 122.

14. Repointing the MT's imperative (*raḥ°qû*) as a perfect (*rāḥ°qû*), along with most modern and some medieval interpreters. See Zimmerli, *Ezekiel*, 1:229.

"drive them out of the city," just as he earlier brought Israel out of the land of Egypt (Ezek. 11:9; cf. Ex. 6:6). Whereas once he promised to deliver Israel from the hand of the Egyptians (Ex. 3:8), now he threatens to give them into the hand of foreigners (Ezek. 11:9). The judgments that once fell on Egypt (Ex. 6:6; 12:12) now fall on the inhabitants of Jerusalem (Ezek. 11:10). In this context, the phrase "the borders of Israel" evokes the division of the land under Joshua, where the borders of all of the tribes were established (Josh. 15–19; cf. Ezek. 48!). Far from the land of Canaan being their "possession" (Ezek. 11:15; cf. Ex. 6:8), which they may divide among themselves without regard to the exiles, the inhabitants of Jerusalem will die outside the land because of their failure to keep the Lord's decrees and laws.[15] It will be shown that they are not a privileged "remnant" after all.

Ezekiel then once more sees enacted in visionary form God's judgment. As in chapter 9, where he saw the idolatrous elders cut down as the firstfruits of God's judgment (9:6), so also here he sees one of the "leaders of the people," Pelatiah, die while Ezekiel is carrying out the Lord's command to prophesy against him (11:4). In both instances, Ezekiel's response to this demonstration of the reality of God's judgment is to fall on his face and cry out the question: "Sovereign LORD! Will you completely destroy the remnant of Israel?" (11:13; cf. 9:8). Up to a point, Ezekiel shares the presuppositions of the Jerusalemites. God's land and God's people are an indivisible unity. Those already in exile are therefore, by definition, "far from God." If then, in addition to the previous catastrophe, comprehensive judgment falls on those who remain in the land, who will be left? Surely the whole house of Israel will then be destroyed. The end of the tunnel will have been reached, with no way out.

The answer to Ezekiel's first cry in 9:8 had been brief and ambiguous: The Lord responded with words of judgment without compassion—yet the reappearance of the priestly figure with his writing kit left room for hope that some righteous remnant might have been found to survive the holocaust (9:9–11). But the response to Ezekiel's second cry (11:13) is a glorious declaration that the future of Israel lies among the exiles: It is Ezekiel and his brothers and "blood relatives"[16]—his fellow exiles—who constitute "the whole house of Israel" (11:15). Yes, they have been sent far away from the land of Israel, but even there they have not been cast out of the Lord's pres-

---

15. Allen has noted the use of motifs from Ex. 6:6–8 in Ezek. 11:17–20 (as well as in 20:30–42) to depict the idea of a new exodus (*Ezekiel 1–19*, 165); however, the use actually starts earlier with the depiction of the anti-exodus from Jerusalem.

16. Lit., this phrase translates "the men of your redemption," i.e., those for whom Ezekiel has responsibility to act as their "redeemer," ensuring that their land remains associated with their name.

ence because "for a little while I have been a sanctuary for them in the countries where they have gone" (11:16). By this we see that the Lord's movement is not simply a departure *from* Jerusalem, on account of the idolatries that have profaned the sanctuary there (8:6), but also a departure *to* Babylon, to be a sanctuary for his true people there.

But the Lord's exile, like that of his true people, is only a temporary state of affairs.[17] The counterpart of the anti-exodus of the Lord's nonpeople from Judah will be a new exodus of the Lord's true people from all the nations to which they have been scattered. They will be brought back once more (11:17; cf. Ex. 6:6); the land that Ezekiel cannot redeem for his redemption relatives (Ezek. 11:15) will be redeemed for them by the Lord (cf. Ex. 6:6).[18] The detestable idols and vile images with which the former inhabitants filled the land (7:20; 8:3–17) will be removed by the new inhabitants (11:18).

The reason for this change in behavior is, quite literally, a change of heart. The Lord will create in his new people "an undivided heart," not so much in the sense of mutual agreement among the people, but rather in the sense of undivided loyalty to the Lord, a single-minded commitment to him (cf. Jer. 32:39). In place of the old spirit, whose mindset resulted in death (Ezek. 11:5–6),[19] God's new people will be given "a new spirit." They will receive "a heart of flesh" that will respond to the Lord in place of their old stony heart (cf. 3:7). In contrast to the present occupants of the land, who neither follow the Lord's decrees nor keep his laws (11:12), his new people will observe both decrees and laws (11:20). The result of such renewal will be nothing less than the fulfillment of the goal of the first exodus: "They will be my people, and I will be their God" (11:20; cf. Ex. 6:7). This is the first substantive indication in Ezekiel of a solid hope for the future for God's people in exile.

There is, however, no such promising hope for those who remain in the land: They remain committed to idolatry and abominations, for which the judgment they receive will be fully deserved (Ezek. 11:21). Thus ends

---

17. *miqdāš mᵉᶜat* can either mean "a little sanctuary" (Greenberg, *Ezekiel 1–20*, 190) or "a sanctuary for a little time" (cf. NIV; RSV). Both translations are possible: for the former, cf. Dan. 11:34, while for the latter, see Hag. 2:6. Nevertheless, in a context where it is immediately followed by a promise of return, it seems best to understand it as a (positive) statement of the temporary nature of the Lord's presence among the exiles rather than a (negative) statement of the incompleteness of the Lord's presence with them (see Carl F. Keil, *Ezekiel*, trans. J. Martin, 2 vol. [Grand Rapids: Eerdmans, 1988 reprint], 1:151). The *waw* consecutive + imperfect thus introduces a logical contrast between the two halves of v. 16.

18. Allen, *Ezekiel 1–19*, 164.

19. Notice how "the thoughts (literally "ascendings") of your spirit" (NIV "what is going through your mind") issue in the murders of 11:6. They form a natural opposition to the Lord's thoughts, which come to the prophet through the descending of the Lord's Spirit, which literally "falls" on Ezekiel (v. 5).

Ezekiel's temple vision: The glory departs from the temple and moves off onto the Mount of Olives, across from Jerusalem, as if waiting to see the judgment on the rebellious city completed, while the prophet is returned to his own people in exile.

DIVINE ABANDONMENT and identification. The temptation to believe that God is statically tied to one location is not one that immediately occurs to us. Yet that difference of perspective is not simply a matter of "evolutionary progress" in our thought, as if modern people like us have advanced beyond such "primitive" ideas. Solomon himself recognized the incongruity of supposing that the One who created the universe would dwell in a house made with human hands (1 Kings 8:27). Yet he also recognized that the Lord had chosen to link himself and his honor in a unique way with the temple in Jerusalem. It was the place he had chosen to set his Name (1 Kings 8:29; cf. Deut. 12:11), the sole place where sacrifices were to be offered to the Lord.

It was therefore no light thing when Solomon's successors repeatedly failed to honor the temple as such, allowing or even encouraging idolatry and syncretistic worship at the high places throughout the land. If God really were the true God and not simply an ineffectual idol, such a history of unfaithfulness and abominations, which culminated in Ezekiel's vision of chapter 8, could only lead to disaster. So it did in 586 B.C. The One who had sovereignly set his Name on Jerusalem could, and finally did, remove his favor and protection.

It is hard for us, as modern people, to relate to the scale of such a catastrophe in the minds of God's people. Yet Ezekiel's message was not simply one of divine abandonment. It was also one of divine identification. God was leaving Jerusalem to its fate but he was not leaving himself without a remnant. The answer to Ezekiel's twice-posed question: "Are you going to destroy the entire remnant of Israel?" was "Yes and No." Yes, the remnant who remained in Judah were slated for further catastrophic judgment, from which the survival of any was an entirely moot prospect.[20] But no, that did not mean the end for God's people. A remnant already existed in exile, who would experience God's presence with them in exile for a little while, after which there would be a new exodus and a return to the Promised Land.

God's true presence among the human race. But even the experience of exile and return did not bring about the full blessings of the covenant. True,

---

20. Compare Jer. 5:1–2, where the prophet Jeremiah, in Jerusalem, is told to search the city for one righteous person. Should even one be found, the Lord will spare the city.

there was a kind of "second exodus" during the time of Cyrus, with the return of many Jews to their homeland (Ezra 1).[21] With the encouragement of the prophets Haggai and Zechariah, the second temple was built. Yet there is a pervasive feeling of incompleteness in the postexilic writings—a sense that there is something more to come.[22] There was no physical manifestation of the Lord's presence in the second temple to match that at the dedication of the first temple (1 Kings 8:11) or that expected by Ezekiel (Ezek. 43:1–5).

That fulfillment awaited the New Testament era. With the coming of Jesus, the presence of God is no longer located in the physical, man-made temple, but the presence once again "made [a] dwelling" (lit., "tabernacled") among his people (John 1:14), just as it had during the desert period and, according to Ezekiel 11:16, during the Exile. In the person of Jesus, God's presence is once more mobile, no longer tied to a mountain, whether Mount Gerazim or Mount Zion; the time has now come when true worshipers will worship the Father in spirit and in truth (John 4:23). In Jesus is also the coming of the glory that Ezekiel looked for. Thus John comments: "We have seen his glory, the glory of the One and Only, who came from the Father, full of grace and truth" (John 1:14). In other words, with the coming of Jesus there is a fundamental redemptive-historical change in the manifestation of God's glory and presence.

If, however, Jesus is the personal manifestation of the divine glory in the New Testament, then this passage in Ezekiel 10–11 casts a fascinating light on Matthew 23:37–24:3. There Jesus laments Jerusalem's history of hardheartedness towards the prophets and her refusal to come to him (23:37). As a result, her house will be left desolate (23:38), and Jerusalem will not see Jesus again until they are willing to welcome his coming (23:39). He then prophesies the forthcoming destruction of the temple (24:1) and removes himself to the Mount of Olives. Once more, the glory has departed from Jerusalem to the Mount of Olives, leaving behind a magnificent but doomed structure.

Names. From our modern perspective, we may also easily miss the appropriateness that marks the personal names of those singled out for judgment. Old Testament narratives often have names that fit and prefigure the action to unfold. Thus when an Old Testament audience read that Esau was given his name because it apparently means "hairy" and Jacob was so-named because it was understood to mean "he grasps the heel" (or "deceives," Gen. 25:25–26), that information would have been immediately recognized as significant for

---

21. Hugh G. M. Williamson, *Ezra-Nehemiah* (WBC 16; Waco, Tex.: Word, 1985), li, 16.

22. Gordon McConville writes: "The books express deep dissatisfaction with the exiles' situation under Persian rule; the situation is perceived as leaving room for a future fulfilment of the most glorious prophecies of Israel's salvation and the cause of the delayed fulfilment is Israel's sin" ("Ezra-Nehemiah and the Fulfilment of Prophecy," *VT* 36 [1986]: 223).

the story that follows, in which Jacob cheats Esau out of his inheritance by pretending to be the hairy brother (27:23). Similarly, the identification "Saul" (meaning "asked for/dedicated to") is on one level deeply appropriate for the king that Israel asked God to provide for them (1 Sam. 8:5), yet raises the question of Saul's dedication to God. At the same time, however, the alert Hebrew reader remembers that 1 Samuel 1:27–28 has already identified Samuel as the one "asked for" from God and "dedicated to" (*šāʾûl*) him, whereby God is suggesting that Samuel may be a better "Saul" than Saul himself.

In the light of this, we should probably not regard the personal names in Ezekiel 8–11 as mere social identifiers. Though the persons involved were presumably real historical figures (like Saul and Jacob), their names underline the message. For if Jaazaniah ben Azzur means "the LORD hears, son of [divine name] helps," it is hardly coincidental that the Lord has indeed heard. He has heard not just what Jaazaniah and the other elders have been saying but even the thoughts of their hearts. The absence of a specific divine name element in his patronym (Azzur) may not immediately appear significant,[23] but is perfectly fitting in this context where the question of which deity these people have been seeking their help from is left open. Moreover, Pelatiah ben Benaiah means "the LORD delivers [causes to escape], son of the LORD builds up," yet he is the one who derides the Lord's command to build and does not escape. In every respect, the judgment of God exactly fits those on whom it falls.[24]

THE VEIL PULLED BACK. In the *Wizard of Oz* Dorothy and her three friends, the tin man, the scarecrow, and the cowardly lion, journey along the yellow brick road until they arrive at the famed city of Oz, where they hope that the powerful wizard will grant them their heart's desire. When they arrive, the enigmatic wizard appears to them in a variety of fearsome and beautiful forms and sends them off on a quest to prove themselves by disposing of the wicked witch of the west; if they succeed, he promises to grant them their wish. However, when they finally

---

23. The equivalent form with theophoric element would be Azariah, "the Lord helps" (1 Kings 4:2), or Azriel, "God helps" (1 Chron. 5:24). The occurrence of such names in variant forms with or without the theophoric element is common in the Old Testament: e.g., Nathan/Nathaniel, Dan/Daniel, Obed/Obadiah.

24. The name Jaazaniah ben Shaphan in Ezekiel 8:11 has an equally appropriate ring to it. Like the other Jaazaniah, the Lord indeed hears what he is saying (8:12), while like a *šāpān* (a hyrax or rock badger) he is buried away in a subterranean cave. Indeed, the hyrax was itself an unclean animal (Lev. 11:5), a fitting image for the idolatrous worshipers to conjure up.

return after having successfully completed their mission and enter the great and mighty wizard's throne room, Dorothy's dog Toto pulls back a curtain in the corner. In that way, the foursome learns that the "great and mighty wizard" is in fact a failed fairground conjurer, who does everything by illusion. With the screen taken away, they discover that the world of Oz is not at all what they thought it was.

In Ezekiel 8–11, the screen is taken away from the course of Judah's history, and it is revealed to the prophet that things are not at all what they had appeared to be. The fundamental reality that Judah had always relied upon, the presence of God in their midst in the temple on Mount Zion, is revealed to be now nothing more than a hollow shell. The glory of God has departed from their midst, leaving the city ripe for destruction. What that means is that those who seem to themselves to be in the better situation—in the frying pan rather than in the fire, those confidently depending on God's commitment to Zion—are actually next on the menu. God has abandoned them to their doom. To continue the culinary metaphor, their goose is cooked.

By contrast, the ones who seem like the offscouring and leftovers—those who seem to be abandoned by God and sent off into exile—are actually the ones with whom the future of God's people rests. For God has not simply departed from Jerusalem, he has departed to the exiles, to be their sanctuary. Because God is with them, they have a future, a future that will bring them back to the land of promise and to receive the goal of the promise: God's dwelling in the midst of his people. The rejected ones are those invited to the banquet, while those who felt secure will be rejected (Luke 14:16–24).

Most of us see life with the screen up. We assume that things are as they appear and that we can easily identify those on whom God's favor rests. We may put our confidence in the traditions of the past, for example, and assume that forms hallowed by repeated usage must be pleasing to God in the present. How far in the past we look may vary from person to person: We may insist on forms that stretch all the way back to the early church, the Reformation, or the Puritans, or simply the forms to which we have been accustomed as individuals. Alternatively, we may place our trust in numbers: If many people attend a particular church or type of church, then surely God's blessing rests on it and we should model our church after that style.

God's presence is not so easily discerned. He does not always continue to bless forms and institutions that he has blessed in the past, nor is he always found in the large and apparently successful churches. In the Bible, he is most often found with the poor and the weak, the despised and rejected, those whom the world regards as castoffs. So when Jesus comes, he visits the temple, but his primary teaching and ministry takes place in the open air. He will eat with the scribes and the Pharisees when they invite him, but he is known rather as the friend of tax collectors and sinners (Matt. 11:19). When he seeks twelve disciples, he goes not to the religious training schools but to the work places of ordinary men and women. The essence of his training program is not a rigorous course of book study, but three years of being in his presence.

The temple in the New Testament era. The reason for this is that in the New Testament the temple has taken human form in the body of Jesus (John 2:19). In him, God's glory lives among us (1:14). Herod's temple, for all its outward glory, is an empty shell, abandoned by God and now simply awaiting its destruction by human hands (Matt. 24:1–2). Ironically, it still stood while Christ experienced the heartrending abandonment on the cross, where his Father forsook him on account of the sins of his people. Its stones remained intact while his physical body was torn down. But that divine abandonment of Christ was only the necessary precursor to its refilling with even greater glory and resurrection as a spiritual body.

As a result of that death and resurrection, the future lies not with the Jerusalem temple but with the body of Christ, the church. In their assembly, they have the presence of God with them in the person of Jesus. This is the significance of Jesus' statement that "where two are three come together in my name, there am I with them" (Matt. 18:20). Paul describes the church in this way: "We are the temple of the living God. As God has said: 'I will live with them and walk among them, and I will be their God, and they will be my people'" (2 Cor. 6:16). Wherever the true church assembles, there God is present in their midst. Or, to put it the other way around, it is the presence of Christ that constitutes the church.

The prerequisite, then, for worship to be possible in the New Testament context is not a building chosen by God and accepted by him, but a people chosen by God and accepted by him. God dwells in the hearts of his people, not in a building made with hands. This surely has implications for how we assess different churches. All too often we make our judgment based on whether the programs a church offers seem to meet our needs or on its denominational label, rather than attempting the harder task of discerning the reality of Christ's presence.

But how do you discern the reality of Christ's presence in a church? The Reformers argued that the marks of the true church were the pure preaching of the Word of God, the sacraments rightly administered, and church discipline properly applied.[25] These are not three entirely separate things, since

---

25. There is some discussion as to the exact number of these marks. Calvin mentions the first two (*Institutes*, 4.1.9) as does the Augsburg Confession, art. 7 and art. 19 of the Church of England. The third is added in the Belgic Confession (art. 29) and the First Scots Confession (ch. 18), while the Westminster Confession reduces them to a single point, "the profession of the true religion" (25.2). Those who mention three marks have

pure preaching ought to result in reformation of sacramental practice, and laxness over church discipline will necessarily affect the administration of the sacraments. However, these marks provide us with a good place to start in assessing the health or otherwise of a church. The ministry of the Word and the sacraments are the two means of grace by which the Lord feeds his people, so that where the Lord is present, we should expect to find both sound preaching and a proper administration of the Lord's Supper and of baptism.

Moreover, Ezekiel's message should underline for us the essential importance of personal and corporate holiness, which is addressed by (among other things) proper church discipline. God's presence in the midst of his people is not to be taken lightly or presumed upon. Those at Pergamum who were treating idolatry and immorality within the church carelessly are warned in Revelation 2:16 to repent, lest Jesus should come and fight against them with the sword of his mouth. God's presence can be removed from a church, just as it abandoned the temple, leading to that church becoming nothing more than a hollow shell. Outwardly, everything may still seem to be in place, but without the internal reality of God's presence it is merely a matter of time before the whole edifice collapses.

Hope for believers. Yet while there is no room for complacency, there is solid hope for the believer in the most trying of times. For even while God may abandon parts of his professing church, he never abandons his covenant commitment to save for himself a people. If the religious leaders of the day and the major denominations turn their backs on him, he will leave them to their fate—but only in order to do a new work through the small and despised, those neglected and considered insignificant. God will choose the weak in order to shame the strong (1 Cor. 1:27). If the Jews will not receive their Messiah, then the gospel will go to the Gentiles. If the West turns its back on Christianity, then God will open up new doors in the other two-thirds of the world. In every generation, God's work of giving to men and women a new spirit and a new heart continues until the full harvest of his people is brought into his kingdom.

The exact formulation of that renewing work in Ezekiel 11:19 is striking. Literally, it reads "I will remove the heart of stone from their flesh and I will give to them a heart of flesh." The stony heart, a heart that is unresponsive to God, is not in the deepest sense something natural to us. Rather a heart that responds joyfully and obediently to God's commands is "flesh of our flesh"—what we were created to be. Yet since the time of Adam's fall into sin

---

included the things they regard as necessary for the *well-being* of the church, while the Westminster Confession has focused simply on the one thing necessary for the *existence* of the church.

our humanity has been so perverted that we have become "by nature objects of [God's] wrath" (Eph. 2:3). Unless God performs divine heart surgery on us, we cannot obey him or please him. What we need is not simply to keep a series of New Year's resolutions or to turn over some new leaves. We need radical surgery, nothing less than a new birth from above (John 3:3). Thanks be to God, therefore, for the gift of Jesus Christ, in whom we are a new creation, reconciled to God (2 Cor. 5:17). As Calvin expressed it, in the form of a prayer:

> Almighty God, as we have completely perished in our father Adam, and no part of us remains uncorrupted so long as we bear in both body and soul grounds for wrath, condemnation, and death, grant that, reborn in your Spirit, we may increasingly set aside our own will and spirit, and so submit ourselves to you that your Spirit may truly reign within us. And then grant, we pray, that we not be ungrateful to you, but, appreciating how invaluable is this blessing, may dedicate and direct our entire life to glorifying to your name in Jesus Christ our Lord. Amen.[26]

---

26. *Ezekiel I*, 280.

Ezekiel 12:1–20

❧

THE WORD OF THE LORD came to me: [2]"Son of man, you are living among a rebellious people. They have eyes to see but do not see and ears to hear but do not hear, for they are a rebellious people.

[3]"Therefore, son of man, pack your belongings for exile and in the daytime, as they watch, set out and go from where you are to another place. Perhaps they will understand, though they are a rebellious house. [4]During the daytime, while they watch, bring out your belongings packed for exile. Then in the evening, while they are watching, go out like those who go into exile. [5]While they watch, dig through the wall and take your belongings out through it. [6]Put them on your shoulder as they are watching and carry them out at dusk. Cover your face so that you cannot see the land, for I have made you a sign to the house of Israel."

[7]So I did as I was commanded. During the day I brought out my things packed for exile. Then in the evening I dug through the wall with my hands. I took my belongings out at dusk, carrying them on my shoulders while they watched.

[8]In the morning the word of the LORD came to me: [9]"Son of man, did not that rebellious house of Israel ask you, 'What are you doing?'

[10]"Say to them, 'This is what the Sovereign LORD says: This oracle concerns the prince in Jerusalem and the whole house of Israel who are there.' [11]Say to them, 'I am a sign to you.'

"As I have done, so it will be done to them. They will go into exile as captives.

[12]"The prince among them will put his things on his shoulder at dusk and leave, and a hole will be dug in the wall for him to go through. He will cover his face so that he cannot see the land. [13]I will spread my net for him, and he will be caught in my snare; I will bring him to Babylonia, the land of the Chaldeans, but he will not see it, and there he will die. [14]I will scatter to the winds all those around him—his staff and all his troops—and I will pursue them with drawn sword.

[15]"They will know that I am the LORD, when I disperse them among the nations and scatter them through the countries.

¹⁶But I will spare a few of them from the sword, famine and plague, so that in the nations where they go they may acknowledge all their detestable practices. Then they will know that I am the LORD."

¹⁷The word of the LORD came to me: ¹⁸"Son of man, tremble as you eat your food, and shudder in fear as you drink your water. ¹⁹Say to the people of the land: 'This is what the Sovereign LORD says about those living in Jerusalem and in the land of Israel: They will eat their food in anxiety and drink their water in despair, for their land will be stripped of everything in it because of the violence of all who live there. ²⁰The inhabited towns will be laid waste and the land will be desolate. Then you will know that I am the LORD.'"

THE MESSAGE OF Ezekiel 8–11 may well be summed up as: "Nothing escapes the Lord's notice." Contrary to public opinion in Jerusalem, which held, "The LORD does not see us; the LORD has forsaken the land" (Ezek. 8:12; cf. 9:9), the Lord had indeed seen everything and laid it out in a vision before his prophet. Likewise, the Lord's acute sense of hearing had picked up the pronouncements of the wicked counselors in 11:3, though he would be signally deaf to any cries for help from his people (8:18). Because of their abominations and idolatry, he would indeed abandon the land, leaving it at the mercy of the Babylonian army. This was the message that Ezekiel was to bring to the exiles; it was a vision intended for their ears (11:25).

But if Ezekiel cherished any hopes of seeing a revolutionary change in the thinking of the exiles as a result of his message, he is quickly disabused of his notions in chapter 12. Like the Jerusalemites, his fellow exiles are a rebellious people. They do not see what the Lord shows them, nor do they hear what the Lord says, not because they lack the physical organs of sight and hearing, but simply because they are rebellious (12:2). They have eyes to see but they do not see; ears to hear but they do not hear (12:2). In the language of 11:19, they are still characterized by the heart of stone, a stubborn will that rejects obedience.

This saying of 12:2 underlies the sign-acts that follow it. This section is made up of a sign-act of exile (12:3–7), the interpretation of this sign-act (12:8–17), and a second sign-act of fear and trembling (12:18–20). The dominant motif throughout is of looking and not seeing. Repeatedly, Ezekiel is instructed to carry out his actions "as they watch" (*l^{ecê}nêhem*, seven times in 12:3–7). His actions are not particularly obscure, depicting as they do an event in which the exiles had all personally taken part. Yet the result of his actions, noted by the Lord in verse 8, is not dawning comprehension on the part of the exiles but inability to understand. They ask him: "What are you doing?" Nor does the second sign-act make things clearer to them. Though they have seen with their eyes what he has done, they still do not get the message.

What is more, even when he delivers the word of the Lord to them, explaining in oracular form what the sign-act means, the people's response is that recorded in 12:27: "The vision he sees is for many years from now, and he prophesies about the distant future." Though they hear every word he speaks, it is clear that they have understood nothing at all. Indeed, they are a rebellious people, who have ears and do not hear, eyes and do not see.

The initial sign-act that the prophet performs depicts the action of going into exile. Ezekiel is first to put together an exile's pack, containing the few belongings an exile might be able to carry along on the long journey. This may consist simply of an animal skin to hold food and act as a pillow, a mat to lie on, and a bowl out of which to eat and drink.[1] These preparations are to be made in the daytime, though the departure is delayed until evening. This delay serves both the practical purpose of allowing time for a crowd to gather to witness the sign-act and a symbolic purpose, representing God's delaying of judgment until the proper time, the gathering gloom of evening (12:4).[2]

The growing darkness provides a frighteningly appropriate backdrop for the drama. At that time, Ezekiel is to dig through the adobe wall of his house and go out through it, taking his pack with him (12:5). Moreover, he is to cover his face so that he cannot see the land (12:6). All of this has symbolic meaning: The Jerusalemites and their prince will go into exile just as he has acted out (v. 11).

The symbolic meaning of the otherwise rather enigmatic sign is expounded in 12:10–16. It concerns the fate of Zedekiah, the prince (*nāśîʾ*), along with the house of Israel in Jerusalem (12:10). Many of the details of the sign-act are capable of more than one interpretation. Does the breaking through the wall symbolize something Zedekiah does in his attempt to escape[3] or the breaches made by the Babylonians through which they bring

---

1. Greenberg, *Ezekiel 1–20*, 209.

2. For darkness/evening as symbolic of judgment see Jer. 13:16 (Greenberg, *Ezekiel 1–20*, 210). The middle of the night is when judgment falls on Egypt (Ex. 12:29).

3. So Cooke, *Ezekiel*, 131.

out their prisoner?[4] Does the covering of his face represent an attempt at concealment,[5] or shame and grief?[6]

Some of these complexities may be due to reading the text in the light of its historical fulfillment recorded in 2 Kings 25:4–7; however, some are due to the prophet's penchant for complex, multivalent images, which involve plays on words and sounds.[7] Thus the prince (*nāśîʾ*) is both the one who "lifts up" (*yiśśāʾ*) his pack and also "the burden" (*maśśāʾ*) to be carried (12:10, 12).[8] He is both the one who goes out and the one who is brought out, as a literal translation of verse 12 makes clear: "As for the prince who is among them, he will lift up [his pack] upon his shoulder in the darkness and he will go out; through the wall they will dig to bring [him] out through it."[9]

Though the imagery is complex, the essential message seems reasonably straightforward. Not only will there be a further exile, bringing out those still remaining in Jerusalem and Judah, but this anti-exodus will center on the person of the prince, Zedekiah. His personal transgressions have not yet been the object of Ezekiel's prophecies (though they will be later on, e.g., in Ezek. 17 and 19).[10] Here he is in view primarily as the representative of the people. Because he shares their inability to see the coming judgment, that judgment will take the form of no longer being able to see the land, that is, he will never return from exile. This motif is found regularly in extrabiblical curses[11] and was fulfilled historically when the Babylonians blinded Zedekiah at Riblah and took him into exile, never to return (2 Kings 25:7).

All this will happen not because of the desire of Nebuchadnezzar for a little more *Lebensraum* ("room to live"), as Adolf Hitler later designated his expansionist ambitions. More fundamentally, it is because the Lord has set a snare for Zedekiah and for the people he represents (Ezek. 12:13). The Lord

---

4. Allen, *Ezekiel 1–19*, 179; Block, *Ezekiel 1–24*, 370.

5. The LXX translates: "So that he might not be seen." Similarly Cooke, *Ezekiel*, 132.

6. So the medieval Jewish commentators Rashi and Kimḥi; similarly, Vawter & Hoppe, *Ezekiel*, 78.

7. Greenberg, *Ezekiel 1–20*, 219.

8. Indeed, "burden" (*maśśāʾ*) involves a further play on words, since it can refer either to a literal load to be carried, as in Ex. 23:5, or to a prophetic oracle, as in Isa. 14:28.

9. This ambiguity may account for the repeated use of the Hiphil of *yāṣāʾ* ("to bring out") often where we would expect the simple Qal ("to go out"). The attraction to this formula may be linked to the idea of the journey into exile as an anti-exodus that we saw also in the previous chapter.

10. See esp. Ezek. 17:19–21, which uses similar language to 12:13–14 in depicting the consequences of Zedekiah's breach of covenant. Some commentators have suggested that Ezek. 17 may actually have been delivered earlier than Ezek. 12. See Thomas Krüger, *Geschichtskonzepte im Ezechielbuch* (BZAW 180; Berlin: de Gruyter, 1989), 404–6.

11. Block, *Ezekiel 1–24*, 376.

is the One who will bring Zedekiah to Babylonia and will scatter his forces to the winds, pursuing him with drawn sword (12:14). The Lord is the One who will disperse his followers among the nations, a mere handful surviving Ezekiel's favorite apocalyptic triad of "sword, famine and plague" (12:15–16). These (lit.) "men of number" (ʾanšê mispār; i.e., a number small enough to be counted) will "acknowledge" (yᵉsappᵉrû) among the nations their abominations and come to acknowledge the Lord's preeminence (12:16). The implication is not necessarily that they will exhibit repentance for their actions but that at least they will recognize that it is the Lord who has acted against them. Their defeat and dispersal are evidence of the Lord's wrath in action, evidence aimed at curing the willful obtuseness of those remaining in Judah.

To this initial sign-act and interpretation, a further one is then added: Ezekiel is to eat and drink with trembling and shuddering, depicting the anxiety that the inhabitants of Jerusalem and Judah will feel. The violence with which they have filled the land will return on their own heads, with the towns being destroyed and the land devastated. This time, however, those emerging from the devastation with a knowledge of the Lord's preeminence are not those in Judah but "the people of the land" (v. 19), that is, the exiles. The land of Judah and all who remain in it are doomed. They are not to be the objects of envy, as the exiles must have been tempted to view them, but rather of horror and pity. At the same time, those whom the inhabitants of Judah would have regarded as landless unfortunates will turn out to be the inheritors of the land (11:16–17).[12]

God is not impotent even in the face of ears that will not hear and eyes that will not see; one way or another, he will get his message through. The exiles will come to see that they indeed are the fortunate ones who have escaped the total judgment of God on his rebellious people. But in order for them to receive their inheritance in the land, God must first of all act in judgment on those who remain. It is this unpalatable truth that they are so reluctant to see.

THE NEED FOR and value of visual aids. In our churches, we are used to preaching to the converted. Few have experience of the difficult task of street preaching, attempting to bring God's message to an audience that, by and large, is not predisposed to listen. Those who do have such experience generally recognize the need to grab people's attention in some way. In some respects, therefore, Ezekiel's sign-acts functioned as a kind of "street theater," a means of drawing a crowd.

---

12. On this general sense of ʿam-hāʾāreṣ, see Talmon, "Judean ʿam-hāʾāreṣ," 71.

Yet Ezekiel's sketches were not merely a prelude to the message, they were themselves the message. Because of their vivid, visual nature, they were able to penetrate past the blind eyes and deaf ears into the consciousness beyond. These visual images would sit there, like the sower's seed, waiting to germinate into an awareness of the reality of God and of his purposes in history. God's self-revelation that "I am the LORD" was written on the life of his prophet; he was their "sign" (12:11). That "sign" would not bear the same kind of fruit in every life. The knowledge that "I am the LORD" was not necessarily a saving knowledge. Yet one way or another, through the actions of God in history, revealed first to his prophets, all would come to know that there is a God and there is a judgment on sin.

This is an unpalatable truth at all times and in all places. It is not just the modern era that finds it hard to accept that "all have sinned and fall short of the glory of God" (Rom. 3:23). But perhaps particularly in the contemporary American setting, where positive thinking carries such weight, the language of sin and judgment is considered out of place. Thus Rabbi Harold Kushner's most recent book seeks to counter the notion "that God holds us to strict standards of Right and Wrong, that God knows every secret, nasty thing we ever do, even our secret, nasty thoughts, and that every sin separates us from God's love."[13] Like the exiles of Ezekiel's day, Rabbi Kushner prefers to think rather more optimistically about the future. But the biblical perspective is ruthlessly honest about our own failures and their consequences. This truth is important because only those whose eyes have been opened to the true danger of their position as objects of God's wrath will be persuaded to flee to the refuge God offers.

God's definitive "visual aids." Supremely, of course, God's self-revelation of his own existence and of the reality of judgment on sin comes through Jesus Christ. His life, death, and resurrection are God's ultimate acts of judgment on sin and salvation of his people. If sin does not separate us from God's love, why was Jesus separated from his Father on the cross? But also the resurrection demonstrates visibly God's acceptance of Jesus' death in place of his people. The cross and the empty tomb are God's definitive visual aids.

In the meantime, through the work of the Holy Spirit, God is opening the eyes and ears of the spiritually blind and deaf to the reality of salvation in Christ. Though his people may be despised and rejected by other people, like their Savior, they are accepted by God and incorporated into his family. On the last day, however, every knee will bow and every tongue will confess that Jesus Christ is Lord, to the glory of God the Father (Phil. 2:10–11). At that time the knowledge of his lordship will be universal.

---

13. *How Good Do We Have to Be?* (Boston and New York: Little, Brown & Co., 1996), 12.

In the meantime, we as the people of Jesus have a unique role to play as signs, as witnesses before a watching world (Acts 1:8). To the world around us, we are a letter from Christ, to use Paul's phrase (2 Cor. 3:3). That testimony, like Ezekiel's witness, must not only be verbal but also visual, aimed at the eye-gate and the ear-gate alike. This will be particularly true in cultures and locations that are not hospitable to our message. Words by themselves may suffice to communicate to those who have ears to hear, but those whose ears are tightly shut must see the Word become flesh again in the lives of his followers. We must speak clearly of the tragic and dangerous state of men and women without Christ: They are sinners under the wrath of God, at risk of eternal lostness. But we must also make visible clearly, in word and deed, the love of God demonstrated in this awesome fact, that while we were still sinners, Christ died for us (Rom. 5:8).

GOD'S WORD BECOMING flesh. How do we demonstrate the reality of the Word who became flesh in our contemporary world? For Ezekiel, the word he received took flesh in his actions— actions that were uncomfortable and costly (breaking through his own wall with his bare hands!), actions that were embarrassingly odd (pretending to go into exile, eating and drinking with violent trembling). Through his actions, along with the accompanying words, a message of judgment on their dearest hopes was imparted to his hearers, so that when God's judgment occurred, the people would know that God was the One who had brought it about. Ezekiel had to tear down the things on which his hearers depended in this present world, in order that they might see the greater thing that God wished to do in and through them.

For Jesus, the Word becoming flesh meant leaving the heavenly glory he shared with the Father to come to earth, taking on himself humanity with all its weaknesses and limitations. He was no armchair warrior; in his incarnation, he was willing to get down and dirty and become part of humankind, bearing the consequences of Adam's sin along with us. He experienced the frustrations of living in a world where things do not work as they ought to; he wept at the graveside of his friend Lazarus, overcome by the pain of human loss. He wrestled with the forces of evil and darkness and death and won the struggle, so that we might be liberated from our bondage to sin and take part in the new exodus of God's people. He died so that we might share in an exodus, not from Egypt or Babylon but out of the kingdom of this world into the kingdom of God. In his crucified flesh, he demonstrated both the judgment of God on sin and the love of God toward sinners.

How though does God's Word take flesh through us? Evangelicals have sometimes been accused of making the Word who became flesh back into words again. We can talk a good talk, but don't always have the walk to match it. A world with ears tightly closed against the truth needs to see the reality of our faith written in changed lives. It needs to see what Harvie Conn calls "show and tell" evangelism: costly witness in word and deed, where our deeds underline the reality of our words, while our words explain the meaning of our deeds.[14]

These actions need not be as peculiar or complex as Ezekiel's sign-acts. One church I know of offered free gift-wrapping at Christmastime at a local store, handing out also a leaflet about the real gift of Christmas. Another might offer a free car wash, while explaining our need as humans for the washing that Jesus offers. The church of which I was pastor in Oxford ministered to older people who had no connection with the church by cutting their grass, as a means of demonstrating in practical ways the love of Jesus.

In this, we were simply following the ancient tradition of the church. The fourth-century emperor Julian complained to the pagan priests of his day that the "impious Galileans" were looking after the pagan poor as well as their own.[15] Free service offered in self-sacrificial ways may indeed seem to many people as bizarre as Ezekiel's actions in an age where so many people are motivated solely by the bottom line. Yet it simply reflects the fact that word and deed together can penetrate to the heart in a way that words alone cannot.

Going out to people. As our culture becomes more and more opposed to the gospel, it will become more and more necessary to take the message out to people rather than waiting for them to come in to the church. Street preaching is one method, while street theater may also be a means of sparking spiritual conversations. These are not in any sense a substitute for the regular ministry of the church, but they are a means of bringing the gospel out to those who are a rebellious people, who have eyes to see but do not see, and ears to hear but do not hear (12:2).

However, even creative communication efforts cannot by themselves open up closed eyes. Even after we have shown the gospel and told the gospel, the fundamental truth remains that those around us are not merely spiritually blind and deaf but dead in their transgressions and sins (Eph. 2:1).

---

14. Harvie Conn, *Evangelism: Doing Justice and Preaching Grace* (Grand Rapids: Zondervan, 1982), 33. See also the examples he gives on pp. 49–56.

15. *Galatians* 305 B, D. See Geoffrey W. H. Lampe, "Diakonia in the Early Church," in *Service in Christ: Essays Presented to Karl Barth on his 80th Birthday*, ed. J. I. McCord and T. H. L. Parker (Grand Rapids: Eerdmans, 1966), 50.

What they need is not simply a vivid depiction of the truth of sin and judgment and God's love; rather, they need new hearts, something only God can give people. Unless the Lord opens their ears and eyes and hearts, all our labors will be in vain.

But what gives us hope in our evangelistic efforts is that God wants to bring men and women to know him, to see his hand as the Prime Mover in everything that happens in this world. Our task is not to sit about debating whether the size of that redeemed remnant will be few in number, but rather to enter the kingdom ourselves and make every effort to encourage others to do likewise in word and deed (Luke 13:23–24).

2 Cor 3:3 ↑ = my Christ aid
lives as a visual
to people -- holy people SEE
- X in my life!

Ezekiel 12:21–13:23

HE WORD OF THE LORD came to me: 22"Son of man, what is this proverb you have in the land of Israel: 'The days go by and every vision comes to nothing'? 23Say to them, 'This is what the Sovereign LORD says: I am going to put an end to this proverb, and they will no longer quote it in Israel.' Say to them, 'The days are near when every vision will be fulfilled. 24For there will be no more false visions or flattering divinations among the people of Israel. 25But I the LORD will speak what I will, and it shall be fulfilled without delay. For in your days, you rebellious house, I will fulfill whatever I say, declares the Sovereign LORD.'"

26The word of the LORD came to me: 27"Son of man, the house of Israel is saying, 'The vision he sees is for many years from now, and he prophesies about the distant future.'

28"Therefore say to them, 'This is what the Sovereign LORD says: None of my words will be delayed any longer; whatever I say will be fulfilled, declares the Sovereign LORD.'"

13:1The word of the LORD came to me: 2"Son of man, prophesy against the prophets of Israel who are now prophesying. Say to those who prophesy out of their own imagination: 'Hear the word of the LORD! 3This is what the Sovereign LORD says: Woe to the foolish prophets who follow their own spirit and have seen nothing! 4Your prophets, O Israel, are like jackals among ruins. 5You have not gone up to the breaks in the wall to repair it for the house of Israel so that it will stand firm in the battle on the day of the LORD. 6Their visions are false and their divinations a lie. They say, "The LORD declares," when the LORD has not sent them; yet they expect their words to be fulfilled. 7Have you not seen false visions and uttered lying divinations when you say, "The LORD declares," though I have not spoken?

8"Therefore this is what the Sovereign LORD says: Because of your false words and lying visions, I am against you, declares the Sovereign LORD. 9My hand will be against the prophets who see false visions and utter lying divinations. They will not belong to the council of my people or be listed in the records of the house of Israel, nor will they enter the land of Israel. Then you will know that I am the Sovereign LORD.

¹⁰"'Because they lead my people astray, saying, "Peace," when there is no peace, and because, when a flimsy wall is built, they cover it with whitewash, ¹¹therefore tell those who cover it with whitewash that it is going to fall. Rain will come in torrents, and I will send hailstones hurtling down, and violent winds will burst forth. ¹²When the wall collapses, will people not ask you, "Where is the whitewash you covered it with?"

¹³"'Therefore this is what the Sovereign LORD says: In my wrath I will unleash a violent wind, and in my anger hailstones and torrents of rain will fall with destructive fury. ¹⁴I will tear down the wall you have covered with whitewash and will level it to the ground so that its foundation will be laid bare. When it falls, you will be destroyed in it; and you will know that I am the LORD. ¹⁵So I will spend my wrath against the wall and against those who covered it with whitewash. I will say to you, "The wall is gone and so are those who whitewashed it, ¹⁶those prophets of Israel who prophesied to Jerusalem and saw visions of peace for her when there was no peace, declares the Sovereign LORD." '

¹⁷"'Now, son of man, set your face against the daughters of your people who prophesy out of their own imagination. Prophesy against them ¹⁸and say, 'This is what the Sovereign LORD says: Woe to the women who sew magic charms on all their wrists and make veils of various lengths for their heads in order to ensnare people. Will you ensnare the lives of my people but preserve your own? ¹⁹You have profaned me among my people for a few handfuls of barley and scraps of bread. By lying to my people, who listen to lies, you have killed those who should not have died and have spared those who should not live.

²⁰"'Therefore this is what the Sovereign LORD says: I am against your magic charms with which you ensnare people like birds and I will tear them from your arms; I will set free the people that you ensnare like birds. ²¹I will tear off your veils and save my people from your hands, and they will no longer fall prey to your power. Then you will know that I am the LORD. ²²Because you disheartened the righteous with your lies, when I had brought them no grief, and because you encouraged the wicked not to turn from their evil ways and so save their lives, ²³therefore you will no longer see false visions or practice divination. I will save my people from your hands. And then you will know that I am the LORD.'"

THE PROBLEM OF distinguishing between true and false prophecy had a long history in Israel. Alongside the true messenger of God, who brought God's word to his people, were many imitators who bore a message of a different stamp. In Ezekiel 13, the prophet addresses the men and women who had appointed themselves Israel's spiritual guardians. First, however, he turns to address a related issue in 12:21–28, the cynicism and general confusion that resulted from the conflicting messages that the people were hearing.

Confusion Over Prophecy (12:21–28)

AS HE DOES on a number of other occasions, Ezekiel addresses these issues by presenting two current popular sayings or slogans. (1) The first "proverb" of the people asserts the ineffectiveness of the prophetic word in general: "The days go by and every vision comes to nothing" (12:22). The people had grown so used to hearing visions proclaimed that never came about that some had come to the conclusion that all prophetic visions were nothing more than empty words. There was no such thing as genuine revelation from God, and the prophets could thus safely be disregarded. Time passed and nothing happened. Therefore, these people reckoned, nothing would ever happen. The Lord's response through Ezekiel to such people was to throw a slightly revised form of their saying back in their faces. By changing the verbs of their formulation, he affirms: "The days are near when [lit., and] every vision will be fulfilled" (12:23).

Indeed, every vision would be fulfilled because of a twofold action on the Lord's part. In the first place, there would be no more false visions or flattering divination among the people of Israel (12:24). The mention of the "false vision" (*ḥ*a*zôn šāw*ʾ) points forward to the worthless activities of the so-called "prophets of Israel," which are criticized in the next chapter (cf. 13:6),[1] while with the expression "no more" (*lō*ʾ ...*ʿôd*), we encounter a characteristic idiom of the prophet's contrast between the way things were in the past and the way they would be in the future.[2] False prophecy would be silenced, so that the people might no longer be led astray by it. In addition, however, true prophecy would be vindicated: The Lord will speak, and what he speaks will happen with no more delay (12:25).

---

1. Johannnes Herrmann suggests that it has been introduced here specifically in order to provide a link with what follows (*Ezechielstudien*, [BWAT 2; Leipzig: Hinrichs, 1908], 19). The connection is certainly not coincidental.

2. Cf. Ezek. 12:23–28; 13:21, 23; 14:11; 16:41–42, 63; 23:27; 34:10, 22, 28–29; 36:12, 14–15, 30; 37:22–23; 39:7, 28; 43:7; 45:8.

The people had grown tired of waiting so long for the Lord to act in fulfillment of the words of the true prophets (Hab. 2:2–3). When the prophesied judgment of Jerusalem took place and the false prophets were cut off, then the people would know who were the true prophets, and that they had indeed spoken at God's command (cf. Ezek. 2:5). This is God's answer to the skeptics of Ezekiel's day.

(2) Yet alongside these unbelievers was apparently a second party, the delayers. This group of people did not deny the effectiveness of the prophetic word in general. They simply hoped that this particular word of judgment would not take effect until a future generation. Their motto was, "The vision he sees is for many years from now, and he prophesies about the distant future" (12:27). Such an attitude was not without historical justification. Isaiah's prophecy to Hezekiah of a future Babylonian invasion of Judah and the enslavement of his descendants at their hands was recognized by Hezekiah as implying "peace in our time" (Isa. 39:5–8). Had not a whole series of prophets foretold the coming doom of Israel down through the years? Might not at least one more generation pass before the ax of judgment descended? This second group also receives a "no more" answer from the Lord: There will be no more delay; the Lord will fulfill whatever he has spoken (12:28).

The Lord's commitment to fulfill *whatever he has spoken* (12:25, 28) brings us to the crux of the issue between the true and the false prophets—the source of their words. Not every word spoken by someone claiming to be a prophet would be fulfilled, for not all spoke the word of the Lord. In order for every prophetic word to be fulfilled, it was necessary that judgment should come to silence the self-proclaimed prophets. This idea, mentioned in passing in 12:24, is unfolded throughout chapter 13 in two halves that show considerable symmetry.[3] Ezekiel first addresses the false prophets ("the prophets of Israel," 13:1–16) and then the false prophetesses ("the daughters of your people who prophesy out of their own imagination," 13:17–23).

Address to the False Prophets of Israel (13:1–16)

THE VERY TITLE Ezekiel gives his opponents—"the prophets of Israel" (13:1)—raises a paradox. In spite of the existence of a body of men who could be addressed thus, their ineffectiveness to accomplish the Lord's purpose is such that he must still raise up someone like Ezekiel so that the people "will know that a prophet has been among them" (2:5).[4] The foundational difference between Ezekiel and "the prophets of Israel" is the *origin* of their prophecy: The false prophets "prophesy out of their own imagination,"

---

3. Greenberg, *Ezekiel 1–20*, 242.
4. Vawter and Hoppe, *Ezekiel*, 82.

whereas Ezekiel declares the vision that the Sovereign Lord has revealed to him (cf. 11:25).

In 13:3 Ezekiel calls these people "foolish prophets [a pun on the similar sounding words *nᵉbîʾîm*, prophets, and *nᵉbālîm*, fools] who follow their own spirit and have seen nothing." They confidently proclaim the divine origin of their words, saying, "Hear the word of the LORD" (13:2), and using the oracle formula, "The LORD declares" (13:6–7). They even hope to see what they have prophesied established (13:6), though in actuality they have no calling from Yahweh (13:7).

Because the message of the false prophets originates in their own hearts rather than in the Lord's revelation, Ezekiel also criticizes the content—or rather, lack of content—of their messages. Their visions are false and their divinations a lie (13:6); this phrase and its variations form a constant refrain in 13:6–9. What their message consists of is revealed in verse 10: They have been prophesying "Peace," when in fact no peace is to be expected.[5]

Such false comfort has had catastrophic results. In speaking according to their own hopes rather than the word of the Lord, they have seduced God's people into a false security that will be devastatingly exposed on the coming day of judgment. This criticism of the prophets is expressed in a series of pictures. (1) They have acted "like jackals among ruins" (13:4). The Hebrew word translated "jackals" (*šûʿālîm*) also covers smaller scavengers such as "foxes."[6] Clearly this is not a positive image. The average jackal is not busy among the ruins with a trowel and construction helmet, rebuilding what has fallen down; rather, his presence there is a matter of self-interest, looking to pounce on any small animals hiding in cracks in the rocks. It seems from other passages in the Bible that the picture may be even more negative than that. The jackal/fox may be thought of as an agent of destruction, as in Nehemiah 4:3: "What they are building—if even a fox (*šûʿāl*) climbed up on it, he would break down their wall of stones!"[7]

(2) Intent on pursuing their own prey, these skulking scavengers have failed to take on the dangerous, but necessary, task of standing in the gaps to build up a solid protection for Israel on the Day of the Lord (13:5). In this verse, the picture is changed to that of a besieged city. In ancient warfare, the attackers would build up a siege ramp, frequently to a corner of the city, in order to breach the walls higher up where they were thinner. Meanwhile

---

5. See v. 16; see also Jer. 6:14; 8:11.

6. Allen suggests that here "jackals" is the more appropriate translation since foxes hunt singly while jackals congregate in groups around ruins (*Ezekiel 1–19*, 201). However, foxes would presumably have found ruins equally conducive to their lifestyle, while the plural simply corresponds to the plural "prophets of Israel."

7. Henry L. Ellison, *Ezekiel: The Man and His Message* (London: Paternoster, 1956), 56. For a similar connection between foxes/jackals and ruins, see Lam. 5:18.

the defenders would build a counter-ramp on the inside to enable the easy supply of materials to repair any breaches that were made.[8] Only the bravest would be found at the breaks in the wall, for there the fighting would be at its fiercest. The false prophets, however, are more interested in their own personal security than the safety of the city.

(3) The third picture Ezekiel uses to describe the "prophets of Israel" also involves a wall. In 13:10–16 the image is of a poorly constructed wall,[9] which the prophets rather than rebuilding properly merely cover with "whitewash,"[10] thus giving it a misleadingly solid appearance. Its true nature will be exposed, however, by the coming of the storm. When the rain comes down in floods, with hailstones and violent winds, the wall will collapse to the destruction of all concerned in the venture (13:12–15).

The concern of the passage is not so much the fate of those who trust in the whitewashed wall, but that of those who have whitewashed it, that is, the false prophets. The divine hand will be raised in judgment on them,[11] and it is decreed that "they will not belong to the council of my people or be listed in the records of the house of Israel, nor will they enter the land of Israel" (13:9). (1) To be excluded from "the council of my people" (sôd ʿammî) was to be cut off from their place in the assembly of the righteous, the true Israel.[12] It is surely a fitting fate that those who have falsely claimed to be prophets, and thus to have access to the council of the Lord (sôd yhwh), will ultimately be excluded even from the council of his people.

(2) Further, their names will not "be listed in the records of the house of Israel" (13:9). To be left off the records of the people means being excluded from full participation in the community. The importance of such a list may be seen from Nehemiah 7, where the finding of a register listing those who first returned from exile became the basis on which certain families were excluded from the priesthood (Neh. 7:63–64 = Ezra 2:62–63).

---

8. This metaphor has been vividly illuminated by the excavations of siege ramps and counter-ramps at Lachish. On these see Israel Eph'al, "The Assyrian Siege Ramp at Lachish," *Tel Aviv* 11 (1984): 60–70; David Ussishkin, "The Assyrian Attack on Lachish: The Archaeological Evidence From the Southwest Corner of the Site," *Tel Aviv* 17 (1990): 53–86.

9. The Hebrew word ḥayiṣ only occurs here in the Old Testament. In the Mishnah, this word denotes a rough stone wall not filled in with earth (Šeb. 3:8).

10. The word used here has been variously rendered and appears to be equivalent to "vanity" or "hogwash" (Block, *Ezekiel 1–24*, 407).

11. This expression of judgment normally occurs with nāṭâ (Ezek. 6:14; 14:9, 13; 16:27; 25:7, 13, 16; 35:3) while here in 13:9 it occurs with hāyâ: "My hand will be against [them]." This construction, which elsewhere indicates the force of divine inspiration, is here used as a pun: Those who never felt the reality of the divine hand in inspiration will now feel it in judgment (see Greenberg, *Ezekiel 1–20*, 237).

12. Block, *Ezekiel 1–24*, 405.

---

(3) They will not "enter the land of Israel" (13:9). When Israel returns from exile, the false prophets will not participate in that return. Like rebellious Israel in the desert, they will not [re-]enter the Promised Land.

Address to the False Prophetesses of Israel (13:17–23)

THE CHARGE AGAINST the women who prophesy in the second part of Ezekiel 13 is both similar to and different from that against the prophets of Israel. In common with Ezekiel's criticism of the prophets of Israel, the source of the women's prophecy is identified as "out of their own imagination" (13:17). However, whereas the prophets of Israel were apparently prophesying in forms indistinguishable from those used by Ezekiel,[13] the practices adopted by the women seem to have had magical overtones. Exactly what those practices are has been a matter for some debate because of the obscure terminology employed. It seems that the women were involved in tying magic bands of some kind (*kᵉsātôt*, 13:18),[14] though whether the object being tied up was the medium herself, the inquirer, or an image of the victim is not clear.

Further, the prophetesses are charged with making *mispāḥôt* for their heads (13:18). *mispāḥôt* occurs only here and in 13:21, and the common translation "veils" is at best a tentative suggestion on the basis of the context; they may equally well have been amulets worn around the neck. How those veils or amulets functioned is also a matter of conjecture. Whatever the precise form of their actions, however, they are not those of a true prophet (or prophetess) of the Lord.

The prophesying women are apparently concerned more with the future of individuals than the fate of the nation. They mediate life and death to "the righteous" and "the wicked" (13:22). There is certainly nothing wrong in such concerns; such themes are part of Ezekiel's own calling to prophetic ministry (see 3:17–21; 33:1–9). The women are not criticized for dealing with the wrong questions but for giving the wrong answers. They "disheartened the righteous with [their] lies, when I had brought them no grief, and . . . encouraged the wicked not to turn from their evil ways and so save their lives" (13:22). In other words, their magically derived oracles are upsetting the moral and spiritual order, afflicting those who ought not to have been afflicted and comforting those who ought not to have been comforted.

---

13. Ezekiel too saw visions and recognized the potential effectiveness of divination. See Duguid, *Ezekiel and the Leaders of Israel*, 94.

14. For the meaning of this *hapax legomenon*, compare the usage of the Akkadian cognate *kasû*, "to bind," often in a magical context (H. W. F. Saggs, "'External Souls' in the Old Testament," *JSS* 19 [1974]: 5).

In doing this, the prophesying women are motivated not by divine calling but by pursuit of personal profit in the form of small payments of barley
and bread.[15] The result of their activities is deadly, killing "those who should
not have died" and sparing "those who should not live" (13:19). They are, in
a graphic image, "ensnar[ing] people like birds" (13:20), that is, regarding both
their clients and their communities as disposable objects, to be exploited in
whatever ways proved profitable. These statements should be read against
the background of Ezekiel's own call to be a watchman, warning the wicked
to turn from their ways and encouraging the righteous to remain steadfast
(3:17–21; 33:1–9). Fulfillment of this role is a means of turning the wicked
from death to life and releases the prophet from responsibility for them. The
women's destructive work in this area, however, prevents the wicked from
becoming aware of their true state, putting both their lives and the women's
own lives in jeopardy (13:18).

As with the condemnation of the prophets of Israel, there is a focus on
the negative results of the activities of the prophesying women. They have
lied to the people, who in turn have listened to their lies (13:19). Out of
concern for the people of Israel, referred to as "my people" five times in this
chapter (Ezek. 13:9, 10, 19, 21, 23), the Lord will act to break the power of
the prophesying women over the people, destroying their equipment so that
the people will no longer be their victims (13:20–21).

The closing verses of the chapter (13:22–23), while still grammatically
addressed to the women, pick up themes from the first section to round off
the whole. The "prophets of Israel" and the "[women] who prophesy" both
oppose in different ways the ministry to which God has called Ezekiel.[16]
The "prophets of Israel" are a stumbling block to the reception of Ezekiel's
message of national judgment by the people, while the "[women] who prophesy" undermine his calling to proclaim life to the righteous and to warn the
wicked to turn from their ways. To be opposed to the prophet God has sent
is to be a false prophet(ess), ensnaring the people rather than setting them
free, causing distress to the righteous and false confidence to the wicked.

In this way, both righteous and wicked are trapped as they come to believe
inaccurate and false ideas about God's plan for his people. Ezekiel asserts
that the future fate of his opponents will show him to have been the true
prophet of the Lord. When the Lord acts to destroy the works of his opponents, then the people "will know that I am the LORD" (Ezek. 13:14, 21, 23)

---

15. On the analogy of 1 Sam. 9:7, where the seer gives his oracle in return for a small
payment of bread, this interpretation of the significance of the barley and bread is to be preferred to that which sees these as the materials for the magical practices. See Zimmerli,
Ezekiel, 1:297.

16. Greenberg, *Ezekiel 1–20*, 245.

and (by implication) that Ezekiel has acted as his true prophet. The coming of the truth will indeed set them free. Then the unbelievers and delayers will be answered in full.

Bridging Contexts

SPEAKING GOD'S WORD TODAY. It may seem as if the world of ancient prophets and prophetesses is very different from ours, until we consider what a wide variety of sources people around us turn to in order to determine the future. We too live in a world where many people claim to speak for God, both inside and outside the church.[17] We too live in a world where people readily turn to superstition for guidance, consulting their daily horoscope in the newspaper or calling "dial a psychic." Though we may not have an officially sponsored "magical" worldview, as the Babylonians did, popular attitudes are often much closer to the old paganism than we might expect.[18] These false ideas trap people by making it harder for them to hear God's Word.

What has changed for us, however, is the form in which God's revelation comes. For Ezekiel, God's word came to him directly. To be sure, in some instances he had God's earlier self-revelation to judge it by. Thus his prophecies are strongly influenced by references to the events of biblical history and in places he adapts the words of other prophets, notably Jeremiah and Zephaniah (e.g., cf. Ezek. 22:25–28 with Zeph. 3:3–4). His prophecies did not come to him in a vacuum, but what marked him out from his opponents was that he spoke as one directly and inerrantly inspired by God. He had stood in God's council, heard his words, and received his commission; therefore he spoke. When Ezekiel said "This is what the Sovereign LORD says...," he spoke the truth.

The false prophets, by contrast, spoke out of their own imagination. They pretended to such inspiration, even adopting similar formulas ("The LORD declares...," 13:6–7), yet there was no reality of revelation to back up their words. The visions they claimed to have seen were empty lies, not the real thing.

Our situation is different from Ezekiel's. We who speak God's word today do so "second-hand," as it were. We do not speak as those who have received a direct, personal message from God, but as those who have the full and

---

17. For one example of this, see Michael G. Maudlin, "Seers in the Heartland: Hot on the Trail of the Kansas City Prophets," *Christianity Today* 35 (Jan. 14, 1991): 18-22.

18. In a survey of Baby Boomers, Wade Clark Roof discovered that 26 percent of them "believed" in astrology (*A Generation of Seekers: The Spiritual Journeys of the Baby Boom Generation* [San Francisco: HarperSanFrancisco, 1993], 72).

completely inspired Word of God, the Scriptures. Our task is to take that word and apply it to our contemporary situation. The contrast in our day between "true prophet" and "false prophet" is not so much as to who has really received the word of God, but rather who is rightly handling the Word of God.

At first sight, it might seem to be a disadvantage to be living in a time of mediate rather than immediate revelation. It might seem attractive to be able to declare to our congregations as the prophets did, "This is what the LORD says ...," and then proceed with God's direct revelation for today. Yet the difficulties experienced by God's people in discerning between true and false prophets and between true and false prophecies, then and now, point us in the other direction. Actually, we are the advantaged ones, for our congregations can test our words against an infallible measuring rod, the completed Scriptures.

However, even though the Scriptures are infallible, our exegesis of them is not. Not everything in the Bible is equally clear, nor is it always clear which particular text is appropriate to a particular situation, or which texts provide the context in the light of which other texts should be read. These facts should lead us to cautious humility when it comes to identifying our opponents as "false prophets." Other believers may, while seeking to apply Scripture to the same situation as ourselves, come to different conclusions from us. The issue between us in this case is not whether there is a revelation from God or whether Scripture applies to a particular situation, but what that revelation requires us to do. With such people, we should be willing to enter patient dialogue, seeking to grow in our mutual understanding of how the Word applies to this particular problem.

Misreading God's Word. But we also encounter in our situation those who disbelieve in the reality of any revelation at all, just as Ezekiel did. Here our concern is not so much with those holding other religious convictions or no religious convictions, but with those who while claiming to be Christians actually undermine the Bible as the basis for theology. This may take the form of a soothing semiorthodoxy, proclaiming a partial message that sounds like the truth, but is actually a distortion. Such preachers may mention only the positive aspect of salvation, while ignoring the uncomfortable realities of God's wrath on sin and the judgment to come.

Or it may take the form of a more radical revisioning of Christianity in the likeness of pagan religions, addressing God as "Divine Father/Mother" or "Sophia."[19] The basis of these first two positions is ultimately a denial of the

---

19. For an example of this, see Donald Bloesch's review of *The New Century Hymnal*, ed. A. G. Clyde in *Christianity Today* (July 15, 1996): 49–50.

reality of the Bible as the ultimate revelation of God and the sole standard for faith and practice.

In addition, we have those who, while recognizing the Bible as a revelation from God, blunt its message by applying it to a time other than our own. This may take the form of an eschatologically overworked imagination, which pushes the significance of the Bible into the future. On this approach, the Bible is seen as a source book for end-times prophecies rather than a message that speaks to us in our everyday life.

However, perhaps more common in our situation is a more subtle form of this problem, which pushes the significance of the Bible back into the past. For such people, the historical and cultural rootedness of the Scriptures provides a reason for abandoning its teaching in our present historical and cultural context. For instance, instead of considering how Paul's teaching on the role of women both challenges and affirms aspects of our own culture, it is held that while Paul may have had something true (and even inspired) to say to the people of his day, before it can say anything to us, his teaching must be brought up to date and into line with the times in which we live.

Even such a well-respected evangelical scholar as F. F. Bruce could fall into this error. In discussing Paul's view of the role of women in the ministry of the church, he concluded: "Whatever in Paul's teaching promotes true freedom is of universal and permanent validity; whatever seems to impose restrictions on true freedom has regard to local and temporary conditions."[20] For Bruce, this extrabiblical criterion—"true freedom"—became the means by which Scripture's less palatable teachings were ruled of no relevance for the present day. Now this is not to suggest that there are not difficult questions to answer about how particular Scriptures should be applied in changed cultural conditions; however, in principle the answer to that difficulty is fundamentally to allow Scripture to interpret Scripture, rather than to submit it to modern consciousness for arbitration.[21]

Such teachings are no less destructive in our era than they were in days of old. The result of both kinds of teaching is that people are confused about what the Bible says and how, if at all, it relates to us. The word of warning to the false prophets and prophetesses is still valid. There is no place among God's people for those who seek to lead them astray. Yet the comfort for God's people remains. When the Lord ultimately acts, it will be seen definitively who has rightly handled his Word.

---

20. "Women in the Church: A Biblical Survey," in Bruce, *A Mind for What Matters* (Grand Rapids: Eerdmans, 1990), 263.

21. See Robert W. Yarbrough, "The Hermeneutics of 1 Timothy 2:9–15," in A. J. Köstenberger, T. R. Schreiner, and H. S. Baldwin (eds.) *Women in the Church: A Fresh Analysis of 1 Timothy 2:9–15* (Grand Rapids: Baker, 1995), 178–85.

RESPONDING TO THE **present Babel.** "If the trumpet does not sound a clear call, who will get ready for battle?" (1 Cor. 14:8). So Paul describes the babble of conflicting voices heard in the Corinthian church. There was no clear message—no "revelation or knowledge or prophecy or word of instruction" (14:6)—and the result was an unedifying confusion. A similar confusion reigns in the church of our day. There have never been more different denominations and factions within denominations, each proclaiming a different message to the world. No wonder the world is confused as to what the essential message of Christianity is!

How should we who make up the church respond to the present Babel? On the one hand, it is more essential than ever that those within the church who affirm the Scriptures as the divinely inspired Word of God, the sole rule of faith and practice, should work together to seek to resolve old problems and bury irrelevant distinctions. Past history should not keep us apart where the Scriptures do not. The force of Jesus' high priestly prayer for the full unity of those who will believe in him should be fully felt (John 17:23), not least because the result of that unity will be the world knowing that the Father has commissioned and sent the Son. It is a travesty when racial, social, and historical differences divide the church of Christ.

On the other hand, however, we should recognize that the current cacophony is not simply the result of a disagreement among family members. Satan's strategy is to imitate God's means of self-revelation in order to confuse the message. Wherever there are prophets, there are also false prophets. Wherever there are those preaching the truth, there are also those propagating lies. Remember the words of Jesus in Matthew 7:22—23: "Many will say to me on that day, 'Lord, Lord, did we not prophesy in your name, and in your name drive out demons and perform many miracles?' Then I will tell them plainly, 'I never knew you. Away from me, you evildoers!'" It is not enough to be sincere; it is not enough to make great claims about yourself; what counts is knowing God and faithfully declaring his Word.

We are therefore not automatically to believe those who claim to be speaking the Word of God to us. As John instructs us, we are to test every spirit (1 John 4:1). If someone is of God, then he or she will confess that Jesus Christ has come in the flesh (4:2). The need to test those who claim to bring God's message to us did not come to an end in Ezekiel's day; it was true in New Testament times and it is true today. We are to apply the test that the Bereans are commended for: They "examined the Scriptures every day to see if what Paul said was true" (Acts 17:11). We are not to be taken in by lofty claims, but rather to test all things by the standard of the Word of God. In some instances, that may mean separating from those who claim to be Christians but fail the test. We should not allow historical accidents to hold us together with those from whom the Scripture insists that we part.

Motivation behind failure to prophesy correctly. What was it, though, that motivated the false prophets? Why would people claim to speak for God when they had received no such commissioning? Why would someone prophesy a peace for which he had no evidence? It's really very simple, isn't it? People want to hear good news. When the terminally ill patient comes to his physician and says, "Tell me the truth, Doctor, is it serious? Am I going to die?" which is easier: to tell the uncomfortable truth or gloss it over with optimistic words? It is much easier to tell people happy news than sad news—especially if that sad news involves a judgment on their lifestyle. The bottom line for the false prophets was comfort for themselves, self-interest rather than telling the people what they really needed to hear. It is so much easier to build on sand than to dig down to the solid rock. But when the flood comes, the difference in foundation is immediately apparent (Matt. 7:24–27).

In truth, all of us who preach or talk to others about Christianity are familiar with the temptation to be a false prophet from time to time. Sometimes the temptation is to be a jackal. As a jackal, the ruins of other people's lives are of no account to you so long as you have the things you need. You have little concern for those around you going to a lost eternity in hell; your own interests are more important.

At other times, perhaps the temptation is to be a draft-dodger, happy to let others stand in the gap rather than you. Your security and safety are what are really important to you. So you do not witness to those at work or at school because they might laugh at you or think you are weird. Not for you a place on the front lines of evangelism. You'd rather watch from the sidelines.

At still other times, the temptation comes to be a whitewasher. You never confront anyone about their sinful lifestyle. Instead, by your silence, you whitewash their wall. Should I witness to that family member who is a Mormon? Why, he lives such a good moral life! Splish, Splash! On goes another coat of whitewash. Should I inquire whether my family members are really trusting in Jesus for their salvation? But they all go to church, don't they? Splish! Splash! The appearance is all that counts. If the truth be told, there is a little bit of each of these categories of false prophet within each of us.

Jesus Christ, the true prophet. We should not leave this passage, however, without considering how Christ has fulfilled the role of true prophet. The man who stood in the gap in the city wall on the day of battle was risking his own life for the good of others. Jesus not only risked his life but gave his own life freely, pouring out his blood on the cross for you and me. Jesus did not let his own security stand in the way of doing God's work, nor did he guard his own comfort. Instead, for the sake of his people, he "made himself nothing, taking the very nature of a servant, being made in human likeness. And being found in appearance as a man, he humbled himself and became obedient to death—even death on a cross!" (Phil. 2:7–8).

Nor was Jesus ever willing to whitewash over people's sins, as a cursory glance at the Gospels will show. He had a better way of dealing with human sins than to cover them with whitewash; he covered them with his atoning blood. As a result, Christ's people are those who have "washed their robes and made them white in the blood of the Lamb" (Rev. 7:14). He is himself both the foundation on which they build and the One who is able to make what they have built stand forever. The wise person is indeed the one who is built on such a rock, which is alone able to withstand the storm of the Final Judgment.

Ezekiel 14:1–11

S OME OF THE ELDERS of Israel came to me and sat down in front of me. ²Then the word of the LORD came to me: ³"Son of man, these men have set up idols in their hearts and put wicked stumbling blocks before their faces. Should I let them inquire of me at all? ⁴Therefore speak to them and tell them, 'This is what the Sovereign LORD says: When any Israelite sets up idols in his heart and puts a wicked stumbling block before his face and then goes to a prophet, I the LORD will answer him myself in keeping with his great idolatry. ⁵I will do this to recapture the hearts of the people of Israel, who have all deserted me for their idols.'

⁶"Therefore say to the house of Israel, 'This is what the Sovereign LORD says: Repent! Turn from your idols and renounce all your detestable practices!

⁷"'When any Israelite or any alien living in Israel separates himself from me and sets up idols in his heart and puts a wicked stumbling block before his face and then goes to a prophet to inquire of me, I the LORD will answer him myself. ⁸I will set my face against that man and make him an example and a byword. I will cut him off from my people. Then you will know that I am the LORD.

⁹"'And if the prophet is enticed to utter a prophecy, I the LORD have enticed that prophet, and I will stretch out my hand against him and destroy him from among my people Israel. ¹⁰They will bear their guilt—the prophet will be as guilty as the one who consults him. ¹¹Then the people of Israel will no longer stray from me, nor will they defile themselves anymore with all their sins. They will be my people, and I will be their God, declares the Sovereign LORD.'"

EVEN IN EXILE, the people were not left without leadership. The vacuum left by the absence of the old structures, built around the monarchy, was filled by "the elders," the heads of the exiled families.[1] Though they had presumably come to the prophet seeking an encouraging oracle from the Lord, Ezekiel turns on these elders with a sharp accusation of idolatry (see also chs. 8 and 20). The charge against them is given in 14:3: "These men have set up idols in their hearts and put wicked stumbling blocks before their faces." The accusation of having set up their "idols in their hearts" is reminiscent of 8:10–12, where the elders are denounced for secret idolatry with "all the idols of the house of Israel."

In other words, the elders in exile are tainted with the same fundamental sin as those left behind in Judah: internal idolatry. Even while externally willing to go through the orthodox motions of inquiring of the Lord, their hearts belonged elsewhere. The phrase "wicked stumbling block," which occurs six times in Ezekiel, is also invariably linked to idolatry.[2] Because the hearts of the exilic elders are divided between the Lord and idols, the Lord will give the elders no answer to their inquiry except an answer of judgment (14:4). By this means, the Lord will "seize" their hearts, arresting them for their sin (14:5).[3] Seeking to serve two masters will result in judgment by the Lord, the only "master" with any real power to act.

The people in exile are equally implicated in this halfheartedness. They may not have given in to the flagrant idolatry going on in Jerusalem, but there was a more subtle form of assault that had affected even those in exile with the prophet in Babylon. They found themselves living in a broken and fallen world, where their regular experience was of dislocation and disorientation, where things were falling apart, where the center could not hold, and where life did not seem to make sense. The temptation they faced was to turn to the idols of this world as a means of, if not making sense out of the world, at least of numbing the pain.

Those who feel abandoned by God find that the pull of seeking out other gods increases, other gods whom they think can deliver the sense of security and significance they seek. If the Lord cannot deliver, why not try Marduk

---

1. See Duguid, *Ezekiel and the Leaders of Israel*, 110. On the strengthened position of the elders during and after the exile see Daniel L. Smith, *Religion of the Landless* (Bloomington, Ind.: Meyer-Stone, 1989), 94–99.

2. Duguid, *Ezekiel and the Leaders of Israel*, 117.

3. The NIV's "I will . . . recapture [their] hearts" is probably too optimistic. *tāpaś* (lay hold of, seize) often has the sense of apprehend, arrest (e.g., Num. 5:13; Jer. 26:8). See Greenberg, *Ezekiel 1–20*, 249.

or one of the other Babylonian gods? Their hearts are torn between two loyalties, and they are attracted by the blessings that the idols seem to promise, the greener grass they offer, the more powerful magic they seem to contain.

The result is that all of the exiles have, in their hearts, deserted the Lord for their idols (14:5). Such people—whether native-born Israelite or proselyte (14:7)[4]—should not expect to receive a word of divine guidance through the prophet. God is not deceived by the orthodoxy of their outward behavior, for he looks on the heart (1 Sam. 16:7). Instead, the Lord will answer them himself (Ezek. 14:7), by direct action rather than through a prophet. Do they want a word from the Lord? The Lord will demonstrate his attitude toward them by making them "an example and a byword" (14:8). Just as Lot's wife has become a proverbial example of the dangers of looking back, so they too will become a "byword," a proverbial warning of the dangers of divided loyalties.

The judgment with which they are threatened is being "cut . . . off from [the LORD's] people" (14:8). This punishment has often been interpreted as a form of excommunication;[5] however, in view of the divine destruction threatened on a prophet in the following verse, the death penalty is more likely indicated here.[6] In any case, it is doubtful that the people would have seen a big distinction between the two fates as we do. In either case, the sinner would be excised from the covenant community, from the realm of life, and sent out into the realm of death, like the scapegoat on the Day of Atonement.[7]

A similar judgment would apply to any prophet who attempted to provide an oracle for them. There were clearly other prophets present in exile apart from Ezekiel, and the temptation to go shopping around for a more favorable word was significant. Yet any such word would be no true word from the Lord, but rather a deceiving word sent as a judgment on the compromising prophet and people alike (14:9). Those who sought false gods rather than the true God would find what they sought—lies in place of the truth. Those who attempted to counteract God's will by speaking when he had not spoken would find that they were doing nothing other than God's will, confirming the guilty ones in their guilt.

---

4. The language of "any Israelite or alien living in Israel" is anachronistic addressed to those in exile. It is used here as an echo of the priestly style of law found in the Pentateuch. For the similarities to Lev. 17, see Greenberg, *Ezekiel 1–20*, 252.

5. Paul Joyce, *Divine Initiative and Human Response in Ezekiel* (JSOTS 51; Sheffield: JSOT Press, 1989), 67; Anthony Phillips, *Ancient Israel's Criminal Law* (Oxford: Blackwell, 1970), 29–30.

6. Greenberg, *Ezekiel 1–20*, 250.

7. In fact, the two practices were frequently linked, with excommunication often acting as a preparation for the covenantal death penalty. See William Horbury, "Extirpation and Excommunication," *VT* 35 (1985): 34.

Yet the fact that they are unwittingly doing the sovereign will of God in no way exempts the prophet, as secondary cause, from responsibility for his own words. In Deuteronomy 13:1–5 both elements are brought together: the will of the Lord to test the people (v. 3), and the will of the prophet to lead the people astray from the way of Yahweh (v. 5). If the people refuse to listen to God's prophets who tell them the truth, the Lord will bring judgment on the people by giving them lying prophets, who will tell them what they want to hear.

A similar judgment fell on Ahab in 1 Kings 22: As a judgment for his refusal to listen to prophetic truth, the Lord promised to send him a deceitful oracle through another prophet. Yet the prophet remains responsible for his own actions. Prophet and idolater alike will each "bear their guilt" (Ezek. 14:10), that is, they will bear the punishment their iniquity deserves. The guilt of each is equal (14:10), and so they are destined for a similar fate, that of being "cut off" or "destroyed" from the covenant people.

Yet the goal of God's judgment on the exiles is not their total extermination, but rather their salvation.[8] There is still room for God's people to repent and return to God (14:6).[9] The result of God's purifying judgment will be a faithful and undefiled people, cleansed from their transgressions (14:11). The goal of the covenant—God's dwelling in the midst of his people—will certainly not be thwarted, not even by Israel's sin (14:11).[10]

DIVINE SOVEREIGNTY and human responsibility. The question of the relationship between divine sovereignty and human responsibility is by no means a new issue. Yet perhaps few eras have been less conducive to the acceptance of divine sovereignty than ours. We live in an age that celebrates human freedom above all things. As my wife once heard it put in a women's Bible study: "The debate between divine sovereignty and human free will is too complex to discuss. But of this one thing we can be sure: Human beings have free will." Previous generations (and indeed many contemporary non-Western cultures) would certainly not have framed their conclusions in similar terms. If there was one thing that was clear to them, it was that the gods did what they wished and human beings were pow-

---

8. Blenkinsopp, *Ezekiel*, 72.

9. Ezekiel uses the Qal and Hiphil forms of šûb together in his appeal. We might capture the flavor best by translating, "Turn and return."

10. Greenberg describes the phrase "they will be my people, and I will be their God" as "the essential expression of the bond between Israel and its God," an expression drawn from the terminology of marriage and adoption (*Ezekiel 1–20*, 254).

erless against them. In consequence, what modern Westerners may perceive as the key interpretive issue in this passage (How can God deceive a prophet and still hold him responsible for his actions?) would probably not have been a difficulty for Ezekiel's audience.

The Old Testament frequently traces actions that we attribute to secondary causes back to their primary cause in the will of God. Thus, whereas we perceive the abundance or lack of rain to be due to a certain combination of meteorological conditions, some of which we now recognize as due to our own mismanagement of the planet, the ancient Israelite saw the rains as a direct expression of the Lord's pleasure or displeasure with his people (Deut. 11:13–14).

In part, this is due to our different position in the redemptive-historical scheme of things. God no longer deals with our nations directly, in the way he did with ancient Israel, for our nations are not in covenant relationship with him as Israel was. So for us, rain is not directly an expression of the blessings and curses of the covenant. But in part, this attitude is also an expression of a modern form of idolatry, whereby nature is crowned with god-like powers and humanity is perceived as the only significant player in the universe.

In contrast, in the Bible it is God who is the only significant player in the universe. All things can ultimately be traced back to his agency and his will. Even the prophecy of a false prophet, which led people astray, could not be given without the Lord's permission and direction. Does that thereby make God responsible for sin? By no means. For God's action in giving the prophet a deceitful oracle is nothing other than giving him and his hearers what they have sought. It is a judgment of God that in no way violates the free will of prophet or people, for they do nothing other than what their nature inclines towards. The vaunted "free will" of sinful humanity turns out to be nothing more than the "free will" of a hungry lion presented with the choice between a juicy piece of meat and a fresh green salad. It is the lion's nature always (freely!) to choose the meat. Should the zookeeper sovereignly choose to present the lion only with fresh meat and to hold back the salad, the lion's "free will" is not thereby violated. He continues to choose what his nature dictates he will choose.

Our natural human inclination and God's grace. Left to themselves, human beings have a similar "taste" for evil. By nature, they will inevitably choose lies in place of the truth and worship the created in place of the Creator (Rom. 1:18–25). Therefore, God is in no way violating their free will when he gives them over to the sinful desires of their hearts and a depraved mind (1:24, 26, 28), or when he sends a powerful delusion on those who have refused to love the truth (2 Thess. 2:11–12). Those New Testament references demonstrate that this is not merely an "Old Testament" doctrine, but one that persists throughout the pages of Scripture.

Indeed, the truly difficult question to answer is not why God sovereignly allows sinners to persist in the delusion they seek, but why God sovereignly chooses to save some of those selfsame sinners! It is not because those saved are more intelligent or richer or more beautiful or more righteous than those who perish. Far from it, all is of grace, not of works, so that no one has any grounds for boasting (Eph. 2:8–10). The sovereignty that changes the lion's nature, enabling him to lie down in peace and eat salad with the lamb, is genuinely astonishing and without cause except for God's electing love! How indeed can it be that sinful men and women can acquire a taste for righteousness? *There* is the true cause for wonder. As Charles Wesley put it in his great hymn:

> And can it be that I should gain
> > An interest in the Savior's blood?
> Died He for me, who caused His pain?
> > For me, who Him to death pursued?
> Amazing love! how can it be
> > That Thou, my God, shouldst die for me?

Contemporary Significance

THE STANDARD OF "just good enough." When I used to work in the oil industry, we had a problem that we called the problem of "just good enough." Things would always be manufactured *just* good enough to meet the standard you set—and no better. If you simply specified a car, what you got was the most basic vehicle on four wheels, not a Mercedes. If you wanted a Mercedes, you had to ask for a Mercedes. Similarly, most people, most of the time, are content to coast through life, doing just enough. We don't in general have a massive urge to push back the frontiers of knowledge and goodness. Most of us are content to live lives that are "just good enough."

But what is "just good enough" when it comes to your commitment to God? Is it enough to be 25 percent committed—you come to church one Sunday out of four and obey two and a half of the Ten Commandments? Is it enough to be 51 percent committed—better than the average pew sitter? Or must you be 100 percent, totally, life-dominatingly committed to God? If this was a multiple-choice test, I'm sure we'd all get the right answer. Everyone within the church knows that you ought to be 100 percent committed to God. So why is it that surveys time and time again show that the majority of Christians behave little differently from their secular counterparts?

Why is it that the statistics on premarital sex and divorce are not radically different for Christians and non-Christians?

The answer is that all of us who claim the name of Christ have divided hearts. Outwardly, our appearance may "fit": We go to church regularly and appear to be decent, religious people. Yet when it comes to the tough decisions in life, there are other standards operating than God's Word, which demonstrates the existence in our hearts of other gods than the true God. We have deep-seated idolatries in our hearts that drive our various behavior patterns. Like the Laodiceans, our deeds prove us to be neither cold nor hot, but lukewarm, fit only to be spit out (Rev. 3:16).

The fundamental issue of idolatry. Yet when trouble comes, we want the Lord to come to our aid. We seek his help, but at the same time we don't want to give up on our other options. We don't want to give up our cherished sins. Ezekiel tells us that such an approach to God is not an option. You cannot serve the true God and keep one foot in the camp of idolatry at the same time. God sees what we are really like on the inside; we cannot hide the truth from him, and the double-minded person stands to receive nothing from God (James 1:7).

Much of the counseling within the church of our day fails to recognize the key significance of the idolatries that remain within our hearts. On the one hand, there is a moralizing approach that focuses purely on the level of behavior. This approach says, "Your problem is that your anger (or lust, or worry, or whatever) is sin. Repent and change your behavior! If you would just do what is right, then good feelings will follow." The problem with this approach is that in focusing on behavior it doesn't go deep enough. It doesn't recognize the reason for the behavior: the idols and false beliefs that are driving it. The reason why this particular person sins in this particular way is because there are idols and false beliefs in his or her life that say, "By doing this, you will gain what is really important and meaningful in life."

On the other hand, there is a psychologizing approach to counseling that says, "Your basic problem is that you don't see that God loves you and accepts you just as you are. If you could just feel good about yourself, right actions will follow." This approach focuses on the feelings rather than the behavior, but still doesn't go deep enough. It doesn't recognize that behind the bad feelings lies an idolatry, a belief that "even if God loves me, yet while I don't have this, I'm not a worthwhile person." Both approaches fail to see the sin behind the sin, the fundamental issue of idolatry.[11]

---

11. David Powlison, "Idols of the Heart and 'Vanity Fair,'" *Journal of Biblical Counseling* 13 (1995): 49. See also Edward T. Welch, *When People Are Big and God Is Small: Overcoming Peer Pressure, Codependency, and the Fear of Man* (Phillipsburg, N.J.: Presbyterian and Reformed, 1997), 44–47.

A better approach is to recognize that driving both our behaviors and our feelings are deep-seated heart idolatries. Our fundamental problem lies in looking to something besides God for our happiness. This is not a new observation. The church father Tertullian put it this way:

> The principle crime of the human race, the highest guilt charged upon the world, the whole procuring cause of judgment, is idolatry. For, although each single fault retains its own proper feature, although it is destined to judgment under its own proper name also, yet it is marked off under the *general* account of idolatry. . . . Thus it comes to pass, that in idolatry all crimes are detected and in all crimes idolatry.[12]

What does Tertullian mean by that? He goes on to explain that all murder is idolatry since the motive for killing is ultimately that something is loved more than God—yet in turn all idolatry is murder for it incurs one's own death. Similarly all idolatry is also adultery because it is unfaithfulness to the truth and to God, while adultery is idolatry because it flows from the inordinate desire for a person or for a sensation, a desire stronger than our love for God and our desire to obey his law.

Idolatry, then, is simply the desire for something other than God at the center of our lives as our guiding star, the source of meaning in our life. As such, idolatry is the sin behind every sin, the life-lie that drives all of our choices and values. The object of that idolatry varies from person to person. There are probably as many different idols as there are human beings. However, the fact that we have idols is an inescapable truth. Our hearts are, in Calvin's vivid image, factories that mass-produce idols.[13]

Repentance and freedom from idolatry. The only way to deal with our idols is to come to God in the simple act of repentance. Repentance turns its back on any other source of hope or self-justification and finds its refuge in the Lord alone. It is the attitude expressed by the hymnwriter Augustus Toplady: "Nothing in my hand I bring; simply to thy cross I cling." This attitude is the ultimate idol-smasher, for every idolatry is at root an effort towards self-justification. Every idol promises us salvation, that is, self-worth, if we will just give in to what it demands. The idol "beauty" says: "I can make you a worthwhile person. Just make the sacrifices I require, and you will never lack friends"; the idol "power" says: "Put in the long hours in pursuit of your career, even though it costs you your family, and I will give you a significant life." Idols make promises to those who can meet their demands.

---

12. "On Idolatry," *The Ante-Nicene Fathers*, ed. A. Roberts & J. Donaldson (Grand Rapids: Eerdmans, 1973), 3.61.

13. *Institutes of the Christian Religion*, 1.11.8.

Christianity offers salvation, meaning, and worth only to those who recognize that they can *never* give what the law demands; their only hope lies in the fact that Christ has fulfilled it for them. "Religion" or "doing good" is a popular idolatry that says: "Be a good person, punish yourself for your sins, turn your back on them, and you will be saved." The difference between Christians and religiously minded idolaters is that Christians repent not only of their sins but also of their very best deeds, their best righteousness, in order to receive in its place the righteousness of Christ, to which they cling single-heartedly.[14]

Even that ability to cling single-heartedly to the Lord is itself the gift of God. The promise of Ezekiel 11:19 is that the Lord will give his people "an undivided heart," a single-minded devotion to the Lord. By nature, all of us desert God and go after idols. But our idols will not ultimately have dominion over us. In order to rescue us from ourselves and from the grasp of our idols, God sent Jesus Christ into the world for us. There is nothing half-hearted about Jesus' commitment to his people. He came down from heaven to live among us—that alone is an astonishing commitment. But his commitment is laid out even more plainly for us to see on the cross. His body was torn apart there because of my sins. His blood was poured out as a fountain to cleanse me from my unrighteousness. There on the cross, Jesus won a complete victory for us. Through his complete obedience, the demands of the law were comprehensively met. That's why his final words on the cross were: "It is finished" (John 19:30). It is complete! His work is done.

Christ's finished work on the cross is what gives us freedom from our idols. Their power to threaten us was broken once and for all, there and then. When our idols say to us, "You are not a worthwhile person if you do not have success or beauty or wealth or children or _____" (fill in the appropriate blank with the demand of your idol), now we can simply point them to the cross. There, God demonstrated his love by declaring me worth the death of his sinless only Son; there, God declared me a valued member of his family; there, God accomplished for me the free gift of salvation. That fact, unlike the moralizing or psychologizing approaches, frees me to recognize the full depth of my sin, because I now recognize the full depth of God's love for me in Christ. I am indeed a far worse sinner than I ever thought, but in Christ I am at the same time far more loved than I ever dared hope.

The result of Jesus' wholehearted sacrifice is the salvation of his people and their restoration to the full covenant relationship with God. What Ezekiel looked forward to, the presence of God in the midst of his sinless people on

---

14. This principle is classically expounded by George Whitefield in "The Method of Grace," *Select Sermons of George Whitefield* (London: Banner of Truth, 1964), 81–82.

the far side of judgment (14:11), is still that to which the church looks forward. Though even now we experience the presence of Jesus in our midst whenever two or three are gathered together (Matt. 18:20), yet we are still strangers and aliens in this world, all too familiar with sin. Remaining sin in the lives of believers serves God's glory by showing that he has not done anything without cause. It continues to remind us of our own weakness and depravity and thus to point us to the Savior. It continues to remind us of the world's depravity, and thus of our neighbors' utter need of Christ if they are ever to be saved.

But sin will not remain our constant companion forever (Ezel. 14:11). Because of the sin-bearer's death in our place, we look forward to the day when we will join perfectly in the worship on the heavenly mountain. There we will join with the whole community of saints of all times and places, along with the heavenly hosts of angels and archangels. On that day, the dwelling of God will be with his people and he will live with them (Rev. 21:3). On that day, our idols will finally be smashed, and we will be able to worship and serve our beloved God with undivided hearts.

Ezekiel 14:12–23

🌿

THE WORD OF THE LORD came to me: ¹³"Son of man, if a country sins against me by being unfaithful and I stretch out my hand against it to cut off its food supply and send famine upon it and kill its men and their animals, ¹⁴even if these three men—Noah, Daniel and Job—were in it, they could save only themselves by their righteousness, declares the Sovereign LORD.

¹⁵"Or if I send wild beasts through that country and they leave it childless and it becomes desolate so that no one can pass through it because of the beasts, ¹⁶as surely as I live, declares the Sovereign LORD, even if these three men were in it, they could not save their own sons or daughters. They alone would be saved, but the land would be desolate.

¹⁷"Or if I bring a sword against that country and say, 'Let the sword pass throughout the land,' and I kill its men and their animals, ¹⁸as surely as I live, declares the Sovereign LORD, even if these three men were in it, they could not save their own sons or daughters. They alone would be saved.

¹⁹"Or if I send a plague into that land and pour out my wrath upon it through bloodshed, killing its men and their animals, ²⁰as surely as I live, declares the Sovereign LORD, even if Noah, Daniel and Job were in it, they could save neither son nor daughter. They would save only themselves by their righteousness.

²¹"For this is what the Sovereign LORD says: How much worse will it be when I send against Jerusalem my four dreadful judgments—sword and famine and wild beasts and plague—to kill its men and their animals! ²²Yet there will be some survivors—sons and daughters who will be brought out of it. They will come to you, and when you see their conduct and their actions, you will be consoled regarding the disaster I have brought upon Jerusalem—every disaster I have brought upon it. ²³You will be consoled when you see their conduct and their actions, for you will know that I have done nothing in it without cause, declares the Sovereign LORD."

THIS SECTION OF Ezekiel's prophecy focuses on the inevitability and justice of God's decision to destroy Jerusalem. The oracle begins by introducing a hypothetical country that is unfaithful to the Lord. The implied universality of the principle is an important element supporting the justice of God's actions: The rules are the same for any nation and have not been applied unfairly to Israel. However, behind the implied universality, the actual reference is clearly to Israel, for the phrase "by being unfaithful" (14:13) refers elsewhere to a breach of a covenant relationship. This may be through marital infidelity (Num. 5:12, 27), misappropriation of an object belonging by rights to the Lord, as in the case of Achan (Josh. 7:1), or other action that violates the covenant between God and his people (e.g., Lev. 26:40; Ezek. 17:20). Such a breach of the covenant inevitably brings on the offending nation (i.e., Israel) the curses attached to the covenant in Leviticus 26.

These covenant curses are itemized individually in the form of four test cases (Ezek. 14:13–14, 15–16, 17–18, 19–20). In each case, a different covenant curse is envisaged: famine, through cutting off the bread supply (Lev. 26:26); wild beasts (26:22); a sword (26:25); and finally plague (26:25). The prophet has already brought together this fearsome foursome in Ezekiel 5, underlining the nature of judgment as nothing arbitrary but simply the just application of the sanctions of a covenant to which Israel subscribed—and then repeatedly broke. Now, therefore, the curses of Leviticus 26 will descend.

What is common to all four cases is the hypothetical presence in the land of three righteous men: Noah, Daniel, and Job. Each of these men was noted for righteous behavior in the midst of a corrupt generation. Noah is described as "a righteous man, blameless among the people of his time" (Gen. 6:9), while Job was held up by God to Satan as a model of righteousness (Job 1:8). The identity of "Daniel" has provoked considerable discussion, with the majority of scholars arguing that he is not the biblical character of that name, which has a different spelling, but rather a heroic figure of antiquity, Danel. This king is known from Ugaritic sources as a just ruler who "judges the cause of the widow and adjudicates the case of the fatherless."[1] He would fit with Noah and Job as ancient figures of international reputation.

Others have argued, however, that this ruler's unquestioned pagan origins would likely have been problematic for a radically theocentric prophet such as Ezekiel, and that the arguments advanced against the traditional identification

---

1. James B. Pritchard, ed., *Ancient Near Eastern Texts*, 2d ed. (Princeton: Princeton Univ. Press, 1955), 151, 153. See John Day, "The Daniel of Ugarit and Ezekiel and the Hero of the Book of Daniel," *VT* 30 (1980): 174–84.

with the biblical figure Daniel are not as strong as they may at first sight appear. He too fits the description of a righteous man in a difficult time, and he would probably have been known, at least by reputation, to Ezekiel's hearers.[2] However, Ezekiel's oracles against the nations (Ezek. 25–32) demonstrate that he is quite capable of utilizing mythical ideas known to his hearers to make his theological points, and in the oracle against the King of Tyre he once again alludes to "Danel" (28:3).[3] The bottom line is that both passages are open to either identification. Fortunately, in neither case does the interpretation of the passage rest on the identification adopted. Whether mythical Danel or biblical Daniel was originally intended, in the passage he functions merely as a cipher for a readily recognized wise and righteous man.[4]

The point in each case is that even three such outstanding citizens would be unable to rescue their closest relatives (sons and daughters) out of the divinely decreed disaster for covenant violation (14:14, 16, 18, 20); their righteousness would suffice merely to save themselves. Here, there is reference to the principle of covenant or corporate solidarity, whereby a family unit often stands or falls together.[5] It may well be that again the apparently universal language serves to deal with a specific situation, for many of those in exile would have left their children behind them and would naturally be concerned for their fate.[6] The source of their hope would be that, as Abraham noted, God would not surely destroy the righteous along with the wicked (Gen. 18:23).

That basic theological statement is not contested in the hypothetical situation of Ezekiel 14; the righteous would themselves escape the judgment. What is contested, however, is the presumption that the presence of men of sufficient righteousness would save a land under the just judgment of God. If even such men could only save themselves and not their closest relatives, then what hope was there for the families of ordinary people? A similar declaration of the hopelessness of Jerusalem's situation is found in Jeremiah 15.

---

2. Harald-Martin Wahl, "Noah, Daniel und Hiob in Ezechiel XIV 12–20 (21–3): Traditionsgechichtliche Hintergrund," *VT* 42 (1992): 551–52; Block, *Ezekiel 1–24*, 448–49.

3. The use of mythical elements is a common feature of the genre of oracles against the nations. See John B. Geyer, "Mythology and Culture in the Oracles Against the Nations," *VT* 36 (1986): 129–45.

4. Baruch Margalit complicates the interpretative possibilities further by arguing that there is an allusion to the nonbiblical Danel in Ezek. 14 but not in Ezek. 28! See *The Ugaritic Poem of AQHT* (Berlin and New York: De Gruyter, 1989), 490.

5. This principle was not an inviolable rule, as Ezekiel's examples themselves show. Noah's children were preserved through the Flood because of their father's righteousness, but Job's children were not protected by his righteousness. However, the latter case is clearly regarded as the exception rather than the rule.

6. Greenberg, *Ezekiel 1–20*, 261.

There the Lord declares that he would not heed the intercession of even such famous prophets as Moses and Samuel. The people's fate is decided. It is too late for any change of heart to occur, and it would be useless for Jeremiah to attempt to avert it.

The repetition of the four cases in which the sentence and the outcome are the same, while only the form of the judgment is different, underlines the inevitability of Jerusalem's destruction (14:21). Her situation is worse on two counts than that of the hypothetical land of 14:12–20. Not only does she lack such righteous men as Noah, Daniel, and Job, but in addition she is faced with not one kind of judgment but all four at once. The statement "How much worse will it be . . ." is obvious; the inevitable outcome to be expected is that none can survive.[7]

Yet the next verse introduces a surprising twist. Indeed, unexpectedly, some will survive the catastrophe. There will be sons and daughters brought out of the ruins (14:22). Their survival, however, is not due to their own righteousness or to the righteousness of relatives imputed to them. Indeed, they are not "saved" (*nāṣal*) from the city but "brought out" (Hophal of *yāṣāʾ*) from it, a term that focuses on them as prisoners of war rather than trophies of grace.[8] The purpose of saving this remnant is not for their sake but to "console" those already in exile by allowing them to see the extent of Jerusalem's depravity. When the exiles see the impious behavior of this "unspiritual remnant," then they will know that the Lord has not acted without cause (14:23). Justice will not only be done; it will be seen to have been done. Every mouth will be stopped by a recognition of just how bad Jerusalem had become, and therefore how clearly God had no other choice but to act.

Bridging Contexts

CORPORATE RESPONSIBILITY. The idea of corporate or familial responsibility is not a familiar one in contemporary culture. We are thoroughly indoctrinated into the idea of individual responsibility, whereby a person who does wrong is the only one who should receive punishment. Thus, when we read the story of Achan's sin in Joshua 7, we find it hard to understand why Achan's whole family should suffer for his sin. In our culture, we would simply have punished Achan, and though that punishment may have had consequences also for his family (in the loss of a husband and father), those consequences would be an unintentional by-product of justice, not its goal.

---

7. Block, *Ezekiel 1–24*, 450.
8. Allen, *Ezekiel 1–19*, 220.

In contrast, the Old Testament is full of examples of corporate responsibility. Representatives of a person's family suffer on account of the sins of the head of that family (e.g., Saul's descendants in 2 Sam. 21:1–9) or are saved on account of the righteous behavior of a family member (e.g., Lot saved out of Sodom because of Abraham's intercession in Gen. 19:29; Rahab's family in Josh. 2:12–13; 6:17).

Nor is this simply an expression of ancient cultural beliefs picked up from the surrounding cultural context, which we can dismiss as irrelevant for us. In the incident of Saul's descendants, God's judgment fell on the people because of Saul's unatoned sin (2 Sam. 21:1), while in the book of Chronicles, Judah's prosperity is inextricably and immediately bound up with the faithfulness of their king. Not only do the people act on the basis of corporate solidarity, so too does God. Indeed, this principle of corporate solidarity is expressed in the very heart of Israel's creed, the Ten Commandments. There the Lord describes himself as "a jealous God, punishing the children for the sin of the fathers to the third and fourth generation of those who hate me, but showing love to a thousand [generations] of those who love me and keep my commandments" (Ex. 20:5–6).

The covenant community. This corporate solidarity is closely connected to the idea of the covenant. When Abraham enters into a covenant with God, he is not the only one to be included in the blessings; they are for his descendants as well (Gen. 17:7). But if his descendants share in the blessings of the covenant as they faithfully follow in Abraham's footsteps, so also they face the consequences that flow from disobedience to the covenant. In the case of the Abrahamic covenant, the curse is simple exclusion from the covenant community (17:14). With the Sinai covenant, however, arrive not only more detailed blessings for obedience (Lev. 26:3–13) but also more extensive sanctions for disobedience (26:14–45). Because of God's covenant with David and his house, the king is assigned a unique place in the economy of Israel, as a channel of God's blessing or curse on his people. The consequences for those who disobey these covenants include not merely themselves but the whole covenant community.

Ultimately, the Bible tells us, the whole world is divided into two communities, under two covenant heads. One community is made up of those who are "in Adam," unregenerate humanity. The other community is made up of those who are "in Christ," God's covenant people. The fate of these two peoples is already determined by the obedience or disobedience of their respective covenant heads: All those in Adam are under sentence of death, while those who are in Christ will reign in life (Rom. 5:12–20).

The point of Ezekiel 14, however, is that this "big picture" of righteousness or sin imputed on the basis of membership of a community must not blind us to the individual demands made on covenant members. Jesus answers the claim of the Jews of his day that they were Abraham's children by saying, "If you were Abraham's children . . . you would do the things Abraham did" (John 8:39). The members of Adam's community prove themselves to be natural children of their father by sinning on their own account; equally, those who claim to be members of the Lord's covenant community must demonstrate a righteousness of their own, reflecting the perfect righteousness they have been given. As the apostle John puts it:

> The man who says, "I know him," but does not do what he commands is a liar, and the truth is not in him. But if anyone obeys his word, God's love is truly made complete in him. This is how we know we are in him: Whoever claims to live in him must walk as Jesus did. (1 John 2:4–6)

We cannot trade on the borrowed righteousness of others while ourselves lacking the marks of regeneration. For we too face a judgment to come on the last day in which God's justice will be poured out in full measure. Only those truly trusting in Jesus Christ as their covenant head will escape, and there can be no assurance apart from obedience. Obedience—genuine, idol-smashing obedience—is the mark of a true work of grace in the heart.

THE MYSTERIOUS SIDE **of providence.** As human beings, one of our persistent traits is the marginalization of evil. We find it hard to believe in the existence of evil inside ourselves and the ones we love; instead, we reserve that sobriquet for the perpetrators of genocide and mass murder. We are ready to recognize that Hitler may have been evil, and perhaps Charles Manson and others of his ilk, but we are reluctant to admit that all of us are tainted with the same brush. We start from the premise that we are all basically good. And if we are basically good, how can a good God permit "bad things" to happen to us?

The Bible has a radically different perspective. All of us are basically bad, as Paul makes clear in Romans 3:23: "All have sinned and fall short of the glory of God." Until we grasp the accuracy of this statement as a description not merely of the worst of people but the very best, we will never understand the nature of the world in which we live. Our hearts will be filled with resentment at the impossible demands that God makes on us and his inexplicable anger at our inevitable failures.

But when we (all too rarely) experience genuine guilt over our actions, then our eyes are finally opened to the truth about our standing in God's sight. We realize that a God who is not moved to anger by what we have done cannot be a good being.[9] If that is so, and we are in fact much worse than we ever thought, then the astonishing aspect of the world is not the bad things that happen to good people but the good things that happen to bad people. Why should God send his rain on good and evil alike? God's patience with sinners is the really mysterious side of providence.

For that reason, the fall of Jerusalem to the Babylonians is not a bad thing happening to good people but a genuinely bad thing (a "dreadful," or more lit., an "evil" judgment; see 14:21), which is deservedly happening to bad people. When the exiles learn the truth of Jerusalem's depravity by observing the survivors of the holocaust, then they will come to recognize that God has indeed not acted without cause (14:23). A city and nation can reach a stage where the presence of a few righteous people, be they the most righteous people who ever lived, cannot save it from God's wrath (14:13–20). As it was in the days of Noah and in the time of Sodom, so now judgment without mercy will descend upon the wicked of Jerusalem.

A God of grace and patience. Yet was Jerusalem really worse in its idolatry and social sins than New York or San Francisco or any of our modern cities? Are our small towns and villages really more God-fearing than the ancient Israelites were? The astonishing fact is not that God judged Jerusalem, but that God allows our contemporary society, with all its sins, flagrant and secret, to continue to exist. We should not regard that patience as inability to act, however. God's "slowness" is patience in order to allow time for all of his chosen people to repent. But once that harvest is complete, the Day of Judgment will come with speed and finality (2 Peter 3:9–10). The sheep will be separated out from the goats, the children of the kingdom from the children of wrath, and there will be no room for quibbling at the justice of God.

All will then see that God has indeed done nothing without cause. When the true extent of the evil in our hearts is revealed, there will be no more marveling over how a good God could send anyone to eternal punishment. Instead, there will only be wonder and adoration at the astonishing grace of God that chose to rescue us from the fate we deserved all too well. We will be truly astonished that he chose from before the foundation of the world to save for himself a people of every tribe and nation and language group, through the death of his only Son on the cross. On that day, our refrain will indeed be, in Charles Wesley's words:

> Died He for me, who caused His pain?
>> For me, who Him to death pursued?
> Amazing love! How can it be?
>> That Thou, my God, shouldst die for me?

---

9. See C. S. Lewis, *The Problem of Pain* (New York: Macmillan, 1962), 59.

Ezekiel 15

THE WORD OF THE LORD came to me: ²"Son of man, how is the wood of a vine better than that of a branch on any of the trees in the forest? ³Is wood ever taken from it to make anything useful? Do they make pegs from it to hang things on? ⁴And after it is thrown on the fire as fuel and the fire burns both ends and chars the middle, is it then useful for anything? ⁵If it was not useful for anything when it was whole, how much less can it be made into something useful when the fire has burned it and it is charred?

⁶"Therefore this is what the Sovereign LORD says: As I have given the wood of the vine among the trees of the forest as fuel for the fire, so will I treat the people living in Jerusalem. ⁷I will set my face against them. Although they have come out of the fire, the fire will yet consume them. And when I set my face against them, you will know that I am the LORD. ⁸I will make the land desolate because they have been unfaithful, declares the Sovereign LORD."

IN THE EARLIER CHAPTERS, we saw how Ezekiel was called to use a variety of sign-acts to illustrate and drive home to the people's hearts the great danger facing Jerusalem. The vision of the abandonment of the temple (chs. 8–11) formed essentially the same message in another format. Chapters 15–19 comprises a series of extended metaphorical units, demonstrating Ezekiel's versatility in pounding home the message with which he has been commissioned.[1]

Ezekiel 15 is a brief parable, a pictorial story with a sting in the tail; the interpretation of the parable that the prophet adds develops the message of chapter 14 concerning the inevitability of Jerusalem's destruction. The link with the preceding section is apparent in the concluding verse (15:8), which picks up the idea of a land acting unfaithfully (māʿal maʿal; 14:13), that is, breaching the covenant relationship, and consequently becoming desolate (šᵉmāmâ; 14:16).[2]

---

1. Lawrence Boadt, "The Poetry of Prophetic Persuasion: Preserving the Prophet's Persona," *CBQ* 59 (1997): 19.

2. Greenberg, *Ezekiel 1–20*, 267. Note also the "how much less . . ." of 15:5, which is the same as "how much worse . . ." in 14:21.

This acts as a kind of inclusio, rounding off this section (14:12–15:8) with its focus on Jerusalem's forthcoming annihilation.[3]

Yet the message of chapter 15 only becomes plain when the interpretation is added to the parable. Like many parables, the meaning is at first concealed in a homely illustration, so obviously true to life that no one can disagree. Once the audience has accepted the self-evident surface message of the parable, then its less palatable deeper significance can be revealed. In a similarly roundabout way, the prophet Nathan confronts King David with his adultery (2 Sam. 12:1–10). First, he tells a story of a rich man who steals his poor neighbor's single lamb rather than kill one of his own. Only after David has recognized the self-evident truth that such behavior is reprehensible ("The man who did this deserves to die") does Nathan reveal its true application: "You are the man!" David is condemned out of his own lips. Similarly in Isaiah's "Song of the Vineyard," the prophet lays out the deplorable state of the Lord's vineyard in metaphorical form before stating explicitly that the vineyard in question is the Lord's vineyard, the house of Israel and the men of Judah (Isa. 5:1–7).

Thus, Ezekiel starts out with a familiar agricultural picture. The prunings cut from the vine were familiar objects, and it is immediately apparent to all that they serve no useful purpose. They cannot be manufactured into anything of value, not even a peg to hang something on—the most basic of all uses. They have neither strength nor beauty to commend them. The only thing therefore to do with these agricultural by-products is to burn them. Now frequently among the ashes of the fire, half-burnt pieces of vine would be found, the ends burned away and the middle charred. Were such pieces thereby made more useful? The conclusion of 15:5 is inescapable: "If it was not useful for anything when it was whole, how much less can it be made into something useful when the fire has burned it and it is charred?" No one can disagree with Ezekiel's presentation thus far.

He then proceeds to apply the metaphor, to press home a less acceptable proposition: Jerusalem is like that vine wood, and its fate is therefore (inevitably) going to be that of half-burnt vine branches, fit for nothing but to be thrown back onto the fire and consumed completely. Just as the Lord has "given" vine wood to be burnt because of its uselessness, so also the inhabitants of Jerusalem have been "given" by the Lord (15:6). This implies not only a comparable divinely determined fate (burning) but a comparable divinely determined assessment of value (useless).

But even this first "burning," the initial defeat of Judah in 597 B.C. and the first exile, has not achieved a redemptive purpose: The people have not been

---

3. Allen, *Ezekiel 1–19*, 214.

made any more fit for God's purposes, but on the contrary even more useless than before. Again, the conclusion is inescapable: "Although they have come out of the fire, the fire will yet consume them" (15:7). Back into the fire they will go, for they are fit for nothing else, and this time the destruction will be complete. As in 14:12–23, the unfaithfulness of the land to its covenant overlord in pursuing idols will result in its being made desolate.

BECAUSE WE ARE not familiar with vines and vine branches in our everyday experience, the temptation for us is to connect this parable too quickly to the usage of that imagery in the rest of Scripture. The Bible is the only place where we are accustomed to encounter vines and branches. Yet in so doing we may miss the point of the parable, which moves from obvious everyday experience to establish unpalatable spiritual truth. Ezekiel's hearers would not immediately have recognized the vine branch as a picture of Israel, and it is important for the effectiveness of the parable that they should not do so until *after* they have accepted the surface meaning as inescapably true. Like David, they must not recognize their reflection in the mirror until they have pronounced sentence on themselves. Parables characteristically pull the rug out from underneath us, sweeping away our comfortable certainties and showing us an unexpectedly unfamiliar landscape where a moment earlier we thought we found ourselves at home.[4]

Having said that, once the application has been made, the parable invites comparison with other traditional uses of similar imagery, notably the vineyard image and that of fire. The vine is a traditional symbol for Israel, expressing God's loving care for that nation as a vinedresser takes care of what he has planted (Ps. 80:8–9; Isa. 5:1–7). The image also expresses God's expectation of return from his people: The vinedresser looks for fruit in return for his labors, an expectation in which he has often been disappointed (Isa. 5:2; Jer. 2:21).

Ezekiel takes this metaphor one stage further by comparing the inhabitants of Jerusalem not to the vine itself, from which fruit was to be expected, but to the prunings from the vine, which were inherently useless and fit only for the fire. This fits with Ezekiel's radical emphasis on the congenital nature of Israel's sin, which comes to expression in the following chapter.[5] There never was a golden age of obedience in the past from which Israel has now

---

4. Diane Gabrielsen Scholl, "Alice Walker's Parable *The Color Purple*," *Christianity and Literature* 40 (1991): 259.

5. Greenberg, *Ezekiel 1–20*, 269.

declined but only one long history of unfaithfulness, and thus judgment is inevitable.

Yet does Ezekiel's message not also invite the hearer to ask the question: "If those remaining in the land are the prunings, is there still a true vine, a real Israel, somewhere else—perhaps even among the exiles?" This fits with Ezekiel's insistence in chapter 11 that God's presence is no longer in Jerusalem but among the exiles. In contrast to the insistence of those left in the land that they were the choice portion, chosen to inherit the land (11:3, 15), they are actually the part destined for burning, while the remnant exists among those in exile (11:7–12, 15–16).

The imagery of fire has a twofold history in the Old Testament, as a purifying force and as a destroying force. The idea of a refiner's fire cleansing the people from their impurities is found in 1 Kings 8:51; Isaiah 1:25; 48:10; and several times in postexilic literature (e.g., Mal. 3:2–3). Yet the fire is also an image of the power of the Lord to destroy the worthless (e.g., Ex. 15:7; Isa. 5:24). It is only natural for the imagery of fire to be applied to the trials of 586 B.C. But the real question was whether that fire had a refining goal, producing a purified people, or a destroying goal, wiping out an impure people. Ezekiel's contention, which runs contrary to the hopes of many of his fellow exiles, was that as far as Jerusalem was concerned, the fire was that of God's judgment, and its goal was not the redemption of his city (as in Isa. 1:25–26) but its total destruction.

WHY DO BAD THINGS happen to people in this life? The destruction coming on Jerusalem is one specific example of a more general problem: If all things in this world come from the hand of the sovereign Lord, why does he send pains and sorrows into the lives of all people, and some more than others? What purpose do these things serve in the world? The answer to that question is that, like fire, they serve a twofold purpose: to purify and to destroy.

There are two mistakes people commonly make in this regard. The first is to assume that all "bad things" have a destructive, punitive purpose. Why did I lose my job? Why did my spouse die? Why did God allow my ex-husband to sexually abuse my child? If we see all of these evils as only the result of God's punitive purpose, then we develop a tragically distorted view of God. God is then seen as a kind of divine policeman, eternally hiding at the roadside to catch us exceeding the speed limit of life.

True, all the evils in this world are the result of sin—for without the Fall there would have been no death or sickness, no cause for tears or mourning.

But not all the evils in my life are the direct result of *my* sin. To take a trivial example, God did not cause it to rain on my picnic because I missed my quiet time yesterday. Jesus addressed this view when his disciples posed the question to him concerning a man blind from birth, as to who sinned: the man himself or his parents. The Lord's response is illuminating: "Neither this man nor his parents sinned . . . but this happened so that the work of God might be displayed in his life" (John 9:3). Jesus' point is not that the man and his parents were sinless; rather, their personal sins were not the determining factor, but God's good purpose.

That purpose may be expressed through profound, life-changing incidents, as in the healing of this man, a sign demonstrating Jesus' power. Pain may indeed be the megaphone through which God speaks in order to get our attention. Or it may be expressed in the apparently trivial disappointments we experience, which cumulatively encourage us to turn our eyes from seeking satisfaction in this fallen world onward to seek our true satisfaction in God's new creation. Without God's redemptive application of the rod of suffering to our lives, we would have no cause to desire something better than this world and thus to turn to God.

Yet not all suffering is inherently redemptive. That was the mistake the exiles had been deceived into making by their eager desire for a better future for their homeland. So also people may imagine that because a person has suffered a great deal, he or she has automatically been made a better person by it. Some suffering may not only result from my sin, it can also confirm me in my sin. Suffering can harden a heart, preparing the person for final destruction, as well as soften it, preparing him or her for final redemption.

What is it, then, that makes suffering fruitful in the life of one person, while in another it is merely a foreshadowing of the wrath to come? This is the question Jesus addresses in his image of the vine and the branches (John 15). Picking up on the Old Testament imagery of Israel as a vine, he declares that he himself is the true vine whom God tends; in other words, he himself is the true Israel (John 15:1). To be "in [him]," that is, to be a member of his body, a living part of the church, is to be part of the true, fruit-bearing Israel (John 15:4), while to be apart from him is to be worthless, fit only to be burned in the fire (15:5–6). There is no place in God's kingdom for the "go it alone" mentality that is so popular in our culture.

Freedom from suffering is precisely *not* the result to be expected from remaining on the vine: on the contrary, fruitful branches are "pruned" just as fruitless ones are cast off (John 15:2, 6). Suffering is a part of every life, but for the Christian it is a "fruitful" part of life, bearing a harvest of righteousness (cf. Heb. 12:11). As we suffer, we are further conformed to the likeness of Christ, the Suffering Servant. As we suffer, we are detached from our passionate absorption with ourselves and this present world and taught to refocus our attention on the glories that await us in the place where suffering will be no more. Suffering teaches us that God's grace is sufficient for easily broken earthen vessels like us (2 Cor. 4:7–10). For the non-Christian, however, suffering ultimately bears no fruit; it brings about no change in one's course of life. Outside the vine, the outlook is as bleak as that which Ezekiel prophesies for Jerusalem: Unbelievers are headed on a course toward certain destruction.

Ezekiel 16

T HE WORD OF THE LORD came to me: ²"Son of man, confront Jerusalem with her detestable practices ³and say, 'This is what the Sovereign LORD says to Jerusalem: Your ancestry and birth were in the land of the Canaanites; your father was an Amorite and your mother a Hittite. ⁴On the day you were born your cord was not cut, nor were you washed with water to make you clean, nor were you rubbed with salt or wrapped in cloths. ⁵No one looked on you with pity or had compassion enough to do any of these things for you. Rather, you were thrown out into the open field, for on the day you were born you were despised.

⁶'''Then I passed by and saw you kicking about in your blood, and as you lay there in your blood I said to you, "Live!" ⁷I made you grow like a plant of the field. You grew up and developed and became the most beautiful of jewels. Your breasts were formed and your hair grew, you who were naked and bare.

⁸'''Later I passed by, and when I looked at you and saw that you were old enough for love, I spread the corner of my garment over you and covered your nakedness. I gave you my solemn oath and entered into a covenant with you, declares the Sovereign LORD, and you became mine.

⁹'''I bathed you with water and washed the blood from you and put ointments on you. ¹⁰I clothed you with an embroidered dress and put leather sandals on you. I dressed you in fine linen and covered you with costly garments. ¹¹I adorned you with jewelry: I put bracelets on your arms and a necklace around your neck, ¹²and I put a ring on your nose, earrings on your ears and a beautiful crown on your head. ¹³So you were adorned with gold and silver; your clothes were of fine linen and costly fabric and embroidered cloth. Your food was fine flour, honey and olive oil. You became very beautiful and rose to be a queen. ¹⁴And your fame spread among the nations on account of your beauty, because the splendor I had given you made your beauty perfect, declares the Sovereign LORD.

¹⁵'''But you trusted in your beauty and used your fame to become a prostitute. You lavished your favors on anyone who

passed by and your beauty became his. ¹⁶You took some of
your garments to make gaudy high places, where you carried
on your prostitution. Such things should not happen, nor
should they ever occur. ¹⁷You also took the fine jewelry I gave
you, the jewelry made of my gold and silver, and you made for
yourself male idols and engaged in prostitution with them.
¹⁸And you took your embroidered clothes to put on them, and
you offered my oil and incense before them. ¹⁹Also the food I
provided for you—the fine flour, olive oil and honey I gave
you to eat—you offered as fragrant incense before them. That
is what happened, declares the Sovereign LORD.

²⁰'''And you took your sons and daughters whom you bore to
me and sacrificed them as food to the idols. Was your prostitution not enough? ²¹You slaughtered my children and sacrificed
them to the idols. ²²In all your detestable practices and your
prostitution you did not remember the days of your youth,
when you were naked and bare, kicking about in your blood.

²³'''Woe! Woe to you, declares the Sovereign LORD. In
addition to all your other wickedness, ²⁴you built a mound for
yourself and made a lofty shrine in every public square. ²⁵At
the head of every street you built your lofty shrines and
degraded your beauty, offering your body with increasing
promiscuity to anyone who passed by. ²⁶You engaged in prostitution with the Egyptians, your lustful neighbors, and provoked me to anger with your increasing promiscuity. ²⁷So I
stretched out my hand against you and reduced your territory;
I gave you over to the greed of your enemies, the daughters
of the Philistines, who were shocked by your lewd conduct.
²⁸You engaged in prostitution with the Assyrians too, because
you were insatiable; and even after that, you still were not satisfied. ²⁹Then you increased your promiscuity to include
Babylonia, a land of merchants, but even with this you were
not satisfied.

³⁰'''How weak-willed you are, declares the Sovereign LORD,
when you do all these things, acting like a brazen prostitute!
³¹When you built your mounds at the head of every street and
made your lofty shrines in every public square, you were
unlike a prostitute, because you scorned payment.

³²'''You adulterous wife! You prefer strangers to your own
husband! ³³Every prostitute receives a fee, but you give gifts
to all your lovers, bribing them to come to you from every-

where for your illicit favors. ³⁴So in your prostitution you are the opposite of others; no one runs after you for your favors. You are the very opposite, for you give payment and none is given to you.

³⁵"Therefore, you prostitute, hear the word of the LORD! ³⁶This is what the Sovereign LORD says: Because you poured out your wealth and exposed your nakedness in your promiscuity with your lovers, and because of all your detestable idols, and because you gave them your children's blood, ³⁷therefore I am going to gather all your lovers, with whom you found pleasure, those you loved as well as those you hated. I will gather them against you from all around and will strip you in front of them, and they will see all your nakedness. ³⁸I will sentence you to the punishment of women who commit adultery and who shed blood; I will bring upon you the blood vengeance of my wrath and jealous anger. ³⁹Then I will hand you over to your lovers, and they will tear down your mounds and destroy your lofty shrines. They will strip you of your clothes and take your fine jewelry and leave you naked and bare. ⁴⁰They will bring a mob against you, who will stone you and hack you to pieces with their swords. ⁴¹They will burn down your houses and inflict punishment on you in the sight of many women. I will put a stop to your prostitution, and you will no longer pay your lovers. ⁴²Then my wrath against you will subside and my jealous anger will turn away from you; I will be calm and no longer angry.

⁴³"Because you did not remember the days of your youth but enraged me with all these things, I will surely bring down on your head what you have done, declares the Sovereign LORD. Did you not add lewdness to all your other detestable practices?

⁴⁴"Everyone who quotes proverbs will quote this proverb about you: "Like mother, like daughter." ⁴⁵You are a true daughter of your mother, who despised her husband and her children; and you are a true sister of your sisters, who despised their husbands and their children. Your mother was a Hittite and your father an Amorite. ⁴⁶Your older sister was Samaria, who lived to the north of you with her daughters; and your younger sister, who lived to the south of you with her daughters, was Sodom. ⁴⁷You not only walked in their ways and copied their detestable practices, but in all your ways you soon

became more depraved than they. [48]As surely as I live, declares
the Sovereign LORD, your sister Sodom and her daughters
never did what you and your daughters have done.

[49]"'Now this was the sin of your sister Sodom: She and her
daughters were arrogant, overfed and unconcerned; they did
not help the poor and needy. [50]They were haughty and did
detestable things before me. Therefore I did away with them
as you have seen. [51]Samaria did not commit half the sins you
did. You have done more detestable things than they, and
have made your sisters seem righteous by all these things you
have done. [52]Bear your disgrace, for you have furnished some
justification for your sisters. Because your sins were more vile
than theirs, they appear more righteous than you. So then, be
ashamed and bear your disgrace, for you have made your sisters appear righteous.

[53]"'However, I will restore the fortunes of Sodom and her
daughters and of Samaria and her daughters, and your fortunes along with them, [54]so that you may bear your disgrace
and be ashamed of all you have done in giving them comfort.
[55]And your sisters, Sodom with her daughters and Samaria
with her daughters, will return to what they were before; and
you and your daughters will return to what you were before.
[56]You would not even mention your sister Sodom in the day
of your pride, [57]before your wickedness was uncovered. Even
so, you are now scorned by the daughters of Edom and all her
neighbors and the daughters of the Philistines—all those
around you who despise you. [58]You will bear the consequences of your lewdness and your detestable practices,
declares the LORD.

[59]"'This is what the Sovereign LORD says: I will deal with
you as you deserve, because you have despised my oath by
breaking the covenant. [60]Yet I will remember the covenant I
made with you in the days of your youth, and I will establish
an everlasting covenant with you. [61]Then you will remember
your ways and be ashamed when you receive your sisters, both
those who are older than you and those who are younger. I will
give them to you as daughters, but not on the basis of my
covenant with you. [62]So I will establish my covenant with you,
and you will know that I am the LORD. [63]Then, when I make
atonement for you for all you have done, you will remember
and be ashamed and never again open your mouth because of
your humiliation, declares the Sovereign LORD.'"

IF EZEKIEL 15 presents an oblique parable, sneaking assent from its hearers before confronting them with the realization that they have just condemned themselves, Ezekiel 16 adopts an altogether different approach. It is an "in-your-face" condemnation of Jerusalem, in which the identity and nature of the central figure of the extended metaphor[1] is never disguised and frequently dictates the inclusion of otherwise incongruous details into the story. With graphic imagination and violent force, Ezekiel strips away the popular fiction of "Jerusalem the Golden" and replaces it with the figure of "Jerusalem the Prostitute." Here we have an exposé of Jerusalem's true nature, with the prophet taking the part of prosecuting counsel in the divine courtroom.[2]

The story starts out by depicting Jerusalem's dubious origins. It began among the Canaanites, of an Amorite father and a Hittite mother (Ezek. 16:3). This was, of course, literally true of the city of Jerusalem. The city predated the arrival of the Israelites in the land of Canaan, and its prior population is called Amorite in Joshua 10:6. The word "Hittite" actually seems to denote two distinct groups of people in the Old Testament. In many passages it describes a local people from Palestine, the descendants of a man named "Heth" (e.g., Ex. 3:8, 17), while in other passages the reference is to the neo-Hittite kingdoms in northern Syria that succeeded the Hittite empire proper (1 Kings 10:29; 2 Chron. 1:17). Here in Ezekiel the reference seems to be to the former group, the native Canaanite variety.[3]

In contrast to Israel, who in her creed traced her heritage back to "a wandering Aramean" (Deut. 26:5) whose arrival in the land of Canaan was the result of God's action in fulfillment of his promise, the city of Jerusalem's roots in the land are entirely natural and pagan.[4] Jerusalem's prominent position is based on the accidents of history, not the acts of God; even before David captured it and made it his capital city, it was an important (pagan) city in its own right.

The child Jerusalem was born to heartless parents, however, who revealed their own depravity by abandoning the newborn infant. None of the usual

---

1. The description of the genre of this passage as an "extended metaphor" or "narrative metaphor" comes from Julie Galambush, *Jerusalem in the Book of Ezekiel: The City As Yahweh's Wife* (SBLDS 130; Atlanta: Scholars, 1992), 11. Although the passage has allegorical features, it is not strictly an allegory, since there is not a point by point correspondence between the elements of the metaphor and the real world referents.

2. "Confront" (*hôda*ᶜ; v. 2) is legal terminology (Greenberg, *Ezekiel 1–20*, 272).

3. On the Hittites, see Gregory McMahon, "Hittites in the Old Testament," *ABD*, 3:231–33.

4. Galambush, *Jerusalem*, 81.

obstetrical practices of cutting the navel cord, washing the child, covering her body in a mixture of salt and oil, and swaddling tightly for a lengthy period of time was carried out. Instead, alone and unloved, she was left in a field to die. The exposure of weak or unwanted children, especially girls, was an all-too-familiar spectacle in the ancient world.

Into that situation of helplessness and hopelessness, however, came God's intervention. Passing by this sorry spectacle, he spoke his life-giving word, causing her to live[5] and thrive like a plant of the field. To adopt our idiom, she grew like a weed. The word of the Lord was all it took to turn the field from a place of death (16:5) to a place of life (16:7). Subsequently, she grew up, reached sexual maturity (16:7),[6] and attained an age appropriate for marriage (16:8). Historically, this period corresponds to the pre-Israelite period of Jerusalem's history, during which time she existed and prospered (at the Lord's command!), but was not yet directly included in his purposes.

At the end of this time, she once again came to the Lord's attention, and he spread a corner of his robe over her, symbolically covering her nakedness (16:8). This was an act with quasi-legal status, affirming the choice of a bride, as in the case of Ruth and Boaz (Ruth 3:9).[7] The Lord then gave an oath and entered into a covenant relationship with Jerusalem. In the terms of the metaphor, he married her. Again, the historical reality lies buried beneath the surface in the establishing of the Davidic covenant, which entails not simply the election of David and his descendants (2 Sam. 7) but also the election of Zion, David's city, as the city of the Great King (Ps. 48:2).

The Lord's choice of Jerusalem was not merely a legal and political convenience, however, but a true love match on his part. He did for the girl what no one else had ever done, washing off her blood, anointing her, and clothing her (16:8–9) in a threefold reversal of the circumstance of her birth, when she was not washed, anointed, or clothed (16:4).[8] He provided her with

---

5. Meir Malul has pointed out the significance of Akkadian parallels in which a child is adopted ("caused to live") while "in its amniotic fluid and birth blood," meaning that the baby can never be reclaimed by its natural parents ("Adoption of Foundlings in the Bible and Mesopotamian Documents: A Study of Some Legal Metaphors in Ezekiel 16.1–7," *JSOT* 46 [1990]: 108–11).

6. NIV: "You . . . became the most beautiful of jewels. Your breasts were formed and your hair grew" should perhaps rather be translated, "You developed the ornament of ornaments, [namely] your breasts were formed and your [pubic] hair sprouted." The point is the physical development that accompanies the onset of puberty. See Greenberg, *Ezekiel 1–20*, 276.

7. Zimmerli, *Ezekiel*, 1:340.

8. Again, the historical realities behind the metaphor peep through in the delay between the time of Jerusalem's birth and the time of the Lord's care for her. This delay is awkward in terms of the imagery of the foundling ("why was she not washed at once?"), but wholly comprehensible in terms of the underlying reality.

a wardrobe fit for a queen, with embroidered dresses and shoes of fine leather (16:10). This is not merely elegant or royal clothing, however. She is clothed in materials that are elsewhere associated with the tabernacle, underlining her symbolic identity as the home of the temple.[9]

In addition, the Lord lavished on her an extensive supply of fine jewelry: bracelets, necklace, nose-ring, earrings, and crown (16:11–12). Virtually every part of the anatomy that could be bejeweled in the ancient Near East was attended to. Finally, she was fed with the very best: fine flour, honey, and olive oil (16:13). On account of her natural beauty (which itself was the result of the Lord's decision to allow her to live in the first place) and of the splendor with which the Lord had endowed her, her fame spread far and wide (16:14).[10]

But another turning point in her fortunes takes place in verse 15. Instead of remembering that it was the Lord who had endowed her with all these blessings, she trusted in her beauty and prostituted her reputation. Like the prodigal son, she wasted her substance in riotous living. The beautiful clothes were used to adorn the high places where idolatrous worship occurred and to clothe the idols housed within. The gold and silver were used to manufacture the idols themselves; the flour, oil, and honey, which had been given to her for food, were offered instead to her idols (16:16–19). Even her children, those whom she had borne to the Lord, were not safe; they were sacrificed to the idols she had made for herself (16:20–21).

Again, this history of idolatry corresponds to the general trend of Israel's behavior according to the account of the book of Kings. Even Solomon used part of his great wealth to build temples for the gods of his foreign wives (1 Kings 11:7–8), and the practice of child sacrifice is attested of Ahaz in 2 Kings 16:3 and Manasseh in 21:6, as well as more widely in the time of Jeremiah (Jer. 7:31; 19:5; 32:35).[11] The high places were a perennial attraction to God's people, repeatedly seducing them away from the worship of the true God (2 Kings 17:9–10).

This depiction of Jerusalem's idolatry in terms of adultery has its roots in Hosea 2:4–14, where the northern kingdom of Israel is described as an ungrateful wife who takes the gifts of her husband and foolishly lavishes them on her lovers. Yet Ezekiel takes the same basic picture and develops it much further than Hosea had. Hosea's Israel was simply a foolishly promiscuous woman; Ezekiel's Jerusalem is a thoroughly depraved and degraded prostitute. Her behavior descends to ever deeper depths in 16:23–34. In

---

9. Galambush, *Jerusalem*, 95.

10. The beauty of Zion/Jerusalem is a central theme of Psalm 48.

11. Zimmerli, *Ezekiel*, 1:344.

place of one type of location for her idolatry (the "high places," *bāmôt;* 16:16), there are now two (the "mound," *geb,* and "lofty shrine," *rāmâ;* 16:24, 31). In place of adultery with idols, there now appear liaisons with human partners, with ever increasing promiscuity.

The language of lust becomes stronger: Jerusalem spread her legs for any who passed by (16:25), not least her "lustful neighbors," the Egyptians (16:26). God's judgment in reducing her territory was of no effect (16:27). Indeed, Jerusalem did not even act like a normal prostitute, for they at least are motivated to sin for material gain or out of financial desperation. Jerusalem, however, has been sinning at her own expense, so perverse in her lust that she pays everyone to join in her depravity (16:34).

Again, the historical background stretches the allegory almost to the breaking point. As a description of a woman, it is beyond the reaches even of the fevered imagination of the tabloid press. Yet as a picture of Judah's political strategy, it fits perfectly. Judah had a history of looking for love in all the wrong places, seeking security not in the Lord but in the arms of a foreign power. In the days of Ahaz, it was Assyria (2 Kings 16:7). In the days of Hezekiah, it was Babylon (20:12–19). In the days of Zedekiah, it was Egypt (Jer. 2:36; Ezek. 17:15). These alliances were frequently costly to Judah, for accepting a major power as overlord carried with it a substantial price tag. The suzerain invariably expected to receive silver and gold as tribute in exchange for protection (2 Kings 16:8). Even then, only rarely did they deliver the hoped-for help.

But far more expensive in the eyes of the Old Testament prophets was the cost in religious terms. An overlord may or may not have forcibly imposed his state religion on the vassal state, but religious effects on the vassal nation were nonetheless real.[12] Behind every act of international diplomacy stood the gods of the nations as guarantors of compliance. For this reason, such international cooperation inevitably involved a measure of recognition of the existence and power of the gods of the nations, along with an implicit affirmation that trusting in the Lord alone was not effective. The temptation to appeal to the gods that had apparently made the other nation great was powerful.

It was therefore not a coincidence that Ahaz introduced Syrian-style innovations into the Jerusalem temple immediately after meeting with Tiglath-Pileser, king of Assyria, in Damascus (2 Kings 16:10–16). What may have seemed to politically oriented kings merely a good, if expensive, insurance policy, a means of covering all the bases, seemed to the biblical prophets

---

12. See the discussion in Morton Cogan, *Imperialism and Religion: Assyria, Judah and Israel in the Eighth and Seventh Centuries B.C.E.* (SBLMS 19; Missoula, Mont.: Scholars, 1974), 44–49.

a clear abandonment of Judah's single-minded covenant commitment to the Lord. For them, imitation was the sincerest form of blasphemy.

For Jerusalem, the natural and inevitable consequence of an adulterous lifestyle was an adulteress's death (Ezek. 16:38). The punishment is in accord with the crime. The normal practice was for adulteresses first to be exposed naked in public (16:37; cf. Nah. 3:5),[13] followed by their stoning by the assembly (Deut. 22:22; Ezek. 16:40).[14] Similarly, Jerusalem's places of idolatry would be torn down, her wealth and possessions stripped away, leaving her in the state in which she began, naked and bare (Ezek. 16:39; cf. 16:7). Only then, when full circle had been reached and the one initially chosen for life had been sentenced to death and executed, would the Lord's wrath finally be turned aside (16:42). Even then, it would be the silence not of mercy but of completion of the judicial sentence: All that she did had been returned on her head (16:43).

In the description of the death sentence to be carried out on Jerusalem, the historical realities are once again dominant. The sentence is executed by an assembly of Jerusalem's peers, including her lovers (16:37). It involves not simply stoning her but death by the sword (16:40) and the burning down of her houses (16:41). Each of these reflects the actual historical downfall of the adulterous city, rather than the normal punishment of an adulterous woman.

In 16:44 the imagery changes from the husband-wife relationship to mother and daughter. Whereas Jerusalem had previously been considered in relationship to her adoptive "family," now her natural genetics are brought to the fore. She has proved herself to be a chip off the old block by despising her husband and children. She is like her mother, the Hittite, who was married to an Amorite (16:45), the people whose sins had led to their expulsion from the land of Canaan at the time of Joshua (Gen. 15:16). This statement serves not only to link this section with the preceding one but also to suggest that she stands to share their fate of being cut off from the land.

In addition, Jerusalem has a family resemblance to her natural sisters, Samaria and Sodom, who are the primary focus of this section. Samaria, the former capital of the northern kingdom of Israel, is described as her older sister—"older" (16:46) refers to her size rather than age. She stands for the larger, northern kingdom, while Sodom, the "younger" (or "littler") sister, is physically smaller.[15] Samaria lives to the north of Jerusalem with her "daughters," that is, in the common Semitic idiom, the surrounding villages, while Sodom is to the south (16:46). Jerusalem is surrounded by sinners and fits naturally into their company, delighting to go along with the crowd.

---

13. Compare the rationale of *Mishnah Sotah* 1:5: "She exposed herself for sin, God therefore exposes her."

14. Allen, *Ezekiel 1–19*, 242.

15. Greenberg, *Ezekiel 1–20*, 288.

What Sodom lacked in size, it more than made up for in reputation. Along with its other ugly sister, Gomorrah, it had become a byword for abomination (Gen. 19:4–9; cf. Isa. 1:10)—and consequent complete destruction (Isa. 1:9). As well as the sexual sin to which it gave its name, which may lie behind the "detestable things" (*tōʿēbâ*) of Ezekiel 16:50, Sodom is here cited for being proud, overfed, and untroubled by the cares of life, while neglecting the needs of the poor and needy (16:49). She is the epitome of social sin.

Samaria's history of cultic sin was too well known to require further elaboration by Ezekiel. Ever since Jeroboam introduced his golden calves to the national shrines at Bethel and Dan and allowed a non-Levitical priesthood to preside over them (1 Kings 12:28–33), the northern kingdom had been regarded as theologically suspect. Samaria too had been judged by God for her aberrations and destroyed by the Assyrians (2 Kings 17:3–23).

Yet according to Ezekiel neither of these twin icons of sin could match Jerusalem's record. She did more detestable things than either of them, making them seem (comparatively) righteous (16:51). In comparison to the pot, the kettle is barely scorched! The conclusion is inescapable: If God judged Sodom because of her sin and if he judged Samaria because of her sin, how will Jerusalem escape from his wrath (cf. 2 Kings 21:13)?

However, if the similarity between Jerusalem and her sisters serves to justify further God's action in completely destroying her (Ezek. 16:58), that is not the only focus of attention here. Rather, the purpose of this comparison with her sisters in crime is designed to evoke a sense of shame on Jerusalem's part (16:52). Just as in her pride Jerusalem once scorned Sodom for her sin, so now that Jerusalem's sin has been uncovered, the surrounding nations scorn her (16:57). Now, instead of looking down her nose at Sodom and Samaria as beyond redemption, she will herself only be redeemed alongside them (16:53). Paradoxically, it is in that redemption itself that shame will be experienced as the inhabitants of Jerusalem realize how much worse they have been than the bywords of iniquity, Sodom and Samaria.

Though they have despised God's oath and broken his covenant and must therefore be judged (16:59), yet judgment is not God's last word. For though Jerusalem does not remember the days of her youth (16:22, 43), the Lord will remember the days of her youth and will therefore establish an everlasting covenant with her (16:60). In so doing, he will create in her the two qualities that are signally lacking in her at present, memory and shame (16:61).[16] On the one hand, she will be profoundly aware of having broken the covenant, shattering it so completely that it can no longer stand as the basis of her self-identity vis-à-vis other nations (16:61). She will recognize

---

16. Ibid., 305.

that there is no goodness within herself to which she can appeal, no obedience that can form the basis for confidence in the presence of the Lord. In the language of Hosea, she will know herself to be "Not My People" (Hos. 1:9). She will be aware of the depths of her sin and ashamed of it.

On the other hand, she can also look back to the days of her youth, the days when, in the imagery of Ezekiel 16:4–6, she was similarly naked and bare before the Lord. If he chose her once, not on the basis of anything in herself but simply his own sovereign will, can he not do so again? If he covenanted with her once, may he not do so once again, this time forever? Were it not for the Lord's own words it would be too much to hope for. Second chances like that simply don't happen in real life. Lightning never strikes twice in the same place.

Yet that is precisely what the Lord affirms. He will remember his original covenant with her and establish it as an everlasting covenant (16:60),[17] a covenant that precisely because it includes wanton sinners is big enough to include Sodom and Samaria alongside Jerusalem. The nations will view Jerusalem as an object lesson of the wideness of God's mercy. On the day when the Lord "makes atonement" (*kipper*)[18] for Jerusalem (16:63), she will remember and be ashamed; her tongue will be stilled[19] and her pride humbled once and for all.

NO DECORUM HERE. It is perhaps not surprising that this chapter is rarely preached on in our churches. In spite of the conclusion of Douglas Stuart that "those who wish to teach or preach on this chapter ... can do so quite successfully and with decorum,"[20] many still concur with the assessment of C. H. Spurgeon: "A minister can scarcely read it in public"![21] While certainly discernment must be exercised—it is understandable, for instance, why this passage is not found in children's Bible storybooks—one wonders if contemporary Christians need to be as shielded

---

17. The word "establish" (Hiphil of *qûm*) is usually used of confirming an already existing covenant rather than originating a new relationship (Greenberg, *Ezekiel 1–20*, 291). It thus serves to underline the continuity between Israel's future relationship with the Lord and his original purpose.

18. For "to atone" (*kipper*) as paying a ransom, see Gordon Wenham, *The Book of Leviticus* (NICOT; Grand Rapids: Eerdmans, 1979), 59.

19. Lit., "There will never again be opening of the mouth (i.e. self-justification) for you." See Greenberg, *Ezekiel 1–20*, 292.

20. *Ezekiel*, 141.

21. Cited in Thomas, *Ezekiel*, 108.

from unpleasant realities as we tend to think. These same Christians are regularly bombarded with similarly shocking stories on the nightly news.

Furthermore, is it possible to teach this passage "with decorum" and not lose an essential element of its message? There are no new *facts* here about Israel's history, and if we read it simply as a historical catalog of crime like 2 Kings 17, we lose all that this passage *distinctively* contributes to the message of Scripture. The whole point is the lack of decorum in Ezekiel's manner. He will not "be polite" about Israel's history of sin; instead, he is instructed to expose it in its full ugliness in the most graphic manner possible. Only thus can he get the point across.[22]

Differences in perspective because of cultural distance. But politeness is not the only thing that holds us back in our understanding of Ezekiel 16. Because of the cultural distance between then and now, we are likely to react to its message in significantly different ways from Ezekiel's original message. They too would have been shocked by his graphic depiction of Jerusalem's depravity. But other aspects of the picture would have struck them differently from the way they strike us. For instance, when we read of a passerby picking up an abandoned baby, it elicits no surprise in our minds. Our response is, "Of course he or she would rescue the baby and find someone to take care of it. What other choice is there?" But in the ancient world there was no "of course" about it. In those days, if you adopted every abandoned baby you found, your house would soon be bursting at the seams. It was an accepted tragedy.

Nor could Ezekiel's audience immediately assume, as we do, that the mysterious stranger had favorable plans for the orphan. It was not unknown in antiquity for girl babies to be rescued for the purpose of prostitution rather than adoption. These differences mean that they would recognize more fully than we do the grace involved in the Lord's action, picking up this stray and not merely allowing her to survive or even adopting her, but marrying her, lavishing on her every good thing.

Nor are we used to a wife being completely dependent on her husband. In these days of equality between husband and wife, the image of marriage conveys something quite different to us than it did back then. Our culture thinks of a coequal partnership, in which each party owns half of everything, unless there is a prenuptial agreement to the contrary. In contemporary society, it is also a relationship that can be dissolved as easily as it is made, if a better offer comes along. Indeed, in Hollywood films, adultery is regularly portrayed not only as acceptable but also as praiseworthy if it allows for

---

22. The tendency to downplay the "shocking" elements of this passage is no modern phenomenon; it is already present in the Targum, which mutes the sexual imagery (see Blenkinsopp, *Ezekiel*, 77).

self-fulfillment. The idea of marriage as a relationship of subordination and obligation on the wife's part is alien to us.

In contrast, it is essential to Ezekiel's metaphor that the wife is not an independent agent, free to seek self-fulfillment in the arms of another, and that death is the appropriate sentence for adultery. Only if we understand those cultural norms will we feel the ingratitude of the woman, who has taken the gifts that were lavished on her by her true husband and squandered them on her many lovers. Only then will we feel the just nature of the sentence imposed on her, feelings that would have been automatic for Ezekiel's original hearers.

The danger is that because we may disagree with the cultural norms of marriage expressed in this chapter, finding them "politically incorrect" and "oppressive to women," we may also therefore dismiss the teaching of the chapter. That would be like dismissing Ezekiel 15 because modern technology has, after all, found a use for charcoal-toasted vine branches. Ezekiel's goal is not to affirm the abiding validity of the details of his picture, nor is he giving any justification to husbands abusing their wives. Rather, he is utilizing conventional norms to illustrate a deeper reality, namely, the relationship between the Lord and his people.

For whatever we conclude concerning the institution of marriage, the relationship of the Lord and his people is not a coequal relationship, in which we "own" whatever he gives us and we are free to choose whether we will serve him or another god. To think that way is to lose sight of the magnitude of his grace and mercy in choosing us in the first place. Every good thing we have, not just in material terms but even in the ability to think rightly about him and act appropriately in obedience, is a fruit of his Spirit in our hearts (1 Cor. 4:7) and a gift from him (James 1:17). Our relationship is a gracious bond, freely entered into on his part without any merit on ours. To be faithful to him is to experience eternal life; to depart from him is reprehensible adultery and depravity, which can only lead to death.

Contemporary Significance

PRESENTING SIN'S **true ugliness.** If the sermons preached in our churches were movies, what rating would the distributors give them? In many churches, every sermon would rate a "G" ("General Audiences"). There is nothing in them to offend anyone, young or old, seeker or convert alike. Like the seeker-sensitive church I mentioned earlier, we are eager to present people with "a delightful, thought-provoking hour." We are concerned, as the quote from Douglas Stuart revealingly admitted, always to preach "with decorum." The presence of Ezekiel 16 in the pages of Scripture urges us, at least in some situations, to pull off the kid gloves and present sin in its full ugliness. Fire and brimstone sermons that focus alone on hell and God's wrath may be a serious misrepresentation of the true God, but so also are a continuous diet of polite, decorous sermons that only mention heaven and God's love. Sin is ugly, offensive, and depraved, and people need to hear that side of the Christian message too.

One might illustrate the point by reference to the movie *Schindler's List*. This film depicted as fully as it could the ugliness of the concentration camps in World War II Germany. It merited the "R" ("Restricted") rating, which it received, limiting it to adult audiences. Now a portrayal of the same facts may perhaps have been made that would have only necessitated a "PG" ("Parental Guidance suggested") rating, by passing over some of the more gruesome details. But the emotional impact of such a film would not have been nearly the same, for only in the details does the full depth of the horror emerge. Only an "R" rating portrayal does justice to the evils of Auschwitz and Belsen; similarly, sometimes only an "R" rated sermon does justice to the outrage of sin.

The ugliness in the cross. How else do you explain the obscenity of the cross? An innocent man—the only truly innocent man who ever lived—is convicted in a rigged trial, abused by his guards until he can scarcely walk, yet forced to carry his own cross on a back that has been flayed raw. Nails are forced through the living flesh of his hands and feet, and he is jerked upright to hang until, too tired to lift himself one more time, he suffocates. What good God could permit such a death? What loving God could permit his own beloved Son to undergo such agony? What awful thing could be so bad that only such an atonement could pay for it?

The answer is *sin*. In the cross, we see sin revealed in its starkest, most abominable ugliness. There, if we sweep away for a second the prettification with which we sentimentalize that terrible moment, we see God's "R" rated answer to my sin. There is the "atonement" that God made (16:63), the ransom that he paid for his people (cf. Mark 10:45). The cost of our salvation was not silver and gold but the precious blood of the Lord Jesus Christ (1 Peter 1:18–19). This is something that we all too easily forget. As Flannery O'Connor reminds us:

> There is something in us ... that demands the redemptive act, that demands that what falls at least be offered the chance to be restored. The reader of today looks for this motion, and rightly so, but what he has forgotten is the cost of it. His sense of evil is diluted or lacking altogether, and so he has forgotten the price of restoration.[23]

23. *Mystery and Manners: Occasional Prose*, ed. Sally Fitzgerald (New York: Farrar, Straus & Giroux, 1969), 48. In a similar vein, the novelist Larry Woiwode is quoted as saying, "If

Remembering in our lives. The realization of the price of restoration should stir in our hearts remembrance and shame (see 16:63). We should remember what we once were—and be ashamed. Perhaps, like the Corinthians, we were ourselves once sexually immoral or idolaters or prostitutes or homosexual offenders or thieves or greedy or drunkards or slanderers or swindlers (1 Cor. 6:9–11). Perhaps we were none of the above and proud of it, as the Jerusalemites prided themselves on not being like the Sodomites and Samaritans (Ezek. 16:56), and the Pharisee prided himself on being better than the tax collector (Luke 18:11). Perhaps we were convinced, like the rich young ruler, that we had fulfilled our obligation to our neighbors perfectly from our youth (18:21).

Whatever our own estimation of our righteousness or lack of it, the Bible tells us that all are alike in this matter. Every mouth is silenced before God, for "all have sinned and fall short of the glory of God" (Rom. 3:23). We were all, good and bad alike, by nature objects of God's wrath (Eph. 2:3). Let us never forget what we once were, for that is the true measure of the greatness of God's work in our lives. As Calvin put it: "If we desire, therefore, our sins to be blotted out before God, and to be buried in the depths of the sea . . . we must recall them often and constantly to our remembrance: for when they are kept before our eyes we then flee seriously to God for mercy, and are properly prepared by humility and fear."[24]

The same reasoning led John Newton to instruct that his epitaph should simply read: "John Newton, Clerk; once an infidel and libertine, a servant of slaves in Africa, was, by the rich mercy of our Lord and Savior, Jesus Christ, preserved, restored, pardoned and appointed to preach the faith he had long labored to destroy."

The cross should also stir us to remember what we are now in Christ. Remembering what we once were is never to be an excuse for slipping back into our old ways. Though we were once objects of wrath, now we have been made alive with Christ, raised with him, and seated with him in the heavenly realms (Eph. 2:5–6). Those who once belonged on the Corinthian list are now "washed . . . sanctified . . . justified in the name of the Lord Jesus Christ and by the Spirit of our God" (1 Cor. 6:11). Such a change in being must inevitably result in a changed lifestyle, so that we no longer do the things we once did. Remembering in Scripture is never simply a mental exercise but one that issues in a particular course of action, based on the truth remembered.

---

sin isn't mentioned or depicted, there's no need for redemption. How can the majesty of God's mighty arm be defined in a saccharin romance? Real sin is the curse we wrestle with every day" (Chris Stamper and Gene Veith, "Get Real," *World* [July 4–11, 1998]: 18).

24. *Ezekiel II*, trans. T. Myers (Grand Rapids: Baker, 1989), 181.

Nor are we left with mere words to help us in our remembering. For we have been given the Lord's Supper, along with its admonition: "Do this . . . in remembrance of me" (1 Cor. 11:25). In the Lord's Supper, the gospel is made visible before our very eyes. In the tokens of broken bread and poured-out wine, we see with our eyes and recall in our hearts the body of Christ broken and the blood of Christ poured out.

But the Lord's Supper is more than a symbol; it is a sacrament, communicating what it depicts. It is not simply the gospel in pictures; it is the gospel made sure to those who partake. Just as the ancient Israelites participated in the "fellowship offering" by eating together the body of the lamb that had been slain for them, so also we participate in Christ as we eat together the bread and drink the wine, the new covenant tokens of the body and blood of the Lamb of God (cf. 1 Cor. 10:16). The Lord's Supper is, to apply more appropriately the words of the beef commercial, "Real food for real people."

But our remembering of what we once were and, by the grace of God, what we are now must also have an evangelistic impact on our lives. If we were saved by our works, then it would be understandable for us to give up on many of those around us. There's no way that they could earn their way into heaven. But there is room for neither pride nor despair when salvation is all of grace; it can reach down to Sodom as easily as to Jerusalem. It can touch the heart of a prostitute more easily than a Pharisee. Though the city is to be judged, yet it can be restored. Even the height of wickedness, whether you call it Sodom, or Jerusalem, or some other more contemporary name, is not beyond the reach of God's grace. Why? Because of the all-sufficiency of the atonement God made in the death of Jesus Christ, the righteous for the unrighteous. The words of Fanny J. Crosby sum up the awesome magnitude of what Christ has done on the cross, and the impact that reality should have upon our hearts:

> O perfect redemption, the purchase of blood!
> > To every believer the promise of God;
> The vilest offender who truly believes,
> > That moment from Jesus a pardon receives.
> Praise the Lord! Praise the Lord! Let the earth hear His voice!
> > Praise the Lord! Praise the Lord! Let the people rejoice!
> O come to the Father, through Jesus the Son:
> > And give Him the glory! Great things He hath done!

Ezekiel 17

THE WORD OF THE LORD came to me: [2]"Son of man, set forth an allegory and tell the house of Israel a parable. [3]Say to them, 'This is what the Sovereign LORD says: A great eagle with powerful wings, long feathers and full plumage of varied colors came to Lebanon. Taking hold of the top of a cedar, [4]he broke off its topmost shoot and carried it away to a land of merchants, where he planted it in a city of traders.

[5]"'He took some of the seed of your land and put it in fertile soil. He planted it like a willow by abundant water, [6]and it sprouted and became a low, spreading vine. Its branches turned toward him, but its roots remained under it. So it became a vine and produced branches and put out leafy boughs.

[7]"'But there was another great eagle with powerful wings and full plumage. The vine now sent out its roots toward him from the plot where it was planted and stretched out its branches to him for water. [8]It had been planted in good soil by abundant water so that it would produce branches, bear fruit and become a splendid vine.'

[9]"Say to them, 'This is what the Sovereign LORD says: Will it thrive? Will it not be uprooted and stripped of its fruit so that it withers? All its new growth will wither. It will not take a strong arm or many people to pull it up by the roots. [10]Even if it is transplanted, will it thrive? Will it not wither completely when the east wind strikes it—wither away in the plot where it grew?'"

[11]Then the word of the LORD came to me: [12]"Say to this rebellious house, 'Do you not know what these things mean?' Say to them: 'The king of Babylon went to Jerusalem and carried off her king and her nobles, bringing them back with him to Babylon. [13]Then he took a member of the royal family and made a treaty with him, putting him under oath. He also carried away the leading men of the land, [14]so that the kingdom would be brought low, unable to rise again, surviving only by keeping his treaty. [15]But the king rebelled against him by sending his envoys to Egypt to get horses and a large army.

Will he succeed? Will he who does such things escape? Will he break the treaty and yet escape?

¹⁶'''As surely as I live, declares the Sovereign LORD, he shall die in Babylon, in the land of the king who put him on the throne, whose oath he despised and whose treaty he broke. ¹⁷Pharaoh with his mighty army and great horde will be of no help to him in war, when ramps are built and siege works erected to destroy many lives. ¹⁸He despised the oath by breaking the covenant. Because he had given his hand in pledge and yet did all these things, he shall not escape.

¹⁹'''Therefore this is what the Sovereign LORD says: As surely as I live, I will bring down on his head my oath that he despised and my covenant that he broke. ²⁰I will spread my net for him, and he will be caught in my snare. I will bring him to Babylon and execute judgment upon him there because he was unfaithful to me. ²¹All his fleeing troops will fall by the sword, and the survivors will be scattered to the winds. Then you will know that I the LORD have spoken.

²²'''This is what the Sovereign LORD says: I myself will take a shoot from the very top of a cedar and plant it; I will break off a tender sprig from its topmost shoots and plant it on a high and lofty mountain. ²³On the mountain heights of Israel I will plant it; it will produce branches and bear fruit and become a splendid cedar. Birds of every kind will nest in it; they will find shelter in the shade of its branches. ²⁴All the trees of the field will know that I the LORD bring down the tall tree and make the low tree grow tall. I dry up the green tree and make the dry tree flourish.

'''I the LORD have spoken, and I will do it.'''

Original Meaning

EZEKIEL HAS ALREADY used a variety of forms of metaphorical language, both subtle and not-so-subtle, with powerful effect. In this chapter, he continues to utilize metaphorical language, this time in a form that combines "riddle" (NIV, "allegory") and "parable" (17:2). A "riddle" (*ḥîdâ*) is a statement that hides the truth it imparts,[1] while a "parable" (*māšāl*) elucidates the truth that underlies it by putting it in a fresh light. In other words,

---

1. William McKane describes it as a statement "whose essence was opaqueness, mystification, enigma" (*Proverbs: A New Approach* [Philadelphia: Westminster, 1970], 267).

this chapter functions both to conceal and reveal. It has a surface meaning that is fairly simple to comprehend, even if its message is not necessarily welcome, but to the discerning reader it also has a deeper, underlying significance. Perhaps this section best fits into the genre of "fable," a story that communicates its concealed message by transposing the realities it describes into the world of plants and animals (cf. Jotham's fable in Judg. 9:7–20).

The story itself concerns two great eagles,[2] a cedar, and a vine. The first eagle came to Lebanon, broke off the newest growth of a mighty cedar, and carried it off to a land of merchants,[3] that is, Babylon (17:4; cf. 16:29). In the cedar's place, the eagle planted a vine, giving it every possible advantage. He provided for it fertile soil and abundant water supply, all the conditions necessary for maximal growth. In those conditions it spread out, producing branches and limbs but remaining low in stature (17:6).

Desiring more from its life, however, and observing that there was an alternative, the vine turned away from its first provider and sent its roots toward the second eagle. This bird is described in similar language to the first eagle—it too was powerful of wing and beautiful of plumage—yet without the same fulsome glory as the first.[4] It had done nothing for the vine, just as the first eagle had left nothing undone, yet the ungrateful vine turned its allegiance from the first to the second (17:7).

The fate of the vine is predictable. In seeking to gain something more, it will instead throw away everything it has been given. Turning its branches toward the second eagle is already a repudiation of its purpose as a fruitful, splendid vine (17:8). The second eagle will do nothing for it; all the vine will succeed in doing is arousing the anger of the first eagle, who will come and tear off its fruit and uproot it from its place. It will not be a difficult task for this powerful eagle to accomplish, whose activity throughout the parable contrasts with the passivity of the second eagle (17:9). The vine's chosen course of action is worse than foolish, it is suicidal.

As in the case of Jotham's fable in Judges 9, the political realities depicted in this fable are little more concealed from the original hearers than when in contemporary American political cartoons the Republican Party is depicted by an elephant and the Democrats by a donkey. So there is a certain irony

---

2. The Hebrew word *nešer* has a semantic range that includes both the griffon-vulture and the eagle. Here the abundance of feathers and the greatness attributed to the bird clearly indicates the latter.

3. Lit., "the land of Canaan." The equation "Canaanites" = "merchants" is due to the particular affinity of the Phoenicians for trade and is found also in Zeph. 1:11 and perhaps in the ambiguous Zech. 14:21.

4. Allen appropriately describes the rival eagle as "somewhat damned by faint praise" (*Ezekiel 1–19*, 257).

in Ezekiel saying to his audience: "Do you not know what these things mean?" (17:12). His hearers could probably have supplied for themselves the inter-pretation that follows. The first eagle is the king of Babylon, while the cedar sprig is Jehoiachin, whom Nebuchadnezzar carried off to Babylon, along with Ezekiel himself. The "seed of your land" whom Nebuchadnezzar put in his place is clearly Zedekiah, Jehoiachin's uncle, whom Nebuchadnezzar installed in Jehoiachin's place. The second eagle is Egypt, from whom Zedekiah was seeking aid to break free from the Babylonian yoke.[5]

The meaning of the parable is therefore self-evident: Zedekiah's foreign policy is worse than foolish, it is suicidal. His revolt cannot stand on the basis of seeking help from a (disinterested) lesser superpower against the dominant superpower in the contemporary ancient Near East. Will he thrive? No way!

But is the fable's meaning as clear as it appears at first sight? Throughout the fable there are slightly discordant notes that do not fit with the straight-forward, surface analysis. These remind us that the fable is a riddle as well as a parable; it conceals a deeper truth as well as reveals an obvious lesson. For instance, Lebanon is not only the proverbial home of all cedars but also the name of one of Solomon's palaces (cf. 1 Kings 7:2; Jer. 22:23). So the dis-cerning reader is invited to consider who planted "the cedar in Lebanon" in the first place. Who established the Davidic dynasty in Jerusalem? Further back still, who was it who had brought them "to the land of Canaan," just as Nebuchadnezzar brought Jehoiachin "to the land of merchants"?

Moreover, the vine planted in conditions suitable for growth is a classic pic-ture of the Lord's provision for Israel (Isa. 5:1–7); indeed, the imagery of "no effort spared," which seems more than a little overdone with reference to Nebuchadnezzar, fits perfectly for the Lord's care. He is the One who, accord-ing to Psalm 80, brought a vine out of Egypt and cleared the ground in order to plant it in the Promised Land (Ps. 80:8–11). Likewise, Ezekiel's address to Judah as "this rebellious house" describes the history of their relationship with the Lord much better than their history (to date) with Babylon.

Taken together, these hints supply a deeper significance to the breaking of Zedekiah's oath of loyalty to Nebuchadnezzar. It is not simply that break-ing an oath lawfully taken is a serious matter. It is not even that the oath Zedekiah was forced to swear was taken in the Lord's name and therefore he would act as guarantor to bring into effect the covenant curses attached to it. It is that there is a fundamental *analogy* between Zedekiah's rebellion against his covenant overlord, Nebuchadnezzar, and Israel's rebellion against her covenant overlord, God himself. If Zedekiah's abandoning of his (rela-

---

5. For a survey of the historical events referred to in this chapter, see the Introduction.

tively) prosperous situation in favor of the Egyptian option is a suicidally foolish breach of the covenant relationship, what may we say about Israel's abandonment of the Lord and their history of rebellion against him?

Thus, at just the moment when it might seem that Ezekiel has unpacked the meaning of the fable, he launches into its *real* meaning with the word "therefore" (17:19).[6] The fundamental significance of the picture is not exhausted by the political observation that a breach of the covenant with Nebuchadnezzar, sworn on oath, is suicide. Rather, as Greenberg notes, "the political transaction is used as a model from which a theological analogy is drawn."[7] The political leadership in Judah has not only despised and broken Nebuchadnezzar's covenant (an act for which they will face the consequences); on a deeper level they have despised and broken the Lord's covenant (17:19; cf. the similar wording of 16:59). The result is that the coming judgment is not merely a harsh taste of *Realpolitik*, but the judgment of God on a rebellious house. If the risk of rousing the Babylonian wrath ought to give pause to plans to send to Egypt for help (and it ought), how much more should the risk of the Lord's wrath give pause to a people willfully headed away from the One who planted them in a land flowing with milk and honey?

The deeper message of the fable thus paints the hopelessness of Zedekiah's revolt against Nebuchadnezzar in its blackest hues, pointing out that he was not just rebelling against the mighty Babylonians, but against the sovereign Lord, the God who made heaven and earth. At the same time, however, the latter part of this chapter also reworks the fable in more positive terms (17:22–24). The Lord himself, no longer acting through intermediaries, will take a new shoot from the cedar and plant it on a high and lofty mountain (17:22). A new cedar will grow on the mountain heights of Israel into a lofty tree, which will provide in its branches shelter for birds of all kinds (17:23). In contrast to the vine, which even in ideal conditions rebelled and failed to fulfill its potential (17:8), the cedar will achieve the eagle's initial purpose. In that way, all the trees of the field (the nations) will be brought to an understanding of the Lord's sovereignty in history, seeing that the rise and fall of empires is entirely his doing (17:24).

The interpretation of this postscript to the earlier fable is a straightforward development from the deeper level of meaning of those verses. What does the future hold after the Lord's judgment on Judah? Is there any hope for the uprooted vine? The logical answer would be no, but Ezekiel affirms, against all logic, that the Lord will intervene to reverse the failures of the past. Just

---

6. Greenberg, *Ezekiel 1–20*, 321.
7. Ibid., 322.

as Nebuchadnezzar once installed Zedekiah, so Yahweh will install his own vassal on Mount Zion.[8] In contrast to the vine that rebelled and would soon wither (17:7–10), the cedar of Yahweh's planting will thrive and bear fruit (17:23).

However, it is not simply a matter of rescuing the cedar sprig that has been carried off to Babylon and restoring Jehoiachin to the throne. The problem lies deeper than that, for the whole history of the monarchy is, from Ezekiel's perspective, one of failure. Yahweh will go back to the source, as it were, for a new shoot, though still from the same cedar tree.[9] Though no hope is held out for the present cedar sprig (Jehoiachin) or the vine (Zedekiah), yet the death of the contemporary Davidides does not mean the end of the road for the Davidic monarchy. The failure of all past Davidic kings to usher in God's kingdom does not mean an abandonment of God's promises to David of an eternal throne (2 Sam. 7:16). A new sprig from that same tree will be planted and will flourish under the blessing of Yahweh's protection. Indeed, his future greatness will far surpass that of the past monarchs of Israel, having a worldwide impact as the nations see God visibly at work establishing his kingdom.

Bridging Contexts

CODED SPEECH AS a tool of communication. In a country where free speech is considered sacrosanct, the vehicle of metaphorical speech is one to which contemporary prophets rarely resort. We can say what we think in plain, unequivocal terms. Such a luxury has not always been afforded to government critics down through the ages and is not permitted to many around the world in the days in which we live. In such situations, various forms of pictorial speech or coded message—parable, riddle, or allegorical or apocalyptic language—become popular. The superficial message may be couched in safely "unreal" terms, while allowing the deeper, coded message to be understood by initiates.[10]

But even in a context where free speech is permitted, metaphors, parables, and allegories can be powerful tools of communication, giving a fresh per-

---

8. This "high and lofty mountain ... of Israel" can only be Mount Zion. See Jon D. Levenson, *Theology of the Program of Restoration of Ezekiel 40–48* (HSM 10; Missoula, Mont.: Scholars, 1976), 7.

9. A similar expectation is found in Isa. 11:1, where a shoot is anticipated, springing "from the stump of Jesse." See Otto Kaiser, *Isaiah 1–12*, trans. R. A. Wilson (Philadelphia: Westminster, 1972), 157. Note also the similarity of Isa. 10:33b and Ezek. 17:24.

10. Walter Brueggemann, *Cadences of Home: Preaching Among Exiles* (Louisville: Westminster/John Knox, 1997), 42.

spective on a familiar situation or bringing to light unrecognized parallels and similarities. That is why art and literature have so often had a critical role in bringing about social change. For example, Harriet Beecher Stowe's famous book, *Uncle Tom's Cabin*, probably had a far greater impact on the future of slavery in America than all the political speeches of her contemporaries. In a similar way, Ezekiel uses the political reality of Zedekiah's covenant with Nebuchadnezzar and its impending breach to bring home the spiritual reality of Israel's broken covenant with the Lord and its impending consequences. Playing fast and loose with one's covenant overlord is never wise and frequently fatal, whether that overlord is Nebuchadnezzar or God himself.

The consequences of breaking an ancient covenant. Yet some aspects of that comparison may well be lost on us as contemporary listeners. Because we are not familiar with the nature of covenant treaty documents, we may be unaware that to break your oath of covenant loyalty was to call down on your own head all of the curses attached to that covenant. It was customary for such self-imprecatory curses to be attached to the end of an ancient Near Eastern covenant treaty document. Thus, after naming the gods who are summoned as witnesses of the oath, the treaty between the Hittite king Mursilis and Duppi-Tessub of Amurru concludes:

> The words of the treaty and the oath that are inscribed on this tablet—should Duppi-Tessub not honor these words of the treaty and the oath—may these gods of the oath destroy Duppi-Tessub together with his person, his wife, his son, his grandson, his house, his land and together with everything that he owns.[11]

It is not clear whether the Babylonians regularly imposed such an oath of allegiance on vassals in the name of their own gods, although the Assyrians clearly adopted that practice.[12] According to 2 Chronicles 36:13, Nebuchadnezzar had indeed made Zedekiah swear an oath in the name of God. When he broke such an oath, Zedekiah could hardly expect God's aid.

But it may well be that, like so many of his predecessors, it was not the Lord's aid he sought anyway, being content if he could merely gain substantial military assistance from Egypt. He hoped to play the two major regional superpowers, Babylon to the east and Egypt to the west, off against one another. It was a dangerous game to play. Similar strategies of seeking help from Egypt were in place in Isaiah's time, with no significant results (Isa. 30:1–7; 31:1–3). Yet in spite of that negative history, hope of help from Egypt sprang eternal in the hearts of those in power in Judah. Turning their

---

11. *ANET*, 205.
12. Morton Cogan, *Imperialism and Religion*, 48–49.

back on their one true refuge, the Lord himself, they placed their hope in the chariots and horses whose ancestors had perished in the Red Sea (Ex. 15:4). Such an attitude was inevitably doomed to disaster.

The monarchy in Israel and Judah. The monarchy itself in Israel and Judah suffered for a similar mismatch between expectations and performance. God had made provision at the outset of Israel's history for that institution: Ancient prophecies had foretold it (Gen. 49:10; Num. 24:17) and the Mosaic Law had regulated it (Deut. 17:14–20). Yet when the people actually made the request for a king, their motivation was entirely wrong. They wanted a king who would lead them and fight their battles for them, so that they could be like all the other nations around them (1 Sam. 8:20). They had forgotten that they were not called to be like the nations around them but to be God's own treasured possession, a kingdom of priests (Ex. 19:6). They had apparently also missed the fact that in the immediately preceding chapter they had fared well enough in the second battle of Ebenezer, with "only" the Lord fighting for them (1 Sam. 7:2–14).

What happened was that they had transferred to the monarchy all the faith that their fathers had placed in the ark of the covenant. At the first battle of Ebenezer in 1 Samuel 4, their fathers looked to the ark to lead them into battle and to bring them automatic victory over their enemies. It did not work. Now their descendants were looking to a king to bring them automatic victory over their enemies. They didn't really trust God as their king, so they wanted to replace him by an earthly king, someone you could see and feel and touch. In that hope, they were going to be disappointed. Their deliverance came not from an ark or an earthly king, but from the Lord, who made heaven and earth.

But God's plan for his people is ultimately gracious. He does not plan to destroy them. Do they want a king? He will give them a king. In fact, he will give them a whole series of kings to rule over them. Over the next five hundred years they will have a succession of all kinds of kings: good kings, bad kings, strong kings, weak kings. They will have more than enough kings for them to see that no earthly king can meet their needs. There will be no king who can provide them lasting shelter against the storms of life, a reality that found poignant expression in Lamentations 4:20: "The LORD's anointed, our very life breath, was caught in their traps. We thought that under his shadow we would live among the nations." What they really need is for the Lord himself to be their king, to establish the monarchy on a new footing as a lofty tree that will produce fruit and shelter, peace and prosperity (Ezek. 17:24).

Having shown the people throughout the pages of the Old Testament what kind of king they need, in Jesus God himself will come to be their king. He is the perfect king, fully obedient to God's laws, a king after God's own heart. He is a king who intercedes for his people like a prophet, a king who offers his own life up as a priest, a king who will not die and pass his kingdom on to a line of depressingly inferior descendants. He is indeed the King of kings.

LACK OF SPIRITUAL **insight.** We live in an age of intense political analysis. The nightly news is filled with the results of the latest polls, which are scrutinized for their potential impact on political thinking. Whenever major political changes take place, such as an election at home, an international trade treaty, or a major event like the dismantling of the Berlin Wall, there is an outpouring of words explaining how these events will affect our lives. In large measure, governments depend on such analysis to make their decisions. Yet in spite of the intense searchlight of analysis, politicians still can and do make phenomenal mistakes. Right up until the moment Saddam Hussein invaded Kuwait in 1990, intelligence reports apparently regarded such an outcome as unlikely. That miscalculation, along with Hussein's estimation that he could safely annex Kuwait, cost many lives on both sides.

Zedekiah's decision to rebel against Babylon was a miscalculation of similarly costly proportions. Encouraged perhaps by the Egyptians under Pharaoh Hophra, he sought to break free, only to discover too late that the Egyptians were freer with their words than with their military might. The intelligence analysis led him astray. Nebuchadnezzar came, as Ezekiel had warned, and judged the covenant-breaker, executing his sons in front of his very eyes and then putting his eyes out before taking him to Babylon in chains. Yet, disastrous as his foreign policy was for Judah, Ezekiel insists that Zedekiah's basic problem was not lack of political insight but lack of spiritual insight. It was not merely Nebuchadnezzar's covenant he had broken but the Lord's.

We suffer from the same rose-tinted myopia that Zedekiah did. On a societal level, we think the problem with our world is essentially political. If we were just able to kick the present set of bums out of office and elect people who agree with us, the world would instantly be a better place. So we pour our time and energy into political campaigns and boycotts and other efforts to bring about change through political means. On a personal level, we think the solution is to pour our time into gathering the information necessary for wise decision-making. We read the consumer reports before we purchase a new car. We do our homework before we invest money in a particular stock, to ensure, as far as possible, that we will get a good rate of return for our money. We plan our careers years in advance, trying to make sure that we are in the right place at the right time to reach the very top. We try to make wise provision for our retirement years so that we will not be in want.

Now all of these things are good things to do, on a personal and societal level. We should work for political change and we should plan for the future. Yet we can be so busy doing the good things that we miss out on the one insight that is really necessary, the best thing: maintaining our personal and corporate spiritual life with God. But as Jesus reminds us: "What good will it be for a man if he gains the whole world, yet forfeits his soul?" (Matt. 16:26).

How many people have planned for every eventuality they can encounter in life, yet have left out of the reckoning entirely their coming great encounter with God in death? Anyone who has ever talked to people in the streets or in their homes and asked them the question "If you were to die tonight, would you be sure of going to heaven?" can testify that many have never thought about their coming appointment with their Creator. Yet for all of us, the ultimate reality is not how much we have reformed the world or how well we have planned our money and our efforts. It is the fact that we will all one day have to stand before God to give account of what we have done.

God's answer to our hopeless situation. Perhaps one reason why we ignore that ultimate reality is that we do not wish to be confronted with the unpleasant truth. It is easier for us, like Zedekiah, to believe in comforting accounts of our own ability to stand on our own merits rather than to face the harsh facts of the untenability of our own position. We want to believe that we can change the world through our own efforts. We want to think that God ought to be impressed, at least somewhat, by our goodness and righteous acts. We prefer not to remember that we are helpless sinners on a collision course with a God of absolute purity and holiness, in whose presence sin cannot be tolerated. But if we accept the fact that we are all covenant-breakers in Adam as well as covenant-breakers on our own account, how shall we stand on that day? Is our ultimate future as bleak as was Zedekiah's?

The answer lies in the new chip off the old block, the sprig of the cedar tree that God will plant. This new beginning from David's line will be a covenant-keeper, not a covenant-breaker like Zedekiah. He will not simply be a slightly improved version of the past, a political retooling of last year's model, but a radically new beginning. As a result, instead of scattering death and destruction in his wake, he will provide shelter and security not merely for Israel but for all of the nations of the earth.

The fulfillment of this prophecy is found in Jesus Christ. The angel Gabriel says of the child to be conceived in Mary's womb: "The Lord God will give him the throne of his father David, and he will reign over the house of Jacob forever; his kingdom will never end" (Luke 1:32–33). Mary herself speaks in the *Magnificat* of a reversal of fortunes, furnishing the evidence of

God's sovereignty: "He has brought down rulers from their thrones but has lifted up the humble" (1:52). Jesus is the coming King, who reverses the fortunes of Israel by his covenant-keeping.

Jesus is definitively not merely a retooling of the past; rather, he is a radically different kind of ruler. He comes as a king—but a king who rides on a donkey (Matt. 21:5). He comes as the Prince of Peace—yet meets a bloody death on the cross. He is himself the Holy One of Israel—yet he eats with tax collectors and sinners (Matt. 9:11). The One who was by nature exalted humbles himself. In the Incarnation, he takes on human form, the form of a servant, and carries it all the way to the death of the cross. But the humble one is paradoxically also exalted.

His kingdom is like the mustard seed, the smallest of all seeds, which grows into a great tree, in whose branches the birds of the air find shade (Mark 4:30–32). Those who come to him receive in him every spiritual blessing (Eph. 1:3). He is not only the new king, he is himself the new temple planted on the high and lofty mountain of Israel (Ezek. 17:22; see 40:2). As the humble one is lifted up on the cross, he draws to himself by his elevation not only God's own people, Israel, but men and women from all nations as well (John 12:32). Because of his humility, he has now been exalted to the highest place and given the name above every name (Phil. 2:9).

In his humiliation and exaltation, Christ gives us a radically different model for leadership—and indeed for life. How much of our leadership style is based on our own abilities and efforts to get others to serve us? We build our kingdoms and our lives around our own analysis of the world, seeking to make the contacts and build the relationships we think will prosper us, heedless of God and his Word. The irony is that so often our efforts do not even achieve what we aimed at on a human, political level. How much more tragic, though, that in the process we have abandoned God and rebelled against him! Will such rebels prosper? By no means!

The good news, however, is that in spite of our weakness and folly, Christ's kingdom continues to grow and develop, based on his goodness and covenant faithfulness, not ours. Our rebellion and failure may have negative consequences in our own lives, but it cannot prevent God from achieving his purposes in the world. He may work slowly, from our perspective, through imperceptible growth from small beginnings rather than radical revolution, but his work is nonetheless effective. His tree provides perfect shelter and security for all of his own people. As he has planned, he will bring men and women from every tribe and nation to know himself, justified in the perfect obedience of their true king, the shoot of David, Jesus Christ.

Ezekiel 18

THE WORD OF THE LORD came to me: 2"What do you
people mean by quoting this proverb about the land
of Israel:

"'The fathers eat sour grapes,
   and the children's teeth are set on edge'?

3"As surely as I live, declares the Sovereign LORD, you will
no longer quote this proverb in Israel. 4For every living soul
belongs to me, the father as well as the son—both alike
belong to me. The soul who sins is the one who will die.

5"Suppose there is a righteous man
   who does what is just and right.
6He does not eat at the mountain shrines
   or look to the idols of the house of Israel.
He does not defile his neighbor's wife
   or lie with a woman during her period.
7He does not oppress anyone,
   but returns what he took in pledge for a loan.
He does not commit robbery
   but gives his food to the hungry
   and provides clothing for the naked.
8He does not lend at usury
   or take excessive interest.
He withholds his hand from doing wrong
   and judges fairly between man and man.
9He follows my decrees
   and faithfully keeps my laws.
That man is righteous;
   he will surely live,

declares the Sovereign LORD.

10"Suppose he has a violent son, who sheds blood or does
any of these other things 11(though the father has done none
of them):

"He eats at the mountain shrines.
He defiles his neighbor's wife.

¹²He oppresses the poor and needy.

He commits robbery.

He does not return what he took in pledge.

He looks to the idols.

He does detestable things.

¹³He lends at usury and takes excessive interest.

Will such a man live? He will not! Because he has done all these detestable things, he will surely be put to death and his blood will be on his own head.

¹⁴"But suppose this son has a son who sees all the sins his father commits, and though he sees them, he does not do such things:

¹⁵"He does not eat at the mountain shrines

or look to the idols of the house of Israel.

He does not defile his neighbor's wife.

¹⁶He does not oppress anyone

or require a pledge for a loan.

He does not commit robbery

but gives his food to the hungry

and provides clothing for the naked.

¹⁷He withholds his hand from sin

and takes no usury or excessive interest.

He keeps my laws and follows my decrees.

He will not die for his father's sin; he will surely live. ¹⁸But his father will die for his own sin, because he practiced extortion, robbed his brother and did what was wrong among his people.

¹⁹"Yet you ask, 'Why does the son not share the guilt of his father?' Since the son has done what is just and right and has been careful to keep all my decrees, he will surely live. ²⁰The soul who sins is the one who will die. The son will not share the guilt of the father, nor will the father share the guilt of the son. The righteousness of the righteous man will be credited to him, and the wickedness of the wicked will be charged against him.

²¹"But if a wicked man turns away from all the sins he has committed and keeps all my decrees and does what is just and right, he will surely live; he will not die. ²²None of the offenses he has committed will be remembered against him. Because of the righteous things he has done, he will live. ²³Do

I take any pleasure in the death of the wicked? declares the Sovereign LORD. Rather, am I not pleased when they turn from their ways and live?

²⁴"But if a righteous man turns from his righteousness and commits sin and does the same detestable things the wicked man does, will he live? None of the righteous things he has done will be remembered. Because of the unfaithfulness he is guilty of and because of the sins he has committed, he will die.

²⁵"Yet you say, 'The way of the Lord is not just.' Hear, O house of Israel: Is my way unjust? Is it not your ways that are unjust? ²⁶If a righteous man turns from his righteousness and commits sin, he will die for it; because of the sin he has committed he will die. ²⁷But if a wicked man turns away from the wickedness he has committed and does what is just and right, he will save his life. ²⁸Because he considers all the offenses he has committed and turns away from them, he will surely live; he will not die. ²⁹Yet the house of Israel says, 'The way of the Lord is not just.' Are my ways unjust, O house of Israel? Is it not your ways that are unjust?

³⁰"Therefore, O house of Israel, I will judge you, each one according to his ways, declares the Sovereign LORD. Repent! Turn away from all your offenses; then sin will not be your downfall. ³¹Rid yourselves of all the offenses you have committed, and get a new heart and a new spirit. Why will you die, O house of Israel? ³²For I take no pleasure in the death of anyone, declares the Sovereign LORD. Repent and live!

Original Meaning

THIS CHAPTER CONTINUES the pattern of pictorial speech found in the preceding chapters, but this time the proverb comes from the mouth of the people, not delivered from the Lord. It is an erroneous proverb—or at least a proverb erroneously applied[1]—and such has been its misuse that the Lord swears that all use of it will be eliminated from Israel (18:3). The proverb runs: "The fathers eat sour grapes, and the children's teeth are set on edge" (18:2), thus affirming that sometimes children suffer for their parent's actions rather than the parents themselves.

---

1. A true proverb applied to the wrong situation will lead to a false conclusion. "A stitch in time saves nine" is a valid proverb, yet if used where the appropriate proverb is rather, "Fools rush in where angels dare to tread," the results may be disastrous. Hence Prov. 26:9 warns: "Like a thornbush in a drunkard's hand is a proverb in the mouth of a fool."

The application to which the people of Ezekiel's time had put the proverb is not hard to discern: "Our fathers sinned against God, but we their children (the generation of the Exile) are the ones paying the price; that's the way the world is and nothing can be done about it." A similar thought is expressed in Lamentations 5:7: "Our fathers sinned and are no more, and we bear their punishment." Jeremiah also confronted the same proverb (Jer. 31:29–30), which suggests that the idea had considerable currency around the time of the Exile.

The Lord's response to this proverb is a categorical denial of its applicability. Both father and son "belong" to the Lord; indeed, everyone belongs to him (18:4). The Lord is not only sovereign over all flesh, but he is also a just judge. There is no unfair attribution of punishment to the next generation for the sins of the fathers; instead, "the soul who sins is the one who will die" (18:4), a maxim that had already been applied to the earthly judicial realm in Deuteronomy 24:16.

These assertions of the sovereignty and especially the justice of God are not random theological statements drawn from a treatise on the attributes of God. Rather, they are specifically designed to meet and address the temptations of those in exile. To the temptation to fatalistic despair, Ezekiel affirms God's sovereignty. Life is not in the hands of blind Kismet, who capriciously dispenses undeserved sufferings. To the temptation to question God's goodness, Ezekiel affirms the justice of God's ways. These specific temptations and their answers underlie the course of the disputation that follows.

The first part of that disputation is a case study covering three successive generations, presented in the form of priestly case law.[2] The formula "If a man ..." followed by the judicial verdict is comparable to that found in Leviticus 20:9–21. The three generations described are a righteous man who is succeeded by a wicked son, who is in turn followed by a repentant, righteous son. The behavior of each is assessed against a "checklist" of righteous behaviors, a kind of miniature Ten Commandments.[3]

This list covers three basic areas of morality, which may be broadly categorized as piety, chastity, and charity. The first man mentioned is orthodox in his religious practice: He does not eat on the mountains (18:6); that is, he is not involved in the idolatrous cults of the high places (see 6:3–7). Nor does

---

2. Zimmerli, *Ezekiel*, 1:375.

3. These kinds of "legal lists" for those who sought nearness to God are found elsewhere in the Old Testament (e.g., Ps. 15; Isa. 33:15) and elsewhere in the ancient Near East. On these lists, see Gordon H. Matties, *Ezekiel 18 and the Rhetoric of Moral Discourse* (SBLDS 126; Atlanta: Scholars, 1990), 88–105, and Moshe Weinfeld, "Instructions for Temple Visitors in the Bible and in Ancient Egypt," *Egyptological Studies* (ScrHier 28; Jerusalem: Magnes, 1982), 224–28.

he lift his eyes to Israel's idols—a gesture suggesting an appeal to the idols for help.[4] As with the Decalogue, undivided commitment to the Lord is the primary token of obedience. Moreover, he does not commit adultery with his neighbor's wife, nor does he lie with a woman during her menstrual period (18:6). The latter was prohibited in Leviticus 18:19 on account of the ritual uncleanness contracted by this flow of blood, as with other bodily discharges.

In addition, this righteous man does not oppress those in debt to him; instead, he returns objects given to him as security for a debt (18:7). This may mean faithfulness in returning the poor man's garment to him by nightfall so that he has something to sleep in, as required in Exodus 22:25, or it may simply mean actually returning the pledge once the debt has been repaid. There were a multitude of ways in which an unscrupulous lender could take advantage of the desperate. Far from robbing, however, this righteous man feeds and clothes the poor out of his own resources (Ezek. 18:7). He does not lend at interest; such "loan sharking" was prohibited in Leviticus 25:36–37, where it is clear that the person concerned was in desperate need and thus open to exploitation. The righteous person draws back from all such wrongdoing and practices true justice between people (Ezek. 18:8). To summarize, this person "follows my decrees and faithfully keeps my laws" (18:9). What is the verdict on such a person? "That man is righteous; he will surely live."

On the other hand, suppose this man's son is the antithesis of all his father stands for. He does everything bad his father abhorred and fails to do any of the good things his father did. Point by point, Ezekiel checks off his sins. What is to be the verdict on such a person? "Will such a man live? He will not!" He will die, and his death will be no one's fault but his own (18:13).

But suppose this second man also has a son who swims against the tide. He is like his grandfather in doing what is good and right, not like his wicked father. He sees what his father does and deliberately follows a different course. His life is again a model of piety, chastity, and charity. What is the verdict on the third generation? According to the proverb of 18:2, he ought to face the inexorable consequences of his father's misdeeds. But according to Ezekiel, "he will surely live" (18:17). His father will be judged on the basis of his sins and die (hence, he will not be rescued by the first generation's righteousness). But the son will be judged on the basis of his own record and will live (hence, he will not die on account of his father's sin). In the heavenly

---

4. Greenberg, *Ezekiel 1–20*, 329. He also points out that the pairing of lifting up the eyes with mountains evokes an apostate version of Ps. 121:1: "I lift up my eyes to the hills—where does my help come from?" In place of the orthodox response, "My help comes from the LORD, the Maker of heaven and earth," the apostate seeks help from the idols whose high places are situated there.

court, as in the earthly court (Deut. 24:16), "the soul who sins is the one who will die" (Ezek. 18:20).[5]

At this point, Ezekiel envisages a hypothetical objection: "What![6] Does the son not share the guilt of the father?" (18:19a, pers. trans.). By providing this *reductio ad absurdum*, the complaint of Ezekiel's audience is undermined.[7] In such a clear case, no one can dispute the justice of Ezekiel's assertion: "Since the son has done what is just and right and has been careful to keep all my decrees, he will surely live. The soul who sins is the one who will die" (Ezek. 18:19b–20). But to accept this as God's way is necessarily to abandon the applicability of the original proverb to their situation. If this generation is experiencing the "death" of exile and if God deals justly with each generation, then the only possible conclusion is that they too must also be tarred with guilt before God.

The point Ezekiel is making is not that the previous generation was any less guilty than the present generation. Far from it! He has already characterized Jerusalem's earliest roots as pagan (16:3), and he will shortly describe the history of Israel from the desert period on as one of continuous rebellion (20:4–29). To make the picture match Israel's history, all three generations have to be identified with the second generation: the epitome of wickedness. But Ezekiel's point is that the present generation is not guiltless. They themselves have shared in the sins of past generations, as 20:30–32 makes explicit. Therefore, although the judgment they are now undergoing is certainly in part a judgment on the result of the sins of previous generations, the present generation are not innocent bystanders but *guilty* bystanders. They too have shared in eating the sour grapes, so they cannot pass the buck for the unpleasant aftertaste onto others. God's dealings with them have been nothing other than perfectly just.

But if that point is accepted, then the possibility of despair becomes real.[8] If God is indeed judging this generation for its sin, what is the point of even trying to please him? If they are condemned sinners, what room is there for

---

5. This succession of three generations (righteous-unrighteous-righteous) is not a purely hypothetical construct but some scholars suggest a correspondence to the historical succession of Josiah-Jehoiakim-Jehoiachin. This perhaps accounts for the placement of chapter 18 between chapters 17 and 19, which focus on the fate of the royal line; Ezekiel 18 would then further justify hope for the future of the exiled Jehoiachin. See Antti Laato, *Josiah and David Redivivus: The Historical Josiah and the Messianic Expectations of Exilic and Postexilic Times* (ConBOT 33; Stockholm: Almqvist & Wiksell, 1992), 358.

6. For *maddûa*ᶜ as a rhetorical device expressing affected surprise (18:19), see BDB 396c. The New Living Translation renders it: "'What?' you ask. 'Doesn't the child pay for the parent's sins?'"

7. Joyce, *Divine Initiative*, 48.

8. Greenberg, *Ezekiel 1–20*, 337.

hope? Since their death sentence is decreed, ought they not simply to eat, drink, and try to be merry in the time that remains to them?

By no means! Ezekiel 18:21–32 addresses that question by propounding another pair of case studies. The first concerns a wicked person who turns from his sins and does what is right (18:21). Will such a person not live? Indeed he will, for the Lord takes no pleasure in putting to death the sinner. Grace is possible for the one who repents; his transgressions will be remembered no more (18:22–23). By contrast, the righteous person who "repents" of his righteousness and abandons his service of God will not escape judgment. Right standing before God is not capital that can be banked, either by oneself or one's ancestors, allowing one to live on the accrued interest. Apostasy is always a fearful possibility to be reckoned with.

Thus, just as this generation is not guiltless but brings on its own head divine judgment, so also as long as it exists, this generation is not fixed on its present course. Change, real change, is always possible—for better or for worse! This is fundamentally the reason for which Ezekiel was appointed a watchman back in chapter 3: so that the wicked might be turned from their ways to a godly way of life, and the righteous be warned not to fall away.

In all this, is God not just? The problem, says Ezekiel, is not God's lack of justice. The problem is with Israel's lack of justice. The problem is not that God has not judged this present generation according to what they deserve. Rather, it is that they deserve all too fully the judgment that has fallen on them. But that is only part of the story. The essential point the prophet is making is introduced by the word "therefore" in verse 30.[9] Judgment is coming! God will judge Israel, not unjustly or capriciously but according to their ways. In the past, he has shown justice abundantly tempered with mercy to Israel. They have repeatedly fallen short of God's standard, loving their transgressions more than they love God. What is more, in the present they continue in the way of their fathers. If the proverb were true, they would be condemned for sure.

But even now it is not too late! Even wicked, condemned sinners can still leave their transgressions behind, repent, and acquire for themselves[10] a new heart and new spirit (18:31). Even now death is not inevitable. They can still return to the God of all grace and live (18:32). If they do so, God will not turn them away but will give them what they seek and what he has already promised: a new heart and a new spirit (11:19).[11] Everything that pre-

---

9. Joyce, *Divine Initiative*, 52.

10. For this translation, see Allen, *Ezekiel 1–19*, 267.

11. The rhetorical device of calling on the hearers to do for themselves something that ultimately only the Lord can do, is also found in Deuteronomy, where Moses tells the peo-

cedes it—the case studies, the declaration of God's justice, the statement of God's mercy—everything leads up to the passionate appeal to turn from death, to choose life and live (cf. Deut. 30:15–20)!

Bridging Contexts

THE CORPORATE NATURE of Ezekiel 18. All too often Ezekiel 18 has been treated as if drawn from the pages of a systematic theology textbook. Frequently, the result of this approach has been to hail the prophet as introducing a new theological idea into Israel, that of "individual responsibility." Previously, so the argument goes, Israelites thought in terms of "corporate responsibility," but Ezekiel cleared the way for the New Testament by asserting the standing of the individual soul before God.[12] Such an idea appeals to our individualistic age, but it is not founded in the text.

In our exposition, we have demonstrated that the case studies, though they describe hypothetical individuals, actually are building an argument that applies to Ezekiel's generation as a whole. It was *the corporate group* (the "house of Israel," 18:25, 29–30) on whom judgment had come and who is urged to repent and turn once more to the Lord. This same corporate emphasis is found elsewhere in Ezekiel. Israel's long history of sin has now made their final doom inevitable (cf. Ezek. 20).

However, that fate does not descend on an innocent generation but one that is also guilty of the same sins as its predecessors. The corporate nature of judgment is not arbitrary, any more than is the corporate aspect of salvation, but it is bound up with the transmission of those same sinful characteristics on to the next generation. Following the example of the fathers, the children have also been eating sour grapes. Just as the blessings of the covenant community are not transmitted to the next generation as something separate from their parent's faith, so also the covenant curse is transmitted in company with unbelief.

A similar theme emerges in the books of Judges to Kings, where repeated cycles of apostasy reach a point of no return with the excesses of Manasseh, from which not even the reform of Josiah can rescue Judah (2 Kings 23:26).[13] Yet at the same time, the generations after Manasseh are not excused. Though Josiah is righteous and receives the reward of at least being buried in his

---

ple both that they must circumcise their hearts (Deut. 10:16) and that God will circumcise their hearts (30:6). The point is that God can be relied upon to act faithfully to his promises and to carry through in us the good work he has begun.

12. For the history of this discussion, see Matties, *Ezekiel 18*, 115–25.

13. See J. Gordon McConville, "Narrative and Theology in the Book of Kings," *Biblica* 70 (1989): 45.

own tomb (23:30), the four kings leading up to the exile (Jehoahaz, Jehoiakim, Jehoiachin, and Zedekiah) each do evil in the eyes of the Lord. Punishment for the sins of their forebears falls not on the heads of the innocent but the guilty. The question being addressed by Ezekiel, then, is not whether judgment is corporate, but whether that corporate judgment is just or not.

Indeed, the very categories Ezekiel utilizes—"righteous/unrighteous," "life/death"—are corporate categories in the Old Testament. The "legal lists" were not expressions of some impersonal entity called "Right" or "Natural Law" or "Truth." The prophets would never have begun their arguments with the words: "We hold these truths to be self-evident. . . ." To be righteous was to be in right relationship with the Lord, to accept him as your overlord, and therefore to accede to his demands on your life.

Necessarily, rightly relating to the Great King involved rightly relating to his friends and enemies as well. Thus, righteousness prohibited idolatry (giving allegiance to any other overlord) and taking advantage of the poor (oppressing the King's people). Chastity and purity were prerequisites to entering his presence. To be unrighteous, on the other hand, was to live as the antithesis of an obedient vassal, consorting with the King's enemies and doing the things he had forbidden. The law was an expression of the wisdom of the Great King that provided opportunity for the vassal to express loyalty.

The one who is faithful to these requirements will "live," that is, enjoy the fullness of relationship with the Great King that flows from obedience.[14] Such life is not merely physical existence, or even the future hope of return from exile, but a place among the people of the King in the presence of the King. Death, on the other hand, means estrangement from both God and the covenant community, along with all of the blessings that went with that status. To be cut off from God's people is to be "dead" even while physically still alive, for one would be separated from the source of life. There is no life apart from the Source and Giver of life; as Deuteronomy 30:20 puts it: "The LORD is your life, and he will give you many years in the land he swore to give to your fathers, Abraham, Isaac and Jacob."

The individual dimension. Yet this stress on the corporate nature of both life and death, of blessing and curse, should not blind us to the fact that these elements have always had an individual dimension to them in the Bible. As early as the Flood, God was concerned to rescue the righteous out of the midst of the judgment (Gen. 6:9). "Righteous" Lot (as Peter calls him in 2 Peter 2:7) was similarly delivered out of the judgment of Sodom and

---

14. On the concepts of "life" and "death," see Walther Zimmerli, "'Leben' und 'Tod' im Buche des Propheten Ezechiel," *ThZ* 13 (1957): 494–508.

Gomorrah, though his unbelieving sons-in-law were consumed in the conflagration. Joshua and Caleb, the two spies to bring a positive report of the Promised Land, were the only two from that generation to enter it (Num. 13–14). When Ahab's sin resulted in drought, God provided supernaturally for Elijah first by means of ravens and then by means of a foreign widow (1 Kings 17). In the midst of the judgment that finally falls on the wicked for their sin, God is able to protect his own.

THE PROBLEM OF EVIL. When I was growing up, two of the top three things we were never allowed to say were, "It's not my fault," and, "It's not fair." (The other was, "I couldn't help it.") Those very phrases are, in effect, what Ezekiel's contemporaries were saying to God by using the parable about the fathers having eaten sour grapes and the children having their teeth set on edge. As they suffered the discipline of God in the Exile, their first response was, "This is not our fault," which in turn led logically to the accusation, "God, that's not fair." Ezekiel's response is to affirm that, along with previous generations, it is indeed their fault. It is not God's unfairness but their sin that is the problem. They are simply in denial about the true nature of their case. But Ezekiel doesn't take away their excuses in order to leave them crushed under the full impact of God's law. He pleads with them even now to turn and live.

The question of why bad things happen in this world is a problem for anyone who thinks about the world at all, who lives beyond the level of momentary feelings. That's why Rabbi Harold Kushner's book *When Bad Things Happen to Good People*[15] was such a best-seller. The issue he posed is a real one—even if the answer he gave to that question was seriously flawed. His solution is that God means well but is ultimately unable to prevent everything bad from hitting home. According to him, God is like a good parent, doing everything in his power to protect his children, but ultimately powerless against the intrusions of chaos into the order of the world and the free expression of evil on the part of those he has created.

Those of us who believe in the God whom the Bible reveals have a problem with Rabbi Kushner's "solution," however.[16] It is based on a wrong picture of God. The Bible portrays God as victorious over the forces of chaos from the beginning of Genesis on. Nothing can stand against his omnipotent, creative word. The mighty Egyptian army is smothered by the Red Sea

15. New York: Schocken, 1981.
16. For a response, see Dan McCartney, *Why Does It Have to Hurt?*

when it seeks to make bad things happen to God's people. As a general principle, the writer of Proverbs teaches us that there is no such thing as chance in this world: "The lot is cast into the lap, but its every decision is from the LORD " (Prov. 16:33). Nor is the Lord helpless even against the decisions of wicked people. Indeed, he declares in Isaiah 8 that he will use the fierce and godless ruler of the Assyrians to execute judgment on his own people. No, the problem is not with God's power.

Recognizing that reality, the temptation is for us to oversimplify in a different direction. We may baldly reply to Rabbi Kushner in words that sound superficially like those of Ezekiel: "Bad things don't happen to good people, for there are no good people. Bad things only happen to bad people, for we are all bad." Certainly there is a strong element of biblical truth in that statement. "All have sinned and fall short of the glory of God," says Paul in Romans 3:23. Thus, we are all bad people, who deserve much more in the way of bad things than we ever receive in this life.

A "pro-life" God. Yet that approach oversimplifies the problem in a different direction by suggesting that there is only one reason why these bad things are happening, which is as a punishment from God because of our sin. Ultimately, this approach leads to the kind of question we find the disciples asking Jesus when they encountered a man born blind: "Who sinned, this man or his parents, that he was born blind?" (John 9:2). In the face of profound personal tragedy, we are content merely to debate suffering as an interesting theological issue, considering our duty done if we prove God "not guilty" of the charge of unfairness.

Not so, says Ezekiel! Certainly he answers the theological issue, but important though the issue is, he doesn't stop there. He is concerned not merely to demonstrate that God is just in condemning his people to death, but also to show that in spite of everything they have done, God is resolutely "pro-life." Even when the "life" in question is the life of those who have rebelled against him, God desires that they should turn and live.[17] He therefore presses on from the abstract theological issue ("Where does this suffering come from?") to the intensely personal issue ("What is your relationship to God?").

You see, though suffering in this life ultimately flows from Adam's sin, a sin in which we corporately share not as innocent bystanders but as guilty coconspirators, yet it also has a multitude of diverse purposes in the provi-

---

17. "Sin is not a cul de sac, nor is guilt a final trap. Sin may be washed away by repentance and return, and beyond guilt is the dawn of forgiveness. The door is never locked, the threat of doom is not the last word" (Abraham Heschel, *The Prophets* [New York: Harper & Row, 1969], 1:174).

dence of God. Some suffering has indeed as its purpose the judgment of sinners, here and now. Those who flout the Word of God find that there is often a price to pay. In other cases, however, suffering has a redemptive purpose, providing the occasion for those outside the kingdom to be brought to an awareness of their need for God. So Ezekiel faces his contemporaries with the challenge posed by their exile. He confronts them passionately with the need to choose between life and death, to choose between repenting and turning to God or continuing on their present course, with all of its ultimate consequences.

What did Jesus say in answer to the disciples' question as to which one had sinned, the man born blind or his parents? His answer was: "Neither this man nor his parents sinned . . . but this happened so that the work of God might be displayed in his life" (John 9:3). This suffering, says Jesus—indeed all suffering—is a work of God in the world. As we have noted, it sometimes has a redemptive purpose and sometimes a purpose of judgment. The latter should indeed not surprise us since we are sinners, born to sinners. God will certainly be glorified in executing judgment on sin. The truly surprising part is the first part: that God, through suffering, works for good in us and others, redeeming us, deepening our devotion to him, and drawing others to himself through us. The real question we face in this topsy-turvy world is: "How can bad things achieve a good purpose in bad people?"

The ultimate answer. The full answer to that question comes only at the cross. There God brought to remembrance my sins and the sins of all of his people so that they might not be remembered finally against us (18:22). Those sins must be dealt with. They cannot simply be swept under the carpet. The death penalty that they deserve must be executed. Someone must surely die for them. But there at Calvary, instead of putting me to death, or even me and my children for my sins, he put to death rather his own Son, his own beloved Son, who had no sin of his own.

We have not begun to grasp the reason why we suffer if we have not first considered the suffering of Christ in our place. For it was on the cross that his suffering made it possible for my suffering to be for good, for God's glory in my redemption, for God's glory in my growth in grace. That doesn't make it any less suffering. It is indeed painful, frequently very painful, as we endure it. But it does mean that for Christians, suffering is not for our judgment but is the means of God's gracious work in our lives, by which we are increasingly conformed to the image of Jesus Christ.

Ezekiel's passion to convey that message of life for everyone who will repent fits the cost paid by Jesus to make it possible. What can we say, however, about our own anemic efforts to share the good news? Faced with the reality of millions going to a lost eternity, do we form debating clubs to bat around the issue of the fate of those who have never heard of Jesus? Do we sit around and argue about the sociological factors that have caused so many fewer people to go to church nowadays than thirty years ago? Or do we rather determine that if sinners will go to hell, it will at least be over our dead bodies? As Charles Haddon Spurgeon put it:

> Oh, my brothers and sisters in Christ, if sinners will be damned, at least let them leap to hell over our bodies; and if they will perish, let them perish with our arms about their knees, imploring them to stay, and not madly to destroy themselves. If hell must be filled, at least let it be filled in the teeth of our exertions, and let no one go there unwarned and unprayed for.[18]

The only appropriate response to the cross is to plead and exhort and pour out our lives to communicate the gospel of Jesus Christ. Like Ezekiel, we must confront men and women here and now with their desperate need to turn from their sins and to receive forgiveness and new life through Christ, and thus live forever with God and his people.

---

18. "The Wailing of Risca," *The New Park Street and Metropolitan Tabernacle Pulpit*, vol. 7 (Pasadena, Tex.: Pilgrim, 1961,1969 reprint), 11.

Ezekiel 19

AKE UP A LAMENT concerning the princes of Israel
²and say:

'''"What a lioness was your mother
    among the lions!
She lay down among the young lions
    and reared her cubs.
³ She brought up one of her cubs,
    and he became a strong lion.
He learned to tear the prey
    and he devoured men.
⁴ The nations heard about him,
    and he was trapped in their pit.
They led him with hooks
    to the land of Egypt.
⁵ '''"When she saw her hope unfulfilled,
    her expectation gone,
she took another of her cubs
    and made him a strong lion.
⁶ He prowled among the lions,
    for he was now a strong lion.
He learned to tear the prey
    and he devoured men.
⁷ He broke down their strongholds
    and devastated their towns.
The land and all who were in it
    were terrified by his roaring.
⁸ Then the nations came against him,
    those from regions round about.
They spread their net for him,
    and he was trapped in their pit.
⁹ With hooks they pulled him into a cage
    and brought him to the king of Babylon.
They put him in prison,
    so his roar was heard no longer
    on the mountains of Israel.
¹⁰ '''"Your mother was like a vine in your vineyard
    planted by the water;

it was fruitful and full of branches
because of abundant water.
¹¹Its branches were strong,
fit for a ruler's scepter.
It towered high
above the thick foliage,
conspicuous for its height
and for its many branches.
¹²But it was uprooted in fury
and thrown to the ground.
The east wind made it shrivel,
it was stripped of its fruit;
its strong branches withered
and fire consumed them.
¹³Now it is planted in the desert,
in a dry and thirsty land.
¹⁴Fire spread from one of its main branches
and consumed its fruit.
No strong branch is left on it
fit for a ruler's scepter.'

This is a lament and is to be used as a lament."

Original Meaning

BY NOW, WE ARE familiar with the versatility with which the prophet delivers his message. Here, while continuing the pictorial speech of the last few chapters, Ezekiel moves from prose into poetry, adopting the form of a lament or dirge.

A lament was a common and distinctive form of song, frequently sung at a funeral, extolling the virtues of the departed and grieving the tragic circumstances surrounding the person's death. A classic example is found in 2 Samuel 1:19–27, where David mourns the deaths of Saul and Jonathan. In the hands of the prophets, however, the genre underwent a change of perspective, for the catalogue of virtues of the departed became a list of faults, while the tragic circumstances of the demise were projected into the future rather than simply recorded from the past.[1] To conduct a "funeral service" for a still-living patient may not always be considered in the best

---

1. Allen, *Ezekiel 1–19*, 285–86. Alternatively, the prophetic use can be described as a "parody" of the lament genre, infusing an incongruous content into a familiar style (Block, *Ezekiel 1–24*, 594).

of taste,[2] but it is an effective way of communicating the certainty with which a death is anticipated! This certainty is particularly striking following on from Ezekiel 18, where the wicked man has been summoned to turn and live.

Ezekiel's lament is made up of two distinct images: a lioness and her cubs, and a vine and its branches. At first sight, these images seem distinct and unconnected. However, both were familiar images for the royal tribe of Judah, and the images are brought together, albeit in a different way, in Jacob's blessing of a ruler who would come from the tribe of Judah (Gen. 49:9–11).[3] When the familiar imagery was combined with the familiar meter (and musical style?) of lament, it would have been immediately apparent to Ezekiel's listeners that what they heard was "a lament concerning the princes of Israel" (Ezek. 19:1).[4]

The first image is of a mother lioness who produces a number of cubs.[5] Out of them, she chooses one to be the leader of the pack. He behaves in lionlike fashion, tearing the prey and even consuming people (19:3). As a result, he is hunted by the nations,[6] captured, and carried off to Egypt (19:4). In his place, she appoints a second cub, who acts with even greater destructiveness (19:6–7). He too is hunted by the nations, captured, and carried into exile, this time to Babylon.

As with the imagery of Ezekiel 16–17, historical facts are built into the picture, resulting in an occasionally incongruous mixture of metaphor and reality. The first cub clearly represents Jehoahaz, who, after a brief three-month reign in 609 B.C., was carried off to Egypt by Pharaoh Neco (2 Kings 23:33–34). His reign is described as tearing the prey and devouring men (Ezek. 19:3). This carnivorous blood lust is sometimes understood not as a blameworthy feature, but simply as describing the normal growth and development of the king within the chosen metaphor.[7] However, given the extension of the metaphor in 19:6 and further in 22:25, where the behavior is

---

2. Ronald M. Hals calls it "incredibly crass" (*Ezekiel* [FOTL 19; Grand Rapids: Eerdmans, 1989], 130).

3. Block demonstrates that there are several lexical links between the two passages (*Ezekiel 1–24*, 603, 608). Ezekiel will also allude to Gen. 49:9–10 in Ezek. 21:27.

4. On Ezekiel's distinctive usage of the phrase "the princes of Israel" (v. 1), see Duguid, *Ezekiel and the Leaders of Israel*, 10–57.

5. Ezek. 19:2a should be translated as a question: "What is your mother? A lioness!" See Block, *Ezekiel 1–24*, 595.

6. Commentators disagree as to the method of hunting. Against the conventional translation of *šaḥat* as "pit," here and in v. 8, Moshe Held has argued that it rather denotes a kind of net, cognate with Akkadian *šētu* ("Pits and Pitfalls in Akkadian and Biblical Hebrew," *JANESCU* 5 [1973]: 173–90). Both methods of hunting lions are attested in antiquity.

7. Zimmerli, *Ezekiel*, 1:394.

clearly reprehensible, that seems unlikely. Rather, it seems probable that Ezekiel exploited an ambiguity that is inherent within the metaphor.

The comparison of kings and lions was old and well established, yet the imagery contains the possibility of powerful men acting like wild beasts that have the capacity to empty the land (2 Kings 17:26). A poetic figure that in some contexts is strongly positive (Gen. 49:9; Deut. 33:20) can in other contexts become a figure of fierce cruelty (Prov. 28:15; Nah. 2:12–13). In terms of the brevity of Jehoahaz's reign, this negative characterization is probably somewhat stylized, yet he may have begun the policies for which his successor Jehoiakim is criticized in Jeremiah 22:13–17.

The second lion behaves similarly to the first, tearing prey and devouring men (19:6). In addition, he "broke down their strongholds[8] and devastated their towns," behavior that breaks out of the metaphorical realm (i.e., behavior appropriate to lions) into the literal realm (i.e., behavior appropriate to kings). The lament is unclear as to whose towns are devastated and which land is terrified of him. Normally, such language would apply to the lion's foes. Yet it is sufficiently ambiguous to cover the actual destruction wreaked on the lion's own country, Judah, whose towns and cities were destroyed as a result of the foolish policies of successive kings.[9] This second lion too, having behaved like a wild animal, was hunted down.

The identity of the second lion has been the object of much debate. The primary choices are Jehoiachin, with whom Ezekiel was exiled, or Zedekiah, his successor, who was exiled in 586 B.C. If the lion metaphor is taken as a separate unit, then Zedekiah is probably the best choice.[10] However, if the entire chapter is viewed as a two-image picture, with a change of metaphor between the first and second images, then Jehoiachin fits best as the second lion, while Zedekiah is then reserved for the second image, that of a vine and its branches.[11] Although much attention has been devoted to the question,

---

8. The NIV here emends a difficult Hebrew text. Taking the MT as it stands, Greenberg explains the literal "he knew his widows" as "he came to know those whom his actions had made widows" (*Ezekiel 1–20*, 351).

9. The Delphic oracle was fond of such ambiguity, as when it told Croesus that if he went to war, he would certainly destroy a great kingdom. The statement was true but deceptive, for the great kingdom he destroyed was not that of his enemies, as he had supposed, but his own.

10. So, most recently, Allen (*Ezekiel 1–19*, 288). Allen argues on the stylistic grounds that the object of a prophetic lament is the future, not the past. The older argument based on identifying the mother lioness as Hamutal, the mother of Jehoahaz and Zedekiah, is less convincing.

11. Block has now suggested Jehoiakim for the second lion, reviving an older interpretation, with Jehoiachin and Zedekiah both represented in the oracle against the vine (*Ezekiel 1–24*, 605). This further underlines the complexity of the task of identification.

the meaning of the passage is not significantly altered by which identification is adopted; the point is that the current rulers of Judah are simply the latest outcroppings of the rock of oppression and pride from which they were hewn.

In the second image, a vine is planted in a vineyard[12] beside abundant waters. The perfect conditions provided for her lead to abundant growth, and in particular many strong branches suitable for a ruler's scepter (19:11). It towers high above the clouds[13] but, as may be expected, pride goes before a fall, and the lofty vine is uprooted, withered by the east wind and stripped of its fruit (19:12). Its strong branches are burned, and the vine is replanted in the desert, in a dry and thirsty land (19:13). Indeed, the destructive fire itself comes from one of the branches and consumes its fruit; the result is that no strong branch is left suitable for a ruler's scepter (19:14).

Once more, the picture is not difficult to decode. The vine is Judah, planted by the Lord in perfect conditions. As a result, she produces many scions capable of ruling. But pride is her downfall. In wrath, the Lord uproots her and withers her, replanting her outside the Promised Land, back in the desert of exile. The fire, which started in one of the branches (Zedekiah), results not simply in a loss of the fruit (destruction of land/people) but also in the annihilation of all the other strong branches (potential rulers). In Zedekiah, the Davidic dynasty will come to a sudden end, at least for the present.

Echoes of chapter 17 are evident throughout this second picture. Both describe a vine planted in conditions suitable for growth (17:5–6), then uprooted in wrath (17:9) and shriveled by the east wind (17:10). The tall tree is brought low (17:24). Though the focus is different, placed on divine action rather than human action, the conclusion for Zedekiah is the same: no escape.

Bridging Contexts

THE OPTIMISM OF contemporary culture. The genre of lament is not a familiar one to contemporary readers, especially in an American context. We live in a culture that is inherently optimistic, which cannot accept the possibility of a definitive verdict of death. We believe in surprising comebacks, in victory snatched from the jaws of defeat, and especially in happy endings. The writer Christopher Lasch comments: "American historical writing takes little account of the

---

12. MT has (lit.) "in your blood" (see NIV note), which may be due to attraction to the similar phrase in Ezek. 16:6, 22. Two Hebrew manuscripts have the reading "your vineyard."

13. NIV "thick foliage" is possible, but Ezekiel uses the same word also in 31:3, 10, 14 to describe a majestic cedar, and there "clouds" seems clearly a better translation. See Greenberg, *Ezekiel 1–20,* 353.

possibility of tragedy—missed opportunities, fatal choices, conclusive and irrevocable defeats. History has to have a happy ending."[14]

Perhaps the closest we normally come to encountering this genre in our culture is in the character of Ebenezer Scrooge, who has become traditional Christmas viewing in one film incarnation or other of Charles Dickens' novel *A Christmas Carol*. Like the princes of Israel, Scrooge hears ahead of time the sound of his own funeral. In keeping with the dictates of our culture, however, Scrooge receives the warning in time and is reformed, resulting in the requisite happy ending.

For Judah under Zedekiah, there is no prospect of a happy ending. Her fate is sealed, along with his; doom, defeat, and despair await them. The lions will be trapped; the vine will be chopped down from its lofty position and replanted not in the Promised Land but in a dry and desert land. The ruler's scepter is gone. Even though there is ultimate hope, as 17:22–24 makes clear, the present situation is one of unmitigated doom. What makes it worse is the fact that it is unmitigated doom in spite of God's good promise. For back in Genesis 49:8–12, a passage with close links in imagery to Ezekiel 19, God promised that the scepter would never depart from the line of Judah, whom he compares to a young lion. But even God's promises cannot be presumed on, if taken out of context. The scepter will indeed depart from Judah, at least for the present time, because of the sins committed by those who held it.

Often the optimism of our culture carries over into the church. During a conversation on the difficulty of church planting in England, an American pastor once remarked to me, "Given $60,000 and two years, I can plant a church here in the United States." Of course, such invincible optimism is not all bad. The pessimism that characterizes my own British culture adopts as its favorite text, "[This is] the day of small things" (Zech. 4:10). It needs to hear the words of Jeremiah: "Ah, Sovereign LORD, you have made the heavens and the earth by your great power and outstretched arm. Nothing is too hard for you" (Jer. 32:17). We should indeed believe that with God all things are possible. But to be true to God's Word, optimism must always be optimism in God's power combined with a healthy pessimism in our own abilities. God can do all things with or without us; without him, we can do nothing (compare Ps. 127:1–3).

Even where that basic point is affirmed in theory, cultural optimism sneaks into our assessment of the church and its mission in practice. Our natural tendency inclines us to believe that small churches ought to grow into larger churches, that missionaries ought to see significant numbers of converts, and that our ministries will certainly prosper, provided we faithfully follow

---

14. *The True and Only Heaven: Progress and Its Critics* (New York: Norton, 1991), 221.

biblical guidelines. This is particularly evident in the exclusive adoption of the biblical imagery of farming and harvest by the church growth movement in their description of missions.

The logic of the argument goes as follows: The church's mission is to gather God's harvest; like any good farmer, God seeks to maximize his production; his strategy (and therefore ours) will be to send workers to where the harvest is most ripe.[15] The possibility of God's calling people to the kind of ministry exercised by Isaiah or Ezekiel may be acknowledged, but it is immediately discounted as an unusual situation.[16] According to this position, the norm *ought* to be successful ministry! But where does such confidence come from? Is it not a version of the view of history described by Christopher Lasch, only given a Christian spin, so that it issues in the conviction that *church* history must have a happy ending?

A reality check. Ultimately, of course, church history does have a happy ending. The final chapters of Revelation assert that no matter what happens in between now and then, the church's position is ultimately secure. In the person of Christ, the promise of God that the scepter will not depart from the line of Judah will be ultimately fulfilled. As the bride of Christ, we are being prepared for the day when Christ will return to make all things new. But does that ultimate optimism allow for, indeed require, a similar optimism for the present, the time between the times? Can we say that we should expect the progress of the church to be smoothly and consistently in a forward direction?

Church history to date hardly seems to support such a notion. What we need is a strong reality check. Areas where the early church was strong are now virtually without a gospel witness; areas that were at the heart of the Reformation now see empty churches and cold hearts. Is that indeed a call for God's workers to go elsewhere? The apostle Paul would not seem to support such an idea. He warned Timothy about the prospect of hard times ahead in ministry, with hearers who would rather turn aside to myths than hear the truth. However, instead of urging him to move on to find "whiter harvests," he told him to keep his head, endure hardship, do the work of an evangelist, and discharge the duties of his ministry (2 Tim. 4:1–5).

The truth is that there is no "norm" in God's work. He calls some to white harvests and notable "success." He calls others to faithful labor with little or no visible reward. Still others live in a day of cold, hard hearts, in which the lack of faithfulness of God's people can only result in disaster for the church,

---

15. For a classic example of this approach, see C. Peter Wagner, *Frontiers in Mission Strategy* (Chicago: Moody, 1971), 41–47.

16. Wagner states confidently, "This is not the norm" (ibid., 47).

unless God graciously sends revival. Sometimes he chooses not to send revival, and a church dies. In the short term, even if not in the long term, the possibility is real that church history may indeed be a record of tragedy— of missed opportunities, of fatal choices, of conclusive and irrevocable defeats. We may need to learn how to lament and weep before the Lord and recognize our sins and those of our fellow Christians that have caused God to depart from our midst. In the midst of the pain of our lamentation, however, our confidence may yet be placed in God's faithfulness. As Lamentations 3:22–24 puts it:

> Because of the LORD's great love we are not consumed,
> for his compassions never fail.
> They are new every morning;
> great is your faithfulness.
> I say to myself, "The LORD is my portion;
> therefore I will wait for him."

GOD'S WONDERFUL PLAN? "God loves you and has a wonderful plan for your life." So runs one part of the presentation of the gospel known as "The Four Spiritual Laws," which has been popularized by Campus Crusade for Christ. This encouraging thought is certainly in line with our culture's optimistic outlook, but is it true? Can we legitimately tell people that God has a wonderful plan for their lives?

Criticism of the statement often runs along the lines that since some of the people to whom we speak are not going to be saved, it is inappropriate to tell them that God's plan for their life is wonderful. What is so wonderful about a plan that ends up in hell? But is it even legitimate to say to Christians, "God has a wonderful plan for your life"? May we legitimately address Christians with the proof text of this position, the Lord's words in Jeremiah 29:11: "I know the plans I have for you ... plans to prosper you and not to harm you, plans to give you hope and a future"?

In one sense, of course, we may. *Ultimately*, God does have a wonderful eternity prepared for his people. "No eye has seen, no ear has heard, no mind has conceived what God has prepared for those who love him" (1 Cor. 2:9). But the more pressing question involves the here and now, the in-between time. The assertion that God has a wonderful plan for our lives often rings hollow when measured up against the realities of day-to-day life. Our lives are frequently more desert than well-watered place. We seem to spend more time at Marah, where the wandering Israelites found the water too bitter to drink, than at Elim, the place of rest with its twelve springs and seventy palm trees, overflowing with abundance (see Ex. 15:22–27).

If we have been sold a promise as Christians that "it's a wonderful life," then we may spend much time struggling with that reality. We may live in permanent denial of life's unpleasant realities or blame ourselves for failing to measure up, because if we were "really spiritual" life wouldn't be this way. The truth is, however, that our present existence is frequently less than wonderful, and the Bible never pretends that it ought to be otherwise. Jeremiah's words were addressed to people living in exile, experiencing in its full harshness the bitterness of life, who needed to be assured that in the midst of the distress, there was still hope for the future. He goes on to denounce those who promise short-term relief (Jer. 29:21–23)! Those who are living comfortably back in Judah, on the other hand, are addressed not with hope but with a message of certain destruction (e.g., 24:8–10).

That destruction was coming on Judah in part because of the sins of their royal leaders. Proud and violent, they had led the people astray from God. Now God was indeed announcing his plan for their life, but it was not what they would call wonderful. Instead, it is a lament, a messenger of sure and certain death. That death would fall not only on the individuals concerned but also on the present Davidic house as a whole. There would be no more second chances, no replacement for Zedekiah as head of the line of David. Just as Isaiah's prophecy of a shoot growing from the stump of Jesse proclaimed the coming of the chain saw of God's judgment on the existing royal line (Isa. 11:1; how else, after all, would you end up with a "stump"?), so also Ezekiel surveys the recent history of the Davidic monarchy and writes on it in large letters, "Failure."

The fulfillment of God's ultimate plan. None of Israel's kings, not even the greatest, David himself, had been able to establish God's kingdom on earth. All of them ultimately failed. None of them could lead God's people into their rest. So the prophet takes out his correction fluid and whites them out as the source of hope. In spite of God's promises, all that is left is a lament. What a depressing truth for Ezekiel's hearers! It means that all of their present hopes in any existing human figure must be crushed, and they must depend entirely on something new that God will do. Nor is there any direct statement in this passage of what form this "new thing" will take.

But the links back to chapter 17 remind us not to forget how that chapter ends, with the promise of a fresh start, a new sprig from the cedar, a new Son of David, who will bring in nothing less than a new world (17:22–24). Isaiah's old prophecy likewise was not simply a statement that God would reduce the house of David to a stump, but that out of that stump a new shoot would grow, through whom God's purposes would be fulfilled (Isa. 11:2–

16). Though Ezekiel laments the fate of the house of David, which is as good as dead, he serves the God who brings life from the dead. God's promises cannot ultimately be destroyed by human weakness and failure, not even by a long history of weakness and failure. In the end, every one of his promises to David will not fail but will be fulfilled in the true Son of David, Jesus Christ.

This passage thus gives both comforting and challenging news for all of us. What makes it challenging news for us is the fact that the same verdict delivered against the house of David stands against us and all of our best efforts. It is not simply the rulers of old who abused their position of power who have fallen short of the glory of God, it is all of us. Like the line of the kings of Israel and Judah, our personal histories are littered with a trail of wrecks. No matter who you are, no matter how squeaky clean your image, when God looks at your life, he writes across it in large letters, "Failure" (cf. Rom. 3:23).

Worst of all, that is true not simply of your most wicked moments, but of your best. It is not just when you are stabbing somebody in the back, or gossiping or stealing or committing adultery that you offend God. It is when you are helping a little old lady across the street, while underneath there is the sneaking thought, "Is anybody seeing what a wonderful person I am?" It is while you are praying in a prayer meeting, or giving to the poor, or feeding the hungry, while all along there is a corner of your heart that is a little impressed with your own goodness and that feels God ought to be impressed too.

Like Judah of old, what you need is not just another (slightly better) version of the same. We make New Year's resolutions and plans to quit this bad habit and abandon that sin and start to do this good thing and generally overhaul our lives. We think, "Next year, I'll be a little better than this. This year wasn't so great, perhaps, but next year things will be different." Ezekiel's lament tells us that New Year's resolutions aren't enough, just as a new Davidic king wouldn't be enough. God will have to do something far more radical to save us.

The good news is that in Jesus Christ God has done precisely such a radical new work. In spite of the failure of all of Judah's kings, good as well as bad, God sent another King, the true "Lion of the tribe of Judah" and "Root of David" (Rev. 5:5). In spite of your personal repeated failure, God has triumphed in Christ to win the salvation of all his people. But this Lion, far from tearing the prey and devouring men (Ezek. 19:6), has conquered by appearing as a Lamb, who has been slain on behalf of his people (Rev. 5:6).

The appearance of this Lamb of God opens a window into heaven that transforms our experience of present realities. Though the present we live in and the immediate future we face may be bleak and forbidding, "a dry and thirsty land" (Ezek. 19:13), that fact no longer devastates us because this world is not our home. It is merely our place of pilgrimage on a journey to our real home. Though now we lament, soon we will go to the place where laments will be no more. Though we now suffer, soon we will be worshiping at the feet of the Lamb in heaven. Though we place no confidence in the flesh, knowing that the glory of this world is passing away and people here will continually disappoint us and fail us, we have full confidence in God and in the efficacy of his promises. We believe that the ruler's scepter has been given into the hand of the Lord Jesus Christ, and ultimately he will rule the nations as King of kings and Lord of lords (Rev. 19:15–16). In that promise lies a sure and certain hope that our failures are not the end of the story. God's faithfulness is.

IN THE SEVENTH YEAR, in the fifth month on the tenth day, some of the elders of Israel came to inquire of the LORD, and they sat down in front of me.

²Then the word of the LORD came to me: ³"Son of man, speak to the elders of Israel and say to them, 'This is what the Sovereign LORD says: Have you come to inquire of me? As surely as I live, I will not let you inquire of me, declares the Sovereign LORD.'

⁴"Will you judge them? Will you judge them, son of man? Then confront them with the detestable practices of their fathers ⁵and say to them: 'This is what the Sovereign LORD says: On the day I chose Israel, I swore with uplifted hand to the descendants of the house of Jacob and revealed myself to them in Egypt. With uplifted hand I said to them, "I am the LORD your God." ⁶On that day I swore to them that I would bring them out of Egypt into a land I had searched out for them, a land flowing with milk and honey, the most beautiful of all lands. ⁷And I said to them, "Each of you, get rid of the vile images you have set your eyes on, and do not defile yourselves with the idols of Egypt. I am the LORD your God."

⁸"'But they rebelled against me and would not listen to me; they did not get rid of the vile images they had set their eyes on, nor did they forsake the idols of Egypt. So I said I would pour out my wrath on them and spend my anger against them in Egypt. ⁹But for the sake of my name I did what would keep it from being profaned in the eyes of the nations they lived among and in whose sight I had revealed myself to the Israelites by bringing them out of Egypt. ¹⁰Therefore I led them out of Egypt and brought them into the desert. ¹¹I gave them my decrees and made known to them my laws, for the man who obeys them will live by them. ¹²Also I gave them my Sabbaths as a sign between us, so they would know that I the LORD made them holy.

¹³"'Yet the people of Israel rebelled against me in the desert. They did not follow my decrees but rejected my laws—although the man who obeys them will live by them— and they utterly desecrated my Sabbaths. So I said I would

pour out my wrath on them and destroy them in the desert.
¹⁴But for the sake of my name I did what would keep it from
being profaned in the eyes of the nations in whose sight I had
brought them out. ¹⁵Also with uplifted hand I swore to them
in the desert that I would not bring them into the land I had
given them—a land flowing with milk and honey, most beautiful of all lands—¹⁶because they rejected my laws and did not
follow my decrees and desecrated my Sabbaths. For their
hearts were devoted to their idols. ¹⁷Yet I looked on them
with pity and did not destroy them or put an end to them in
the desert. ¹⁸I said to their children in the desert, "Do not follow the statutes of your fathers or keep their laws or defile
yourselves with their idols. ¹⁹I am the LORD your God; follow
my decrees and be careful to keep my laws. ²⁰Keep my Sabbaths holy, that they may be a sign between us. Then you will
know that I am the LORD your God."

²¹'"But the children rebelled against me: They did not follow my decrees, they were not careful to keep my laws—
although the man who obeys them will live by them—and
they desecrated my Sabbaths. So I said I would pour out my
wrath on them and spend my anger against them in the desert.
²²But I withheld my hand, and for the sake of my name I did
what would keep it from being profaned in the eyes of the
nations in whose sight I had brought them out. ²³Also with
uplifted hand I swore to them in the desert that I would disperse them among the nations and scatter them through the
countries, ²⁴because they had not obeyed my laws but had
rejected my decrees and desecrated my Sabbaths, and their
eyes lusted after their fathers' idols. ²⁵I also gave them over to
statutes that were not good and laws they could not live by;
²⁶I let them become defiled through their gifts—the sacrifice
of every firstborn—that I might fill them with horror so they
would know that I am the LORD.'

²⁷"Therefore, son of man, speak to the people of Israel and
say to them, 'This is what the Sovereign LORD says: In this
also your fathers blasphemed me by forsaking me: ²⁸When I
brought them into the land I had sworn to give them and they
saw any high hill or any leafy tree, there they offered their sacrifices, made offerings that provoked me to anger, presented
their fragrant incense and poured out their drink offerings.
²⁹Then I said to them: What is this high place you go to?'" (It
is called Bamah to this day.)

³⁰"Therefore say to the house of Israel: 'This is what the Sovereign LORD says: Will you defile yourselves the way your fathers did and lust after their vile images? ³¹When you offer your gifts—the sacrifice of your sons in the fire—you continue to defile yourselves with all your idols to this day. Am I to let you inquire of me, O house of Israel? As surely as I live, declares the Sovereign LORD, I will not let you inquire of me.

³²"'You say, "We want to be like the nations, like the peoples of the world, who serve wood and stone." But what you have in mind will never happen. ³³As surely as I live, declares the Sovereign LORD, I will rule over you with a mighty hand and an outstretched arm and with outpoured wrath. ³⁴I will bring you from the nations and gather you from the countries where you have been scattered—with a mighty hand and an outstretched arm and with outpoured wrath. ³⁵I will bring you into the desert of the nations and there, face to face, I will execute judgment upon you. ³⁶As I judged your fathers in the desert of the land of Egypt, so I will judge you, declares the Sovereign LORD. ³⁷I will take note of you as you pass under my rod, and I will bring you into the bond of the covenant. ³⁸I will purge you of those who revolt and rebel against me. Although I will bring them out of the land where they are living, yet they will not enter the land of Israel. Then you will know that I am the LORD.

³⁹"'As for you, O house of Israel, this is what the Sovereign LORD says: Go and serve your idols, every one of you! But afterward you will surely listen to me and no longer profane my holy name with your gifts and idols. ⁴⁰For on my holy mountain, the high mountain of Israel, declares the Sovereign LORD, there in the land the entire house of Israel will serve me, and there I will accept them. There I will require your offerings and your choice gifts, along with all your holy sacrifices. ⁴¹I will accept you as fragrant incense when I bring you out from the nations and gather you from the countries where you have been scattered, and I will show myself holy among you in the sight of the nations. ⁴²Then you will know that I am the LORD, when I bring you into the land of Israel, the land I had sworn with uplifted hand to give to your fathers. ⁴³There you will remember your conduct and all the actions by which you have defiled yourselves, and you will loathe yourselves for all the evil you have done. ⁴⁴You will know that I am the

LORD, when I deal with you for my name's sake and not
according to your evil ways and your corrupt practices,
O house of Israel, declares the Sovereign LORD.'"

AFTER FIVE CHAPTERS of largely pictorial speech—
proverbs, riddles, parables, and laments—the
prophet returns to the language of straightforward history. This change is marked by a renewed
interaction between the prophet and his public. In Ezekiel 15–19, the word
of the Lord comes to the prophet unsought, though in some cases in response
to sayings that had become common currency among God's people. Now,
however, the prophetic speech is triggered by an attempt on the part of the
"elders of Israel" to inquire of the Lord, as in Ezekiel 14.

The "elders of Israel"[1] were the lay leaders of the exilic community (see
Jer. 29:1), and they appear at key points of Ezekiel's indictment of the people (Ezek. 8:1; 14:1; 20:1). In each case, the charge leveled against the elders
is secret idolatry (8:11; 14:3), a sin they share with the people at large. The
very ones who once led the people in receiving a foretaste of the pouring out
of the Spirit (Num. 11:24–25) now lead the people in their spiritual adultery.[2]

It is now the summer of 591 B.C. The elders have assembled before Ezekiel
in order to "inquire of the LORD" (20:1). Now, as a life-stance, "inquiring of
the LORD" or "seeking the LORD" would have been commendable; indeed, in
Amos 5:4 the Lord addresses the house of Israel in precisely those terms:
"Seek me and live." But as Amos goes on to point out, seeking the Lord can
never be simply one part of a broadly based religious strategy. Seeking the
Lord is, by definition, exclusive: To seek the Lord means not to seek the calf
idols of Bethel (Amos 5:5). But this is precisely where the elders fail the test.
Because they are involved in the idolatrous practices of their ancestors, the
Lord will not answer them.[3] The door is so firmly closed in their faces that
the prophet does not even bother to record the substance of their request.

---

1. The exact title given to this group varies. In Ezek. 8:11 they are called the "elders of
the house of Israel," while 14:1 and 20:1, 3 speak of the "elders of Israel." Probably the same
group is indicated by the "elders of Judah" in 8:1 (Duguid, *Ezekiel and the Leaders of Israel*, 112).

2. Ibid., 113–18.

3. The niphal of *dāraš* (seek, inquire of) in the Lord's statement is often translated as a
"tolerative Niphal" ("I will not allow them to inquire of me"). However, as Bruce Waltke and
Michael O'Connor point out, "the tolerative *Niphal* often involves the element of efficacy:
what the subject allows to happen can indeed be carried through" (*An Introduction to Biblical
Hebrew Syntax* [Winona Lake, Ind.: Eisenbrauns, 1990], 23.4g). Thus, the point is not so much
that the Lord will put a stop to their seeking but their seeking will be ineffective; they will
seek but not find.

They might just as well not have said a word. In fact, they may not even have reached the point of framing their question before they are cut off. It is not *what they ask* that the Lord finds unacceptable but *who they are*.[4]

Yet (perhaps surprisingly) the chapter does not end here. Although the Lord will not answer them in terms of what they are seeking, he has a message for them to hear, addressed directly to their sin (20:4–5; cf. 14:4). Ezekiel is called to join God in judging the elders by confronting them with their sin. He is to present to them a history of Israel from God's perspective. That is, it is a history that focuses not on Israel's history of cultural and political achievements but rather on their history of idolatry. Ezekiel is to confront the elders with "the detestable practices of their fathers" (20:4).[5]

The way in which Ezekiel challenges the elders with Israel's history has more than a little in common with chapter 18. It is essentially a story of three consecutive generations, with intended application to the present generation. The choice laid before each generation is obedience to the Lord's life-giving laws (Ezek. 20:11, 21; cf. 18:9) or death-dealing disobedience (20:23–25; cf. 18:13). The three generations Ezekiel chooses here for his case study are the generation who lived in Egypt at the time of the Exodus (20:5–10), the desert generation (vv. 11–15), and their children (vv. 18–23). Each generation's history is presented as a six-stage cycle:[6]

(1) The Lord's self-revelation (vv. 5–6, 11, 18–19)
(2) A challenge to exclusive devotion (vv. 7, 12, 19–20)
(3) Israel's rebellion (vv. 8, 13, 21)
(4) The threat of the Lord's wrath (vv. 8b, 13b, 21b)
(5) Wrath limited/deferred for the sake of the divine name (vv. 9, 14, 22)
(6) Act of limited judgment (vv. 10, 17, 23)

According to this schema, each new generation is confronted for itself with a fresh revelation of the Lord. To each comes the gracious self-announcement "I am the LORD" (20:12, 20, cf. v. 5). The basis for this self-revelation is not Israel's merit but divine election and a covenant oath sworn by God to bring

---

4. Commentators have made many ingenious suggestions as to the substance of their query, based on inferences drawn from Ezekiel's response to them. But the whole point is that Ezekiel's response is not an answer to their inquiry! See Greenberg, *Ezekiel 1–20*, 387–88.

5. The phrase "the detestable practices of their fathers" is itself a striking inversion of the regular Deuteronomic phrase "the detestable ways of the nations" (Deut. 18:9). At the outset, Ezekiel's charge is clear: Israel's ancestors were no better than the pagan nations they replaced in Canaan (Block, *Ezekiel 1–24*, 620).

6. My analysis is broadly the same as that of Franz Sedlmeier, *Studien zu Komposition und Theologie von Ezechiel 20* (Stuttgarter Biblische Beiträge 21; Stuttgart: Verlag Katholisches Bibelwerk, 1990), 212.

them to the Promised Land (Ezek. 20:5).[7] His care for them was demonstrated in "searching out"[8] the perfect location for them to inhabit, "a land flowing with milk and honey, the most beautiful of all lands" (20:6). But this decisive act in Israel's history required a response on the part of Israel of exclusive devotion to the Lord. To the first generation, it meant getting rid of their vile images and the idols of Egypt (20:7).[9] To the second generation, it meant obeying the Lord's decrees and laws given at Sinai (20:11–12).

Of these decrees, Ezekiel singles out for particular mention the Sabbath law. The Sabbath was foundational to the Israelite view of sacred time and community. In Exodus 31:16–17, the Lord said to Moses:

> The Israelites are to observe the Sabbath, celebrating it for the generations to come as a lasting covenant. It will be a sign between me and the Israelites forever. . . .

With its regular one day in seven observance, the Sabbath cut across the nature-based calendars of the pagans, which revolved solely around phases of the moon and agricultural seasons. Instead, it called God's people to march to the beat of a different drum, as a mark of submission to their covenant overlord.[10] It was a sign of their liberation from bondage (for slaves are not in control of their schedule) but also a sign of their distinctiveness from other nations who had not been similarly redeemed. To profane the Sabbath was thus to abandon an essential element of their distinctiveness as the people of the Lord and to attempt, in effect, to "become like the nations around us." It is to refuse to follow the example that God himself set in Genesis 2:1–4. This same requirement ("Follow my decrees and be careful to keep my laws. Keep my Sabbaths holy") is reiterated to the next generation as well (Ezek. 20:18–20).

But Israel's consistent response to this gracious self-revelation was rebellion. Three times that rebellion is detailed, not simply in general terms but

---

7. This is the only use in Ezekiel of the verb *bāḥar* ("he chose"). This verb is a favorite of Deuteronomic literature to express the relationship between the Lord and Israel; see Moshe Weinfeld, *Deuteronomy and the Deuteronomic School* (Oxford: Clarendon, 1972), 327.

8. *tûr* is earlier used of the Lord's preparing campsites in the desert ahead of his people (Deut. 1:33) and of the spies reconnoitering the land (Num. 13:1–2). These echoes underline the history of Israel's perverseness: Before the spies searched out the land and by a majority vote declared it unsuitable, God had already searched it out and declared it good.

9. The historical validity of this representation is frequently questioned (e.g., by Zimmerli, *Ezekiel*, 1:409). However, the rapidity with which the people slid into idolatry in the desert, constructing a golden calf barely three months after their departure from Egypt (Ex. 32), hardly suggests that their pre-exodus state was one of untarnished devotion to the Lord!

10. Walter J. Harrelson, *From Fertility Cult to Worship* (Garden City, N.Y.: Doubleday, 1969), 30. Compare Matitiyahu Tsevat, "The Basic Meaning of the Biblical Sabbath," *ZAW* 84 (1972): 455.

specifically as the failure to keep themselves distinct in the terms of the requirements of stage (2) of the cycle (20:7, 12, 19–20). Three times the Lord threatened[11] to pour out his wrath on them once and for all, destroying them utterly. Yet each time he held back his hand, not because such a judgment was in any sense undeserved, but for the honor of his name, lest the nations around Israel read her destruction as the Lord's inability to protect his own (cf. Num. 14:15–16).

Nonetheless, in each case limited judgment does fall: First-generation Israel exits Egypt and finds itself not in a beautiful land flowing with milk and honey but in the desert (20:10). The next generation does not inherit the Promised Land either but are doomed to die in the desert (20:15). The third generation not only fails to inherit the Promised Land but will be scattered among the nations (20:23). The upraised hand, swearing on oath to bring the chosen people into the land of promise (20:5), now becomes an upraised hand swearing on oath that this generation shall never enter (20:15), and finally swearing that they will rather go into exile (20:23). The unfaithful elect experience the covenant curses, not the covenant blessings.

In addition, in place of God's good decrees and statutes (20:11), this generation is handed over to "not good" statutes, laws that led not to right-eousness and life but to defilement and death (20:25).[12] These "not good" statutes meant not only death for them but death for their firstborn sons, offered up in the fire to Molech.[13] The end point of Israel's story is thus the utter reverse of the goal at the beginning. Israel, the Lord's "firstborn son" (Ex. 4:22), was to be freed from Egypt so that he could offer pure worship in the Promised Land (4:23). But through their rebellion the Israelites instead end up sacrificing their own firstborn sons in the pursuit of defiled worship, with the threat of inevitable exile hanging over them like a Damoclean sword.

To this threefold cycle of gracious election, rebellion, and limited judgment, a coda is added in 20:27–29, briefly bringing the story up to date. Lest anyone should argue that Ezekiel is raking up old history long forgotten, he replies that the history of Israel's occupation of Canaan is similarly depressing. Their ongoing love affair with the high places and their defiled worship proves that they are under God's judgment, even in the sworn land

---

11. The NIV's "So I said ..." (20:8, 13, 21) is too weak. For *ʾāmar* as "threaten" see BDB 56c, which cites also Deut. 9:25; see also NLT.

12. Note that these "not good" statutes and laws are not termed "my decrees and ... laws" by the Lord (in contrast to the "good" statutes and laws that they rejected (vv. 11, 19, 24). See Leslie C. Allen, *Ezekiel 20–48* (WBC 29; Dallas: Word, 1990), 12.

13. On this practice, see George C. Heider, *The Cult of Molek: A Reassessment* (JSOTS 43; Sheffield: JSOT, 1985).

of promise (20:28), down to this very day (*ᶜad hayyôm hazzeh*, the last words of 20:29). Today is, after all, Ezekiel's interest, as the repetition of the phrase in 20:31 makes clear. Israel's present is exactly the same as Israel's past: vile images, child sacrifice, and idolatry (20:31). Surely Israel is a rebellious house, not just in times past but in the present, as the Lord had made clear to Ezekiel in 2:3. Such people need not expect any reply to their attempts to inquire of the Lord (20:31).

But what should they expect from the Lord? The answer given in 20:32–44 may surprise us, though it is already implicit in the account Ezekiel has given of Israel's history. God will act, not to destroy his people utterly but rather to fulfill his original purposes in election: to establish a purified people to worship him (20:40–41). He will do this through a new exodus, not because of any merit on Israel's part but for the sake of his own name (20:44).

This answer, as we have said, is already implicit in Ezekiel's rendering of history. The reason for the focus on the generations around the Exodus rather than the generation of the patriarchs or those during the occupation of the land now becomes clear. There is an analogy to be drawn between the Exodus/desert generation and his own. The present position of the exilic generation in the six-part cycle of sin and judgment is (6): Israel's rebellion has led to a limited judgment on the Lord's part—specifically, the scattering among the nations, mentioned in 20:23. But as the three-generation cycle makes clear, *(6) can never be the end of the story!* God's people cannot be destroyed completely, not because they do not deserve it but because God has staked the reputation of his own name on the covenant promises made to them. He may and indeed does chastise them and judge them, but he can never abandon them utterly. His divine nature requires faithfulness to his promise, even in the face of unrelenting human sin (cf. Hos. 11:8–11).

Therefore, there must necessarily be a new act of salvation on God's part, a new exodus. Israel cannot be abandoned to "be like the nations, like the peoples of the world, who serve wood and stone," as the elders had thought (Ezek. 20:32)! Whether that thought is one of desire ("We want to be like the nations ...")[14] or of despair ("We are become like the nations ...")[15] is not really the issue; rather, the focus is on the impossibility of such a thing happening for God has staked his reputation on them (cf. 36:22–23).

Divine election cannot be revoked; the Lord will reign over them (20:33). The echoes of 1 Samuel 8 are not coincidental. There, too, the people had sought to become "such as all the other nations" by having a king (8:5), which is interpreted as a rejection of the Lord's reign over them (8:7). They

---

14. So NIV; Greenberg, *Ezekiel 1–20*, 371.
15. Zimmerli, *Ezekiel*, 1:414.

are warned of the real consequences of their choice (8:11–18), yet ultimately their election is not revocable. They do not, indeed cannot, become like the nations around them: instead, even their rebellious wish for a monarchy is subsumed in the providence of God. The Lord himself gives them the kings of his own choosing, good and bad, to prepare the way for the coming of the King of kings.

Similarly, the message of God's kingship exercised in a new exodus is not necessarily good news. Yes, his reign comes with a mighty hand and outstretched arm, as in the first exodus (Deut. 4:34 and frequently); yes, he will bring them out of the nations and gather them just as he once brought them out of Egypt (Ezek. 20:34). But in addition, his reign comes with outpoured wrath. Just as the unfaithful Israelites were brought up out of Egypt only to die in the desert, so too the regathered Israel will be purged in the "desert of the nations" (20:35). There God will meet with his people "face to face," just as he met with Moses "face to face" in the tent of meeting (Ex. 33:11).

But this face-to-face meeting will not be that of two friends, as it was with Moses, but rather a meeting of personal judgment. The use of the Niphal of *šāpaṭ* underlines the legal nature of this encounter.[16] God will go to court against the rebels among his people, singling out the transgressors from the faithful just as a shepherd counts and separates his sheep by passing them one by one under his rod (Ezek. 20:37).

The application to the present generation comes in 20:39. The choice is, in one sense, theirs to make. They may go and serve their idols, if they wish. But they must remember this: that God's purpose in the election of Israel will stand. A time is coming when in place of the profane worship offered on every high hill and under every leafy tree there will be pure worship offered in the one true place, God's holy mountain, the high mountain of Israel (20:40).

This looks forward in seed form to the full description of the renewed Israel at worship on a high mountain in chapters 40–48. The positive result of the new exodus will be pure worship offered by a purified people, in whom the Lord's holiness is publicly displayed to the eyes of the nations. There the oath made in Egypt (20:5) will be fulfilled (20:42), and there the remnant who survived the desert judgment—not on merit but by grace—will appreciate the immensity of their own sin and the faithfulness of God to his covenant promises (20:44). The future for Israel depends entirely on God and his commitment to his Word. But those who refuse to trust God to fulfill his promises and instead have turned their backs on him will never enter the new Promised Land.

---

16. Block, *Ezekiel 1–24*, 651.

Bridging Contexts

CONTEMPORARY CHOICES. In a world of disposable relationships, it is hard for us to grasp the meaning of a covenant bond. We live increasingly in a culture where people change spouses like former generations used to trade in their cars—whenever they start making noises we don't care for, or after three to five years, whichever comes sooner. As a culture, we tend to make and break friendships frequently, as we or our friends move on to new places or as we grow apart from one another. As a culture, we are inclined to abandon the older generation to nursing homes when they become too much of a burden to us. The idea of sticking with a long-term relationship through thick and thin is, if not yet utterly foreign to our experience, at least becoming a rarity. We are, after all, the consumer generation; we tend to view people as products—commodities to be used as long as they meet our needs and fulfill our desires, but always likely to become obsolete or superseded by a "new and improved" product.[17]

This attitude has filtered through into our understanding of religion. Thus, we do not have a lifetime commitment to one church or even to one denomination, but change our churches whenever we find one that better meets our needs. According to George Barna, in the near future "people will no longer have a single church home but multiple church homes. On any given Sunday they will wake up and choose a particular church which they feel will meet the needs they feel most keenly that morning."[18]

This attitude holds true not merely of one's choice of church but across religions as well. Perhaps as never before people are "choosing their religion," not on the basis of whether the religion is "true" or "false" but whether that particular religious perspective "works for them." In the marketplace of religious ideas, all perspectives are regarded as being equally valid; may the best marketer win![19]

The one nonnegotiable in this process, from a contemporary perspective, is personal choice.[20] As the bumper sticker expounds it: "Attend the church or synagogue of your choice this week!" Which church or synagogue most

---

17. See Rodney Clapp, "Why the Devil Takes Visa: A Christian Response to the Triumph of Consumerism," *Christianity Today* 40 (Oct. 7, 1996): 19–33.

18. "The Church of the 90's: Meeting the Needs of a Changing Culture," *Reformed Seminary Journal* (September 1990), 11. This trend is already visible. Wade Clark Roof cites the case of a man who described himself as "primarily Catholic," who as well as attending weekly Mass also belongs to an ecumenical prayer group and frequently worships at a local evangelical church because of its "good preaching" (*A Generation of Seekers*, 245).

19. See R. C. Sproul, *Choosing My Religion* (Grand Rapids: Baker, 1995).

20. Roof states: "Personal autonomy rather than family heritage or religious background will increasingly be the basis on which one relates to the sacred. What a person chooses rather than is born into will be decisive" (*A Generation of Seekers*, 259).

fully expounds the truth about God is apparently not an issue; for many, it is not even a relevant question. The important factor is that this is the religion and church that you have chosen.

Not our choice but the Lord's. It is hard to imagine a viewpoint more radically different from that of Ezekiel 20. For Ezekiel, what is definitive is not Israel's choice but *the Lord's* choice. Israel in the past had frequently, even invariably, chosen wrongly. "Attending the church or synagogue of their choice" had led to worshiping idols in Egypt and the pagan gods and goddesses in the land of Canaan. Such idolatrous worship frequently had the marketing edge on true worship. People voted with their feet in favor of the false rather than the true. Yet even though the people were unfaithful, God remained faithful to his covenant promises and his own character. God could not walk away from Israel like a manufacturer who simply discontinues an unprofitable or defect-prone line and retools a product to meet the demand of changing times.

The one nonnegotiable for Ezekiel, therefore, is God's choice: Israel's "choice" only occurs in the context of their prior chosenness as the covenant community. They can choose to fulfill their calling, to be a blessing and so to receive life. Or they can choose to rebel against that calling, seeking to be free of that chosenness like the nations around them, and face the consequences. If they choose to be like the nations, by God himself (note the oath formula of 20:33) there will be hell to pay. God's judgment will certainly fall on those who choose the false worship over the true. The salvific event of a new exodus will bring nothing but judgment for them, just as the first exodus led to judgment in the desert for a whole generation. Yet, in spite of that, God's salvation purposes are unshakable: He will establish his chosen ones not in the "church of their choice" but in the holy mountain of his choosing, the new city of God (20:40).[21]

THE WORLD REVOLVES around God. John Corrie identifies the following trends as typical of postmodern culture:

It is a culture characterized by freedom of choice in which we are invited to "pick'n'mix" our own philosophy of life. Furthermore ... it is hedonistic and materialistic; it generates a breakdown of respect for

---

21. Ezekiel never uses the terminology of the "new Jerusalem" for the visionary city of the future, probably because of his negative portrayal of its past. For him, Jerusalem is the Great Prostitute (cf. Ezek. 16; 23). But it is clear what city he has in mind, in purified form, and the language of Revelation 21:2 suggests that such a designation is appropriate for our use.

authority, confusion on moral absolutes and a fierce individualism which destroys community values. It is a culture in search of meaning, significance and purpose, since it breaks down any unified sense of reality, creating anonymity and atomization.[22]

Ezekiel has some hard words for such a generation that has institutionalized and glorified rebellion under the banner of "choice." It summons a people who think that the world revolves around themselves to a Copernican change in their thought: We are called to accept the truth that the world rather revolves around God.

But what are the implications for us, who are called to proclaim the gospel in this culture? We need to remind people that what matters is not what we think about God but what he thinks of us.[23] I once met a woman who told me that she kept a Bible and literature from Mormons and Jehovah's Witnesses alongside her child's bed so that when he grew up he could choose for himself what to believe. Such a view is frequently regarded as highly enlightened in our day and age, where everything is tolerated except intolerance.[24] Ezekiel would not have been greatly surprised by such a view, for already in his day people sought to match the "enlightened attitudes" of those around them. He has another word for it than broad-mindedness, though: For him, it is rebellion against the one true and living God.

The true nature of rebellion. Rebellion is never simply against an abstract conception of God, however, but against the personal God of grace. Satan always seeks to persuade us, as he did our first parents, that God is a harsh taskmaster who will exploit us and abuse us if we allow him, and that he seeks to deny us things that are good (Gen. 3:1).[25] The reality is exactly the opposite, for them and for us. God had made a perfect world for Adam and Eve to live in and placed them in the most perfect spot within it, a paradise. Their area of personal freedom was large; the restriction minuscule. Yet being deceived into reading that minuscule restriction as bondage, they gave in to Satan's temptation, only to discover too late what true bondage was.

Similarly, God came to Israel in the midst of their miserable bondage and offered them the way to the total freedom of pure worship. He promised

---

22. "A New Way of Being the Church? Liberation Theology and the Mission of the Church in a Postmodern Context," *Evangel* 14 (Summer 1996): 50.

23. C. S. Lewis, *The Weight of Glory and Other Addresses* (Grand Rapids: Eerdmans, 1972), 10.

24. A study of attitudes among members of Generation X (those born between 1963 and 1977) cites " lack of dogmatism" as one of five main characteristics that Xers are looking for in faith groups. See Andrés Tapia, "Reaching the First Post-Christian Generation," *Christianity Today* 38 (Sept. 12, 1994): 18–23.

25. This portrayal of God as an abuser and exploiter is not merely an ancient heresy; it is precisely the picture of God that David Halperin reads into this passage (*Seeking Ezekiel*, 170).

them not just any land but a beautiful land for their own (Ezek. 20:6). Only the very best would do for God's people. They, however, sought only half-freedom. They wanted freedom from the unpleasant circumstances of their sin and from its messy complications, but not freedom from the sin itself. They would rather keep their idols and perish in the desert than enter the Promised Land without them.

So also in our day many seek meaning, significance, and purpose—but only on their own terms. Spirituality is a growth market. We are surrounded by a generation of seekers, who assume that God can be found whenever and wherever they choose to seek him. For them, "seeking" is another word for "shopping." But, as the elders discovered, God is not a cosmic merchandiser, for whom "the customer is always right." It is possible, indeed inevitable, that the determinedly open-minded seeker will not find an answer from Israel's God.

A downward spiral. What is more, left to itself rebellion naturally heads into a downward spiral. From Adam to Cain is only one generation, but in that time we move from humankind having to be talked into sin by Satan (Gen. 3:1) to humankind unwilling to be talked out of sin by God (4:6–7). By the time we arrive at Lamech, seven generations from Adam, we have already reached the poetic glorification of gratuitous violence, a kind of primeval version of "gangsta rap" (4:23–24). Not even the cosmic judgment of the Flood can reverse the downward trend of sin.

So too for Israel. As the generations pass, Israel's idolatry goes from bad to worse, moving from idolatry in Egypt and disobedience to God's life-giving law in the desert, to culminate in perverse obedience to laws and statutes that lead to death, even to the sacrifice of their firstborn children. What then shall we say of our own era, in which idolatry is not so much tolerated as celebrated? The cover of a New Age mail order catalog declares as their slogan, "Live fully; laugh often; love all ways; look within."[26] The biblical command to love always (Eph. 5:2) is now enculturated as the injunction to "love all ways."

But at the same time as our society embraces a tolerance that freely encompasses even the intolerable, we also see the growth of death-giving statutes. The idea of euthanasia is finding growing acceptance in this country, as in many others around the world.[27] At present, it operates around the fringes of legality, but its supporters continue to press for legal recognition. We too have adopted our own form of child sacrifice, slaughtering countless unborn

---

26. The Red Rose Collection, San Francisco, Calif.; October 1996.

27. See *Religion and Medical Ethics*, ed. Allen Verhey (Grand Rapids: Eerdmans, 1996), 135–38.

babies on the altars of the secular gods of convenience and comfort, of reputation and respectability.[28]

We find ourselves today, then, perhaps more clearly than our parents did, in the midst of a society that is in headlong rebellion against God and is reaping the fruits of that rebellion in seared consciences and irrationally self-destructive behaviors. We live in the midst of a society of adults and children suffering the traumatic effects of broken relationships, in some cases ending up in alcohol and drug addiction as a means of deadening the pain of their deep sense of rejection and alienation. Others have buried themselves in their work and career, seeking some kind of significance for their lives. Thus far Ezekiel's words address us clearly.

Implications of rebellion for contemporary society. What, then, are the implications of Ezekiel 20 for such a generation? Two things come across clearly in this chapter. (1) On the one hand, rebellion will inevitably be punished. Israel can never simply choose to be like the nations and thus remove herself from God's authority. There are only two choices for Israel: She can choose to accept her election and live on the basis of God's laws, or she can rebel as she has so often before and face the consequences of certain death. Likewise, our generation needs people within the covenant community who are prophetically willing to call a spade a spade, to call sin sin, to speak of death and hell and the judgment to come. We need to confront the socially acceptable idols of comfort and success and career progress, which many in our churches attempt to combine with a commitment to Christ, as well as the more blatantly pagan idolatries.

We need to confront in our own hearts the continual temptation to remake our understanding of God into a comfortable reflection of our own image instead of submitting unreservedly to his self-revelation in Scripture. It is not a comfortable message to proclaim in an age that calls idols of wood and stone "different paths to God" and the high places "the church of your choice." But God has not changed and the reality of his wrath must be recognized. Otherwise, we are simply deceiving ourselves and those around us with lies about God.

(2) On the other hand, Ezekiel 20 should also fill Christians with profound optimism. For it asserts that, come hell or high water, with or without the help of his church, God's kingdom will come. His purposes in election are so sure that not even Israel's continual history of sin can thwart them. Though in the providence of God his first exodus did not bring to fruition his purpose of a pure, worshiping people, the second exodus will.

---

28. As Frederica Mathewes-Green points out, the idolatry is not always on the part of the women who have the abortion; frequently, family or peer pressure are significant factors ("Why Women Choose Abortion," *Christianity Today* 39 (Jan. 9, 1995): 21—25.

What, however, is this second exodus of which Ezekiel speaks? In some postexilic literature the return to Judah under Cyrus is portrayed as a second exodus,[29] yet the tone of partial fulfillment predominates in these books. Those who participated in the return were well aware of how far short it fell of the extravagant language of the prophets. It is more of a first stage in the second exodus that the exodus itself. Not until Jesus comes proclaiming the good news of liberation does the exodus start in earnest (Luke 4:18—19). Yet, as Ezekiel makes clear, the goal of the second exodus, like that of the first exodus, is not simply liberation. This is the problem with much liberation theology. Though the exodus from Egypt is proclaimed as the paradigm,[30] the goal of that exodus is lost from view. The people are redeemed and purified from Babylon and Egypt *so that they can worship*. The goal of exodus, indeed of all salvation, is a purified people worshiping the one true God.

Ezekiel describes that pure worship in typical Old Testament terms: sacrifices offered in a restored temple. But even though at the return to the land the temple was rebuilt and sacrifices were offered, something was still missing. The fulfillment of Ezekiel's worship, as for all Old Testament worship, is found in Jesus Christ, who affirmed to the woman of Samaria a new era of worship. In this new era, people will worship neither on Mount Gerizim nor in Jerusalem, nor even on Ezekiel's high mountain, but in spirit and in truth. With the coming of Jesus, as the mediator of the new covenant, the true "new age" of worship has dawned, the age of the worship of the redeemed community in the presence of God himself (Heb. 12:22—24).

---

29. Williamson, *Ezra, Nehemiah*, li.

30. See, for example, Gustavo Gutiérrez, *A Theology of Liberation*, trans. C. I. & J. Eagleson (Maryknoll, N.Y.: Orbis, 1973), 159.

Ezekiel 20:45–21:32

୧

THE WORD OF THE LORD came to me: ⁴⁶"Son of man, set your face toward the south; preach against the south and prophesy against the forest of the southland. ⁴⁷Say to the southern forest: 'Hear the word of the LORD. This is what the Sovereign LORD says: I am about to set fire to you, and it will consume all your trees, both green and dry. The blazing flame will not be quenched, and every face from south to north will be scorched by it. ⁴⁸Everyone will see that I the LORD have kindled it; it will not be quenched.'"

⁴⁹Then I said, "Ah, Sovereign LORD! They are saying of me, 'Isn't he just telling parables?'"

²¹:¹The word of the LORD came to me: ²"Son of man, set your face against Jerusalem and preach against the sanctuary. Prophesy against the land of Israel ³and say to her: 'This is what the LORD says: I am against you. I will draw my sword from its scabbard and cut off from you both the righteous and the wicked. ⁴Because I am going to cut off the righteous and the wicked, my sword will be unsheathed against everyone from south to north. ⁵Then all people will know that I the LORD have drawn my sword from its scabbard; it will not return again.'

⁶"Therefore groan, son of man! Groan before them with broken heart and bitter grief. ⁷And when they ask you, 'Why are you groaning?' you shall say, 'Because of the news that is coming. Every heart will melt and every hand go limp; every spirit will become faint and every knee become as weak as water.' It is coming! It will surely take place, declares the Sovereign LORD."

⁸The word of the LORD came to me: ⁹"Son of man, prophesy and say, 'This is what the Lord says:

"'A sword, a sword,
    sharpened and polished—
¹⁰sharpened for the slaughter,
    polished to flash like lightning!

"'Shall we rejoice in the scepter of my son Judah? The sword despises every such stick.

¹¹ "'The sword is appointed to be polished,
    to be grasped with the hand;

271

it is sharpened and polished,
    made ready for the hand of the slayer.
¹² Cry out and wail, son of man,
    for it is against my people;
    it is against all the princes of Israel.
They are thrown to the sword
    along with my people.
Therefore beat your breast.

¹³"Testing will surely come. And what if the scepter ˻of Judah˼, which the sword despises, does not continue? declares the Sovereign LORD.'

¹⁴"So then, son of man, prophesy
    and strike your hands together.
Let the sword strike twice,
    even three times.
It is a sword for slaughter—
    a sword for great slaughter,
    closing in on them from every side.
¹⁵ So that hearts may melt
    and the fallen be many,
I have stationed the sword for slaughter
    at all their gates.
Oh! It is made to flash like lightning,
    it is grasped for slaughter.
¹⁶ O sword, slash to the right,
    then to the left,
    wherever your blade is turned.
¹⁷ I too will strike my hands together,
    and my wrath will subside.
I the LORD have spoken."

¹⁸The word of the LORD came to me: ¹⁹"Son of man, mark out two roads for the sword of the king of Babylon to take, both starting from the same country. Make a signpost where the road branches off to the city. ²⁰Mark out one road for the sword to come against Rabbah of the Ammonites and another against Judah and fortified Jerusalem. ²¹For the king of Babylon will stop at the fork in the road, at the junction of the two roads, to seek an omen: He will cast lots with arrows, he will consult his idols, he will examine the liver. ²²Into his right hand will come the lot for Jerusalem, where he is to set up

battering rams, to give the command to slaughter, to sound
the battle cry, to set battering rams against the gates, to build
a ramp and to erect siege works. ²³It will seem like a false
omen to those who have sworn allegiance to him, but he will
remind them of their guilt and take them captive.

²⁴"Therefore this is what the Sovereign LORD says: 'Because
you people have brought to mind your guilt by your open
rebellion, revealing your sins in all that you do—because you
have done this, you will be taken captive.

²⁵"'O profane and wicked prince of Israel, whose day has
come, whose time of punishment has reached its climax, ²⁶this
is what the Sovereign LORD says: Take off the turban, remove
the crown. It will not be as it was: The lowly will be exalted
and the exalted will be brought low. ²⁷A ruin! A ruin! I will
make it a ruin! It will not be restored until he comes to whom
it rightfully belongs; to him I will give it.'

²⁸"And you, son of man, prophesy and say, 'This is what the
Sovereign LORD says about the Ammonites and their insults:

"'A sword, a sword,
    drawn for the slaughter,
polished to consume
    and to flash like lightning!
²⁹Despite false visions concerning you
    and lying divinations about you,
it will be laid on the necks
    of the wicked who are to be slain,
whose day has come,
    whose time of punishment has reached its climax.
³⁰Return the sword to its scabbard.
    In the place where you were created,
in the land of your ancestry,
    I will judge you.
³¹I will pour out my wrath upon you
    and breathe out my fiery anger against you;
I will hand you over to brutal men,
    men skilled in destruction.
³²You will be fuel for the fire,
    your blood will be shed in your land,
you will be remembered no more;
    for I the LORD have spoken.'"

273

THIS SECTION OF Ezekiel's prophecy, all one chapter in the Hebrew versification,[1] divides up into four subsections:

(1) A parable and its interpretation (20:45–21:7)
(2) The song of the sword (21:8–17)
(3) An oracle of judgment against Jerusalem and her prince (21:18–27)
(4) An oracle of judgment against Ammon and against the sword (21:28–32)

The common theme that binds these sections together is the catchword "sword" as an image of God's judgment, which together with the associated image of fire, falls first on God's people, then on the not-so-innocent bystanders, and finally on the agent of judgment, the Babylonians.

The passage begins with the command to Ezekiel to face toward the south of Israel and preach against it (20:46); fire is coming on the southern forest, which will consume every tree, "both green and dry" (20:47). The conflagration will consume the entire land from south to north and scorch the faces of all who are present. It will be publicly recognized as the work of the Lord and will not be extinguished (20:48). But the people's response to this message is apparently total lack of comprehension: They say of Ezekiel, "Isn't he just telling parables?" (20:49).

Like all parables, this one both conceals and reveals. Some things are immediately clear from the parable, for it concerns an all-consuming judgment of the Lord. The judgment is all-consuming in its *content*, both green tree (i.e., not normally suitable for burning) and dry (i.e., naturally fit for the fire); in its *geographical scope* (from the south northwards); and in its *temporal scope* (it has been kindled and will not be extinguished). Yet the precise focus of the parable is not immediately clear: Who is the "southern forest" (20:47)? Without that critical piece of information, the parable remains an obscure riddle.

That information is supplied in the interpretation that follows: The three Hebrew terms for "south" in the parable (*têmān; dārôm; negeb*) are matched by three objects of judgment: Jerusalem, the sanctuary,[2] and the land of Israel (21:2). With that identification in place, other elements of the parable are put into sharper focus. Israel is the southland from the perspective of the traditional "enemy from the north," a motif introduced already in 1:4. The image

---

1. The Hebrew versification is five verses different in this chapter from the English; the references in the commentary are to the English verse numbers.

2. MT has the indefinite *miqdāšîm* ("sanctuaries"); this is frequently repointed *miqdāšām* ("their sanctuary"), a reading actually found in a few manuscripts (Allen, *Ezekiel 20–48*, 19). Others identify the plural sanctuaries as the pagan shrines of Israel (see Wevers, *Ezekiel*, 1623).

of fire is linked with that of the sword of the Lord, which is coming against the land to cut off both righteous (the green tree) and wicked (the dry tree), from the south to the north of the land. The sword has been drawn from its scabbard and will not return there.

The focus of the interpretation, like that of the parable, is the all-encompassing nature of the coming judgment. "Righteous" and "wicked," like "green tree" and "dry tree," operate together as a merism, a pair of opposites that includes everything in between. These two are not, however, a randomly chosen pair, which could be replaced by another stock pairing such as "young" and "old."[3] If the judgment includes even the *righteous*, whom one would expect normally to be spared (9:4), then indeed no one will escape. The coming judgment on Jerusalem will not be selective and short-lived, as was the invasion of 597 B.C., but all-encompassing and all-consuming. Nor is there any hope of a reprieve: The fire is kindled; the sword is drawn; there is only the fearful expectation of judgment.

To underline that fearful certainty, Ezekiel is instructed to perform a sign-act of publicly sighing and groaning with a broken spirit (21:6).[4] When people ask him why he is sighing, he is to respond with a somewhat cryptic statement: "Because of the news that is coming. Every heart will melt and every hand go limp; every spirit will become faint and every knee become as weak as water" (21:7). What event has come that merits such a response? Ezekiel's hearers would have to think back to Ezekiel 7, where the final judgment was threatened in virtually identical language.[5] The threatened judgment is now a present reality.

The prophet then receives a poetic oracle concerning the sword.[6] The twin judgment images of cutting (the sword) and burning (the fire) are maintained in the twin actions of sharpening and burnishing (note the connection

---

3. Moshe Greenberg, *Ezekiel* 21–37 (AB; New York: Doubleday, 1997), 420.

4. Lit., "with crushing of the loins"; the loins were considered the seat of internal strength in the ancient Near East.

5. Many commentators, along with the NIV, assume that it is "the news" that has come. However, in view of the obvious connection of the following phrase to 7:14, it is better to see in the "it has come" (*bāʾâ*) a reference back to the repeated prophecy of the judgment that would come (*bāʾâ*; 7:5, 7, 10; cf. the masculine *bāʾ* in 7:6, 12). See the translations adopted in the KJV, RSV, and NEB.

6. The Hebrew of this oracle is in places very obscure. Particularly difficult are v. 10b, which the NIV renders, "Shall we rejoice in the scepter of my son Judah? The sword despises every such stick," and v. 13, where the NIV has, "Testing will surely come. And what if the scepter ,of Judah,, which the sword despises, does not continue? declares the Sovereign LORD." These verses have so far defied the ability of commentators to make grammatical or logical sense of them; they may be marginal notes that have crept into the text (so Allen, *Ezekiel* 20–48, 19–20).

between polishing and lightning in 21:10, 15). Together, these actions serve to prepare the weapon for action. Once prepared, the sword is handed over to the executioner to use against God's people and the princes of Israel. Ezekiel is to strike his hands together in a threatening gesture,[7] not once or twice but three times, symbolizing the totality of the judgment (21:14). Israel will be surrounded, hemmed in on all sides with no place to run and no place to hide (21:14–16). The prophet's threatening gesture is merely a public display of the Lord's own threatening gesture and determination to satisfy his wrath[8] in his decimation of the people.

Thus far "the sword" of the Lord has been an entirely figurative image of divine judgment. In 21:18–27, however, we are introduced to the human agency that executes the divine will, the sword of the king of Babylon. The prophet is instructed to perform another sign-act, this time marking out a three-way road junction with a signpost.[9] One way comes from Babylon; the other two go to Rabbah, the capital of the Ammonites, and to Jerusalem, the capital of Judah. Ezekiel is to act out the forces of the king of Babylon coming to this parting of the ways and deciding which route to follow. To which of those two rebellious cities should they go?

Ezekiel pictures the king utilizing all the pagan means of decision-making: drawing arrows from a quiver (somewhat akin to our practice of drawing straws), consulting the household gods, and examining the liver of a sacrificial animal (21:21). These three means belong properly to different cultural contexts: divination by arrows was typically Arabian (though see 2 Kings 13:15–19), consulting household gods was known in an Israelite context (Hos. 3:4), while the examination of livers was a Babylonian specialty. It may be that Nebuchadnezzar actually used such diverse practices;[10] however, given the prominence of the number three as representative of completeness in this section, it is perhaps more likely that the multiplication of oracles represents comprehensive consultation of the gods. Where three separate oracles agree on a single course of action, is not divine approval sure?

The irony is that this use of pagan means of discerning the will of the gods is here an accurate discernment of the will of the true God. The "lying div-

---

7. Clapping the hands can have a variety of meanings in the Old Testament, and the gesture has been variously interpreted. However, here, as in 6:11, it introduces a proclamation of judgment and is best interpreted as evincing anger (Block, *Ezekiel 1–24*, 679).

8. NIV: "and my wrath will subside" (v. 17) sounds as if the cooling of God's anger is not directly related to Israel's punishment; in fact, it is precisely through executing judgment on his people that his wrath will be satisfied.

9. *yād* here refers to an inscribed stone monument that simply served to mark the division of two routes (see Zimmerli, *Ezekiel*, 1:442).

10. As Allen suggests (*Ezekiel 20–48*, 27).

inations" that had found such favor with God's people (Ezek. 13:7) now become the very means through which judgment comes on them (21:23). Their broken oath to the Lord is punished by the one with whom they have broken a human covenant. In this way, the king of Babylon is acting as divine prosecution counsel (*mazkîr*),[11] bringing out into the open Israel's guilt and arresting them for it.[12] As in a court of law, the point is not so much that the guilty party is "reminded" of their sins, as the NIV suggests, but rather that they are made public and therefore subject to the punishment they deserve (21:24).

That punishment falls not only on the people but also upon Zedekiah, rather dismissively addressed as "O profane and wicked prince." By introducing him by that title rather than by name, Ezekiel puts the focus of the judgment on the office, not the person.[13] It is not simply that Zedekiah will be stripped of the insignia of royalty, the turban and the crown (21:26), but that in him the old order of things has reached a conclusion. A divine reordering of society is called for, in which the Lord will exalt the lowly and bring down the exalted (21:26; cf. 17:24).[14] His guilt (*ʿāwōn*) is complete; so, with a fittingness that the Hebrew pun brings out, he will be made completely a "ruin" (*ʿawwâ*, repeated three times).

This ruinous state will persist until the coming of him to whom judgment (*mišpāṭ*) belongs, to whom it has been assigned by the Lord. In traditional exegesis, this has been seen as a reference to the coming of the Messiah, the one to whom the "right" (*mišpāṭ*) of kingship belongs.[15] However, since in 23:24b *nātattî mišpāṭ* refers to the Lord's handing over judgment to the Babylonians, the traditional exegesis seems unlikely.[16] Rather, it seems that Ezekiel has reshaped the traditional messianic oracle of Genesis 49:10 into a threatening oracle of judgment. Now the scepter will not depart from Judah until the coming of the judge . . . Nebuchadnezzar![17]

---

11. On the office of *mazkîr*, see Henning G. Reventlow, "Das Amt des Mazkir: Zur Rechtsstruktur des öffentlichen Lebens in Israel," *ThZ* 15 (1959): 161–75.

12. Like *mazkîr*, *tāpaś* stems from the sphere of law and order. See Zimmerli, *Ezekiel*, 1:445.

13. There may also be a pun intended on Zedekiah's name, which means "The LORD is righteous."

14. This theme of the reversal of the status of a vassal as an exercise of royal power on the part of the Great King is also attested in Assyrian sources. See Donald J. Wiseman, *The Vassal-Treaties of Esarhaddon* (London: The British School of Archaeology in Iraq, 1958), 44, lines 191–92.

15. This understanding is already present in the Targum and was widespread in the earlier part of this century; hence Cooke translates "to whom the right belongs" and adds, "a hint at the coming of one who will have the right to wear the crown, who will be the true king" (*Ezekiel*, 235). However, *mišpāṭ* nowhere else in Ezekiel has this sense of "right, claim."

16. See William Moran, "Gen 49:10 and Its Use in Ezekiel 21:32," *Bib* 39 (1958): 405–25.

17. Compare the similar reshaping of Gen. 49:9–10 in Ezek. 19, noted above.

Yet precisely this method of framing the judgment oracle reminds us of the Judge behind the judge, the Coming One behind the coming one. Heathen Nebuchadnezzar may be God's chosen instrument of judgment in Ezekiel 21, just as heathen Cyrus may be God's "anointed," his chosen instrument of salvation, in Isaiah 45. Yet the dominant reality in both cases is the plan and purpose of God. God's promise to Judah in Genesis 49 is not retracted in Ezekiel 21, though it may be reshaped because of the sin of God's people. The departure of the scepter may be necessary and appropriate because of the history of sin of the "princes of Israel," which culminates in Zedekiah; yet its departure can only be temporary, because the defining reality is God's election, not humanity's sin.

Judgment is not limited to Judah, however. The (pagan) oracle that directed Nebuchadnezzar toward Jerusalem is more a stay of execution for Ammon than a reprieve. They too, like Zedekiah, are among the profane wicked whose time of punishment has come (cf. 21:29 with 21:25). Therefore they too will feel the cutting edge of the sword of God's judgment. As the initial parable made clear, God's judgment is comprehensive in scope. Indeed, that judgment will eventually include the sword itself. The sword that was drawn from the Lord's scabbard, "not [to] return again" in 21:5, will at last be returned to its sheath in 21:30. There, in the place where it was created, it will be judged (21:30).

Babylon is neither above God nor independent of God in its furious power. Rather, it is merely his creation, a tool to be taken up and used for his purposes and then put down when its usefulness is over. What the Lord has lifted up, the Lord can also reduce once more to nothing. In that way it will become clear that it is the Lord who has raised her up and put her down, not any supposed power of her own gods.

 FIRE AND SWORD. The images of fire and sword for God's judgment have a venerable history. They come together already in Genesis 3:24, where the cherubim assigned to guard the entrance to Eden are accompanied by a flaming sword. The flashing sword is God's instrument of judgment on his enemies in Deuteronomy 32:41; his sword is poised against Assyria (Isa. 31:8) and Edom (34:5–6), and the angel of the Lord appears to Joshua with a drawn sword before the battle of Jericho (Josh. 5:13).

But the Lord can fight against his people as well as for them. In 1 Chronicles 21:16 the angel is poised with drawn sword over Jerusalem rather than an enemy city, while Jeremiah prophesies the coming of the sword of the

Lord against the whole land from one end to the other (Jer. 12:12). Equally, the Lord's fire continually threatens his unholy people: It burns up those who rebel against him in the desert (Num. 11:1; 16:35) and hangs over the head of their unholy descendants (Jer. 15:14; 17:4).

In no instance, however, is either the sword or fire an entity with a mind of its own. Even when they are figurative representations of human agencies of destruction, they operate entirely within the realm of God's sovereignty as agents of his judgment. He kindles the fire and brings the sword down on his enemies in his wrath. Nor is that simply an Old Testament concept of God. In fact, Jesus describes his ministry on earth in precisely those terms. He came not "to bring peace to the earth . . . but a sword" (Matt. 10:34). In the parallel passage in Luke's Gospel, the sword is replaced by fire as Jesus exclaims: "I have come to bring fire on the earth, and how I wish it were already kindled!" (Luke 12:49). His mission is one of executing God's judgment on earth.

This indeed was what the Old Testament prophesied: Malachi spoke of the appearance of the Lord like a refiner's fire or launderer's soap (Mal. 3:1–2). But if Jesus has come to bring about judgment, how can any survive? Will his judgment not be as comprehensive as that which Ezekiel described, leading to the total destruction of all flesh?

Surviving the refiner's fire. How can the refiner's fire of God's wrath pass over us and not burn us alive? The answer is because it has already passed over Jesus and poured its heat out on him. How can the avenging sword of the Lord pass by us without destroying us? Because it was sheathed in the body of Jesus on the cross so that it cannot further harm his people. God has raised his sword of judgment and brought it down on the shepherd in place of the sheep (Zech. 13:7).[18] His death in our place makes it possible for us to come close to the avenging God of justice and not be destroyed by him. Through Jesus, a safe way has been made for us to approach God, whereby the fire of God's wrath is transformed into the refiner's fire, which purifies and tests but does not destroy (13:9). Because of him, we may return to God and find him coming near to us also.

That is not to say that we do not experience the testing work of God's fire as believers. We do. The quality of all of our work will be tested by that medium, which will expose its true nature (1 Cor. 3:13). If we have built with lasting materials upon the only foundation of our lives as Christians, the finished work of Christ, there will be rewards stored up for us. But if we have

---

18. Iain Duguid, "Messianic Themes in Zechariah 9–14," in *The Lord's Anointed: Interpretation of Old Testament Messianic Texts*, ed. P. E. Satterthwaite, R. S. Hess, and G. J. Wenham (Grand Rapids: Baker, 1995), 278.

built only with shoddy, temporary materials, all that we have labored for on earth will be destroyed. The prospect of the fire to come is a sobering challenge to the believer to examine whether he or she is building suitably for the test. Yet even that believer who has built the least-enduring structure on the foundation of Christ will not be destroyed by the testing fire (1 Cor. 3:15). Though his or her work may count for nothing, he or she will still be saved because the destructive power of the fire has all been absorbed by Jesus.

But that safety is only for those for whom Christ died. Those outside Christ are left exposed to the full weight of the crushing, piercing, burning wrath of God. The fire of God's anger against sin has not been extinguished, nor has the sword of his wrath been blunted. There are no innocent bystanders; none will excuse their actions by reference to God's sovereignty. A day is established for God's final and complete judgment of all flesh, when Jesus Christ will ride forth to battle with a sharp sword, treading the winepress of the fury of God's wrath (Rev. 19:15). He will make war on all the forces that oppose God and anyone whose name has not been written in the book of life will be thrown into the lake of fire (20:14–15).

Imagery and propositional statements. The Bible is a book filled with images and imagery. God delivers his message not in the cold tones of propositional statements (although we may certainly deduce from the Bible propositions about who God is and what he is like) but in a welter of pictures. Supremely, his self-communication takes the form of the visible enactments of the prophets and most particularly of the final prophet, Jesus Christ, the Word become flesh.

Ironically, however, much expository preaching, which seeks to faithfully deliver the message of the Bible, begins by abstracting the proposition (the so-called "big idea of the passage") from its surrounding imagery. That imagery is then tossed away like so much used wrapping paper, while the "big idea" is repackaged in an entirely new format for its delivery to the contemporary congregation. Could that be one reason why people find so much of our preaching boring? We have lost the vivid directness of the fire-filled Word of God, replacing it by the cool logical flow of classical rhetoric. If we wish to regain the power of the original proclamation, we would do well to consider more fully how we can deliver messages about fires that burn and words about the sword that cut to the heart.[19]

---

19. For more help in understanding biblical images, see L. Ryken, J. C. Wilhoit, and T. Longman III, eds. *Dictionary of Biblical Imagery* (Downer's Grove, Ill.: InterVarsity, 1998).

THE QUESTION OF JUSTICE. One of the biggest questions in contemporary society is the question of justice. Where is the God of justice in our modern world? When children are gunned down on our streets in drive-by shootings, what is God doing about it? Where is God in Bosnia and Rwanda, in the midst of ethnic cleansing and tribal genocide? Deep in their hearts, people are outraged by the lack of justice in this world. Instinctively, they long for justice to reign and have an innate desire to see strong action against the wicked, with right triumphing and evil defeated. Isn't that why virtually every politician is on the side of law and order? Isn't that why there is a whole genre of popular vigilante movies, in which a strong individual establishes justice and peace by shooting, stabbing, or otherwise disposing of a formidable array of bad guys?

But if a standard of complete justice were actually to be imposed, each of us would face a very real problem: The justice for which we say we long would condemn each one of us as transgressors. Far from saving us, Superman would be implacably opposed to our way of life. All would stand condemned and guilty; all would face the fearful prospect of immediate and complete reckoning, with the Man of Steel dedicated to putting us out of circulation.

Imagine yourself as the villain rather than as the innocent bystander in the vigilante movie, and you begin to understand the horror of Judah's situation. They stood condemned as guilty, and now the prophet declared the onset of immediate and complete judgment at the hands of the king of Babylon, Nebuchadnezzar. Nor was it simply the might of Babylon that was dedicated to crushing the life out of them. The sword of the Lord himself was raised against them; the fire of his wrath had been kindled and would not be extinguished. What a fearful prospect! This is Jerusalem's *Nightmare on Elm Street*, with the Lord himself playing the part of Freddy Krueger.

The fire of eternal punishment. Yet is the situation of modern men and women who are without Christ any more secure? Not at all! Unless they hear the gospel and trust in the death of Christ on the cross, turning from their sins, they face the eternal prospect of the fire and the sword, God's wrath poured out on them. They are, to use the language of Jonathan Edwards, "sinners in the hands of an angry God," suspended over the pit of eternity by a narrow thread of life, in perpetual danger of falling to eternal destruction.

The destruction of Jerusalem in 586 B.C. was terribly comprehensive when God handed over judgment to the sword of Babylon. However, it was merely a sideshow when compared to the comprehensive judgment of the world that awaits the coming of the one to whom judgment belongs. God's wrath is aroused at the rebellious thoughts, deeds, and words of those whom he has created. When the Judge of all the earth comes to settle final accounts, the sword will fall on uncleansed sinners, to their eternal doom.

The doctrine of eternal torment in hell is not popular these days. In fact, it probably never has been, even in the heyday of Puritan preaching. In the modern world in particular, however, it is rarely the topic of sermons. Far more often, it is the subject of attempts to present the biblical teaching in a kinder, gentler light. As John Gerstner so aptly put it: "Modern theology has tended to take either the pain out of eternity or the eternity out of pain."[20] Like the erstwhile inhabitants of Jerusalem, we are convinced that the Judge will choose the other road and we will be spared. We don't really believe that the Bible's teaching on eternal punishment should be taken literally, at least not with reference to ourselves. But it is precisely with reference to ourselves that we should consider this doctrine. As C. S. Lewis reminds us:

> In all our discussions of Hell we should keep steadily before our eyes the possible damnation, not of our enemies nor of our friends (since both these disturb the reason) but of ourselves. This [doctrine] is not about your wife or son, nor about Nero or Judas Iscariot; it is about you and me.[21]

The fire of purification. What then are we to do? Is there any hope that we can survive his coming? Is there any future for you and me? The answer, incredibly, is yes! Yes! The fire will descend with purifying power as well as destructive force. Yes, the sword will cut away impurity as well as cut off the impure. A remnant, a purified remnant, will emerge, refined like gold and silver, ready to serve the Lord in righteousness.

So what is the answer to the problem of evil and injustice in this world? On one level, there is no answer. God does not give us information simply to satisfy our philosophical questions. What he does do is to bring the question home personally to each person: What is the answer to *your* evil and lack of justice? The Christian's answer is to point to the cross: there, once and for all time, the eternal wrath of God that I deserved was poured out completely on Jesus Christ, God's only Son. In that act is God's final answer to the problem of my evil: The Son of God was bruised for my transgression and broken for my iniquity. Because of that death, and only because of that death, I can look forward without fear to the coming again of the heavenly Judge to judge all nations of the earth with righteousness and truth.

---

20. *Jonathan Edwards on Heaven and Hell* (Grand Rapids: Baker, 1980), 91. For a good recent defense of the traditional position, see Robert A. Peterson, *Hell on Trial: The Case for Eternal Punishment* (Phillipsburg, N.J.: Presbyterian and Reformed, 1995).

21. *The Problem of Pain*, 116.

But lack of fear of the coming of the fire and the sword does not mean that we can sit back and relax. Our works will be tested by fire as believers, and much of what we spend our time on is far from fireproof. We fill our lives with the trivial, passing our time instead of spending it, living alongside people aimlessly instead of living with them purposefully. Even those closest to us may hardly ever be affected by the ideas that we claim are closest to our hearts. Instead of burning out for God, we are heaping up empty actions for God's grand bonfire. From the perspective of eternity, how wasted will so much of our lives seem to have been?

Ezekiel 22

T HE WORD OF THE LORD came to me: ²"Son of man, will you judge her? Will you judge this city of bloodshed? Then confront her with all her detestable practices ³and say: 'This is what the Sovereign LORD says: O city that brings on herself doom by shedding blood in her midst and defiles herself by making idols, ⁴you have become guilty because of the blood you have shed and have become defiled by the idols you have made. You have brought your days to a close, and the end of your years has come. Therefore I will make you an object of scorn to the nations and a laughing-stock to all the countries. ⁵Those who are near and those who are far away will mock you, O infamous city, full of turmoil.

⁶"'See how each of the princes of Israel who are in you uses his power to shed blood. ⁷In you they have treated father and mother with contempt; in you they have oppressed the alien and mistreated the fatherless and the widow. ⁸You have despised my holy things and desecrated my Sabbaths. ⁹In you are slanderous men bent on shedding blood; in you are those who eat at the mountain shrines and commit lewd acts. ¹⁰In you are those who dishonor their fathers' bed; in you are those who violate women during their period, when they are ceremonially unclean. ¹¹In you one man commits a detestable offense with his neighbor's wife, another shamefully defiles his daughter-in-law, and another violates his sister, his own father's daughter. ¹²In you men accept bribes to shed blood; you take usury and excessive interest and make unjust gain from your neighbors by extortion. And you have forgotten me, declares the Sovereign LORD.

¹³"'I will surely strike my hands together at the unjust gain you have made and at the blood you have shed in your midst. ¹⁴Will your courage endure or your hands be strong in the day I deal with you? I the LORD have spoken, and I will do it. ¹⁵I will disperse you among the nations and scatter you through the countries; and I will put an end to your uncleanness. ¹⁶When you have been defiled in the eyes of the nations, you will know that I am the LORD.'"

¹⁷Then the word of the LORD came to me: ¹⁸"Son of man, the house of Israel has become dross to me; all of them are the

copper, tin, iron and lead left inside a furnace. They are but the dross of silver. ¹⁹Therefore this is what the Sovereign LORD says: 'Because you have all become dross, I will gather you into Jerusalem. ²⁰As men gather silver, copper, iron, lead and tin into a furnace to melt it with a fiery blast, so will I gather you in my anger and my wrath and put you inside the city and melt you. ²¹I will gather you and I will blow on you with my fiery wrath, and you will be melted inside her. ²²As silver is melted in a furnace, so you will be melted inside her, and you will know that I the LORD have poured out my wrath upon you.'"

²³Again the word of the LORD came to me: ²⁴"Son of man, say to the land, 'You are a land that has had no rain or showers in the day of wrath.' ²⁵There is a conspiracy of her princes within her like a roaring lion tearing its prey; they devour people, take treasures and precious things and make many widows within her. ²⁶Her priests do violence to my law and profane my holy things; they do not distinguish between the holy and the common; they teach that there is no difference between the unclean and the clean; and they shut their eyes to the keeping of my Sabbaths, so that I am profaned among them. ²⁷Her officials within her are like wolves tearing their prey; they shed blood and kill people to make unjust gain. ²⁸Her prophets whitewash these deeds for them by false visions and lying divinations. They say, 'This is what the Sovereign LORD says'—when the LORD has not spoken. ²⁹The people of the land practice extortion and commit robbery; they oppress the poor and needy and mistreat the alien, denying them justice.

³⁰"I looked for a man among them who would build up the wall and stand before me in the gap on behalf of the land so I would not have to destroy it, but I found none. ³¹So I will pour out my wrath on them and consume them with my fiery anger, bringing down on their own heads all they have done, declares the Sovereign LORD."

Original Meaning

THE IDEA OF comprehensive judgment descending on God's people was already present in Ezekiel 21, but in chapter 22 it moves into the foreground. In this chapter, the prophet is called on to act as prosecuting counsel, making known to Jerusalem in detail her detestable ways, which form the basis for both the actuality and the immediacy of divine judgment. The comprehensive nature of her sins means that judgment is *necessary* and judgment is *now*.

The prophet begins by presenting his indictment in outline form (22:3–5): Jerusalem's sins involve both social sins—that is, sins against humanity (e.g., "shedding blood," 22:3)—and cultic sins—that is, sins against God (e.g., the manufacture of idols, 22:3). These two broad classes of sins have resulted in two respective consequences: social sins lead to "guilt" (ʾāšam, 22:4), the forensic state of deserving punishment, while cultic sins lead to "defilement" (ṭāmēʾ, 22:4), the ritual state of being unfit to appear in the presence of God. The combination of these in Jerusalem's case means that she has brought on herself her "doom," or more literally, "her time" (ʿittāh, 22:3); her days have come to a close, and the end of her years have come (v. 4).

Like a virus in the bloodstream, Jerusalem's defilement and guilt have built up to the point where they now initiate a life-threatening crisis.[1] Now the hour of her judgment has struck. The result of that judgment will make Jerusalem into an "object of scorn" to the nations around her. Both those near at hand and those far away will mock her as being an "infamous city" (22:5), that is, famous for her cultic and social sins, which have led to her downfall.

Verses 6–12 give the first catalogue of Jerusalem's crimes, showing how she has offended against God's law. The charges are directed against the "princes of Israel," a phrase normally understood as designating the former kings of Judah. Thus in view are not merely present sins but a continuing history of sin on the part of Judah's leadership.[2] The kings are specifically indicted because it was their responsibility to establish justice in the community, especially by protecting the poor and weak (Ps. 72:1–4).

The sins listed here are not a random collection of charges, but specifically an accusation of having violated the laws of the Pentateuch, especially those of the so-called "Holiness Code" of Leviticus 18–20; 25.[3] Thus in Ezekiel 22:7, the accusation that "they have treated father and mother with contempt" has a basis in Leviticus 20:9, while the claim that they oppressed the alien is based on Leviticus 19:33. The same is true of the remainder of the charges made by the prophet: "despis[ing] my holy things and desecrat[ing] my Sabbaths" (see 19:30), slandering (see 19:16), eating "at the mountain shrines" (see 19:26, LXX),[4] "commit[ting] lewd acts" (see 20:14), "dishonor[ing] their fathers' bed" (see 20:11), "violat[ing] women during their

---

1. Zimmerli, *Ezekiel*, 1:456.
2. Duguid, *Ezekiel and the Leaders of Israel*, 38.
3. Reventlow, *Wächter über Israel*, 101–6.
4. MT has "with the blood." Ezek. 18:6, 11, 15 correspond to 22:9, but cf. 33:25.

period" (see 18:19), "commit[ting] a detestable offense with [one's] neighbor's wife" (see 20:10), "defil[ing one's] daughter-in-law" (see 20:12), "violat[ing one's] sister" (see 20:17), "tak[ing] usury and excessive interest" (see 25:36)," and "mak[ing] unjust gain from your neighbors" (see 19:13).

Though the charges themselves are largely drawn from the Holiness Code, the specific turn of phrase is in many places influenced by Deuteronomy, for instance, in the final concluding phrase: "You have forgotten me" (Ezek. 22:12; cf. Deut. 8:14, 19). The end result, then, is a comprehensive indictment of the former rulers of Judah on the basis of the law of Moses; the covenant bond forged on Mount Sinai has been broken.[5] The "holy nation" (Ex. 19:6) has become thoroughly unholy.

Such a comprehensive catalogue of sins can have only one outcome. As Deuteronomy 8:19 makes clear: "If you ever forget the LORD your God . . . you will surely be destroyed." So the next two sections (Ezek. 22:13–16, 17–22) deal with the Lord's response to his people's sin under the twin images of *judgment by scattering* and *judgment by gathering*. The literary device of using two diametrically opposite images together underscores once again the comprehensive nature of Judah's doom.

Verse 13 acts as the link between the accusation and the threat of punishment, summarizing the accusation by putting together the last charge ("unjust gain") with the first ("blood you have shed in your midst," cf. v. 3) in a reversed arrangement to form a chiasm. Because of these things the Lord will now act, dispersing Judah among the nations and scattering them through the countries (22:15). In this way, the Lord will bring an end to Judah's uncleanness (22:15). Though such a fate for the Lord's people would be "defiling" to the Lord[6] in front of the nations, it was a necessary price to pay. As Leslie Allen puts it, the Lord's defilement through Judah's exile "was the lesser of two evils that he was prepared to endure as the price to pay for making his forgetful people remember who and what he was."[7]

But this scattering is not the only dimension of judgment threatened. Paradoxically, there appears also a "gathering for judgment," as the house of Israel is gathered into Jerusalem, into the heart of the smelter's furnace, to experience the destructive impact of the full outpouring of the Lord's wrath (22:18–22). This is paradoxical not merely because "gathering" is the logical

---

5. To "forget" the Lord is distinctively covenantal language; see Willi Schottroff, "שָׁכַה," *THAT*, 902.

6. Reading *w⁽nihaltî*, "I will be defiled" for MT *w⁽nihalt*, "you will be defiled." The versions also have the first person singular, though they derive their translations from the root *nāhal*, "to inherit." See Zimmerli, *Ezekiel*, 1:454; and compare 36:20 for the same idea.

7. *Ezekiel 20–48*, 37. The theme of God's scattering and dispersing his people among the nations is prominent in Ezekiel, being found also in 12:15; 20:23; 36:19.

opposite of "scattering," but also because the terminology of gathering is elsewhere normally used in a positive sense.

The conventional use of the imagery envisages first a scattering of God's people in his wrath and then, after the judgment has had a purifying effect, a gathering of God's people in his mercy. For instance, in 11:17 the Sovereign Lord promises to gather his people from the countries where they have been scattered.[8] Although he frequently uses "gathering" in this conventional, positive sense, Ezekiel has already indicated a possible negative aspect of gathering as a precondition for judgment rather than salvation in 20:34. Here in chapter 22, however, it functions together with its opposite "scattering" to underline the comprehensive nature of the coming judgment.

Nor is this the only conventionally positive theme given a negative twist in Ezekiel 22. The image of judgment as the refiner's fire, purifying the dross to leave only the pure metal, appears several times in the Bible (notably in Isa. 1:21–31; 48:10; Mal. 3:2–3). But in Ezekiel 22, as in Jeremiah 6:27–30, the refining process has a purely negative product, with nothing but unpurged molten dross produced. The purpose of this divine act of judgment, then, is not to purify his people, but merely to pour out on rebellious sinners his fiery wrath.

This outpouring of God's wrath has not yet happened to Judah, notwithstanding the disasters of 605 and 597 B.C. She remains "a land not cleansed[9] or showered in the day of wrath" (Ezek. 22:24). Most commentators understand this as the removal of the covenant blessing of rain, an idea that is certainly common in the Old Testament (e.g., Lev. 26:19).[10] However, in context the "day of wrath" is a future event, so the absence of rain must refer to the absence of an element of judgment. The concept of rain on the land as an element of judgment is present in the Flood narrative (Gen. 7:4, 11), and the expectation of a future destructive flood is reflected in Ezekiel 13:11 and 38:22.[11] It may therefore be better to understand 22:24 as the absence of a

---

8. Other examples of gathering as the redemptive reversal of scattering in Jeremiah and Ezekiel include Jer. 23:3; 29:14; 31:8, 10; 32:37; 49:5; Ezek. 20:41; 28:25; 29:13; 34:13; 36:24; 37:21; 38:8; 39:27.

9. The NIV, following the LXX and most commentators, reads *lōʾ humtʿrâ* ("not rained on") rather than *lōʾ mᵉṭōhārâ* ("not cleansed") on the grounds that it fits the parallelism better. See Allen, *Ezekiel* 20–48, 32. This emendation is possible but not required, especially if the "showering" is a negative rather than a positive image.

10. Allen, *Ezekiel* 20–48, 38; Zimmerli, *Ezekiel*, 1:467.

11. Rabbinic commentators discussed whether this verse implies that the great flood bypassed Israel (*b. Zebaḥ.* 113a). Such expectations of a future flood were apparently also present in Babylon; see Moshe Anbar, "Une nouvelle allusion à une tradition babylonienne dans Ezechiel (22:24)," *VT* 29 (1979): 352–53.

---

cleansing deluge, like the great Flood, which would have purged the land of evildoers in one great day of destruction. Because of this lack of cleansing in the past, the land remains full of oppression, detailed in the following verses, which will lead to a final pouring out of indignation on the people (22:31).

If the first catalogue of the sins of Jerusalem was detailed with reference to the law (esp. Lev. 18–20; 25), the second catalogue of Jerusalem's sins is detailed with reference to one of the prophets, namely, Zephaniah 3:3–4.[12] Though Zephaniah's four categories of leaders charged with wrongdoing (officials, rulers, prophets, and priests) are expanded to five (princes, priests, officials, prophets, and people of the land), the underlying continuity between the charges is clear: All of the leadership classes in Judah are charged and found guilty of wrongdoing.

The "princes," described as being like "a roaring lion," have wreaked havoc through a series of social sins (Ezek. 22:25). In effect, they preenacted the societal devastation that the Babylonians would bring to full measure when they destroyed Jerusalem.[13]

The "officials," described as "wolves," have likewise misused their power for the purpose of "unjust gain" (22:27).

Even the "priests," who elsewhere in Ezekiel are not singled out for any blame, except in the explicit reversal of this charge in 44:23–24, did "violence to my law and profane my holy things" (22:26). They have failed in their task of protecting Yahweh's holy things by not teaching the proper distinction between holy and unholy, clean and unclean. The unusual phrase "they shut their eyes to the keeping of my Sabbaths" seems to indicate the priests' failure to prosecute those who transgressed the law (cf. a similar phrase in Lev. 20:4).

Meanwhile the "prophets" are condemned in terms similar to Ezekiel 13 as unreliable whitewashers, telling people what they wanted to hear in the Lord's name, when he had not sent them (22:28).

The "people of the land," who in this context should be identified as a group of powerful men in Jerusalem with close ties to the Davidic house,[14] have also been taking advantage of their position. They have been exploiting those unable to defend themselves: "the poor and needy and ... the alien" (22:29).

After the conclusion of the second catalogue of sins, we again read of the Lord's twofold response. He first of all sought for "a man among them who would build up the wall and stand before me in the gap on behalf of the

---

12. The *fact* of a relationship between these two passages has been generally recognized for over a century. The *direction* of the dependence has been debated, but to my mind the clinching argument in favor of the priority of Zephaniah is the use of *bᵉqirbāh* in v. 27 rather than *betôkāh*, which is found frequently elsewhere in this chapter.

13. Greenberg, *Ezekiel 21–37*, 462.

14. For this sense of ʿam-hāʾāreṣ, see Talmon, "ʿam-hāʾāreṣ," 68–78.

land" (22:30). In other words, he sought a true prophet (cf. 13:5)—someone who would take on the difficult and dangerous task of interceding for the people, just as Moses did successfully after the incident of the golden calf (Ps. 106:23). But this time no one was found to deflect God's wrath, and thus the all-consuming fiery anger of God will descend on Jerusalem (Ezek. 22:31). As if to emphasize the connection to the destruction of Jerusalem depicted in chapters 9–11, the last, ominous words of the Lord are the same in both cases: "[I will bring] down on their own heads all they have done" (22:31; cf. 11:21).

Bridging Contexts

JERUSALEM AS SPIRITUAL CENTER. Few contemporary readers are aware of the unique place that Jerusalem occupied in preexilic Israel. She was not merely the ancient equivalent of London or Washington, D.C., the seat of government and power; she was the spiritual center of God's people, the one place in all the earth where God had chosen to place his name. Thus in Psalm 48 the praise of God and the praise of Zion go hand in hand. Jerusalem is "the city of our God," Mount Zion is "his holy mountain," the unique place of God's presence (Ps. 48:1, 3).

To describe its significance the psalmist borrows the language of Canaanite mythology: It is exalted above the other mountains, like the uttermost heights of Mount Zaphon, the supposed home of the Canaanite pantheon.[15] It was the very center of the earth, both geographically and theologically (Ezek. 5:5).[16] Of course, Jerusalem gained that spiritual significance from its role as the home of the temple built by Solomon, on which the Lord had promised to set his name (1 Kings 9:3). But the city itself stood within the aura of holiness created by the temple, so that her walls and towers became objects of spiritual meditation (Ps. 48:12–13) and she herself was a place of pilgrimage and a subject of prayer (Ps. 122).

But as a consequence of that unique significance, Jerusalem was also required to be a place of radical holiness. As the psalmist says: "Who may ascend the hill of the LORD? Who may stand in his holy place?" (Ps. 24:3; cf. Ps. 15). The laws governing the entrance ways into the temple and the offering of the sacrifices were designed to prevent the intrusion of the profane into the place of the sacred. The accusation of Ezekiel 22 was that the barriers

---

15. See Richard J. Clifford, *The Cosmic Mountain in Canaan and the Old Testament* (HSM 4; Cambridge, Mass.: Harvard Univ. Press, 1972), 3.

16. This idea was more fully developed in the rabbinic sources than in the Old Testament, but it is present in the idea of Jerusalem as the "center" or "navel" (Ezek. 38:12) of the earth, that is, the point from which the creation of the earth proceeded. See Jon D. Levenson, *Sinai and Zion* (San Francisco: Harper & Row, 1985), 115.

against the profane had comprehensively broken down. The entirely "holy city" had become the entirely "unholy city." The very heart of Judah, geographically and theologically, had become corrupted by sin. In place of the assertion of the psalmist "God is within her," from which followed the assurance "she will not fall" (Ps. 46:5), Ezekiel charged, with the repeated use of the catchwords *dām* ("blood[shed]") and *bᵉtōkēk* ("in your midst"), that "you have shed [blood] in your midst" (Ezek. 22:13), from which followed the certainty that God's wrath would fall. There could be no escape for the radically polluted "city of God."

The contaminating nature of blood in ancient Israel. The other aspect of Ezekiel 22 that will not be readily recognized by contemporary readers is the specially contaminating nature of blood in ancient Israel. To be sure, the idea of bloodstained hands being repellent is familiar to us. We need only think of Shakespeare's depiction of Lady Macbeth, a figure tormented by the vision of hands indelibly stained with the blood of her victim, so that even though she washed her hands repeatedly the foul spots could not be removed. But the revulsion in ancient Israelite society to the shedding of innocent blood was even stronger. The blood, whether of an animal or of a person, contained the life and was therefore to be treated with special reverence (Lev. 17:11). When a domestic animal was sacrificed, this reverence required that the blood was to be sprinkled on the altar (17:6); if a wild animal were killed for food, its blood was to be drained onto the ground before the meat could be consumed (17:13).

Anyone failing to observe these measures was deemed "guilty of bloodshed" and was to be cut off from the covenant people. This requirement was intended to underline the sacredness of all life, both animal and human.[17] Those who failed to show respect for the life of others would be excluded from the covenant community, the place where life was to be found. What prospect then awaits the city that has become as deeply defiled as it is possible to be, filled with bloodshed (Ezek. 22:3–4)? It is only a matter of time before she will be cut off—and Ezekiel affirms that the time of Jerusalem's complete destruction has now indeed come.

DIES IRAE. When I was a university student I participated in a performance of Mozart's *Requiem*. We were told the story of how, while seriously ill, Mozart was approached by a mysterious stranger who commissioned him to write a Requiem Mass. Mozart became

---

17. See Jacob Milgrom, *Leviticus 1–16* (AB; New York: Doubleday, 1991), 713.

convinced that this was an angelic visitation, telling him to write a Requiem for himself. Though he did not live to complete his final work—it was finished from his notes by one of his students—the result is a powerful and compelling piece of music. One of the most emotionally charged parts of the *Requiem* for me was his rendition of the ancient Latin hymn *Dies Irae*. To the accompaniment of crashing chords, the fortissimo voices cry out, "Dies irae, dies illa, solvet saeclum in favilla, teste David cum Sibylla. . . ." Although I did not really understand the words (one year of high school Latin will only take you so far), I knew it had something to do with the Judgment Day, and the thought of a desperately ill genius composing the music with which to face his own Maker gave it a powerful emotional appeal.

I recently discovered an English translation of the *Dies Irae*, and realized that I had barely begun to understand the power of its conviction:

> Day of wrath! O day of mourning!
> See fulfilled the prophet's warning—
> Heaven and earth in ashes burning!
> Oh, what fear man's bosom rendeth,
> When from heav'n the Judge descendeth,
> On Whose sentence all dependeth!
> Wondrous sound the trumpet flingeth,
> Through earth's sepulchers it ringeth,
> All before the throne it bringeth.
> Death is struck and nature quaking,
> All Creation is awaking,
> To its Judge an answer making.
> Lo! the book exactly worded,
> Wherein all hath been recorded;
> Thence shall judgment be awarded.
> When the Judge His seat attaineth,
> And each hidden deed arraigneth,
> Nothing unavenged remaineth.[18]

Such a stirring vision of the final judgment is not found in many contemporary worship songs, nor indeed in many hymnbooks in current use. These days we sing of the love of God and of the mercy and grace of God, but not, it seems, of the wrath of God and of the reality and certainty of final judgment. Why not?

---

18. The original Latin poem dates back to around the thirteenth century. This translation is by W. J. Irons, printed in *Hymns Ancient and Modern*. For its appropriateness in connection with this passage, see Millard Lind, *Ezekiel* (Believer's Church Bible Commentary; Scottdale, Pa.: Herald, 1996), 191.

Taking sin seriously. I think that the answer lies in our failure to under-stand the *reality* and the *comprehensiveness* of our sin. The person unconvinced of the reality and comprehensiveness of Jerusalem's sin, when faced with its destruction in 586 B.C., asks, "Why wouldn't God save her?" Ezekiel seeks to redirect that question so that the questioner asks: "How could a holy God do anything other than condemn her?" His method was simply to demon-strate the fact and the scope of her sin.

Modern people are equally unconvinced of the reality of their sin. The message of Paul that "all have sinned and fall short of the glory of God" (Rom. 3:23) is not one that finds a ready hearing in today's society. We tend to redefine sin out of existence as dysfunction or psychological weakness. What used to be called sin is now merely an "alternative lifestyle." Our cul-ture has "defined deviancy down" to the point that what used to be consid-ered deviant behavior is the new "normal."[19]

This is true not merely in society at large but also in the churches. In a recent television interview, the Archbishop of Canterbury, George Carey, bewailed the fact that Britain was in danger of losing its Christian values and complained that the nation had "lost the language of sin." But earlier in the same interview, when questioned about the marital difficulties of Prince Charles, he reportedly responded: "He is a man who takes faith seriously, who attends worship and someone who has struggled as many people struggle with . . . brokenness in relationships. Therefore it's wrong for you and I to sit in judgment on people who are, as we are, people made in the image of God."[20] Apparently persistent adultery and divorce are no longer to be described as "sin"; now they are "brokenness in relationships."

Even those who still talk about sins have frequently lost the sense of the comprehensive nature of our sin. Preachers (and churches) tend to have a shortened list of actual sins that they preach against. Some churches are strong against sexual sins, foul language, and drunkenness but have little to say about the economic sins of unjust business practices or the societal sins of racism that are endemic around us. Other churches speak strongly against structural evils but almost completely neglect the area of private morality. Per-haps we all have a tendency to dwell more on the sins that dog the lives of others than the faults of our own congregations. Not so Ezekiel: No one can escape the range of the charges he addresses.

Along with the loss of the sense of sin goes the loss of understanding of God's wrath. Paul understood that: "We were by nature objects of [God's]

---

19. Daniel Patrick Moynihan, "Defining Deviancy Down," *The American Scholar* (Winter 1993). See also Gertrude Himmelfarb, *The De-Moralization of Society: From Victorian Virtues to Modern Values* (New York: Alfred Knopf, 1995), 234–37.

20. "Prince's Faith Receives Carey's Blessing," *The [London] Times* (Dec. 23, 1996).

wrath" (Eph. 2:3). Why? Because we "were dead in [our] transgressions and sins" (2:1). A knowledge of sin and the understanding of God's wrath go together. It should therefore be no surprise that in a society where sin is no longer believed in, the wrath of God is not understood.[21] We increasingly ask the question, "Why would a good God sentence anyone to eternal punishment?" instead of the question, "How can a holy God do anything other than condemn me to the depths of hell?"

Sin and redemption in "the city." The reality of sin, however, is an everyday fact for all of us, perhaps especially for those who live in our major cities. Just as ancient Jerusalem had drawn to itself all manner of detestable practices, so typically the major cities of our world are hotbeds of every kind of vice. This is merely what one would expect, given the origins that the Bible ascribes to the city. In Genesis, the city is Cain's natural territory. It is archetypally the place where no one is his or her brother's keeper. In a small town, everybody not only knows your name and the state of your marriage, they know everything about you, down to how often you change your underwear. That intimate knowledge acts as a powerful brake on public sin. In a big city, by contrast, you can be surrounded by a million people and not know a single soul. Few people know what you do, and fewer still care.

Cain's line is the one that excels in farming, in engineering, and in the arts (Gen. 4:20–22). It increases in power, wealth, and luxury. But paradoxically as it prospers materially it also declines in morals. The problem with the city is not population density but sin. Put a lot of sinners close together and it is not surprising that you will reap degradation. The city draws out what is in humanity, good and bad. It is the place of progress, of technology, of the arts—all of which are good gifts of God, but all of which can so easily be perverted.

Yet God can redeem even the city. The place that in Genesis 1–11 is the home of Cain's descendants and the builders of the tower of Babel becomes in Revelation 21–22 the new Jerusalem, the place where God lives with his people. It will be in a heavenly city that we will know God and be fully known by him, and live in intimate and untroubled fellowship with our brothers and sisters. We were created for society; we were not created to live alone. After the Fall, to be sure, society becomes a mixed blessing. Sin has societal consequences. God's solution, however, is not to call his redeemed people to live a hermit existence in the desert but to form them into a new society, the church, where we share fellowship with those who are our siblings in Christ.

Awakening a sense of sin and presenting God's grace. But how can we awaken a sense of sin in those around us who are as yet outside the church?

---

21. For a contemporary writer not afraid to speak of sin and the wrath of God, see D. Martyn Lloyd-Jones, *Romans 3:20–4:25; Atonement and Justification* (Grand Rapids: Zondervan, 1970), 6–10.

In one sense, we cannot. At the heart of the problem is the fact that those outside Christ are dead in their transgressions and sins. How do you wake the dead? Only the Holy Spirit can perform that miracle. Nonetheless, in our preaching we need to have a balance of preaching the law and preaching the gospel.

Ezekiel's methodology for addressing the people of his own day was to show them how far short they had fallen of the standards laid down in God's Word. He indicted his hearers comprehensively of crimes against the Law and the Prophets. The standards he used were not those of contemporary society, with which they might compare favorably, but God's perfect law, before which all stood condemned. He showed them the extent to which sin had contaminated the very heart of their society. He charged them not merely with sin in general, but of detailed specific sins of comprehensive range. Only after they had been confronted with the reality and depth of their sin could they come to an understanding of the rightness of God's wrath against them. Only then could the good news of God's grace be preached to them.

On the basis of the approach of Ezekiel and some of the other prophets, it has sometimes been insisted that the law is a necessary first step toward understanding the gospel, as if only after first understanding fully the claims of the law can one come to Christ.[22] In fact, however, law and grace belong together in contributing to our understanding of sin and thus our understanding of our need for Christ. If we merely understand the law without seeing God's grace, we can fall into the trap of seeing God as the cosmic policeman, upholding apparently arbitrary standards that get in the way of our self-fulfillment. This view of God was the serpent's goal in his questioning of Eve in the Garden of Eden. He sought to maximize the restrictiveness of God's law ("Did God really say, 'You must not eat from *any* tree in the garden'?" Gen. 3:1) and to minimize God's gracious goodness ("God knows that when you eat of it . . . you will be like God, knowing good and evil," 3:5).

Equally, if we merely understand grace without seeing the place of the law, then we may view God as the cosmic grandfather, understanding all and there-

---

22. This principle of law first and then gospel was laid out in the original Puritan manual of preaching, William Perkins' *The Art of Prophesying* (Carlisle, Pa.: Banner of Truth, 1996, reprint of 1606 original). Its continuing influence is clear in C. H. Spurgeon's "A Plain Man's Sermon," where he asserts: "The law is the needle, and you cannot draw the silken thread of the gospel through a man's heart, unless you first send the needle of the law through the center thereof, to make way for it" (*Metropolitan Tabernacle Pulpit: Sermons Preached and Revised in 1886*, vol. 32 [London: Banner of Truth, 1969], 27). Similarly, R. B. Kuiper states: "The call to repentance must come first in evangelism" (*God-Centered Evangelism* [Grand Rapids: Baker, 1961], 134).

fore forgiving all. What is important is not so much the order in which law and grace are proclaimed but the fact that both are clearly proclaimed. Perhaps rather than a fixed order of proclamation, it would be better to view their relationship as a dynamic relationship, more of a circle than a straight line.

Law and grace understood together point us to our need for Christ. In Christ, we see that God's law is good and perfect, designed for our utmost fulfillment as human beings; the only utterly fulfilled person who ever lived is also the only person who ever fully kept God's law. Yet in Christ we see the full meaning of God's grace—that grace is (in the children's acronym) God's Riches At Christ's Expense. Forgiveness for us is complete, full, and free. But it was not without cost. The cost of free forgiveness was borne for us on the cross, where Jesus purchased the blood-filled Jerusalem and her (un)spiritual descendants in order to rehab her into his heavenly bride, the new Jerusalem, in whom God can dwell forever.

The author of the *Dies Irae* understood clearly that law and grace go together. Thus, having trumpeted the threats of the law, he goes on:

> What shall I, frail man, be pleading,
> Who for me be interceding,
> When the just are mercy needing?
> King of majesty tremendous,
> Who dost free salvation send us,
> Fount of pity, then befriend us!
> Think, good Jesus! My salvation
> Caused thy wondrous Incarnation;
> Leave me not to reprobation.
> Faint and weary Thou hast sought me
> On the cross of suffering bought me;
> Shall such grace be vainly brought me?
> Righteous Judge! For sin's pollution
> Grant Thy gift of absolution,
> Ere that day of retribution.
> Guilty, now I pour my moaning,
> All my shame with anguish owning,
> Spare, O God, Thy suppliant groaning.

Someone to stand in the gap. The problem facing Ezekiel was not simply that he encountered a few defiled individuals, who needed to hear the gospel. Jerusalem herself, the holy city, was completely defiled. There was no righteous remnant; no one in the catalogue of leaders was left free from the taint of sin, not even the priests. There was literally no one to stand in the gap for her. In Abraham's day, a quorum of ten righteous men might have saved Sodom. In Jerusalem, the new Sodom (Ezek. 16:46), there is not even left one righteous Lot who will escape.

Such too is the world in which we live. The best of our righteousness is as filthy rags in the presence of a holy God. As Christians we know that we are saved not by our righteousness, but by the One who stood in the gap for us, Jesus Christ himself, who bore the full weight of the true *dies irae*, the day of God's wrath. On that day, the sun was turned to darkness while he suffered the full weight of the punishment our sins deserved (Matt. 27:45). The earth itself convulsed and the curtain in the temple, the barrier closing off the presence of God in the Most Holy Place, was torn in two, opening up a gap for us to come to God. As we come, we in turn are called to share in the prophetic ministry of "standing in the gap." We are called to intercede in prayer for the lost, taking the risk of rejection and persecution as we warn them of the wrath to come, and to live lives of purity as we wait so that nothing may hinder the message of life that is proclaimed through us.

Ezekiel 23

THE WORD OF THE LORD came to me: ²"Son of man, there were two women, daughters of the same mother. ³They became prostitutes in Egypt, engaging in prostitution from their youth. In that land their breasts were fondled and their virgin bosoms caressed. ⁴The older was named Oholah, and her sister was Oholibah. They were mine and gave birth to sons and daughters. Oholah is Samaria, and Oholibah is Jerusalem.

⁵"Oholah engaged in prostitution while she was still mine; and she lusted after her lovers, the Assyrians—warriors ⁶clothed in blue, governors and commanders, all of them handsome young men, and mounted horsemen. ⁷She gave herself as a prostitute to all the elite of the Assyrians and defiled herself with all the idols of everyone she lusted after. ⁸She did not give up the prostitution she began in Egypt, when during her youth men slept with her, caressed her virgin bosom and poured out their lust upon her.

⁹"Therefore I handed her over to her lovers, the Assyrians, for whom she lusted. ¹⁰They stripped her naked, took away her sons and daughters and killed her with the sword. She became a byword among women, and punishment was inflicted on her.

¹¹"Her sister Oholibah saw this, yet in her lust and prostitution she was more depraved than her sister. ¹²She too lusted after the Assyrians—governors and commanders, warriors in full dress, mounted horsemen, all handsome young men. ¹³I saw that she too defiled herself; both of them went the same way.

¹⁴"But she carried her prostitution still further. She saw men portrayed on a wall, figures of Chaldeans portrayed in red, ¹⁵with belts around their waists and flowing turbans on their heads; all of them looked like Babylonian chariot officers, natives of Chaldea. ¹⁶As soon as she saw them, she lusted after them and sent messengers to them in Chaldea. ¹⁷Then the Babylonians came to her, to the bed of love, and in their lust they defiled her. After she had been defiled by them, she turned away from them in disgust. ¹⁸When she carried on her prostitution openly and exposed her nakedness, I turned away

from her in disgust, just as I had turned away from her sister.
[19]Yet she became more and more promiscuous as she recalled
the days of her youth, when she was a prostitute in Egypt.
[20]There she lusted after her lovers, whose genitals were like
those of donkeys and whose emission was like that of horses.
[21]So you longed for the lewdness of your youth, when in Egypt
your bosom was caressed and your young breasts fondled.

[22]"Therefore, Oholibah, this is what the Sovereign LORD
says: I will stir up your lovers against you, those you turned
away from in disgust, and I will bring them against you from
every side—[23]the Babylonians and all the Chaldeans, the men
of Pekod and Shoa and Koa, and all the Assyrians with them,
handsome young men, all of them governors and commanders,
chariot officers and men of high rank, all mounted on horses.
[24]They will come against you with weapons, chariots and wagons and with a throng of people; they will take up positions
against you on every side with large and small shields and with
helmets. I will turn you over to them for punishment, and they
will punish you according to their standards. [25]I will direct my
jealous anger against you, and they will deal with you in fury.
They will cut off your noses and your ears, and those of you
who are left will fall by the sword. They will take away your
sons and daughters, and those of you who are left will be consumed by fire. [26]They will also strip you of your clothes and
take your fine jewelry. [27]So I will put a stop to the lewdness
and prostitution you began in Egypt. You will not look on
these things with longing or remember Egypt anymore.

[28]"For this is what the Sovereign LORD says: I am about to
hand you over to those you hate, to those you turned away
from in disgust. [29]They will deal with you in hatred and take
away everything you have worked for. They will leave you
naked and bare, and the shame of your prostitution will be
exposed. Your lewdness and promiscuity [30]have brought this
upon you, because you lusted after the nations and defiled
yourself with their idols. [31]You have gone the way of your sister; so I will put her cup into your hand.

[32]"This is what the Sovereign LORD says:

"You will drink your sister's cup,
    a cup large and deep;
it will bring scorn and derision,
    for it holds so much.

> ³³You will be filled with drunkenness and sorrow,
>   the cup of ruin and desolation,
>   the cup of your sister Samaria.
> ³⁴You will drink it and drain it dry;
>   you will dash it to pieces
>   and tear your breasts.

I have spoken, declares the Sovereign LORD.

³⁵"Therefore this is what the Sovereign LORD says: Since you have forgotten me and thrust me behind your back, you must bear the consequences of your lewdness and prostitution."

³⁶The LORD said to me: "Son of man, will you judge Oholah and Oholibah? Then confront them with their detestable practices, ³⁷for they have committed adultery and blood is on their hands. They committed adultery with their idols; they even sacrificed their children, whom they bore to me, as food for them. ³⁸They have also done this to me: At that same time they defiled my sanctuary and desecrated my Sabbaths. ³⁹On the very day they sacrificed their children to their idols, they entered my sanctuary and desecrated it. That is what they did in my house.

⁴⁰"They even sent messengers for men who came from far away, and when they arrived you bathed yourself for them, painted your eyes and put on your jewelry. ⁴¹You sat on an elegant couch, with a table spread before it on which you had placed the incense and oil that belonged to me.

⁴²"The noise of a carefree crowd was around her; Sabeans were brought from the desert along with men from the rabble, and they put bracelets on the arms of the woman and her sister and beautiful crowns on their heads. ⁴³Then I said about the one worn out by adultery, 'Now let them use her as a prostitute, for that is all she is.' ⁴⁴And they slept with her. As men sleep with a prostitute, so they slept with those lewd women, Oholah and Oholibah. ⁴⁵But righteous men will sentence them to the punishment of women who commit adultery and shed blood, because they are adulterous and blood is on their hands.

⁴⁶"This is what the Sovereign LORD says: Bring a mob against them and give them over to terror and plunder. ⁴⁷The mob will stone them and cut them down with their swords; they will kill their sons and daughters and burn down their houses.

⁴⁸"So I will put an end to lewdness in the land, that all women may take warning and not imitate you. ⁴⁹You will suffer the penalty for your lewdness and bear the consequences of your sins of idolatry. Then you will know that I am the Sovereign LORD."

AS IN CHAPTER 16, the prophet depicts the history and future of Judah by means of an extended metaphor, picturing Jerusalem and Samaria as two exceedingly wanton women. The shockingly explicit language and not particularly disguised identities of the cities combine to give the resulting picture an "in-your-face" effect, whose emotional impact is far greater than a similar indictment in dry legal terminology would have been. If, as Paul Ricoeur has argued, metaphor involves the "felt participation" of the reader,[1] then in Ezekiel 23 the prophet harnesses all of the emotional impact of a graphic portrayal of sexual perversion to drive home the point that Jerusalem's coming destruction is both the deserved and the inevitable consequence of her past actions.

Two women are introduced in the opening verses as sisters, sharing a common mother (23:2). This is intended to denote not merely the historical fact of a shared heredity between the northern and southern kingdoms but a deeper commonality: Though they are two in number, they are one in nature, living parallel lives.[2] This essential identity is underlined by the names they are given: Samaria is designated "Oholah" while Jerusalem is named "Oholibah." The meaning of these names ("her tent" and "my tent is in her") does not seem to be in this case of any particular significance; rather, it is the similarity of their names that draws our attention. Oholah and Oholibah go together like Tweedledum and Tweedledee.[3]

These sisters have behaved alike from their youth. Already in Egypt they gave themselves over to prostitution (23:3). But in spite of that, the Lord "made honest women of them" (to use a Victorian phrase): He married them and they became the mothers of his children (23:4). Thus far, there is nothing controversial about Ezekiel's retelling of history. God had entered an exclusive relationship of overlordship, a covenant, with Israel, in spite of Israel's checkered history. Israel's undistinguished past in terms of their

---

1. Paul Ricoeur, "The Metaphorical Process As Cognition, Imagination and Feeling," *On Metaphor*, ed. S. Sacks (Chicago: Univ. of Chicago Press, 1978), 154, cited in Galambush, *Jerusalem*, 8.

2. Galambush, *Jerusalem*, 110.

3. Allen, *Ezekiel 20–48*, 48.

faithfulness to the Lord was not particularly news to those familiar with the events recounted in Exodus and Numbers: the grumbling at Marah (Ex. 15:23–24), the golden calf (Ex. 32), the bad report of the spies (Num. 13:26–33), Korah's rebellion (Num. 16), the immorality with the Moabites (Num. 25).[4] Besides, that was all ancient history.

In the next verses, however, Ezekiel brings his hearers down to the present in a hurry with a brief sketch of the history of the older sister, Oholah (i.e., Samaria, the northern kingdom; 23:5–10). Not content with the Lord, she traded her attentions elsewhere. She lusted after the Assyrians, seeking to enter a covenant with them, a politico-religious alliance that implied a repudiation of trust in the Lord as her sole provider. What attracted her to the Assyrians was their power and prestige. They all appeared to her as warriors—horsemen and charioteers, governors and commanders, dressed in splendid garments of blue (23:6).

The historical background of this assertion is not hard to trace. From around 841–840 B.C., Israel was involved in an alliance with Assyria when Shalmaneser III received a substantial tribute from Jehu.[5] Climbing into bed with Assyria may have seemed the logical—perhaps the only possible—political option to Israel's leadership, but it was also tantamount to a rejection of trust in the Lord in favor of Assyria's idols, with which Israel now defiled herself (23:7). It was a return to her former way of life in Egypt, from which the Lord had redeemed her (23:8).[6] The consequences of her lifestyle choice were severe, yet fitting. The Lord gave her over into the hand of her lovers, the Assyrians (23:9). The very things that attracted her to them rebounded against her. Their warrior power was exerted against her, and far from clothing her in similar manner to themselves they stripped her naked and killed her (23:10).

But Oholah is not Ezekiel's real interest. The brief sketch of her history merely sets up a paradigm of sin and punishment to which the subsequent history of her southern sister can be compared. Oholah became a "byword" (lit., a "name") among women, and judgments were done to her (23:10). This is her function in the chapter: Her history is known and (from a southern perspective) regarded as a just fate for her sin. But the question is, "Has her younger sister applied to herself the lessons to be drawn from the older sister's fate?"

---

4. For a similar list of Israel's failings in the desert, see Ps. 106:7–39.

5. The details are recorded on the Black Obelisk of Shalmaneser III; see *ANET*, 280–81.

6. Galambush sees here a reference to Israel's subsequent rebellion against Assyria on the strength of Egyptian support (*Jerusalem*, 112). However, although this was certainly a further manifestation of the same mindset, seeking human deliverers instead of the Lord, this does not seem to be in the prophet's mind; it is Oholah's Egyptian *lifestyle* that she does not abandon (lit., "her adultery from Egypt"), not her Egyptian *lover*.

As the chapter unfolds, it is evident that she has not. Oholibah is not merely like her sister; she is *worse* than her sister. Nor is this depravity the result of ignorance: Her sister "saw" and yet still became more depraved in her lust, committing more adulteries than her sister (23:11). She first sinned in exactly the same way with the Assyrians (23:12, which closely recapitulates 23:5–6), and then added to her little black book the Babylonians (23:14). She was worse in her wantonness than her sister not merely in the number of her lovers (two as against one) but in the nature of their relationship. She was attracted to the Babylonians by a mere wall depiction; entranced by the vision of them she herself sent messengers to Babylon to get them (23:16). She was thus not merely willing to be seduced but was herself the active seductress. They thus became idols come to life for her: Like the idols of the house of Israel in 8:10, they are described as "portrayed on a wall, figures of Chaldeans" (23:14). Though they may be attractively dressed up, they are merely an old idolatry warmed over.

Once more, the historical details lie not far below the surface of the metaphor. Judah's relationship with Assyria went back to at least 734 B.C., when Ahaz appealed to Tiglath-Pileser for assistance against Pekah of Israel and Rezin of Damascus (2 Kings 16:5–7; Isa. 7:1–2). In 714 B.C., Hezekiah entertained ambassadors from the Babylonian ruler Merodach-Baladan, who was seeking to rally support against the Assyrians (2 Kings 20:12–19). When the Babylonian-led resistance crumbled, Hezekiah once again apparently sent tribute to the Assyrians.[7] But by 605 B.C. Babylon had established itself as the dominant power in the region, and Judah was in a vassal relationship toward them.

What his compatriots may have read as political necessity, however, Ezekiel presents in a different light: Submission to these relationships is nothing less than spiritual adultery against their true covenant head, the Lord himself. Once again, the prophet seeks to challenge Judah's complacent sense of moral and spiritual superiority to her former northern neighbor.

Her adulterous liaisons did not satisfy Oholibah. Having been defiled by her lovers, she became disgusted with them and turned away from them (23:17). But in turning away from her adulterous lovers, she still did not turn away from her love of adultery. She continued her prostitution openly, so that the Lord turned away from her, just as he had earlier turned away from her sister (23:18).

Yet even this did not deter her from her course; it was a case of "train a child in the way [s]he should go, and when [s]he is old [s]he will not turn from it" (Prov. 22:6). She remembered the days of her youth in Egypt, not as the time

---

7. Alan R. Millard, "Sennacherib's Attack on Hezekiah," *TynBul* 36 (1985): 71.

when the Lord delivered her from bondage (as the book of Deuteronomy repeatedly urges Israel to remember Egypt[8]) but as the time when they enjoyed pleasures no longer theirs (cf. Num. 11:5). As DeVries puts it: "She had forgotten what she should have remembered and remembered what she should have forgotten."[9] In her lust, she was not even limited by natural relationships; instead, she sought those whose sexual capacities were not merely superhuman but positively bestial ("whose genitals were like those of donkeys and whose emission [lit., floods] was like that of horses," Ezek. 23:20).

The result of such thoroughgoing depravity is predictable: A fitting judgment will fall on the head of the wanton woman. The Lord "will stir up"[10] her lovers against her from all around (23:22), not merely the Babylonians and Assyrians but men from Pekod, Shoa, and Koa as well.[11] As with Oholah, the things that attracted Oholibah to her lovers are now used against her. Their strength and military prowess now become the means of assaulting her on every side; weaponry, chariotry, armor, and numbers are now turned against Jerusalem (23:24). God will "turn [his wayward people] over to them for punishment," and as a result their enemies will be allowed to "punish [them] according to their standards."

This combination of divine and human judgment is further developed in the following verses. The Lord says, "I will direct my jealous anger against you, and they will deal with you in fury" (23:25). As Jerusalem's sins were worse than her sister's, so also will her punishment be. She will not only be stripped but also disfigured, and her children will not only be taken from her but will also fall by the sword and be consumed by fire (23:25).[12] The goal of this judgment is a proper amnesia: forgetting the prostitution begun in Egypt (23:27). Her lovers have now become her enemies, who will strip her and plunder her (23:28–29). As she followed in the pattern of her elder sister, so now she will share her elder sister's fate and drink from the same bitter cup of sorrow, all the way down to its dregs (23:32–34). In her shame, she will tear out the bodily members that led her into sin in the first place, her breasts.[13]

---

8. Deut. 7:18; 15:15; 16:3, 12; 24:18, 22.

9. Simon J. DeVries, "Remembrance in Ezekiel: A Study of an Old Testament Theme," *Int* 16 (1962): 64.

10. Is it significant that the Hiphil of *ʿûr* can have a sexual connotation, as in Song 2:7; 3:5; 8:4? See BDB, 735c.

11. Whether these last three are historical allies of Judah or Chaldean tribes is debated. The three names suggest a sinister wordplay, sounding like "punish," "cry for help," and "shriek" (Allen, *Ezekiel 20–48*, 50).

12. This is presumably metaphorical "overkill" since all three fates cannot simultaneously occur to individuals. Alternatively, three different (though equivalent) fates may be in view; compare the use of the same three modes of death in 5:2.

13. Greenberg, *Ezekiel 21–37*, 484.

In the remaining verses (23:36–49), Ezekiel is once more cast into the role of prosecuting attorney ("Son of man, will you judge. . . ?") as the point of the metaphor is driven home. Jerusalem[14] is to be confronted with her adultery and bloodshed. This section links together the political charges of the earlier part of chapter 23 with the social and cultic charges of chapter 22. Adultery has taken place at home and on the road, with domestic and foreign idols. At home, sanctuary and Sabbath have been defiled, and even their children have been sacrificed (23:38–39). Not content with such "homegrown" heresies, they have sent messengers far and wide to all comers (23:40). But in spite of their beauty preparations and makeup, their true nature is becoming clear to all: an aging, worn-out prostitute, desired not for her charms but for her availability and price (23:43).

Once more, the conclusion of the sisters' activities is clearly stated: An army will come, plundering them, stoning them, and putting them to the sword. Their children will be slaughtered, their homes burned (23:47). Thus the Lord will bring to an end all such adultery. This time the object lesson will be heeded (unlike in v. 10), and "all women"[15] will be chastened and not do likewise (23:48). The chapter closes with the recognition formula: "Then you will know that I am the Sovereign LORD" (23:49).

Bridging Contexts

THE NATURE OF METAPHOR. Metaphors and related forms of pictorial speech are among the most culture-specific means of expression. Is it truly possible to explain to anyone not brought up in a cricketing nation what it means to be "playing on a sticky wicket"?[16] The entire effectiveness of the metaphor depends on shared "commonplaces,"

---

14. Rhetorically, the charge is addressed to Oholah as well as Oholibah. However, as with the metaphor itself, the focus is clearly on Jerusalem (Oholibah) as the charge of "defil[ing] my sanctuary" (23:38) makes clear.

15. The reference to "women" here is not a moralizing application to women and adultery in general (so Zimmerli, *Ezekiel*, 1:492) but rather figurative, as in v. 10. However, it can scarcely be figurative of the nations (so Eichrodt, *Ezekiel*, 333; Allen, *Ezekiel 20–48*, 51) since they do not exist in the same covenant relationship to the Lord in Ezekiel. If a specific application is to be sought, they are surely figurative of future generations within the covenant people, who will learn from the fall of Samaria and Jerusalem the lesson that the generation prior to the Exile was unable or unwilling to learn from the fall of Samaria.

16. For the curious, in former days cricket pitches were left uncovered during rain delays. During the period after a rain delay, as the pitch (or "wicket") was drying out, the ball would frequently bounce or spin unexpectedly off a damp spot, causing great difficulties to the unfortunate batsman. In recent years, with pitches fully covered to ensure rapid resumption of play after a rain delay, "sticky wickets" are only a memory.

a range of ideas associated with the image used in the metaphor.[17] These ideas are culturally determined. The metaphor "the LORD is my shepherd" naturally means something slightly different in an ancient Near Eastern context from what it does in a Scottish context because Scottish shepherds are associated with a different set of ideas from ancient Near Eastern shepherds—for instance, the use of sheep dogs.

This difficulty may, of course, be overcome in many cases if readers immerse themselves sufficiently in the source culture to understand the ideas associated with the image in question. It becomes problematic, however, when the reader finds the image adopted is not merely alien but antagonistic. The perspective of the metaphor is not simply different from their perspective but is positively repulsive to it. This situation tends to trigger an instinctive response in the reader of rejection toward the metaphor.

This process may happen on a personal level, as when a person who has a bad relationship with his or her own human father finds it hard to accept the biblical image of God as "Father." But this same process can also happen on a cultural level. For example, the Sawi people of Irian Jaya celebrated men who formed friendships with the express purpose of later betraying the befriended one in order to be killed and eaten.[18] This cultural association naturally made it hard for them to understand the gospel, for on their cultural reading Judas was evidently the hero of the story.

By the same token, the metaphor of Ezekiel 23 is not merely alien to our twentieth-century Western culture, it is, to many people, antagonistic. That antagonism may be expressed in mild language ("We cannot but feel ill at ease with the harsh way in which guilt and blame for sexual misconduct is presented ... as primarily a female responsibility")[19] or in harsh language ("a pornographic fantasy"),[20] but it is there in most contemporary expositions. What is alien is not so much the message itself—for the message of Ezekiel 23 is not fundamentally different from that of the preceding chapters—but the form in which the message is delivered, the metaphor itself. It is the envelope in which the letter comes that causes offense, not the letter itself.

Understanding the ancient marital metaphor. What shall we say about this envelope? Perhaps in the face of contemporary revulsion, we do well to

---

17. See Max Black, *Models and Metaphors: Studies in Language and Philosophy* (Ithaca, N.Y.: Cornell Univ. Press, 1962).

18. See Don Richardson, *Peace Child* (Glendale: Regal, 1974).

19. Ronald E. Clements, *Ezekiel* (Louisville: Westminster/John Knox, 1996), 108.

20. Athalya Brenner, "Pornoprophetics Revisited: Some Additional Reflections" *JSOT* 70 (1996): 63–86. J. Cheryl Exum terms this chapter "the most pornographic example of divine violence" (*Plotted, Shot and Painted: Cultural Representations of Biblical Women* [JSOTS 215; Sheffield: Sheffield Academic Press, 1996], 109).

---

recognize how accurately it communicated truth within its own cultural context. It relied on certain cultural commonplaces. It assumed (1) the idea of the capital city as the "wife" of the deity,[21] (2) the idea that political alliances with foreign nations were a breach of that covenant relationship, analogous to adultery,[22] (3) the idea that multiple adultery on the part of a woman was shocking and perverse, and (4) the idea that the appropriate punishment for adultery was death (Lev. 20:10). If those presuppositions are affirmed, then Ezekiel makes his case with considerable logic and great emotional power that the city of Jerusalem has become polluted by her adultery and God is entirely justified in bringing in the agents of his choice. To be sure, attention is uniquely focused in this chapter on the punishment of the adulteress rather than that of her lovers, but the remaining chapters of Ezekiel make it clear that the other nations will not escape God's judgment either (Ezek. 25–32; cf. 21:30–32).

However, we should also recognize that the cultural "commonplaces" affirmed above are different from those generally accepted today. Multiple adultery is now often regarded as self-fulfillment. It is depicted positively in novels and movies as something to be envied and emulated. Violence against women, on the other hand, is one of the few remaining taboos, an act that rightly generates strong feelings of revulsion. What is more, many people in our society question the use of the death penalty for any crime, let alone for adultery. Indeed, most within the church would rightly be uncomfortable with the idea of executing adulterers.[23] So we have to recognize that the envelope in which it is packaged makes it hard for contemporary readers to "hear" the message of Ezekiel 23.

This fact was illustrated personally for me at a recent scholarly conference where a paper was presented on Ezekiel 23. The presenter argued that on close examination the chapter deconstructed its own message, a message the presenter herself found to be theologically problematic. In personal conversation after the lecture, it transpired that part of the presenter's interest in and concern over this particular passage stemmed from her own experience in hearing it used to justify the abuse of women. Because of her experiences and feminist perspective, the metaphor adopted by the prophet was deeply troubling to her, leading her to reject the message contained by the metaphor.

Two ways of using metaphors. However, there are actually two ways of using metaphors to address an audience. One way is to use to the full extent

---

21. Galambush, *Jerusalem*, 23.

22. Ibid., 59.

23. For a thoughtful study of the issues, see Vern Poythress, "Just Penalties for Sexual Crimes," *The Shadow of Christ in the Law of Moses* (Brentwood, Tenn.: Wolgemuth & Hyatt, 1991), 193–221.

the accepted cultural commonplaces to drive home an unpalatable truth in an inescapable way. That is how the story of the poor man with one ewe lamb, which the prophet Nathan recounted to King David, works (2 Sam. 12:1–4). An inescapable straightforward logic drives the story to its conclusion, at which point the application is made. Alternatively, a metaphor may be used to turn upside down expectations, thus challenging the "cultural commonplaces." So in the parable of the good Samaritan, the "cultural commonplace" that all Samaritans were filthy scoundrels is challenged by placing the expected villain in what turns out to be the hero's role.

To its original audience, Ezekiel 23 was an example of the first category of usage. Though the women were outrageously unlike any that Ezekiel's audience knew, the metaphor itself was unproblematic: There would have been no question in their minds that the fate of the women was thoroughly deserved. No matter how unpalatable the message that Jerusalem would inevitably be destroyed because of the people's unfaithfulness to God, demonstrated in foreign political alliances, the metaphor clearly worked in that setting.

To a contemporary audience, however, it will be difficult to use it in that way unless considerable work is done first, explaining the ancient Near Eastern perspective.[24] It may be more profitable to use it in the second mode, to undermine the contemporary cultural commonplaces that what used to be called sin is simply harmless fun, so long as it takes place between consenting adults. Sin is always a serious business, whether it takes the form of actual adultery or spiritual adultery, the worship of literal false gods of wood and gold or the spiritual false gods of materialism, capitalism, socialism, and every other "ism" that seems to offer a way of "salvation." Sin has serious consequences. It has wages that must always be paid, whether by ourselves in eternity or by Christ on the cross. That belief is far from being a contemporary commonplace. It is, nonetheless, true.

ELIMINATING THE CONCEPT **of sin.** Sin is an unfashionable concept. Christian counselor John Bettler has pointed out how our very language of sexual sins softens the idea of sin: "We don't commit adultery anymore. We have affairs. . . . Adultery sounds harsh and ugly and destructive. An affair sounds kind of gentle and nice and almost acceptable. In the same way, we don't have homosexuals anymore. We have peo-

---

24. Paradoxically, the parable of the good Samaritan has become equally hard to expound in a context where the adjective "good" is entirely comfortable, even expected, next to the noun "Samaritan."

ple with alternative sexual preferences. We've softened the concept of sin."[25] But if we don't have sin, we are no longer sinners. And if we are not sinners, we don't need salvation; we need recovery instead.

Jerusalem was beyond help or recovery. She was a sinner of truly shocking proportions: a multiple-timing, "cheating wife" sort of sinner. There was no "twelve-step" program that could bring about her recovery from her sexual addiction. The "Higher Power" was not there to assist her but to pour out his justified wrath on her for her sin. The Babylonians would come—the very ones in whom she had trusted—and they would bring to an end her existence. It was time to write her sorry obituary: She was a sinner from her youth and a sinner to the end. She belonged together with the sexually immoral, the idolaters, the adulterers, the male prostitutes, the homosexual offenders, the thieves, the greedy, the drunkards, the slanderers, and the swindlers; like them, she would certainly not "inherit the kingdom of God" (1 Cor. 6:9–10). It may be countercultural today to assert that "the wages of sin is death" and that those who offend in the smallest way against a pure and holy God deserve to spend an eternity experiencing his wrath, but it is not because that is an unscriptural notion.

All too often in our proclamation of the gospel we shy away from shocking our neighbors with the radical truth of the horrible, hell-deserving nature of sin. In that, we may be motivated by our desire not to put a stumbling block in our neighbor's path. Perhaps we are also motivated by our desire to forget the fact that the personal sins we have ourselves committed are equally hell-deserving. Yet in eliminating the awfulness of sin, we simultaneously eliminate the meaning of the cross, the very heart of the gospel. For if sin is not really all that bad, why did the Son of God have to die to pay the debt that sinners owed?

God's actions to save us. What is the truly remarkable, world-shaking notion in Scripture is not that God's wrath is revealed against all ungodliness (Rom. 1:18). That is simply the logical consequence of his infinite holiness and purity. Rather, what is astonishing is that when that wrath is revealed from heaven against all ungodliness, not all will share Jerusalem's fate. Certainly it is not because some especially righteous human beings do not deserve to share her fate. We all deserve the same judgment. We too are among those on Paul's 1 Corinthians 6:9–10 list—certainly in our thoughts and, in some cases, also in our acts. Paul is speaking of us when he says, "That is what some of you were" (6:11). But God intervened. He acted to save us: "You were washed, you were sanctified, you were justified in the name of the Lord Jesus

---

25. John F. Bettler, "Counseling and the Doctrine of Sin," *Journal of Biblical Counseling* 13 (1994): 2.

Christ and by the Spirit of our God." We were sinners, but now in Christ we are saints. What an amazing change!

But once again Ezekiel 23 reminds us that that change cannot be wrought without the payment of a price. A penalty for sin must be borne (23:49); someone must cover my debt. For me to be reclothed in Christ's righteousness, he had to be stripped naked. For me to be crowned with glory, he had to wear the crown of thorns. For me to live, he had to die. The violence I deserved fell on him; it is by his stripes that I am healed. The wrath to come is real, and if it did not fall on Jesus in my place, then I must bear it myself.

Ezekiel 23 is incorporated into Scripture not to give its readers some kind of salacious fantasy of sex and violence, as some contemporary commentators imagine. Certainly it is intended to shock, as was the case with the other "R-rated" section of Ezekiel's prophecy (ch. 16). But the shock is designed to jolt the comfortable into a recognition of the reality and inevitability of the judgment to come so that we might see the utter folly of trusting in anything—or anyone—less than the living God. It is intended to strip away the pretensions of the pseudo-righteous and expose the naked truth that they too deserve the full weight of God's wrath.

There is no message of hope in Ezekiel 23. The stone is rolled away to reveal the gaping mouth of the tomb, which is ready to swallow up defiled Jerusalem, just as it had earlier swallowed up defiled Samaria. But for those reading Ezekiel 23 from a New Testament perspective, the opened mouth of another tomb speaks a word of comfort even to those as defiled as Jerusalem. Because Christ has died in our place, and more than that has risen from the dead, there is now no condemnation for us who are in Christ Jesus! My death is swallowed up in his victory; my defilement is replaced by his purity, credited to my account. In the name of the Lord Jesus Christ, I too have been washed, I have been justified, and I am being sanctified. What is more, this is true in spite of the sins that I continue to commit daily. Although I am unfaithful to my commitment to God and continue to sin against him regularly in thought, word, and deed, the gospel continues to be good news for me, a sinner. In the words of William Cowper's hymn:

> There is a fountain filled with blood drawn from Immanuel's veins;
> And sinners plunged beneath that flood lose all their guilty stains.
>
> The dying thief rejoiced to see that fountain in his day;
> And there may I, though vile as he, wash all my sins away.
>
> Dear dying Lamb, Thy precious blood shall never lose its power,
> Till all the ransomed church of God be saved, to sin no more.
>
> E'er since by faith I saw the stream Thy flowing wounds supply,
> Redeeming love has been my theme, and shall be till I die.

Ezekiel 24

❧

I N THE NINTH YEAR, in the tenth month on the tenth day, the
word of the LORD came to me: [2]"Son of man, record this
date, this very date, because the king of Babylon has laid
siege to Jerusalem this very day. [3]Tell this rebellious house a
parable and say to them: 'This is what the Sovereign LORD says:

"'Put on the cooking pot; put it on
    and pour water into it.
[4]Put into it the pieces of meat,
    all the choice pieces—the leg and the shoulder.
Fill it with the best of these bones;
[5]   take the pick of the flock.
Pile wood beneath it for the bones;
    bring it to a boil
    and cook the bones in it.

[6]"'For this is what the Sovereign LORD says:

"'Woe to the city of bloodshed,
    to the pot now encrusted,
    whose deposit will not go away!
Empty it piece by piece
    without casting lots for them.
[7]"'For the blood she shed is in her midst:
    She poured it on the bare rock;
she did not pour it on the ground,
    where the dust would cover it.
[8]To stir up wrath and take revenge
    I put her blood on the bare rock,
    so that it would not be covered.

[9]"'Therefore this is what the Sovereign LORD says:

"'Woe to the city of bloodshed!
    I, too, will pile the wood high.
[10]So heap on the wood
    and kindle the fire.
Cook the meat well,
    mixing in the spices;
    and let the bones be charred.

¹¹ Then set the empty pot on the coals
    till it becomes hot and its copper glows
so its impurities may be melted
    and its deposit burned away.
¹² It has frustrated all efforts;
    its heavy deposit has not been removed,
    not even by fire.

¹³"'Now your impurity is lewdness. Because I tried to cleanse you but you would not be cleansed from your impurity, you will not be clean again until my wrath against you has subsided.

¹⁴"'I the LORD have spoken. The time has come for me to act. I will not hold back; I will not have pity, nor will I relent. You will be judged according to your conduct and your actions, declares the Sovereign LORD.'"

¹⁵The word of the LORD came to me: ¹⁶"Son of man, with one blow I am about to take away from you the delight of your eyes. Yet do not lament or weep or shed any tears. ¹⁷Groan quietly; do not mourn for the dead. Keep your turban fastened and your sandals on your feet; do not cover the lower part of your face or eat the customary food ⌐of mourners⌐."

¹⁸So I spoke to the people in the morning, and in the evening my wife died. The next morning I did as I had been commanded.

¹⁹Then the people asked me, "Won't you tell us what these things have to do with us?"

²⁰So I said to them, "The word of the LORD came to me: ²¹Say to the house of Israel, 'This is what the Sovereign LORD says: I am about to desecrate my sanctuary—the stronghold in which you take pride, the delight of your eyes, the object of your affection. The sons and daughters you left behind will fall by the sword. ²²And you will do as I have done. You will not cover the lower part of your face or eat the customary food ⌐of mourners⌐. ²³You will keep your turbans on your heads and your sandals on your feet. You will not mourn or weep but will waste away because of your sins and groan among yourselves. ²⁴Ezekiel will be a sign to you; you will do just as he has done. When this happens, you will know that I am the Sovereign LORD.'

²⁵"And you, son of man, on the day I take away their stronghold, their joy and glory, the delight of their eyes, their

heart's desire, and their sons and daughters as well—²⁶on that day a fugitive will come to tell you the news. ²⁷At that time your mouth will be opened; you will speak with him and will no longer be silent. So you will be a sign to them, and they will know that I am the LORD."

FOR TWENTY-THREE CHAPTERS now, Ezekiel has been proclaiming the wrath to come on Jerusalem. Finally, in Ezekiel 24, the sword of judgment descends on the city. Verses 1–14 are an oracle delivered to the prophet by God on the very day when Nebuchadnezzar's assault on the city began. The message is received by the prophet on the tenth of the tenth month, and the prophet is to make note of this date, which on our reckoning is January 15, 587 B.C., because this is the day on which the king of Babylon laid siege to Jerusalem (24:2).[1] This date is to be noted because it will subsequently provide further "objective" evidence of the prophet's veracity.

The Day of Reckoning for Jerusalem (24:1–14)

FOLLOWING THE HEBREW more literally, this is the day when Nebuchadnezzar "leaned on" (*sāmak*) Jerusalem, a word with overtones of the sacrificial system. A worshiper approaching the sanctuary designated the animal to be sacrificed as his through a ritual "leaning on of hands" (Lev. 1:4; 3:2).[2] By Ezekiel's use of this terminology, Nebuchadnezzar is depicted as designating Jerusalem as the sacrificial lamb—though hardly one without spot or blemish, as the law required—ready to be dismembered for the glory of God.

This sacrificial language leads into a parable to be delivered to[3] the "rebellious house" (*bêt hammerî*, 24:3). This is a favorite expression for Judah in Ezekiel,[4] one that indicates that their rebellion against Nebuchadnezzar is not a glorious (if doomed) fight for freedom and self-determination but rather an expression of their basic rebellious nature—a rebellion fundamentally directed against God. In the parable, Jerusalem is compared to a cooking pot (*sîr*) in which abundant meat has been placed to be cooked (24:3), an image familiar already from 11:7–12. The sacrificial animal has been cut up

---

1. On the date, see Block, *Ezekiel 1–24*, 772–73.

2. Wenham, *Leviticus*, 63.

3. *ʾel* is ambiguous and can either mean the parable is to be addressed "to" the rebellious house or that it is "about" the rebellious house (Greenberg, *Ezekiel 21–37*, 497).

4. It occurs fourteen times in the book: 2:5–6; 3:9, 26–27; 12:2–3, 9, 25; 17:12; 44:6.

and all of its pieces "gathered"[5] to be boiled, presumably as a fellowship offering. The wood[6] has been piled up under the pot and the pot has been brought to a nice simmer.[7]

Thus far the expectations of the audience have been moved in a positive direction. But in a classic twist, typical of the genre of parable, what ought to be a tasty sacred meal is, in fact, a foul, profane mess. The "choice pieces" and "the best of these bones" from the "pick of the flock" (24:4–5) turn out to be nothing but defiled filth (ḥeᵖātâ, 24:6).[8] This filth that is inside her will not "come out" (yāṣāᵖ; 24:6; NIV, "go away"), a phrase that has a double meaning. In terms of the imagery of the pot, the filth that will not come out reflects the frustration of a burned-on mess that cannot be removed. On the level of the metaphorical meaning, "come out" is precisely what Jerusalem's inhabitants hope to do at the end of the siege.

As in chapter 11, however, the pot will not protect them; they have defiled the city by their evil and so they (the filth) will not come out from her safely. Their only exit from the pot will be when they are "brought out" (Hiphil of yāṣāᵖ) for judgment (24:6; cf. 11:9). Nor will this judgment be partial, with some selected to die and some to live, as when the lot was cast over the two goats on the Day of Atonement, with one chosen for the altar and the other to be driven off into the desert (Lev. 16:8). No lots will be cast over the pot, for all the meat is destined for the same end, reprobation (Ezek. 24:6). There will be no escape.

The blood Jerusalem has shed in her midst is left uncovered, poured out on a bare rock rather than on the ground (24:7). Covering the blood with earth (Lev. 17:13) was required for the blood of all animals slaughtered for meat in Deuteronomy 12:16, 24. Blood left exposed would provoke the wrath of God, so their action was nothing less than a deliberate act of sacrilege. Like the blood of Abel, the blood of the innocent victims of the bloody city cries out for justice, and in consequence Jerusalem's blood will also be poured out uncovered (Ezek. 24:8).

---

5. "To gather" is usually the language of restoration. Here, however, as in 22:19–22, the language has been diverted to speak of destruction.

6. MT has the word for "bones," but the bones are in the pot, not underneath it. It should be a similar word meaning "wood," as in verse 10.

7. The Hebrew for "put ... on" (šᵉpōṯ, 24:3) sounds almost exactly like "judge" (šāpaṭ).

8. This rather obscure word, which occurs only in this chapter, is normally translated "rust" (RSV) or "corrosion" (Allen), a condition affecting the pot itself. Thus the NIV renders it "the pot now encrusted." However, it may rather be referring to the contamination wrought by what is inside the vessel ("the pot whose filth is in her") rather than on the vessel itself (Block, *Ezekiel 1–24*, 778). This fits better with the depiction of the city of bloodshed in Ezekiel 22, which stresses repeatedly the defilement "in her."

Returning to the imagery of the pot, the Lord declares: "Heap on the wood and kindle the fire. Cook the meat well, removing the broth,[9] and let the bones be charred" (24:10). The empty pot is now transformed into a kind of refiner's furnace in a final attempt to try to melt away the impurities (24:11), as in 22:20–22. But once again, all efforts to remove the defilement have proved ineffective. God's wrath must be satisfied on Jerusalem if she is ever to be clean again (24:13), and it is time for that definitive final action to begin. The time for words has ended; now it is time for deeds (24:14).

The Death of Ezekiel's Wife (24:15–27)

THE SECOND HALF of the chapter shows that the oracle of painful destruction is not delivered from the safety of an armchair in distant Babylon. The sword that is going to strike Jerusalem first strikes the prophet himself in the most painful and personal of his prophetic sign-acts. His own wife, the delight of his eyes, is suddenly taken from him (24:16). This is no random turn of fate, but a sudden stroke directly from God. Yet Ezekiel is not permitted to mourn publicly in the traditional ways, by lamentation and tears, disheveled clothing, and special food (24:17). All he can do is "groan quietly," that is, mourn in privacy and isolation without the usual rites invoking social solidarity and sympathy.[10] Outwardly, he is to behave as if nothing has happened.

This strange behavior is to be a sign to the people of the significance of what is to come (24:24). The temple in Jerusalem was their pride and joy; it had become as precious to the Jerusalemites as the closest of relations (24:21). This building, the delight of their eyes, will be desecrated by God. It will be destroyed along with the sons and daughters whom the exiles had left behind. Yet the people will not weep or wail or mourn publicly for the temple (24:22). This is not because of any absence of grief on their part, but because in the face of such a devastating, all-encompassing judgment, the usual social structures of mourning rites will be overwhelmed. The normal channels of community support will be gone in the face of such universal loss; only inward grief will be possible (24:23).

But in the deepest depths of the gloom comes hope of a turning point in Judah's fortunes. On the very day when the blow falls on Ezekiel's compatriots, when the news of the fall of Jerusalem is confirmed by a fugitive,

---

9. The NIV, following MT, renders this "mixing in the spices." However, this translation does not fit the context, and the LXX and some manuscripts support the possibility that metathesis of Hebrew letters has occurred, so that the text should read, "remove the broth." The removal of broth leaves the meat dry in the cauldron, ready to be burned. See Block, *Ezekiel 1–24*, 767.

10. Greenberg, *Ezekiel 21–37*, 509.

Ezekiel's lips will be opened and he will be dumb no more (24:27). This dumbness was imposed on him at the outset of his ministry (see 3:26). He was thereby unable to intercede for the people, indeed, unable to speak anything at all except words of judgment. But a time is coming when his dumbness will be removed. With the destruction of Jerusalem, his words of judgment for the city will come to an end; their time will be complete.

Here ends the first lesson, we might say—the lesson of inevitable and incredible judgment poured out on sinners. The prophet's dumbness will be ended, and God's favor will once again be extended toward his people. This promise marks a shift in the nature of Ezekiel's proclamation. In the chapters that follow, it will be time for the prophet to speak words of judgment on the surrounding nations, Israel's enemies (chs. 25–32), and then, when the promise of the removal of dumbness is fulfilled (ch. 33), words of hope to God's chosen people (chs. 34–48).

Bridging Contexts

MEAT AND BLOOD. Filthy pots encrusted with burnt food are familiar to all places and times. Even modern technology has produced little answer to the basic problem; in my experience, the "potscrubber" cycle on the average dishwasher is a hopelessly over-optimistic designation. Old-fashioned elbow grease is required to try and shift the carbonated remains of serious culinary disasters, and even then sometimes all efforts are in vain.

But the moral and cultic dimensions of the intended meal of Ezekiel 24 may easily be lost on us. We are used to eating meat as a daily experience, unless we are vegetarian. In an ancient culture, however, unless you were exceptionally wealthy, eating meat was a rare experience, usually associated with a sacrifice.[11] On this occasion, Jerusalem's inhabitants are themselves the sacrifice, but the end result is unfit for consumption because of the city's defilement. All that is produced at the end of the fiery trial is a defiled pot, filled with a blackened mess, which even the most extreme measures cannot cleanse.

The concern to handle blood appropriately is also rather distant from us. Blood was regarded as a peculiarly sacred liquid in Israel. It contained the life of the creature (Lev. 17:11) and in consequence had to be disposed of properly. If it was the blood of a clean animal, slaughtered as a sacrifice, it was

---

11. The cultic overtones of the intended meal are further underlined by the use of a copper caldron as opposed to the standard domestic cookware made of pottery (Block, *Ezekiel 1–24*, 776).

poured out beside the altar (Deut. 12:27). If it was the blood of a profane animal, slaughtered for meat, it was to be poured out on the ground (12:16, 24) and covered with earth (Lev. 17:13). In this way, proper respect was shown for the agent of animate life.

In its original intention, blood was a taboo that emphasized Israel's calling to be "pro-life" in the fullest sense. But Jerusalem had proved careless about bloodshed, even the shedding of human blood. It was a place where life was cheap. Her inhabitants had neglected their responsibility to take seriously the requirement of Genesis 9:6, that human bloodshed be regarded as a crime of utmost seriousness, because of the nature of human beings as created in the image of God. In consequence, her blood also would be shed by God without pity and her life held to be cheap.

The hidden wisdom of God's set purposes. Much more problematic for the contemporary reader is the death of Ezekiel's wife and his prohibition from mourning. On the one hand, the conception is prevalent among Christians that "God loves you and has a wonderful plan for your life." Even though we may steer clear of its excesses, the health and wealth gospel ("God loves you and wants to give you a Cadillac and a mansion by the Country Club") still influences our thinking. We tend to believe that God's loving plan for our lives must surely include reasonable health, a job, a spouse, and a decent standard of living. If any of these things are absent from our lives, we tend to place the responsibility not on God but on the forces of evil in the world. God wants us to have these things, we theorize, but we are caught in the crossfire of the cosmic battle.

Nowhere in his Word does God promise us such an easy ride through life. Nor does he pass off responsibility on others. He is the sovereign Lord, which means that even on the battleground, the buck stops with him. Ezekiel's wife dies not because God is powerless to prevent such a thing happening, but because God has a significant purpose to accomplish through that "evil" also. It is a painful providence for the prophet to bear, but nonetheless he must receive this bitter cup too from the hand of his loving Father. As Job, another Old Testament figure equally tormented by God, put it so succinctly: "Shall we accept good from God, and not trouble?" (Job 2:10).

That God takes such dramatic action to highlight the situation is a measure of the seriousness of Judah's sin and the pain level of the coming judgment—both for Judah and for Judah's God. But what God asks his people to undergo for his sake is no more than what he himself is willing to go through for their sake. His beloved Son, Jesus, is nailed to the cross, the ultimate act of wicked men in consort together, but this itself is nothing other than God's "set purpose" (Acts 2:23). God has the right to do with his creatures as he sees fit. It may not have been the course of events we would have chosen, but that is hardly the point. The point is that God's purposes are determined with a wisdom that is above our wisdom, on the basis of thoughts that are above our thoughts. Submitting to the will of such a good God, who did not spare his own Son but freely gave him up for us, is no stoic fatalism but the freeing dependence of a trusting child.

Ancient mourning patterns. But how could God ask Ezekiel not to mourn for his wife? Isn't this an inhuman demand? Again, our unfamiliarity with the ancient culture leads us to undue psychologizing. In fact, what God asks of Ezekiel is hardly a unique occurrence. As a priest, Ezekiel would have been familiar with the restrictions on public mourning for priests in active service prescribed in Leviticus 21. A priest was not permitted to make himself ritually unclean—as formal mourning would require—for any except the closest of his relatives (21:1–4), while the high priest was not even permitted to mourn for his father or mother (21:11). Similarly, after the deaths of Nadab and Abihu in Leviticus 10, their father Aaron and their brothers Eleazar and Ithamar were forbidden to mourn for them, even though the rest of Israel could (10:6).

That does not mean that they could not feel the pain of the loss in their hearts—undoubtedly they would have—but public mourning was not permitted for the sacred person. Thus what the Lord asks of Ezekiel is not an unfeeling psychological imposition ("your wife whom you love will die and you must pretend nothing has happened") but simply a refraining from the normal social customs. His behavior was certainly regarded as odd, so that the people ask him why he is acting in this way (24:19), but it was not inhuman.

THE CERTAINTY OF **God's just judgment.** When judgment comes it will always be unexpected, no matter how clearly and often God's messengers have warned of its coming. So it was in the case of Jerusalem. Ezekiel had warned repeatedly of its certain doom, and now he speaks for the final time before that doom was realized. The fire was now kindled, ready to consume the contaminated mess that filled Jerusalem. This fire would not purify the inhabitants of the city, for they were beyond such help. It was designed simply to destroy.

What has this ancient history to do with us? The fall of Jerusalem in 586 B.C. acts as a picture of the ultimate destruction of the world. Though the scoffers may doubt that such a day of the Lord will ever happen, seeing the delay on God's part as evidence that judgment will never come (2 Peter 3:3–4), God's wrath will be poured out on the world in due season. It will come like a thief in the night (3:10), and the visible universe will disappear. God's patience, long-suffering though it is, will ultimately be exhausted, and the fire of his wrath will be poured out on the world.

Why? It is because there is no other suitable means for dealing with recalcitrant, impenitent sinners. Justice must ultimately be done, and it will be. As Abraham put it in Genesis 18:25, "Will not the Judge of all the earth do right?" Indeed he will, and the end result will be destruction for the world, as it was for Sodom and Gomorrah. The purpose of this fiery conflagration is not the purification of the wicked. Having refused to be cleansed (Ezek. 24:13), now God's people have nothing to expect but payment in full for what their actions deserve, which is God's wrath poured out without pity or holding back (24:14).

Living in the light of God's judgment. Is this just an "Old Testament" perspective on God that is out of step with the fullness of "New Testament" revelation of God's love? Not at all. The writer to the Hebrews warns of the fearful fate that awaits anyone who turns his or her back on the revelation of God in Christ:

> If we deliberately keep on sinning after we have received the knowledge of the truth, no sacrifice for sins is left, but only a fearful expectation of judgment and of raging fire that will consume the enemies of God. Anyone who rejected the law of Moses died without mercy on the testimony of two or three witnesses. How much more severely do you think a man deserves to be punished who has trampled the Son of God under foot, who has treated as an unholy thing the blood of the covenant that sanctified him, and who has insulted the Spirit of grace? For we know him who said, "It is mine to avenge; I will repay," and again, "The Lord will judge his people." It is a dreadful thing to fall into the hands of the living God. (Heb. 10:26–31)

In the face of this fearful prospect, how should we then live? Unquestionably, the passing away of this present age should be the dominant reality in our thinking. As Paul tells the Corinthians, this knowledge should affect our attitudes to all our relationships, our emotions, and our possessions.

> What I mean, brothers, is that the time is short. From now on those who have wives should live as if they had none; those who mourn, as if they did not; those who are happy, as if they were not; those who buy something, as if it were not theirs to keep; those who use the things of the world, as if not engrossed in them. For this world in its present form is passing away. (1 Cor. 7:29–31)

There will come a day for all of us as individuals and for this world as a whole when "time" will be called on mercy and God's wrath will be let loose.

In the meantime we live as Ezekiel did, as men and women under orders. We have been commissioned for the battle, and even the most precious things we possess here on earth we have merely as stewards. We do not own our children, or our wives, or even our own bodies. Bearing God's message to the world can be a costly business for us, just as it was for Ezekiel. This level of commitment is something that the world finds hard to understand.

The fact that Hollywood fails to grasp this level of self-giving was graphically demonstrated to me by a scene in the film *At Play in the Fields of the Lord*. In this scene, a missionary to South America was depicted burying his only child, who had died of blackwater fever. As the rain came pouring down, he cried out to the heavens, "I didn't give my permission!" Though there may be those whose faith has been shaken to the core by the costly nature of missionary service, the history of centuries of Christian martyr-witnesses[12] is that over and over again Christians *have* given God "permission"—as if such permission were required! As Martin Luther put it in his great hymn:

> And though they take my life, goods, honor, children, wife,
> Yet is their profit small: these things shall vanish all
> The city of God remaineth.

Nor is it simply missionaries who are mere stewards of the things of this world. The same is true for all of us who name the name of Christ. God has the right at any moment to take from any of us the things that we hold dearest of all in this world. After all, he created both them and us. But more profoundly still, God has the right because he was willing to give up into the hands of sinful people the delight of his eyes, his only Son, the Lord Jesus Christ. He "gave his permission" for Jesus to be beaten and tortured and mocked. What is more, as Jesus hung on that cross, God himself did not show him mercy but instead poured out the full weight of his wrath over our sins on him. The consuming fire of God's wrath against sin was kindled on Jesus, without pity or holding back.

God and the cross of his Son. Yet just as the deepest night for Jerusalem is the beginning of the end of God's wrath on his people and the turning point to hope in Ezekiel's message, so also the death of Jesus Christ on the cross is the turning point in the history of redemption. The blackness of Good Friday causes the light of Easter Sunday to break out with fresh power for Christ's disciples. The taking away of their Lord, the delight of their eyes, to lay him in a tomb, paradoxically, is the means by which they may be enabled to enjoy him forever.

---

12. The English words "witness" and "martyr" can both be used to translate a single Greek word, and in the early church the concepts frequently became synonymous.

Since God did not spare his own Son, surely he has the right to ask us not to spare even the delight of our eyes, whatever that is. We should be willing to give it up freely for the sake of spreading the good news and for the sake of the glory of this great God. Nor is it enough merely to be willing; sometimes, God actually takes from us that which is most precious to us. In those moments, as we are enabled by his grace to say, "Not my will, but yours be done, Lord," we become living signs to the world around us of God's grace and glory. We become living demonstrations of the fact that we do not regard God as our accomplice, whose job is to ensure that we live comfortable and fulfilling lives. Rather, he is our Lord, who has bought us with a price and owns us and everything we have. Moreover, we do not mourn as the world mourns, for in the midst of our sadness and real sense of painful loss, we know the assurance that just as our Lord has risen, so also will all his people.

But the cross also reminds us of the certainty of judgment on all who refuse its offer of life. It is this reality that lends urgency to our proclamation of the gospel. For us there is still time. The end of the world has not yet been pronounced. Our tongues have not been silenced. Far from it, we have been given a gospel to share with every creature under heaven that there is one name given to people by which they may yet be saved, the name of Jesus Christ. We have been commanded to preach the good news to all freely, that many may come to Christ and experience his forgiveness and mercy. However, we must never forget that the time we have been given is not unlimited, and the final judgment announced repeatedly in the Scriptures will one day become a reality—a joyful reality for all who are in Christ, but a fearful reality for those who remain outside.

Ezekiel 25

THE WORD OF THE LORD came to me: [2]"Son of man, set your face against the Ammonites and prophesy against them. [3]Say to them, 'Hear the word of the Sovereign LORD. This is what the Sovereign LORD says: Because you said "Aha!" over my sanctuary when it was desecrated and over the land of Israel when it was laid waste and over the people of Judah when they went into exile, [4]therefore I am going to give you to the people of the East as a possession. They will set up their camps and pitch their tents among you; they will eat your fruit and drink your milk. [5]I will turn Rabbah into a pasture for camels and Ammon into a resting place for sheep. Then you will know that I am the LORD. [6]For this is what the Sovereign LORD says: Because you have clapped your hands and stamped your feet, rejoicing with all the malice of your heart against the land of Israel, [7]therefore I will stretch out my hand against you and give you as plunder to the nations. I will cut you off from the nations and exterminate you from the countries. I will destroy you, and you will know that I am the LORD.'"

[8]"This is what the Sovereign LORD says: 'Because Moab and Seir said, "Look, the house of Judah has become like all the other nations," [9]therefore I will expose the flank of Moab, beginning at its frontier towns—Beth Jeshimoth, Baal Meon and Kiriathaim—the glory of that land. [10]I will give Moab along with the Ammonites to the people of the East as a possession, so that the Ammonites will not be remembered among the nations; [11]and I will inflict punishment on Moab. Then they will know that I am the LORD.'"

[12]"This is what the Sovereign LORD says: 'Because Edom took revenge on the house of Judah and became very guilty by doing so, [13]therefore this is what the Sovereign LORD says: I will stretch out my hand against Edom and kill its men and their animals. I will lay it waste, and from Teman to Dedan they will fall by the sword. [14]I will take vengeance on Edom by the hand of my people Israel, and they will deal with Edom in accordance with my anger and my wrath; they will know my vengeance, declares the Sovereign LORD.'"

15"This is what the Sovereign LORD says: 'Because the Philistines acted in vengeance and took revenge with malice in their hearts, and with ancient hostility sought to destroy Judah, 16therefore this is what the Sovereign LORD says: I am about to stretch out my hand against the Philistines, and I will cut off the Kerethites and destroy those remaining along the coast. 17I will carry out great vengeance on them and punish them in my wrath. Then they will know that I am the LORD, when I take vengeance on them.'"

WITH THIS CHAPTER, we move into a new section of Ezekiel's prophecy: a series of oracles against the surrounding nations (chs. 25–32). They are arranged as a series of six oracles addressed to Judah's immediate neighbors (chs. 25–29, the first four in ch. 25), followed by a climactic seventh oracle against the traditional enemy, Egypt (chs. 30–32). The nations around Judah are addressed in clockwise order, starting with Ammon in the Transjordan to the east of the northern kingdom of Israel, and moving south to the other Transjordanian foes, Moab and Edom. After that, the prophet turns his attention west to Philistia in the southern coastal plain and then north to the coastal cities of Tyre and Sidon.[1]

Oracles against foreign nations are a common genre in the prophets and typically include a direct address by God to the nation concerned, charges of arrogant attitudes and/or actions (esp. against Israel), and a prediction of the nation's doom.[2] All of these elements are found in classical form in the oracle against Ammon (25:1–7).

In this oracle the Lord tells the prophet to set his face toward the Ammonites and prophesy against them (25:2), charging them with rejoicing over Judah's downfall. They exulted in noisy triumph, saying "Aha!" (heʾāḥ, the ancient equivalent of cheering) when the sanctuary was desecrated, the land of Israel laid waste, and the people of Judah exiled (25:3). Instead of being appalled at the tragedy that had overcome the sacred place, the holy land, and the chosen people, they regarded their destruction as a cause for celebration. They saw it as proof positive that the triangular relationship between the nation of Israel, her land, and her deity was broken forever.[3] Judah's fall demonstrated to them the superiority of their gods over Yahweh. Hands, feet,

---

1. Daniel I. Block, *Ezekiel 25–48* (NICOT; Grand Rapids: Eerdmans, 1998), 5.
2. Stuart, *Ezekiel*, 249.
3. Block, *Ezekiel 25–48*, 17.

and inner emotions were all united in celebration of the Ammonites' hatred of Israel (25:6).[4]

Because of that attitude, the Ammonites too would experience judgment. Their own land would be laid waste, given to invaders from the East, a perpetual threat for those who inhabited the towns of the Transjordan (25:4). Their produce would be eaten by others and their people cut off, exterminated, and destroyed—a threefold fate to match their threefold rejoicing (25:4, 7).

As a result of this judgment the Ammonites "will know that I am the LORD" (25:7). This recognition formula, which occurs over sixty times in Ezekiel as a whole, is a dominant theme in these foreign nation oracles. The nations will recognize the Lord's sovereignty when he acts to judge not only his own people but them as well. In so doing, he will demonstrate that he is the only one with power to judge or to deliver; in the face of the Lord's fury, their gods are impotent to save them.

The oracle against Moab (25:8–11) charges them with saying, "Look, the house of Judah has become like all the other nations" (v. 8). The irony is that there was not a little truth in that statement: Judah had indeed in large measure become like the nations in the way she lived, giving herself over to idolatry (20:32). But it could never be true in the sense in which Moab had intended, so that this statement is nothing short of blasphemy on her lips. They meant, "Judah's fall demonstrates that her claims to elect status by the Lord are worthless; she is a reject nation, thrown onto the scrap heap of history along with her god."[5] Instead, it is Moab who will be utterly destroyed, along with Ammon. They are the ones who will be left unremembered on the stage of world history, along with their gods, thus demonstrating the reality and uniqueness of the Lord's existence and sovereign power to act (25:10).

The Edomites (25:12–14) seem not merely to have gloated over the downfall of Judah but to have actively participated in it. The brief statement of verse 12 that "Edom took revenge on the house of Judah" is fleshed out in more detail in the book of Obadiah. There Edom is accused of aiding and abetting the Babylonians, seizing Judah's wealth, cutting down the fugitives, and handing over the survivors (Obad. 11–14). Although they were from a biblical perspective close kin of the Israelites (Num. 20:14–15; Deut. 23:7–8), they had no compassion on their brothers. Moreover, instead of the Lord's judgment on his people putting the fear of Israel's God into their neighbors, they viewed it simply as an opportunity for personal gain and the settling of old scores. The result of their seeking revenge on Judah, however, will be God's execution of vengeance on them, using his own people to do so (Ezek. 25:14).

---

4. Allen, *Ezekiel 20–48*, 67.
5. Greenberg, *Ezekiel 21–37*, 526.

In 25:15–17 the Philistines are likewise charged with trying to settle old scores, taking revenge with malice in their hearts, and seeking to work out their "ancient hostility" (lit., "eternal enmity") toward Israel in the destruction of the chosen people. They too will experience the vengeance of God: The Kerethites will be cut off (Kereth sounds like *kārat*, the Hebrew word for "cut off") and the Philistines destroyed. It will be vengeance for vengeance. Then they too will recognize the Lord's sovereign power (25:17).

Bridging Contexts

WHY SHOULD A PROPHET who has spent so much time addressing the sins of his own people suddenly turn around and address the surrounding nations? Was it any of his business what these other nations thought and did? Even if the prophet had made it his business, what does it concern us, especially when the nations addressed have long since crumbled into the dust? What possible relevance could these chapters have for the twentieth-century reader? In practice, if not in theory, these chapters tend to be bracketed off and ignored in our thinking about the book of Ezekiel. If the book as a whole is rarely preached, that is doubly true of the oracles against the nations.

Intended audience and message. One answer to the question of relevance might be to see the prophet as a kind of international diplomat, a one-man precursor of the United Nations, addressing war crimes on a transnational level. The problem with that approach, however, is that there is no evidence that these oracles were actually delivered to the nations addressed or were ever intended to be.[6] The real audience for these oracles is the Judean listener, not the putative listener in the nation addressed.[7]

So what message is contained in these foreign nation oracles for the Judean listener? (1) They are being assured that God does not operate on a double standard, whereby he judges only Israel's sins while the nations are free to behave as they like. Judgment may begin with the house of God, but it doesn't end there. The outpouring of God's wrath extends not simply to the rebels in his own house but also to all those who refuse to recognize his sovereignty. They too must come to "know that I am the LORD"; that is, they must and will ultimately acknowledge that he is the only true God, the one who holds the nations in the palm of his hand, who raises up kingdoms and brings them down again according to his own good pleasure (cf. Isa. 40:15–24).

---

6. An exception to this general rule is Jeremiah's prophecy against Babylon, which he entrusted to the staff officer Seraiah to read when he got to Babylon (Jer. 51:59–64). This is the exception that proves the rule, however.

7. Skinner, *Ezekiel*, 217.

(2) In spite of the outpouring of God's wrath on his people, they nonetheless remain his people, who are infinitely precious to him. It is noteworthy that the charge leveled against each of the foreign nations in Ezekiel 25 is that they have persecuted or insulted God's chosen people, and thereby insulted God. To take God's people lightly is never a safe thing to do in the Old Testament. In spite of the pattern of sin among Abraham's offspring, God's word to Abraham was still effective: "I will bless those who bless you, and whoever curses you I will curse; and all peoples on earth will be blessed through you" (Gen. 12:3). Those who rejoice over Israel's downfall—even over her downfall at the hands of the Lord himself—are simply inviting a curse on their own heads, a curse that Ezekiel pronounces effective.

(3) Ezekiel's Judean hearers are reminded that God has his own consistent designs behind all the events of history, the prime purpose of which is to bring glory to himself. Judgment will fall on these nations who mock and abuse Judah in her hour of distress for the same reason that it fell originally on Judah herself: The Lord will thereby be recognized as a powerful and holy God, who acts in and through history.

This consistency of design on God's part is itself a message of encouragement to God's people. The one who said, "Whoever curses you I will curse," is the same one who said, "All peoples on earth will be blessed through you." If the first statement is still operative, then so also is the second. The fact that this goal had not yet been achieved indicated to the people of Judah that God's purposes were not yet at an end as far as their nation was concerned, no matter how bleak her future outlook may have seemed from a human perspective.

SATAN'S STRATEGIES. The assaults of Satan on the church come in a number of different forms. Essentially, however, they boil down to three basic strategies: persecution, seduction, and deception. When he adopts the strategy of persecution, Satan appears as a roaring lion, seeking whom he may devour (1 Peter 5:8). But he can also just as easily dress himself as an angel of light, seeking to deceive God's people (2 Cor. 11:14), or he can utilize the Great Prostitute to seduce God's people (Rev. 18). All three of these strategies have been at work in his assault on Judah through the surrounding nations, as we will see in the next few chapters, and the oracles against the foreign nations give God's answers to Satan's assaults in order to fortify his people.

The nations immediately surrounding Judah, which are the focus in Ezekiel 25, have been Satan's willing tools in persecuting God's people. Taking advantage of God's acts of judgment, they rejoiced at her downfall and made it worse. God's answer to his people's cry of "How long, Sovereign Lord?" (cf. Rev. 6:10) is a declaration of judgment on the persecutors. The blood of the martyrs cries out for justice, and justice it will receive. The message to the church or the Christian undergoing persecution is that God sees what is happening and in due season will act and judge.

The certainty of judgment on those who lift a finger against God's elect applies not merely to Satan's human agents but to the spiritual forces of evil as well. They will ultimately be thrown into the lake of burning sulfur, where they will be tormented day and night forever (Rev. 20:10). Such an eternal punishment is a fitting end for Satan, the one whose "eternal enmity" toward God and his people finds merely a faint echo in the "eternal enmity" between the Philistines and Israel (Ezek. 25:15).

God's delay in judgment. But if God will ultimately act to break the teeth of the wicked, why does he wait so long? Why does he not immediately intervene to bring on them the judgment they deserve, just as he acted to judge Jerusalem? Sometimes, of course, he does, as in the case of Sodom and Gomorrah, but those cases seem to be the exception rather than the rule. One answer to the question of why God delays is so that he may show mercy even to the wicked. The persecutors themselves may yet be shown mercy. Thus Peter answers those who accuse God of tardiness in keeping his promises of justice by the assertion that "[God] is patient with you, not wanting anyone to perish, but everyone to come to repentance" (2 Peter 3:9). God delays the coming of judgment so that Saul the persecutor can be turned into Paul the apostle.

However, the display of God's mercy is not the only reason for his delay. The persecution of the church and the martyrdom of Christians is not simply a means to an end—a way of strengthening the church and bringing about conversions—it is an end in itself. Simply put, martyrs bring glory to God as they lay down their lives. As people freely give up their lives in the service of the gospel, they demonstrate that, for them at least, the Lord is God. He is more precious to them than life itself. In some cases, persecution may strengthen the church. In others, it may seem to succeed in stamping it out.[8] But in every case, it brings about a testimony to the lordship of Jesus Christ. That testimony may be accepted or rejected by the persecutors here and now. But ultimately God will not be ashamed to be known as the God of those who have suffered for him, and the knowledge of his universal lordship will then be universally recognized even by those who sought unremittingly here on earth to stamp that knowledge out.

---

8. Mark Galli, "Is Persecution Good for the Church?" *Christianity Today* 41 (May 19, 1997): 16–19.

A warning. However, it may also be that in some cases we fill the role of the surrounding nations rather than that of God's suffering people. For a common theme in God's accusation of the nations is that they rejoiced at the divine judgment falling on others. Perhaps we too have been heedless or even happy when our opponents have apparently received their "comeuppance" at the hands of God, whether those opponents be inside or outside the Christian community. We have perhaps been secretly, or not so secretly, glad over the fall of prominent televangelists; some have even gleefully proclaimed that the AIDS virus is a judgment from God against homosexuals.

God's judgment is real in history as well as beyond history, but it should never be contemplated lightly. We would do well to remember the words of Jesus that the measure we use in judging others will be the same one used on us (Luke 6:38). Rather, with reverent fear and trembling before the awful reality of the judgment of God, we should seek to persuade all people to flee the wrath to come (2 Cor. 5:10–11).

Ezekiel 26–27

☙

IN THE ELEVENTH YEAR, on the first day of the month, the word of the LORD came to me: ²"Son of man, because Tyre has said of Jerusalem, 'Aha! The gate to the nations is broken, and its doors have swung open to me; now that she lies in ruins I will prosper,' ³therefore this is what the Sovereign LORD says: I am against you, O Tyre, and I will bring many nations against you, like the sea casting up its waves. ⁴They will destroy the walls of Tyre and pull down her towers; I will scrape away her rubble and make her a bare rock. ⁵Out in the sea she will become a place to spread fishnets, for I have spoken, declares the Sovereign LORD. She will become plunder for the nations, ⁶and her settlements on the mainland will be ravaged by the sword. Then they will know that I am the LORD.

⁷"For this is what the Sovereign LORD says: From the north I am going to bring against Tyre Nebuchadnezzar king of Babylon, king of kings, with horses and chariots, with horsemen and a great army. ⁸He will ravage your settlements on the mainland with the sword; he will set up siege works against you, build a ramp up to your walls and raise his shields against you. ⁹He will direct the blows of his battering rams against your walls and demolish your towers with his weapons. ¹⁰His horses will be so many that they will cover you with dust. Your walls will tremble at the noise of the war horses, wagons and chariots when he enters your gates as men enter a city whose walls have been broken through. ¹¹The hoofs of his horses will trample all your streets; he will kill your people with the sword, and your strong pillars will fall to the ground. ¹²They will plunder your wealth and loot your merchandise; they will break down your walls and demolish your fine houses and throw your stones, timber and rubble into the sea. ¹³I will put an end to your noisy songs, and the music of your harps will be heard no more. ¹⁴I will make you a bare rock, and you will become a place to spread fishnets. You will never be rebuilt, for I the LORD have spoken, declares the Sovereign LORD.

¹⁵"This is what the Sovereign LORD says to Tyre: Will not the coastlands tremble at the sound of your fall, when the wounded groan and the slaughter takes place in you? ¹⁶Then

all the princes of the coast will step down from their thrones and lay aside their robes and take off their embroidered garments. Clothed with terror, they will sit on the ground, trembling every moment, appalled at you. [17]Then they will take up a lament concerning you and say to you:

> "'How you are destroyed, O city of renown,
>   peopled by men of the sea!
> You were a power on the seas,
>   you and your citizens;
> you put your terror
>   on all who lived there.
> [18]Now the coastlands tremble
>   on the day of your fall;
> the islands in the sea
>   are terrified at your collapse.'

[19]"This is what the Sovereign LORD says: When I make you a desolate city, like cities no longer inhabited, and when I bring the ocean depths over you and its vast waters cover you, [20]then I will bring you down with those who go down to the pit, to the people of long ago. I will make you dwell in the earth below, as in ancient ruins, with those who go down to the pit, and you will not return or take your place in the land of the living. [21]I will bring you to a horrible end and you will be no more. You will be sought, but you will never again be found, declares the Sovereign LORD."

[27:1]The word of the LORD came to me: [2]"Son of man, take up a lament concerning Tyre. [3]Say to Tyre, situated at the gateway to the sea, merchant of peoples on many coasts, 'This is what the Sovereign LORD says:

> "'You say, O Tyre,
>   "I am perfect in beauty."
> [4]Your domain was on the high seas;
>   your builders brought your beauty to perfection.
> [5]They made all your timbers
>   of pine trees from Senir;
> they took a cedar from Lebanon
>   to make a mast for you.
> [6]Of oaks from Bashan
>   they made your oars;
> of cypress wood from the coasts of Cyprus
>   they made your deck, inlaid with ivory.

⁷ Fine embroidered linen from Egypt was your sail
   and served as your banner;
 your awnings were of blue and purple
   from the coasts of Elishah.
⁸ Men of Sidon and Arvad were your oarsmen;
   your skilled men, O Tyre, were aboard as your seamen.
⁹ Veteran craftsmen of Gebal were on board
   as shipwrights to caulk your seams.
 All the ships of the sea and their sailors
   came alongside to trade for your wares.
¹⁰‴Men of Persia, Lydia and Put
   served as soldiers in your army.
 They hung their shields and helmets on your walls,
   bringing you splendor.
¹¹ Men of Arvad and Helech
   manned your walls on every side;
 men of Gammad
   were in your towers.
 They hung their shields around your walls;
   they brought your beauty to perfection.

¹²‴Tarshish did business with you because of your great
wealth of goods; they exchanged silver, iron, tin and lead for
your merchandise.

¹³‴Greece, Tubal and Meshech traded with you; they
exchanged slaves and articles of bronze for your wares.

¹⁴‴Men of Beth Togarmah exchanged work horses, war
horses and mules for your merchandise.

¹⁵‴The men of Rhodes traded with you, and many coastlands were your customers; they paid you with ivory tusks and
ebony.

¹⁶‴Aram did business with you because of your many products; they exchanged turquoise, purple fabric, embroidered
work, fine linen, coral and rubies for your merchandise.

¹⁷‴Judah and Israel traded with you; they exchanged wheat
from Minnith and confections, honey, oil and balm for your
wares.

¹⁸‴Damascus, because of your many products and great
wealth of goods, did business with you in wine from Helbon
and wool from Zahar.

¹⁹‴Danites and Greeks from Uzal bought your merchandise; they exchanged wrought iron, cassia and calamus for
your wares.

²⁰"'Dedan traded in saddle blankets with you.

²¹"'Arabia and all the princes of Kedar were your customers; they did business with you in lambs, rams and goats.

²²"'The merchants of Sheba and Raamah traded with you; for your merchandise they exchanged the finest of all kinds of spices and precious stones, and gold.

²³"'Haran, Canneh and Eden and merchants of Sheba, Asshur and Kilmad traded with you. ²⁴In your marketplace they traded with you beautiful garments, blue fabric, embroidered work and multicolored rugs with cords twisted and tightly knotted.

²⁵"'The ships of Tarshish serve
    as carriers for your wares.
You are filled with heavy cargo
    in the heart of the sea.
²⁶Your oarsmen take you
    out to the high seas.
But the east wind will break you to pieces
    in the heart of the sea.
²⁷Your wealth, merchandise and wares,
    your mariners, seamen and shipwrights,
your merchants and all your soldiers,
    and everyone else on board
will sink into the heart of the sea
    on the day of your shipwreck.
²⁸The shorelands will quake
    when your seamen cry out.
²⁹All who handle the oars
    will abandon their ships;
the mariners and all the seamen
    will stand on the shore.
³⁰They will raise their voice
    and cry bitterly over you;
they will sprinkle dust on their heads
    and roll in ashes.
³¹They will shave their heads because of you
    and will put on sackcloth.
They will weep over you with anguish of soul
    and with bitter mourning.
³²As they wail and mourn over you,
    they will take up a lament concerning you:

"Who was ever silenced like Tyre,
surrounded by the sea?"
³³ When your merchandise went out on the seas,
you satisfied many nations;
with your great wealth and your wares
you enriched the kings of the earth.
³⁴ Now you are shattered by the sea
in the depths of the waters;
your wares and all your company
have gone down with you.
³⁵ All who live in the coastlands
are appalled at you;
their kings shudder with horror
and their faces are distorted with fear.
³⁶ The merchants among the nations hiss at you;
you have come to a horrible end
and will be no more.'"

Original Meaning

IN CONTRAST TO the short oracles against the nations in Ezekiel 25, the oracle against Tyre covers almost three chapters (26:1–28:19). The remainder of chapter 28 is taken up by a brief oracle against Tyre's companion town Sidon (28:20–23) and then an oracle of encouragement to Israel (28:24–26), which draws together the oracles to Israel's immediate neighbors. Rather than study such a large section in one piece, we will break it into two parts (chs. 26–27 and ch. 28), but because of the style of composition of the oracle we should remember that the three chapters form a single unit. In that way, we will be reminded to see the scope of the whole as well as the significance of the individual parts.

The oracle against Tyre is composed of three distinct but essentially parallel literary panels, each of which ends with the same concluding phrase about Tyre's going down to the realm of the dead: It will come "to a horrible end" (*ballahôt*) and "will be no more" (*ʾênēk ʿad-ʿôlām*; see 26:21; 27:36; 28:19). The purpose of this panel construction is not to present three separate and different oracles but to invite the reader to place the three oracles side by side and see essentially the same message presented in three different ways.

The First Panel (26:2–21)

THE FIRST PANEL is a straightforward prophecy against the city of Tyre. It is introduced by a date, the first day of an unnamed month in the eleventh year (v. 1).[1] This places the oracle close to the fall of Jerusalem, which occurred in the middle of the eleventh year (cf. 40:1). The charge against Tyre is similar to that raised against Judah's other neighbors: She rejoiced when Jerusalem fell, seeing in that event the opportunity for personal gain: "The gate to the nations is broken, and its doors have swung open to me" (26:2). A potential rival for her trading empire has been eliminated, opening up new avenues to prosperity.[2]

Ezekiel is quick to point out the flaw in Tyre's thinking. The God who brought judgment on Jerusalem is also against Tyre and will judge her in an almost exactly corresponding manner (26:3). Does Tyre hope to become the new meeting place for the nations? The Lord will bring many nations against her (26:3). Did Tyre rejoice to see Jerusalem's doors shattered? Her walls will be destroyed and her towers torn down (26:4). Did Tyre expect to prosper? She will become plunder for the nations (26:5). Point by point, Tyre's positive expectations are turned on their heads.

The assault of the nations on Tyre is described as being like the waves of a stormy sea (26:3), which is a peculiarly apt image for the city of Tyre. It was originally built on a coastal island about a mile long and half a mile wide, whose strength came from its position surrounded by water. These metaphorical possibilities of Tyre's geographical situation will be utilized to the full in the second panel, where she is described as a great ship.

The second part of the first oracle against Tyre adds specificity to the picture. The general expression "many nations" (26:3) resolves into the specific figure of Nebuchadnezzar, king of Babylon (26:7). The assault and destruction of Tyre is described in great, if rather stereotypical, detail (26:8–12).[3] But the end result is exactly the same: Tyre will be reduced to a bare rock,

---

1. The absence of a specific month is unusual since most of Ezekiel's dated oracles contain day, month, and year. The proposal of *BHS* that an original reference to the eleventh month has dropped out because the numeral was the same as that of the year is the most plausible (Cooke, *Ezekiel*, 294). Alternatively, Allen proposes that the unusual form of eleven is itself a corruption of the twelfth year (*Ezekiel 20–48*, 71). He leaves the month indeterminate.

2. Allen suggests that Tyre stood to benefit from Jerusalem's fall primarily in political rather than economic terms (*Ezekiel 20–48*, 75). That may be a correct observation in historical terms, but the oracles themselves focus entirely on Tyre as a leader in international commerce.

3. The description shows no interest in the peculiar difficulties of assaulting an island city, where the conventional means of siege walls and ramps and formations protected from above by shields (26:8) are rather problematic. Though Nebuchadnezzar's assault greatly reduced Tyre's significance and power, the city itself was not destroyed until the time of Alexander the Great (332 B.C.), who built a causeway out from the mainland to the island in order to be able to capture the city.

the haunt of local fishermen rather than of long-distance trading vessels (26:5, 14). Her former glory will never be regained (26:14).

The terrible fall of Tyre will have an impact on her maritime trading partners, the "coastlands" or "islands" (26:15). They will tremble and adopt the customs of mourning, with their rulers coming down from their thrones and setting aside their fine robes (26:16), taking up a lament for the fallen city. It will be as if the island city has sunk into the heart of the chaotic "ocean depths" (*tᵉhôm*, 26:19), its inhabitants condemned to "the pit" (*bôr*, 26:20), never to return again. These are terms with mythical overtones, though as elsewhere in Scripture the mythical symbols have been completely subjugated in a universe under God's control. The "deep" was an element of the primeval chaos that God transformed into cosmos in Genesis 1, while "the pit" was the shadowy underworld of the dead, the nightmare end of those abandoned by God (see Ps. 28:1; 30:3; 88:4; 143:7). Though people seek for Tyre, she will have utterly vanished, sunk by God's torpedoes, never again to be found (Ezek. 26:21).

The Second Panel (27:1–36)

THE SECOND PANEL (27:1–36) proclaims essentially the same message as the first, but in the form of a lament. The lament genre typically contrasts past glory with present loss, and Ezekiel exploits this format to the full. He describes in great detail the glory of Tyre under the metaphor of a majestic ship. She was a legend in her own mind, beautiful to the point of perfection (27:3), created out of the best resources of the surrounding nations. She was fitted out with prime timbers for her construction, fine cloth for her sails and awnings (27:5–7). Her crew had been recruited from the best manpower available: skilled seamen to form her crew, experienced craftsmen to make necessary repairs, and highly trained soldiers to act as her company of marines (27:8–11b), bringing her beauty to perfection (27:11c). Could there ever have been a more perfect ship?

Nor was her beauty merely cosmetic. The merchant ship Tyre is depicted as a highly efficient business machine, trading in all kinds of costly goods. The seemingly interminable list of her trading partners, whether borrowed from an extant source or modeled after that form, makes clear the astonishing array of her wares. The cargo list seems to be organized by geographic areas, starting with Mediterranean locations and those in Asia Minor (27:12–15) and moving on through Palestinian regions from south to north (27:16–17) to Syria (27:18–19), Arabia (27:20–22), and finally Mesopotamia (27:23–24).[4] By covering all points of the compass and virtually every imaginable precious

---

4. Zimmerli, *Ezekiel*, 2:71.

commodity, the picture is established of Tyre as the commercial crossroads of the world, the Hong Kong of the ancient Near East.

But the paean of praise for her beauty and commercial importance only heightens the tragedy of her downfall. Like the *Titanic*, she fell victim to her own self-propaganda. Her apparent invincibility contains the seeds of her own downfall. She is "filled with heavy cargo in the heart of the sea" (27:25), a description that fits the city Tyre literally as well as the ship Tyre metaphorically. But when the stormy wind blows, the sea that provides the source of the mariner's wealth can easily become an enemy. An east wind (from Babylon) will start to blow, and the mighty vessel will founder with the loss of all hands (27:26–27). The rapidity with which her demise can be described contrasts starkly with the lengthy description of her beauty. Her beauty and security count for nothing when the storm strikes.

As in the first panel, once again those who watch from the sidelines tremble, and a lament is raised for the doomed city. This time those who adopt the customary forms of mourning—weeping, wailing, sackcloth, dust and ashes, shaving their heads—are the sailors and seafaring people in company with the kings of the coastlands and the merchants (27:28–36). Tyre's joy over the destruction of "the gate to the nations" (26:2) is seen to be thoroughly misplaced, for the one who judged Jerusalem will also judge Tyre, the marketplace of the "nations" (27:33, 36). The end result for Tyre is the same as the first panel: Tyre will "come to a horrible end and will be no more" (27:36).

Bridging Contexts

THE GOAL OF TYRE. This oracle against Tyre is distinctively different from the other oracles against the foreign nations. The remainder of the nations immediately surrounding Israel (Ammon, Moab, Edom, Philistia, and—after Tyre—Sidon) set themselves up in opposition to God's people. Tyre, however, thought to substitute herself for God's city, Jerusalem, and take her place. She thought that the downfall of the chosen city was her opportunity to become the center of the universe, "the gate to the nations" (26:2). It was a role for which she seemed admirably naturally gifted, as the oracle and lament make clear. She possessed not only a strategic location but also great beauty and wealth. She was the Hong Kong of the ancient world, a bustling trading city at the crossroads of east and west.

Indeed, in terms of natural advantages, Tyre was far more suited to the description "the gate to the nations" (26:2) than was Jerusalem. Jerusalem may have been poetically described by the psalmist as being "beautiful in its loftiness, the joy of the whole earth" (Ps. 48:2). However, we should not assume that this is an "objective" description that could equally well have been found on the pages of an ancient *Architectural Digest* as on the pages of Scripture. Jerusalem's beauty was spiritually discerned, based on her election as "the city of our God" (Ps. 48:1). So too was her security, which rested not on the supposed impregnability of being an island, dwelling in the midst of the seas, but rather on the presence of God within her (Ps. 48:3). The result of that indwelling presence is described by the psalmist in an image that matches exactly that of Ezekiel 27: When the kings of the earth gathered against Jerusalem, "you destroyed them like ships of Tarshish shattered by an east wind" (Ps. 48:7).

But the psalmist's confidence must have seemed to the exiles to have been ill-founded. Jerusalem had not survived the assault of the nations, but on the contrary had herself been shattered. Ezekiel had been called to give the reasons for this in the first part of his prophecy: Jerusalem lay under God's judgment for her sins and as a result had been abandoned by his presence. God was no longer within her, which explained her destruction. But in the nature of the case, with the destruction of God's own city, the attractions of her rivals must have increased. It is one thing to proclaim that God is greater than mammon to people who are comfortably off; it is another to proclaim that to a people who feel themselves to have been abandoned by their God.

The symbolism of the sea. It is to such people that the prophet addresses his oracle against Tyre. To those tempted to be seduced by Tyre's prosperity, he proclaims Tyre's ultimate doom. The city whose strength comes from her location in the heart of the seas will be drowned in the heart of the seas. This is an image far more potent for the ancient reader than for the modern. The sea may impress us with its power when whipped up into a storm, but for the ancient reader it possessed a mythological status as the personification of the forces of chaos that continually opposed the forces of order and threatened to overwhelm them.

In ancient creation narratives, the Sea (Yam) was one of the principal opponents of the gods, who had to be overcome before the world could be established. The Deep (*tᵉhôm*) appears similarly in Genesis 1, albeit in demythologized form, as the precreation state of void and wilderness that God transforms into a place of order and beauty and life (Gen. 1:2; cf. Ezek. 26:19). In the Psalms, the seas frequently represent the forces of chaos that are ranged against God, though the psalmist affirms that God is mightier than the seas (e.g., Ps. 93:3–4). In the new heavens and new earth there will be no more sea (Rev. 21:1), for all chaos will be finally and permanently overcome.

Therefore, Tyre's fate of foundering like a ship in a great storm, going down with all hands, perhaps carries more affective weight for its original readers than it does for us. The sea was a more emotive image for them than it is for us. Yet even to us, the oracle underlines once more that even the most destructive, out-of-control forces in the world operate under the direct control of God. He is the One who brings many nations against Tyre, "like the sea casting up its waves" (Ezek. 26:3), and natural defenses and strength will avail nothing against God's judgment. The seductive power of wealth is thus defused by showing its ultimate insecurity and final end. Like those who traveled first class on the *Titanic*, with all its unparalleled grandeur, those who place their trust in this world are traveling on a comfortable one-way trip to nowhere. As John Newton put it in one of his greatest hymns:

> Fading is the worldling's pleasure,
> all his boasted pomp and show.
> Solid joys and lasting treasure,
> none but Zion's children know."

SEDUCED BY SATAN. We mentioned in the comments on chapter 25 that Satan has three basic strategies for undermining the faith of God's people: persecution, seduction, and deception. All three are addressed in Ezekiel's oracles against the foreign nations. Several of Israel's neighbors have acted in a hostile manner towards her, persecuting her in her hour of difficulty, as we saw in chapter 25. But in the form of Tyre, we see especially the second strategy: seduction. The greater space devoted by Ezekiel to addressing this strategy perhaps demonstrates its relative significance as a temptation to his audience.

We would do well similarly to ponder the particular combination of strategies that Satan favors against us and those around us. For those who live in affluent Western culture, seduction is certainly a prominent element in his armory. We should therefore take particular note of the fact that in Revelation 2–3, the letters to the seven churches of Asia Minor, the two churches about which Jesus is purely positive are those experiencing persecution. Those about which Jesus is purely negative, by contrast, all face the assault of Satan in the form of seduction. All too often, while persecution purifies, seduction sedates.

The heart of seduction lies in the promise of prosperity and wealth. In the temptations of Jesus, Satan offered him "all the kingdoms of the world and their splendor" if Jesus would simply bow down to him (Matt. 4:8). So too he comes to contemporary people and offers comfort, peace, and security through material prosperity: Get a good job with a good salary and fringe benefits and you'll be set up for life. This is the philosophy adopted by many around us. As the bumper sticker puts it: "He who dies with the most toys wins." Never mind about questions of right or wrong, of ultimate significance or values; do whatever it takes to feel good and to win. That is seduction.

God's answer to Satan's seduction. The answer to seduction is not to offer people a different way to feel better and win more, as some imitation versions of Christianity proclaim. The health and wealth gospel declares that faith is the key to unlocking your full potential, so that you can have whatever you want here and now. All you have to do is "name it and claim it." In a materialistic society such an approach will always find followers, but it is merely another brand of seduction.

The true answer to seduction is to open people's eyes to the shallowness of the "beauty" on offer. The Great Prostitute of Revelation 17–18, "Babylon," is modeled in many respects after Ezekiel's description of Tyre. She sits on many waters (17:1), she is the ultimate trading nation (18:12–13), and when she falls the kings of the earth and the sailors mourn (18:9, 17). "Babylon" here is a cipher for Rome, and her trump card is wealth and luxury, in short, materialism. She is the front cover of *Cosmopolitan* and *Vogue* rolled into one. However beautiful and powerful Rome may appear, however, the book of Revelation reveals the truth that her beauty is only skin deep and her power is merely temporary. Judgment is coming, which will uncover the true nature of all things and put them into proper perspective.

Today the Great Prostitute lives not in Tyre or Rome, but in Hollywood and along Madison Avenue; her seductive voice speaks not in Latin but with an American accent, drawing the world away from God and towards materialistic excesses. Her power is seen in the fact that the good news of Coca Cola is more widely proclaimed than the good news of Jesus Christ. Consumerism is making disciples in all nations through its seductive charms.

At the heart of seduction, however, is a lie: that what you see is what you get. And Satan, the eternal liar, is skilled at making us see things from their most attractive perspective. Like an artful angler, he hides the hook and shows us only the juicy worm. Not until too late does the fish discover the steel within. So also Satan attempts to seduce us by showing us beautiful things that compete for our attention, hiding the bitter fruit they bear. He offers the pleasures of adultery, hiding the pain of broken relationships that follow. He persuades us that our children can do just as well in day care, while to succeed in our careers requires us to put in long hours at the office or shop. He persuades us that we really "need" a bigger house, a newer car, and more clothes. He counsels us that we should buy now and pay later. Satan's tackle box is well equipped with lures, but the truth in each of these cases is that we will indeed pay later for what we buy now.

How does God wean our hearts from the seductiveness of this world? (1) One way is through what the Puritans would call the "strokes" and "crosses" of life, the ways in which God causes things not to go as we had hoped. Like a good father, God does not allow us to run wild, but graciously disciplines us, sometimes by opening our eyes to see the hook before we bite and sometimes by using the pain of the hook to bring us to our senses. Thomas Boston described the power of a "cross providence" to bring powerful conviction of sin in these terms:

> As when one walking heedlessly is suddenly taken ill of a lameness: his going halting the rest of the way convinces him of having made a wrong step; and every new painful step brings it afresh to his mind. So God makes a crook in one's lot, to convince him of some false step he has made or course he has taken.[5]

These are never the pleasant experiences of our spiritual walk, but as the writer to the Hebrews reminds us, such discipline "produces a harvest of righteousness and peace for those who have been trained by it" (Heb. 12:11).

(2) The other way for us to learn to resist the attractiveness of Satan's seduction is to learn to fix our eyes on the truth, on Jesus. If Jerusalem's beauty was spiritually discerned even during its prosperous days, then it was not surprising that many would be seduced away by the apparent beauty of its rival during her humiliation at the time of the Exile. So also there are many today who are unable to discern the beauty of Christ crucified. Their eyes are blinded to the truth. The world still seems to offer far more attractive alternatives than the Son of Man.

But for all her attractiveness, the seductiveness of the Great Prostitute does not deliver long-term satisfaction. For the prostitute and her partners, sex is not an expression of a deep relationship, it is itself the relationship. When the sex is over, so is the relationship.[6] So it is also with the seductive attraction of false worship. The false worshiper bows down to his or her idols—be they sex, power, family, or whatever—and says, "So long as you bless me and give me tangible rewards, I will give you worship in return." It is a fundamentally commercial deal. When idolatry ceases to "work for you," however, you go out in search of a new idolatry, a more attractive prostitute, who will give you the high you seek. But the true worshiper says with Job, "Though he slay me, yet will I hope in him" (Job 13:15). Such worship flows naturally and inevitably from a deep relationship and is not based on calculations of what the worshiper gets in return.

---

5. Thomas Boston, *The Crook in the Lot* (Wilmington, Del.: Sovereign Grace, 1972 reprint), 12. John Flavel similarly poses the question to the one experiencing affliction: "What if by the loss of outward comforts God preserves your soul from the ruining power of temptation?" (*The Works of John Flavel*, vol. 5 [London: Banner of Truth, 1968 reprint], 443).

6. Peterson, *Reversed Thunder*, 146.

Faithfulness. The irony is that faithfulness is a better deal in the long run than idolatry. Adultery does not pay; the future belongs not to the Great Prostitute but to the Bride of the Lamb. She is the One who will come down from heaven adorned for her marriage to the Lamb. In heaven, the true beauty and splendor of Christ will finally be clear to all, but will be enjoyed only by those whose eyes have been opened by God to the beauty of Christ in his humiliation. They have come to know the grace of God demonstrated to us in this: that he who was rich became poor for us, that we might share his riches; that he who was glorious was humiliated for us, that we might share his glory; that he who was all-powerful became weak, that in him we might become strong. Those who are truly feasting their eyes on the beauty of the true Lamb of God, the Lamb that was slain, will not be so easily seduced by the tawdry imitations Satan offers.

Ezekiel 28

THE WORD OF THE LORD came to me: ²"Son of man, say to the ruler of Tyre, 'This is what the Sovereign LORD says:

> "'In the pride of your heart
> you say, "I am a god;
> I sit on the throne of a god
> in the heart of the seas."
> But you are a man and not a god,
> though you think you are as wise as a god.
> ³Are you wiser than Daniel?
> Is no secret hidden from you?
> ⁴By your wisdom and understanding
> you have gained wealth for yourself
> and amassed gold and silver
> in your treasuries.
> ⁵By your great skill in trading
> you have increased your wealth,
> and because of your wealth
> your heart has grown proud.

⁶"'Therefore this is what the Sovereign LORD says:

> "'Because you think you are wise,
> as wise as a god,
> ⁷I am going to bring foreigners against you,
> the most ruthless of nations;
> they will draw their swords against your beauty
> and wisdom
> and pierce your shining splendor.
> ⁸They will bring you down to the pit,
> and you will die a violent death
> in the heart of the seas.
> ⁹Will you then say, "I am a god,"
> in the presence of those who kill you?
> You will be but a man, not a god,
> in the hands of those who slay you.
> ¹⁰You will die the death of the uncircumcised
> at the hands of foreigners.

I have spoken, declares the Sovereign LORD.'"

¹¹The word of the LORD came to me: ¹²"Son of man, take
up a lament concerning the king of Tyre and say to him: 'This
is what the Sovereign LORD says:

    "'You were the model of perfection,
        full of wisdom and perfect in beauty.
¹³You were in Eden,
        the garden of God;
    every precious stone adorned you:
        ruby, topaz and emerald,
        chrysolite, onyx and jasper,
        sapphire, turquoise and beryl.
    Your settings and mountings were made of gold;
        on the day you were created they were prepared.
¹⁴You were anointed as a guardian cherub,
        for so I ordained you.
    You were on the holy mount of God;
        you walked among the fiery stones.
¹⁵You were blameless in your ways
        from the day you were created
        till wickedness was found in you.
¹⁶Through your widespread trade
        you were filled with violence,
        and you sinned.
    So I drove you in disgrace from the mount of God,
        and I expelled you, O guardian cherub,
        from among the fiery stones.
¹⁷Your heart became proud
        on account of your beauty,
    and you corrupted your wisdom
        because of your splendor.
    So I threw you to the earth;
        I made a spectacle of you before kings.
¹⁸By your many sins and dishonest trade
        you have desecrated your sanctuaries.
    So I made a fire come out from you,
        and it consumed you,
    and I reduced you to ashes on the ground
        in the sight of all who were watching.
¹⁹All the nations who knew you
        are appalled at you;
    you have come to a horrible end
        and will be no more.'"

²⁰The word of the LORD came to me: ²¹"Son of man, set your face against Sidon; prophesy against her ²²and say: 'This is what the Sovereign LORD says:

"'I am against you, O Sidon,
    and I will gain glory within you.
They will know that I am the LORD,
    when I inflict punishment on her
    and show myself holy within her.
²³ I will send a plague upon her
    and make blood flow in her streets.
The slain will fall within her,
    with the sword against her on every side.
Then they will know that I am the LORD.

²⁴"'No longer will the people of Israel have malicious neighbors who are painful briers and sharp thorns. Then they will know that I am the Sovereign LORD.

²⁵"'This is what the Sovereign LORD says: When I gather the people of Israel from the nations where they have been scattered, I will show myself holy among them in the sight of the nations. Then they will live in their own land, which I gave to my servant Jacob. ²⁶They will live there in safety and will build houses and plant vineyards; they will live in safety when I inflict punishment on all their neighbors who maligned them. Then they will know that I am the LORD their God.'"

EZEKIEL 28:1–19 COMPLETES what the prophet has to say against Tyre. Then in verses 20–23 Ezekiel prophesies against the sister city of Tyre, namely, Sidon. He closes this chapter with a brief address to the Lord's own people (vv. 24–26).

The Third Panel (28:1–19)

CONTINUING THE THEMES found in the first two panels of Ezekiel's prophecy against Tyre (chs. 26–27), the third panel combines both straightforward prophecy and lament, this time directed at the ruler of Tyre, who in his person and fate acts as a kind of personification of the city.[1] He is accused of overweening pride, of saying in his heart, "I am a god; I sit on the throne of

---

1. Allen, *Ezekiel 20–48*, 93.

a god in the heart of the seas" (28:2). He claims to exercise the divine authority that comes from sitting on the throne of the gods.[2]

The evidence on which the king of Tyre rests his claim to the status of a divine being is twofold: his wisdom and his wealth. In the first place, he claims to be as wise as a god, wiser than the ancient hero Danel (28:3). As we pointed out with reference to Ezekiel 14, it is disputed whether this is a reference to the famous biblical character Daniel, or to a person known from the Ugaritic Aqhat epic. The mythical Danel is a character of proverbial wisdom,[3] but so also is the biblical figure, and he better fits the description as the one "from whom no secrets are hid," to borrow the language of the *Book of Common Prayer* (Ezek. 28:3; cf. Dan. 2:21–23, 47; 4:6, 18; 5:12).[4] The king of Tyre apparently thinks of himself as surpassing this all-time great in the wisdom "Hall of Fame" and achieving levels of wisdom and knowledge that are reserved to the gods. This enormous wisdom, in his estimation, is what has brought him his great wealth. That his treasuries are full of gold and silver is attributed to his skill in trading (28:4–5); thus, along with his wealth his pride has grown enormously (28:5).

The Sovereign Lord will quickly put the king of Tyre in his place. His vaunted wisdom and claimed divine status will not help him when the true God brings the nations against him; they will draw their swords against his wisdom and beauty and quickly cut him down to size (28:6–8). The most objective demonstration of his human status will be his helplessness in the hands of those who capture him as they put him to death (28:8–10). What kind of god is he if he can be so easily slain? Far from being a god, he will go down to "the pit," dying the death of the slain in the chaotic heart of the seas (28:8). Here there is a clear echo of the fate of the city of Tyre itself in Ezekiel 26:19–20.

The king's destiny is underlined in the command to the prophet to raise a lament for the king of Tyre (28:12). A lament presupposes the death of the person concerned, thus emphasizing from the outset his humanity. Yet the lament (with perhaps more than a hint of sarcasm?) in its eulogy appears at the outset to take his claims of divinity seriously. It describes him as a "model of perfection" or, as the Hebrew translates literally, the "very seal of proportion." This phrase seems to identify the king of Tyre as the very epitome of perfection, full of wisdom and consummate in beauty (28:12).

In keeping with his claims of semidivine status, as one who sits on the seat of the gods (28:2), the king of Tyre is described as having been present at the

---

2. Block, *Ezekiel 25–48*, 95.
3. See *ANET*, 149–55; Day, "The Daniel of Ugarit and Ezekiel," 174–84.
4. Greenberg, *Ezekiel 21–37*, 574; Block, *Ezekiel 25–48*, 96.

beginning of the world in Eden, the garden of God, adorned with every precious stone (28:13).[5] He was even anointed as a "guardian cherub" (28:14), one of the heavenly beings described as the Lord's throne-bearers in Ezekiel 1 and 10 and known from the account in Genesis 3 as the guardians of the sacred garden. He had access to the center of the divine presence, being "on the holy mount of God"[6] and walking about among the stones of fire (28:14).[7] These numerous, if sometimes oblique, references to the creation narrative set up the picture of the king of Tyre as the first (and therefore foremost) of all men, an *Urmensch* become *Übermensch* (original man become superman). Greater even than Adam, he has not been made "a little lower than angels"; he claims to rank right up there among the divine beings.

But his greatness and privilege as the protological man simply serves to underline the greatness of his fall from grace. This possibility is inherently present in the Edenic imagery. Just as the image of the heavily laden merchant ship in Ezekiel 27 lends itself naturally to the image of the sinking ship, so the image of the Man in Paradise leads almost inevitably to the picture of Paradise Lost. The abundance of his trade brought with it not merely riches but also violence and pride; his "wisdom" became corrupt and led him into wickedness (28:16–17).

This wickedness, and the judgment it subsequently incurred, exposed the pretension of his pride. Far from being a self-sufficient divinity, his humanity and derivative status were laid bare when at the command of the one true God he was banished from the garden and from the presence of God (28:16). Far from being a god, who by a theophany might sanctify a piece of ground as a suitable site for a sanctuary, his very presence had the opposite effect, defiling sanctuaries (28:18). Cast down to the ground, he was made a public spectacle before the kings of the earth and consumed by fire from within (28:18).

The end result of this judgment is that the king of Tyre, like his city, will come to a horrible end and will be no more (26:19). Like the second panel,

---

5. Nine of the twelve stones from the high priest's breastplate are listed here, with the third set of three from the list in Ex. 28 omitted, perhaps accidentally during the course of the transmission of the text.

6. The Hebrew may also be read, "you were on the holy mount, you were a divine being" (Greenberg, *Ezekiel 21–37*, 584), emphasizing the essence of the sin of the king of Tyre. Like the original sin, it involved the claim to have "be[come] like God" (Gen. 3:5).

7. "Walking about" (*hithallāk*) occurs frequently in the context of the sanctuary. See Gordon Wenham, "Sanctuary Symbolism in the Garden of Eden Story," in *I Studied Inscriptions From Before the Flood: Ancient Near Eastern Literary and Linguistic Approaches to Genesis 1–11*, ed. R. S. Hess and D. T. Tsumura (Winona Lake, Ind.: Eisenbrauns, 1994), 400–401. The reference to "stones of fire" is obscure but may refer to a hedge of sparkling gemstones around the garden.

then, the third panel paints a glorious, hyperbolic picture of Tyre's present splendor. But that present glory merely serves to underline the depth of Tyre's fall when it comes, a fall that will affect both Tyre and her king. When the great ship Tyre sinks, her captain will go down to the depths along with her.

Oracle Against Sidon (28:20–23)

AFTER THE THREE-PANEL depiction of Tyre's judgment comes a brief oracle against Tyre's neighbor, Sidon (28:20–23). There is no particular charge leveled against her; presumably she is included in the general charges of rejoicing in Jerusalem's downfall and profiting from it. But her rejoicing will be short-lived, for she, like the other nations, will find that Judah's God is not to be trifled with. The Lord will gain glory for himself by executing judgments on Sidon—plague, bloodshed, and the sword on every side (28:22–23). As in the Exodus, he will gain glory from his execution of judgment on his people's foes (Ex. 14:4, 17–18).[8] Then indeed the nations will experience personally the Lord's holiness and power.

This is, in fact, a significant aspect of the judgment on the nations. The power of the Lord's holiness has already been demonstrated in his execution of judgment on his own people. But his faithful love for his people requires him to demonstrate that Jerusalem is not finally cast off. The promise to Abraham that "whoever curses you I will curse" (Gen. 12:3) is still in force.

Address to the Lord's People (28:24–26)

AS WE CONCLUDE the circular tour of judgment on Israel's immediate neighbors, the prophet is instructed once again to address the Lord's own people so that they may understand the reason for what they see happening. These words of hope form the central fulcrum for the oracles against the nations, showing that their purpose is to build hope in Ezekiel's immediate audience.[9] The judgments on the nations that the prophet describes are ultimately for Israel's own good, so that when the full regathering of the nation takes place, she may dwell in safety, free from prickly neighbors (28:24).

Indeed, God will demonstrate his holiness—the distinctiveness of his being—not only by judging the nations but also by once again gathering his own people to the Promised Land. He will demonstrate his power by giving them peace and security in the land promised to the patriarchs in the sight of the nations all around (28:25). The people will once again be able to build houses and plant vineyards (28:26), long-term projects that speak of settled

8. Allen, *Ezekiel 20–48*, 99.
9. Block, *Ezekiel 25–48*, 4.

security. Then all nations will see that Israel is God's people and he is their God, which has been the goal of his covenant relationship with them from the outset (Ex. 6:7). This point is underlined in the modified version of the recognition formula used. Instead of the usual "then they will know that I am the LORD," the oracle closes, "Then they will know that I am the LORD their God" (Ezek. 28:26). Paradise, which the king of Tyre claimed and lost, may still be regained by God's own people.

A HEAVENLY CONFLICT DEPICTED? This passage has suffered from imaginative exegesis at the hands of the early church fathers, whose ideas have been given renewed currency in some contemporary expositions. These writers interpreted the depiction of Ezekiel 28, along with a similar passage addressed to the king of Babylon in Isaiah 14, as describing literally a heavenly conflict between God and the forces of evil. This conflict resulted in the fall of "Lucifer" and his followers from a primary place in the heavenly realms to the earth.

Such an interpretation ignores the metaphorical context of both passages, however. The king of Tyre is no more literally the first creature, the cherub of the garden, than Tyre itself is literally a merchant ship in Ezekiel 27. These images exploit the possibilities that are inherent in the situation of Tyre as an island or the claims of the king of Tyre to be a divine being in order to show that each image has a dark side. Ships can sink; paradise can be lost. In each case, the perfection of the initial state is magnified to hyperbolic proportions in order to underscore the calamity when it comes.

This means that just as there was never a literal ship that fit the description of the ship Tyre that actually sank (though it is in the nature of ships to sink), so also there need not here be reference to an actual perfect creature exactly matching the description of the guardian cherub, who was cast down to the earth. It is enough that there is a general knowledge of the fact that paradise, the home of the perfect, can be lost, an idea expressed not only in the biblical account of Genesis but in ancient Near Eastern myths. To use a contemporary analogy, the proverb "Pride goes before a fall" depends not on any particular fall, but simply on the fact that it is the general nature of the world in which we live for hybris to bear bitter fruit.

Agents of Satan. Nevertheless, it is also true that the powers that exist in this world do not always act alone. In some cases, they may act as agents of Satan in concerted opposition to Christianity. Jesus speaks of Christians being persecuted and brought before kings and governors for the sake of his name (Luke 21:12). The modern state may arrogate to itself semidivine status, claiming and receiving the ultimate allegiance of all citizens, just as Herod received the worship of the people of Tyre and Sidon (!) in Acts 12:22.[10] In so doing, it is nothing other than a mask for the assaults of Satan on God's people.

But Christians will always own no other king than King Jesus, in the assurance that ultimately his is the name to which every knee will bow. Like the pretensions of the king of Tyre or King Herod, the pride that launches such totalitarian claims will inevitably ultimately be brought low by God. Such confidence in God's ultimate triumph, which is legitimately founded on this passage, is far more important to Christian perseverance than obscure metaphysical speculations about the origins and early history of the evil one.

THE SEDUCTIVE POWER **of wisdom.** We have already addressed in our discussion of chapters 26–27 the seductive power of material prosperity. What this section adds is the seductive power of wisdom and of power itself. The king of Tyre prided himself on his god-like "wisdom" as being the source of all his material prosperity. We too, in the modern world, are often in awe of the wisdom of "experts."

We live in a culture of specialization and increasing dependence on expertise.[11] When we get sick, we no longer go just to a doctor but to a specialist family practitioner. If it is something serious, then we are immediately referred to a cardiologist or urologist or whichever specialist is appropriate. Even auto mechanics now specialize in particular makes of car or in oil changes or tune-ups. As a result, we have become dependent on the advice of "experts" in every sphere of life, from investments to child-rearing and marriage. We attend their seminars and rely on their expertise, often reassured by their impressive array of credentials.[12]

But the pursuit of wisdom on its own is not necessarily good. It was divine wisdom that the serpent promised our first parents in the garden: "You will

---

10. On the connection between these two passages, see Mark R. Strom, "An Old Testament Background to Acts 12:20–23," *NTS* 32 (1986): 289–92.

11. See Os Guinness, *Dining With the Devil: The Megachurch Movement Flirts With Modernity* (Grand Rapids: Baker, 1993), 71.

12. Our addiction to experts is prominent even where the results of our dependence are less than impressive. Anne Cassidy notes that this generation of children has been raised more by the advice of experts than any that preceded it. In spite of that fact, parents seem to be more bewildered and children more out of control than ever. Her radical solution is less, not more, dependence on "child development experts" ("Best Parenting Instructions Are Built in," *Chicago Tribune* [July 31, 1998], 1/25).

be like God, knowing good and evil" (Gen. 3:5). The offer of autonomous wisdom was a lie, and the result was Paradise Lost. Yet men and women still seek to establish their own wisdom apart from God, whether by listening to an internal voice or seeking the guidance of the experts. In the New Age movement, the trends are often combined as "experts" charge $500 or more for weekend seminars that promise inner enlightenment, an empowering knowledge of self and the world, through which health, wealth, and wholeness may be attained.

The wisdom of the world may offer a God-like ability to succeed in everything we attempt while living lives free of pain and sickness. It offers a seductively attractive path to those who are suffering physically or otherwise lacking in some area of their lives. The wisdom of the world, however, is foolishness to God (1 Cor. 1:20). For the Christian, wisdom consists neither in consulting the experts nor in seeking inner enlightenment, but in consulting God and in living according to his Word. This way makes no promises of present wealth, health, or ease. The way of God's wisdom, however, is the only safe path back to Paradise Regained.

The seductive power of power. Nor is it enough to avoid being seduced by the wisdom of the world. Christians are also frequently seduced by the power of the world. The powers that be, whether political, intellectual, or economic, frequently oppose the truth of the Scriptures. In many conflicts, the gods of this age seem able to put more battalions onto the field than the God of the Bible. The temptation that faces the church in such situations is to attempt to fight power with power. In response to pagan political agendas, it is easy to get sucked into believing that the only correct response is a Christian political agenda.[13] In response to the power of a consumer culture, many are persuaded that the answer is better marketing for the church.

The love of power can also infiltrate the church. Church leaders or denominational structures can easily be elevated six feet above contradiction. I was once told by a church leader with whom I disagreed over whether a practice was right, "The denomination has decided. What gives you the right to disagree?" The answer to his question (though unfortunately I did not have it on my lips at the time) is that Jesus is our king, not the church, and his wisdom is expressed in the Scriptures. If the Bible says so, I must believe it, no matter what the experts or the powers say. If the Bible denies it, then I may not think so, though all the world agrees. As Martin Luther put it in his famous declaration to the Diet of Worms: "Here I stand. My conscience is captive to the Word of God. I can do no other."

---

13. For the pitfalls of such politicization, see Charles W. Colson, "The Power Illusion," in Michael C. Horton (ed.) *Power Religion* (Chicago: Moody, 1992), 25–38.

Jesus as the power and wisdom of God. The assurance of Ezekiel 28 is that it is those who take their stand on the Word of God and the wisdom of God who will ultimately stand, not those who kowtow to the wisdom and the powers of this world. Their strength is but a show, no matter how impressive it appears. It contains within itself the seeds of its own demise. But those who trust in Jesus have built their house on the solid Rock, who is more solid than even the contemporary rock of ages, Tyre.

That fact is true because Jesus Christ is both the power of God and the wisdom of God (1 Cor. 1:24). The message of the cross may be despised by those who are perishing, because it seems the way of weakness, but in reality it is the power of God (1 Cor. 1:18). The way of weakness that the crucified Christ represents is stronger by far than any human strength. He is the true model of perfection, who was with the Father in the beginning, the exact image of the invisible God (Col. 1:15). He was the one who was actually present in Eden, yet without sin. The king of Tyre might make great boasts of his divine status, but Jesus Christ really is one with the Father (John 10:30). He is the reality to which the king of Tyre blasphemously aspired.

But there was one key similarity between Jesus and the king of Tyre: Both died in humiliation, under the judgment of God. Yet even in this similarity is a crucial difference: Although Jesus was banished from the Father's presence on the cross, in his case the cause was not his pride but ours. Mine was the transgression that deserved the fate of the uncircumcised, under God's curse. His was the payment of the penalty that my desire to "be like God" incurred.

The ultimate destiny of Jesus and the king of Tyre are also radically divergent. The king of Tyre will fall to the underworld, never to return. Jesus has ascended to the right hand of the Father in glory. There he is crowned with many crowns and exalted above all names. What is more, he is united forever to his people, whom he won for himself through his death and resurrection. Therein lies our assurance and our hope. If we are exalted by the world like the king of Tyre, there are no guarantees of our remaining at the top. Those who reject the way of Christ in favor of the wisdom of the world are destined for the pit. But if instead we follow the way of suffering and affliction in company with Jesus, we will also be exalted with him and be with him for all eternity.

Jesus, the second Adam, the eschatological God-man, has paid for our original and actual sin once and for all on the cross. Through his death, he has regained Paradise on our behalf. As a result, we are assured of immortality in him (1 Cor. 15:45–54). Here and now we may only experience a foretaste, but some day we will experience the fullness of rest and blessing when the Lord reveals himself in the sight of the nations as "the LORD [our] God" (Ezek. 28:26).

Ezekiel 29:1–30:19

I N THE TENTH YEAR, in the tenth month on the twelfth day,
the word of the LORD came to me: [2]"Son of man, set your
face against Pharaoh king of Egypt and prophesy against
him and against all Egypt. [3]Speak to him and say: 'This is what
the Sovereign LORD says:

> "'I am against you, Pharaoh king of Egypt,
>   you great monster lying among your streams.
> You say, "The Nile is mine;
>   I made it for myself."
> [4]But I will put hooks in your jaws
>   and make the fish of your streams stick to your scales.
> I will pull you out from among your streams,
>   with all the fish sticking to your scales.
> [5]I will leave you in the desert,
>   you and all the fish of your streams.
> You will fall on the open field
>   and not be gathered or picked up.
> I will give you as food
>   to the beasts of the earth and the birds of the air.

[6]Then all who live in Egypt will know that I am the LORD.

"'You have been a staff of reed for the house of Israel.
[7]When they grasped you with their hands, you splintered and
you tore open their shoulders; when they leaned on you, you
broke and their backs were wrenched.

[8]"'Therefore this is what the Sovereign LORD says: I will
bring a sword against you and kill your men and their animals.
[9]Egypt will become a desolate wasteland. Then they will know
that I am the LORD.

"'Because you said, "The Nile is mine; I made it," [10]there-
fore I am against you and against your streams, and I will
make the land of Egypt a ruin and a desolate waste from
Migdol to Aswan, as far as the border of Cush. [11]No foot of
man or animal will pass through it; no one will live there for
forty years. [12]I will make the land of Egypt desolate among
devastated lands, and her cities will lie desolate forty years
among ruined cities. And I will disperse the Egyptians among
the nations and scatter them through the countries.

¹³"'Yet this is what the Sovereign LORD says: At the end of forty years I will gather the Egyptians from the nations where they were scattered. ¹⁴I will bring them back from captivity and return them to Upper Egypt, the land of their ancestry. There they will be a lowly kingdom. ¹⁵It will be the lowliest of kingdoms and will never again exalt itself above the other nations. I will make it so weak that it will never again rule over the nations. ¹⁶Egypt will no longer be a source of confidence for the people of Israel but will be a reminder of their sin in turning to her for help. Then they will know that I am the Sovereign LORD.'"

¹⁷In the twenty-seventh year, in the first month on the first day, the word of the LORD came to me: ¹⁸"Son of man, Nebuchadnezzar king of Babylon drove his army in a hard campaign against Tyre; every head was rubbed bare and every shoulder made raw. Yet he and his army got no reward from the campaign he led against Tyre. ¹⁹Therefore this is what the Sovereign LORD says: I am going to give Egypt to Nebuchadnezzar king of Babylon, and he will carry off its wealth. He will loot and plunder the land as pay for his army. ²⁰I have given him Egypt as a reward for his efforts because he and his army did it for me, declares the Sovereign LORD.

²¹"On that day I will make a horn grow for the house of Israel, and I will open your mouth among them. Then they will know that I am the LORD."

³⁰:¹The word of the LORD came to me: ²"Son of man, prophesy and say: 'This is what the Sovereign LORD says:

> "'Wail and say,
>   "Alas for that day!"
> ³ For the day is near,
>   the day of the LORD is near—
> a day of clouds,
>   a time of doom for the nations.
> ⁴ A sword will come against Egypt,
>   and anguish will come upon Cush.
> When the slain fall in Egypt,
>   her wealth will be carried away
>   and her foundations torn down.

⁵Cush and Put, Lydia and all Arabia, Libya and the people of the covenant land will fall by the sword along with Egypt.

⁶′′′This is what the LORD says:

> ′′′The allies of Egypt will fall
> and her proud strength will fail.
> From Migdol to Aswan
> they will fall by the sword within her,
> > declares the Sovereign LORD.
> ⁷′′′They will be desolate
> among desolate lands,
> and their cities will lie
> among ruined cities.
> ⁸Then they will know that I am the LORD,
> when I set fire to Egypt
> and all her helpers are crushed.

⁹′′′On that day messengers will go out from me in ships to frighten Cush out of her complacency. Anguish will take hold of them on the day of Egypt's doom, for it is sure to come.

¹⁰′′′This is what the Sovereign LORD says:

> ′′′I will put an end to the hordes of Egypt
> by the hand of Nebuchadnezzar king of Babylon.
> ¹¹He and his army—the most ruthless of nations—
> will be brought in to destroy the land.
> They will draw their swords against Egypt
> and fill the land with the slain.
> ¹²I will dry up the streams of the Nile
> and sell the land to evil men;
> by the hand of foreigners
> I will lay waste the land and everything in it.

I the LORD have spoken.

¹³′′′This is what the Sovereign LORD says:

> ′′′I will destroy the idols
> and put an end to the images in Memphis.
> No longer will there be a prince in Egypt,
> and I will spread fear throughout the land.
> ¹⁴I will lay waste Upper Egypt,
> set fire to Zoan
> and inflict punishment on Thebes.
> ¹⁵I will pour out my wrath on Pelusium,
> the stronghold of Egypt,
> and cut off the hordes of Thebes.

¹⁶ I will set fire to Egypt;
  Pelusium will writhe in agony.
 Thebes will be taken by storm;
  Memphis will be in constant distress.
¹⁷ The young men of Heliopolis and Bubastis
  will fall by the sword,
  and the cities themselves will go into captivity.
¹⁸ Dark will be the day at Tahpanhes
  when I break the yoke of Egypt;
  there her proud strength will come to an end.
 She will be covered with clouds,
  and her villages will go into captivity.
¹⁹ So I will inflict punishment on Egypt,
  and they will know that I am the LORD.'"

AFTER THE SIX ORACLES against Israel's immediate neighbors (chs. 25–28), we reach the seventh, climactic oracle, which is delivered against Egypt (chs. 29–32). This oracle is itself made up of seven subunits (29:1–16; 29:17–21; 30:1–19; 30:20–26; 31:1–18; 32:1–16; 32:17–32).[1] Like the substantial oracle against Tyre that preceded it, the word against Egypt addresses both the land of Egypt and its ruler and threatens judgment on both.

The First Oracle (29:1–16)

EZEKIEL 29 OPENS with a word of judgment against Pharaoh, who is addressed under the figure of a great sea monster (*tannîn*).[2] This sea monster was a well-known element of ancient Near Eastern mythology, a force of chaos that had to be tamed before the world could be created.[3] The prophet Isaiah had already utilized the imagery of the sea monster to describe God's defeat of Egypt at the time of the Exodus (Isa. 51:9), while in Genesis 1:21 the great sea monster appears in demythologized form as simply another of God's creatures.

---

1. Block, *Ezekiel 25–48*, 128. In each case, the new section is introduced by the formula "The word of the LORD came to me . . ." and in every case except 30:1 the oracle is dated.

2. The MT has *tannîm* ("jackals") but the rest of the water-based imagery requires reading *tannîn* ("sea monster"), along with many manuscripts and versions. The MT may be the result of a scribal error or an otherwise unknown variant form (Allen, *Ezekiel 20–48*, 102).

3. John Day, *God's Conflict With the Dragon and the Sea* (Cambridge: Cambridge Univ. Press, 1985), 94–95.

In Ezekiel, the mythical picture blends with the geographically appropriate image of Pharaoh as a great crocodile, resting secure amid the Nile streams, to give a picture of the ruler of Egypt as a superhuman, supernatural force of destruction. Thus far, Pharaoh would probably not have disputed the description. According to Egyptian records, the god Amon-Re said to Pharaoh Thutmoses III, "I cause them to see thy majesty as a crocodile, the lord of fear in the water, who cannot be approached."[4] But just as the positive metaphor of the ship of Tyre in full sail lends itself to the negative picture of the ship of Tyre catastrophically wrecked, so also the image of Pharaoh as a powerful crocodile, even one of mythical proportions, lends itself to the picture of Pharaoh as the trapped crocodile, subdued by the Great Hunter. For both the ship and the crocodile, their watery fortress proves to be less than impregnable. Tyre's home "in the midst of the seas" ($b^e t \hat{o} k$ $hayy \bar{a} m$) was no secure defense, and neither will Pharaoh's abode "in the midst of the Nile/streams" ($b^e t \hat{o} k$ $y^e \hat{o} r$).[5]

Thus, for all Pharaoh's boasts of divine power, claiming to have created for his own purposes the Nile, the source of all of Egypt's prosperity, he will be trapped with hooks like an ordinary crocodile (29:4). He will be brought out into the desert, the place of judgment (20:35), and there executed along with "all the fish of your streams," that is, either the nations allied to him or the members of his armed forces. Their bodies will be left dishonorably exposed to become food for wild animals, rather than being gathered for decent burial.[6] Such a fate was commonly invoked as a curse in ancient Near Eastern treaties.

The reason for this act of judgment becomes clear in verses 6–7. Egypt has been an unstable support, a "staff of reed" to Judah. The term "staff of reed" is an oxymoron: A staff needs to be strong and reliable to support the weight placed on it, while a reed is by definition something thin and fragile (1 Kings 14:15). Egypt's sin was to appear to be a source of military support in Judah's struggle against Babylon, encouraging her to rebel against her overlords. Once the battle was joined, however, she stood at a distance, leaving Judah to her fate.

The image of Egypt as a "splintered reed of a staff" was already used centuries earlier in the Assyrian field commander's speech to Hezekiah's emissaries (2 Kings 18:21; Isa. 36:6). In that instance, it was an unfair and

---

4. *ANET*, 374; cited in Lind, *Ezekiel*, 244.

5. The Egyptian loanword $y^e \hat{o} r$ can be translated either "Nile" or "streams." The NIV, like many modern translations, utilizes both English words in this chapter to translate this single Hebrew word.

6. RSV reads $l\bar{o}^{\ni}$ $tiqq\bar{a}b\bar{e}r$ ("you shall ... not be ... buried") along with many Hebrew manuscripts and the Targum, for the MT $l\bar{o}^{\ni}$ $tiqq\bar{a}b\bar{e}\d{s}$ ("you will not be collected"). Whether or not this emendation is correct, it at least underscores the purpose of the gathering: This is not the gathering of return from exile but merely of bodies for burial, as in 2 Sam. 21:13–14.

inaccurate assessment of the situation since Hezekiah had placed his trust in a much firmer support, the Lord (2 Kings 18:5). Nevertheless, as a judgment of the political dangers of trusting in Egypt, it was a true statement at most points in Israel's history.[7]

Though the sin of trusting in the staff of reed was primarily Judah's sin, yet the object of that trust is judged along with her. God's people should indeed have known better than to trust in Egypt, but Egypt too is not guiltless for soliciting their trust and then proving dangerously unstable, causing (in the imagery of leaning on an unstable support) their shoulders to become shattered and their hips to totter (Ezek. 29:7). Egypt's arrogant claims to creator status are a contributory factor in Judah's sin (29:9). As a result, she too will be judged by God and turned into an utter devastation, a devastated land in the midst of devastated lands. This total destruction will extend from Migdol on the northeast frontier all the way down to Aswan in the far south (29:10). The whole of Egypt will be uninhabited for forty years (29:11), which is not only the standard length of a generation in biblical terminology but is also the length of the Judean exile Ezekiel had prophesied in 4:6.

To underline the symmetry of Egypt's fate with those who trusted in her, her people will be scattered among the nations and dispersed among the peoples, just like Judah (12:15; 20:23; 22:15). Even more strikingly, they too will be gathered by the Lord from among the nations, brought back from captivity, and returned to the land from which they originated (29:14). But these similarities only serve to highlight the differences in their ultimate fates. Egypt will not be fully restored but merely reestablished as a shadow of her former self, confined to the distant areas of Upper Egypt (29:16). There it will no longer act as a source of temptation for Judah in her foreign policy. In their weakened state, they too will come to an awareness of God's sovereign power. Her "restoration" is not so much an act of grace on the Lord's part for Egypt's sake as it is a reminder of Israel's past faithlessness, which will never again be repeated.

The Second Oracle (29:17–21)

THE SECOND ORACLE in the sequence against Egypt is the latest of all the dated oracles, coming from the beginning of the twenty-seventh year of the Exile (29:17). It recognizes the relative fruitlessness of Nebuchadnezzar's campaign against Tyre, of which Ezekiel had spoken in chapters 26–28. Though the effort expended was great, with both helmet and shield leaving their marks on the relevant parts of the anatomy, the booty achieved at the end of the campaign was minimal (29:18). In compensation, since they were

---

7. Greenberg cites Sargon II of Assyria's statement that his contemporary counterpart in Egypt was "a king who cannot save" (*Ezekiel 21–37*, 604).

working for the Lord (29:20), the Lord will give Egypt's wealth as plunder for Nebuchadnezzar's army (29:19).

It has become almost a shibboleth in commentaries to see the purpose of this oracle as Ezekiel's explaining away the failure of his earlier prophecy against Tyre.[8] According to Josephus, Nebuchadnezzar did indeed besiege Tyre for some thirteen years (586–573 B.C.).[9] By the end of that time, Tyre's economic and political importance was destroyed, and the king of Tyre became a vassal of Nebuchadnezzar.[10] The siege appears to have been a success, as Ezekiel had prophesied. However, the material rewards were not, according to Ezekiel, appropriate to the energy expended. It is this imbalance that the Lord now promises to redress.

If the passage had been intended as an apologetic against a failure of literal fulfillment, it is extraordinary that the prophet chooses such a minor part of his prophecy to defend. If he were confronted by literalists, insisting on a word-for-word fulfillment of his prophecy, one would have expected them to press Ezekiel on the major point that Tyre had not actually been reduced to a bare rock (26:4) but was still a viable city, rather than on the minor point that Tyre had not provided significant booty for her captors. In addition, an oracle with such a purpose would belong properly after the Tyre oracles, not in the middle of the oracles against Egypt.

In fact, the purpose of the oracle is quite different.[11] There is no mention as such of any "failure" of an earlier oracle; on the contrary, the essential success of the oracle against Tyre is presupposed. Nebuchadnezzar did indeed, as Ezekiel prophesied, assault Tyre and bring her to ruin. The point being made here is simple: The worker is worthy of his hire, and Nebuchadnezzar is acting as the Lord's worker in his conquests, both of Tyre and Egypt. Just as he had succeeded against Tyre, so also he will succeed against Egypt, and this time he will receive payment in full.

Chapter 29 then closes with a brief oracle that reminds us that Israel remains the central focus of the prophet's interest, even in the oracles against the foreign nations. Commensurate with Egypt's reduction in significance will

---

8. Donald Gowan is typical when he writes: the prophet "does not find it necessary to defend or explain away his earlier prophecy; in effect he just admits that it didn't happen" (*When Man Becomes God* [Pittsburgh: Pickwick, 1975], 103. Similarly, Greenberg, *Ezekiel 21–37*, 617; Block, *Ezekiel 25–48*, 149.

9. *Contra Apionem*, 1.156; *Antiquities*, 10.228.

10. *Cambridge Ancient History*, 2d ed., 235.

11. Leslie Allen, having accepted that this oracle originates in the failure of the earlier prophecy, then goes on to note that "the redactional agenda of these verses is a different one" (*Ezekiel 20–48*, 111). It is the "redacted" (i.e., inscripturated) agenda with which we are concerned here.

be a strengthening of the house of Israel. This turn in Israel's fortunes will result both in a recognition of the Lord as the agent of this change and in a recognition that Ezekiel has been the Lord's prophet: The Lord will "open your mouth"; that is, Ezekiel's testimony will be validated (29:21).[12]

The Third Oracle (30:1–19)

IN THIS THIRD oracle, the content of the prophecy of the first oracle (29:1–16) is essentially replayed in the form of a lament. The prophet is instructed to wail and mourn for the coming of the day of the Lord's judgment on Egypt (30:3–4). Egypt's allies, which were mentioned as sharing her downfall in the first oracle under the image of the "fish of your streams" (29:4), now come into focus as distinct nations. Ethiopia (Cush), Libya (Put), Lydia, all Arabia, Cub,[13] and the people of the land in covenant with them[14] will fall along with Egypt (30:5–6). The entire confederacy will be reduced to a shattered and burned ruin (30:6–9), made desolate at the hand of Nebuchadnezzar and his ruthless army (30:10–12). From Memphis, Tahpanhes, and Heliopolis in the north of Egypt to Thebes in the south, the cities of Egypt will be destroyed (30:13–19).

The summary statement in 30:19, "So I will inflict punishment on Egypt, and they will know that I am the LORD," evokes repeated themes of the Exodus narrative, where both "doing judgments" against Egypt (Ex. 6:6; 7:4; 12:12; Num. 33:4) and the knowledge of God (Ex. 7:5; 14:4, 18) are prominent. As in the Exodus, this act of judgment will strike at both the gods of Egypt and their earthly rulers (Ezek. 30:13). In the imagery of the cosmic Day of the Lord, the light will be turned to darkness and the proud strength of Egypt brought to an end (30:18). By this means, God will demonstrate conclusively his existence and power in front of a watching world.

Bridging Contexts

COMFORTING THE AFFLICTED. One of the dangers against which I warn aspiring preachers in our seminary is that of preaching against all the sins with which no one in their congregation struggles. It is relatively easy to warn the heterosexuals about the dangers of

---

12. Greenberg, *Ezekiel 21–37*, 616.

13. See NIV note. This nation is otherwise unknown from the ancient Near Eastern sources, unless it is a mistake for Lub, which is another term for (part of) Libya.

14. "The people of the covenant land" is frequently taken as an oblique reference to Judah (e.g., Allen, *Ezekiel 20–48*, 115; Block, *Ezekiel 25–48*, 159). However, the phrase "the land of the covenant," despite its biblical sounding overtones, nowhere else occurs to designate the Promised Land. The closest parallel is in Obad. 7, which speaks of "the men of your covenant," which the NIV appropriately renders "your allies."

homosexuality, the teetotaler about the snare of alcoholism, the politically conservative about the hazards of liberalism, the rigidly orthodox about the perils of false teaching. All of these are indeed real concerns, but insofar as they are not a part of your congregation, to preach against them will merely instill a comfortable sense of "us" versus "them." "We" are those who are right-eous, holy and free from sin (at least, from those sins); "they" are the filthy, abhorrent sinners. Like the Pharisee in the temple, we continually remind God and ourselves of the sins of others, rather than recognizing the reality of our own sins (Luke 18:11). In the meantime, our more subtle sins of pride, self-centeredness, and lack of love may go completely unchallenged.

At first sight, it may appear that the oracle against Egypt falls into this cat-egory of sermon. Does it not address someone else's sins and threaten judg-ment on them, to the exclusion of any interest in Judah's misdeeds? Is Ezekiel selling out his responsibility as a prophet? Those who have read this far through the book will hardly think that a likely scenario. If the preacher's task is both to afflict the comfortable and to comfort the afflicted, few will accuse Ezekiel of unduly sparing the comfortable. But now it is time for Ezekiel to turn to the task of comforting the afflicted. The foreign nation oracles are part of that ministry of comfort.

But how precisely does this oracle against Egypt encourage the exiles of Judah? The first way is by assuring them of God's continuing concern for his own people. Egypt's fault lay not in a general tendency to raise false hopes of deliverance in people, but specifically in having falsely raised the hopes of God's people. Presumably, the Egyptian policy of encouraging rebellion against Babylon extended to all of the small nation states of the Levant. Indeed, the oracle mentions a number of nations who had, like Judah, thrown their lot in with Egypt, with what would prove to be fatal consequences. Yet God is not equally concerned with all of the peoples. It is not because Egypt had been a source of false hopes to Libya or the Arabians that she is judged, but because she had been the source of false hope to the house of Israel. God has a special concern with the fate of his own people.

God's concern for his covenant people. In the New Testament, the covenant people with whom God is concerned is no longer merely national, ethnic Israel but the spiritual "Israel of God" (Gal. 6:16), a new creation in which circumcision and uncircumcision are no longer of importance (6:15). In one sense, nothing has changed. God's people remain those whom he has called, claimed as his own, and redeemed out of bondage. The Old Testa-ment people of God had experienced his salvation in the liberation from Egypt; the New Testament people of God are those who have experienced the new exodus accomplished by Jesus, leading his people out of their bondage to sin.

But the fullness of blessing achieved in Jesus is too great to be contained within ethnic lines. His calling is to be a light also to the Gentiles (Isa. 42:6; 49:6). He came so that those who were afar off under the old covenant might be brought near in him (Eph. 2:13), made heirs of the promised Holy Spirit (Acts 2:38–39), and ingrafted into the olive tree that represents the covenant community (Rom. 11:17–24). Now the Gentiles are no longer strangers and aliens but in Christ are fellow citizens with the Jews as God's people (Eph. 2:19). Israel has not been abolished or sidelined with the coming of Christ but rather has been eschatologically expanded by the inclusion of Jews and Gentiles together into the one new people of God, the church.[15]

God's anger continues to be expressed against those who lead his people astray. Egypt acted as a source of temptation for Judah; therefore she, along with Judah, will experience the weight of God's wrath. Similarly, Jesus warns his disciples, "Things that cause people to sin are bound to come, but woe to that person through whom they come. It would be better for him to be thrown into the sea with a millstone tied around his neck than for him to cause one of these little ones to sin. So watch yourselves" (Luke 17:1–3). Peter speaks of the swift destruction that awaits those who are false teachers (2 Peter 2:1). It is a fearful thing to lead astray from the true paths one of Christ's sheep, whether by our words or actions. God's action against Egypt will be swift and decisive, and will result in her removal as a source of temptation; even after her "restoration" she will never again be a stumbling block for God's people.

Factors in Egypt's downfall. But God's motivation to act against Egypt is not merely concern to punish those who led the house of Israel astray. He is also motivated by a concern for his own glory. Egypt, in the person of Pharaoh, had set herself up as a rival to the true God. Pharaoh depicted himself in semimythical terms as a godlike creature, who made and controlled the forces of blessing in nature, namely, the Nile. Such claims cannot be tolerated. God must and will act to cut the idols of Egypt down to size, just as he did earlier during the Exodus.

This time, however, it is not Israel but Egypt who will be brought up through the waters out into the desert, which will prove for them a place of judgment rather than salvation (29:4–5). Pharaoh's creatureliness will be demonstrated in the most incontrovertible of ways, death, followed by the dishonorable exposure of his body to the appetites of scavenging beasts. To a culture like Egypt, where postmortem care of the body, especially the body

---

15. See Edmund P. Clowney, "The New Israel," in Carl E. Armerding and W. Ward Gasque, ed., *Dreams, Visions and Oracles: The Layman's Guide to Biblical Prophecy* (Grand Rapids: Baker, 1977), 207–20.

of a pharaoh, was regarded as a matter of nothing less than cosmic significance, this was the ultimate judgment.

Egypt's downfall will also provide the rewards for God's worker in the judgment, Nebuchadnezzar (29:17–21). God will be in no one's debt; even the unrighteous laborer is worthy of his hire. How much more, then, may the righteous and faithful servant expect to see a reward! Ezekiel himself serves as an example of this. His words of hope of restoration for Israel will be fulfilled, and then he will be honored accordingly as a true prophet (29:21). God's ultimate purpose will be seen to be not merely the destruction of the unrighteous but the salvation of a people for himself, through the fulfillment of the prophetic word.

The lament over Egypt. But what does chapter 30 add to Ezekiel's argument? We have noted above that in terms of content it essentially repeats the message of chapter 29. However, the format is different, in that the message is expressed in the form of a lament. Repetition is a device used frequently in the Bible to underscore the importance of a point and to drive it home. But this is not simply repetition, it is repetition with a twist: By repeating the threat of Egypt's downfall in the form of a lament, the message gains affective strength, impacting the emotions as well as the mind.

Because of the association with death and the sense of pain and loss that that event brings, laments carry strong emotional overtones. In this case, the playing of the funeral dirge before the actual death is a token and surety that the death will ultimately occur. Egypt and all her allies will certainly fall. This message is particularly important for the exiles to hear and learn because it underlines once again the reason for Judah's demise. Instead of trusting in the Lord as her strength and Redeemer, she turned to other supports, allying herself to Egypt. She is therefore directly comparable to Egypt's allies who are mentioned here by name, for the fate of all those in covenant with Egypt is to fall by the sword (30:6).

Contemporary Significance

THE ATTRACTIVENESS OF **the world.** Egypt was always an attractive place, seen from an Israelite perspective. In the minds of those in the desert generation, it was the place of a varied abundance of food: of meat and fish, of cucumbers, melons, leeks, onions, and garlic (Num. 11:5). Nostalgia overcame reality in painting the glories of their past existence before the Lord stepped in and saved them. Somehow the memories of the overseer's lash faded, drowned out in the aroma of spicy food. By comparison, their "saved" existence in the desert, with only manna to eat, seemed altogether bland.

The dangerous attractiveness of Egypt is a theme even as early as the patriarchal narratives. When there was nothing to eat in the Promised Land, there was food enough in Egypt (Gen. 12:10). When Lot chose the most promising land (even though it was outside the Promised Land), it bore a striking resemblance to Egypt (13:10). When the wife of promise was barren, her Egyptian maidservant turned out to be easily fertile (16:1–4). The way of obedience was always hard, while the way of Egypt always seemed easy.[16] Similarly, when danger threatened during the period of the monarchy, Egypt was never far from Judah's thoughts as a potential savior. She, after all, had virtually unlimited resources of chariots and horses and men at her disposal, as Israel had experienced firsthand. Pharaoh Shishak, for instance, was once able to muster against Rehoboam twelve hundred chariots, sixty thousand horsemen, and men without number (2 Chron. 12:3). In comparison to the Egyptian option, what had the Lord to offer?

So too for us, the world has many powerful attractions, many idolatries that seem to offer us easy routes to security and success. There is the pursuit of political power, which says to us, "What could you not do if only you controlled the legislative process?" There is the pursuit of financial gain, which seems to offer personal comfort and the power to control your own destiny. There is the pursuit of fame and personal importance, which is perhaps a particular temptation to preachers and teachers. "What great things you could accomplish," it whispers, "if only you could preach in a larger church, where your message would be heard by more people."

Like Egypt, each of these idolatries promises us safety and success, if we will only throw in our lot with them. Like Egypt, however, if we place our trust in them, each of these will prove to be a broken reed, twisting and destroying our lives. For all their godlike claims to be able to create and sustain a prosperous universe, the reality never matches up to the prospectus.

How not to be deceived by Satan. Like Israel before him, Jesus faced the alluring attractiveness of the ways of the world. During a forty-day spell in the desert, Jesus was tempted to trust in alternative means of reaching his goals (Matt. 4:1–11). Even the form of the temptations that he faced echoed the temptations of Israel in the desert. Jesus' hunger paralleled Israel's need for bread in the desert, which the Lord answered by providing manna (Ex. 16). Unlike the grumbling response of his ancestors, Jesus replied to Satan, "Man does not live on bread alone, but on every word that comes from the mouth of God" (Matt. 4:4, citing Deut. 8:3).

Next the Israelites were thirsty, and we are told that "they tested the LORD" at Massah (Ex. 17:7); Jesus responded to Satan's second temptation

---

16. For this, see Iain Duguid, "Hagar the Egyptian: A Note on the Allure of Egypt in the Abraham Cycle," *WTJ* 56 (1994): 419–21.

by saying, "Do not put the Lord your God to the test" (Matt. 4:7, citing Deut. 6:16).

Then the Israelites made for themselves a golden calf and bowed down to it (Ex. 32), exactly what the devil wanted Jesus to do to him. Unlike his ancestors, Jesus was not willing to comply with Satan's request. He replied, "Worship the Lord your God, and serve him only" (Matt. 4:10, citing Deut. 6:13). Whereas Israel failed in the desert, striking out three times, Jesus endured faithfully, resisting the attractive but fatally flawed "Egyptian option."

He did so because he was not deceived by Satan. He saw clearly that things are not always as they appear. Satan offers a solution for our felt needs, immediate relief for the blister points of life. However, our felt needs are not always our real needs. Sometimes what offers temporary relief causes long-term problems. Jesus rejected Satan's quick-fix solutions in favor of a life lived in obedience to God's call, a path that led all the way to the cross. Why did he do so? Because he saw the ultimate realities of life: that men and women would be eternally lost without a Savior, someone who lived the life of perfect obedience in their place and who died the death their sins deserved. For Jesus, there was no "Egyptian option" in accomplishing our salvation, and so he followed the hard road.

Our thinking is often much more clouded. We feel the pain of the blister points of life and are tempted to find relief in whatever form it may be offered. Yet all too often that "relief" involves a compromise with the world. When danger threatens, we run to Egypt, not to the Lord. We do so only because we have forgotten the ultimate realities of life—that sin never ultimately delivers what it promises, that those who make a compact with the world will see the source of their hopes burned up. Like most purist anglers, Satan prefers fly-fishing to bait-fishing. He would rather hook you with something that looks good but is an absolute lie than allow you even the pleasure that he promised you while he is reeling you in. But if he has to, he will place a real worm on the hook and offer you "real" relief—a relief that lasts only until the hook is firmly embedded in your jaw.

Surviving the Day of the Lord. For the destiny of this world is ultimate destruction, just like Egypt. The Day of the Lord is coming, when this present world will be burned up, a day of judgment and destruction for the ungodly (2 Peter 3:7). The true nature of all things will be revealed. The "staff of reed" in which we have placed our trust will be shown up as a false hope. The remembrance of this judgment to come should have the same salutary effect on us as Ezekiel's prophecy of Egypt's destruction was intended to have on his original audience: "Since everything will be destroyed in this way, what kind of people ought you to be? You ought to live holy and godly lives ... mak[ing] every effort to be found spotless, blameless and at peace with him" (2 Peter 3:11, 14). Egypt and all who trust in her will be destroyed.

Those who trust in the Lord will endure, however. The true prophet and the faithful servant of God may have to endure mockery and disbelief in the present. In the long run, however, God is not mocked, and he will be in no one's debt. At the same time as the true nature of the fickle reed is revealed, so also will be revealed the solid refuge that Christ represents for his saints. What he began with his obedience in our place in the desert, he completed with his obedience in our place on the cross, establishing redemption for his people and raising a horn of salvation for us, just as Zechariah, the father of John the Baptist, prophesied (Luke 1:68—69).

Ezekiel 30:20–32:32

I N THE ELEVENTH YEAR, in the first month on the seventh day, the word of the LORD came to me: ²¹"Son of man, I have broken the arm of Pharaoh king of Egypt. It has not been bound up for healing or put in a splint so as to become strong enough to hold a sword. ²²Therefore this is what the Sovereign LORD says: I am against Pharaoh king of Egypt. I will break both his arms, the good arm as well as the broken one, and make the sword fall from his hand. ²³I will disperse the Egyptians among the nations and scatter them through the countries. ²⁴I will strengthen the arms of the king of Babylon and put my sword in his hand, but I will break the arms of Pharaoh, and he will groan before him like a mortally wounded man. ²⁵I will strengthen the arms of the king of Babylon, but the arms of Pharaoh will fall limp. Then they will know that I am the LORD, when I put my sword into the hand of the king of Babylon and he brandishes it against Egypt. ²⁶I will disperse the Egyptians among the nations and scatter them through the countries. Then they will know that I am the LORD."

^{31:1}In the eleventh year, in the third month on the first day, the word of the LORD came to me: ²"Son of man, say to Pharaoh king of Egypt and to his hordes:

"'Who can be compared with you in majesty?
³ Consider Assyria, once a cedar in Lebanon,
     with beautiful branches overshadowing the forest;
  it towered on high,
     its top above the thick foliage.
⁴ The waters nourished it,
     deep springs made it grow tall;
  their streams flowed
     all around its base
  and sent their channels
     to all the trees of the field.
⁵ So it towered higher
     than all the trees of the field;
  its boughs increased
     and its branches grew long,
     spreading because of abundant waters.

⁶All the birds of the air
    nested in its boughs,
all the beasts of the field
    gave birth under its branches;
all the great nations
    lived in its shade.
⁷It was majestic in beauty,
    with its spreading boughs,
for its roots went down
    to abundant waters.
⁸The cedars in the garden of God
    could not rival it,
nor could the pine trees
    equal its boughs,
nor could the pine trees
    compare with its branches—
no tree in the garden of God
    could match its beauty.
⁹I made it beautiful
    with abundant branches,
the envy of all the trees of Eden
    in the garden of God.

¹⁰'''Therefore this is what the Sovereign LORD says: Because it towered on high, lifting its top above the thick foliage, and because it was proud of its height, ¹¹I handed it over to the ruler of the nations, for him to deal with according to its wickedness. I cast it aside, ¹²and the most ruthless of foreign nations cut it down and left it. Its boughs fell on the mountains and in all the valleys; its branches lay broken in all the ravines of the land. All the nations of the earth came out from under its shade and left it. ¹³All the birds of the air settled on the fallen tree, and all the beasts of the field were among its branches. ¹⁴Therefore no other trees by the waters are ever to tower proudly on high, lifting their tops above the thick foliage. No other trees so well-watered are ever to reach such a height; they are all destined for death, for the earth below, among mortal men, with those who go down to the pit.

¹⁵'''This is what the Sovereign LORD says: On the day it was brought down to the grave I covered the deep springs with mourning for it; I held back its streams, and its abundant

waters were restrained. Because of it I clothed Lebanon with gloom, and all the trees of the field withered away. ¹⁶I made the nations tremble at the sound of its fall when I brought it down to the grave with those who go down to the pit. Then all the trees of Eden, the choicest and best of Lebanon, all the trees that were well-watered, were consoled in the earth below. ¹⁷Those who lived in its shade, its allies among the nations, had also gone down to the grave with it, joining those killed by the sword.

¹⁸"Which of the trees of Eden can be compared with you in splendor and majesty? Yet you, too, will be brought down with the trees of Eden to the earth below; you will lie among the uncircumcised, with those killed by the sword.

"'This is Pharaoh and all his hordes, declares the Sovereign LORD.'"

³²:¹In the twelfth year, in the twelfth month on the first day, the word of the LORD came to me: ²"Son of man, take up a lament concerning Pharaoh king of Egypt and say to him:

"'You are like a lion among the nations;
    you are like a monster in the seas
thrashing about in your streams,
    churning the water with your feet
    and muddying the streams.

³"'This is what the Sovereign LORD says:

"'With a great throng of people
    I will cast my net over you,
    and they will haul you up in my net.
⁴I will throw you on the land
    and hurl you on the open field.
I will let all the birds of the air settle on you
    and all the beasts of the earth gorge themselves on you.
⁵I will spread your flesh on the mountains
    and fill the valleys with your remains.
⁶I will drench the land with your flowing blood
    all the way to the mountains,
    and the ravines will be filled with your flesh.
⁷When I snuff you out, I will cover the heavens
    and darken their stars;
I will cover the sun with a cloud,
    and the moon will not give its light.

⁸ All the shining lights in the heavens
    I will darken over you;
    I will bring darkness over your land,
                    declares the Sovereign LORD.
⁹ I will trouble the hearts of many peoples
    when I bring about your destruction among the nations,
    among lands you have not known.
¹⁰ I will cause many peoples to be appalled at you,
    and their kings will shudder with horror because of you
    when I brandish my sword before them.
On the day of your downfall
    each of them will tremble
    every moment for his life.

¹¹ "For this is what the Sovereign LORD says:

"'The sword of the king of Babylon
    will come against you.
¹² I will cause your hordes to fall
    by the swords of mighty men—
    the most ruthless of all nations.
They will shatter the pride of Egypt,
    and all her hordes will be overthrown.
¹³ I will destroy all her cattle
    from beside abundant waters
no longer to be stirred by the foot of man
    or muddied by the hoofs of cattle.
¹⁴ Then I will let her waters settle
    and make her streams flow like oil,
                    declares the Sovereign LORD.
¹⁵ When I make Egypt desolate
    and strip the land of everything in it,
when I strike down all who live there,
    then they will know that I am the LORD.'

¹⁶ "This is the lament they will chant for her. The daughters of the nations will chant it; for Egypt and all her hordes they will chant it, declares the Sovereign LORD."

¹⁷ In the twelfth year, on the fifteenth day of the month, the word of the LORD came to me: ¹⁸ "Son of man, wail for the hordes of Egypt and consign to the earth below both her and the daughters of mighty nations, with those who go down to the pit. ¹⁹ Say to them, 'Are you more favored than others? Go

down and be laid among the uncircumcised.' ²⁰They will fall
among those killed by the sword. The sword is drawn; let her
be dragged off with all her hordes. ²¹From within the grave
the mighty leaders will say of Egypt and her allies, 'They have
come down and they lie with the uncircumcised, with those
killed by the sword.'

²²"Assyria is there with her whole army; she is surrounded
by the graves of all her slain, all who have fallen by the sword.
²³Their graves are in the depths of the pit and her army lies
around her grave. All who had spread terror in the land of the
living are slain, fallen by the sword.

²⁴"Elam is there, with all her hordes around her grave. All
of them are slain, fallen by the sword. All who had spread terror in the land of the living went down uncircumcised to the
earth below. They bear their shame with those who go down
to the pit. ²⁵A bed is made for her among the slain, with all
her hordes around her grave. All of them are uncircumcised,
killed by the sword. Because their terror had spread in the
land of the living, they bear their shame with those who go
down to the pit; they are laid among the slain.

²⁶"Meshech and Tubal are there, with all their hordes
around their graves. All of them are uncircumcised, killed by
the sword because they spread their terror in the land of the
living. ²⁷Do they not lie with the other uncircumcised warriors
who have fallen, who went down to the grave with their
weapons of war, whose swords were placed under their heads?
The punishment for their sins rested on their bones, though
the terror of these warriors had stalked through the land of
the living.

²⁸"You too, O Pharaoh, will be broken and will lie among
the uncircumcised, with those killed by the sword.

²⁹"Edom is there, her kings and all her princes; despite their
power, they are laid with those killed by the sword. They lie
with the uncircumcised, with those who go down to the pit.

³⁰"All the princes of the north and all the Sidonians are
there; they went down with the slain in disgrace despite the
terror caused by their power. They lie uncircumcised with
those killed by the sword and bear their shame with those who
go down to the pit.

³¹"Pharaoh—he and all his army—will see them and he will
be consoled for all his hordes that were killed by the sword,

declares the Sovereign LORD. ³²Although I had him spread terror in the land of the living, Pharaoh and all his hordes will be
laid among the uncircumcised, with those killed by the sword,
declares the Sovereign LORD."

IN THE PREVIOUS unit we examined the first three
of the seven oracles that Ezekiel utters against
Egypt. This present unit looks at the last four oracles. This section brings to a close the prophet's
round of oracles against the nations.

The Fourth Oracle (30:20–26)

THE FOURTH OF the seven oracles against Egypt declares that God has already
begun to act. The date formula in 30:20 places it shortly before the fall of
Jerusalem; the oracle itself rules out the possibility of any relief coming from
the Egyptian direction, since the Lord has "broken the arm of Pharaoh king
of Egypt" (30:21). The historical background of this oracle lies in an apparent attempt by Pharaoh Hophra to intervene in the crisis of his day (Jer.
37:5); however, though this led to a withdrawal of Nebuchadnezzar's army
in the short term, the hopes raised in the Judean capital were soon to be
dashed. After dealing with the Egyptians, Nebuchadnezzar returned to finish what he had started in Jerusalem (Jer. 39:1).

The defeat of Egypt is described in terms of a breaking of Pharaoh's arm
(Ezek. 30:21). The "arm" in the Old Testament is the part of the body through
which a person acts. It is therefore a symbol of strength: A strong arm enables
effective action, while a broken arm renders a person helpless (cf. Job 22:9;
Ps. 10:15).[1] The fundamental contrast in this oracle is between the broken
arms of Pharaoh and the arms of Nebuchadnezzar that have been strengthened by the Lord (Ezek. 30:25). This bout is clearly not an equal contest.
Ezekiel even anticipates potential objections that though Pharaoh's arm has
been broken, it may be healed (30:21), or that though one arm has been
broken Pharaoh still has another arm with which to fight (30:22). Even the
faintest source of hope must be removed; the broken arm will not receive the
medical treatment necessary for it to be healed. On the contrary, it will be
broken again, along with the sound arm that remains (30:22).[2] Egypt's power

---

1. It is interesting to note in passing that the "strong-armed man" was apparently a title
appropriated by the Pharaoh of the day. See James K. Hoffmeier, "The Arm of God Versus the Arm of Pharaoh in the Exodus Narratives," *Bib* 67 (1986): 378–87.

2. Some have seen in the breaking of the two arms of Pharaoh, a reference to an attack
launched by the Egyptian on two fronts, by land and by sea. One of these attacks had been

will be comprehensively destroyed, a prediction ultimately fulfilled in the conquest of Egypt by Cambyses in 525 B.C.

In the background of this struggle between two world powers, however, there is another actor. The "arm" that acts most frequently in the Old Testament is the arm of the Lord, notably in the Exodus, when he brought his people out of Egypt "by a mighty hand and an outstretched arm" (Deut. 4:34). This formula is a constant refrain throughout the Old Testament; in this passage the arm of the Lord is not directly referred to, but the Lord's action is everywhere evident. He is the one who will break Pharaoh's arms and strengthen Nebuchadnezzar's (Ezek. 30:22, 25). It is the Lord's sword that Nebuchadnezzar will draw against Egypt (30:25). It is the Lord who will scatter the Egyptians among the nations (30:26). The clash of the superpowers is under his control.

The Fifth Oracle (31:1–18)

THE FIFTH ORACLE against Egypt compares Pharaoh to a massive tree that is felled because of its pride. Who is comparable to Pharaoh in greatness? He himself recognized no equal, and in what follows Ezekiel takes his claims of greatness seriously. He is like a cypress (31:3)[3] or a mighty cedar in Lebanon; there follows a graphic picture of a tree of supernatural proportions. The myth of a tree that constitutes the heart of ordered existence, with its roots in the subterranean depths and its topmost branches in the sublime heights, providing shelter for the entire animal world, was part of the lore of the surrounding nations.[4]

Here Ezekiel puts this mythical picture to use as a description of Egypt's greatness, like a mighty cedar in Lebanon, with its topmost branches in the clouds (31:3).[5] Her roots were fed by the deep springs under the earth (*tᵉhôm*,

---

defeated, and the other would likewise come to nothing (Kenneth S. Freedy and Donald B. Redford, "The Dates in Ezekiel in Relation to Biblical, Babylonian and Egyptian Sources," *JAOS* 90 [1970]: 471 n.39; Lawrence Boadt, *Ezekiel's Oracles Against Egypt: A Literary and Philological Study of Ezekiel 29–32* [Biblica et Orientalia 37; Rome: Biblical Institute, 1980], 85). However, this seems unnecessarily subtle and takes no account of the rebreaking of the good arm. It is better to see these as two separate defeats for Egypt, one past and one future.

3. The NIV follows the MT and versions and reads "Assyria," a reading defended by Greenberg (*Ezekiel 21–37*, 637). In each of these word pictures of Ezekiel, however, the object of the oracle is first described in glorious terms and then brought low, which makes the oracle more appropriately directed at Egypt. The reference to Assyria presumably came in through a miswriting of *tᵉʾaššûr*, "cypress," or possibly of a misreading of a variant form (Allen, *Ezekiel 20–48*, 122). The difference in overall interpretation of the passage is slight: either Pharaoh is being compared to Assyria, the great tree that flourished and was cut down, or Pharaoh is directly compared to a mighty tree that flourished and was cut down.

4. Zimmerli, *Ezekiel*, 2:146.

5. Rather than NIV's "thick foliage" (see comments on Ezek. 19:11).

31:4). As a result, she grew higher than all the other trees of the earth, providing shelter for all the birds of the air and the beasts of the field (31:5–6; cf. Dan. 4:10–12). In plain language, she became the greatest of nations, the overlord of all the nations. In fact, her greatness surpassed earthly proportions; not even the trees of the jewel of original creation, Eden itself, could match Egypt's beauty. Here are echoes of the same exalted status attributed to the king of Tyre (28:13–14), and also of the same fundamental sin: pride (28:17; 31:10).

Pride once again precedes a fall from grace. In all the vivid word pictures used by Ezekiel in the oracles against the foreign nations, the nature of the glorious object described contains within it the seeds of its own destruction. Tyre was a majestic ship, but is now sunk (ch. 27). Her king was as glorious as the first man, a semidivine being in the Garden of Eden, but like Adam he was driven out (28:1–19). Pharaoh is a crocodile of mythical proportions, but will be hunted down like an ordinary reptile (29:1–16). Here now, Egypt is a great world tree, but it will be felled by the cosmic lumberjack.

It was the Lord who had raised Egypt to her elevated status ("I made it beautiful with abundant branches," 31:9), but she considered her attainments something of which to be proud (31:10). The Lord can just as easily cast her down, as the personal pronouns indicate: "I handed it over . . . I cast it aside" (31:11). The agency of execution is human ("the ruler of the nations," 31:11), but the instructions come from on high. Broken and shattered, the tree no longer provides shade and protection for the birds and the beasts, as a king might for his people (Lam. 4:20); instead, its fallen branches are merely a convenient resting place for them (Ezek. 31:13). Just as her height was unparalleled in her time, so it will never again be surpassed; for all the dominant nations that come after her will share her mortality, treading along with her the way to destruction, bound for the underworld (31:14).[6]

The cosmic scale of the tree is matched by cosmic mourning at its fall and descent into Sheol, the home of the unworthy dead.[7] The cosmic springs are

---

6. The NIV's "the earth below" is a misleading translation of *'ereṣ taḥtît;* it is clearly part of the underworld, perhaps even the lowest part.

7. Sheol is often described as the home of all who die, hence the frequent English translation "the grave." This is not strictly accurate. Though in the Old Testament the godly may fear being abandoned by God to Sheol (Ps. 88:3), nowhere is a righteous man actually said to have gone down into Sheol. Perhaps the contrast between the fate of the righteous and the unrighteous after death is most clearly evident in Ps. 49, where those who trust in themselves are destined for Sheol (49:14), while the psalmist expects something different for himself. What that "something" is may not always be clear in the Old Testament, but in several places there is evidence of such a hope. On Sheol, see Philip S. Johnston, *The Underworld and the Dead in the Old Testament* (Ph.D. diss.; Cambridge Univ., 1993).

shut up, while Lebanon, the home of the mighty cedar, is darkened (31:15). The heights and the depths, the sources of light and subterranean water, are thus both clothed in mourning, a state also affecting those in between.

The nations of the world trembled at the sound of the tree's fall, whose echoes reverberated even into the underworld. Those of its predecessors who had envied it, described as "the trees of Eden, the choicest and best of Lebanon" (31:16), were gratified in its sharing of their demise, while those who had allied themselves to it went down with it to Sheol (31:17). There they joined those killed by the sword, whose unpeaceful end was thought in some way to carry over to their state beyond death. Ezekiel brings out the point of the word picture explicitly in 31:18. Though Egypt's splendor and majesty were unrivaled in all the powerful nations who went before (i.e., the "trees of Eden"), she too will share their fate in the underworld among those outside the peaceful community, among the uncircumcised and those slain by the sword.

The Sixth Oracle (32:1–16)

IN HIS SIXTH oracle against Egypt, Ezekiel returns to the image of Pharaoh as crocodile. This time the image is combined with that of a lion, with the emphasis more on the natural aspect of the imagery than the supernatural overtones of chapter 29. The lion and crocodile are two mighty beasts, who appear all-powerful (32:2). Indeed, both images were regularly appropriated by the pharaohs as positive self-descriptions.

Yet in spite of their strength, both may be hunted and killed. Though Pharaoh considers himself like a lion, the great Hunter has him in his sights.[8] Once more through human agency ("with a great throng of people," 32:3), the Lord will cast his net over Pharaoh, a method of hunting suitable to either crocodiles or lions (cf. 19:8). His corpse will be thrown to the ground to provide a home and food for the birds of the air and beasts of the field, much as was the fallen cosmic tree in 31:13. At this point, the scale of Pharaoh's demise takes on semimythical proportions: His body is big enough to be spread on the mountains and fill the valleys, his blood enough to water the land and fill the ravines (32:5–6).

The images of cosmic darkness and universal mourning are invoked, both of which were present in the previous oracle (31:15–16). In an echo of the penultimate Exodus plague on Egypt, the plague of darkness (Ex. 10:21–

---

8. The root *dāmâ* ("to be like") does not normally occur in the Niphal; most translations assume a reflexive sense for it "you consider yourself like . . ." (Boadt, *Ezekiel's Oracles*, 129). *dāmâ* ("be cut off, destroyed") does occur in the Niphal, however, and there may well be a play on words here: "You consider yourself a lion of the nations" sounds exactly like "you are destroyed, O lion of the nations."

22), the heavens will be darkened, and sun, moon, and stars will fail to give light (Ezek. 32:7). The peoples will be appalled, and their kings will shudder because of the scale of Egypt's devastation, fearing for their own lives (32:9–10).

In this final onslaught against Egypt, the king of Babylon will shatter her pride (32:11–12). The night of the first Passover was a mere firstfruits in comparison to this full harvest of God's judgment, for on that occasion only the firstborn of human beings and animals died (Ex. 12:29). Here, however, all people and animals are cut off from the land (Ezek. 32:13). The demise of the great animal-human of verse 2 is underlined by the ceasing of his thrashing around, muddying the streams (32:13). Now the waters of Egypt will flow as clear and smooth as oil, untroubled by any disturbance (32:14). Egypt will once again recognize the sovereign power of the Lord when he acts to strike down all who live there, this time with no exceptions (32:15). The lament is prepared; all that waits is the execution of the divine decree (32:16).

The Seventh Oracle (32:17–32)

THE FINAL ORACLE against Egypt, and the final oracle in the sequence of oracles against the nations, sums up everything that has gone before by means of a comprehensive tour of the underworld, which is to be Egypt's new home. Six nations are named as already there: Assyria, Elam, Meshech-Tubal, Edom, the princes of the north, and Sidon. Egypt is the climactic and completing seventh nation of the underworld.

Once again, the oracle draws out and expands an idea present in an earlier pronouncement (31:17–18), which spoke of Egypt's descent into the underworld and the company she would keep there. Here, however, the picture is presented in graphic detail. Egypt's future home will be among the unquiet dead—with those outside the covenant ("the uncircumcised")[9] and those who fell by the sword (32:21). Though all these other nations were once mighty and had administered a reign of terror while they lived, now they bear the reproach for their iniquity. A place of punishment—"the pit" (32:24)—is prepared for all such, and Pharaoh certainly qualifies to join the club (32:28). For the time of the Lord's appointing, he too spread terror in the land of the living (32:32), but soon he will become merely a part of the terror that is the land of the dead. The Sovereign Lord has spoken (32:32).

---

9. The description of Egypt as "uncircumcised" is a theological rather than literal assessment. Like the Edomites and Sidonians, it appears that the Egyptians practiced circumcision (Jack M. Sasson, "Circumcision in the Ancient Near East," *JBL* 85 [1966]: 473–76). However, from Ezekiel's perspective, though they may have been physically circumcised, in God's eyes they remained "uncircumcised."

THE FANTASY OF EGYPT. As with the preceding oracles against Egypt, so also these oracles only make sense against the background of what Egypt represented to Israel. Egypt frequently figured in Judean fantasies as a substitute for the Lord, providing chariots and horses to prop up Judean efforts to secure independence from the great world powers of the East. These fantasies must be shattered before the people can be restored; they need to see that only the Lord is able to deliver them from all dangers.

Ezekiel shatters the Judean illusions about Egypt by opening the people's eyes to Egypt's coming fate. Even though her present powers were indeed of mythical proportions—hence the use of mythical images of the great sea monster or world tree—her end will be the eminently unmythical fate of death. In fact, the situation is even worse than that, for her present power is much diminished. The Lord has already broken one of Pharaoh's arms and before long will break the remaining arm, as well as rebreak the broken limb, thus leaving Egypt helpless and unable to offer help to others. In the conflict between the Lord and the world powers, the Lord is always victorious. Moreover, in that struggle the Lord employs human agents to do his bidding, and Nebuchadnezzar is nothing less than the servant of the Lord, equipped with the sword of the Lord to execute judgment on the Lord's enemies (30:24). To stand against Nebuchadnezzar is to stand against the Lord and to incur certain death, as Egypt's allies will find out.

Ezekiel's description of the underworld draws on what would then have been a widely accepted three-layer view of the universe. The upper layer (heaven) was the home of the divine beings; the center layer was the "land of the living," while underneath lay Sheol, the realm of death and the dead. The Old Testament descriptions of this place are relatively sparse compared to the fullness of New Testament revelation. It is more accurate to characterize it as a place of "underlife" than a place of "afterlife," for there is nothing in that realm that deserves the epithet of "life." It is a place of shadows, of the experiencing by the unrighteous of the unsuffered consequences of a lifetime.[10] If Egypt and her pharaoh rightly belong there, so also do all who trust in her. The unexpressed implication is that it will not be so for those who trust in the Lord.

The deceit of contemporary Egypts. In our context, Egypt does not hold the same attractions as it did for Ezekiel's hearers. For us, it is merely a geographical region, not a spiritual entity. However, the same basic temptations

---

10. See Daniel I. Block, "Beyond the Grave: Ezekiel's Vision of Death and the Afterlife," *BBR* 2 (1992): 113–41.

assail us, for we too have our earthly strongholds in which we place our trust, blindly worshiping and serving created things rather than the Creator (Rom. 1:25). The end of Egypt as a factor in our spirituality is not the end of the lie of self-sufficiency; rather, the lie has endless power to change into a new form and reshape for maximum appeal in each of our lives. For example, for some contemporary people the allure of Egypt is replaced by the allure of wealth. For those people, money seems to offer the same things that Egypt offered Judah: independence, freedom from outside controls and limits, the power to choose, and comfortable affluence. The core lie is the same; only the packaging has changed.

Yet the new idol is just as deceitful as the old—and for the same reasons. On the one hand, its power is not as great as we are tempted to believe. The mythical aura of invincibility that wealth carries in our society is just that: a myth. God can bankrupt the richest person, or in allowing them to possess wealth he can still deny them the blessings they thought it would give them: freedom, happiness, and independence. Many people who achieve great wealth nonetheless find their lives filled with a pervasive boredom. God continues to shatter the arms of the strongest idols of this world.

Yet even if the power of money were as great as its advertising copy claims, so that it really could buy happiness and satisfaction in life, death still remains as the great leveler and relativizer of all of this world's goods. As the grim Spanish proverb puts it: "There are no pockets in the shroud." On the day of death, the inability of wealth to deliver lasting blessings will become thoroughly evident, as deceased millionaires rub shoulders in the grave with paupers. There are no exclusive country club areas in either heaven or hell.

Wealth is, of course, not the only contemporary "Egypt substitute." There are perhaps as many claimants to the title as there are people. On all sides, we are presented with products and ideologies, philosophies and relationships, each of which asserts that it alone offers true freedom. Some are more self-evidently illusory in the present than others: the alcoholic's bottle and the crack addict's needle are more obviously deceptive in what they offer than the respectable middle-class idols of career, reputation, family, and possessions.

Yet ultimately any refuge apart from God is a delusion, professing a power that it does not have, promising much and delivering little. The most profound work of God in our lives is the Spirit's work of unmasking our own personal idolatries, the refuges in which we have come to trust rather than him. Often he does so by bringing us through repeated trials in a particular area of our lives that expose the true nature and impotence of our idols. Though the process may be painful, it is nonetheless an act of God's grace when he exposes the destitution of our idols in this life, lest we share their fate in death.

IN WHAT DO we trust? The declaration on U.S. bank notes is unequivocal: "In God we trust." Unfortunately, it is a single-mindedness that few of us, even as Christians, live out in practice. The temptation to trust in the paper on which the slogan is written rather than in the God of whom the slogan speaks is real. Yet on what does our faith in that piece of paper rest? The paper can be burned up, lost, or stolen. Even if the paper is retained, its value can be devastated through runaway inflation to the point where the note itself is virtually worthless. Moreover, even if none of these things happen, U.S. dollars are not the local currency beyond the grave. How foolish we are, then, to place our trust in money! Yet how many of us still believe unflinchingly in its power to bless us, and that possessing more of it will make our life more meaningful and desirable! The number of people who participate weekly in the various state and local lotteries demonstrates the power of that myth in our society.

Or consider the power of the myth of career. How many people have devoted their lives to finding a fulfilling and rewarding job? In the process, they may sacrifice precious relationships and outside interests on the altar of success, which they have defined as career progress. How many find, if they finally reach the top of the ladder, that they wish they had climbed a different one? Even if they are content with the ladder they have climbed and they receive the benediction of their idol, do its blessings last? Sooner or later, through retirement or death, the ladder is put away. The job is turned over to someone else. Where will they be then?

But perhaps these are altogether too obvious idols to deceive us. Perhaps we have instead sacrificed everything on the altar of family. What could be more noble than laying down our lives for the sake of our loved ones? Yet if our trust is in our family to provide meaning and value in our lives, then we too are headed for disappointment sooner or later. In the short term, we should remember that we are investing our love in fallen sinners. Even faithful Christians see their spouses commit adultery or their children rebel and run away, in spite of their best efforts. The pain and sorrow of such traumas are real and intense. But in the life of someone for whom family has become the controlling myth, they are more than intense; they are devastating. Life loses all its meaning, for meaning was determined by the sense of family.

Yet, tragic though it is, such a painful loss may be God's way of demonstrating the powerlessness of "family" to save. It is a broken reed, which wounds those who lean on it. Even those who do not experience that kind of disillusionment through broken family relationships must still face up to the reality of death. The ultimate dissolution of all earthly relationships is a fact that cannot be gainsaid. Relationships by blood or marriage may serve to gain us citizenship in earthly kingdoms, but they will avail us nothing when it comes to citizenship in the kingdom of heaven.

Escape from ultimate disappointment. In his book *The Great Divorce,* C. S. Lewis imagines a group of people on a day trip from hell to the borders of heaven. Hell is depicted as a gray, shadowy place, full of ordinary things like bus stops and fish-and-chip shops, but ultimately unreal. Heaven, on the other hand, is bright, sharp, and real. It is an uncomfortable place for the shadowy, unsubstantial people on the day trip. On their arrival, they are each faced with the choice of whether to stay in heaven and so gradually, painfully become "real," or to return to the comfortable shadowland. In each case, the decision boils down to a choice between retaining an idol and gradually becoming nothing more than a pale reflection of the idol itself, or allowing the idol to be killed, thus being set free to a new dimension of life. Lewis's allegory describes well the choice that we are faced within life: Follow the true God along the real path—often a painful decision but ultimately the way to life—or believe our idols when they tell us that we cannot live without them and settle for an empty promise now and ultimate disappointment.

I wonder how many of the painful experiences we encounter in life are God's direct challenges to the "Egypts" in our lives? Though they are painful, yet these "frowning providences" (as the Puritans called them) are still evidence of God's goodness and love for us. Thanks be to God that he often acts sooner rather than later to expose the powerlessness of that in which we have trusted to save ourselves. But how slow we often are to learn!

Ezekiel 33

THE WORD OF THE LORD came to me: ²"Son of man, speak to your countrymen and say to them: 'When I bring the sword against a land, and the people of the land choose one of their men and make him their watchman, ³and he sees the sword coming against the land and blows the trumpet to warn the people, ⁴then if anyone hears the trumpet but does not take warning and the sword comes and takes his life, his blood will be on his own head. ⁵Since he heard the sound of the trumpet but did not take warning, his blood will be on his own head. If he had taken warning, he would have saved himself. ⁶But if the watchman sees the sword coming and does not blow the trumpet to warn the people and the sword comes and takes the life of one of them, that man will be taken away because of his sin, but I will hold the watchman accountable for his blood.'

⁷"Son of man, I have made you a watchman for the house of Israel; so hear the word I speak and give them warning from me. ⁸When I say to the wicked, 'O wicked man, you will surely die,' and you do not speak out to dissuade him from his ways, that wicked man will die for his sin, and I will hold you accountable for his blood. ⁹But if you do warn the wicked man to turn from his ways and he does not do so, he will die for his sin, but you will have saved yourself.

¹⁰"Son of man, say to the house of Israel, 'This is what you are saying: "Our offenses and sins weigh us down, and we are wasting away because of them. How then can we live?" ' ¹¹Say to them, 'As surely as I live, declares the Sovereign LORD, I take no pleasure in the death of the wicked, but rather that they turn from their ways and live. Turn! Turn from your evil ways! Why will you die, O house of Israel?'

¹²"Therefore, son of man, say to your countrymen, 'The righteousness of the righteous man will not save him when he disobeys, and the wickedness of the wicked man will not cause him to fall when he turns from it. The righteous man, if he sins, will not be allowed to live because of his former right-eousness.' ¹³If I tell the righteous man that he will surely live, but then he trusts in his righteousness and does evil, none of

the righteous things he has done will be remembered; he will die for the evil he has done. ¹⁴And if I say to the wicked man, 'You will surely die,' but he then turns away from his sin and does what is just and right—¹⁵if he gives back what he took in pledge for a loan, returns what he has stolen, follows the decrees that give life, and does no evil, he will surely live; he will not die. ¹⁶None of the sins he has committed will be remembered against him. He has done what is just and right; he will surely live.

¹⁷"Yet your countrymen say, 'The way of the Lord is not just.' But it is their way that is not just. ¹⁸If a righteous man turns from his righteousness and does evil, he will die for it. ¹⁹And if a wicked man turns away from his wickedness and does what is just and right, he will live by doing so. ²⁰Yet, O house of Israel, you say, 'The way of the Lord is not just.' But I will judge each of you according to his own ways."

²¹In the twelfth year of our exile, in the tenth month on the fifth day, a man who had escaped from Jerusalem came to me and said, "The city has fallen!" ²²Now the evening before the man arrived, the hand of the LORD was upon me, and he opened my mouth before the man came to me in the morning. So my mouth was opened and I was no longer silent.

²³Then the word of the LORD came to me: ²⁴"Son of man, the people living in those ruins in the land of Israel are saying, 'Abraham was only one man, yet he possessed the land. But we are many; surely the land has been given to us as our possession.' ²⁵Therefore say to them, 'This is what the Sovereign LORD says: Since you eat meat with the blood still in it and look to your idols and shed blood, should you then possess the land? ²⁶You rely on your sword, you do detestable things, and each of you defiles his neighbor's wife. Should you then possess the land?'

²⁷"Say this to them: 'This is what the Sovereign LORD says: As surely as I live, those who are left in the ruins will fall by the sword, those out in the country I will give to the wild animals to be devoured, and those in strongholds and caves will die of a plague. ²⁸I will make the land a desolate waste, and her proud strength will come to an end, and the mountains of Israel will become desolate so that no one will cross them. ²⁹Then they will know that I am the LORD, when I have made the land a desolate waste because of all the detestable things they have done.'

³⁰"As for you, son of man, your countrymen are talking together about you by the walls and at the doors of the houses, saying to each other, 'Come and hear the message that has come from the LORD.' ³¹My people come to you, as they usually do, and sit before you to listen to your words, but they do not put them into practice. With their mouths they express devotion, but their hearts are greedy for unjust gain. ³²Indeed, to them you are nothing more than one who sings love songs with a beautiful voice and plays an instrument well, for they hear your words but do not put them into practice.

³³"When all this comes true—and it surely will—then they will know that a prophet has been among them."

AFTER THE JUDGMENT oracles of Ezekiel 1–24 and the oracles against the foreign nations in chapters 25–32, we finally get to the good news in chapters 34–48. The turning point in the saga is chapter 33, and it comes with the arrival among the exiles of the news of Jerusalem's fall. That bad news clears the ground for the proclamation of something new. Ezekiel 33 is a carefully constructed whole, with a chiastic movement that hinges around the confirmation of the fall of Jerusalem (33:21–22). Verses 1–11 find a counterpart in verses 30–33, with their emphasis on hearing or not hearing the prophetic word, while verses 12–20 share similar emphases on moral behavior with verses 23–29.[1] The whole chapter should thus be seen as a response to the news of that central event of Jerusalem's fall.

In that respect, this chapter continues logically on from the end of chapter 24, where Ezekiel was told to expect a survivor (*pālîṭ*)[2] to come bringing news of Jerusalem's demise (24:26). In chapter 33, the survivor arrives. Similarly, the removal of the prophet's dumbness, anticipated in 24:27, becomes a reality in 33:22. These references bracket off the oracles against the foreign nations (chs. 25–32) as a separate section that completes the judgment oracles of the prophet. In chapters 34–48 the prophet's focus is placed on oracles

---

1. Allen, *Ezekiel 20–48*, 153.

2. Here we should think of *pālîṭ* as a "survivor" rather than a "fugitive." It probably referred to someone surviving the fall of Jerusalem (Zimmerli, *Ezekiel*, 2:192), rather than someone who had escaped deportation by the Babylonian forces (Stuart, *Ezekiel*, 315). Why should someone in the latter category make the arduous journey to Babylonia on his own, to the very place to which the Babylonians wished to deport him? As Clements puts it: "No right minded survivor would have sought refuge in the enemy homeland" (*Ezekiel*, 147).

proclaiming the salvation and restoration of Israel. These distinctions are not absolute, of course; there is hope of salvation in chapters 1–32 and words of judgment in chapters 34–48. But the whole tenor of the prophet's ministry undergoes a dramatic paradigm shift, now that Jerusalem has fallen.

Ezekiel 33 opens with the depiction of the prophet as "watchman," just as did his oracles of destruction in chapter 3. On one level, this functions as a means of renewing the prophet's commission for his new ministry.[3] However, the similarities between the two sections should not be overpressed. In chapter 3, the image functioned as part of a private message to the prophet, pressing on him the importance of taking his task seriously. In chapter 33, it is part of a public proclamation (33:2, 7), pressing in on the people their own responsibility for their fate and the real possibility, even now, of repentance and return.

The proclamation starts from the general statement of a commonly accepted fact, that when the Lord sent a judgment against a land, the watchman was responsible for the consequences only if he did not warn the people (33:2–6). From this general principle, Ezekiel moves to the specific case facing the people in verses 7–9: Clearly the Lord has sent judgment against his people, and Ezekiel was appointed as his watchman (33:7). No one who has read chapters 4–32 can doubt the prophet's faithfulness to proclaiming the judgment to come; he is free from any culpability in the death of the wicked.

But does this mean that there is now no hope for God's rebellious people? Having failed to heed the prophetic word of warning, does that mean that since judgment has come, they are as good as dead? This seems to have been the thought among at least some of the exiles. They are saying to one another: "Our offenses and sins weigh us down, and we are wasting away because of them. How then can we live?" (33:10). Now that Jerusalem is on the brink of destruction and they are finally taking the possibility of judgment seriously, despair is a real danger.

Ezekiel's answer to that was that the living God takes no pleasure in the death of the wicked but rather seeks their repentance that they may live (33:11; cf. 18:31–32). God's judgment is not a fixed, deterministic fate that operates regardless of human action, but rather is a response to actual human behavior. Even now, it is not too late to turn and be saved. The fundamental covenant choice of life or death is still open to the people (33:11). The prophet illustrates the reality of that choice by appealing to two case studies, familiar from chapter 18. In the first case, a righteous man "trusts in his [past] righteousness" and does evil; he will surely die and not live (33:13). In the second, a wicked man turns from his sins and does what is right; he will surely live and not die (33:14).

---

3. Taylor, *Ezekiel*, 213.

Although these are presented as two equal and opposite cases, it is evident from the context that the primary interest is the second case—the wicked person who may yet live. That is the situation in which the people find themselves in 33:10. The prophet's point is that neither judgment nor salvation is an automatic process, but each works itself out through a life of "righteousness" or "wickedness"—that is, a life lived in accordance with the terms of the covenant ("the decrees that give life," 33:15) or in violation of it.

The problem that the people face is not that of God's justice, of which they complain in 33:17. His ways are indeed just, even more than just, since the path to life is continuously held open to rebels. The problem is with the people's lack of righteousness; they have followed an unjust way (33:17). They have consistently chosen the path to death over the path to life. That is what makes it bad news that God will judge each according to his own way (33:20)! Nonetheless, the point of the case studies is that there is a remedy for the bad news. The possibility of repentance is Ezekiel's answer to despair, though the need for perseverance is also there to counteract any tendency toward presumption.

This is the context in which Ezekiel places the news of Jerusalem's destruction (33:21–22). A survivor brings an eyewitness testimony of the city's fall. This is the radical turning point in the fortunes of God's people and in Ezekiel's own life. His dumbness, which has been with him since his commissioning as a prophet in 3:26–27, is now removed, just as the Lord promised in chapter 24. The prophet has finally been released from his divinely imposed bondage. The possibility of a new beginning for God's people similarly exists. But which will they choose: life or death?

The prophet is not left long in suspense. The following two sections make it clear that the hearts of God's people have not been fundamentally changed even by this radical act of judgment. Both back home in Judah (33:23–29) and among the exiles (33:30–33), it is business as usual. Those who remain behind in Judah, inhabiting the ruins of God's judgment, see the situation as an opportunity for economic gain rather than personal and societal repentance. Claiming to be Abraham's children, they interpret God's covenant promise of the land to Abraham as an inalienable right, an unconditional covenant. If Abraham as one man was able to possess the land, how much more his many descendants still living in the land (33:24)?

Indeed, the example of Abraham was a pertinent one to those who experienced the devastation of the Promised Land. The prophet Isaiah had urged the people to

> Look to Abraham, your father,
>   and to Sarah, who gave you birth.

When I called him he was but one,
>   and I blessed him and made him many.
The LORD will surely comfort Zion
>   and will look with compassion on all her ruins;
he will make her deserts like Eden,
>   her wastelands like the garden of the LORD. (Isa. 51:2–3)

The promise to Abraham should indeed act as an assurance that God would not completely abandon Israel but would comfort Zion and look with compassion on all her ruins (cf. Mic. 7:18–19). But this assurance of God's covenant faithfulness is only relevant for those who are, like Abraham, covenant-keepers. Those who do not continue in Abraham's faithful ways cannot expect to experience the blessings of the covenant.

The people are, in fact, corporately in a situation analogous to the first case study described by Ezekiel. They are relying on earlier righteousness—in this case, that of Abraham—to see them through in the face of present disobedience. The prophet describes their disobedience in the stereotypical terms of "eat[ing] meat with the blood still in it[4] and look[ing] to ... idols and shed[ding] blood" (33:25), or "you rely on your sword, you do detestable things, and each of you defiles his neighbor's wife" (33:26). Should such covenant-breakers inherit the blessings of the covenant and possess the land? By no means! Rather, these covenant-breakers will continue to inherit the three classic curses of the covenant: the sword, wild animals, and plague (33:27; cf. Lev. 26:22, 25).[5] The land will continue to suffer God's judgment until it becomes a desolate wasteland (Ezek. 33:28–29; cf. Lev. 26:32–33). All their hopes will come to nothing.

Nor are matters any better among the exiles. The news of Jerusalem's fall appears to have given Ezekiel's message a certain popularity and topicality. He is now the subject of conversation in the cities and doorways (33:30). To use a contemporary analogy, he is the toast of the talk shows. But the interest is superficial: The people listen to his words but do not put them into practice, regarding them as an intriguing phenomenon rather than a life-changing reality. His fame is like that of a pop star, whose declarations on spiritual matters may arouse curiosity but are scarcely accorded authoritative status. People may have been humming along to his tune, but they are paying no attention to the true meaning of his lyrics.

Time, however, will prove the power of the word of the Lord through Ezekiel: "When all this comes true—and it surely will—then they will know

---

4. Or perhaps "eating over blood," a proscribed form of divination (Greenberg, *Ezekiel 21–37*, 684).

5. Allen, *Ezekiel 20–48*, 153.

that a prophet has been among them" (33:33). In that day, just as all will know experientially the power of the Lord, so they will also be forced to recognize the authenticity of the Lord's prophet.

THE HARSH REALITIES of life. The people of Ezekiel's day were a people whose physical and psychological world had collapsed. The news of the destruction of Jerusalem was a paradigm-shaking reality. It was as if the sky had fallen on their heads. The central belief structures of their world crumbled, causing many of them to be faced with the temptations of overwhelming doubt and despair. These are not issues that are often addressed from the pulpits of our churches, where a relentlessly upbeat image of the Christian life is presented as the norm. "Smile, Jesus loves you!" is our slogan. Yet for many people, the outward smile conceals teeth gritted to endure the harsh realities of life. The temptations to doubt and despair are still there under the surface, but in our contemporary circles they are "the temptation that dare not speak its name."

The reality that life is not uniformly wonderful has, of course, always been true. However, the willingness to face up to that fact is something that varies from culture to culture and generation to generation, depending on that generation's experience. Thus the generation that grew up in Europe around the turn of the century possessed a strong corporate faith in the progress and perfectibility of humankind—only to have that faith decisively shattered in the trenches of the Somme and the mud of Passchendaele. The post-First World War generation knew firsthand what doubt and despair were. They knew how hard faith in the reality and love of God was in a brutal and bloody world.

On a smaller scale, a similar shift in the cultural landscape is taking place in our time. The Baby Boomers (those born between the end of the Second World War and 1960) have grown up in an age of unprecedented economic growth and social improvement. As a generation, they came to expect endless opportunities and affluence; in general, they believe that through hard work and education, anything is possible. Theirs is an essentially optimistic outlook on life, which is mirrored by the upbeat, "self-help" approach of many sermons.

The generation that followed them, however, commonly dubbed the "Baby Busters" or "Generation X," has grown up in a world of recession and divorce, of global warming and downsizing.[6] As a result, in spite of their rel-

---

6. They are perhaps (stereo)typified by the three main characters in Douglas Coupland's book *Generation X: Tales for an Accelerated Culture* (New York: St. Martin's, 1991). These are

ative affluence, they are not an optimistic generation, but rather cynical and bored, bereft of meaning and purpose.[7] Such a generation is not likely to be reached by pop psychology and pat answers, for they know all too well the meaning of doubt and despair. Douglas Coupland expresses his own experience of doubt and despair in these terms:

> Is feeling nothing the inevitable result of believing in nothing? And then I got to feeling frightened—thinking that there might not actually be anything to believe in, in particular. I thought it would be such a sick joke to have to remain alive for decades and not believe in or feel anything.[8]

Not everyone of his generation shares these same feelings, of course. Personal experiences significantly shape each person in different ways. However, the church must recognize the general shift in cultural outlook to address the unchanging gospel in ways that still communicate. Part of that shift in our day will be learning to preach to the despairing in ways that speak to their particular needs and temptations.

A deep awareness of sin. The despair felt among the exiles was not simply the result of the hand fate had dealt them, however. It was the result of the evidence of God's judgment on his people. They despaired not simply because of their situation but because of their sin (33:10). Such a depth of awareness of sin is not common in our day. Few today ever reach the point of crying out in recognition of God's holiness, "How then can we live?" (33:10). Few come to the deep conviction that there is a God and there is judgment for sin and there may even be salvation, but that *it may not be for them!*

Such, however, was the experience of some past ages. For example, in the classic eighteenth-century work *Human Nature in Its Fourfold State*, Thomas Boston described the eleventh (!) stage in the conversion process in the following terms:

> The man being thus far humbled ... looks on himself as unworthy of Christ, and unworthy of the favour of God. ... If you now tell him he is welcome to Christ, if he will come to him, he is apt to say, "Can such a vile and unworthy wretch as I be welcome to the holy Jesus?[9]

---

described on the back of the book as having "been handed a society priced beyond their means. Twentysomethings, brought up with divorce, Watergate and Three Mile Island, and scarred by the 80's fallout of yuppies, recession, crack and Ronald Reagan, they represent the new lost generation—Generation X."

7. Jock McGregor: "Generation X: The 'Lost' Generation," *L'Abri Lectures* 11 (Summer 1997). See also Stanley Grenz, *A Primer on Postmodernism* (Grand Rapids: Eerdmans, 1996), 13.

8. *Life After God* (New York: Pocket Books, 1994), 178.

9. *Human Nature in Its Fourfold State*, 277.

Here, doubtless drawing on his own extensive pastoral experience in a rural congregation in Scotland, Boston depicts a man who has been so crushed by the preaching of the law that he feels a sense of total despair. He feels his sin to be so great that even Jesus will not welcome him. Of course, at the root of such despair is pride rather than true humility, as Boston goes on to show. It is precisely such vile wretches that the Son of Man came to seek and save (Matt. 9:12–13). However, it is a mark of the prominent preaching by Boston and his contemporaries of the claims of the law of God on all people and the certainty of God's wrath against unbelievers that such feelings of despair were produced.

Boston was far from being a legalist, but he was not afraid to say from his pulpit, "O wicked man, you will surely die" (33:8). Sometimes the pendulum may indeed have swung too far in that direction, so that genuine believers lacked assurance of salvation, but that is scarcely a danger in most contemporary pulpits. We need to learn from the past how to preach for deep heart conviction of sin, until people cry out in our churches also, "What must I do to be saved?"

Are we getting through? Of course, not everyone will respond in such positive terms to the plain preaching of the law. There will be those who, like the remnant left in Judah, feel that all this preaching has nothing to do with them. Instead of appealing to Abraham, as Ezekiel's contemporaries did (33:24), in our churches they may appeal to the fact that they have grown up in the church, as have their parents before them. Such an appeal to tradition is not enough. Even though God promises to deal faithfully with the children of his people (Gen. 17:8; Acts 2:39), that promise does not work *apart from* their faith but *through* their faith. It is as the next generation is brought by the Holy Spirit to their own expression of faith in the God of their fathers that they inherit the promises of their fathers' God.

Others may respond in a superficially favorable way, praising the clarity with which the Word is being preached. They listen and listen, but never learn or do. For them, as for some of Ezekiel's hearers, the preacher is merely an entertainer, not a conveyer of life-changing truth. Like the seed that fell on rocky ground in the parable of the sower (Matt. 13:5–6), there is no substance to their claim to faith. Time will demonstrate that fact, as they wilt under the pressures of life.

SUPERFICIAL OR GENUINE? What do we say to those whose world has caved in? What specific temptations and problems do such people face? Those living through the aftermath of personal or societal disaster face the danger of false hope of shallow and easy answers. Many people seem to think that suffering inevitably prepares one for sainthood. Suffering is not automatically redemptive, however, nor are all the promises of God's Word available equally to all without distinction. The blessings of a covenant relationship with God come only to those within the covenant community who are living a life of obedience to the covenant.

This means that there is no automatic salvation to be found in having prayed a particular prayer, or in having been received into the membership of a particular church, or in having been baptized (whether as a child or an adult). The promises made to Abraham are real and substantial, but they are only effective for those who are genuinely Abraham's spiritual children. Such people are justified by faith, just as he was, but specifically they are justified by a faith that works itself out in action, just as his did (James 2:20–24). A claim of faith without the works that go along with it is a false claim, and the hope that is based on it is a false hope. True saints are those who persevere in faith and action to the end. In an age of "easy-believism," this is a note that needs to be sounded more clearly in our churches. The law needs to be clearly preached to those who consider themselves comfortably within the covenant community, even though their lives demonstrate no evidence to back up their claim, to press in on them their need of Christ.

For some, a major life crisis may cause them to attend church, but only as superficial hearers. Like Ezekiel's audience, they may find the form of the message interesting and stimulating, but they never feel its power in their hearts as a life-changing reality. Those of us who are preachers need to be careful that we do not foster such shallow attention. In our day, there is a focus on "seeker-sensitive" services that will present the gospel in a way that will be attractive to such people. The task of the church, however, is not to assemble seekers but to make disciples.

The task of the preacher. We should certainly have services that are open and understandable to all who come, but we should never forget that our goal is to see these people move beyond being seekers to being those who are found in Christ. The seriousness of the message must never be obscured by the desire to make the medium more attractive. The preacher's task is not to entertain or inform but to plead passionately with men and women to flee the wrath that is to come on account of sin. The preacher is commissioned to call clearly for repentance and turning to Christ, to be a watchman rather than an entertainer.

But preachers must not only preach the law to confront the hypocrite, they must also preach the gospel to woo the lost sheep. They must answer the pressing question of the justice of God (33:17). In times of personal or societal meltdown, the question for many is, "Why are these things happening to me? What did I ever do to deserve it?" In Judah's case, the answer to that question was apparently simple: It is not the Lord's way that is unjust, but rather their own ways are unjust (33:20). The disaster that had befallen Jerusalem was the consequence of Jerusalem's sin, as Ezekiel had gone to considerable lengths to demonstrate before the city fell. But God's purpose even in this painful judgment was not death for the errant sheep but life; after all, the Lord has no pleasure in the death of the wicked. He does not commission his prophet to say: "Turn or burn; take it or leave it; the choice is entirely yours." Instead, he instructs his watchman to cry out: "Turn! Turn from your evil ways! Why will you die, O house of Israel?" (33:11).

Responding to life's struggles. Sometimes, as with Jerusalem, the catastrophic things that happen to you are the results of your own sin. In other cases, they are not directly the result of your own sin. In either event, however, your responsibility is the same: to heed the call to respond to the glory of God. Painful experiences may be the occasion for our eyes being opened to God for the first time, or they may be the call to demonstrate perseverance in the midst of the depths of our suffering. As Christians they are never, however, simply designed to crush us. In our deepest and most desperate struggles, the problem lies not in God's unfairness in placing these burdens on us, but rather in our unrighteousness that makes us resent our particular providence.

The profound news of the gospel is that whatever bad things happen to us in this life, God does *not* judge us as Christians on the basis of our own ways but rather on the basis of Christ's righteousness. The gospel is therefore good news to the despairing. Since God has loved us so profoundly as to send Jesus to die on the cross for us, what will he not give to us? The bruised reed he will not break; the smoldering wick he will not extinguish.

This was the painful truth to which Horatio Spafford testified in his famous hymn, "It Is Well With My Soul." After the death of his only son, he suffered the loss of his business holdings in the Great Fire of Chicago in 1871. Just two years later, his wife and four daughters were on board a passenger ship that sank in mid-Atlantic; only his wife survived. In a short period, virtually his entire world had been destroyed. Yet as he sailed to be with his wife, at the very spot where his daughters had drowned, he wrote these immortal words of faith in God's goodness to his people, no matter what happens:

When peace like a river attendeth my way,
When sorrows like sea billows roll,
Whatever my lot, thou hast taught me to say,
"It is well, it is well with my soul."

Chorus:
It is well with my soul,
It is well, it is well with my soul.

Though Satan should buffet, though trials should come,
Let this blest assurance control:
That Christ has regarded my helpless estate,
And has shed his own blood for my soul.

My sin—O, the bliss of this glorious thought,
My sin—not in part but the whole,
Is nailed to the cross and I bear it no more:
Praise the Lord, praise the Lord, O my soul!

And, Lord, haste the day when my faith shall be sight,
The clouds be rolled back as a scroll,
The trump shall resound and the Lord shall descend:
Even so—it is well with my soul.

Ezekiel 34

THE WORD OF THE LORD came to me: ²"Son of man, prophesy against the shepherds of Israel; prophesy and say to them: 'This is what the Sovereign LORD says: Woe to the shepherds of Israel who only take care of themselves! Should not shepherds take care of the flock? ³You eat the curds, clothe yourselves with the wool and slaughter the choice animals, but you do not take care of the flock. ⁴You have not strengthened the weak or healed the sick or bound up the injured. You have not brought back the strays or searched for the lost. You have ruled them harshly and brutally. ⁵So they were scattered because there was no shepherd, and when they were scattered they became food for all the wild animals. ⁶My sheep wandered over all the mountains and on every high hill. They were scattered over the whole earth, and no one searched or looked for them.

⁷"'Therefore, you shepherds, hear the word of the LORD: ⁸As surely as I live, declares the Sovereign LORD, because my flock lacks a shepherd and so has been plundered and has become food for all the wild animals, and because my shepherds did not search for my flock but cared for themselves rather than for my flock, ⁹therefore, O shepherds, hear the word of the LORD: ¹⁰This is what the Sovereign LORD says: I am against the shepherds and will hold them accountable for my flock. I will remove them from tending the flock so that the shepherds can no longer feed themselves. I will rescue my flock from their mouths, and it will no longer be food for them.

¹¹"'For this is what the Sovereign LORD says: I myself will search for my sheep and look after them. ¹²As a shepherd looks after his scattered flock when he is with them, so will I look after my sheep. I will rescue them from all the places where they were scattered on a day of clouds and darkness. ¹³I will bring them out from the nations and gather them from the countries, and I will bring them into their own land. I will pasture them on the mountains of Israel, in the ravines and in all the settlements in the land. ¹⁴I will tend them in a good pasture, and the mountain heights of Israel will be their grazing land. There they will lie down in good grazing land, and there

they will feed in a rich pasture on the mountains of Israel. ¹⁵I
myself will tend my sheep and have them lie down, declares
the Sovereign LORD. ¹⁶I will search for the lost and bring back
the strays. I will bind up the injured and strengthen the weak,
but the sleek and the strong I will destroy. I will shepherd the
flock with justice.

¹⁷''''As for you, my flock, this is what the Sovereign LORD
says: I will judge between one sheep and another, and
between rams and goats. ¹⁸Is it not enough for you to feed on
the good pasture? Must you also trample the rest of your pasture with your feet? Is it not enough for you to drink clear
water? Must you also muddy the rest with your feet? ¹⁹Must
my flock feed on what you have trampled and drink what you
have muddied with your feet?

²⁰''''Therefore this is what the Sovereign LORD says to them:
See, I myself will judge between the fat sheep and the lean
sheep. ²¹Because you shove with flank and shoulder, butting
all the weak sheep with your horns until you have driven them
away, ²²I will save my flock, and they will no longer be plundered. I will judge between one sheep and another. ²³I will
place over them one shepherd, my servant David, and he will
tend them; he will tend them and be their shepherd. ²⁴I the
LORD will be their God, and my servant David will be prince
among them. I the LORD have spoken.

²⁵''''I will make a covenant of peace with them and rid the
land of wild beasts so that they may live in the desert and sleep
in the forests in safety. ²⁶I will bless them and the places surrounding my hill. I will send down showers in season; there will
be showers of blessing. ²⁷The trees of the field will yield their
fruit and the ground will yield its crops; the people will be
secure in their land. They will know that I am the LORD, when I
break the bars of their yoke and rescue them from the hands of
those who enslaved them. ²⁸They will no longer be plundered
by the nations, nor will wild animals devour them. They will live
in safety, and no one will make them afraid. ²⁹I will provide for
them a land renowned for its crops, and they will no longer be
victims of famine in the land or bear the scorn of the nations.
³⁰Then they will know that I, the LORD their God, am with
them and that they, the house of Israel, are my people, declares
the Sovereign LORD. ³¹You my sheep, the sheep of my pasture,
are people, and I am your God, declares the Sovereign LORD.'''

Original Meaning

EZEKIEL 34 IS a dual oracle of judgment and salvation. It is an oracle of judgment on the shepherds and fat sheep who have oppressed the flock, and of salvation for the rest of the flock through the personal intervention of the Lord as their shepherd.

This chapter opens with an oracle against "the shepherds of Israel" (34:1–16). The title *shepherd* was a well-known ascription of both kings and gods in the ancient Near East. For example, the second millennium Babylonian king Hammurabi describes himself as "the shepherd who brings salvation and whose staff is righteous," while his much later successor Merodoch-Baladan II is called "the shepherd who gathers together again those who have strayed."[1] Frequently, in this role the earthly king stood as a representative of the divine shepherd who had appointed him.[2] A similar notion of the relationship between the king and God was present in Israel. Thus, when the tribes came to David at Hebron to make him king over them, the basis of their action was the Lord's declaration concerning David: "You will shepherd my people Israel, and you will become their ruler" (2 Sam. 5:2).

In Ezekiel's oracle of judgment, however, the Lord is coming *against* his shepherds—the former kings of Judah—because they have failed to fulfill their role of shepherd properly. The proper task of a shepherd was to care for the flock, that is, to protect it from dangers on the outside and dissension within—gathering those who strayed, leading the flock to good pasture and clean drinking water, and taking special care of the poor and the weak. On the contrary, these shepherds have viewed their position as an opportunity for personal gain, ruling harshly and brutally, feeding only themselves, not the flock, and even slaughtering the choicest animals (34:2–6). The phrase "to rule ... brutally" (34:4) is only found in two other passages in the Old Testament. In Exodus 1:13–14 it refers to the way the Egyptians treated their Hebrew slaves, while in Leviticus 25:43, 46 it is forbidden to treat a fellow Israelite in this manner. Ezekiel thus accuses the "rulers of doing what their own history should have taught them to abhor and what the law of Moses expressly forbade."[3]

Because of the shepherds' sinful self-interest, judgment is coming on them (34:7–10). In the absence of a true shepherd, the flock has been scattered and plundered (34:8). But now the Lord will step in and remove the false shepherds from their office so that they can no longer feed themselves at the flock's expense. Their shepherding will be brought to an end as the Lord acts to rescue his sheep

---

1. Lorenz Dürr, *Ursprung und Ausbau der israelitisch-jüdischen Heilandserwartung: Ein Beitrag zur Theologie des Alten Testamentes* (Berlin: Schwetscke, 1925), 118–19.

2. Zimmerli, *Ezekiel*, 2:213.

3. Werner Lemke, "Life in the Present and Hope for the Future," *Interp* 38 (1984): 173 n.10.

(34:10). Now the Lord will himself search out the flock and take care of them, gathering them from all the places where they were scattered (34:12).

This metaphorical image of shepherd and sheep is made from a concrete promise of return from exile in verse 13: "I will bring them out from the nations and gather them from the countries, and I will bring them into their own land. I will pasture them on the mountains of Israel, in the ravines and in all the settlements in the land." The day of clouds and darkness when they were scattered, the day of judgment,[4] is over; now they can look forward to a return to the "mountains of Israel," the heart of the Promised Land. There they will experience the full blessing of the Lord's shepherding: He will feed them on rich pasture and cause them to lie down in safety; he will search for the lost and bind up the injured; he will establish justice, punishing the oppressors and strengthening the weak (34:16).

This last thought leads into a further oracle of judgment (34:17–22) against the "rams and goats" (v. 17) or the "fat sheep" (v. 20). These are the broader class of leaders of the community, who had oppressed the weak with violence and grasped the limited resources for themselves without considering the needs of those without influence or power.[5] Even what they did not need for themselves they spoiled, thus denying it to others (vv. 18–19). They had abandoned the traditional responsibility of the upper class for the social well-being of the other classes.[6] In the desperate times leading up to the Exile, the weakest went to the wall. To prevent that happening again in future, the Lord will intervene to execute judgment within his flock, judging between sheep and sheep (v. 22). He will thus deal with both external and internal dangers to the peace and security of his flock.[7]

As elsewhere in Ezekiel, we see in this chapter a double critique of the failures of the past: the divine response of punishing those responsible and the divine promise of intervention to reverse those failures.[8] In concrete form, the intervention takes the form of setting up over them "one shepherd, my servant David," who will act as their "prince" (*nāśî*, 34:23–24). This figure of a *nāśî* is often taken as something less than a king, a kind of "apolitical messiah," who rules "among" rather than "over" the people.[9] However, such a

---

4. See Joel 2:2, Zeph. 1:15 for the same phrase in the context of the Day of the Lord. See Allen, *Ezekiel 20–48*, 162.

5. Duguid, *Ezekiel and the Leaders of Israel*, 122.

6. Bernd Willmes, *Die sogenannte Hirtenallegorie Ezekiel 34: Studien zum Bild des Hirten im AT* (Beiträge zur biblischen Exegese und Theologie 19; Frankfurt: Peter Lang, 1984), 511.

7. Block, *Ezekiel 25–48*, 292.

8. Jon D. Levenson, *Theology*, 86.

9. See Zimmerli, *Ezekiel*, 2:219; Ralph W. Klein, *Ezekiel: The Prophet and His Message* (Columbia, S.C.: Univ. of South Carolina Press, 1988), 241.

---

stress fails to note that the new shepherd *is* placed over the people (34:23). His relationship to them is not simply *primus inter pares* (first among equals) but shepherd to sheep, a relationship that involves authority as well as service.

Indeed, the change to be wrought in Israel's situation is not so much a change in the nature of the office as in the nature of the occupant. God's solution to a history of bad shepherds is not to replace shepherding with a better system, but to replace the bad shepherds with a good shepherd.[10] This good shepherd will be like the great king David, the king after God's own heart (1 Sam. 13:14), the archetypal picture of a strong king ruling with justice and fairness.[11]

This future ruler is not merely an ad hoc solution to the necessities of governing the restored people. On the contrary, it is nothing less than the fulfillment of the covenant with David. God promised David that he would "raise up" (Hiphil of *qwm*) his offspring to succeed him and that he would establish his kingdom (2 Sam. 7:12, 25). Solomon subsequently received the promise that, if he followed the pattern of his father David, his throne would be established (Hiphil of *qwm*) forever. Now that dynastic oracle will be fulfilled with the raising up (Hiphil of *qwm*) of a new David (Ezek. 34:23; cf. Jer. 33:14; Amos 9:11), who would be the Lord's servant and his people's shepherd.

In addition, the Lord will make "a covenant of peace" with his flock (34:25). In place of the curses of the Sinai covenant, which they have experienced while being under the judgment of God—wild animals, drought, famine, and the sword (Lev. 26:14–35)—they will now experience the blessings of the covenant: safety, rain in its season, fruitfulness, and peace (26:4–13). The state of experiencing the blessings that flow from a harmonious relationship with God is what makes this distinctively a "covenant of peace."

This covenant is thus not so much a "new" covenant as it is the experience of the blessings promised in the original covenant. In place of the monarchy divided by sin, God's people will be united under one shepherd. In place of an undistinguished procession of monarchs, they will be given a ruler after God's own heart, a new David. In place of famine, plague, drought, and the sword, they will see a new level of peace and prosperity so that they will no longer bear the reproach of the nations (Ezek. 34:29).[12] Then indeed they will know that the Lord their God is with them—for blessing and not for

---

10. Duguid, *Ezekiel and the Leaders of Israel*, 47.

11. J. David Pleins, "From the Stump of Jesse: The Image of King David As a Social Force in the Writings of the Hebrew Prophets," *Proceedings of the Eastern Great Lakes and Midwest Bible Society* 6 (1986): 162.

12. Greenberg notes the significance of the absence of the blessing of victory in war; the new community is now directly under divine protection, as will become clearer in chapters 38–39 (*Ezekiel 21–37*, 707).

curse—and that they are his people. They will be his sheep and he will be their God, the harmonious relationship celebrated in Psalm 100:3.[13]

THE SHEPHERD METAPHOR. Who is my shepherd? The answer to that question should be known even by Sunday school children. As Psalm 23:1 affirms: "The LORD is my shepherd." But the New Testament unfolds the answer further when Jesus asserts in John 10:11: "I am the good shepherd." Jesus is the tough yet tender leader of his flock, who protects his sheep against the dangers of marauders and knows each one by name (10:11–14). He is the one shepherd who unites in himself his flock (10:16). He is the good shepherd, who leaves the ninety-nine sheep on the hillside to search for the one lost sheep, and when it is found, brings it home rejoicing (Luke 15:4–6). Jesus is also the discerning shepherd, who separates the sheep from the goats on the final Day of Judgment (Matt. 25:32).

However, just as in the Old Testament the notion of God as the Chief Shepherd was combined with that of the king as the shepherd of the people, so also Christ presently rules through the leaders of the church, who are appointed as undershepherds (1 Peter 5:2–4). As Peter makes clear, this is a position that combines authority with service: They are to "oversee" the flock but not "lord it" over them. Unlike the bad shepherds of Ezekiel 34, they are not to serve for their own benefit. Like the Chief Shepherd, they will have to be on the lookout for marauding wolves while watching tenderly over the flock, committed to their care (Acts 20:28–29).

It is this special combination of toughness and tenderness that the image of shepherd is uniquely fitted to convey. Of the two aspects, the toughness involved in being a shepherd is easily missed today. We must heed the helpful insight of Alastair Campbell: "[In the Bible, the shepherd's] unsettled and dangerous life makes him a slightly ambiguous figure—more perhaps like the cowboy of the 'Wild West' than the modern shepherd in a settled farming community."[14]

---

13. The text of v. 31 has aroused some suspicion since *ʾādām* ("people") is absent from the original text of the Septuagint. It is normally read as a clumsy secondary gloss, identifying the Lord's flock as being human, connecting this passage with 36:38 (Zimmerli, *Ezekiel*, 2:221). Alternatively, it has been argued that the words call attention to the depth and greatness of the divine condescension in meeting with a human being who is taken from the earth and returns to it again (Hengstenberg, *Ezekiel*, 305). But in the context that has just mentioned the fulfillment of the covenant with David and the Sinai covenant, might it not reasonably reach further back and affirm the restoration of the original covenant of creation, so that it is affirmed of the restored people, "You are 'Adam' and I am your God"?

14. Alastair V. Campbell, *Rediscovering Pastoral Care* (London: Darton, Longman & Todd, 1981), 27.

The blessings of the new covenant. In addition, we should note that the blessings of the covenant we experience as Christians are different from those that believers experienced under the old covenant because we have a different relationship to the land in which we live. For them, the land of Canaan was in a special way "God's land," which they inhabited as his tenants. For that reason, the fertility of the land functioned, in Chris Wright's phrase, as a "spiritual thermometer" of the relationship between Israel and her God.[15] When they were obedient to their covenant obligations, God's goodness was demonstrated in rainfall and abundant harvests; when they were disobedient, his displeasure made itself manifest in the lack of these things (Deut. 28). This provided a pictorial prefiguring of the final eschatological state of blessing for the righteous and curse for the covenant-breakers.[16]

Under the new covenant, what is decisive for us as Christians is the perfect obedience of Christ in our place (Heb. 2:17–18; 4:15–16). For this reason, even though by nature we are covenant-breakers, we may still possess every spiritual blessing in Christ (Eph. 1:3). The heart of these blessings is nothing less than peace, life in all its fullness. Now we have peace with God and with our fellow human beings, as Jews and Gentiles united together in Christ, who is our peace (2:14). Through his death on the cross, those who were once in separate sheepfolds—those "far away" and those "near" (2:13)—have now been welded into a single flock, "one new man" (2:15). Through that death, this peace is already a present reality in our lives (Rom. 5:1).

However, at present we only experience that blessing in a partial way; our lives are an ongoing struggle against sin, and we continue to live in a fallen world. This world is a place of ongoing tribulation (John 16:33). Sometimes those trials are the result of our own disobedience, sometimes not. Sometimes obedience results in material blessing, sometimes in persecution and hardship. But even in the midst of the trials of this life we may yet experience incomprehensible peace and inexpressible joy because of the nearness of the Shepherd (Phil. 4:5, 7).

CEO OR PASTOR? In the contemporary church, the image of minister as shepherd is rapidly becoming an endangered species. Our models of leadership are increasingly borrowed from business. In place of the traditional view of the minister as a "pastor," the minister is now viewed as the equivalent of the CEO of a major corporation or,

---

15. Christopher J. H. Wright, *An Eye for an Eye: The Place of Old Testament Ethics Today* (Downer's Grove, Ill.: InterVarsity, 1983), 59.

16. Poythress, *The Shadow of Christ*, 72.

to continue the agricultural metaphor, as a "rancher" overseeing a large sheep-producing enterprise.[17] It is argued, perhaps correctly, that only thus can large churches be established and maintained.

But what is the theological cost of viewing ministry as management and pastors as professional organizers, albeit in charge of spiritual organizations? What is lost in the switch is the biblical vision of the pastor as a shepherd of a flock of souls. Such a vision is far from being a peripheral matter; in Thomas Oden's words, the shepherd image is the "pivotal analogy" for leadership in the Scriptures.[18] As we have moved from being pastors to ranchers, we have traded in the vocation of handcrafting saints for the business of mass-producing sheep.[19]

But what does it mean for a pastor to be a shepherd? It is a unique combination of afflicting the comfortable and comforting the afflicted. The bad shepherds of Ezekiel 34 were criticized because they ignored the fat sheep who were oppressing the other sheep, while they lived comfortably off the products of the flock. In contrast, the good shepherd will both confront the fat sheep and tenderly care for the weak sheep (34:16).

Most of us who are shepherds fall far short of this standard. Sometimes, we don't challenge those who are comfortable for fear of stirring up conflict—after all, the fat sheep are often big givers who underwrite the church's budget (and pay our salaries). Nor do we always comfort the weak sheep as we should. Taking care of the weak sheep is hard, painful, time-consuming work, and we have been told that there are more important things to do with our time. As a result, we gradually turn into managers of the flock, and as long as the flock is growing in numbers, no one around us complains. God is against such shepherds, however. He is the one to whom we are ultimately accountable, and what will it profit us if we grow a sizable megachurch, yet neglect our calling to shepherd the sheep? We will stand under his condemnation.

The good shepherd. The good shepherd will know his flock by name; he will know their strengths and their weaknesses, their joys and their sorrows. He will be there to share in the joy of their wedding celebrations, to celebrate the birth of their children, to comfort them in their sickness, and to be there when they die. Like being a watchman, being a shepherd is a heavily responsible task;

---

17. Thus Leith Anderson writes: "The style switch [from traditional to 'shopping center' church] moves from 'farmer,' where one person does everything, to 'rancher,' where a leader works with and through others" (*A Church for the 21ˢᵗ Century: How to Bring Change to Your Church* [Minneapolis: Bethany House, 1992], 178). The distinction seems to have originated with Lyle Schaller, "Looking at the Small Church: A Frame of Reference," *The Christian Ministry* 8 (1977).

18. Thomas C. Oden, *Pastoral Theology: Essentials of Ministry* (San Francisco: Harper & Row, 1983), 49.

19. For a voice crying out against this trend, see the countercultural vision of Eugene Peterson in "The Business of Making Saints," *Leadership* 18 (Spring 1997): 20–28.

it is not a job where you punch in and out and work "professional hours" (see Gen. 31:38–40). But it is also a profoundly rewarding task. Who else gets to share in all of these profoundly important moments in people's lives? Who else gets to shape and influence people's lives in such a deeply significant way?

If we are to return to truly being shepherds, perhaps we need to reconsider our love affair with big churches. It is possible to lord it over a flock of thousands; it is possible to herd a flock of hundreds; but is it really possible to pastor a congregation of more than about two hundred?[20] At the very least, within larger churches we need consciously to create subcongregations of this size or smaller, in which real shepherding takes place, where loving concern and care is expressed and strong, scriptural accountability is exercised.

In our organizational chart, someone must be shepherding our sheep. Moreover, the leader of the larger congregation must resist the pressures to retreat into the role of superstar preacher or of vision-casting executive. Though such people may not be able to shepherd all of the people all of the time, they should certainly be shepherding *some* of the people all of the time and *all* of the people some of the time. Otherwise, there is a real danger that contemporary pastors will lose touch with their sheep and they with them.[21]

Jesus, the model. In all of this, Jesus is our supreme model of what it means to shepherd the flock. He did not act as the rancher of a large herd, comfortably managing a megaflock from a distance through intermediaries. He picked a small group of twelve disciples and lived together with them in a way that completely changed their lives. He ate with them and slept with them; he sweated with them and sat with them; he laughed with them and cried with them. He was their pastor.

In addition, Jesus also had a ministry to a larger group of people, to the thousands who followed him around. He confronted the self-righteous Pharisees boldly, pointing out how far the righteousness of which they were so proud fell short of God's standards. But the needs of the multitudes moved him to compassion, for he saw that they were "like sheep without a shepherd" (Matt. 9:36). As a result, he was never too busy to sit with ordinary people, even with tax collectors and sinners, finding out their concerns and worries while pointing them to their deeper spiritual needs.

In Jesus we see the perfect balance of comforting the afflicted and afflicting the comfortable that is the shepherd's task. He afflicted the comfortable. That is, to those who relied on their own righteousness, he was unmerciful

---

20. Church growth books generally identify the number at which a dramatic shift in church dynamics becomes necessary as somewhere between 120 and 200. See Kent R. Hunter, *Foundations for Church Growth* (New Haven, Mo.: Leader, 1983), 155.

21. For helpful comments on how the pastor of a large church can still exercise the ministry of a pastor, see Eugene Peterson, "The Business of Making Saints," 27.

in tearing away the fig leaves of their excuses, driving them to see their utter need of the gospel. But he also comforted the afflicted. The sinners and outcasts did not need to have the law preached to them; they had heard it too often on the lips of the Pharisees. They needed instead to be drawn to God. They needed to hear that God did not delight in their extermination but rather was wooing them to come to him so that they might live. They needed to know that there was a place in his flock for the adulterer and homosexual, the alcoholic and the drug addict.

Most of us who are pastors will naturally gravitate toward one style of pastoral ministry or the other. By temperament, we typically either draw people to Christ or we drive them to Christ. But the image of the shepherd calls us to a richer, more balanced view of our calling: as drawers and drivers, drivers and drawers, by all means winning those whom God, the Great Shepherd, is adding to his flock.

Jesus, the fulfillment of Ezekiel 34. But Jesus is not merely the model shepherd who makes contemporary pastors feel guilty by how far short we fall. He is himself the One of whom Ezekiel 34 speaks. He is the One in whom all the covenants of the Old Testament find their fulfillment. He is the ultimate Shepherd-King, who fulfills the Davidic covenant, as the crowds recognized during his triumphal entry into Jerusalem (Matt. 21:9). He fulfills the Mosaic covenant both as the Lawgiver, who speaks his authoritative word from the mountain (Matt. 5–7), and also as the One who has come to fulfill the law given from Sinai (Matt. 5:17). He is the Second Adam, who through his obedient life, death, and resurrection fulfills the covenant of creation (1 Cor. 15:45–49). He is the One who ushers in for his people the blessings of the covenant by being the covenant-keeper in our place. In him, we have peace with God; in him, we have peace with one another; in him, all creation finds peace.

All of these blessings have both a "now" and a "not yet" aspect to them. We see them in part now, but we do not yet see them in all their fullness. Creation still groans with anticipation as it awaits the revelation of the new heavens and the new earth and of ourselves as sons and daughters of God (Rom. 8:19–23). In the meantime our experience frequently continues to be "trouble or hardship or persecution or famine or nakedness or danger or sword" (8:35). But these are momentary light afflictions in comparison to the glory that awaits us (8:18). One day Christ will return, and all will be gloriously fulfilled as God gathers his worldwide flock from many nations into his presence. Then there will be no more suffering, no more pain, no more disharmony with God, my neighbor, or the world. As Revelation 7:17 puts it:

> For the Lamb at the center of the throne will be their shepherd;
>> he will lead them to springs of living water.
> And God will wipe away every tear from their eyes.

Ezekiel 35:1–36:15

THE WORD OF THE LORD came to me: [2]"Son of man, set your face against Mount Seir; prophesy against it [3]and say: 'This is what the Sovereign LORD says: I am against you, Mount Seir, and I will stretch out my hand against you and make you a desolate waste. [4]I will turn your towns into ruins and you will be desolate. Then you will know that I am the LORD.

[5]"'Because you harbored an ancient hostility and delivered the Israelites over to the sword at the time of their calamity, the time their punishment reached its climax, [6]therefore as surely as I live, declares the Sovereign LORD, I will give you over to bloodshed and it will pursue you. Since you did not hate bloodshed, bloodshed will pursue you. [7]I will make Mount Seir a desolate waste and cut off from it all who come and go. [8]I will fill your mountains with the slain; those killed by the sword will fall on your hills and in your valleys and in all your ravines. [9]I will make you desolate forever; your towns will not be inhabited. Then you will know that I am the LORD.

[10]"'Because you have said, "These two nations and countries will be ours and we will take possession of them," even though I the LORD was there, [11]therefore as surely as I live, declares the Sovereign LORD, I will treat you in accordance with the anger and jealousy you showed in your hatred of them and I will make myself known among them when I judge you. [12]Then you will know that I the LORD have heard all the contemptible things you have said against the mountains of Israel. You said, "They have been laid waste and have been given over to us to devour." [13]You boasted against me and spoke against me without restraint, and I heard it. [14]This is what the Sovereign LORD says: While the whole earth rejoices, I will make you desolate. [15]Because you rejoiced when the inheritance of the house of Israel became desolate, that is how I will treat you. You will be desolate, O Mount Seir, you and all of Edom. Then they will know that I am the LORD.'"

[36:1]"Son of man, prophesy to the mountains of Israel and say, 'O mountains of Israel, hear the word of the LORD. [2]This is

what the Sovereign LORD says: The enemy said of you, "Aha!
The ancient heights have become our possession." ' ³Therefore
prophesy and say, 'This is what the Sovereign LORD says:
Because they ravaged and hounded you from every side so that
you became the possession of the rest of the nations and the
object of people's malicious talk and slander, ⁴therefore, O
mountains of Israel, hear the word of the Sovereign LORD: This
is what the Sovereign LORD says to the mountains and hills, to
the ravines and valleys, to the desolate ruins and the deserted
towns that have been plundered and ridiculed by the rest of
the nations around you—⁵this is what the Sovereign LORD
says: In my burning zeal I have spoken against the rest of the
nations, and against all Edom, for with glee and with malice in
their hearts they made my land their own possession so that
they might plunder its pastureland.' ⁶Therefore prophesy concerning the land of Israel and say to the mountains and hills, to
the ravines and valleys: 'This is what the Sovereign LORD says:
I speak in my jealous wrath because you have suffered the
scorn of the nations. ⁷Therefore this is what the Sovereign
LORD says: I swear with uplifted hand that the nations around
you will also suffer scorn.

⁸'"But you, O mountains of Israel, will produce branches
and fruit for my people Israel, for they will soon come home.
⁹I am concerned for you and will look on you with favor; you
will be plowed and sown, ¹⁰and I will multiply the number of
people upon you, even the whole house of Israel. The towns
will be inhabited and the ruins rebuilt. ¹¹I will increase the
number of men and animals upon you, and they will be fruitful and become numerous. I will settle people on you as in the
past and will make you prosper more than before. Then you
will know that I am the LORD. ¹²I will cause people, my people
Israel, to walk upon you. They will possess you, and you will
be their inheritance; you will never again deprive them of
their children.

¹³'"This is what the Sovereign LORD says: Because people
say to you, "You devour men and deprive your nation of its
children," ¹⁴therefore you will no longer devour men or make
your nation childless, declares the Sovereign LORD. ¹⁵No
longer will I make you hear the taunts of the nations, and no
longer will you suffer the scorn of the peoples or cause your
nation to fall, declares the Sovereign LORD.'"

EZEKIEL 35 COMPRISES an oracle against the nation of Edom, under the figure of its central mountain, Mount Seir. At first sight, it might seem out of place among the surrounding chapters that speak of Israel's restoration. Ezekiel had already delivered a brief oracle against Edom in the oracles against the foreign nations (25:12–14), where Edom appears as one of the seven hostile neighbors of God's people. However, this larger oracle against Edom is linked together with the oracle that follows it (36:1–15) as a pair of contrasting panels of darkness and light.

Having spoken of the restoration of the monarchy in chapter 34, the central feature of the Davidic covenant, Ezekiel now addresses the future of the land of Canaan, the central feature of the covenant with Abraham. The issue at stake between Israel and Edom is nothing less than the possession of the Promised Land.[1] As in chapter 34, where the prophet begins by critiquing the existing bad situation and announcing judgment on it (the panel of doom), after which he announces a message of the reversal of the situation (the panel of salvation), so here first comes doom pronounced on Mount Seir, followed by salvation pronounced on the mountains of Israel.[2] The judgment of Edom is a necessary prerequisite for the restoration of Judah.

The chapter opens with an address through the prophet against Mount Seir, the symbol of Edom (35:2). Edom, the nation to the southeast of Judah, had apparently taken advantage of the power vacuum left by the destruction of Jerusalem to move into Judean territory and take it over. Her fortunes seemed on the rise, but that was not God's final word. Ultimately, God would act to bring Edom down. The Lord declared that judgment would come on Mount Seir, so that she would become "a desolate waste" (35:3), exactly the same fate he had earlier brought on the mountains of Israel (6:14).[3]

The reason for God's judgment is given in 35:5: Because of the "ancient hostility" (*ʾêbat-ʿôlām*) between the two nations, the Edomites gave the Israelites over to the sword in their time of judgment. This hostility reached all the way back to the time of their progenitors, Jacob and Esau (also known as Edom), as recorded in Genesis 27–28. Even the establishment of peace between these two individuals (Gen. 33) did not allay the deep-seated grievances among their descendants, which stretched down throughout history, amplified rather than diminished by the passage of time. Thus, when Judah

---

1. Clements, *Ezekiel*, 158. The question of who will possess the land given to Abraham has already been raised in 33:24–29.

2. Lind, *Ezekiel*, 281.

3. Bernard Gosse, "Ézéchiel 35–36,1–15 et Ézéchiel 6: La désolation de la montagne de Séir et le renouveau des montagnes d'Israël," *RB* 96 (1989): 511–17.

was under God's wrath and Jerusalem was judged, Edom saw an opportunity to reclaim the stolen birthright by helping the Babylonians. But their animosity will rebound on their own heads, says the Lord. Because of their "bloodthirsty hatred" (Ezek. 35:6),[4] blood will in turn pursue them until they are utterly cut off. To match their perpetual enmity toward Israel, now they will become "desolate forever" (šimmôt-ʿôlām, 35:9).

The source of Edom's perpetual enmity toward God's people becomes clear in 35:10. The Edomites desired to possess the two lands[5] of Israel and Judah for themselves and thus to reclaim by force the stolen birthright, in spite of the Lord's past presence there. This ambition will be thwarted by the Lord's intervention to protect the honor of his own name, which was linked to the gift of Canaan to his people (35:11–12; cf. Ex. 32:11–14). Far from their possessing the traditional Israelite inheritance, their own inheritance will be wiped out; just as they rejoiced at Israel's downfall, many nations will rejoice at theirs (Ezek. 35:15). Then indeed they will know that the Lord is the One who stands behind the assignment of the land of Canaan to Israel as a lasting inheritance (Num. 34:2); his present abandonment of the land is not permanent.

Lasting possession of the land is not achieved by Edomite power, nor indeed by Jacob's tricky strategies, but by sovereign divine election, backed up by the Lord's commitment to honor his own name (Ezek. 35:11). It is that divine election that makes the mountains of Israel the permanent "inheritance of the house of Israel" (35:15). Though the vassal Israel has been temporarily removed, the land of Canaan remains the rightful property of the Lord.[6] The living God will not be mocked or trifled with (35:13). Edom's foolish boasting will ultimately be seen as the empty words of the godless, who think to overthrow God's kingdom, only to find themselves the object first of God's mirth and then of his wrath (Ps. 2).

If Ezekiel 35 gives the dark side of the future (i.e., the destruction of presently ascendant Edom), 36:1–15 gives the bright side: the return of God's people to the land of promise. The address to the "mountains of Israel" parallels the address to Mount Seir, as well as the earlier oracle of destruction to those selfsame mountains in chapter 6. Whereas Edom sought to

---

4. This is the NJPS translation. The NIV has "since you did not hate bloodshed . . ."; however, the oath formula with ʾim-lōʾ normally introduces a positive statement. See Joüon-Muraoka, §165.

5. From Ezekiel's theological perspective, there were not in actuality two lands and two nations but one. Yet the de facto situation of two separate nations was what appeared to outsiders, such as the Edomites. But this de facto situation would not persist forever, as 37:15–23 makes clear.

6. Block, *Ezekiel 25–48*, 322.

possess the mountains of Israel, the "ancient heights" (*bāmôt ʿôlām*, 36:2), and will be brought down to the depths, Israel will return to possess the land that is now in the hands of many nations (36:3).

It becomes clear as the oracle progresses that Edom in Ezekiel 35 is merely one representative of the nations at large who oppose Israel and her God.[7] Her fate is therefore representative of all who oppose God's plan; all who seek to benefit from Israel's misfortune will meet the same end at the hands of Israel's jealous God (36:5). Though the promise of the land to Israel may at present be in abeyance because of Israel's unfaithfulness, it has not been abrogated and ultimately will be fulfilled because of the Lord's concern for his name.[8]

Whereas in the past God's jealousy and wrath were poured out on the mountains of Israel so that they became the object of scorn for the nations, that scorn will be returned on the head of the nations (36:7). Israel has once again become "my people" (*ʿammî*, 36:8). The mountains of Israel will burst forth with a primeval fruitfulness as the Lord turns his face toward them in blessing (36:9). People and animals will multiply and be fruitful for the Israelites (36:11), an echo of the creation mandate in Genesis 1:28. This re-creation will not merely be a return to the former status quo but will be something even better than their original state (36:11).

Historically, the mountains of Israel had not always been experienced as a land that "does flow with milk and honey" (Num. 13:27). Sometimes it had seemed to be, as the ten timid spies falsely reported, a "land [that] devours those living in it" (13:32). But just as this report was essentially false then, so also it continued to be false as it was repeated by the nations around Israel (Ezek. 36:13). The mountains of Israel, Israel's heartland, would once again be a place of prosperity and blessing, experiencing the positive fruits of divine election; no longer would it be a barren and undesirable place, under God's curse because of the people's unfaithfulness to their covenant overlord.

Bridging Contexts

EDOM AS A **theological entity.** To contemporary readers, Edom is a geographical entity, not a theological one. It may be faintly recognized as the name of one of Israel's neighboring states, and the diligent student or pastor may even be interested enough to look it up on the map printed in the back of a Bible to ascertain its precise location. But this approach misses the theological overtones that the term *Edom* had for the ancient reader. Edom was not merely another bothersome neighbor, engaged

---

7. Stuart, *Ezekiel*, 331.

8. Allen, *Ezekiel 20–48*, 173.

in occasional border skirmishes over disputed territory; Edom was *the* archetype of the nonelect, the very paragon of a nation raging against the Lord and against his anointed.

This relationship of antagonism between Israel and Edom was long-standing. It extended all the way back to the founders of the two nations, Jacob and Esau, who struggled with one another in the womb (Gen. 25:22). It was revealed to their mother, Rebekah, that this struggle was not a simple brotherly squabble, such as is known to all those who have more than one son, but was rather the consequence of a profound theological difference. The Lord said to her, "Two nations are in your womb, and two peoples from within you will be separated; one people will be stronger than the other, and the older will serve the younger" (25:23). In other words, the Lord had chosen for the line of promise to descend through the younger son, Jacob, so that the path of blessing for the older son, Esau, would lie in submitting to God's choice.

Unfortunately, Esau was not willing to follow that path. Although he counted his birthright and the promise that (humanly speaking) went with it such a light thing that he was willing to trade it for a bowl of stew (Gen. 25:29–34), yet when Jacob craftily tricked him out of his father's blessing, his thoughts turned to murder (27:41). Of course, Jacob himself was far from blameless in all of this; he was seeking to attain the promise by strategy rather than by faith. But from before the outset of his life, Esau appears as a man passed over by God, uninterested in the things of God and antagonistic toward the chosen line.

This remained Edom's subsequent posture toward Israel. When the Israelites were coming up out of Egypt, they asked simply for right of passage through Edomite territory, offering to pay for whatever they consumed. The Edomites, however, refused and sent out a large army to turn them back (Num. 20:14–21). Later on, in the time of David, the tables were turned, and Edom was conquered by Israel (2 Sam. 8:14). They remained subject to Israel until the time of Jehoram, at which point they rebelled and reestablished their independence (2 Kings 8:20). Given that history, it is perhaps understandable that they rejoiced over the fall of Jerusalem and cheered on the Babylonian destroyers (Ps. 137:7). But to oppose God's chosen people and to rejoice at their fall is to incur God's wrath, a wrath that in due time will be poured out on Edom as an example to all who oppose God.

Thus, when Isaiah depicts the coming world-shaking judgment on all nations, his language moves from cosmic destruction to the devastation of Edom (Isa. 34:2–10). Edom will be consigned to the eternally unquenchable lake of fire, whose smoke ascends forever and ever (Isa. 34:9–10), a judgment that is preparatory to God's ultimate acts of cosmic salvation (Isa. 63). Likewise, in Malachi 1, the ultimate proof of God's love for Israel is the destruction of Edom, who is termed "the Wicked Land, a people always under the wrath of the LORD" (Mal. 1:4; cf. Obad.). None of this extreme language can be properly understood outside the representative role of Edom as the symbol of the nonelect, who perpetually range themselves against the Lord and his people and will ultimately face the consequences.[9]

This ongoing conflict provides the background for Paul's use of the example of Jacob and Esau in Romans 9. Paul appeals to the two brothers as an example of sovereign election: God chose Jacob over Esau before the twins had done anything good or bad (Rom. 9:11). Jacob is the archetype of the one chosen by God for blessing in spite of who he was; Esau is the archetype of the nonelect, passed over by God, who then proceeds to live out his life in enmity toward God and his people. The fruit of election is salvation by grace for the elect; the fruit of reprobation is a life of enmity against God that leads to final judgment. Both of these outcomes are, however, the result of the antecedent decision of God to have mercy on those on whom he will have mercy and to harden those whom he will harden (9:18).

Yet even though Edom as a nation is implacably opposed to God, the Lord's electing mercy is still experienced by individuals from that nation. For Deuteronomy 23:7–8 declares: "Do not abhor an Edomite, for he is your brother.... The third generation of children born to them may enter the assembly of the LORD." In other words, even the "hated" Edomite may be engrafted into the family tree of Israel, and the one who was "not my people" by grace may yet become "my people" (cf. Hos. 2:23). The electing grace of God knows no limits.

The land of Israel as a theological entity. In contrast to the destruction to be poured out on Edom and thus on all that Edom represents, the land of Israel is promised unparalleled fertility. Should we see a fulfillment of this in the present agricultural development of the desert areas of Palestine? To do so is to miss the significance of the Edenic overtones of the promise. It is not merely fruitfulness that is being promised to the mountains of Israel but specifically a return to the Eden-like conditions of blessing that accompany the presence of the Lord in the midst of his people. What is promised is nothing short of complete fulfillment of the blessings promised to the patriarch Abraham, of a land and its people blessed by the immediate presence of their God.[10]

The multiplication of people envisaged by Ezekiel (36:10–12) finds a partial fulfillment in the adding of multitudes to the kingdom of God through the carrying out of the Great Commission to make disciples of all nations

---

9. In that respect, it is interesting to note that King Herod, who sought so desperately to kill Jesus as a baby, was himself an Idumean, or Edomite.

10. Block, *Ezekiel 25–48*, 336.

(Matt. 28:19). This is the New Testament analogue of the creation mandate given to humanity in Eden to be fruitful and multiply (Gen. 1:28). Its ultimate fulfillment, however, still lies in the future, where the Edenic fruitfulness of the earth will be restored in the new heavens and a new earth, where God's presence is in the midst of his people forever (Rev. 21:1–3).

ALL IS OF **God's electing grace.** God's people have never lacked for enemies. Throughout history, there have always been those only too eager to oppose and hurt God's chosen ones. At times, it may seem as if the oppressors of the church have the upper hand and are about to crush her utterly. How can believers know for sure during those hard times that such an outcome can never happen? The answer is the assurance of God's election and promise. God has determined from all eternity to save a people for himself, and that purpose must stand in spite of all that the forces of the evil one can throw against it.

Our assurance cannot rest on our own merits and strength or on our heredity; God did not choose Jacob because he was better than Esau or Israel because she was better than Edom. He chose them simply because of his own good pleasure and purpose. Nor did he choose the nation of Israel because he foresaw that they would be strong enough to withstand the fiery furnace of trials. Rather, in Israel's case they were in the fiery furnace precisely because of their own long history of sin. Not all the descendants of Israel are part of the true Israel (Rom. 9:6). Even some who by descent are from the elect people will prove themselves to be nonelect individuals by their unrepentant sin. Some of the vine branches will refuse to abide in the vine, to their own eternal destruction (John 15:6).

But in spite of Israel's sin and rebellion against God, the honor of his name required him to act to preserve for himself a people. Astonishingly, the way in which he has chosen to do so is by engrafting the Gentiles into a new nonethnic entity, the true Israel of God (Rom. 11:17, 26; Gal. 6:16). We were engrafted into the vine not because we chose him but because he chose us to bear lasting fruit for him (John 15:16). All is of grace, even our fruitfulness, so that no one can boast in the presence of God.

Hatred from the world. Even while we are assured of God's love, however, we may rest equally assured of the world's hatred. It will hate us because it hated our master, Jesus, first (John 15:18). Esau cannot abide God's election of Jacob, and the world cannot abide God's love for his saints. We do not belong to the world or fit in it; therefore, we should expect the world to exhibit an "eternal hostility" toward us for the sake of Christ (cf. John 15:20–21).

Those who oppose God and arrogantly attempt to injure his people face the certainty of judgment, however. God will act to protect his own people, and even where he temporarily withholds his protecting hand and allows painful experiences to befall us, that is not God's ultimate word. Jesus' ultimate word to those who are his people is, "Come, you who are blessed by my Father; take your inheritance" (Matt. 25:34). By contrast, his ultimate word to those who oppose him is, "Depart from me, you who are cursed, into the eternal fire prepared for the devil and his angels" (25:41).

There is, literally, no future in fighting God. This is true not simply for the irreligious Edomite, but for the most sincerely religious individuals who range themselves against God's people. Edom's problem was not that they lacked sincerity in their religious beliefs in their gods, but rather that their sincerely held beliefs were misguided. In the experience of the outpouring of God's wrath on them, they would come at last to acknowledge the painful truth of the reality and power of Israel's God, the Lord (Ezek. 35:15).

We can be thankful, however, that just as "not all who are descended from Israel are Israel" (Rom. 9:6; in other words, not all of the elect nation are elect individuals), so also not all who are descended from Edom are Edom (i.e., not all those who wickedly oppose God are headed for eternal torment). Otherwise, we would all be lost. But alongside God's sternness exists his mercy (11:22). God's present patience with unbelievers serves his purposes in election, for some of those who are at present blasphemers against God and persecutors of the church will ultimately be found among the elect, trophies of redeeming grace, which can extend even to darkest Edom.

The apostle Paul himself was evidence of this powerful work of God (1 Tim. 1:13), and church history abounds with similar examples. To give just one, the very Auca Indians who speared to death Jim Elliot and his four friends—missionaries who had come to share the gospel with them—were subsequently converted and discipled through the ministry of two of the widows, Elisabeth Elliot and Rachel Saint. Those who once sought to destroy the gospel of God were by grace ultimately brought to love the same gospel.[11]

Properly understood, this electing grace of God should cause us as Christians to be lost in wonder, love, and praise that we have been chosen by God to become part of his people. We have been chosen not because of anything in us or because of what we can do for him, but simply because of his mercy. We who were once not his people have by grace been incorporated into the community of God's saints. As former Edomites who have been engrafted into the Israel of God, we of all people should therefore sing Charles Wesley's great hymn with renewed amazement:

---

11. See the remarkable testimonies of those involved in the massacre recorded by Steve Saint in "Did They Have to Die?" *Christianity Today* 40 (Sept. 16, 1996): 20–27.

And can it be, that I should gain an interest
    in the Savior's blood?
Died He for me, who caused His pain?
    For me, who Him to death pursued?
Amazing love! How can it be?
    That Thou, my God should'st die for me?

Ezekiel 36:16–38

A GAIN THE WORD of the LORD came to me: ¹⁷"Son of man, when the people of Israel were living in their own land, they defiled it by their conduct and their actions. Their conduct was like a woman's monthly uncleanness in my sight. ¹⁸So I poured out my wrath on them because they had shed blood in the land and because they had defiled it with their idols. ¹⁹I dispersed them among the nations, and they were scattered through the countries; I judged them according to their conduct and their actions. ²⁰And wherever they went among the nations they profaned my holy name, for it was said of them, 'These are the LORD's people, and yet they had to leave his land.' ²¹I had concern for my holy name, which the house of Israel profaned among the nations where they had gone.

²²"Therefore say to the house of Israel, 'This is what the Sovereign LORD says: It is not for your sake, O house of Israel, that I am going to do these things, but for the sake of my holy name, which you have profaned among the nations where you have gone. ²³I will show the holiness of my great name, which has been profaned among the nations, the name you have profaned among them. Then the nations will know that I am the LORD, declares the Sovereign LORD, when I show myself holy through you before their eyes.

²⁴"'For I will take you out of the nations; I will gather you from all the countries and bring you back into your own land. ²⁵I will sprinkle clean water on you, and you will be clean; I will cleanse you from all your impurities and from all your idols. ²⁶I will give you a new heart and put a new spirit in you; I will remove from you your heart of stone and give you a heart of flesh. ²⁷And I will put my Spirit in you and move you to follow my decrees and be careful to keep my laws. ²⁸You will live in the land I gave your forefathers; you will be my people, and I will be your God. ²⁹I will save you from all your uncleanness. I will call for the grain and make it plentiful and will not bring famine upon you. ³⁰I will increase the fruit of the trees and the crops of the field, so that you will no longer suffer disgrace among the nations because of famine. ³¹Then you will remember your evil ways and wicked deeds, and you

will loathe yourselves for your sins and detestable practices. ³²I want you to know that I am not doing this for your sake, declares the Sovereign LORD. Be ashamed and disgraced for your conduct, O house of Israel!

³³"'This is what the Sovereign LORD says: On the day I cleanse you from all your sins, I will resettle your towns, and the ruins will be rebuilt. ³⁴The desolate land will be cultivated instead of lying desolate in the sight of all who pass through it. ³⁵They will say, "This land that was laid waste has become like the garden of Eden; the cities that were lying in ruins, desolate and destroyed, are now fortified and inhabited." ³⁶Then the nations around you that remain will know that I the LORD have rebuilt what was destroyed and have replanted what was desolate. I the LORD have spoken, and I will do it.'

³⁷"'This is what the Sovereign LORD says: Once again I will yield to the plea of the house of Israel and do this for them: I will make their people as numerous as sheep, ³⁸as numerous as the flocks for offerings at Jerusalem during her appointed feasts. So will the ruined cities be filled with flocks of people. Then they will know that I am the LORD."

IT IS NOT ENOUGH for God merely to give Israel a new shepherd-leader and a renewed land. The nation had had good kings in the past and had lived in the land God had promised to Abraham, Isaac, and Jacob. But the people themselves had proved unworthy to inhabit the land. A total transformation was required if the regathering and return were to be a success. It is this subject to which the prophet now turns, giving the reasons why judgment was necessary in the first place and the reasons why mercy will surely follow.

The prophet begins by pointing out the motivation for God's wrath in the past. The people, while they lived in their own land, polluted it by their actions (36:17). As a result they could not remain in God's presence and he could not remain in their midst. They were unclean, which the prophet describes in terms of the ceremonial uncleanness caused by menstruation. In the law of Moses, this process was considered defiling to a woman, making her unable to take part in religious activities (Lev. 15:19–24). This is not because it was in any sense sinful but because any contact with the realm of death, through the loss of bodily life-fluids (e.g., blood or semen) or through contact with a corpse, renders one unfit to be in contact with the realm of life.[1] Communication with the living God through the various Old Testament means of grace was impossible as long as one was in a state of impurity as a result of contact with death.

What Israel had done while they lived in their land was to turn it into a permanent place of death, thoroughly defiling it by means of bloodshed and idolatry, making it a place unfit for divine habitation by the living God (Ezek. 36:18). God had no choice but to bring on them the curses of the covenant they had broken, in wrath scattering them among the nations, just as he had threatened when they first entered the land (Deut. 29:22–28).

This action, however, created a new problem for God. He had promised to bring this people, who were called by his name, into the land of Canaan to possess it. He had established a relationship between himself, his people, and the land. Yet now the nations could see that the Lord's people were absent from his land (Ezek. 36:21). That three-way relationship had been broken. The conclusion drawn by the surrounding nations would be natural: The Lord's power was insufficient to bring about that which he promised.[2] He had given up on his people as a bad job. The final elimination of those people for their sins—what Moses had feared in Numbers 14:15–16 and had prayed against—had finally become a reality.[3]

Thus, as long as Israel was scattered among the nations, they continually profaned the divine name (Ezek. 36:20). This was now not because of anything particular they were doing, although there is no suggestion that the shock of exile in and of itself brought about a radical change in their behavior. Rather, they profaned God's name *simply by being in exile instead of in the land of promise!*[4]

All of which brings Ezekiel to the reasons for God's future mercy. If there had been no other reasoning involved for God than the necessity of dealing with Israel's sin, permanent wrath would have sufficed.[5] Israel could simply and deservedly have been blotted out from the pages of history as an example of the power of God's holiness and his anger against sin. It is not because God shrinks from dealing out such judgment that he stays his hand from crushing Israel comprehensively and finally. After all, he had earlier repeatedly declared that he would not have compassion (*ḥāmal*) on sinners (5:11; 7:4; 8:18; 9:5, 10).[6] As was the case for the people of Noah's day, the inhabitants of Sodom and Gomorrah, or the Amorites living in the land at the

---

1. See Milgrom, *Leviticus 1–16*, 1004.
2. Block, *Ezekiel 25–48*, 348.
3. Zimmerli, *Ezekiel*, 2:247.
4. Lind, *Ezekiel*, 290.
5. Fairbairn, *Ezekiel*, 191.
6. Allen, *Ezekiel 20–48*, 178.

time of Joshua's assault, those whose sins were full could simply have been totally destroyed.

However, the Israelites of Ezekiel's day were not completely destroyed. Why not? Because though he has no compassion on them, God will nonetheless have concern (ḥāmal) for his name, which he had inextricably linked to Israel by entering covenant with them. Because of that sovereign, irrevocable act, mercy not only may but must be shown to Israel. The honor of God's name will be vindicated by a show of power among the nations when he brings Israel back to her land (36:21–23). The Lord will act, not for Israel's sake, but for the sake of his own name. The root of God's action in restoring his people is grounded not in his love (which might suggest something lovable about the object of his affections) but in a demonstration of his holiness.

But this act through which God's power is demonstrated involves not merely bringing Israel back physically to the land but also a total change in their nature. His people must be redeemed not merely outwardly but inwardly, effectively. Israel will indeed be gathered and returned from the nations to their own land (36:24). Then she will be sprinkled with clean water, symbolizing her cleansing from all her past impurities and idolatries, the things that had made the land unclean (36:25). In a similar way, Leviticus 15 prescribed washing with water to cleanse that which is unclean.

This outward act of initiation is then followed by a deeper, internal change, whereby Israel's heart and spirit will be made new. The "heart" and the "spirit" are the seats of thought and will from which actions flow. Unresponsive, unyielding stone will be replaced by warm, living, responsive flesh (Ezek. 36:26). That which has been defiled will be made clean. The Spirit of God, which brings life and power, will indwell them and create in them both the will and the ability to follow God's decrees and laws (36:27). Then, finally, they will be fit to live in God's land and be his people, and he in turn will not be ashamed to be called their God (36:28).

Then the Israelites will experience the blessings of the covenant, the fruitfulness of the land, rather than the covenant curse of famine that had made them a reproach among the nations (36:30). Such a salvation will not bring about pride in the renewed nation but rather a profound sense of shame, for they will realize that their salvation is not something they have merited or deserved in any sense. Rather, it is a free gift of sovereign grace. Nothing short of such radical divine intervention could have saved such a people.

In addition to the act of self-glorification that results in the restored people being returned to the land, God will also restore the land to a "better-than-original" state. It will become "like the garden of Eden," the ultimate symbol of fertility and fruitfulness (36:35; cf. Isa. 51:3; Joel 2:3). The garden land will be filled with restored cities; the places that once were torn down and desolate will be inhabited and fortified (Ezek. 36:35).[7] In place of the one original *ʾādām* and his wife, the new garden land will be filled with "flocks of *ʾādām*," that is, numerous "people" who will fill the cities to overflowing (36:38). The fertility and fruitfulness will thus encompass the people as well as the land itself, to the point where it will be as crowded as Jerusalem used to be on the great annual festivals, when her streets were crammed with a mass of people and animals (36:38).

The chief blessing, however, will be that God will once more be responsive to Israel's petitions. In the past, he refused to be sought by the elders of his adulterous people (14:3; 20:3).[8] His face was turned away from them and no intercession was possible. But in the future, that too will change. As a mark of Israel's restored status as God's people, he will permit himself to be sought by them to act on their behalf (36:37). To adapt the familiar language of 2 Chronicles 7:14, his people, who are once again called by his name, can now seek his face and God will hear from heaven and heal their land. The abundance of population will be proof of this favor of God that now rests on his people. Then indeed, they and the nations will know that the Lord has rebuilt that which he destroyed and replanted that which he desolated (Ezek. 36:36). God's holiness will then have been displayed fully both in the judgment of the wicked and in the gracious salvation and transformation of the people called by his name.

Bridging Contexts

CEREMONIAL CLEANNESS AND **uncleanness.** The concept of ceremonial uncleanness is a distinctive feature of the Old Testament law. People and things were divided by nature into the categories of "clean" and "unclean," of "sacred" and "profane." Sheep, for example, were "clean" animals, which could be eaten, while camels were "unclean" and could not be eaten (Lev. 11:4).

These were not random divisions within the animal kingdom, nor were they categories motivated by hygienic considerations, a reflection of the relative safety of the meat of the animals concerned. Rather, the animals func-

---

7. We need not see a contradiction between the "fortified" cities of 36:35 and the "unwalled" cities of 38:11. The rhetorical contexts are entirely different. "Fortified" frequently functions as the opposite state for a city to that of "destroyed" (e.g., Isa. 25:2), while the idiom of a people living in "unwalled cities" denotes a people who live without fear of attack (Jer. 49:31). As Greenberg put it, Ezekiel was "not working to a systematic theology, but for immediate rhetorical effect" (*Ezekiel 21–37*, 732).

8. Zimmerli, *Ezekiel*, 2:251.

tioned as a means of holding up a mirror to society. Unclean animals formed the outer circle of the natural order. They were neither to be eaten nor sacrificed to God. Clean animals formed an intermediate category: All clean animals were fit to be eaten, but only some clean animals qualified for inclusion in the central circle, those that could be used for a "sacred" purpose by being sacrificed to God. Those that fit the criteria for this function had to be unblemished animals from a limited number of groups.

A similar ordering prevailed in the social realm and in the realm of sacred geography. On the outside of the circle were the nations, those who lived outside the Promised Land. They could observe God's great acts and act as witnesses of his mighty deeds. But unless they converted, they could not enter the inner circle of God's covenant people, Israel, and live permanently in the land. Even this inner group was subdivided, however, with a "sacred" minority who served as priests and had access to the inner areas of the tabernacle and temple. Membership of this group was limited to unblemished members of a particular subgroup (Levites who were descendants of Aaron).[9] Only these people were qualified for the sacred purpose of approaching God.[10] One of the responsibilities of the priests was to teach clearly to the people these distinctions between "clean" and "unclean" (Lev. 10:10–11; Ezek. 22:26; 44:23).

These were not entirely fixed categories, however. What was clean could become unclean, either temporarily or permanently. For example, a man could become unclean through a bodily discharge or through contact with a person so afflicted (Lev. 15:2–15). Anyone who thus came into contact with the realm of death was temporarily unfit for contact with the living God. Moreover, anyone who had incurred a certain kind of skin disease might become permanently unclean and be cut off from the covenant community (13:45–46). Likewise, what was holy could become profane through inappropriate contact with the profane; and if the priests failed to be holy, they profaned the holy name of the Lord (21:6; 22:2).

What Israel had done through her idolatry and bloodshed was to move themselves as a nation from the category of "clean" to "unclean." The land had become defiled by their presence, just as a woman was defiled (temporarily) by her monthly flow of blood. They were therefore no longer able to inhabit the inner circle, the land of promise, from which they had necessarily been scattered (Ezek. 36:18–19). The punishment fit the crime: Having behaved like the unclean (the nations), they were now scattered among them.

---

9. Ezekiel's further restriction of this group to descendants of Zadok will be discussed in reference to Ezek. 44.

10. For a fuller discussion of the diet laws, see Milgrom, *Leviticus 1–16*, 718–36.

But this was not—indeed, could not be—the final word. For the holiness of God's name was linked to his people, and therefore he would act to move them back from the outer circle to the inner circle. Physically, they would be regathered from among the nations. Spiritually, they would be purified with clean water to cleanse them from existing impurities and changed from the inside out to prevent a recurrence of uncleanness. Then they would be fit to live in the presence of the Holy One and to commune with him.

In the New Testament, the old categories of "clean" and "unclean" are radically revised. This epochal change was revealed in a vision to Peter in Acts 10, when he was shown all kinds of unclean food that he was instructed to eat. But his initial refusal, itself an echo of Ezekiel's refusal to eat unclean food in Ezekiel 4, was rebuked by God with the words: "Do not call anything impure that God has made clean" (Acts 10:15). A radical change had taken place in redemptive history with the death and resurrection of Christ and the pouring out of the Spirit on the church. At a stroke, the old barriers were broken down. The motivation for change was not that the dietary restrictions would form a barrier to the effective evangelization of Gentiles but that the old wall of separation between Jew and Gentile as God's people and outsiders had gone in Christ (Eph. 2:11–22). Now the nations could be included in the people of God, and the line between "clean" and "unclean" is determined not by ethnic origins but by faith in Jesus Christ.

It is important that we recognize the nature of this change, however. It is not that the line between clean and unclean, between holy and profane, has been abolished. Rather, it has moved. In Christ, men and women from all nations become "clean" and "holy." The goal of Exodus 19:6, the creation of a kingdom of priests and a holy people, is fulfilled in the church (Rev. 5:10). No longer are there any gradations of holiness within the holy people: All who are in Christ are sacred, and there is a genuine priesthood that belongs to all believers. For Christians every activity in life is sacred—from reading the Scriptures to emptying the garbage—for all is done to the glory of God. But all those outside of Christ are unclean and profane, no matter their genetic background or their religious fervor. Outside of Christ, their best and most self-denying endeavors are unfit for God's presence, suited only for the trash heap.

Concern for the name of God. In a similar fashion to the concept of ritual cleanliness, the concern for the "name" of God is likewise a distinctive concern of the Old Testament. The divine name Yahweh was revealed to Moses on Mount Horeb (Ex. 3:14), a decisive progress in the self-revelation of God.[11] God's name was placed on the angel who went ahead of the Israelites

---

11. On this, see R. W. L. Moberly, *The Old Testament of the Old Testament: Patriarchal Narratives and Mosaic Yahwism* (Minneapolis: Fortress, 1992).

into the Promised Land, which means that rebellion against him was tantamount to rebellion against God himself (Ex. 23:21). God's name also appeared as a virtual hypostasis of the Lord himself, whether coming against his people in judgment (Isa. 30:27) or dwelling in their midst in blessing at the central place of worship (Deut. 12:5, 11). The Aaronic blessing was intended as a means of putting God's name on the Israelites, so that they might receive his blessing (Num. 6:27).

In the New Testament, concern for God's name remains a central category. The Lord's Prayer includes the petition: "Our Father in heaven, hallowed be your name" (Matt. 6:9). The precise focus, however, has shifted. Now the name placed on God's people is the triune name of Father, Son, and Holy Spirit (28:19). There is no longer a central place of worship on which the divine name is placed and where the divine presence is experienced; instead, whenever two or three of his people gather in the name of Jesus, they experience his presence with them (18:20). God's children are all those who believe in the name of Jesus (John 1:12). Gentiles too are included in this people whom God has chosen for his name (Acts 15:14). By this act of salvation, accomplished through Jesus' death on the cross, the Father will glorify his name (John 12:28).

God's exclusive concern with his own name and glory may seem offensively self-absorbed to contemporary readers. We are used to beginning our theological reflection "from below" and celebrating the God who is "for us." But God is only for us because it brings glory to himself. Moreover, such self-absorption is as great a virtue in God as it is a flaw in human beings. For God to delight in his own perfections is entirely appropriate, since there is no one and nothing greater in which he can delight. To delight in anything less than himself would be idolatry, just as surely as it is idolatry for us as creatures to delight in anything less than our great Creator. Sanctifying his great name, exalting God above all things, is the only task fit for God himself and for humankind, whom he has created in his image.[12]

LIFE CHANGES. The traditional sea shanty "What Shall We Do With the Drunken Sailor?" considers a number of methods of bringing about behavioral change in the inebriate. "Drag him in the longboat until he's sober" is one possibility; another is, "Put him in the scuppers and hose him all over." One doubts, however, that the methods adopted

---

12. See John Piper, *Desiring God: Meditations of a Christian Hedonist* (Portland, Ore.: Multnomah, 1986), 23–38.

will bring about lasting life-change in the person. Other, more serious, methods of attempting to bring about change in people's lives exist in the contemporary world. These include Alcoholics Anonymous, "twelve-step" programs for those with various addictions, Weight Watchers and other programs for those whose problem is with eating, and a plethora of counseling resources for behavioral difficulties. Many people spend hours of their time and countless dollars of resources in seeking effective, lasting change.

The motivation for seeking change on the part of the person concerned is frequently the perception that their life is in some way *dysfunctional*. Such people feel they are not living life to the full, but instead are engaging in lifestyle choices that result in a diminished quality of life. If only they could solve their behavioral problem or find and fix its underlying psychological root, their life will surely be fuller and more meaningful. Then they will be "cured."

In contrast to this essentially medical model of the human predicament, Ezekiel has presented the Lord's diagnosis of Israel's situation. She is not so much sick and in need of a cure, as sinful and in need of purification. Through her past history of sin, she has made herself totally unfit to inhabit God's land and to exist in his presence. Because of her sin, she is offensive to a holy God. In the language that the apostle Paul applies to all of us, she is "by nature [the] object of [God's] wrath" (Eph. 2:3). Her lifestyle change is necessary not so much because she is missing out on living life to the full, but because she has forfeited the right to life itself. God's judgment has descended on her, and she has been scattered among the nations.

This raises the question, "Is such radical change possible?" In contemporary life-change programs, this question is invariably answered in the affirmative: Because of the infinite power of the human spirit, you *can* kick that habit, lose those pounds, win friends and influence people—at least, so the brochures assure us. This humanistic optimism often carries over into the church. So we assure people, "God loves you and has a wonderful plan for your life," as if that were the most natural and self-evident truth in the world. In consequence, it is not surprising to find that many people approach Christianity as if they were interviewing God for a job, checking out whether as a Deity he is up to the task of being "Lord of their life." They are seeking to determine whether Christianity will "work for them," on the assumption that God will be only too pleased to welcome them should they decide in his favor.

The Bible, however, gives us no reason to be so automatically sanguine about the prospect of our acceptance by God. Ever since the fall of Adam and Eve, there has been no "of course" when it comes to the question of the future of the human race. We have collectively walked the tightrope of total destruction by God's wrath several times. That we have survived as a race is not because we somehow merited God's favor or because God's love is more powerful than his wrath and he could not bear to see such delightful creatures as us utterly exterminated. The *only* reason for the continued existence of human beings on this planet is God's commitment to his eternal plan sovereignly to save for himself a people.[13]

What is more, just as Israel was maintained alive by God's firm determination to glorify himself in and through the people he had chosen, so it is also for us who make up the church. There is no "of course" about our salvation. By nature, we are deservedly dead and have no prospect apart from God's wrath. It might be a more biblical approach if instead of starting with the love of God, we begin our presentation of the gospel where Paul does in Romans: "The wrath of God is being revealed from heaven against all the godlessness and wickedness of men" (Rom. 1:18). That there is another way, as Paul goes on to unfold in what follows, is an astonishing testimony to God's determination to finish what he started, for his own glory and not for ours. Our salvation is entirely by grace.

Purification *and* renovation. Because of God's determination to finish what he started, we can be sure not only that his people will be saved but also that they will be fully sanctified. Israel must be cleansed and made holy if she is to stand in his presence. So also the church, God's new covenant people, must be purified from their sins and perfected in righteousness. The people who are saved not *by* works are saved *through* God's work, *for* good works (Eph. 2:9–10).

This work of God in believers is a two-stage process, just as it is depicted in Ezekiel 36.[14] First there is an initial work of *purification*, which corresponds to the outward sprinkling of water on the restored Israel (36:25). Then there is an ongoing work of internal *renovation*, which Ezekiel describes under the figure of receiving the new heart and new spirit through the internal work of the divine Spirit (36:26–27). These two stages are both necessary to being a Christian, and this passage may well be the one that lies behind Jesus' statement to

---

13. John Murray comments: "No treatment of the atonement can be properly oriented that does not trace its source to the free and sovereign love of God. . . . God was pleased to set his invincible and everlasting love upon a countless multitude and it is the determinate purpose of this love that the atonement secures" (*Redemption Accomplished and Applied* [Grand Rapids: Eerdmans, 1955], 9–10).

14. It can also be broken down differently, as in 1 Cor. 6:11, where the salvation experience is described as having three aspects: "You were washed, you were sanctified, you were justified in the name of the Lord Jesus Christ and by the Spirit of our God." In Rom. 8:30, Paul mentions four aspects: "Those he predestined, he also called; those he called, he also justified; those he justified, he also glorified."

Nicodemus, "No one can enter the kingdom of God unless he is born of water and the Spirit" (John 3:5).[15]

(1) God's initial work involves the purification of our sins. In this work, we are the passive recipients of his action in washing away our sins, applying to us the merits of Jesus' work on the cross (Eph. 5:26). It is the necessity of this cleansing regeneration to which baptism points: When we are baptized, whether as adults or children, we testify to the need we all have for Jesus Christ, whose cleansing blood is symbolized in the water. Baptism points to the need for a change that can only come from the outside, for it can only be done by someone else. It is not so much a testimony of my decision for Jesus as an act of wondering faith that Jesus has decided for me.

Baptism is an act of faith in God's promises. When Abraham circumcised his children, he knew it was a circumcision of the heart that counted, not an external ceremony. This is the logic behind the baptism of the children of believers in Reformed and Presbyterian churches. When we baptize our children, we know that a baptism of the heart, a new birth through the Holy Spirit, is necessary. Simply applying water to the outside will not save. But in baptism we lay hold by faith of the goodness of God and claim for our children the promise of the Holy Spirit.

What grounds do any of us have as Christians for hoping that our children will grow up to believe the same things that we do? Perhaps some would say, "Well, I send my little Joshua to church; I read the Bible with him; I set him an example in Christian living." Now all of those things are good, but the only thing you can do for your child by yourself is make your child religious. Only God can give your child the new heart he or she requires. "Well, of course, he'll do that," you reply. But why should there be any "of course" about it? The only thing we pass on to our children as "a matter of course" is a sinful nature and a flawed example.

We can be grateful, however, that God has revealed himself as a covenant God, who deals faithfully with us as families as well as individuals (Gen. 17:7). This self-commitment is not simply a blessing for the old covenant order. As Peter told his hearers on the first day of Pentecost: "The promise [of the Holy Spirit] is for you and your children and for all who are far off" (Acts 2:39). That is what people in the Reformed tradition proclaim joyfully to the world when they baptize little ones—that they too have a promise that they can look to God in repentance and faith and receive the promised Holy Spirit. They are acknowledging to themselves and their children that they cannot save themselves—but also that God can, and will, if they look to

---

15. Linda L. Belleville, "'Born of Water and Spirit': John 3:5," *Trinity Journal* 1 (1980): 125–40.

him in repentance and faith. He will do so, because he is a covenant-keeping God, who does not change and who brings about his determined purpose to save and sanctify a people for himself.[16]

(2) Thus, God's "wonderful plan" for our lives is not limited to taking us to heaven; it also includes bringing heaven into us, remaking us into a holy people. He is not content merely to wash his people of their past sins and to impute to them the righteousness of Jesus Christ, he also wills to work a perfect holiness in them. This is the second stage of God's great work in redeemed humanity: renovation. God's determinate plan is that we be perfect as he is perfect (Matt. 5:48), that when Jesus Christ returns, we be completely purified from all sin (1 John 3:2–6). To be sure, that purpose is not yet a present reality. Everyone living in this world does, in fact, still sin (1 John 1:8). But the Spirit has been poured out into our hearts, in a measure that Old Testament saints could only dream about, in order that the process might begin in us here and now in full assurance that on that day it will be completed.

To be sure, Old Testament saints also experienced the renewing work of the Spirit of God (Ps. 51:10–11).[17] But in their experience the work was always partial, always provisional. Now that Christ has died and risen, the Spirit of God has been given to us in full measure, so that by him we might put to death the misdeeds of the body (Rom. 8:13). At present, we may experience only the firstfruits of the Spirit's work, and we await with eagerness the fullness of redemption (8:23). But just as we look forward to the day when we will be done with sin and long for its coming, so also that promise of God provides the incentive to holy living here and now (1 John 3:3).

A feeling of shame. Finally, God's "wonderful plan" for our lives does not exclude the possibility of shame over past sins. Renewed Israel was to "be ashamed and disgraced" over their conduct, even to the point of self-loathing for their "sins and detestable practices" (Ezek. 36:31–32). Modern people may view such self-loathing as psychologically unhealthy, urging the foundational importance of a high self-esteem.[18]

The Bible takes a different view of our position, however. As we grow in our appreciation of the gospel, we do not view ourselves in a better and

---

16. I appreciate the fact that many thoughtful Christians will disagree with me on this point; however, the above provides a strong rationale for why many in the evangelical camp baptize their children.

17. Block, *Ezekiel 25–48*, 360.

18. An example of this attitude within the Christian community would be Robert Schuller, whose "theology of self-esteem" defines salvation as "rescue from shame to glory" (*Self Esteem: The New Reformation* [Waco, Tex.: Word, 1982], 151). For Schuller, unlike Ezekiel, shame and salvation are mutually exclusive categories. A better perspective on shame and self-esteem is found in Welch, *When People Are Big and God Is Small*, 24–36.

better light. Rather, with Paul, we understand the true offensiveness of our sin, so that we come to view ourselves as the worst of sinners (1 Tim. 1:15). We grow to understand that, by nature, we are far worse than we ever could have imagined, that the wrath of God against my personal sin is fully justified, and that even in my best moments, in my most righteous acts, I deserve nothing other than utter damnation. My heart is indeed deceitful above all things and beyond cure (Jer. 17:9). As a Christian, the first thing I need to know, as the Heidelberg Catechism reminds us, is how great are my sin and misery.[19] That knowledge should induce an appropriate level of sorrow and shame over my sin.

However, as Paul says in a different context, we should not grieve as those who have no hope (1 Thess. 4:13). Though we are indeed far worse than we could have imagined, the gospel reminds us also that in Christ we are far more loved than we could have imagined. It reminds us that though we are and remain sinners all our days on earth, we are at the same time as Christians *justified* sinners, who will one day certainly be *glorified* sinners, perfect in holiness. This is certain because it rests on God's unchanging and eternal decree, not on my fallible and failing efforts. And if God is for us, though the present struggle may be hard and long, the eternal outcome is secure.

---

19. Q.2 What must you know to live and die in the joy of this comfort?

A. Three things: first, how great my sin and misery are; second, how I am set free from my sin and misery; third, how I am to thank God for such deliverance (*The Heidelberg Catechism* [Grand Rapids: CRC Publications, 1989], 12).

Ezekiel 37:1-14

THE HAND OF THE LORD was upon me, and he brought me out by the Spirit of the LORD and set me in the middle of a valley; it was full of bones. ²He led me back and forth among them, and I saw a great many bones on the floor of the valley, bones that were very dry. ³He asked me, "Son of man, can these bones live?"

I said, "O Sovereign LORD, you alone know."

⁴Then he said to me, "Prophesy to these bones and say to them, 'Dry bones, hear the word of the LORD! ⁵This is what the Sovereign LORD says to these bones: I will make breath enter you, and you will come to life. ⁶I will attach tendons to you and make flesh come upon you and cover you with skin; I will put breath in you, and you will come to life. Then you will know that I am the LORD.'"

⁷So I prophesied as I was commanded. And as I was prophesying, there was a noise, a rattling sound, and the bones came together, bone to bone. ⁸I looked, and tendons and flesh appeared on them and skin covered them, but there was no breath in them.

⁹Then he said to me, "Prophesy to the breath; prophesy, son of man, and say to it, 'This is what the Sovereign LORD says: Come from the four winds, O breath, and breathe into these slain, that they may live.'" ¹⁰So I prophesied as he commanded me, and breath entered them; they came to life and stood up on their feet—a vast army.

¹¹Then he said to me: "Son of man, these bones are the whole house of Israel. They say, 'Our bones are dried up and our hope is gone; we are cut off.' ¹²Therefore prophesy and say to them: 'This is what the Sovereign LORD says: O my people, I am going to open your graves and bring you up from them; I will bring you back to the land of Israel. ¹³Then you, my people, will know that I am the LORD, when I open your graves and bring you up from them. ¹⁴I will put my Spirit in you and you will live, and I will settle you in your own land. Then you will know that I the LORD have spoken, and I have done it, declares the LORD.'"

Original Meaning

FROM AN ORACLE depicting flourishing garden-cities filled with vibrantly alive people (36:33–38), the prophet is transported into the darkness of the valley of the shadow of death in chapter 37. This is not the first time that the Spirit has led him out into "a valley" (37:1); this location also provided the backdrop for the prophet's vision of God's glory in 3:22. However, this time the sight that greets him is a scene of total desolation: The valley is full of bones, bones that are many in number and very dry in nature (37:2). But even "Death Valley" must be swallowed up in victory as Ezekiel sees the Lord fulfill in visionary form the promise of 36:27 to put his vivifying Spirit within his people.

The statement that "the hand of the LORD was upon me" (v. 1) links this vision together with the prophet's other visions (1:3; 3:14; 8:1; 40:1), inviting us to view this scene in their light. In the light of 3:22–23, it becomes clear that the valley was not just a random geographical location but a valley in exile. Yet, viewing the vision in the light of chapters 40–48 suggests the significance of the fact that it is a *valley*: The valley in exile forms the ultimate contrast to the "very high mountain" within the land of Israel (40:2).[1] It is the place of death, from which Israel must be delivered before they can be brought into the land of life. This contrast is underlined by the verbs of motion by which the prophet is transported: He is "brought out" (Hiphil of *yāṣā'*) to the valley of death in 37:1 but "brought in" (Hiphil of *bô'*) to the land of life in 40:2.[2]

First the prophet is confronted with a scene of total death. He is "led ... back and forth" over the piles of bones (37:2); there must be no question of his having missed some flicker of life among the bones through having made merely a superficial inspection. Ezekiel's examination is thorough, his conclusions irrefutable: The situation is inimical to life. The valley is filled not merely with slain corpses, but with skeletal remains, and dry skeletal remains at that.

The Lord's question to the prophet, "Son of man, can these bones live?" (37:3a), seems redundant. Certainly, by the power of God corpses have been resuscitated before this in Israel, but only shortly after death, before decomposition occurred (1 Kings 17:17–24; 2 Kings 4:18–37; 13:21).[3] It seems as

---

1. *biqʿâ* ("valley") appears as the antonym of *har* in several places in the Old Testament, notably Deut. 8:7; 11:11; Ps. 104:8. For the "very high mountain" as a theological rather than geographical concept, see Levenson, *Theology*, 41. Intriguingly, perhaps underlining the contrast between the Babylonian *biqʿâ* and the Israelite *har*, the builders of the tower of Babel locate their false place of worship on the *biqʿâ bᵉʾereṣ šinʿār* ("a plain in [the land of] Shinar") in Gen. 11:2. In terms of the spiritual geography of the Old Testament, such a location is inappropriate for divine worship.

2. Renz, *Rhetorical Function*, 163.

3. Block, *Ezekiel 25–48*, 374.

if the prophet's earlier question, "Will you completely destroy the remnant of Israel?" (11:13), has now been answered in the affirmative. God's people have been utterly destroyed for their sin. The covenant curses have been executed and the corpses of the slain left unburied. No life remains in the bones. End of story.

Recognizing the sovereign power of God, however, the prophet is unwilling to give a negative answer. Rather, he turns the question back to God: "O Sovereign LORD, you alone know" (37:3b). In view of the overwhelming outpouring of God's wrath, he cannot answer, "Of course, Lord." Since the destruction of Jerusalem, which was the just judgment on her sins, there can be no "of course." God certainly has the power to bring the dry bones back to life; the question remains as to whether it is his will to do so. That question is swiftly answered in the affirmative: God wills that the dry bones shall indeed live.

The second question to be answered is then, "How shall these bones live?" The means by which that regeneration is brought about is through an infusion of the Spirit (*rûaḥ*) in response to the prophetic word. Thus, Ezekiel is told to prophesy to the bones and require them to listen to the word of the Lord; in response, the Lord will make breath (*rûaḥ*) enter them and bring them back to life, not as ghostly skeletons but as living flesh (37:5–6). Then the bones will know God's lordship.

The prophet obediently speaks the word and sees the power of God instantly unleashed. While he is prophesying, the bones come together and are clothed in flesh and skin—but still without life; there was no breath (*rûaḥ*) in them. It seems as if God's word has failed, as if the bones are after all too dry even for God. But almost before the thought has been framed, it is answered by a second command to prophesy. This time he is to prophesy to the wind (*rûaḥ*), which is invoked to come from afar, bringing life-giving breath to the people. Like the creation of the first *ʾādām* in Genesis 2, which was a two-stage process involving first his formation and then his filling with the breath of life, so the re-creation of this mighty army is a two-stage process of forming and filling. This underlines the difficulty of the re-creation process and the central role of the Spirit in bringing new life to the restored people.[4]

But if the Spirit gives the power through which regeneration takes place, Ezekiel himself is the channel through whom that power is brought to bear. He himself personally experienced a similar infusion of the Spirit at the outset of his ministry. Twice, confronted with the awesome majesty of God, he was reduced to prostration (1:28; 3:23); each time the Spirit entered (*bôʾ*) him, raising him to his feet (2:2; 3:24). This is exactly what happens to the dry bones

---

4. The word *rûaḥ* occurs ten times in 37:1–14, a fact obscured by the necessity of using three different English words to translate it (wind/spirit/breath), and reference to *rûaḥ* in verses 1 and 14 form an *inclusio.*

after they have been re-formed into bodies: The Spirit enters (*bô²*) them, raising them to their feet (37:10). What had first happened in his own life now happens to the renewed Israel through the means of the powerful prophetic word.

Another parallel with the earlier visions helps to make the power of the word even clearer. In Ezekiel 11, the prophet was shown a scene and commanded to prophesy to those involved. On that occasion, it was a word of judgment against the twenty-five men at the east gate of the temple (11:4). In both cases, while Ezekiel "was prophesying" (11:13; 37:7), the words had immediate effect, demonstrated in the death of Pelatiah (11:13) and the coming together of the bones (37:7). Just as the death of Pelatiah served as a graphic demonstration of the certainty of the coming judgment on Jerusalem, so also here the re-creation and restoration of the bones serves as a guarantee of what it symbolizes, the ultimate restoration of Israel as a nation.[5]

The oracle that follows the vision (37:11—14) merely serves to make explicit what the vision has already recounted. The dry bones are the whole house of Israel, who have come to recognize the seriousness of their situation. They are helpless and hopeless, cut off from God's life-giving presence (37:11). Without in the least contradicting this self-perception that their present situation is hopeless—indeed, reinforcing the accurateness of the idea—the Lord still affirms that there is nonetheless hope for the future.

There is a sure and certain future based not on what Israel can do but on God's determination to save his people. Twice, the Lord addresses them as "my people" (37:12—13). Though they are indeed dead, God can and will tear open their graves (shifting the metaphor slightly) and bring them up from the dead, giving them life through his Spirit and resettling them in their land (37:14). The promises of a new spirit and a return to the land made in Ezekiel 36:27—36 will indeed be fulfilled. Then they will know that the Lord not only speaks but acts, thus disproving the proverb of the skeptic, quoted in 12:22: "The days go by and every vision comes to nothing." Ezekiel's visions will come about, and the people will be restored to their land and revitalized, through the internal work of God's Spirit.

FAMILIARITY LEADS TO **misinterpretation.** Of all of the prophecies of Ezekiel, this section is perhaps the most familiar to the average reader. This is not necessarily an advantage, however, because it means that common misconceptions may first have to be cleared away before the constructive work can be done.

---

5. Duguid, *Ezekiel and the Leaders of Israel,* 104.

At first sight, for example, Ezekiel 37 seems to be a proof text for the resurrection of the body, as many of the early church fathers (and early rabbinic interpreters) understood it to be.[6] However, what the prophet is depicting is certainly not an expected universal resurrection. Otherwise, his answer to the question "Can these bones live?" would have been, "Most certainly," or, in similar vein to Martha's response to Jesus, "I know [they] will rise again in the resurrection at the last day" (John 11:24). The question posed by God to the prophet is not a universal philosophical one, "Will bones in general be resurrected?" In the context, it is the intensely particular question, "Will *these* bones live?"

The fact that this passage has been so widely misunderstood by interpreters from such a wide range of backgrounds raises a further point about the nature of visions. Visions, like parables, tend to be open-ended, full of imagery that is capable of diverse interpretations. The precision of logically constructed syllogisms is traded for the affective power of symbols. Some visions are deliberately open-ended, especially those dealing with the future. To avoid such misunderstanding, therefore, it is especially important to read visions within their context. If the vision itself is removed from the context of the biblical book in which it stands, as if it were a timeless statement of universal truths, misunderstanding is likely.

In a similar way, a single still photograph taken from a film might be open to many different interpretations, although, seen within the flow of the movie, its meaning may be univocal. In the case of Ezekiel 37, the context is twofold. The narrower context is the interpretation of the vision given by the Lord himself in 37:11–14. The broader context is the place of the vision within the book itself, as part of the message of restoration to a people who have experienced a full outpouring of the wrath of God.

Exactly what the Old Testament writers understood about life after death in general is still a much-debated topic.[7] Certainly, there was no widespread expectation of bodily resurrection of the kind that appears in the New Testament. The shadowy underground land of Sheol was feared as a place of continued existence, though it can hardly be called life, from which the righteous hoped to be delivered by the Lord (Ps. 49:14–15). The righteous are never actually said to go there, however; though they may fear it as a possibility, it is ultimately the destination of those without God. But in general the Old Testament is vague about the future of the righteous.

---

6. From the Christian side, Zimmerli cites Justin, Irenaeus, Tertullian, Cyprian, Cyril of Jerusalem, Epiphanius of Constantine, Ambrose, Severus, and John of Damascus (*Ezekiel,* 2:264). For the history of Jewish interpretation of the passage, see Greenberg, *Ezekiel 21– 37,* 749–50.

7. For the scholarly consensus, see R. Martin-Achard, "Resurrection," *ABD,* 5:680–84.

In principle, the Old Testament is not opposed to the idea of a resurrection. Indeed, Jesus himself argued for the idea of resurrection from the fundamental Old Testament credo that the God who is the God of Abraham, Isaac, and Jacob is the God of the living, not of the dead (Matt. 22:32). But the focus of the Old Testament is more centrally on the Lord's power over death, whether by rescuing the saints from its clutches (Ps. 18:4—19) or by the miraculous resuscitation of the dead (1 Kings 17:17—24; 2 Kings 4:31—37; 13:20—21). The resurrection (or, more precisely, resuscitation) of the bones in Ezekiel 37 has much more in common with the latter incidents from the ministry of Elijah and Elisha than it does with later ideas of a general resurrection of the dead on the last day.[8]

Neither is there a simple line of connection between this passage and the eschatological outpouring of the Spirit in the last days, predicted in Joel 2:28—29 and fulfilled on the day of Pentecost in Acts 2. *That* outpouring of the Spirit resulted in an extension of the gift of prophecy to all, as Moses had longed to see in Numbers 11:29. The infusion of the Spirit in Ezekiel results instead in renewed life and new power for right living, which is itself a promised prerequisite for life in the land (Ezek. 36:27—28).

Re-creating Israel. In summary, then, this passage is about the divine work of re-creating Israel through the prophetic word and Spirit. Though God's people have been justly judged and handed over into the realm of death for their sins, so that, humanly speaking, there is now no hope for them, yet God can bring life out of death. Because of his wrath, their death is real; because of his grace and his sovereign will to have a people of his own, however, their future prospect of life may be equally real. It is this that the prophet is called to proclaim to them. What he has first experienced himself he now announces to others: life in the Spirit through the power of God. The new creation that was begun in him will assuredly be brought to fulfillment by God.

What precisely does re-creating Israel mean, however? Does it directly anticipate the formation of the present political state of Israel, as some have supposed? To argue in this way is to miss the spiritual significance of the prophecy. For what is in view here, as the connections back to 36:24—38 make clear, is something more than political autonomy for the descendants of Abraham. It is nothing short of the fulfillment of all Old Testament anticipations of eschatological fullness, all of which are fulfilled in Christ. It is in him that the new Spirit-filled Israel of God takes shape, an identity that is no longer governed by ethnic origins and circumcision, as the old Israel was, but rather by faith in the cross of Christ (Gal. 6:12—16).

---

8. This is merely one of a series of connections between Ezekiel and these two prophets. See Keith Carley, *Ezekiel Among the Prophets* (SBT 31; London: SCM, 1975), 13—47.

Is "LIFE AFTER **death**" possible? What happens when you die? This topic has ignited a great deal of interest in recent years, especially through the publication of several books recounting "near-death" experiences, in which a person felt as if he or she had died briefly and then returned to tell the tale.

What Israel faced, however, was not a "near-death" experience, but a "total-death" experience. It was not simply that their heart had stopped beating for a few moments and their brain waves had ceased; they had died and decomposed; their flesh had disintegrated, leaving only bones behind; and then those bones themselves had been left out in the sun to bleach. They were as dead as it was possible to be—and that while physically still alive, for they themselves said, "Our bones are dried up and our hope is gone; we are cut off" (37:11). They knew themselves to be dead while they lived, for they were cut off from the life-giving presence of the living God and therefore without hope.

That is a spiritual condition that by nature we all share. Paul reminds the Ephesians, and along with them all of us, "You were dead in your transgressions and sins, in which you used to live when you followed the ways of this world and of the ruler of the kingdom of the air" (Eph. 2:1—2). By nature, we are all cut off from God's life-giving presence. Subjectively, we may or may not be aware of that fact. We may feel that we are on top of the world and that life couldn't possibly be better, or we may despair of making any sense of the world in which we live. Objectively, however, we are equally dead, no matter how we feel.

Can such dead people live? Is it possible, not merely theoretically but actually, for people like us to be resuscitated and brought back to life toward God? That question cannot simply be answered, "Of course!" as if it were a trivial matter. Because of our sin we are under God's wrath, so the question is not merely "*Can* God in general raise dead people to life?" but rather "*Will* he raise rebels like us to life?" Thanks be to God, the answer for us is positive, as it was for Israel. Thus Paul tells the Colossians, "When you were dead in your sins and in the uncircumcision of your sinful nature, God made you alive with Christ" (Col. 2:13). In Christ, there is life for the spiritually dead.

How, though, is this new life received? It is received through union with Christ. In the preceding verse (Col. 2:12), Paul talks about how as Christians we have been buried with Christ in baptism and raised with him through faith in the power of God, who raised him from the dead. In other words, it is as we share an experience that Christ first experienced for us that we are brought from death to life. For Ezekiel, what happened to the bones had first happened to him. So it is with us: What God does for the Christian, he has first of all done for Jesus.

Jesus took on himself our death. The death that he died on the cross was no mere accident, nor even a means of demonstrating graphically the extent of his love for humanity. There on the cross, he took on himself the sins of his people and was cut off for them. The Lord of life was laid in the tomb; the body of the one who created the universe was laid alongside the bones of those whom he had made. Why? It is because God's wrath against sin demanded that a just penalty be paid. God could not simply wave a magic wand and make sin disappear. Sin had to be paid for. In order to accomplish that, Jesus was, as it were, laid among the dry bones of the valley for my sake. So now my baptism is a burial with him in that death, an identification with his death in my place.

But just as the dry bones in Ezekiel did not remain dead, so also Christ did not remain in the tomb! He burst forth with resurrection power, raised from the dead by God! Just as surely, if we have been truly buried with him in baptism, receiving the reality as well as the sign, we also are made alive in Christ. Our sins are forgiven; the hold of the law over us is broken, nailed to the cross (Col. 2:14). We are not dry bones any longer, but living, breathing, Spirit-infused children of God (Rom. 8:16). What Ezekiel saw in visionary form has now become a reality!

The consequences of life after death. What are the consequences of this fact? (1) There is no reason for Christians to despair. Once again, subjectively we may or may not be aware of that fact. We may feel inside every bit as despairing as Ezekiel's hearers of making sense of our circumstances. Yet that inner confusion does not shake the objective fact to which Scripture points us: If we have died with Christ, we will certainly live with him (Rom. 6:8). To be sure, we do not yet see the full implications of this identification with our resurrected Lord. We still wait for the redemption of our bodies from this sin-tarnished world, where things fall apart and people become sick and die. We cry out in pain because of the tragedies we experience. Yet in the midst of our pain we are called to wait with confident hope (Rom. 8:23–24).

The objective fact of Christ's resurrection is the source of our confidence. Indeed, the importance of the physical resurrection of Christ is not simply that it proves the survival of the soul in general, or that life goes on in some sense beyond the grave. Otherwise, the resurrection of Christ would have no more significance than other resurrections recorded in Scripture, such as that of Lazarus. On the contrary, the New Testament teaching is that the resurrection of Christ is something entirely new, something of pivotal importance for our faith as Christians (1 Cor. 15:12). C. S. Lewis puts it like this:

The New Testament writers speak as if Christ's achievement in rising from the dead was the first event of its kind in the whole history of the universe. He is the "first fruits," the "pioneer of life." He has forced open a door that has been locked since the death of the first man. He has met, fought and beaten the King of Death. Everything is different because He has done so. This is the beginning of the New Creation: a new chapter in cosmic history has opened.[9]

Because Christ has been raised physically and gloriously to life, so also we will be raised physically and gloriously to life; the firstfruits provide the assurance of the full harvest (1 Cor. 15:20–23). Christian hope is therefore focused concretely on Christ in us, the hope of glory (Col. 1:27). Our sure and certain hope is that God's energy is at work in us to present us perfect in Christ (Col. 1:28). Even now we are indwelt by the Spirit of Christ who is at work in us, changing us into what we ought to be (Rom. 8:11).

(2) Since we are indwelt by the Spirit, we should walk according to the Spirit (Rom. 8:4, 12). Ezekiel was filled with the Spirit in Ezekiel 2–3 to equip him for his task; likewise, when the resuscitated bones came together, they became an army, not a debating club or a beach party. They were raised for a purpose. In a similar way, we as Christians have been regenerated and Spirit-filled in order that we too may serve, equipped by the gifts of the Spirit and dressed in the armor of God so that we may do his bidding in the world. We were re-created in Christ Jesus to do good works, which God prepared in advance for us to do (Eph. 2:10). In the appropriately martial imagery of Charles Wesley's hymn, our commission is as follows:

Soldiers of Christ, arise and put your armor on,
Strong in the strength which God supplies, through his eternal Son.
Strong in the Lord of Hosts, and in his mighty power,
Who in the strength of Jesus trusts is more than conqueror.

Stand, then, in his great might, with all his strength endued;
And take to arm you for the fight, the panoply of God.
That, having all things done and all your conflicts past,
Ye may o'ercome through Christ alone and stand complete at last.

Leave no unguarded place, no weakness of the soul;
Take every virtue, every grace and fortify the whole.
From strength to strength go on; wrestle and fight and pray;
Tread all the powers of darkness down and win the well-fought day.

---

9. *Miracles: A Preliminary Study* (New York: Macmillan, 1963), 150.

Ezekiel 37:15-28

THE WORD OF THE LORD came to me: [16]"Son of man, take a stick of wood and write on it, 'Belonging to Judah and the Israelites associated with him.' Then take another stick of wood, and write on it, 'Ephraim's stick, belonging to Joseph and all the house of Israel associated with him.' [17]Join them together into one stick so that they will become one in your hand.

[18]"When your countrymen ask you, 'Won't you tell us what you mean by this?' [19]say to them, 'This is what the Sovereign LORD says: I am going to take the stick of Joseph—which is in Ephraim's hand—and of the Israelite tribes associated with him, and join it to Judah's stick, making them a single stick of wood, and they will become one in my hand.' [20]Hold before their eyes the sticks you have written on [21]and say to them, 'This is what the Sovereign LORD says: I will take the Israelites out of the nations where they have gone. I will gather them from all around and bring them back into their own land. [22]I will make them one nation in the land, on the mountains of Israel. There will be one king over all of them and they will never again be two nations or be divided into two kingdoms. [23]They will no longer defile themselves with their idols and vile images or with any of their offenses, for I will save them from all their sinful backsliding, and I will cleanse them. They will be my people, and I will be their God.

[24]"'My servant David will be king over them, and they will all have one shepherd. They will follow my laws and be careful to keep my decrees. [25]They will live in the land I gave to my servant Jacob, the land where your fathers lived. They and their children and their children's children will live there forever, and David my servant will be their prince forever. [26]I will make a covenant of peace with them; it will be an everlasting covenant. I will establish them and increase their numbers, and I will put my sanctuary among them forever. [27]My dwelling place will be with them; I will be their God, and they will be my people. [28]Then the nations will know that I the

LORD make Israel holy, when my sanctuary is among them forever.'"

THIS PASSAGE CONTAINS a sign-act and a related oracle concerning the future reunification of God's people. It acts as a hinge, both summing up the oracles of hope in chapters 34–37 and looking forward to the establishment of the new sanctuary (chs. 40–48) after the final convulsion of evil in chapters 38–39.

The sign-act involves the prophet's taking two sticks, each of which he is to inscribe with a name (37:16). One is to be designated "Belonging to Judah and the Israelites associated with him" (i.e., the southern kingdom), while the other is to bear the message, "Ephraim's stick, belonging to Joseph and all the house of Israel associated with him" (i.e., the northern kingdom). Strictly speaking, the two rivals for first place among Jacob's sons are Judah and Joseph; hence the proper designation of the sticks as "Belonging to Judah/belonging to Joseph." Historically, however, the rivalry had become essentially a struggle between (the tribes of) Judah and Ephraim, who was Joseph's younger son and the dominant tribe in the northern part of Israel. For that reason, after the schism at the time of Rehoboam, the northern kingdom based in Samaria is frequently referred to as "Ephraim." This historical reality is reflected in the description of the second stick as "Ephraim's stick." Ezekiel is then instructed to join the sticks together in his hand so that they become one stick (37:17).

The writing on the sticks makes the symbolism of the act entirely transparent. Clearly, the reunification of northern and southern kingdoms is anticipated. The sticks (ʿēṣ) inscribed with names of tribes recall the incident of Numbers 17:6–10, where the staffs (maṭṭeh) of the tribal princes are placed before the Lord and Aaron's staff is chosen.[1] Here, however, far from choosing one from the many, the two sticks (scepters?)[2] will be merged into a single, united entity. Not only will the events of recent history be reversed, as has been the focus of chapters 34–37 so far; in addition, the events of much ear-

---

1. Zimmerli, *Ezekiel*, 2:273. Though the Hebrew words are different, the translators of the Septuagint rendered both by *rhabdos*, rod, scepter.

2. Allen, *Ezekiel 20–48*, 193. Greenberg sees the choice of ʿēṣ as being due to its ambiguity, representing both king and kingdom (*Ezekiel 21–37*, 753).

3. Lind, *Ezekiel*, 303. Interestingly, this is the same number of times as the key word *rûaḥ* occurred in 37:1–14.

lier history will be undone. The divided kingdom will once again be undivided. The key word in this section is the word "one" (*ʾeḥād*), which occurs ten times.[3]

Because the action itself is so transparent, the expected question from the audience, "Won't you tell us what you mean by this?" (37:18), is not a request for illumination about the import of the various symbols. Rather, it is a question about the deeper significance of the sign. The Lord's reply, therefore, merely reiterates the sign without further explication, while adding the emphasis that "I" will accomplish all this.[4] The solution to Israel's lengthy history of internal division is not to be found in the appointment of a binational committee to develop a "peace process" but in the divine act of reuniting his people.

What is more, the divinely effected reunion will address the issues raised by the original schism. Just as the division was caused by a failure in the area of servant leadership, with Rehoboam unwilling to serve the people as the older counselors advised (1 Kings 12:7), so also the reunion will be effected by the Lord's providing a single servant-leader, "my servant David" (Ezek. 37:24). Just as the division resulted in the setting up of separate sanctuaries (1 Kings 12:25–33), so also the reunion will result in a return to a single, divinely approved sanctuary in their midst (Ezek. 37:26). There will be no glossing over the differences; the reunion will be established on the basis of a fundamental new spiritual unity, effected by God in the hearts of his people. The Lord's hand is the place where the sticks are rejoined.

Unlike chapter 34, then, the mention of "my servant David" focuses not so much on the nature of the leader as on his significance as the foundation of unity. Just as David had earlier welded the disparate tribes into a united kingdom, so this new David will bring about renewed unity: one kingdom under one king (37:22).[5] He will rule over a renewed people, who will no longer defile themselves with their idols and images, whether in the defiled Jerusalem temple (Ezek. 8) or in the dual temples that Jeroboam set up in Bethel and Dan (1 Kings 12:28–33). These temples, which the biblical writers viewed as idolatrous from the outset, will disappear altogether. The nation will be purified and cleansed by God, thus allowing for a restoration of the covenant relationship between God and his people (Ezek. 37:23) and the blessings that flow from such a relationship (37:25). What is more, those blessings will be enduring, to "their children and their children's children . . . forever" (37:25). The covenant of peace will be "an everlasting covenant"; the sanctuary will be restored to their midst "forever" (37:26).[6]

---

4. Zimmerli, *Ezekiel*, 2:274–75.
5. Compare Hos. 1:11, which speaks of Israel and Judah being reunited under one head (*rōʾš*).
6. The key word *ʿôlām* occurs five times in these verses.

Because the work of purification and reunification is the Lord's, so also the glory will be his. Just as the destruction of the temple and the scattering of the people led to the Lord's name being profaned among the nations, so also the permanent restoration of the sanctuary to Israel's midst will result in the nations' recognizing that the Lord has endowed his people with a new level of holiness (37:28). The significance of the temple's restoration as crowning blessing, then, is this: It is objective evidence of the successful completion of the Lord's purposes to make for himself a holy people, a purpose announced already in 36:27 as the expected result of the outpouring of the Lord's Spirit. The enduring existence of the temple is a marker of that transforming work, for the sanctuary can only exist securely forever in the midst of a thoroughly sanctified community.

This chapter (and with it the section comprising chs. 34–37) closes with the prospect of renewed Israel's living at peace within their own land (37:26). This is the necessary precondition for the final onslaught of the forces of evil in chapters 38–39, in which God will demonstrate his power and commitment to his people by decisively rescuing them from their enemies. However, it is also the necessary prerequisite for the temple building plan of chapters 40–48.

In Deuteronomy 12:10, the Lord promised to give rest (Hiphil of *nwḥ*) to his people from their enemies all around them in the land, after which it would be time to build the central sanctuary. In accordance with that command, "after the LORD had given [David] rest" (Hiphil of *nwḥ*, 2 Sam. 7:1), he started to think about building a temple for the Lord in Jerusalem. Similarly, once the new, united Israel has been settled (Hiphil of *nwḥ*) in the land (37:14) and is at peace, then the nation's thoughts will naturally turn to temple building. Thus the promise of the Lord's sanctuary in the midst of his settled people is a fitting capstone to the prophecies of restoration. Though her enemies will once more descend on her (chs. 38–39), it is so that they may be defeated by the Lord, who will then establish his final temple (chs. 40–48).

Bridging Contexts

THE THEOLOGICAL SIGNIFICANCE of the temple. The temple is not a central category in contemporary Christian thinking. Where we do think of the Old Testament temple, we tend to think of it as simply the forerunner of the modern church building. Its broader political, social, and theological significance is largely lost on us.

---

7. See Carol Meyers, "David As Temple Builder," *Ancient Israelite Religion: Essays in Honor of Frank Moore Cross*, ed. P. D. Miller Jr., P. D. Hanson, and S. D. McBride (Philadelphia: Fortress, 1987), 365–66.

In the ancient Near East, however, the state of a society's temples was considered a measure of its health and wealth and an indication of the favor of its gods. When a king was strong and prosperous, "blessed" by his god, that fact would often be publicly demonstrated through an ambitious program of public building works, of which a temple was a prime example. The building program itself could act as a focus of national unity and a sign of divine approval.[7] In this context, a restoration of a people and of their monarchy without the visible symbol of divine presence provided by the temple would have been unthinkable.

In a similar way, the White House, the Capitol, and the other buildings in Washington, D.C., have a significance for Americans that goes far beyond their mere function as the seat of government. In a real sense, the buildings represent America, and to let them crumble would be unthinkable, even if other equivalent buildings had been erected to carry out their practical function. Thus, when the original presidential palace was destroyed in the War of 1812, it was a matter of national pride to replace it with a bigger and better building as soon as possible.

But there is more than one symbol of God's presence with his people in the Old Testament. The patriarchs experienced his presence in various ways, all of which were occasional rather than permanent. God's permanent dwelling in the midst of his people was not established until Mount Sinai, where Moses received the instructions for the tabernacle (Ex. 25–40). This dwelling was a mobile tent, appropriate for the people's condition as wanderers in the desert and for the early years of conquering the Promised Land. The temple that Solomon constructed at God's command was different. It was not merely the tabernacle on a larger scale, it was a glorious building, exuding permanence and stability—the suitable symbol for God's people at rest in God's land (1 Kings 6).

Ezekiel's vision of God's presence in the midst of his people is different again: It revolves around the establishment of a *sanctuary* (*miqdãs*), a place where they experience and respect God's holiness. It is the symbol of a holy God living in the midst of a holy people. This theme will emerge more clearly in the detailed description of the temple in chapters 40–48, but it is adumbrated already in 37:28, where it is announced that the nations will come to recognize that the Lord sanctifies (*mᵉqaddẽs*) Israel when his sanctuary (*miqdãs*) is among them forever.

The idea of the holy. This connection between the "sanctuary" and "sanctity" or "holiness" has been largely lost today. It was strongly present in medieval and pre-Reformation cathedrals and churches, which were nor-

---

8. See Harold Turner, *From Temple to Meeting House: The Phenomenology and Theology of Places of Worship* (The Hague: Mouton, 1975), 185.

mally divided into three parts. There was the nave, which was accessible to everybody; the chancel, which was only accessible to priest and choir; and the sanctuary, which housed the altar, where only the priest entered.[8] This medieval layout directly reflects the design of the Old Testament temple.

Reformation churches, which rightly emphasized the priesthood—and thus sanctity—of all believers, did away with these distinctions. They recognized that, as we saw in our discussion of Ezekiel 36, the old division of sacred and profane no longer runs through God's people, separating sacred priest from secular congregation, but rather now divides a people who are all holy in Christ from a profane world. The church building was assigned its proper new covenant role as the meeting house of the saints, not the house of God. In place of the central (but remote) altar, the building was redesigned to gather the people around the pulpit and communion table, reflecting the vision of God's people assembled to receive his Word rightly preached and the sacraments duly administered.[9]

The danger of this arrangement, however, is that we lose the necessary sense of holiness when we gather as God's people. As we will see in our study of Ezekiel 40–48, holiness is one of the dominating principles of the new temple. Certainly, in revising the architecture of their churches, nobody intended to lose the idea of holiness. The intention of the Reformers was rather to assert the holiness of all of life. In practice, however, we have all too often profaned all of life instead, leveling everything down rather than up.

Thus we may call the room in which we meet the "sanctuary," yet there is no sense of awe when we gather together as the church, no sense that it is the almighty and holy God himself with whom we are meeting. As a result, our individual lives are often similarly devoid of contact with the Holy One. Because we do not recognize the meeting together of the saints as a "sanctuary" in the biblical sense, we do not live the lives of sanctity that we ought.

JESUS AS OUR TEMPLE. Church unity has become, in some quarters, the modern equivalent of the Holy Grail. It is the revered object of earnest searching and eager desire. There is good reason for this enthusiasm among Christians. Jesus himself prayed for his postapostolic followers to be one, just as he and the Father are one. His desire

---

9. To be fair, it should be admitted that in many "reformed" church buildings the pulpit was far more dominant than the communion table and the baptismal font, reflecting an unbalanced focus on the preaching of the Word to the exclusion of the other means of grace.

10. See "God's Plan for Reunion" in John Frame, *Evangelical Reunion: Denominations and the Body of Christ* (Grand Rapids: Baker, 1991), 67–71.

was that we might be brought to complete unity so that the world may know that the Father sent the Son (John 17:21–23). Though in the present we live in a world where Christians are fragmented and separated from one another, on the basis of the Scriptures we should be repeatedly saying to ourselves and to others: "This is not how the church ought to be."[10] But it is not enough to be in favor of unity in the abstract; we must also be clear about the basis for this unity. In what is the unity of God's people to be grounded? Ezekiel 37 gives us the key answers.

Ezekiel's sign pointing to the reunification of God's people was grounded in the sovereign act of God's establishing one king over his people and one temple at the center of their worship. So also our desired unity as Christians, if it is to be genuine, must be grounded not in ecumenical study commissions and interchurch potluck dinners, but in Jesus Christ, who fulfills both aspects of Ezekiel 37 as our true temple and our true king. True Christian unity does not flow from the top down, with high-level ecclesiastical committees and denominational leaders showing the way, nor does it flow from the bottom up, coming by means of grass-roots initiatives by individual church members. Rather, it flows from the center out: It comes from Christ-centered people discovering that they are, in fact, servants of a common Lord and King.

Christ himself is our true temple because he accomplished in himself everything to which the tabernacle and temple of the Old Testament pointed. When the Word became flesh, he "made his dwelling [lit., tabernacled] among us" (John 1:14), manifesting God's glory in our midst, just as the Mosaic tabernacle was the place where God's glory was manifested in the desert (Ex. 40:34). In him, God's glorious presence is experienced in the midst of his people. Moreover, to act against his person is to do nothing less than to assault God's temple. That is why, referring to his own body in John 2:19, Jesus said, "Destroy this temple, and I will raise it again in three days."

Because Jesus is our temple, he himself is what unites his people together in worship. When Jesus met with the woman of Samaria, he prophesied an end to the divisions between Jews and Samaritans founded on their separate temples: "A time is coming when you will worship the Father neither on this mountain [at the Samaritan temple located on Mount Gerizim] nor in Jerusalem [at the temple on Mount Zion] ... [but] in spirit and in truth" (John 4:21–24). This marks a radical change in the old order of things, which anticipated the nations' coming to worship God at Mount Zion. With the coming

---

11. It is likely that Paul has in mind the actual physical wall that divided Jew and Gentile in the Jerusalem temple in Eph. 2:14. Certainly the passage is filled with temple language, even apart from the explicit reference to the church as the new temple in Eph. 2:22. See Klyne Snodgrass, *Ephesians* (NIVAC; Grand Rapids: Zondervan, 1996), 132–39.

of Christ, the old division between Jew and Samaritan in worship is broken down, not by Samaritans coming to the temple in Jerusalem but by Jew and Samaritan alike being incorporated into Christ himself, as the final temple.

Likewise, Christ has broken down the old wall between Jews and Gentiles through his death on the cross, building both together into a new, holy temple to the Lord (Eph. 2:14–22).[11] There is but one temple of God in this age, the church, the body of Jesus Christ, in which Jews, Samaritans, and Gentiles are all brought together as one. As Galatians 3:28 puts it: "There is neither Jew nor Greek, slave nor free, male nor female, for you are all one in Christ Jesus."

True unity in the church. It is therefore necessarily a contradiction in terms when the church is divided on racial or ethnic lines. Churches and denominations ought not to be "homogeneous units," where Christians choose to meet together with others exactly like them. Rather, each church should strive to be a heterogeneous mixture of those for whom Christ died, an entity that transcends racial, ethnic, cultural, and class barriers, giving expression as a worshiping community to the unity that is ours in our common adoption into God's family. As J. K. S. Reid puts it:

> The church is not an association or corporation of like-minded individuals; and its unity does not have only such strength as their like-mindedness possesses and so can confer. On the contrary, its unity rests upon what Christ has done and is thus complete and inviolate.[12]

Jesus as our king. Our unity as God's people is also rooted in the kingship of Christ. Our fundamental, most basic Christian confession is "Jesus is Lord" (Rom. 10:9; 1 Cor. 12:3). It is because Jesus is the chief cornerstone that the entire building holds together (Eph. 2:20). The church is only one flock, because we are all under the one Shepherd (John 10:16). Jesus Christ is the true and only Head of the church, the One from whom all authority flows. The ascended Lord is the One who provides pastors and teachers for his church, so that we may all "reach unity in the faith and in the knowledge of the Son of God" (Eph. 4:13).

The division of Israel in Ezekiel's day was not between two equally valid opinions, between allegiance to two equally legitimate kings. There was no doubt in the minds of the biblical writers that the line of David was the legitimate line, so that unity could only come in the person of that line. The northern kingdom had to surrender their erroneous views for true peace to be established. In the same way, the age-old dispute between the Samaritans and Jews of Jesus' day was not a moot issue. There was a right answer to the

---

12. *Our Life in Christ* (Philadelphia: Westminster, 1963), 99.

theological issue as to where one should worship: Mount Gerizim or Jerusalem. The Jews had historically been right (John 4:22). Unity would come not through Jews and Samaritans forging a balanced compromise, representing the middle ground between them. Rather, it would be established through the Samaritans coming to the salvation that had been proclaimed to the Jews from the beginning and that had now found its fulfillment in Christ.

For that reason, there can be no unity or compromise with those who deny the lordship of Christ, whether through theological statements that deny the reality of Jesus as the Son of God, or through practice that demonstrates effective unbelief. We are not to welcome all professing Christians indiscriminately, as if what you believe was a matter of small importance. Instead, the New Testament teaches us that we are to refuse to have anything to do with those who teach false doctrine (2 John 10–11). Nor are we to ignore gross sin in our midst, but rather we should exercise appropriate church discipline on those who have sinned, for the sake of their souls (1 Cor. 5:1–5). For our oneness as God's people is based on the rule of Christ over his church and his work of building his saints together into a holy temple, fit for his habitation.

Some divisions may therefore continue to be necessary "to show which of you have God's approval," as Paul puts it (1 Cor. 11:19). There will presumably also continue to be doctrines about which real Christians disagree, which for the sake of peace and harmony in the present may necessitate different denominations. Nonetheless, we should not be in any doubt about God's desire for the church and his eternal purpose for the church—that we may all be one even as the Father and the Son are one (John 17:21).

That purpose will ultimately be accomplished by Christ's work of complete sanctification of his people. There will be no doctrinal disagreements in heaven, for we will all understand perfectly, even as we are perfectly understood (cf. 1 Cor. 13:12). In the meantime, given the clear biblical statements of God's purpose and plan, we all need to search our hearts and consider what we personally have done and are doing to give true biblical unity its fullest possible present expression. How are we responding to Paul's admonition to the divided Corinthians in 1 Corinthians 1:10?

> I appeal to you, brothers, in the name of our Lord Jesus Christ, that all of you agree with one another so that there may be no divisions among you and that you may be perfectly united in mind and thought.

But Ezek prophesies (and details) construction of a physical temple in Jerusalem.

Ezekiel 38-39

THE WORD OF THE LORD came to me: ²"Son of man, set your face against Gog, of the land of Magog, the chief prince of Meshech and Tubal; prophesy against him ³and say: 'This is what the Sovereign LORD says: I am against you, O Gog, chief prince of Meshech and Tubal. ⁴I will turn you around, put hooks in your jaws and bring you out with your whole army—your horses, your horsemen fully armed, and a great horde with large and small shields, all of them brandishing their swords. ⁵Persia, Cush and Put will be with them, all with shields and helmets, ⁶also Gomer with all its troops, and Beth Togarmah from the far north with all its troops—the many nations with you.

⁷"'Get ready; be prepared, you and all the hordes gathered about you, and take command of them. ⁸After many days you will be called to arms. In future years you will invade a land that has recovered from war, whose people were gathered from many nations to the mountains of Israel, which had long been desolate. They had been brought out from the nations, and now all of them live in safety. ⁹You and all your troops and the many nations with you will go up, advancing like a storm; you will be like a cloud covering the land.

¹⁰"'This is what the Sovereign LORD says: On that day thoughts will come into your mind and you will devise an evil scheme. ¹¹You will say, "I will invade a land of unwalled villages; I will attack a peaceful and unsuspecting people—all of them living without walls and without gates and bars. ¹²I will plunder and loot and turn my hand against the resettled ruins and the people gathered from the nations, rich in livestock and goods, living at the center of the land." ¹³Sheba and Dedan and the merchants of Tarshish and all her villages will say to you, "Have you come to plunder? Have you gathered your hordes to loot, to carry off silver and gold, to take away livestock and goods and to seize much plunder?"'

¹⁴"Therefore, son of man, prophesy and say to Gog: 'This is what the Sovereign LORD says: In that day, when my people Israel are living in safety, will you not take notice of it? ¹⁵You

will come from your place in the far north, you and many nations with you, all of them riding on horses, a great horde, a mighty army. [16]You will advance against my people Israel like a cloud that covers the land. In days to come, O Gog, I will bring you against my land, so that the nations may know me when I show myself holy through you before their eyes.

[17]"'This is what the Sovereign LORD says: Are you not the one I spoke of in former days by my servants the prophets of Israel? At that time they prophesied for years that I would bring you against them. [18]This is what will happen in that day: When Gog attacks the land of Israel, my hot anger will be aroused, declares the Sovereign LORD. [19] In my zeal and fiery wrath I declare that at that time there shall be a great earthquake in the land of Israel. [20]The fish of the sea, the birds of the air, the beasts of the field, every creature that moves along the ground, and all the people on the face of the earth will tremble at my presence. The mountains will be overturned, the cliffs will crumble and every wall will fall to the ground. [21]I will summon a sword against Gog on all my mountains, declares the Sovereign LORD. Every man's sword will be against his brother. [22]I will execute judgment upon him with plague and bloodshed; I will pour down torrents of rain, hailstones and burning sulfur on him and on his troops and on the many nations with him. [23]And so I will show my greatness and my holiness, and I will make myself known in the sight of many nations. Then they will know that I am the LORD.'

[39:1]"Son of man, prophesy against Gog and say: 'This is what the Sovereign LORD says: I am against you, O Gog, chief prince of Meshech and Tubal. [2]I will turn you around and drag you along. I will bring you from the far north and send you against the mountains of Israel. [3]Then I will strike your bow from your left hand and make your arrows drop from your right hand. [4]On the mountains of Israel you will fall, you and all your troops and the nations with you. I will give you as food to all kinds of carrion birds and to the wild animals. [5]You will fall in the open field, for I have spoken, declares the Sovereign LORD. [6]I will send fire on Magog and on those who live in safety in the coastlands, and they will know that I am the LORD.

[7]"'I will make known my holy name among my people Israel. I will no longer let my holy name be profaned, and the

nations will know that I the LORD am the Holy One in Israel. ⁸It is coming! It will surely take place, declares the Sovereign LORD. This is the day I have spoken of.

⁹‴Then those who live in the towns of Israel will go out and use the weapons for fuel and burn them up—the small and large shields, the bows and arrows, the war clubs and spears. For seven years they will use them for fuel. ¹⁰They will not need to gather wood from the fields or cut it from the forests, because they will use the weapons for fuel. And they will plunder those who plundered them and loot those who looted them, declares the Sovereign LORD.

¹¹‴On that day I will give Gog a burial place in Israel, in the valley of those who travel east toward the Sea. It will block the way of travelers, because Gog and all his hordes will be buried there. So it will be called the Valley of Hamon Gog.

¹²‴For seven months the house of Israel will be burying them in order to cleanse the land. ¹³All the people of the land will bury them, and the day I am glorified will be a memorable day for them, declares the Sovereign LORD.

¹⁴‴Men will be regularly employed to cleanse the land. Some will go throughout the land and, in addition to them, others will bury those that remain on the ground. At the end of the seven months they will begin their search. ¹⁵As they go through the land and one of them sees a human bone, he will set up a marker beside it until the gravediggers have buried it in the Valley of Hamon Gog. ¹⁶(Also a town called Hamonah will be there.) And so they will cleanse the land.'

¹⁷‴Son of man, this is what the Sovereign LORD says: Call out to every kind of bird and all the wild animals: 'Assemble and come together from all around to the sacrifice I am preparing for you, the great sacrifice on the mountains of Israel. There you will eat flesh and drink blood. ¹⁸You will eat the flesh of mighty men and drink the blood of the princes of the earth as if they were rams and lambs, goats and bulls—all of them fattened animals from Bashan. ¹⁹At the sacrifice I am preparing for you, you will eat fat till you are glutted and drink blood till you are drunk. ²⁰At my table you will eat your fill of horses and riders, mighty men and soldiers of every kind,' declares the Sovereign LORD.

²¹‴I will display my glory among the nations, and all the nations will see the punishment I inflict and the hand I lay

upon them. ²²From that day forward the house of Israel will know that I am the LORD their God. ²³And the nations will know that the people of Israel went into exile for their sin, because they were unfaithful to me. So I hid my face from them and handed them over to their enemies, and they all fell by the sword. ²⁴I dealt with them according to their uncleanness and their offenses, and I hid my face from them.

²⁵"Therefore this is what the Sovereign LORD says: I will now bring Jacob back from captivity and will have compassion on all the people of Israel, and I will be zealous for my holy name. ²⁶They will forget their shame and all the unfaithfulness they showed toward me when they lived in safety in their land with no one to make them afraid. ²⁷When I have brought them back from the nations and have gathered them from the countries of their enemies, I will show myself holy through them in the sight of many nations. ²⁸Then they will know that I am the LORD their God, for though I sent them into exile among the nations, I will gather them to their own land, not leaving any behind. ²⁹I will no longer hide my face from them, for I will pour out my Spirit on the house of Israel, declares the Sovereign LORD."

Original Meaning

EZEKIEL 38 AND 39 form a single unit made up of two panels that describe the defeat of Gog (38:1–23) and the disposal of Gog (39:1–29).[1] Together, the two panels depict the ultimate onslaught of evil against God's apparently helpless people and God's decisive intervention to deliver them from the threat to end all threats. While this depiction may not seem as likely to induce hope in the hearts of Ezekiel's readers as the idyllic descriptions of the future that precede it, it nonetheless serves the same essential purpose. If an enemy such as Gog cannot separate God's people from the good future he has planned for them, then neither can any lesser evil. In the words of Paul in Romans 8:35–39, as he reflects on the significance for daily life of the resurrection of Christ, which demonstrated God's victory over the final enemy, death:

> Who shall separate us from the love of Christ? Shall trouble or hardship or persecution or famine or nakedness or danger or sword? . . .

---

1. Daniel I. Block, "Gog in Prophetic Tradition: A New Look at Ezekiel 38:17," *VT* 42 (1992): 157.

No, in all these things we are more than conquerors through him who loved us. For I am convinced that neither death nor life, neither angels nor demons, neither the present nor the future, nor any powers, neither height nor depth, nor anything else in all creation, will be able to separate us from the love of God that is in Christ Jesus our Lord.

The Defeat of Gog (38:1–23)

THE ORACLE OPENS with a summons to Gog and his allies to arm themselves and to prepare an assault against God's people dwelling peacefully on the mountains of Israel (38:2–9). Gog has frequently been identified with a seventh-century B.C. king of Lydia, who appears under the name *gûgu* in the *Annals of Ashurbanipal*, also known to us as Gyges in the writings of the ancient Greek historian Herodotus.[2] However, in neither instance do the supposed comparisons shed much light on the biblical Gog: *gûgu* is merely one more in a line of minor kings who initially assisted the Assyrians, then rebelled against them, and was destroyed by the steamroller of the Assyrian army. From the perspective of the Assyrian annalist, he is a mere roadkill on the highway of empire.

Herodotus, on the other hand, seems more interested in the bizarre way in which Gyges acquired his throne than what he did after he gained it. He records in detail how Candaules, the king of Lydia, forced Gyges, who was his general, to view his queen in a state of undress in order to convince him of her outstanding beauty. The queen, when she became aware of what had transpired, was understandably distressed by her husband's unseemly behavior. In a response appropriate for a Greek history, she then required Gyges to kill his master, which he in turn accomplished fittingly by hiding in the very same spot where he saw her naked. This is how Gyges became king of Lydia.[3]

Now this is material that has the elements of a splendid Shakespearean play (sex, violence, intrigue, a foreign location) but really doesn't help us much with our understanding of Gog. In neither of the above cases does the historical figure seem to justify the language of commentators describing Gog as "a great figure of the past . . . as we might speak fearfully of a new Hitler."[4] Rather, the Gog of Ezekiel transcends historical categories and takes on mythical proportions, rather like the figure of Arnold Schwarzenegger in the movie *The Terminator*.[5] He is the sort of person who when he drives up to

---

2. Zimmerli, *Ezekiel*, 2:301.
3. See Herodotus, *Hist.* 1.8–13.
4. Allen, *Ezekiel 20–48*, 204.
5. Block fittingly describes Gog as the "archetypal enemy" (*Ezekiel 25–48*, 436).

your house would deliberately drive over your kid's toy truck in the driveway, just for fun. Gog is thoroughly "bad to the bone." You can easily imagine Ezekiel's Gog saying *"Hasta la vista,* baby!" before he blows someone away.

The biblical Gog is no mere historical figure, then, but rather a fear-inducing figure of cosmic proportions; and to make matters worse, he is not alone. He is the commander-in-chief *(nᵉśîʾ rōʾš)*[6] of a coalition of forces gathered from the ends of the earth. He himself is from the land of Magog, and he rules over Meshech-Tubal. His allies include Persia, Cush, and Put (38:5), along with Gomer and Beth Togarmah (38:6). It is no coincidence that together these make up a total of seven nations, and it is significant that they are gathered from the uttermost parts of the world known to the prophet. Meshech-Tubal, Gomer, and Beth Togarmah come from the north, Put (northwest Egypt) and Cush (southern Egypt) from the south and west, while Persia is to the east of Judah.[7]

There is a kind of cosmic reversal of Isaiah 2:2–4 here. Here Ezekiel foresees the nations streaming towards God's holy land in the latter days, not (as in Isaiah) to receive his law or to turn their swords into plowshares and spears into pruning hooks, but to take up their weapons in the "mother of all battles" against the Sovereign Lord and his people. But even such an act of rebellion is itself instigated by God. Though Gog and his allies are far from unwilling participants in the coming conflict, yet the controlling force in all this is the Lord, who directs them by "hooks in your jaws" (Ezek. 38:4).

Once the unholy alliance has been prepared by God, he will summon them against his restored people at a time of his own choosing. Israel is depicted in terms borrowed from Ezekiel 34–37: They have been regathered from the nations to the mountains of Israel; now they live in safety (38:8), a peaceful, unsuspecting, and undefended people (38:11), grown rich in livestock and goods (38:12). They are dwelling "at the center of the land [earth]" (38:12), a description that is theological rather than geographical. Literally, they are dwelling "at the navel of the earth," the loca-

---

6. This phrase has been frequently translated as "prince of Rosh" (cf. NIV note), where Rosh is understood as a place-name, ever since the time of the Septuagint. This translation is grammatically possible, but in the absence of any biblical evidence for such a place-name, it is better to see it as a hierarchical title, as in the similar examples of Num. 3:32 and 1 Chron. 7:40. See Duguid, *Ezekiel and the Leaders of Israel,* 20. In addition, if *rōʾš* is part of the title, then Gog rules over a seven-nation coalition, which underlines the symbolic completeness of the forces arrayed against Israel (cf. the kinds of weapons that are subsequently burned for seven years, while the burial of Gog's army takes seven months). If *rōʾš* is a place-name, however, that symbolism is lost. For the best defense of the view that *rōʾš* is a place-name, see James D. Price, "Rosh: An Ancient Land Known to Ezekiel," *GTJ* 6 (1985): 67–89.

7. Lind, *Ezekiel,* 315.

tion that had expressed Jerusalem's election in 5:5. This position at the center of God's favor, which Jerusalem had forfeited through her sin, has now been restored to the land.[8]

This description of the state of God's people underlines the motives of the evil alliance. They find no justification for their assault in Israel's behavior. Israel is at rest, trusting in the Lord, not in alliances with foreign nations. In that trust she is prospering, experiencing the blessings of covenant faithfulness. Yet trust in the Lord does not eliminate the possibility of conflict. The ungodly, who dwell in "the far north" (38:6, 15; 39:2),[9] will cast greedy eyes in Israel's direction, encouraged by the traders from east and west (38:13), and will advance against them like an overshadowing cloud (38:9, 16).

But in spite of all his planning and preparation, Gog has fundamentally misread the match-up. It is not a matter, as he supposes, of his vast and well-equipped army ranged against a defenseless nation (38:14–16). Rather, by tangling with Israel Gog is taking on Israel's God; this is "my people" and "my land" that he is assaulting. The relationship between God, his people, and his land has been restored, and such an assault on the Lord's name will not pass unchallenged. Indeed, the only reason for Gog's being permitted to come— or, to put it positively as the text does, the reason for which Gog and his allies are brought against Israel—is so that the Lord may demonstrate his greatness and his holiness in defeating this monstrous alliance (38:16). As in the days of Pharaoh, Gog will serve as an object lesson for the nations of the Lord's power and of his love for his people.

Therefore, the judgment of God falls on Gog in 38:17–22. The question of verse 17, "Are you . . . the one I spoke of in former days by my servants the prophets of Israel?" asks whether Gog is the "foe from the north" depicted in passages such as Jeremiah 4–6. The answer to that question has been variously rendered. The NIV, along with many commentators, clearly presupposes the positive answer: "Yes, you are."[10] However, the form of the Hebrew question is entirely open and can be equally easily answered, "No, you are not!"[11] Had Gog been the prophesied "foe from the north," he would have been coming at the Lord's commissioning to bring judgment on his faithless

---

8. Allen, *Ezekiel 1–19*, 72.

9. Note that this expression too, which can also be translated (lit.) as the "heights of [Mount] Zaphon," is a theological rather than geographical description. It is a description of the mythological cosmic mountain, the home of the gods (Clifford, *Cosmic Mountain*, 148). In Ps. 48:2 and Isa. 14:13 the terminology is taken over and applied to the heavenly residence of the Lord; here, however, it may refer to its original signification as the home of the (pagan) gods.

10. So Zimmerli, *Ezekiel*, 2:288; Allen, *Ezekiel 20–48*, 198. Both delete the interrogative *hē* as due to dittography, following the versions.

11. Block, "Gog in Prophetic Tradition," 170–72.

people. Nothing and no one would have been able to stand against him. But this foe, though geographically from the north, is coming not to bring judgment but to be judged. The prophecies of Jeremiah 4–6 have already found their fulfillment in the coming of the Babylonians; never again will God deal with his people in that way.

Instead, the judgments that earlier fell on his people now fall on their enemies. God's hot anger, zeal, and fiery wrath are all emotions of which Israel has felt the weight in the earlier chapters of Ezekiel. Now these same feelings are turned against Gog (38:18–19). The divine warrior will let loose a mighty earthquake, which will cause all creatures to tremble in his presence (38:19–20). The sword, plague, bloodshed, torrential rain, hail, burning sulfur—judgments, most of which were experienced first by Israel—are now experienced by her enemies (38:21–22). Now God will reveal his power and holiness to the nations not by the destruction of his unholy people but by the protection of his restored people (38:23).

The Disposal of Gog (39:1–29)

IN EZEKIEL 39 the focus shifts from the Lord's emotions to his actions, from the protection of his people to the utter destruction of his enemies. Ezekiel begins by announcing the slaughter of Gog (39:1–8). Like Goliath before him, his seemingly invincible power will be broken and his body left exposed for the birds of the air and the beasts of the field (39:4; cf. 1 Sam. 17:46). The fire of God's wrath will be poured out on his homeland and the homelands of his allies (Ezek. 39:6). The destruction they had planned to wreak on a people living "in safety" will return on their own heads (39:6; cf. 38:8).

Unlike past times when, because of his people's sins, the Lord had allowed his name to be profaned by bringing on them the catastrophe of exile (36:22–23), this time the Lord will act to prevent such profanation by defending his people against all assault. This too will demonstrate the holiness of his name by showing that his power to save is as mighty as his power to judge (39:7). The future salvation is as secure as the past catastrophic judgment: "It is coming! It will surely take place" (39:8; cf. 21:7).

Once God has decisively dealt with Gog as a threat, then for the first time Israel is called to act. She plays no part in winning the victory; she merely carries out the mopping-up operation of spoiling the corpses and disposing of the remains (39:9–16). The Israelites collect six kinds of weapons, which for seven years serve them for fuel (39:9). Ironically, these flammable materials seem to have been the only things not harmed by the descent of God's fiery wrath! Those who came to plunder are now plundered (39:10).

In addition to plundering the fallen, however, Israel will also be active in purifying the land by burying the corpses. The holy land must not be defiled by the ongoing presence of death. The whole house of Israel will be engaged in this burial process (39:12). After that, there will be a further period in which two squads of professional morticians will pass through the land, the first squad tagging human remains for the second squad to inter (39:15), until the whole of Gog's army is safely laid to rest "in the Valley of Hamon [the Horde of] Gog." Although the vocabulary is different, it is tempting to see in this army reduced to a valley of bones through the death-dealing activity of the Lord a reversal of Ezekiel 37, where the Lord's life-giving Spirit turned a valley of dry bones into a living army.

The dramatic, though not the chronological, climax comes in 39:17–20. Here the birds and the beasts are invited to come to join in a kind of gruesome "messianic banquet." But on this occasion, instead of animals being slain to feed the appetites of the human guests from north and south and east and west, here the humans have been slain to feed the animals from all around.[12]

The lesson Israel is to draw from these chapters is explicitly laid out for them in 39:21–29. The Lord is sovereign in history, a sovereignty that is displayed before the nations in two separate movements. (1) In the first, God demonstrated his sovereignty by sending his own people into exile because of their sin and unfaithfulness (39:23). He hid his face from them, and as a result they became easy prey for all their enemies.

(2) But in the days to come a new period in Israel's history is beginning. God's people will return from exile; he will have compassion on them. This change in their fortunes will cause them to "bear their shame" ($w^e n \bar{a} \acute{s} \hat{u}$ $^{\jmath} et$-$k^e limm \bar{a} t \bar{a} m$, 39:26).[13] That is, they will take responsibility for their past actions when they are restored to their land and dwell in safety. Then they will know that it is the Lord their God who sent them into exile, and the Lord their God who returns them from exile (39:28). The tragic events of 586 B.C. will never repeat themselves, for the covenant-keeping God will pour out his Spirit on his people, as he once poured out his wrath on them, and he will never again hide his face from them (39:29).

---

12. Lind, *Ezekiel*, 318.

13. NIV "they will forget their shame" emends the MT to $w^e n \bar{a} \acute{s} \hat{u}$. The translation "they will bear their shame," attested by all the versions and the Qere, assumes that $w^e n \bar{a} \acute{s} \hat{u}$ is a shortened form of $w^e n \bar{a} \acute{s}^{e \jmath} \hat{u}$. The Qal of $n \bar{a} \acute{s} \hat{a}$ is rare and occurs nowhere else in Ezekiel, whereas $n \bar{a} \acute{s} \bar{a}^{\jmath}$ $k^e limm \hat{a}$ is frequent in Ezekiel and occurs in a virtually identical context in 16:54. See Zimmerli, *Ezekiel*, 2:295.

Bridging Contexts

IDENTIFICATIONS THROUGHOUT HISTORY. Perhaps few Old Testament passages have seen so many attempts to interpret them in the light of current events as Ezekiel 38–39. This is hardly a new phe-nomenon. The church father Ambrose, writing in the late fourth century, confidently identified Gog as the Goths.[14] In the seventh century, Gog and Magog were the Arab armies that threatened the Holy Land.[15] By the thir-teenth century, Gog had become a cipher for the Mongol hordes from the East.[16] William Greenhill, writing in the seventeenth century, records the opinion of some contemporaries who identified Gog as the Roman emperor, the Pope, or the Turks.[17] In the nineteenth century, against the background of the tensions in Asia Minor that culminated in the Crimean War, Wilhelm Gesenius identified Rosh as Russia.[18] This view was subsequently popular-ized by the *Scofield Reference Bible*, along with the idea taken from other sources that "Meshech" and "Tubal" are the Russian cities of Moscow and Tobolsk.[19] During the First World War, Arno Gaebelein argued that Gomer was Germany.[20]

More recently, in response to the rise of Communism, these ideas have become the staples of popular dispensational end-times literature, to which has

---

14. Ambrose, *De fide ad Gratianum* 2.16, 138. Taking an alternative view, Augustine already protested against such a specific identification of Gog and his allies with particular histor-ical nations in *The City of God* 20.11.

15. Robert L. Wilken, *The Land Called Holy: Palestine in Christian History and Thought* (New Haven: Yale Univ. Press, 1992), 244–45.

16. Bernard McGinn, *Visions of the End: Apocalyptic Traditions in the Middle Ages* (New York: Columbia Univ. Press, 1979), 151.

17. *Ezekiel*, 754.

18. *Hebrew and Chaldee Lexicon*, trans. S. P. Tregelles (Grand Rapids: Eerdmans, 1949; reprint of 1857). The Crimean War was fought between 1853 and 1856 as France and Britain sought to prevent Russian expansionism southeast into Turkey.

19. *Scofield Reference Bible* (New York: Oxford Univ., 1909). The view that Rosh is Russia is maintained in *The New Scofield Reference Bible* (New York: Oxford Univ., 1967), though Moscow and Tobolsk are no longer mentioned.

20. *The Prophet Ezekiel*, 2d ed. (Neptune, N.J.: Loizeaux Brothers, 1972; reprint of 1918), 259.

21. Hal Lindsey's book *The Late Great Planet Earth* (Grand Rapids: Zondervan, 1970) includes chapters entitled "Russia Is a Gog" and "The Yellow Peril." Substantially similar sce-narios are depicted in Harry Ironside, *Ezekiel the Prophet* (Neptune, N.J.: Loizeaux Brothers, 1949), 266–67; David Egner, *The Bear Goes South* (Grand Rapids: Radio Bible Class, 1979); and Clarence E. Mason Jr., "Gog and Magog, Who and When?" *Prophecy and the Seventies* (Chicago: Moody, 1971), 221–32. It should, however, be pointed out that not all dispen-sationalists have accepted the identification of Rosh with Russia; see, for example, Ralph H. Alexander, "A Fresh Look at Ezekiel 38 and 39," *JETS* 17 (1974): 157–69; Charles L. Fein-berg, *The Prophecy of Ezekiel* (Chicago: Moody, 1969), 220.

in some cases been added the contemporary threat of the Red Chinese, usually identified as "the kings from the East" in Revelation 16:12.[21] With its vivid imagery and pictorial language, apocalyptic (or more precisely, proto-apocalyptic) literature such as Ezekiel 38–39 lends itself to a flexible application to whatever the contemporary dangers to world peace are perceived to be. In a world of much tribulation, there will always be a plausible explanation of why these times in particular fit the description of the biblical "end times."

There are numerous factual flaws in these identifications. In the first place, the earliest attestation of the name "Rus" (Russia) dates back to the mid-ninth century A.D. and is thought to have been brought to the area around Kiev by the Vikings.[22] It is etymologically unrelated to the Hebrew term, and modern lexicons have universally rejected Gesenius's claim.[23] Nor can Meshech and Tubal be linked with Moscow and Tobolsk. Rather, they are to be linked with the *Mushku* and *Tabal* peoples of central and eastern Anatolia, who are well known in cuneiform texts from the first half of the first millennium B.C.[24]

Gomer is similarly known to us from cuneiform texts as the warlike *gimir-rai* (known from Greek sources as "Cimmerians"). This people apparently originated in the Crimea, but were pushed southward across the Caucasus by the Scythians at the end of the eighth century B.C.[25] Though the Babylonian Talmud does identify Gomer as the area of "Germania" (or "Kermania"),[26] the Targum Neofiti on Genesis 10:2 rather identifies Germania as the district of Magog! In addition, although Gomer may etymologically be related equally well to the Welsh (*cymri*) as to the proto-Germanic tribes,[27] yet one may observe that the Welsh have not typically played a significant role in the descriptions of the last days.

However, even if correct identifications were to be made on the basis of sound linguistic and archaeological data, attempts to isolate particular nations as "Israel's last enemies" fly in the face of what the text is saying. The point of

---

22. Edwin M. Yamauchi, *Foes From the Northern Frontier: Invading Hordes From the Russian Steppes* (Grand Rapids: Baker, 1982), 20.

23. BDB, 912c recognizes both possible translations of *rō'š*, as a title or a country, but says of the latter "not identified"; this change is already evident in the 1906 edition. Ludwig Koehler and Walter Baumgartner, *Lexicon in Veteris Testamenti libros*, 2d ed. (Leiden: Brill, 1958), 866a, list it as "unknown." Lindsey also cites C. F. Keil as a supporter of the view that Rosh is Russia (*Late Great Planet*, 65); however, though Keil does read *rō'š* as a place-name, he describes the attempt to link it with Russia as "a doubtful conjecture" (*Ezekiel*, 2:160).

24. Edwin Yamauchi, "Meshech, Tubal, and Company: A Review Article," *JETS* 19 (1976): 243–45.

25. Yamauchi, *Foes From the Northern Frontier*, 51.

26. *b. Yoma* 10a.

27. Ephraim A. Speiser, *Genesis* (AB; Garden City, N.Y.: Doubleday, 1962), 66.

Ezekiel 38–39 is not that at some distant point in future history these *particular* nations will oppose Israel, while others (America? Britain?) will rally to her aid. Rather, these seven nations from the ends of the earth, from all four points of the compass, represent symbolically a supreme attempt by the united forces of evil to crush the peace of God's people. This, not coincidentally, is the interpretation given to "Gog and Magog" in Revelation 20:8: They represent "the nations in the four corners of the earth," whom Satan gathers for the final battle against God's people, the city he loves.[28] Their defeat in Revelation is the prerequisite for the establishment of the new Jerusalem, the heavenly city of Revelation 21, which itself has many points of contact with Ezekiel's visionary temple in Ezekiel 40–48.

Ezekiel 38–39 in biblical context. The key to understanding what Ezekiel 38–39 are about—both for its original hearers and for us—lies in recognizing whereabouts in the book of Ezekiel we are at this point. The first twenty-four chapters of Ezekiel, after a brief record of the initial call of the prophet, prophesy an unmitigated pronouncement of judgment on God's people and city. Jerusalem and her inhabitants are finished because of their idolatry and other sins. The Lord has abandoned his people, and it is only a matter of time before they experience the full outpouring of his wrath through the Babylonians.

Ezekiel 25–32 then gives a series of oracles against the foreign nations, pronouncing judgment on those who participated or delighted in Israel's downfall. The presence of these oracles affirms that God has not turned his back on his people utterly. He has not switched sides and gone over to her enemies. The promise to Abraham given in Genesis 12:3, that "I will bless those who bless you, and whoever curses you I will curse," is still in effect— at least, the second half of the promise.

Then Ezekiel 33 records the turning point in the fortunes of God's people when the news of Jerusalem's fall comes to the prophet. Now God's wrath has been satisfied and there is a prospect of a new beginning. That new beginning is outlined in terms of a restoration of the leadership of the people (the shepherds, ch. 34), the land itself (35:1–36:15), and the people who indwell the land (chs. 36–37), culminating in the glorious statements of 37:24–28:

> My servant David will be king over them, and they will all have one shepherd. They will follow my laws and be careful to keep my decrees. They will live in the land I gave to my servant Jacob, the land where your fathers lived. They and their children and their children's children will live there forever, and David my servant will be their prince forever. I will make a covenant of peace with them; it will be an ever-

---

28. Ellison, *Ezekiel*, 134.

lasting covenant. I will establish them and increase their numbers, and I will put my sanctuary among them forever. My dwelling place will be with them; I will be their God, and they will be my people. Then the nations will know that I the LORD make Israel holy, when my sanctuary is among them forever.

But there is a potential problem at this point. Perhaps Israel can be restored and returned to her own land. But what happens then? What is to say that the whole weary cycle of sin and judgment in the shape of an invading army will not begin all over again, as in the days of the book of Judges? It is this question that Ezekiel 38–39 seeks to answer. The purpose of the oracle against Gog becomes clear in 39:21–29; it is intended as a word of reassurance to Israel that the new order of existence promised in chapters 34–37 is not reversible. God will never again turn his face away from his people (39:29). Though trials of all kinds, even the worst imaginable kind, may and will come, they will do so only under God's good and sovereign hand.

The symbolism in Ezekiel 38–39. In fact, even identifying Ezekiel 38–39 as "proto-apocalyptic" may be leading us down the wrong interpretative path. For though these two chapters share a number of features with later apocalyptic, such as symbolism and a schematic view of history, they also have a great deal in common with nonapocalyptic writings. It is especially close thematically to the psalms of Zion's security, where the nations gather together against Jerusalem, only to be repulsed by the Lord (Ps. 2; 46; 48; 76).[29]

The common motif of the attack by the nations against the Lord's dwelling place, the center of the earth, has been transferred by the prophet from Jerusalem itself to the mountains of Israel. This fits with his avoidance of the name of Jerusalem in his prophecies of restoration: Even the city of Ezekiel 48 bears a different name, while the mountains of Israel are for Ezekiel the heart of the Promised Land. The timeless present of the psalm has been transposed to the indefinite future of "after many days" (38:8), but the essential message of the psalmist remains unchanged. The conclusion of Psalm 46 sums up Ezekiel 38–39 equally well:

> Come and see the works of the LORD,
> > the desolations he has brought on the earth.
> He makes wars cease to the ends of the earth;
> > he breaks the bow and shatters the spear,
> > he burns the shields with fire.
> "Be still, and know that I am God;
> > I will be exalted among the nations,

---

29. Stephen L. Cook, *Prophecy and Apocalypticism: The Postexilic Social Setting* (Minneapolis: Fortress, 1995), 88–96.

> I will be exalted in the earth."
> The LORD Almighty is with us;
> the God of Jacob is our fortress. (Ps. 46:8–11)

The significance in this correlation lies in the fact that the "last battle," as depicted in Ezekiel 38–39, is not *qualitatively* different from the everyday battles that face us. The "mother of all battles" differs only in terms of size from the ongoing battles that we as believers face from day to day, not in terms of kind. Just as "the Antichrist" is merely the last and greatest in a constant stream of "antichrists" (1 John 2:18), so also Gog and his foul friends who seek to destroy the restored Israel are simply the ultimate expression of a continual struggle in which Satan seeks to destroy the people of God (cf. Rev. 12:17).

Therefore, the message of Ezekiel 38–39 is not a coded message for those who live in "the last days,"[30] who by carefully unlocking its secrets will be able to determine the symbolic identity of the key participants in the final struggle. Rather, it is a word of encouragement to all the saints of all times and places that no matter what the forces of evil may do, God's purpose and victory stands secure. If God can defeat the combined forces of Gog and his allies and turn them into fodder for the crows and carrion-eaters, how much more can he take care of us, whatever historical manifestation of the enmity of Satan we face.

The ultimate problem with the approach to the Bible that reads Ezekiel 38–39 alongside the morning newspaper in an attempt to correlate the events described in the two documents is that it assumes that unless we are living in the end times, these passages have nothing to say to us. In fact, whether or not these happen to be the final days of God's plan for the world, Ezekiel 38–39 addresses believers with a powerful message of hope. As we noted at the outset of this section, it functions in a thematically similar way to the empty tomb in the New Testament: It is God's ultimate demonstration of power and care for his people in the face of the worst possible scenario. In the light of the resurrection of Christ, why should we fear the more everyday challenges that life throws at us? Even death cannot separate us from such love.

---

30. This phrase is perhaps significantly absent from Ezekiel 38–39. The more general "after many days" (38:8) and "in that day" (38:18; cf. 39:11) do not carry the same eschatological weight (Block, *Ezekiel 25–48*, 428).

CONTEMPORARY DOOMSDAY SCENARIOS. As we approach the end of the second millennium A.D., secular "apocalypses" abound. In our time, we see growing numbers of doomsday scenarios propounded, based around environmental or other perceived hazards to the future of life on planet earth. We worry about global warming and El Niño, about asteroids colliding with the earth, or about political instability in the Balkans, the Middle East, and the former Soviet Union. We fear the possibility of a holocaust created by nuclear or bacteriological warfare. As a reflex of our fears, we dream up cataclysmic adventures on the big screen, in which world peace and "life as we know it" is dramatically threatened, and then against all odds finally saved.[31]

This theme is treated in classic form in the movies *The Terminator* and its sequel *Terminator 2: Judgment Day*.[32] In these popular films, Skynet, a computerized defense system in the "Star Wars" mold, reaches self-awareness and in response to attempts by humans to power it down, triggers a nuclear holocaust. Human resistance against the autonomous machines is led by the feisty messianic figure, John Connor (whose initials are hardly coincidental).[33] In an effort at a preemptive strike, the Skynet sends a mechanical assassin, one of the seemingly all-powerful terminators, back from the future to terminate his mother's life before his birth. Having failed with its initial attempt, in the sequel the system makes a second attempt on John Connor's life when he is a young adolescent.

Such popular apocalyptic scenarios have been around for a while. Over a century ago, in *The War of the Worlds*, H. G. Wells painted a chilling picture of an invasion of a hostile superior life-form from Mars, against which all human military technology was powerless, instantly vaporized by their "heat

---

31. These are not true "apocalypses," however, since many key features are missing. Particularly striking is the fact that in almost all of these Hollywood scenarios the desired goal of the intervention by the [human] savior figure is not the radical transformation of our existence but simply the preservation of the American way of life. Thus in the recent movies *Armageddon* and *Deep Impact*, the savior figures sacrifice themselves in destroying the asteroids that threaten the earth simply to enable life to carry on much as before, symbolized in the latter film by the reconstruction of the Capitol building in Washington, D.C.

32. "The issues raised by the *Terminator* movies are the issues explored by Isaiah, Jeremiah and Ezekiel. How is humankind to avoid extinction... ?" (Gaye Ortiz and Maggie Roux, "The *Terminator* Movies: Hi-Tech Holiness and the Human Condition," in *Explorations in Theology and Film*, ed. Clive Marsh and Gaye Ortiz [Oxford: Blackwell, 1997], 142).

33. In addition to the initials of Connor's name, calling his mother "Sarah" evokes the Old Testament mother of the promised child, further inviting us to explore the religious dimensions of the film.

ray." This life-form fed on human blood and began a program of world domination, which would inevitably (it appeared) mean the end of any recognizable human civilization. Only the intervention of common bacteria, against which the advanced Martians had long ceased to require immunity, prevented the total massacre of the human race.

Wells was ahead of his time, out of step with the general optimism of the Victorian and Edwardian eras. Probably the first significant chink in the armor of a near-universal hope of invincible human progress occurred on April 15, 1912 with the sinking of the *Titanic*. With its descent into the icy depths of the North Atlantic, it took the lives of 1,513 people and created a fault line in the belief of unstoppable progress. The First World War and the depression that followed crushed forever the naive optimism of the previous generation. Together, those events brought us into the era in which we now live, which W. H. Auden dubbed the "Age of Anxiety."[34] Since then, we have lived in the shadow of the end of the world.

Of course, as we noted above, we are by no means the first generation to have this experience. In the fifth century, when the Goths sacked Rome, those who lived through the event felt as if it was the end of the world. Similar threats to "life as we know it" in medieval Europe came from the Moors in the early Middle Ages and the Mongols in the late Middle Ages, and marked out those time periods also as ones of great anxiety. Throughout the course of human history the end of the world has been regularly threatened and has occasionally happened. To date, life goes on.

Living in the shadow of the end of the world. It is the habit of those who live in the shadow of the end of the world, or whose world seems to be ending, to tell themselves stories. These stories, in general, focus on how the end of the world is to be avoided. In *The War of the Worlds*, the final cataclysm is averted unexpectedly, almost accidentally (from a human perspective), through the protective forces of Nature, represented by the all-powerful microbes. In contrast, in the *Terminator* movies human ingenuity and determination triumph over brute strength, and thus humanity is saved.

Christians naturally, and rightly, respond to the general atmosphere of end-of-the-world anxieties by turning from the world's stories to God's stories. At times like this, many turn to the apocalyptic literature of the Scriptures, such as Ezekiel 38–39 or the books of Daniel and Revelation, seeking an infallible word from the Lord. But what do you do with these stories? Many contemporary Christians treat these passages as checklists on the road to Armageddon, providing a countdown on the road to the end of the world.

---

34. See Ulrich H. J. Körtner, *The End of the World*, trans. D. W. Stott (Louisville: Westminster/John Knox, 1995), 1.

However, as we have shown above, this is not how the passage was intended to be read. Rather, it is a dramatic statement of the central truth that no matter what the forces of evil may throw at God's people, in the final analysis God's purpose and victory stand secure. For all Gog's bravado, ultimately it is God who says, "Go ahead; make my day!"

Do you see how comforting this truth is for all of us? Christians have, historically, suffered a great deal for their faith. From the time of Nero, when Christians were dipped in pitch and set alight to illumine the emperor's pleasure gardens, down to the present day, when believers continue to be tortured and killed for their faith in Sudan and elsewhere, the spiritual forces of opposition are real. Often those forces are institutional rather than individual, an organized and orchestrated attempt to destroy the church. For those enduring such times of persecution, Ezekiel 38–39 provides a powerful message of hope.

(1) Although this world is a place of tribulation, God is in control. Gog has his own evil reasons for acting (38:10), but even his wickedly motivated plans can achieve nothing other than what God purposes (38:4). Gog comes intent on plunder, but he does so only because God's plan and purpose is to bring him. Gog's free will is the free will of a shackled lion. If you offer a lion a choice between a fresh green salad and a juicy piece of raw meat, he will choose the latter every time, without compulsion; it is his nature to eat raw meat. But the shackled lion only gets to eat raw meat when his keeper chooses to allow him to.

This is a perspective on persecution and martyrdom that we are not used to thinking about. We tend to assume that martyrdom is an unfortunate but necessary by-product of human free will, a sad fact of life in some parts of the world, but a sign that the world is out of order. Our problem is that we live in a dangerous world populated by lions roaming on the loose, so we tend to think. Not so. The Bible tells us that the lions are real, but they are shackled, or rather, to change the image slightly, they are leashed. They can assault Christians only whenever and wherever God allows them to exercise their natural appetites. What this means is that martyrdom is not merely an occasional abnormality in the church's existence with evangelistic possibilities; it is, at times, nothing less than the will of God for his church.

In other words, God himself may bring tribulation on his people, just as he brings Gog. The reason for that apparently strange fact is that the blood of the martyrs is not merely the seed of the church, but is a sign of the kingdom. It is not merely by our love that the world will know that Christians are Christ's disciples, but by our blood. The disciples are not greater than their master, who was brutally beaten and savagely murdered on a cruel cross. Jesus himself said:

If anyone would come after me, he must deny himself and take up his cross and follow me. For whoever wants to save his life will lose it, but whoever loses his life for me and for the gospel will save it. (Mark 8:34–35)

Jesus was not exaggerating or using hyperbole here. He meant exactly what he said. Martyrdom is a central part of God's strategy for bringing glory to himself through the church.

Thus, in Revelation 6:10, the martyrs under the altar cry out, "How long, Sovereign Lord, holy and true, until you judge the inhabitants of the earth and avenge our blood?" You might expect that the answer given to their question would be: "Until the salvation of the full number of the elect. There must be more time for the evangelization of the world." Indeed, that is not a wrong answer; as Peter says concerning the Second Coming, "The Lord is not slow in keeping his promise, as some understand slowness. He is patient with you, not wanting anyone to perish, but everyone to come to repentance" (2 Peter 3:9). But this is not the answer given to the martyred saints: They are told to wait until the full number of *martyrs* have been killed.

Our view of the world is turned on its head. Our automatic assumption is that God's will for us is peace and prosperity, at least if we are being good Christians, and that the obedient church should grow and prosper just like any well-run business. But we are wrong. God loves you and has a wonderful plan for your life ... but that wonderful plan might mean torture and death for the faith, or simply a life that seems, from the world's perspective, "wasted" ("lost," in Jesus' terms). Ezekiel 38–39 reminds us that even the restored, renewed people of God can expect tribulation, not because the world is out of control but precisely because the world is in God's control; for when God's people cling to him in their darkest hour, against all odds, it brings him glory. God's glory is the primary goal of history, not our happiness and comfort.

This focus requires us always to lift our eyes above the human plane of activity to the divine. When we stay on the human level in our consideration of our sufferings and the sufferings of others, we end up like Job's friends, searching for some hidden reason within us for the suffering. Philip Yancey lists some of the reasons people come up with:

- God is trying to teach you something. You should feel privileged, not bitter, about your opportunity to lean on him in faith.
- Meditate on the blessings you still enjoy—at least you are still alive. Are you a fair-weather believer?

---

35. *Disappointment With God* (Grand Rapids: Zondervan, 1988), 181.

- You are under-going a training regimen, a chance to exercise new muscles of faith. Don't worry—God will not test you beyond your endurance.
- Don't complain so loudly! You will forfeit this opportunity to demonstrate your faithfulness to unbelievers.
- Someone is always worse off than you. Give thanks despite your circumstances.[35]

The problem is that each of these approaches seeks to find some good that the suffering will accomplish within us or within our circle of friends and acquaintances. In the providence of God, that may be the case. But it may not. We are also the players in a cosmic drama acted out before the heavenly hosts. In that play, "every act of faith by every one of the people of God is like the tolling of a bell, and a faith like Job's reverberates throughout the universe."[36] God himself may bring tribulation into our life to bring himself glory through our obedient submission, following in the footsteps of our Master.

(2) God is going to win. This may seem a simple, even simplistic, point, but it is central to the thrust of the Gog narrative. No matter how big the opposition, how well organized they are, how powerful their weaponry, or how paltry the resources of God's people, ultimately the plans of God's enemies will come to nothing. As in Psalm 2, the nations may conspire together and the kings of the earth take a stand against God, but all their posturing causes mirth rather than worry in the heart of the Most High. Ultimately, no matter what Satan throws against the church, the full number of the elect from the north and south and east and west will be brought in and will sit down together at God's table to share in the heavenly feast.

(3) God's victory means the ultimate destruction of all those who oppose him. Gog and his army end up as a massive array of corpses, scattered on the face of the earth. Their weaponry is useless against God's cosmic arsenal of fire and earthquake, hailstones and burning sulfur (38:19–22). Those who came to plunder will end up themselves plundered. Once again adopting the language of Psalm 2, Gog will be terrified in God's wrath, dashed in pieces like pottery, and destroyed along the way. It is foolishness to oppose God, and all who do so will come to a sticky end. Those who turn away from God and refuse the sacrifice of Christ have nothing to expect except certain judgment and the raging fire that will consume the enemies of God (Heb.

---

36. Ibid., 174.

37. Joni Eareckson Tada, "A Stone Cold Fact," *Moody Monthly* 98 (May/June 1998): 71. See also John Kramp, "Spiritual Search and Rescue: The Effort We Make Reflects Our Sense of Urgency," *Moody Monthly* 97 (May/June 1997): 18–19.

10:27). We need to take seriously his admonition: "It is a dreadful thing to fall into the hands of the living God" (10:31).

Do we fathom the significance of this reality for our neighbors, coworkers, and relatives who do not know Christ? In her article "A Stone Cold Fact," Joni Eareckson Tada presses us to see in concrete terms what this means:

> Lord, do you mean my third-grade teacher? The women who run the day-care center where I take my child? My mailman? My housekeeper? The lady who teaches the quilting class down the street? The bank teller who's always telling me jokes? If these people don't know Jesus, they won't "rise to live."[37]

(4) God's victory means the ultimate security of those who trust in him. In Ezekiel 38–39, Israel does not have to lift a finger in her own defense. Those who take refuge in the Lord find blessing and security (Ps. 2:12); God is their refuge and strength, an ever present help in time of trouble (46:1). The certainty of God's victory should be a source of confidence for the believer as he or she faces an uncertain world: You are God's special property and he knows how to take care of his own. You are the apple of his eye, as Zechariah 2 expresses it. As the apostle Paul put it: "If God is for us, who can be against us? He who did not spare his own Son, but gave him up for us all—how will he not also, along with him, graciously give us all things?" (Rom. 8:31–32). Your confidence rests in this: that Almighty God has committed himself to those who trust in him and he will never give them up. Paul reminds us in another place: "I know whom I have believed, and am convinced that he is able guard what I have entrusted to him for that day" (2 Tim. 1:12). The God who will defeat the evil empire of Gog can take care of you also.

The central point. This last point is, it seems to me, the central thrust of Ezekiel 38–39, as the final verses of chapter 39 make clear. Why was Ezekiel 38–39 good news for Ezekiel's original audience? Because it made clear the fact that the events of 586 B.C. could never be repeated. Israel had once because of her sin so polluted the land that it had become totally unfit for divine habitation (39:23). But when God reverses that situation and regathers his people, he will pour out his Spirit in the same measure as he once poured out his wrath (39:29). This will bring about a radical change in the hearts of his people and in the security of his presence with them, such that he will never again hide his face from them. Though tribulations, such as the assault by Gog, will continue, they will no longer be marks of God's wrath but opportunities for God to uncover his power to the world.

Why is Ezekiel 38–39 good news for us? It is because this is precisely the relationship with God in which we, as Christians, stand. Once we too were objects of God's wrath because of our sins (Eph. 2:2–3). Our hearts were too polluted to receive his presence. But now, because of the work of Christ on the cross, we too have been gathered into God's people. We are no longer under condemnation, but have received the Spirit, by whom we have been adopted into God's family. Therefore, we have the settled assurance that God will never leave us nor forsake us (Heb. 13:5–6). Troubles may and will come. No matter where we are on God's "prophetic timetable," that reality remains unchanged. But to us as Christians, troubles come now not as visitations of God's wrath on us but as opportunities for God to uncover his power to the world.

There are two ways in which God may uncover his power to the world in our situation of distress. (1) That power may be uncovered by means of a remarkable deliverance, whereby we are rescued from the midst of our trials, as when Daniel was kept safe in the lions' den or Peter was set free from prison. In that case, we will have the testimony that will launch a thousand books.

(2) But that is not the only way in which God reveals his existence and power in the world. In other cases, God's power may be uncovered by enabling us to withstand tribulation firmly until the end, as when Stephen was given a vision of the ascended Jesus to strengthen him as the murderous stones pounded his body. Either way—whether we are delivered from our trials or endure suffering to the end for the sake of King Jesus—we find out for ourselves and demonstrate to the world and to the cosmic hosts the truth of the Lord's statement: "My grace is sufficient for you, for my power is made perfect in weakness" (2 Cor. 12:9).

Ezekiel 40-42

‎❧

IN THE TWENTY-FIFTH YEAR of our exile, at the beginning of the year, on the tenth of the month, in the fourteenth year after the fall of the city—on that very day the hand of the LORD was upon me and he took me there. ²In visions of God he took me to the land of Israel and set me on a very high mountain, on whose south side were some buildings that looked like a city. ³He took me there, and I saw a man whose appearance was like bronze; he was standing in the gateway with a linen cord and a measuring rod in his hand. ⁴The man said to me, "Son of man, look with your eyes and hear with your ears and pay attention to everything I am going to show you, for that is why you have been brought here. Tell the house of Israel everything you see."

⁵I saw a wall completely surrounding the temple area. The length of the measuring rod in the man's hand was six long cubits, each of which was a cubit and a handbreadth. He measured the wall; it was one measuring rod thick and one rod high.

⁶Then he went to the gate facing east. He climbed its steps and measured the threshold of the gate; it was one rod deep. ⁷The alcoves for the guards were one rod long and one rod wide, and the projecting walls between the alcoves were five cubits thick. And the threshold of the gate next to the portico facing the temple was one rod deep.

⁸Then he measured the portico of the gateway; ⁹it was eight cubits deep and its jambs were two cubits thick. The portico of the gateway faced the temple.

¹⁰Inside the east gate were three alcoves on each side; the three had the same measurements, and the faces of the projecting walls on each side had the same measurements. ¹¹Then he measured the width of the entrance to the gateway; it was ten cubits and its length was thirteen cubits. ¹²In front of each alcove was a wall one cubit high, and the alcoves were six cubits square. ¹³Then he measured the gateway from the top of the rear wall of one alcove to the top of the opposite one; the distance was twenty-five cubits from one parapet opening to the opposite one. ¹⁴He measured along the faces of the

projecting walls all around the inside of the gateway—sixty cubits. The measurement was up to the portico facing the courtyard. ¹⁵The distance from the entrance of the gateway to the far end of its portico was fifty cubits. ¹⁶The alcoves and the projecting walls inside the gateway were surmounted by narrow parapet openings all around, as was the portico; the openings all around faced inward. The faces of the projecting walls were decorated with palm trees.

¹⁷Then he brought me into the outer court. There I saw some rooms and a pavement that had been constructed all around the court; there were thirty rooms along the pavement. ¹⁸It abutted the sides of the gateways and was as wide as they were long; this was the lower pavement. ¹⁹Then he measured the distance from the inside of the lower gateway to the outside of the inner court; it was a hundred cubits on the east side as well as on the north.

²⁰Then he measured the length and width of the gate facing north, leading into the outer court. ²¹ Its alcoves—three on each side—its projecting walls and its portico had the same measurements as those of the first gateway. It was fifty cubits long and twenty-five cubits wide. ²²Its openings, its portico and its palm tree decorations had the same measurements as those of the gate facing east. Seven steps led up to it, with its portico opposite them. ²³There was a gate to the inner court facing the north gate, just as there was on the east. He measured from one gate to the opposite one; it was a hundred cubits.

²⁴Then he led me to the south side and I saw a gate facing south. He measured its jambs and its portico, and they had the same measurements as the others. ²⁵The gateway and its portico had narrow openings all around, like the openings of the others. It was fifty cubits long and twenty-five cubits wide. ²⁶Seven steps led up to it, with its portico opposite them; it had palm tree decorations on the faces of the projecting walls on each side. ²⁷The inner court also had a gate facing south, and he measured from this gate to the outer gate on the south side; it was a hundred cubits.

²⁸Then he brought me into the inner court through the south gate, and he measured the south gate; it had the same measurements as the others. ²⁹Its alcoves, its projecting walls and its portico had the same measurements as the others.

The gateway and its portico had openings all around. It was fifty cubits long and twenty-five cubits wide. ³⁰(The porticoes of the gateways around the inner court were twenty-five cubits wide and five cubits deep.) ³¹Its portico faced the outer court; palm trees decorated its jambs, and eight steps led up to it.

³²Then he brought me to the inner court on the east side, and he measured the gateway; it had the same measurements as the others. ³³Its alcoves, its projecting walls and its portico had the same measurements as the others. The gateway and its portico had openings all around. It was fifty cubits long and twenty-five cubits wide. ³⁴Its portico faced the outer court; palm trees decorated the jambs on either side, and eight steps led up to it.

³⁵Then he brought me to the north gate and measured it. It had the same measurements as the others, ³⁶as did its alcoves, its projecting walls and its portico, and it had openings all around. It was fifty cubits long and twenty-five cubits wide. ³⁷Its portico faced the outer court; palm trees decorated the jambs on either side, and eight steps led up to it.

³⁸A room with a doorway was by the portico in each of the inner gateways, where the burnt offerings were washed. ³⁹In the portico of the gateway were two tables on each side, on which the burnt offerings, sin offerings and guilt offerings were slaughtered. ⁴⁰By the outside wall of the portico of the gateway, near the steps at the entrance to the north gateway were two tables, and on the other side of the steps were two tables. ⁴¹So there were four tables on one side of the gateway and four on the other—eight tables in all—on which the sacrifices were slaughtered. ⁴² There were also four tables of dressed stone for the burnt offerings, each a cubit and a half long, a cubit and a half wide and a cubit high. On them were placed the utensils for slaughtering the burnt offerings and the other sacrifices. ⁴³And double-pronged hooks, each a handbreadth long, were attached to the wall all around. The tables were for the flesh of the offerings.

⁴⁴Outside the inner gate, within the inner court, were two rooms, one at the side of the north gate and facing south, and another at the side of the south gate and facing north. ⁴⁵He said to me, "The room facing south is for the priests who have charge of the temple, ⁴⁶and the room facing north is for the

priests who have charge of the altar. These are the sons of Zadok, who are the only Levites who may draw near to the LORD to minister before him."

⁴⁷Then he measured the court: It was square—a hundred cubits long and a hundred cubits wide. And the altar was in front of the temple.

⁴⁸He brought me to the portico of the temple and measured the jambs of the portico; they were five cubits wide on either side. The width of the entrance was fourteen cubits and its projecting walls were three cubits wide on either side. ⁴⁹The portico was twenty cubits wide, and twelve cubits from front to back. It was reached by a flight of stairs, and there were pillars on each side of the jambs.

⁴¹:¹Then the man brought me to the outer sanctuary and measured the jambs; the width of the jambs was six cubits on each side. ²The entrance was ten cubits wide, and the projecting walls on each side of it were five cubits wide. He also measured the outer sanctuary; it was forty cubits long and twenty cubits wide.

³Then he went into the inner sanctuary and measured the jambs of the entrance; each was two cubits wide. The entrance was six cubits wide, and the projecting walls on each side of it were seven cubits wide. ⁴And he measured the length of the inner sanctuary; it was twenty cubits, and its width was twenty cubits across the end of the outer sanctuary. He said to me, "This is the Most Holy Place."

⁵Then he measured the wall of the temple; it was six cubits thick, and each side room around the temple was four cubits wide. ⁶The side rooms were on three levels, one above another, thirty on each level. There were ledges all around the wall of the temple to serve as supports for the side rooms, so that the supports were not inserted into the wall of the temple. ⁷The side rooms all around the temple were wider at each successive level. The structure surrounding the temple was built in ascending stages, so that the rooms widened as one went upward. A stairway went up from the lowest floor to the top floor through the middle floor.

⁸I saw that the temple had a raised base all around it, forming the foundation of the side rooms. It was the length of the rod, six long cubits. ⁹The outer wall of the side rooms was five cubits thick. The open area between the side rooms of the

temple [10]and the priests' rooms was twenty cubits wide all around the temple. [11] There were entrances to the side rooms from the open area, one on the north and another on the south; and the base adjoining the open area was five cubits wide all around.

[12]The building facing the temple courtyard on the west side was seventy cubits wide. The wall of the building was five cubits thick all around, and its length was ninety cubits.

[13]Then he measured the temple; it was a hundred cubits long, and the temple courtyard and the building with its walls were also a hundred cubits long. [14]The width of the temple courtyard on the east, including the front of the temple, was a hundred cubits.

[15]Then he measured the length of the building facing the courtyard at the rear of the temple, including its galleries on each side; it was a hundred cubits.

The outer sanctuary, the inner sanctuary and the portico facing the court, [16]as well as the thresholds and the narrow windows and galleries around the three of them—everything beyond and including the threshold was covered with wood. The floor, the wall up to the windows, and the windows were covered. [17]In the space above the outside of the entrance to the inner sanctuary and on the walls at regular intervals all around the inner and outer sanctuary [18]were carved cherubim and palm trees. Palm trees alternated with cherubim. Each cherub had two faces: [19]the face of a man toward the palm tree on one side and the face of a lion toward the palm tree on the other. They were carved all around the whole temple. [20]From the floor to the area above the entrance, cherubim and palm trees were carved on the wall of the outer sanctuary.

[21]The outer sanctuary had a rectangular doorframe, and the one at the front of the Most Holy Place was similar. [22]There was a wooden altar three cubits high and two cubits square; its corners, its base and its sides were of wood. The man said to me, "This is the table that is before the LORD." [23]Both the outer sanctuary and the Most Holy Place had double doors. [24]Each door had two leaves—two hinged leaves for each door. [25]And on the doors of the outer sanctuary were carved cherubim and palm trees like those carved on the walls, and there was a wooden overhang on the front of the portico. [26]On the sidewalls

of the portico were narrow windows with palm trees carved on each side. The side rooms of the temple also had overhangs.

⁴²:¹Then the man led me northward into the outer court and brought me to the rooms opposite the temple courtyard and opposite the outer wall on the north side. ²The building whose door faced north was a hundred cubits long and fifty cubits wide. ³Both in the section twenty cubits from the inner court and in the section opposite the pavement of the outer court, gallery faced gallery at the three levels. ⁴In front of the rooms was an inner passageway ten cubits wide and a hundred cubits long. Their doors were on the north. ⁵Now the upper rooms were narrower, for the galleries took more space from them than from the rooms on the lower and middle floors of the building. ⁶The rooms on the third floor had no pillars, as the courts had; so they were smaller in floor space than those on the lower and middle floors. ⁷There was an outer wall parallel to the rooms and the outer court; it extended in front of the rooms for fifty cubits. ⁸While the row of rooms on the side next to the outer court was fifty cubits long, the row on the side nearest the sanctuary was a hundred cubits long. ⁹The lower rooms had an entrance on the east side as one enters them from the outer court.

¹⁰On the south side along the length of the wall of the outer court, adjoining the temple courtyard and opposite the outer wall, were rooms ¹¹with a passageway in front of them. These were like the rooms on the north; they had the same length and width, with similar exits and dimensions. Similar to the doorways on the north ¹²were the doorways of the rooms on the south. There was a doorway at the beginning of the passageway that was parallel to the corresponding wall extending eastward, by which one enters the rooms.

¹³Then he said to me, "The north and south rooms facing the temple courtyard are the priests' rooms, where the priests who approach the LORD will eat the most holy offerings. There they will put the most holy offerings—the grain offerings, the sin offerings and the guilt offerings—for the place is holy. ¹⁴Once the priests enter the holy precincts, they are not to go into the outer court until they leave behind the garments in which they minister, for these are holy. They are to put on other clothes before they go near the places that are for the people."

¹⁵When he had finished measuring what was inside the temple area, he led me out by the east gate and measured the area all around: ¹⁶He measured the east side with the measuring rod; it was five hundred cubits. ¹⁷He measured the north side; it was five hundred cubits by the measuring rod. ¹⁸He measured the south side; it was five hundred cubits by the measuring rod. ¹⁹Then he turned to the west side and measured; it was five hundred cubits by the measuring rod. ²⁰So he measured the area on all four sides. It had a wall around it, five hundred cubits long and five hundred cubits wide, to separate the holy from the common.

IT IS CUSTOMARY for commentators, evangelical and critical alike, to apologize for Ezekiel 40–48. After the heady excitement of the re-creation of Israel in Ezekiel 37 and the apocalyptic battle of Ezekiel 38–39, worthy of the climax to an action-thriller movie of the *Die Hard* genre, the description of the dimensions of the new temple and the regulations for what kinds of sacrifices the prince can offer may seem tame stuff. However, this final vision forms the capstone and climax of the entire book and will, if properly understood, amply repay the labor of study.

As with the opening vision of Ezekiel (1:1–2), the present one opens with a double date formula: "In the twenty-fifth year of our exile, at the beginning of the year, on the tenth of the month, in the fourteenth year after the fall of the city—on that very day the hand of the LORD was upon me and he took me there" (40:1). Whereas the opening vision of the heavenly King on his throne had been dated from the exile of the earthly king, Jehoiachin, this vision of the heavenly city is dated from the destruction of the earthly city, Jerusalem.

Fourteen years have passed since that momentous, earth-shattering event, twenty-five since the beginning of the Exile. In these dates, especially the fact that the vision took place on the tenth of the first month, a reference to the Jubilee year is generally seen. On the tenth day of the seventh month, the Day of Atonement, every fiftieth year, the trumpets were to be blown announcing a specially holy year, a year of proclaiming liberty throughout the land (Lev. 25:8–13). All land bought and sold in the intervening period was to be returned to its original owners, so that those who had lost their land and been reduced to slave status might return to their ancestral heritage (25:13).

It is not too hard to see what correlation might be drawn by the exiles between their present landless, enslaved state and the predicament of many in former times who lived in between Jubilees. The tenth day of the first month of the twenty-fifth year of exile, as the halfway point to the next Jubilee, was a natural time of looking forward to the release that the Lord had announced in chapters 34–37.[1]

It was on this very day that Ezekiel saw his "visions of God," whereby he was taken up to a high mountain in the land of Israel (40:2). This journey to a high mountain has several precursors in Israelite history. It is equivalent to Moses' ascent up Mount Sinai to receive the law of God; indeed, Ezekiel is the only person in the Old Testament apart from Moses who imparts God's legislation to the people.[2] But Moses also received on the mountaintop a detailed design for building the tabernacle and establishing its worship; Ezekiel is likewise shown a heavenly sanctuary and instructed about the requirements for its worship.[3] As with another mountaintop experience of Moses, this time on Mount Nebo in the Abarim Range (Deut. 32:48–52), Ezekiel surveys the Promised Land that has been prepared for God's people, though he himself will never enter it.[4] But the "very high mountain" also represents Mount Zion, the mountain of the temple, concerning which Isaiah had prophesied (Isa. 2:2–3):

> In the last days
> the mountain of the LORD's temple will be established
> > as chief among the mountains;
> it will be raised above the hills,
> > and all nations will stream to it.
> > Many peoples will come and say,
> "Come, let us go up to the mountain of the LORD,
> > to the house of the God of Jacob.
> He will teach us his ways,
> > so that we may walk in his paths."
> The law will go out from Zion,
> > the word of the LORD from Jerusalem.

---

1. Note that the year of liberation is explicitly mentioned in 46:17, and the number twenty-five and its multiples occur frequently in the dimensions of the temple. See Zimmerli, *Ezekiel*, 2:346. Medieval Jewish commentators also linked the date with the Jubilee year but in a different way, arguing that the "thirtieth year" of Ezek. 1 was the thirtieth year since the last Jubilee. Since the thirtieth year was also the fifth year of the prophet's exile (1:2), then the twenty-fifth year of the prophet's exile must be the Jubilee year. See Abraham J. Rosenberg, *Ezekiel: A Translation of Text, Rashi and Commentary* (New York: Judaica, 1991), 2:342.

2. Levenson, *Theology*, 39.

3. Ibid., 40.

4. Ibid., 42.

The literal Mount Zion was never particularly conspicuous for its physical elevation. But here, as in Ezekiel 38–39, we are dealing with theological geography rather than literal geography. The new temple, which appears "like a city" (40:2), is located in the theologically opposite terrain to the dry bones of Ezekiel 37: Just as there the dead are raised to new life, so also here the valley has been exalted and transformed into a "city" on a hill.

There on the mountaintop Ezekiel is met by an angelic figure, who will be his tour guide around the temple. This is not his first visionary guided tour of a temple; in chapter 8 he received a similar tour of the defiled Jerusalem temple and all its abominations, conducted by a similar figure. That vision culminated in the departure of "the glory of the LORD" from the temple (10:18), just as the vision in chapters 40–42 culminates in the return of that glory to the new temple (43:1–5). The focus of the temple vision, then, is the reversal of the divine abandonment of God's people that had culminated in the destruction of Jerusalem.

The angel is equipped with a linen cord (which is not again mentioned) and a measuring rod, to enable him to measure the various parts of the temple (40:3). The linen cord was presumably marked off in multiples of the measuring rod, to enable the measurement of longer distances.[5] This measuring process is intended for Ezekiel's benefit; he is instructed to look and hear, to pay attention to all that he is shown so that he can tell the house of Israel what he sees (40:4). In other words, the purpose of his vision is instructional: He will see things he can then relate to his contemporaries, which will have meaningful content for them (see 43:10–12).

It is highly significant that the first thing the prophet sees on his tour is a wall surrounding the whole temple area (40:5). Walls have as their purpose regulating and defining space; they are there to mark territory as "inside" or "outside" and to regulate access to the "inside" space.[6] Nor is this wall a minor obstacle; it is some ten and a half feet tall and ten and a half feet thick, providing a solid dividing line between the "holy," the area of the temple itself, and the "profane," the area outside. The function of this wall as a wall of separation between these two realms is apparent from the fact that the wall's height is mentioned, a dimension not provided for the other spaces. A wall depends on its height and thickness for its effectiveness in keeping people out, so these dimensions take on a particular importance.

If the wall is too thick to be broken and too high to be scaled, its effectiveness in restricting access will depend on its gates. But what gates this wall possesses! The three sides that permit access (there is no entry on the

---

5. Block, *Ezekiel 25–48*, 515.

6. Kalinda R. Stevenson, *The Vision of Transformation: The Territorial Rhetoric of Ezekiel 40–48* (SBLDS 154; Atlanta: Scholars, 1996), 19.

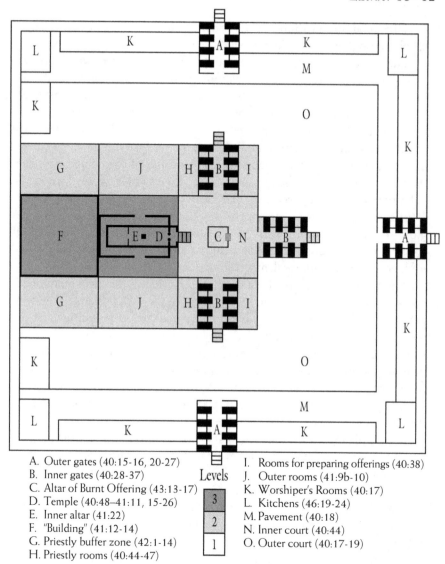

A. Outer gates (40:15-16, 20-27)
B. Inner gates (40:28-37)
C. Altar of Burnt Offering (43:13-17)
D. Temple (40:48–41:11, 15-26)
E. Inner altar (41:22)
F. "Building" (41:12-14)
G. Priestly buffer zone (42:1-14)
H. Priestly rooms (40:44-47)

Levels

I. Rooms for preparing offerings (40:38)
J. Outer rooms (41:9b-10)
K. Worshiper's Rooms (40:17)
L. Kitchens (46:19-24)
M. Pavement (40:18)
N. Inner court (40:44)
O. Outer court (40:17-19)

Figure 1. The Plan of Ezekiel's Temple

west side) are dominated by massive fortress-style gatehouses, almost forty-five feet wide and ninety feet deep (40:13, 15). The defensive nature of these gates is underlined by the fact that they have a portico or vestibule not on the outside, where one would expect it (and where it is on the inner gatehouses) but on the inside.

The gatehouses are further specified as having no fewer than six rooms for guards, three on each side. Similarly constructed gates have been excavated from the preexilic defenses of Megiddo, Hazor, and (probably) Gezer, though these gates were all smaller in scale than that which Ezekiel sees.[7] To add to the sense of inaccessibility, there is a flight of seven steps to be climbed before the worshiper even reaches the gate (40:6, 22, 26). There is no doubt as to the initial impression that Ezekiel's temple is intended to have: It is a mighty fortress that clearly separates the sacred from the profane.[8]

The area of the outer court (O) is of little interest to the prophet or his angelic guide. It is passed over with a brief reference to a paved area (M) all around the court, with thirty rooms (K) opening off from it (40:17–19). These rooms are not sufficiently important to require definition of their measurements or purpose, though commentators have not been slow to fill in Ezekiel's silence. The single key measurement in the outer court is its breadth: one hundred cubits, or roughly 175 feet, from outer gateway to inner gateway (40:19). This substantial dimension is intended not so much to provide space for a massive throng of worshipers[9] as to provide a substantial buffer zone around the holy things in the inner courtyard.

The inner courtyard (N) itself is strongly separated off from the outer courtyard. It is defended by gates (B) exactly identical to those of the outer court, though with the portico on the outside rather than the inside (40:28–37). It is further elevated, probably by about eight feet, with the gates being approached by a flight of eight steps (40:31, 34, 37). There is no mention of a wall around the inner court. Some commentators have assumed that there must have been such a wall on the basis of the massive gatehouses controlling access to the inner court.[10] However, K. Stevenson has pointed out that it was unnecessary to control access to the inner court by means of a wall because of its significantly higher elevation than the outer court. Absence of a wall would have allowed the worshipers there to view the ritual taking place at the altar of the inner court.[11]

At this point, the prophet's progress inward is briefly halted, while his attention is drawn to the purpose of some of the spaces in the inner courtyard.

---

7. According to Yigael Yadin, these gates were roughly seventy feet deep by twenty feet wide. See Zimmerli, *Ezekiel*, 2:352–55.

8. Steven S. Tuell, *The Law of the Temple in Ezekiel 40–48* (HSM 49; Atlanta: Scholars, 1992), 59.

9. So Stuart, *Ezekiel*, 372.

10. Zimmerli, *Ezekiel*, 2:355; Stuart, *Ezekiel*, 375.

11. *Vision of Transformation*, 44.

12. "Burnt offerings" (ʿōlôt) here and in v. 42 appear to represent all the sacrificial offerings that would be made (Allen, *Ezekiel 20–48*, 230).

There are rooms (I) beside the portico of each of the gates for washing the sacrifices (40:38),[12] while the porticoes themselves were used for slaughtering the sacrifices (40:39–43). The precise details concerning the function of these rooms underline the fact already that the primary function of this temple is as a place of offering sacrifice. In the exilic and postexilic situation the need for a sacrifice to atone for the people's sins and enable them to stand in God's presence became a dominant theme. In contrast, key descriptions of Solomon's temple highlight its importance not only as the location for sacrifice but also as the center for prayer (1 Kings 8:28–54; Isa. 56:7).

In addition to these rooms, the prophet also sees two[13] rooms for the Zadokite priests (H), who have overall responsibility for temple and altar (40:44–46).[14] These Zadokites are further defined as "the only Levites who may draw near to the LORD to minister before him" (40:46). Thus the function of both sets of spaces specifically identified within the inner court serves the overall thrust of the vision: separating off access to a restricted space, which is reserved for the priests, so that proper sacrifices may be offered. Both ideas of holiness and sacrifice are present in the summary statement of 40:47. (1) The inner courtyard is a perfect square, a hundred cubits in each direction, for the square is the shape of the holy.[15] (2) At its geometric center is the altar (C), the only piece of furniture noted in the courtyard, which is the place of sacrifice.[16]

Having briefly described the outer and inner courts, Ezekiel is led on to the central feature of the new temple complex, the temple structure (D) itself (40:48; 41:26). Its importance is marked in three ways. (1) It is located as the protected center at the heart of the complex, with walls and zones of controlled access all around it. Although it is the most protected area of the

---

13. MT has *lškôt šārîm* ("rooms for the singers"). The NIV follows most commentators in emending to *lškôt šᵉtayim* ("two rooms"), on the basis of the LXX.

14. This passage, along with others that refer to the Zadokites, has frequently been assigned by commentators to a separate "Zadokite stratum." However, the evidence does not support such "stratification." See Duguid, *Ezekiel and the Leaders of Israel*, 87–90.

15. Stevenson points out the predominance of square shapes in the realm of the holy and their absence in the profane areas (*Vision of Transformation*, 42). Similarly, as you move toward the center of the tabernacle, the spaces become progressively more square until you reach the Most Holy Place, which is a perfect cube. See Menahem Haran, *Temples and Temple Service in Ancient Israel* (Oxford: Oxford Univ. Press, 1978), 152.

16. Zimmerli locates the altar off-center, in front of the temple building, as a mark of the temple building being the center of gravity of the whole (*Ezekiel*, 2:355). However, comparison with Haran's diagram of the tabernacle (*Temple Service*, 152) encourages locating it in the center of the inner court. In that structure, even though the altar is not the "center of gravity" (that privilege belongs to the ark of the covenant), it still sits at the center of the courtyard.

sanctuary, doors are sufficient in place of gates to protect its sanctity, since only the priests have access to the inner court.

(2) The temple building is conspicuous in its elevation, as the highest point of an edifice that is itself on top of the high mountain. It is reached by ascending ten steps (see NIV note on 40:49), whereas going up to the outer court only took seven steps and up to the inner court from the outer court a further eight steps.[17]

(3) Its key significance is reflected in the extent and nature of the description accorded to the building. It is the space of the temple complex that is described in most detail and with the most precise measurements; even the "open area" around it is defined as being twenty cubits (thirty-five feet) wide. The building itself and associated spaces make up another hundred-cubit square.[18]

The temple building is a tripartite structure, comprising portico, outer sanctuary, and inner sanctuary, whose architecture focuses attention on the inner sanctuary, that is, "the Most Holy Place" (41:4). This is the only square space within the temple building itself, and it is reached by passing through three openings of increasing narrowness. The door from the inner court into the portico is fourteen cubits (almost twenty-five feet) wide; the door from there into the outer sanctuary is ten cubits (seventeen feet) wide, while the door into the inner sanctuary is a mere six cubits (ten feet) wide. This design feature underlines the sanctity of the Most Holy Place,[19] a sanctity so great (even before the return of God's glory!) that Ezekiel himself is not permitted to enter it. Instead, he remains outside, while the guiding angel goes in alone and measures it (41:3–4).

All around the temple building are no fewer than ninety rooms (J), on three levels (41:5–11), while behind the temple to the west there was a restricted area of twenty cubits breadth and a "building" (F) of unspecified purpose (41:10, 12). The rationale for this building may simply have been to protect the rear approach to the temple building; from now on no one would approach God "from behind," as it were.[20] Notice that no door or entranceway into the "building" is specified.

Returning to the description of the temple building itself, it is described as completely paneled with wood and decorated with images of palm trees and cherubim (41:17–18). This makes it more ornamented than the gates of the courtyards, which were simply adorned by palm trees (40:16). Palm trees

---

17. The total number of steps is, not coincidentally, twenty-five (Allen, *Ezekiel 20–48*, 235).

18. Stevenson, *Vision of Transformation*, 27.

19. Moshe Greenberg, "The Design and Themes of Ezekiel's Program of Restoration" *Interp* 38 (1984): 193.

20. Zimmerli, *Ezekiel*, 2:380.

were a common symbol of fertility and, along with cherubim, had been part of the decoration scheme of the first temple (1 Kings 6:29), which had also been wood-paneled. However, Ezekiel's decoration scheme is simpler than that of the first temple, which had a wide variety of other symbols carved on it, and the focus on the cherubim recalls the ominous presence of these enforcers of divine judgment in Ezekiel's opening vision.

The only piece of furniture mentioned within the temple building is an "altar" of wood in the outer sanctuary (E), which is designated "the table that is before the LORD" (Ezek. 41:22). This is presumably the table on which the "bread of the Presence" was laid out before the Lord (1 Kings 7:48). It is mentioned here because it will later be referred to as one of the places at which the Zadokite priests have the privilege of ministering (Ezek. 44:16), a situation that is the necessary corollary of its location in the outer sanctuary, where only they had access.

Having described the temple building, Ezekiel is now headed outward once more in his description of the complex. His attention is first drawn to a series of rooms for the priests (G), located north and south of the unnamed building behind the temple. The details of the construction of these rooms are not entirely clear, but they are built on three levels and it appears that the priests could enter at the top from the inner court (42:12) and emerge from the bottom into the outer court (42:9). This serves to underline the status of the rooms as boundary areas for activities that, if not properly contained, might violate the gradation of holiness.[21] These, therefore, are the rooms where the sacrifices and sacred offerings were to be consumed (42:13).

Eating these offerings was both a privilege and a responsibility. It was a *privilege* in that it was a means of providing for the physical needs of the priests, who as Levites had no land of their own to farm (44:28–30). But it was also a *responsibility*, since the consumption of the sin offerings was the required way of disposing of the low-grade contaminated material produced by the purification process. The carcass of the animal was regarded as having absorbed impurities during the sacrificial ritual, which were then dealt with by being ingested by the priest.[22]

In addition to eating the sacred offerings here, the priests were also required to leave the sacred clothes in which they had ministered in these rooms (42:14), so that they might not bring that which was holy into dangerous contact with the profane. Both of these restrictions represent a sig-

---

21. Greenberg, "Design and Themes," 193.
22. See Milgrom, *Leviticus 1–16*, 637.
23. Ibid., 447–52.

nificant raising of the differential between priest and nonpriest when they are compared with the perspective of the book of Leviticus.[23]

Having completed his tour of the inner court, Ezekiel was brought back out to survey the temple from the outside. Its overall dimensions are square, five hundred cubits by five hundred cubits (42:16–20). It might seem only natural that a sacred building would adopt the most sacred shape, but once more the stakes have been raised from the arrangements of the Mosaic and Solomonic eras. In the tabernacle, for example, only the Most Holy Place is square; the other external spaces are increasingly nonsquare. In Ezekiel's temple, however, the entire structure bears an increased level of sanctity that is expressed in its overall shape.

The final note on the layout of the temple brings us back to where we started, to the wall (42:20). This inclusion highlights the wall and its function: It serves "to separate the holy from the common" (42:20). Never again will the profane intrude on the realm of the holy as it did in the past. In the future, the lines will be clearly drawn. The walls must be clearly established, with a place for everyone and everyone in his or her place, so that the Lord can return to his place at the center of his people.

THE ESSENCE OF Ezekiel's vision. Many commentators treat this portion of Ezekiel's prophecy as if it were the work of a harmless eccentric. Ezekiel, being a priest, was naturally interested in temples, just as some other people are interested in classical music, fly fishing, or motorcycles,[24] and so when it comes time to express his vision for the future, he lapses into what is for him the most accessible form of description. This is normally regarded as a somewhat regrettable choice on the priest-prophet's part, an unfortunate mode of self-expression. After all, who today is into temples?

The reader is thus frequently left with the distinct impression of the prophet as being at heart an earnest but dull bureaucrat, of the kind that in popular British mythology are associated with the European Community in Brussels. These faceless officials are believed to spend their time formulating endless petty regulations on how curved bananas are permitted to be or the maximum noise levels that may be emitted by domestic lawnmowers. True, there may possibly be some meaning and value to the work of these individuals, but precisely what that value is tends to escape us. In the same way,

---

24. The examples are from Thomas, *God Strengthens*, 267; Peter C. Craigie, *Ezekiel* (Daily Study Bible; Philadelphia: Westminster, 1983), 278.

because this is part of sacred Scripture, commentators tend to affirm that there is meaning and value in this passage, but precisely what it is for ordinary people is frequently not clear.

Alternatively, on a dispensational interpretation, the significance of this detailed description of the temple building by the prophet is held to be self-evidently clear. These details form the necessary ground plan for the future millennial temple in Jerusalem. It is usually maintained that a competent architect could construct a building from Ezekiel's description.[25] This is undoubtedly true, though the architect would have to use a consecrated imagination to supply the many details that are lacking, most notably the height dimensions and construction materials,[26] and the present temple site in Jerusalem would need to have its topography radically revised.[27] However, on this interpretation, it appears similarly inevitable that contemporary Christian believers, who will by then (*ex hypothesi*) have been raptured, can find little of edification here.

Neither approach, it seems to me, has captured the sense of what Ezekiel is trying to do in these chapters. What we have in Ezekiel 40–48 is nothing less than the visionary reordering of an entire new world, following on the creation of the new people of God in chapter 37 and the birth pangs of chapters 38–39.[28] It is a view of heaven from halfway there, as the semi-Jubilee date indicates, showing a people living with the absence of God a vision of what his presence would be like. It is, in time-honored ancient Near Eastern tradition, a tour of the house that the divine warrior built on completion of his cosmic victory.[29]

Like the account of Genesis 1–11, this cosmogony revolves around the idea of separation and order, but this is significantly a new Eden without a fall. This is a paradise with walls,[30] to prevent new humankind from being driven from the presence of God (as in Gen. 3), or from driving God from their midst (as in Ezek. 8–11). Though the form may be unfamiliar to us, it is nei-

---

25. Feinberg, *Ezekiel*, 242; Ironside, *Ezekiel*, 284.

26. The absence of specified building materials is a particular problem for literal interpretation, since these are precisely described in other situations where God instructs his servants to construct such edifices as the tabernacle and Solomon's temple. Of course, it should also be noted that Ezekiel is not instructed to build anything; he merely has to observe and recount to his fellow exiles what he has seen. The building he sees is already in existence.

27. If indeed the site in Jerusalem is intended. See below on the division of the land in chapters 47–48 on the problems that are posed there for a "literal" interpretation.

28. Susan Niditch, "Ezekiel 40–48 in a Visionary Context," *CBQ* 48 (1986): 216.

29. Ibid., 221.

30. The image comes from Katheryn P. Darr, "The Wall Around Paradise," *VT* 37 (1987): 271–79, though her concern is rather with the (invisible) wall around the new Promised Land than the (very concrete) wall surrounding Ezekiel's temple.

ther the nostalgic musings of a frustrated priest nor the precise notations of an inspired architect. It is a literary piece describing, in symbols drawn from temple categories, the brave new world of the future as a challenge and encouragement to God's people in Ezekiel's day and for us in the present (43:10–12).

A theology of Bible "worlds." Since Ezekiel 40–48 is a description of a new "temple-centered" world, in order to understand its significance we need to read it in the light of the other "worlds" the Bible describes. The first "world" was, of course, the world as originally created, a garden world without walls (Gen. 2). There was no fence there around the forbidden tree of the knowledge of good and evil. There was only the fence of God's word, which said: "You are free to eat from any tree in the garden; but you must not eat from the tree of the knowledge of good and evil, for when you eat of it you will surely die" (2:16–17). There was no sacrifice in that world, for there was no sin to be atoned for or impurity to be cleansed.

But then sin entered the world. The man and the woman were driven from the Garden of Eden, and the presence of God was closed off to them. All of humanity was placed on the outside because of sin, and they were barred from returning by the cherubim, though God promised that this state of alienation would not persist forever, for he would win back a people for himself (Gen. 3:15). It was at this time, after the Fall, that sacrifices began to be offered, though ironically the first sacrifice resulted in further sin and a further driving away from God's presence (4:11–12). The human race had started out on a path that would lead them ever further away from God, as the "progress" of Genesis 1–11 shows.

But with the world of Abraham, God began to reverse this trend. He called this patriarch out from his pagan roots and brought him into the land of promise, where God appeared to him. Abraham responded by setting up altars and offering sacrifices (Gen. 12). God promised to be his God and the God of his descendants after him (17:7). But God's presence with the patriarchs was spontaneous and sporadic. He appeared to them only briefly and intermittently. He did not live permanently with his people until after the exodus from Egypt. At Sinai he gave instructions for a tabernacle, a building with (flimsy) walls and regulations limiting access to protect his sanctity, so that he might live in the midst of his people. Now only the priests had access to the Holy Place and only the high priest to the Most Holy Place— and that only once a year. When the temple was built in Solomon's time, the flimsy walls were made permanent, and the rules of access were solidified.

By Ezekiel's day, however, all of that had broken down. The rules limiting access to God's presence had been flouted, allowing uncircumcised foreigners to penetrate the very heart of the temple (Ezek. 44:7). What is more, the wall of separation between the residence of the earthly king and the heavenly king had never been clearly drawn (43:8), so that the Jerusalem temple frequently functioned as if it were the private royal chapel under the control of the reigning king. To cap it all, the persistent idolatry of the people throughout the land had penetrated the sanctuary and totally defiled it (chs. 8–11). Simply returning to the old ways of doing things was not a possibility. Thus, Ezekiel was given a vision describing an entirely new kind of temple, a temple with radically raised walls, radically heightened standards of holiness, and a radical focus on sacrifice.

When the Jews returned from exile and rebuilt the temple, what they constructed did not resemble Ezekiel's ground plan. This was true not simply in terms of scale, where practical necessities would have been a hindrance. Even in terms of the regulations and perspectives that could easily have been adopted, Ezekiel's plan was not embraced by those who constructed the second temple.[31] Should we therefore look to a future millennial temple in which to see these provisions of heightened sanctity fulfilled? I don't think so. Rather, we should do what it seems to me the New Testament does and see how the goal of Ezekiel's temple finds its fulfillment in Jesus Christ.

Christ as the fulfillment of Ezekiel's temple. For Christ himself *is* the new temple.[32] He is the dwelling of God among humankind, the glory of God made manifest (John 1:14). In one sense, with the incarnation of Jesus, the solid walls of the Old Testament temple have once again become flimsy material for the sake of portability, just as was the case with the tabernacle. Thus John states, "The Word became flesh and made his dwelling [*eskenosen,* lit., tabernacled] among us" (John 1:14). But the walls needed to be flimsy not just for the sake of mobility but also so that they could be torn down in a final cataclysmic temple-cleansing, achieved through the breaking of his body on the cross. That was the "temple" of whose destruction Jesus spoke in John 2:19, when he said: "Destroy this temple, and I will raise it again in three days." There on the cross the radical focus on sacrifice of Ezekiel's temple found its full expression, as the new temple itself was made a complete sacrifice for sin, by which God's people were cleansed once and for all.

But in Christ the radical separation of the holy from the profane of Ezekiel's temple also found its fullest expression. Just as the temple of Ezekiel was in the midst of the people, yet was no longer able to be defiled by them,

---

31. Note that Haggai, writing after the Exile, refers to priestly clothing as having a noncontagious holiness (Hag. 2:12), whereas in Ezekiel's vision the priests' clothes *can* transmit holiness (Ezek. 44:19). A higher standard of precautions is therefore necessary in the design of Ezekiel's temple.

32. For a rich development of this theme, see Edmund P. Clowney, "The Final Temple," *WTJ* 35 (1972): 166–77.

so also the Son of God lived in the midst of a sinful world, yet remained unde-filed (Heb. 4:15). In him the light shone out clearly in the darkness, and the darkness could not in the least compromise it (John 1:5).

In addition, since the church is Christ's body, it is also the new temple. This means that we too as the church are called to share the radical focus on sacrifice of Ezekiel's temple. We do this not by reintroducing the physical sac-rifices of the old order, which pointed forward to the coming of Christ, but by celebrating their fulfillment in the once-for-all sacrifice of Christ. Our lives and our proclamation must center on the message of the cross: the reality of Jesus Christ crucified for us (1 Cor. 1:18–23). Reflecting the order of Ezekiel's temple, we too are called to recognize the difference between the holy and the profane, to separate ourselves from the sin that so easily besets us (Heb. 12:1) and the ties that improperly bind us to unbelievers, who keep us apart from God (2 Cor. 6:14–7:1).

There are, however, differences between our position as Christians and the arrangement of Ezekiel's temple. Most notably, the walls have been moved. While we are to build a wall of separation between ourselves and sin, and even in some situations between ourselves and sinners, now the walls between Christians have been torn down. Now there are no privileged classes of priests who have closer access to God, while ordinary Christians are stuck in the outer court. Now we are all part of a holy priesthood (1 Peter 2:5). Now the greatest wall of all, the wall separating Jew and Gentile, has been torn down. As they are incorporated into Christ, both are together on the inside of the new temple (Eph. 2:14–22).

These similarities and differences find striking focus in the new Jerusalem of Revelation 21, the final, eschatological "world" of biblical revelation. That this visionary "Holy City" is modeled on the temple of Ezekiel 40–48 is indisputable: John is carried away to a great and high mountain to see this city (Rev. 21:10), and he too is accompanied by an angel with a measuring rod (21:15). The city is square, with a great high wall around it and promi-nent gates, while a river of life flows from its center (22:1). All of these fea-tures come directly from Ezekiel 40–48. Yet the differences from Ezekiel's vision are equally striking. The city of Revelation has no temple (21:22), there are twelve gates around the perimeter (not three, as in Ezekiel's tem-ple), and they stand perpetually wide open to the nations (21:12, 25).

What has John done with his predecessor's vision? He has shown how the same themes (separation of the holy from profane and sacrifice) look when they are viewed through the lens of fulfillment in Christ. There is still the same radical separation between the holy and the unholy on which Ezekiel insisted. The wall around Paradise has not been knocked down but has been raised even higher and made even thicker (Rev. 21:17). But now, in place of

Ezekiel's multiplicity of walls, there is only one wall. The final separation has taken place between the righteous and the unrighteous. The righteous—those "whose names are written in the Lamb's book of life" (21:27) and "who wash their robes" (22:14)—have completely free access through the gates of the city to its very heart, the tree of life before the throne of God (22:2, 14). The unrighteous, the cowardly, the unbelieving, the vile, the murderers, the sexually immoral, those who practice magic arts, the idolaters, and all liars (21:8, 27; 22:15)—all of these are permanently on the outside (22:15).

The reason why there is no temple and no walls inside the city is because the entire city has become a giant Most Holy Place, a perfect cube in shape (Rev. 21:16) and covered with pure gold (21:18), just like the original tabernacle. The place to which no one had access in Ezekiel's temple, not even Ezekiel himself, is the place to which all Christians have access in the new Jerusalem. Unlike Ezekiel's temple, there is no altar in this "new world" because the sacrifice has been accomplished once and for all on the cross. The Lamb has been slain, and, risen from the dead, is at the heart of heavenly worship.

Thus, Ezekiel's temple points forward clearly and unequivocally to the salvation that God accomplished in Christ. Ezekiel's vision is not a heavenly construction plan that we are to establish on earth as part of a program of building the kingdom. Rather, the prophet saw something that already exists in heavenly form as a depiction of the kingdom that God himself is constantly engaged in building. This is not "spiritualizing" in the conventional sense of the word, whereby heavenly truths are deduced from earthly realities, but rather the reverse. Ezekiel's vision is precisely a vision of a heavenly truth that found its earthly realization in the incarnation of Jesus Christ. As Edmund Clowney put it: "It is not so much that Christ fulfills what the temple means; rather Christ is the meaning for which the temple existed."[33] If this statement is true of the literal temple of the Old Testament, how much more for the symbolic temple of Ezekiel's vision: Christ is the meaning for which Ezekiel's vision exists.

A NEW KIND of SOCIETY. In Robert Bly's new book, he argues that we have entered an entirely new kind of society in the 1990s, which he calls "the sibling society."[34] We live in a world, he argues, where grown-ups act like adolescents and adolescents see no reason to grow up. It is a society where hierarchical barriers are increasingly swept away in an across-the-board leveling-down process. Parents no longer hold author-

---

33. Ibid., 177.
34. Robert W. Bly, *The Sibling Society* (San Francisco: Perseus, 1996).

ity over their children, husbands no longer hold authority over their wives, bosses no longer hold authority over their employees. Everyone is now leveled out into one great egalitarian mass.

One aspect of this change, functioning as both cause and effect, is the rise of day care and a distinct youth culture. Both of these modern innovations tend to move children from a network of relationships that revolve around home and family into a network of relationships that revolve around peers. The home with its historic authority structures and natural formative influence of the behavior of parents on their children has been replaced by the peer group. For better or worse, I am what I am largely because I copied or rebelled against the example of my parents. For many in the next generation, this will no longer be the case. One of the producers of *Melrose Place* put it like this:

> This generation has the ability to socialize in packs.... At age two, they were taught to get along with others [in day care] and what it means to respect others and somebody's space. So they value those friendships more than family because they spend so much time with them. The people I know from that age group just love being in groups.[35]

This societal change is reflected in the television shows created for them. It is no surprise that we have gone from the family-centered genre of shows like *Leave It to Beaver* and *The Brady Bunch* to the pack-centered genre of *Friends* and *Seinfeld*. We have moved from the old patriarchal society, with its inherent structures, into an amorphous sibling society.

Of course, not everything about this change is bad, as Bly recognizes. The old patriarchal structures in some cases permitted and even encouraged the abuse of wives, children, and employees. If you doubt that, just read a few nineteenth-century novels. In *Wuthering Heights*, for instance, there is a multigenerational pattern of systematic and public wife and child abuse, which would be barely conceivable in modern society. It is no loss that there are laws to protect workers against bosses like Ebenezer Scrooge in Dicken's *A Christmas Carol*.

Nor was the old patriarchal society necessarily more "Christian" than the new sibling society. In the patriarchal society God was frequently conceived as distant and remote, so that for many people (in practice if not always blatantly proclaimed to be such) it could be said, "God is dead." In the 1990s no one except the old-fashioned proclaims the death of God. Instead, for the average non-Christian, God has been absorbed into myself—hence the rise in introspective spiritualities of self-awareness and self-realization. In both

---

35. Kimberly Costello, cited in Rob Owen, *Gen X TV*, 11.

cases, however, God is still experienced as being absent. Because of sin and idolatry, there is no experience of the living presence of God in their lives or in their surroundings, and nothing else can ultimately fill that hole. Beauty can never be beautiful enough, relationships can never be strong enough, money can never make you rich enough, power can never be absolute enough; in all of us, in whatever kind of society we live, there is a deep-seated sense of loss and absence caused by the absence of God.

Responding to the "absence" of God. Ezekiel's visionary temple addresses the believer who lives in a world in which God seems absent. His answer is to lift the veil and show us the black-and-white realities of the world as it really is, the heavenly order of things. In this world there is a place for everything, and everything (and everyone) is in its place. In Ezekiel's vision, society has been reordered and transformed. But most significantly, it is a world where God is once more in his place, for the entire description of Ezekiel 40–42 leads up to the climactic reentry of the glory to the temple in chapter 43.

What does it mean for God not to be "in his place"? For the exiles, it meant a world that had fallen apart, a world that like Humpty-Dumpty had toppled off the wall, and all the king's horses and all the king's men could never simply put him back together again. God had packed his bags and left. God had abandoned them. The sky had fallen and they walked in thick darkness.

This is a description of reality that Ezekiel does not counter. Instead, he affirms that all this is true, but there is more. To the exiles who cry out in pain, "Our bones are dried up and our hope is gone; we are cut off" (37:11), he responds with a vision in which the bones are not merely dry, but *very* dry. To a people sick and tired of invaders, he reports the future approach of the invader to end all invaders, Gog of Magog (chs. 38–39). But in each instance, as also in his description of the new temple, God is active to restore his people. The dry bones can yet live. The hordes of Gog will end up as mounds of corpses. The temple they had defiled can and will be restored.

But the future is not, and cannot be, simply the past rewritten. Instead, in the new order of things there will be high walls built around Paradise to keep the sins of the past from being rewritten. In an adapted symbolism, the cherubim are stationed again to keep the sinners out, aided by high walls and (human) guards. God's holiness will not, and must not, be compromised in any way. The new temple is supremely the place where sacrifices are offered to maintain the renewed covenant relationship between God and his people.

How is this encouraging for Ezekiel's hearers or for us? How is it good news to hear that there will now be a high wall between God and all who lack perfect holiness? The answer is that it is not good news—unless you have considered the unthinkable alternative: that God would no longer be present in the midst of his people *at all*. To those who knew that it was their total depravity and defilement of the temple that caused God to depart from them, even this limited presence was good news indeed.

Yet we who are in Christ have been given far more! We have direct access to the very throne of grace, where Jesus himself intercedes for us at the right hand of the Father (Heb. 4:16; 7:25; 8:1). There are no walls that keep us out of God's presence, not because we are more holy in ourselves than Ezekiel and his hearers but because we have been credited with the perfect right-eousness of Christ in place of our filthy rags. His once-for-all sacrifice has effected the transition that turned us from aliens and strangers, without God and without hope in the world (Eph. 2:12), to insiders who are able to "approach . . . with confidence" (Heb. 4:16). Should we not therefore rejoice at the greatness of the salvation accomplished for us and strive to be pure, even as our Lord Jesus was pure?

But we should also remember that one wall still remains and that many are still outsiders to God's grace. Some live beyond the sound of gospel proclamation. Others have heard the gospel proclaimed over and over again, yet have repeatedly rejected it. Nothing and no one impure can ever enter God's heavenly holy city. Even the most moral person, if he or she does not believe in Christ, is outside the wall; left to themselves, such people must per-ish utterly. Our calling as priests of the new temple is to teach these people too the one way to holiness through trusting in Christ, seeking to draw them into the new world we have been given, where Paradise once more stands open to God's people and the tree of life is freely accessible to all.

Ezekiel 43

THEN THE MAN brought me to the gate facing east, ²and I
saw the glory of the God of Israel coming from the
east. His voice was like the roar of rushing waters, and
the land was radiant with his glory. ³The vision I saw was like
the vision I had seen when he came to destroy the city and like
the visions I had seen by the Kebar River, and I fell facedown.
⁴The glory of the LORD entered the temple through the gate
facing east. ⁵Then the Spirit lifted me up and brought me into
the inner court, and the glory of the LORD filled the temple.

⁶While the man was standing beside me, I heard someone
speaking to me from inside the temple. ⁷He said: "Son of man,
this is the place of my throne and the place for the soles of my
feet. This is where I will live among the Israelites forever. The
house of Israel will never again defile my holy name—neither
they nor their kings—by their prostitution and the lifeless
idols of their kings at their high places. ⁸When they placed
their threshold next to my threshold and their doorposts
beside my doorposts, with only a wall between me and them,
they defiled my holy name by their detestable practices. So I
destroyed them in my anger. ⁹Now let them put away from me
their prostitution and the lifeless idols of their kings, and I will
live among them forever.

¹⁰"Son of man, describe the temple to the people of Israel,
that they may be ashamed of their sins. Let them consider the
plan, ¹¹ and if they are ashamed of all they have done, make
known to them the design of the temple—its arrangement, its
exits and entrances—its whole design and all its regulations
and laws. Write these down before them so that they may be
faithful to its design and follow all its regulations.

¹²"This is the law of the temple: All the surrounding area
on top of the mountain will be most holy. Such is the law of
the temple.

¹³"These are the measurements of the altar in long cubits,
that cubit being a cubit and a handbreadth: Its gutter is a cubit
deep and a cubit wide, with a rim of one span around the edge.
And this is the height of the altar: ¹⁴From the gutter on the
ground up to the lower ledge it is two cubits high and a cubit

wide, and from the smaller ledge up to the larger ledge it is four cubits high and a cubit wide. [15]The altar hearth is four cubits high, and four horns project upward from the hearth. [16]The altar hearth is square, twelve cubits long and twelve cubits wide. [17]The upper ledge also is square, fourteen cubits long and fourteen cubits wide, with a rim of half a cubit and a gutter of a cubit all around. The steps of the altar face east."

[18]Then he said to me, "Son of man, this is what the Sovereign LORD says: These will be the regulations for sacrificing burnt offerings and sprinkling blood upon the altar when it is built: [19]You are to give a young bull as a sin offering to the priests, who are Levites, of the family of Zadok, who come near to minister before me, declares the Sovereign LORD. [20]You are to take some of its blood and put it on the four horns of the altar and on the four corners of the upper ledge and all around the rim, and so purify the altar and make atonement for it. [21]You are to take the bull for the sin offering and burn it in the designated part of the temple area outside the sanctuary.

[22]"On the second day you are to offer a male goat without defect for a sin offering, and the altar is to be purified as it was purified with the bull. [23]When you have finished purifying it, you are to offer a young bull and a ram from the flock, both without defect. [24]You are to offer them before the LORD, and the priests are to sprinkle salt on them and sacrifice them as a burnt offering to the LORD.

[25]"For seven days you are to provide a male goat daily for a sin offering; you are also to provide a young bull and a ram from the flock, both without defect. [26]For seven days they are to make atonement for the altar and cleanse it; thus they will dedicate it. [27]At the end of these days, from the eighth day on, the priests are to present your burnt offerings and fellowship offerings on the altar. Then I will accept you, declares the Sovereign LORD."

Original Meaning

WE NOTED IN the previous section the similarities between the world-constructing vision of Ezekiel 40–48 and Genesis 1–2. A further similarity emerges in Ezekiel 43–46 as the account of the formation of the different spaces in chapters 40–42 is followed by an account of their filling, just as the spaces formed in days 1–3 of Genesis 1 were sub-sequently filled in days 4–6.[1] An empty temple is, by itself, worthless; it was made to be occupied. The logic of the description starts from the center with the filling of the Most Holy Place (43:1–9) and ends at the corners of the outer court, with the description of the activities in the kitchens (46:24).

The return of the glory of the Lord to the new temple is the high point of chapters 43–46. This return, which reverses the abandonment of the temple and its destruction described in equally visionary form in chapters 8–11, is the fulfillment of the central promise of restoration: the Lord dwelling in the midst of his people forever (37:26–28). The connection with the previous visions is made explicit in 43:3: "The vision I saw was like the vision I had seen when he came to destroy the city and like the visions I had seen by the Kebar River."

The glory returns to the temple through the east gate, from the same direction in which it had earlier left (10:18–19).[2] Whereas its departure was slow and halting, however, its return is rapid and direct. On its return, the glory of God not only fills the temple, as it had filled the Solomonic temple at its consecration (1 Kings 8:10–11), it even causes the land itself to shine (Ezek. 43:2). As with the other visions, the prophet's response to the revelation of God's glory is to fall on his face (43:3b).

The overwhelmed prophet is once again picked up by the Spirit and dropped in the inner court, in order for him to hear the word of the Lord (43:5). That word is an assertion of the Lord's kingship and of his "liv[ing] among the Israelites forever" (43:7). As King, the Lord is marking out his territorial claim to the areas defined in the vision, with the new temple as his throne room and footstool.[3] But what is new is not the Lord's claim to kingship or the area over which he makes that claim, it is the assertion that his kingship will be exercised there *forever*.

In order to ensure that his reigning presence remains with his people forever, it is necessary to guard against any repetition of the abuses of the past. This involves once more redefining the nature of the areas around the divine throne room and limiting access that might endanger their sacredness. In the past, the house of Israel and their kings had defiled the Lord's name by their

---

1. A similar pattern has been observed in the construction of the tabernacle. See Frank H. Gorman Jr., *The Ideology of Ritual: Space, Time and Status in the Priestly Theology* (JSOTS 91; Sheffield: JSOT, 1990), 48.

2. This also means that it travels along the east-west spine of the temple, a line of special sanctity in Ezekiel's temple (Block, *Ezekiel 25–48*, 578).

3. Stevenson, *Vision of Transformation*, 50. It may be, however, that the identification of the entire temple rather than the ark as the Lord's footstool represents once again a raising of the standards of holiness compared with the older traditions.

prostitution (i.e., their spiritual adultery with the gods of other nations, as in ch. 23) and by setting up memorial stelae[4] to their monarchs within the temple grounds (43:7–8).[5]

There is no room for these stelae in honor of the human king in the place dedicated to the worship of the divine King. Henceforth they will be banished. Indeed, the whole former social geography of the temple mount, where the house of the divine King was merely a (smaller) neighboring residence to the palace of the human king, will be swept away. Because the former kings defiled the Lord's name by their detestable practices, their position in the future kingdom will be further removed from the center.[6] This is a necessary precondition for the Lord's perpetual dwelling in the midst of his people (43:9).

Verses 10–12 sum up the rationale for the temple vision: Ezekiel is being shown these things so that he can relay them to his own generation. They must consider the design and "be ashamed of their [former] sins." The temple vision is not a building plan or a prediction of the future but rather a powerful symbol that addresses the people in Ezekiel's day. What specifically about the temple design is to move them to shame? They must consider in particular its "plan" (43:10), its "arrangement," its "exits and entrances," along with its "regulations and laws" (43:11). In other words, the temple vision is a pedagogical tool that speaks by its shape and size, and particularly by its permission or denial of access ("exits and entrances").[7] These regulations all serve a single overriding purpose: that the whole area all around the temple may be most holy. In order for God to continue to live in their midst forever,

---

4. NIV translates the Heb. phrase used here as "the lifeless idols of their kings." Various translations of this phrase have been defended in recent literature. The RSV takes it as a literal reference to the corpses of the kings (so also Elizabeth Bloch-Smith, *Judahite Burial Practices and Beliefs About the Dead* [JSOTS 123; Sheffield: Sheffield Academic Press, 1992], 116). Jürgen H. Ebach argued for their identification as offerings for the dead ("PGR = (Toten-)Opfer," *UF* 3 (1971): 365–68. However, the majority opinion has continued to accept D. Neiman's older view that these were memorial stelae erected in honor of the earthly king ("PGR: A Canaanite Cult Object in the Old Testament," *JBL* 67 [1948]: 55–60). See now the discussion in Theodore J. Lewis, *Cults of the Dead in Ancient Israel and Ugarit* (HSM 39; Atlanta: Scholars, 1989), 141.

5. NIV follows the MT in reading *bāmôtām* ("their high places"). However, this introduces a separate location for their idolatry in a context that seems centered around the temple mount. It seems better to revocalize with a number of Hebrew manuscripts and read *bᵉmôtām* ("at their death").

6. On the relationship of the terms *melek* ("king") and *nāśîʾ* ("prince") in Ezekiel, see Duguid, *Ezekiel and the Leaders of Israel*.

7. Stevenson, *Vision of Transformation*, 18–19.

regard for his holiness must govern not simply access to the Most Holy Place, but the entire temple mount (43:12).

Removal of sinners to a safe distance is only one aspect of maintaining the holiness of the temple area; the other, more positive, aspect is through the reestablishment of the sacrificial system. For this reason, Ezekiel's attention is now drawn once more to the altar in the inner court, the central piece of furniture mentioned in the earlier tour. The importance of this altar to Ezekiel's plan is evident not merely from its detailed description but also from its place at the geometric center of the temple complex. The contrast is made clearer by the fact that in the tabernacle the altar was the least sacred of the cultic articles, located in the outer court; its geometric center pointed rather to the ark.[8] Once more this represents an overall raising of the standards of holiness compared to the old ways, assigning the altar an equal sanctity to the furnishings of the Most Holy Place.

The nature of this altar is a three- or four-layer square construction, depending on whether the *ḥêq* (v. 13) is interpreted as a "gutter" (NIV) or a "base" (NRSV). The dimensions of the altar are 18 cubits by 18 cubits (31.5 feet square) at the lowest level and 14 cubits by 14 cubits (24.5 feet square) at the highest (43:13–17). At each corner of the top level there are projections, or "horns," to which blood is applied during some aspects of the ritual (43:20). The whole edifice stands nine cubits (about fifteen feet) high and is approached by a flight of steps from the east. This is a reversal of the normal ancient Near Eastern practice whereby the priest faces east when offering sacrifices. In Ezekiel's temple the priest faces west, toward the Most Holy Place, thus avoiding any suggestion of a repetition of the sun worship of 8:16, the crowning abomination of the earlier temple vision.

Having described the new altar, Ezekiel is then given instructions for the eight-day purification process that fits the altar for sacred use (43:19–27). He himself is assigned a key role in this consecration process, just as Moses had instituted the cult given on Mount Sinai.[9] On the first day he is to offer an unblemished bull as a purification offering (*ḥaṭṭāʾt*),[10] while on days 2–8 he is to offer a male goat as a purification offering and a bull and a ram as burnt offerings. The blood of the purification offerings is to be applied to the altar at the

---

8. Milgrom, *Leviticus 1–16*, 452. The overall tabernacle complex was not a square, as Ezekiel's temple was, but rather two adjoining squares, one comprising the inner court and the other the outer court.

9. J. Gordon McConville, "Priests and Levites in Ezekiel: A Crux in the Interpretation of Israel's History," *TynBul* 34 (1983): 28.

10. NIV translates "sin offering" following the older terminology. However, the purpose of the *ḥaṭṭāʾt* is not the forgiveness of sins but rather the purification of a place. For the terminology and the purpose of the *ḥaṭṭāʾt*, see Milgrom, *Leviticus 1–16*, 253–61.

topmost extremities (the four horns), the lowest extremities (all around the rim), and four middle extremities (the four corners of the upper ledge, 43:20).

Zimmerli notes a parallel between this procedure and the ordination of Aaron and his sons to the priesthood, in which blood is smeared on the right ear, the thumb of the right hand, and the big toe of the right foot (Lev. 8:22–23).[11] The body of the purification sacrifice is then disposed of by burning it outside the sanctuary. The burnt offerings are also to be offered with salt (Ezek. 43:24). Salt was the preservative par excellence in the ancient Near East and seems to have featured prominently in covenant ceremonies.[12] Although it is elsewhere only specifically required in the regulations for the cereal offering (Lev. 2:13), it may well have formed part of all of the offerings made by fire.

The purpose of this ritual with the repeated presentation of purification offerings is to "purify the altar and make atonement [*kipper*] for it," so that the holy space can be used for the regular ministry of offering sacrifices (43:20). The concept of making atonement (or expiation) expresses the idea of ritually wiping away the impurities and sins that adhere to a person or object.[13] Israel's past sins have penetrated even to this heavenly sanctuary and must be cleansed before the work of the cult can be restarted. Without a spiritual spring cleaning of the altar, none of the offerings made on it will be acceptable to God. Once Ezekiel has completed his inaugural ministry, assisted by the Zadokite priests (43:19), the priests will be able to carry out their task of offering burnt offerings and fellowship offerings on the altar, the ongoing means of assuring God's blessing on his people. They will once more be acceptable to God (43:27).

Bridging Contexts

PRECONDITIONS FOR THE **return of God's glory.** The glory of God is an intangible concept for most contemporary Christians. We may pray for God to be glorified in us and in the world, but the idea of glory tends to be somewhat ethereal. In contrast, in the Old Testament the glory of God was a substantial, even tangible, presence. When Moses went up on Mount Sinai, he had an encounter with God's glory that made his face radiant (Ex. 33:18–23; 34:29–30). At the completion of the tabernacle, the glory filled it to such an extent that even Moses could not

---

11. *Ezekiel*, 2:433.

12. Milgrom, *Leviticus 1–16*, 191.

13. Baruch Levine, *Leviticus* (JPS Torah Commentary; Philadelphia: Jewish Publication Society, 1989), 23.

enter (40:34–35). When Solomon finished constructing his temple and dedicated it, God's response was to descend in glory to fill it (1 Kings 8:11). In Old Testament times, God's glory was the visible manifestation of his presence in the midst of his people. Thus Isaiah's vision of the glory of God filling the temple (Isa. 6) forms the basis for his confident assertion in the following chapter of "God with us" ("Immanuel," Isa. 7:14; 8:8).

But the immanent presence of God with us is not necessarily good news for sinners. That is why Isaiah fell on his face, proclaiming the covenant curse on himself: "Woe to me! . . . I am ruined! For I am a man of unclean lips, and I live among a people of unclean lips, and my eyes have seen the King, the LORD Almighty" (Isa. 6:5). He was afraid that the vision of God's glory would not merely make his face shine but would incinerate him. In Isaiah's case, the solution to his needs was at hand in a fully functional altar, from which the seraph brought a live coal to touch his lips and purify him of his sins (Isa. 6:7).

In Ezekiel's vision, although the fundamental concepts are similar, the situation is more complex. The danger with which he is concerned is not so much the presence of God as the absence of God. Though the wrathful presence of God had already led to the destruction of Jerusalem for her sins, the permanent absence of God is an equally fearful prospect. Without the presence of God at the center of the life of the community, there can be no life. There will simply be a collection of dry bones. Ezekiel's vision of the return of God's glory is the theological prerequisite for the restoration of the people, just as surely as his vision of the departure of God's glory from the Jerusalem temple was a theological prerequisite for its destruction. It is a statement that the Lord is still King—an issue addressed in his victory over the nations in chapters 38–39. Specifically, the Lord is King over Israel and will continue to be their King forever. Never again will they experience total abandonment, the absence of God.

Just as God cannot speak through a prophet with unclean lips, however, but must first cleanse them (Isa. 6:7), so he cannot dwell in an unpurified house. The altar is as necessary in Ezekiel 43 as it was in Isaiah 6. But whereas in Isaiah 6 the prophet saw a fully functional heavenly cult that merely needed to be applied to his condition, in Ezekiel the heavenly cult itself is in abeyance and needs to be reconstituted. In Ezekiel, it is not just the prophet who needs to be cleansed; the heavenly altar itself has been defiled

---

14. Behind all of the Old Testament shadows lies a heavenly reality, a reality that in Christ has now come down from heaven to earth, ushering in the New Testament epoch. For a fuller outworking of this principle, see Geerhardus Vos, *The Teaching of the Epistle to the Hebrews* (Grand Rapids: Eerdmans, 1956), 55–65.

by the sins of the people and needs to be ritually purified before true worship can begin once again.[14]

This is a task in which Ezekiel is called to share. Having been faithful in his commission as a watchman in the earlier part of the book, his reward is access to the heavenly altar and a key role in the reinauguration of heavenly worship. It is as if the worship of heaven itself has been halted while God's people are in exile and Jerusalem is in ruins. But now, the vision depicts the resumption of heaven's worship, which carries with it the assurance of a new era in the earthly worship of God's people.

Jesus and God's glory. The testimony of the New Testament is that the new era has dawned in the coming of Jesus Christ. The glories of heaven, depicted in shadowy forms throughout the Old Testament, have now broken into history. Jesus is the fulfillment of the promise of Immanuel; in him, God is with us (Matt. 1:23). In Jesus, the glory of the high and holy God has come and lived in our midst, just as Ezekiel foresaw. As the apostle John testifies, "the Word became flesh and made his dwelling among us. We have seen his glory" (John 1:14). In the language of the writer to the Hebrews, "The Son is the radiance of God's glory and the exact representation of his being (Heb. 1:3). The first of Jesus' miracles, in which he turned water into wine, was not merely an exercise in fulfilling the felt needs of those around him; it was nothing less than a display of his glory (John 2:11).

In general, Christ's glory was veiled even from his closest associates, but on the Mount of Transfiguration the veil was taken away for a moment and the three disciples beheld his radiant presence (Matt. 17:2). On the first Palm Sunday, Jesus entered Jerusalem in kingly triumph—from the east!—and then entered the temple. There he exercised his royal authority over it by throwing out the merchants and the money changers (Matt. 21:1–13).

But in order for his presence with sinful humanity to be for their blessing and not judgment, before his work was complete, Jesus had to offer the perfect sacrifice on the cross. The purpose of this sacrifice was to provide the cleansing blood that might be applied not only to sinners, but also to the heavenly sanctuary itself so that it might be purified (Heb. 9:23). From the perspective of the writer of Hebrews, Jesus is the one who fulfills the prophet's actions in purifying the heavenly altar, only he does his work not with the blood of bulls and goats but with his own blood (9:12). That once-for-all sacrifice is fully efficacious; it does not merely cleanse the sanctuary so that the endless round of animal sacrifices may begin again; rather, it brings that endless round to a final stop (10:11–12).

This is a sacrifice with power beyond the wildest dreams of the Old Testament prophet. Yet it is a sacrifice that brings about precisely what Ezekiel envisages, for now we may have confidence in God's lasting presence with us forever. Indeed, having sent them out to accomplish the task of proclaiming his lordship over all nations, Jesus' final words to his disciples are these: "Surely I am with you always, to the very end of the age" (Matt. 28:20).

CONTEMPORARY UNDERSTANDINGS OF **God**. The modern world believes increasingly in a God who is not there. Though the opinion polls repeatedly demonstrate that a high proportion of people in the West still "believe in God," the nature of that God has shifted dramatically. In place of the old certainties of a transcendent God, people have come to believe more in an immanent God, a God who is not "there" any more than he (or she) is "here." God is now perceived more as a universal life force than as a personality.[15] The heart of such a creed is expressed in the familiar benediction from the *Star Wars* films: "May the Force be with you."

One of the consequences of that societal shift is a loss of belief in moral absolutes and a correlative absence of any sense of guilt over personal wrong-doing. If God is not outside me, then there is no basis for a morality outside me. Whereas the "modern" generation sought empowerment to live lives that were "good" according to some objective standard, the "postmodern" generation seeks freedom to follow whatever personal whim drives them. Although the postmodern generation might not find the music to its taste, their attitude is admirably summed up in the lyric from *The Sound of Music*: "Climb every mountain; ford every stream; follow every byway; 'til you find your dream." The idea that God is absent from us because of our sin and cannot be found by us no matter how diligently we search is alien to our contemporaries.

In contrast to the vague pantheism of so much postmodernism, Christians believe in "the God who is there," in Francis Schaeffer's classic phrase.[16] A life lived without reference to this God is a life lived without its center. He is the mountain peak for which all climbers are unwittingly looking, the country on the other side that the forders seek, the goal in search of which those wandering the byways travel, the reality behind every dream. This, however, does *not* mean that "all roads lead to God." Far from it; because of sin, the most accessible and well-traveled roads lead away from God (Matt. 7:14). Left to ourselves, the natural result of all of our searching is futile thinking and dark-

---

15. Peter Jones, *Spirit Wars: Pagan Revival in Christian America* (Mukilteo, Wash.: Wine Press, 1997), 26–29.

16. *The God Who Is There* (Chicago: InterVarsity, 1968).

ened hearts. By nature, we continually suppress the truth, exchanging God's glory for diverse idolatries (Rom. 1:21–23).

However, the truth of God's existence does mean that we can proclaim to the restless wanderers of the postmodern generation that there is rest and real freedom to be found only in Christ. God is neither dead nor absent, nor is he silent. He is there and constantly speaking to us, addressing us through the glories of creation and the powerful proclamation of his Word (Ps. 19). As creatures we were made to serve somebody, and we cannot escape that destiny. Whatever we value in this world becomes our idol and master, even the pursuit of freedom and liberty itself. True freedom and true fulfillment come ironically only as we submit ourselves to the One we were made to serve. As John Donne put it:

> Take me to you, imprison me, for I,
> Except you enthrall me, never shall be free,
> Nor ever chaste, except you ravish me.[17]

Approaching the God who is there. But if God is objectively there, if his Word is objectively true, and if life may only be found through his presence in our hearts, then the question of how we may approach such a God becomes pressing. Here the need of the postmodern person is the same as the modern, the notorious sinner the same as the righteous-living Pharisee, for "all have sinned and fall short of the glory of God" (Rom. 3:23). All have sinned, and the least sin is sufficient to drive away the life-giving presence of the only true God. How then can we stand in his presence? The only way is to come to the altar. If God is to dwell in our hearts, those hearts must first be cleansed by him. We need the blood of purification applied to our hearts and lives by Jesus Christ, wiping away our sin.

It is that blood that cleanses us of all unrighteousness, making our hearts fit places for God to indwell. It is that blood that is at work in our lives, erecting a wall between us and sin so that sin will not have dominion over us (Rom. 6:14). To be sure, that wall is not yet complete in this life, as we might wish. Sin remains ever with us, our constant unwelcome companion. But the assurance of the new temple is that if Christ has entered our hearts and begun the good work of purification, he will not stop until the wall between us and sin is higher and more effective than that which Ezekiel saw in his new temple.

But when Christ comes into our lives, he does so in only one role: as King. One of the problems that existed in Judah was a confusion over who was really sovereign, a confusion that demonstrated itself in the proliferation

---

17. *Holy Sonnets*, xiv.

of memorial stelae glorifying earthly kings in a building intended to glorify the heavenly King. That may seem an alien problem to us until we start to examine our own hearts and ask how much of our lives are lived to our own glory and how much to God's glory. Who is really sovereign in your decision-making? Who calls the shots in how you spend your money and your time? Who is Lord in how you arrange your priorities? Who occupies the center of your thoughts? All of a sudden, the questions strike closer to home. Although we may confess with our mouths that our bodies are temples of the Holy Spirit, all too often our lives tell a different story.

We can also ask the same question of our churches. Who is really being glorified in what goes on in our worship services? How many of our songs and hymns focus on ourselves, on how good knowing God makes us feel? How many, on the other hand, exalt him for who he is and for what he has done for us in Christ? How often do we emerge from a service more impressed by the skills of the preacher, the musicians, or the soloist than we are overwhelmed by the grace and glory of God? How much of our church's activities are focused on bringing glory to God, compared to how much time, effort, and money are focused on meeting our various needs?

I suspect that we too have our memorial stelae that need to be swept away, if we wish to experience the Spirit of God powerfully at work in our midst. We too have domesticated the church of God, turning it from his kingdom into a little extension of our own kingdoms. But God will live in our midst only as the King, nothing less.

Ezekiel 44

THEN THE MAN brought me back to the outer gate of the sanctuary, the one facing east, and it was shut. ²The LORD said to me, "This gate is to remain shut. It must not be opened; no one may enter through it. It is to remain shut because the LORD, the God of Israel, has entered through it. ³The prince himself is the only one who may sit inside the gateway to eat in the presence of the LORD. He is to enter by way of the portico of the gateway and go out the same way."

⁴Then the man brought me by way of the north gate to the front of the temple. I looked and saw the glory of the LORD filling the temple of the LORD, and I fell facedown.

⁵The LORD said to me, "Son of man, look carefully, listen closely and give attention to everything I tell you concerning all the regulations regarding the temple of the LORD. Give attention to the entrance of the temple and all the exits of the sanctuary. ⁶Say to the rebellious house of Israel, 'This is what the Sovereign LORD says: Enough of your detestable practices, O house of Israel! ⁷In addition to all your other detestable practices, you brought foreigners uncircumcised in heart and flesh into my sanctuary, desecrating my temple while you offered me food, fat and blood, and you broke my covenant. ⁸Instead of carrying out your duty in regard to my holy things, you put others in charge of my sanctuary. ⁹This is what the Sovereign LORD says: No foreigner uncircumcised in heart and flesh is to enter my sanctuary, not even the foreigners who live among the Israelites.

¹⁰"The Levites who went far from me when Israel went astray and who wandered from me after their idols must bear the consequences of their sin. ¹¹They may serve in my sanctuary, having charge of the gates of the temple and serving in it; they may slaughter the burnt offerings and sacrifices for the people and stand before the people and serve them. ¹²But because they served them in the presence of their idols and made the house of Israel fall into sin, therefore I have sworn with uplifted hand that they must bear the consequences of

their sin, declares the Sovereign LORD. ¹³They are not to come near to serve me as priests or come near any of my holy things or my most holy offerings; they must bear the shame of their detestable practices. ¹⁴Yet I will put them in charge of the duties of the temple and all the work that is to be done in it.

¹⁵'''But the priests, who are Levites and descendants of Zadok and who faithfully carried out the duties of my sanctuary when the Israelites went astray from me, are to come near to minister before me; they are to stand before me to offer sacrifices of fat and blood, declares the Sovereign LORD. ¹⁶They alone are to enter my sanctuary; they alone are to come near my table to minister before me and perform my service.

¹⁷'''When they enter the gates of the inner court, they are to wear linen clothes; they must not wear any woolen garment while ministering at the gates of the inner court or inside the temple. ¹⁸They are to wear linen turbans on their heads and linen undergarments around their waists. They must not wear anything that makes them perspire. ¹⁹When they go out into the outer court where the people are, they are to take off the clothes they have been ministering in and are to leave them in the sacred rooms, and put on other clothes, so that they do not consecrate the people by means of their garments.

²⁰'''They must not shave their heads or let their hair grow long, but they are to keep the hair of their heads trimmed. ²¹No priest is to drink wine when he enters the inner court. ²²They must not marry widows or divorced women; they may marry only virgins of Israelite descent or widows of priests. ²³They are to teach my people the difference between the holy and the common and show them how to distinguish between the unclean and the clean.

²⁴'''In any dispute, the priests are to serve as judges and decide it according to my ordinances. They are to keep my laws and my decrees for all my appointed feasts, and they are to keep my Sabbaths holy.

²⁵'''A priest must not defile himself by going near a dead person; however, if the dead person was his father or mother, son or daughter, brother or unmarried sister, then he may defile himself. ²⁶After he is cleansed, he must wait seven days. ²⁷On the day he goes into the inner court of the sanctuary to

minister in the sanctuary, he is to offer a sin offering for himself, declares the Sovereign LORD.

²⁸'''I am to be the only inheritance the priests have. You are to give them no possession in Israel; I will be their possession. ²⁹They will eat the grain offerings, the sin offerings and the guilt offerings; and everything in Israel devoted to the LORD will belong to them. ³⁰The best of all the firstfruits and of all your special gifts will belong to the priests. You are to give them the first portion of your ground meal so that a blessing may rest on your household. ³¹The priests must not eat anything, bird or animal, found dead or torn by wild animals.

Original Meaning

FOLLOWING ON THE description of the return of the glory of the Lord to fill the central space of the temple, Ezekiel 44 continues the process of the filling of the various spaces described in chapters 40–42. No one is allowed access to the Most Holy Place itself, but who may be permitted to enter into the inner court of this holy God?[1] The question of access to God is, of course, not a new one in Ezekiel's day. The tabernacle had strict regulations governing access to the different areas,[2] as had Mount Sinai itself before that (Ex. 24). What is new about Ezekiel's vision, however, is that the rules of access are tighter than those of the tabernacle, and the basis for those rules is now bound up in the past obedience of the parties concerned. Those who have proved themselves obedient are rewarded with the closest access to the center, while those who have strayed are allowed only a more limited access.[3] It is the outworking in visionary, graded form of the question and answer of Psalm 24:3–4:

Who may ascend the hill of the LORD?
    Who may stand in his holy place?
He who has clean hands and a pure heart,
    who does not lift up his soul to an idol
    or swear by what is false.

This section begins with an absolute prohibition of access: the outer east gate is closed and will forever remain closed (44:1–2). Because the Lord entered through it on his return to the Most Holy Place, it has acquired a special sanctity and may not be used by anyone else. However, the space within

---

1. Greenberg, "Design and Themes," 194.
2. Milgrom, *Leviticus 1–16*, 451.
3. Duguid, *Ezekiel and the Leaders of Israel*, 133–39.

the gate may be used by the prince for his sacral meals before the Lord. When he does so, he is to enter this space from the outer court, not from outside the temple complex, in order that the outer gate may remain perpetually closed (44:3).

In this way, both the privilege and restriction of the prince's position is emphasized. On the one hand, he holds a unique position among the laity with special privileges, including access to a private room in part of the central east-west spine of the new temple, an especially holy location.[4] On the other hand, this room is in the outer part of that region, and the prince has no access to the inner court. Thus, compared to the past, when the kings frequently treated the sanctuary as a royal chapel, as if it were their own preserve in which they might establish whatever innovations they wished (e.g., 2 Kings 16:10–18), in future the royal figure has a limited, though still honorable, position.

That the concern of this section is with access—or, to use the language of the passage, "exits and entrances" (Ezek. 43:11)—is further underlined by the brief recapitulation in 44:4–5. Ezekiel sees again the glory of the Lord filling the temple and is thereupon instructed to pay attention to the statutes of the house of the Lord and its laws concerning entrance to the house and its exits. The continued presence of God is contingent on the proper control of access to these areas.

It was a failure to control access in the past that leads to the condemnation of the house of Israel in 44:6. Since Wellhausen used this passage as the heart of his reconstruction of the history of Israelite religion, it has been common to see this passage as a tendentious program aimed at downgrading the Levites from priestly status to that of temple servants.[5] However, it is important to note that the prime target of accusation is the house of Israel as a whole; they (i.e., the laity) are primarily to blame and are therefore the ones who are "downgraded." The Levites are involved only secondarily and therefore receive only a partial exclusion.[6]

The sin of the past lay in bringing "foreigners uncircumcised in heart and flesh into my sanctuary, desecrating my temple" (44:7). This probably refers to the well-attested practice of employing foreign guards in the temple (2 Kings 11:14–19). The people failed in "carrying out [their] duty in regard to my holy things" (*šᵉmartem mišmeret qodāšāy*, Ezek. 44:8); instead, they assigned that charge to others. This view is confirmed by the observation that in tem-

---

4. Stevenson, *Vision of Transformation*, 121.

5. Julius Wellhausen, *Prolegomena to the History of Israel*, trans. J. S. Black and A. Menzies (New York: Meridian Library, 1957), 121–51.

6. Duguid, *Ezekiel and the Leaders of Israel*, 127–29; Stevenson, *Vision of Transformation*, 76.

7. Jacob Milgrom, *Studies in Levitical Terminology I: The Encroacher and the Levite; The Term ᶜaboda* (Berkeley: Univ. of California Press, 1970), 8–10.

ple or tabernacle contexts *šāmar mišmeret* is virtually synonymous with the task of guarding the holy things (Lev. 8:35; 2 Kings 11:5).[7] This sin will be repeated no more; uncircumcised foreigners will have no right of access into the sanctuary (Ezek. 44:9).

Unfortunately, the NIV, like most English translations, obscures the flow of thought in the passage by placing a paragraph break after 44:9, as if verse 10 introduces a new subject. In fact, verse 10 continues the thought of what precedes by identifying the legitimate temple guards, the Levites.[8] The flow of the main train of thought is as follows: The foreigners will not enter the sanctuary (v. 9), but the Levites will (v. 10); they will be in my sanctuary serving as armed guards at the gates of the house (v. 11).

To be sure, the Levites are not exonerated from blame; they served the people in the presence of their idols and must bear the consequences of their sin (44:10). Because they are tainted with the corruption of the preexilic sins of the people, they may not enter the inner court, serve as priests, or have any contact with the sacred offerings (44:13). But their ministry is extended rather than restricted when compared with the preexilic situation. Now they must slaughter the burnt offerings and sacrifices on behalf of the people (44:11), something the people had previously done for themselves.[9]

Once again the walls of separation have been raised in Ezekiel's temple in comparison to the preexilic situation. The sin of the Levites, whatever its precise form,[10] has consequences in terms of restriction on access and service. The greater sin of the people has even greater consequences in more strictly regulated access to the sanctuary and its service. The purpose of these regulations is to induce shame in the hearers as they consider their detestable practices (44:13), yet it is a shame mixed with an appreciation of grace, for the sinners have not been excluded utterly from the presence of the holy God, as their sins deserved.

In contrast to the Levites and the people, whose access is restricted because of their sin, the Zadokite priests receive the privilege of sole access to the inner court and the offering of all sacrifices at the altar and the service at the table inside the sanctuary itself (44:15–16). This privilege is explained as being due to their faithful service in the time of Israel's apostasy (44:15). This is not because the narrator in Ezekiel 44 is unaware of the criticisms aimed at the priesthood in 22:26. In fact, it is precisely these sins that he insists will be done away with in the future, when the priests observe God's law

---

8. Compare the NJPS translation, which places the paragraph break after verse 8. See Rodney K. Duke, "Punishment or Restoration: Another Look at the Levites of Ezekiel 44.6–16," *JSOT* 40 (1988): 65.

9. Cooke, *Ezekiel*, 481.

10. See my *Ezekiel and the Leaders of Israel*, 79–80.

and keep his Sabbaths holy (44:24). The righteousness of the Zadokites is relative, not absolute, just as their access is relative: They are permitted to go closer to the inner sanctum than anyone else, but even they are not allowed to enter the Most Holy Place, not even for the annual Day of Atonement ceremony.[11] Just as sin has spatial consequences of restricted access in Ezekiel's vision of the future, so also righteousness brings with it the spatial rewards of greater access.[12]

But greater access into the realm of the holy carries with it also greater responsibilities and limitations. Because the Zadokite priests penetrate closer to the Most Holy Place than any others, they face additional restrictions on their behavior (44:17–27). They must wear linen rather than woolen clothing when they minister so that they do not defile the inner court with their sweat (44:17–18). Sweat may have been undesirable because it was regarded as belonging to the general category of bodily emissions that rendered one unclean (Deut. 23:9–14).[13] Moreover, they are to distinguish between the "sacred" clothes they wear for ministry and the "other [profane] clothes" they wear for the rest of life. The former are to remain within the inner court, housed in the special rooms described in Ezekiel 42:13–14, so that holiness might not be accidentally transmitted to the people (44:19).

In Israelite law, holiness was not dangerous by itself. It was dangerous only to one who was contaminated with impurity or who acted in contravention of its laws.[14] Therefore the priest, who daily handled the holy things, had to take special care with regard to his ritual cleanliness and actions. The fate of Nadab and Abihu stood as a solemn warning of the dangers attending the ministry of serving a holy God (Lev. 10:1–3). Of particular danger was the contamination associated with contact with the realm of death, either through contact with a corpse (Ezek. 44:25) or through the ritual mourning practices of shaving or loosing the hair of the head (44:20).[15] The possibility of potentially fatal errors induced by the consumption of alcoholic beverages is also taken into account (44:21).[16]

The need for pure priestly stock, which flows from restricting access to the descendants of the seed of Zadok, is present in the restriction of priestly

---

11. Ibid., 82.

12. Stevenson describes this as the genre of "territorial rhetoric" (*Vision of Transformation*, 11–13).

13. Block, *Ezekiel 25–48*, 640.

14. Milgrom, *Leviticus 1–16*, 978–85.

15. It is not so much letting the hair grow long (NIV) as letting it hang uncared for, as in 24:17, 23 (Zimmerli, *Ezekiel*, 2:460).

16. Midrashic sources claimed that alcohol abuse was a factor in the deaths of Nadab and Abihu. See *Pesiq. Rab Kah.* 26:9; *Midr. Lev. Rab.* 20:9.

marriage to unmarried Israelite women or to the widows of priests (44:22). That provision assured that no offspring conceived by a former husband of a different tribe would be accidentally assumed to be of priestly stock.[17] In all these ways, the priests are to be living models of what they teach—that there is a difference between holy and profane, between clean and unclean (44:23).

Since the priests belong to the Lord, they are to have the Lord as their inheritance alone (44:28). Unlike the other tribes, they are to be allotted no territory of their own in the new Promised Land. Instead, they are to be provided for through the sacrificial system. They are to eat the grain offering, the sin and guilt offerings, and all the things vowed to the Lord that cannot be redeemed (as in Lev. 27:28), along with all "the firstfruits" and the "special gifts" (lit., "the sacred contribution from all your sacred contributions," Ezek. 44:30). This last item seems to be related to the "tithe of the tithe," which the Levites are instructed to pass on to the priests in Numbers 18:25–29 (see RSV). This "holy food" from the life-giving altar and the gifts of God's people is to be their sustenance. Birds or animals found dead or torn by wild animals are not to be eaten, however (Ezek. 44:31).

Throughout this chapter, the concern over the holiness of those having access to the central regions of the sanctuary is evident. Those who enter the inner parts of the sanctuary to minister in God's service must have a past history of faithfulness and must continue to walk in the ways of the holy, lest they be destroyed in an instant by the holy God whom they serve.

Bridging Contexts

THE CONCERN FOR and protection of the holy. In ancient Israel, as elsewhere in the ancient Near East, a sanctuary was not a place to be entered lightly and unthinkingly. Rather, the sanctuary was seen as a danger zone, somewhat comparable to a nuclear power plant. In a nuclear power station, strict precautions have to be taken because of the special dangers of radioactivity, which can cause catastrophic effects if it is handled carelessly. Access to some areas of the site is strictly limited, and special clothing has to be worn for some processes to prevent lethal contact between those operating the plant and the radioactive material, and to prevent radioactivity being transmitted by them to the outside world. In an analogous way, the priests had to take special care in their dress and their conduct to avoid danger to themselves and to prevent dangerous levels of holiness being brought into contact with the general public.

---

17. Where these laws differ from the Pentateuchal provisions, Ezekiel seems to be universally more stringent (Skinner, *Ezekiel*, 438).

Nowhere is this caution more evident than in Ezekiel's vision. This is hardly surprising, given Ezekiel's own experience of seeing the Jerusalem temple defiled and subsequently destroyed by God's holy wrath. Anyone who personally witnessed the carnage caused by the meltdown at the Chernobyl nuclear power station would understandably be concerned to tighten up regulations to guard against its repetition. In precisely the same way, Ezekiel's vision represents a tightening of the "holiness code of practice," a raising of the walls and reinforcing the steel of the containment chamber around the temple. Ezekiel is all too aware of something distant from our contemporary thinking: that it is a fearful thing for sinners to fall into the hands of the all-holy God.

But since we are all sinners, who among us can enter the inner court as a reward for our faithfulness? Who has a "righteousness" great enough to stand in God's presence? As Christians, our natural answer, in terms of the New Testament terminology, is "no one." As Romans 3:23 puts it: "All have sinned and fall short of the glory of God." How then do we explain the "righteousness" of the Zadokites, on the strength of which they are granted access and privileges not granted to others? The answer lies in an understanding of the ancient Near Eastern treaty form known as a "covenant of grant."[18]

In this type of treaty, known from Hittite and Akkadian sources as well as in biblical parallels, the faithfulness and loyalty of the ancestor secures the rights of all of his subsequent descendants. Unlike suzerainty treaties, where the covenant acts as a motivation to each generation to show loyalty, a covenant of grant is a simple reward for past loyalty. This loyalty is typically described in the terminology of having walked before the Lord (Gen. 17:1; 24:40; 1 Kings 8:25; 9:4; Isa. 38:3), of having a perfect heart (1 Chron. 28:9; Isa. 38:3), and of having kept God's commands (Gen. 26:5; 1 Kings 2:3). Thus, when the Zadokites are described as having "faithfully carried out the duties of [God's] sanctuary" (Ezek. 44:15), the key issue is their loyalty. They are not implied to be without moral blemish, any more than an Abraham was (Gen. 26:5); however, having been found faithful to God in a day of small things, their reward for loyal service is a place of responsible service in the kingdom (Matt. 25:21).

The question of rewards. The question of reward is a frequent theme in exilic writings, for obvious reasons. The Exile was, from the perspective of the exiles, a world turned upside down. The men in the black hats, the icons of evil, appeared to have won a convincing victory. The temptation to despair and to assimilate, to accommodate oneself to the "new realities," was strong,

---

18. Moshe Weinfeld, "The Covenant of Grant in the Old Testament and in the Ancient Near East," *JAOS* 90 (1970): 184–205.

almost overpowering. How was this to be prevented? How could the exiles be helped to avoid this fate? The answer is by showing them how to don interpretive spectacles that turned reality the right way up and reminded them that ultimately the good would triumph.

This could be done in a number of different ways. For example, the "hero stories" of Daniel, Esther, and Nehemiah show a member of the exiled group triumphing in the midst of the exilic situation, living in the world but not of it, succeeding through wisdom or through the direct intervention of God on their behalf.[19] In a different way, Ezekiel's temple vision turns the world right side up for his hearers, showing them a world in which faithful service of Israel's God receives its due reward.

That reward is, in Ezekiel's vision, a graded reward. Those who have been most faithful (the Zadokites) are rewarded with the greatest access to God; those who have been less faithful (Levites, princes, people) are progressively further at a distance from the throne. This gradation of reward should be neither overstressed nor understressed; there is real differentiation on the basis of merit, yet all the renewed people receive the fundamental blessing of being restored to God's land, with God dwelling in their midst.

Both of these aspects of Ezekiel's teaching are present in the New Testament. (1) In the vision of the new Jerusalem in Revelation 21, the fundamental equality of the saints is stressed. All are made perfect and granted standing in the presence of God himself, the heavenly Most Holy Place, which is the entire city. This is true because of the "covenant of grant" given to all of us who are in Christ; his righteousness is the basis for our full inheritance. In him, through faith, every Christian receives the righteousness of God (Rom. 3:22). In the parable of the workers in the vineyard, those who have worked hardest and longest receive the same reward as those who are hired at the eleventh hour (Matt. 20:1–16).

(2) Yet there are also texts that seem to affirm gradation in reward. In 1 Corinthians 3, Paul draws a contrast between two types of builders. Both are Christians, building up God's church on the only available foundation, Jesus Christ (1 Cor. 3:11); but one builds with gold, silver, and precious stones, while the other builds with wood, hay, and straw (3:12). The works of each will be exposed on the Day of Judgment, its quality tested with fire (3:13). If what a person has built survives, he or she will receive a reward. If it is burned up, he or she will suffer loss (3:14–15). Both are equally saved (3:15), but they receive different rewards.[20]

---

19. On the sociological function of these stories, see Smith, *Religion of the Landless,* 162–64.
20. Anthony A. Hoekema, *The Bible and the Future* (Grand Rapids: Eerdmans, 1979), 263.

Intriguingly, the two Synoptic versions of the parable of the talents present complementary pictures. In Matthew, the focus is on the sameness of the reward that the faithful stewards receive: The man who has been faithful with two talents hears his master say exactly the same words as the one who was faithful with five: "Well done, good and faithful servant! You have been faithful with a few things; I will put you in charge of many things. Come and share your master's happiness!" (Matt. 25:21, 23). Both have been equally responsible with different amounts and so receive the same reward. In Luke's account, however, the one who faithfully achieved a tenfold increase in the money is rewarded with charge of ten cities, while the servant whose stewardship resulted in a fivefold increase is awarded charge over five cities (Luke 19:17, 19). Starting off with the same amount, their differing fruitfulness receives a graded reward.

There is also a desire throughout the Old Testament for a fully righteous priest who will be able to stand before God on the basis of his faithfulness. In 1 Samuel 2:35, in response to the unfaithfulness of the priests of the day, Hophni and Phinehas, God promised that in the future he would raise up "a faithful priest, who will do according to what is in my heart and mind." Ultimately, both that promise and that desire find their fulfillment in the coming of Jesus, the merciful and faithful high priest of God's appointing (Heb. 2:17). He is the only one who ever has stood, or ever will be able to stand, before God in his own righteousness, to offer to him the prayers and praises of his people. As a result, he is the high priest whom we need to enable us to approach the heavenly throne with boldness (Heb. 4:15–16). Our privileged access comes not from our own righteousness but from his.

ON REWARDS. "What's in it for me?" may seem a crass approach to discerning religious truth. Such an approach smacks too much of health, wealth, and prosperity teachers, who promise an immediate cash payoff for acts of devotion to God. In reaction, Christians have sometimes wanted to discuss the questions of faith "more objectively," as if we should be able to delight in a religion that is true, even though its truth is of no benefit to us personally. An extreme position in this direction was developed by Samuel Hopkins in late eighteenth-century New England,

---

21. Joseph A. Conforti, *Samuel Hopkins and the New Divinity Movement: Calvinism, the Congregational Ministry and Reform in New England Between the Great Awakenings* (Grand Rapids: Christian Univ. Press, 1981), 120. This view of Hopkins represents a conscious distancing from the view of Jonathan Edwards, cited below.

who held that a Christian should be willing to be damned for the glory of God.[21] The true believer should, so the argument went, desire to serve God even in the absence of any reward.

Scripture is more balanced than either the health-and-wealth extreme or the Samuel Hopkins extreme. Jesus himself asks us to consider carefully the payoff involved in different allegiances when he says, "What good will it be for a man if he gains the whole world, yet forfeits his soul?" (Matt. 16:26). He urges us to expend ourselves to store up treasure in heaven (Luke 12:33). Paul stresses repeatedly that our sonship makes us heirs—heirs of God and joint heirs with Christ (Rom. 8:17); it is this future reward that makes our present sufferings of little account (8:18). The world may consider that promise of little account, disdainfully describing it as "pie in the sky when you die," but for Paul it is the basis for a hope that engenders patience in the present (8:25). This hope is not mercenary; it is simply the natural desire of love to possess its object.[22] The person who disdains "pie in the sky" is probably a person with no love of pie.

The function of the scriptural teaching of rewards is twofold: It stresses the accountability of the saints to God as well as their future vindication by him.[23] On the one hand, God expects fruitfulness from his servants and will hold everyone accountable for the use of the resources and opportunities entrusted to each one. Much is expected of the one to whom much is given. On the other hand, it is *God* to whom we are accountable and to whom we are to look for our reward.

This latter aspect of the Bible's teaching is particularly important for those in exile like Ezekiel's readers and for us, who struggle to live in a world where it seems that the immoral thrive while the godly struggle to make ends meet. It speaks to those who, like the psalmist, are tempted to envy the arrogant on account of the prosperity of the wicked (Ps. 73:3). It speaks to all of us who have bought into the ancient lie, presently promoted vigorously from Madison Avenue, that "a man's life . . . consist[s] in the abundance of his possessions" (Luke 12:15).

The answer for Ezekiel, as for the psalmist, comes from a visit to the sanctuary, the place of God's presence with his people. There he is shown that what really counts in life are not the toys of this world but the joys of life in the presence of God. Ezekiel could have echoed the psalmist's words of Psalm 73:25–28:

> Whom have I in heaven but you?
>   And earth has nothing I desire besides you.
> My flesh and my heart may fail,

---

22. C. S. Lewis, *The Problem of Pain*, 145.

23. Darrell L. Bock, *Luke* (NIVAC; Grand Rapids: Zondervan, 1996), 488.

but God is the strength of my heart and my portion forever.
Those who are far from you will perish;
   you destroy all who are unfaithful to you.
But as for me, it is good to be near God.
   I have made the Sovereign LORD my refuge;
   I will tell of all your deeds.

In biblical terms, the reward that Christians look for and will receive is not a material one. We do not long for bigger and better mansions in heaven,[24] still less for Cadillacs and country club homes here on earth. Our heart's desire is rather to approach the presence of Almighty God and to stand before him, to be able to cast down our crowns at his feet and worship, lost in wonder, love, and praise. For us, as for the psalmist, it is simply good to be near God. That is the "pie in the sky" for which we long so passionately, and we could never be content to be eternally without it. As Jonathan Edwards put it:

> Love to God . . . will make a man forever unwilling, utterly and finally, to be deprived of that part of his own happiness which he has in God's being blessed and glorified, and the more he loves him, the more unwilling he will be. So that this supposition, that a man can be willing to be perfectly and utterly miserable out of love to God, is inconsistent with itself.[25]

The way of the cross. There is only one way to enter this reward of eternal life in the close presence of God: the way of the cross. When James and John sought the privilege of sitting at Jesus' right and left hand in glory, the problem was not what they sought but the way in which they sought it. To be close to Jesus is indeed the ultimate reward that heaven offers, but it is not to be had for the asking. Rather, it belongs to those who have drunk the cup of Jesus and shared in his baptism (Mark 10:38). Such privilege is opened up to all Christians through his death in our place. When we are baptized, we are baptized into his death and the fruits that flow from his drinking of the cup in our place (Rom. 6:4). Yet the Scriptures also teach of a special reward reserved for those who have followed closely after the way of the suffering

---

24. Thus there is something fundamentally sub-Christian about the popular old gospel song by Ira Stamphill, "I've Got a Mansion Just Over the Hilltop." This song asserts "I'm satisfied with just a cottage below / A little silver and a little gold / But in that city where the ransomed will shine / I want a gold one that's silver lined." It is striking that in the entire description of the joys of heaven in this song, God is not even mentioned!

25. Cited in Conforti, *Samuel Hopkins and the New Divinity Movement*, 121.

servant in this life (Mark 10:45). We are heirs of his glory in the world to come insofar as we share in his sufferings in the present (Rom. 8:17).

However, the privilege of close access to God is a reward we do not have to wait for eternity to begin to experience. We get to sample the firstfruits of the pie ahead of time. Even now, we can approach the throne of God with boldness, presenting our praises and our petitions, basking in the glory of his love. But if we expect to experience the full blessing of communion with God, our behavior must reflect his holiness. For the Zadokites, access to God's presence meant heavy restrictions on their lifestyle. There were things they could not touch, places they could not go to, food they could not eat, and clothes they could not wear if they were to minister in the presence of the all-holy God. So too for us, if we expect to experience the blessing of God's presence with us, then our lifestyle will be (from the world's perspective) restricted.

People around us will undoubtedly think us strange, "narrow" people because we do not do the things they delight to do (1 Peter 4:4). They will find us odd in our commitment to the truth over convenient lies, to God's Word over more fashionable contemporary perspectives, to morality in an age in which anything goes. But we are not accountable to them and their scale of values. Our scale of values should be centered around the glory of communion with God in the present and eternal life in his presence in the days to come, both of which should motivate us to lives of purity (1 John 3:3). Our world is turned right side up. As John Newton put it:

> What words can express the privilege and honor of believers, who, whenever they please, have audience of the King of kings, whose compassion, mercy and power are, like his majesty, infinite. The world wonders at their indifference to the vain pursuits and amusements by which others are engrossed; that they are so patient in trouble, so inflexible in their conduct, so well satisfied with that state of poverty and obscurity which the Lord, for the most part, allots them, but the wonder would cease if what passes in secret were publicly known. They have obtained the pearl of great price; they have communion with God; they derive their wisdom, strength and comfort from on

---

26. "Communion with God," *Select Letters of John Newton* (Edinburgh: Banner of Truth, 1960 reprint), 34.

high, and cast all their cares on him who, they assuredly know, vouch-

safes to take care of them.[26]

Ezekiel 45-46

\(\)

WHEN YOU ALLOT the land as an inheritance, you are to present to the LORD a portion of the land as a sacred district, 25,000 cubits long and 20,000 cubits wide; the entire area will be holy. ²Of this, a section 500 cubits square is to be for the sanctuary, with 50 cubits around it for open land. ³In the sacred district, measure off a section 25,000 cubits long and 10,000 cubits wide. In it will be the sanctuary, the Most Holy Place. ⁴It will be the sacred portion of the land for the priests, who minister in the sanctuary and who draw near to minister before the LORD. It will be a place for their houses as well as a holy place for the sanctuary. ⁵An area 25,000 cubits long and 10,000 cubits wide will belong to the Levites, who serve in the temple, as their possession for towns to live in.

⁶'''You are to give the city as its property an area 5,000 cubits wide and 25,000 cubits long, adjoining the sacred portion; it will belong to the whole house of Israel.

⁷'''The prince will have the land bordering each side of the area formed by the sacred district and the property of the city. It will extend westward from the west side and eastward from the east side, running lengthwise from the western to the eastern border parallel to one of the tribal portions. ⁸This land will be his possession in Israel. And my princes will no longer oppress my people but will allow the house of Israel to possess the land according to their tribes.

⁹'''This is what the Sovereign LORD says: You have gone far enough, O princes of Israel! Give up your violence and oppression and do what is just and right. Stop dispossessing my people, declares the Sovereign LORD. ¹⁰You are to use accurate scales, an accurate ephah and an accurate bath. ¹¹The ephah and the bath are to be the same size, the bath containing a tenth of a homer and the ephah a tenth of a homer; the homer is to be the standard measure for both. ¹²The shekel is to consist of twenty gerahs. Twenty shekels plus twenty-five shekels plus fifteen shekels equal one mina.

¹³"'This is the special gift you are to offer: a sixth of an ephah from each homer of wheat and a sixth of an ephah from each homer of barley. ¹⁴The prescribed portion of oil, measured by the bath, is a tenth of a bath from each cor (which consists of ten baths or one homer, for ten baths are equivalent to a homer). ¹⁵Also one sheep is to be taken from every flock of two hundred from the well-watered pastures of Israel. These will be used for the grain offerings, burnt offerings and fellowship offerings to make atonement for the people, declares the Sovereign LORD. ¹⁶All the people of the land will participate in this special gift for the use of the prince in Israel. ¹⁷It will be the duty of the prince to provide the burnt offerings, grain offerings and drink offerings at the festivals, the New Moons and the Sabbaths—at all the appointed feasts of the house of Israel. He will provide the sin offerings, grain offerings, burnt offerings and fellowship offerings to make atonement for the house of Israel.

¹⁸"'This is what the Sovereign LORD says: In the first month on the first day you are to take a young bull without defect and purify the sanctuary. ¹⁹The priest is to take some of the blood of the sin offering and put it on the doorposts of the temple, on the four corners of the upper ledge of the altar and on the gateposts of the inner court. ²⁰You are to do the same on the seventh day of the month for anyone who sins unintentionally or through ignorance; so you are to make atonement for the temple.

²¹"'In the first month on the fourteenth day you are to observe the Passover, a feast lasting seven days, during which you shall eat bread made without yeast. ²²On that day the prince is to provide a bull as a sin offering for himself and for all the people of the land. ²³Every day during the seven days of the Feast he is to provide seven bulls and seven rams without defect as a burnt offering to the LORD, and a male goat for a sin offering. ²⁴He is to provide as a grain offering an ephah for each bull and an ephah for each ram, along with a hin of oil for each ephah.

²⁵"'During the seven days of the Feast, which begins in the seventh month on the fifteenth day, he is to make the same provision for sin offerings, burnt offerings, grain offerings and oil.

⁴⁶:¹"'This is what the Sovereign LORD says: The gate of the inner court facing east is to be shut on the six working days, but on the Sabbath day and on the day of the New Moon it is to be opened. ²The prince is to enter from the outside through the portico of the gateway and stand by the gatepost. The priests are to sacrifice his burnt offering and his fellowship offerings. He is to worship at the threshold of the gateway and then go out, but the gate will not be shut until evening. ³On the Sabbaths and New Moons the people of the land are to worship in the presence of the LORD at the entrance to that gateway. ⁴The burnt offering the prince brings to the LORD on the Sabbath day is to be six male lambs and a ram, all without defect. ⁵The grain offering given with the ram is to be an ephah, and the grain offering with the lambs is to be as much as he pleases, along with a hin of oil for each ephah. ⁶On the day of the New Moon he is to offer a young bull, six lambs and a ram, all without defect. ⁷He is to provide as a grain offering one ephah with the bull, one ephah with the ram, and with the lambs as much as he wants to give, along with a hin of oil with each ephah. ⁸When the prince enters, he is to go in through the portico of the gateway, and he is to come out the same way.

⁹"'When the people of the land come before the LORD at the appointed feasts, whoever enters by the north gate to worship is to go out the south gate; and whoever enters by the south gate is to go out the north gate. No one is to return through the gate by which he entered, but each is to go out the opposite gate. ¹⁰The prince is to be among them, going in when they go in and going out when they go out.

¹¹"'At the festivals and the appointed feasts, the grain offering is to be an ephah with a bull, an ephah with a ram, and with the lambs as much as one pleases, along with a hin of oil for each ephah. ¹²When the prince provides a freewill offering to the LORD—whether a burnt offering or fellowship offerings—the gate facing east is to be opened for him. He shall offer his burnt offering or his fellowship offerings as he does on the Sabbath day. Then he shall go out, and after he has gone out, the gate will be shut.

¹³"'Every day you are to provide a year-old lamb without defect for a burnt offering to the LORD; morning by morning

you shall provide it. [14]You are also to provide with it morning by morning a grain offering, consisting of a sixth of an ephah with a third of a hin of oil to moisten the flour. The presenting of this grain offering to the LORD is a lasting ordinance. [15]So the lamb and the grain offering and the oil shall be provided morning by morning for a regular burnt offering.

[16]"'This is what the Sovereign LORD says: If the prince makes a gift from his inheritance to one of his sons, it will also belong to his descendants; it is to be their property by inheritance. [17]If, however, he makes a gift from his inheritance to one of his servants, the servant may keep it until the year of freedom; then it will revert to the prince. His inheritance belongs to his sons only; it is theirs. [18]The prince must not take any of the inheritance of the people, driving them off their property. He is to give his sons their inheritance out of his own property, so that none of my people will be separated from his property.'"

[19]Then the man brought me through the entrance at the side of the gate to the sacred rooms facing north, which belonged to the priests, and showed me a place at the western end. [20]He said to me, "This is the place where the priests will cook the guilt offering and the sin offering and bake the grain offering, to avoid bringing them into the outer court and consecrating the people."

---

1. The unit of measure is unexpressed throughout this passage, except for the buffer zone around the sanctuary, which is explicitly 50 cubits. The KJV inserted "reeds," on the basis of 42:16–20, which identified the temple as 500 reeds square, but which has text-critical problems of its own. The overall description of the temple dimensions in chs. 40–42 seems predicated on the basis of a temple complex 500 cubits square. This makes the entire central portion about 8 miles square (25,000 cubits by 25,000 cubits). If the dimensions are in reeds, the central square is closer to 50 miles by 50 miles, which would leave virtually no land on either side for the prince before you arrive at the Mediterranean on the west and the Jordan on the east.

2. According to the NIV, which follows the Septuagint. The MT gives 25,000 by 10,000, restricting this "sacred district" to that occupied by the priests. Whichever is original, the difference is not merely the result of a visual error but of an exegetical difference over whether this refers to the inner, priestly portion, or includes the parallel strip assigned to the Levites. In favor of the Septuagint, 45:3 seems to suggest that the priestly area comprises only one part of the "sacred district," and 48:20 suggests that the overall 25,000 square is made up of the sacred area and the 5,000 by 25,000 strip assigned to the city. In favor of the MT, see Stevenson, *Vision of Transformation*, 31–32.

3. E. G. King, "The Prince in Ezekiel," *Old Testament Student* 5 (1885): 115.

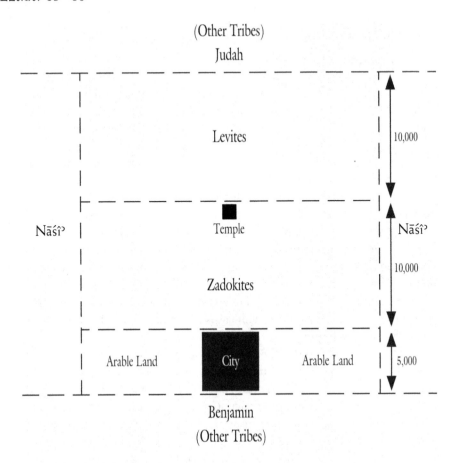

(Other Tribes)

Judah

Levites

10,000

Nāśîʾ

Temple

Nāśîʾ

10,000

Zadokites

Arable Land

City

Arable Land

5,000

Benjamin

(Other Tribes)

Figure 2.
Distribution of land in the sacred portion

²¹He then brought me to the outer court and led me around to its four corners, and I saw in each corner another court. ²²In the four corners of the outer court were enclosed courts, forty cubits long and thirty cubits wide; each of the courts in the four corners was the same size. ²³Around the inside of each of the four courts was a ledge of stone, with places for fire built all around under the ledge. ²⁴He said to me, "These are the kitchens where those who minister at the temple will cook the sacrifices of the people."

---

4. The arrangement of the levitical and priestly strips is not given explicitly, causing some to argue that the sequence moves from north to south (priestly portion, levitical portion,

 IN EZEKIEL 44:28 the priests were promised no
"inheritance" or "possession" in Israel, for the Lord
would be their inheritance and possession.
Ezekiel 45:1–8 follows up this reference to a new
division of the land with a preliminary description of the central area of this
land, a sacred strip running from the Mediterranean Sea in the west to the
eastern edge of the Promised Land. The division of the land as a whole will
be outlined in much greater detail in 47:13–48:35, but the central elements
are clear already in chapter 45.

The issue of possession of the land was, of course, a pressing concern to
the landless exiles. It had already surfaced as a problem in 33:24–29. The
echoes of the theme of Jubilee that we noted at the outset of the vision in
chapter 40 would also naturally have raised the question of a redistribution
of the land. But the prophet was concerned about more than simply assuring the exiles that there would be an equitable reallocation of the land at some
point in the future. Ezekiel wanted to reorient his hearers' focus onto what
the original idea of a Promised Land was all about: a land in which God
would dwell in their midst.

The primary focus of the division of the land for the prophet here is not
safeguarding human equality and land rights, but rather asserting divine sovereignty and safeguarding the divine presence in their midst. Hence, Ezekiel's
first concern in introducing the concept of a new division of the land is to
insist that the people are to "present to the LORD" as an offering the central
portion of the land as a "sacred district" (*qōdeš*, 45:1). This district is to measure 25,000 cubits[1] by 20,000 cubits, comprising the land assigned to the
priests (25,000 cubits by 10,000 cubits) and a similar area assigned to the
Levites.[2]

---

city portion; e.g., Cameron M. Mackay, "Why Study Ezekiel 40–48," *EvQ* 37 [1965]: 161;
Greenberg, "Design and Themes," 202). If, however, the motion is from the inside outward,
as in the tour of the temple, then the priestly portion would be in the center, flanked on
the north by the levitical portion and on the south by the city portion. Given the importance of geometric center in the square design of Ezekiel's temple, it seems most probable
that the temple is located at the geometric center of the sacred portion.

5. This may be the only equitable way of distributing the land among the twelve tribes,
given the topography of the Promised Land, as Greenberg asserts ("Idealism and Practicality
in Numbers 35:4–5 and Ezekiel 48," *JAOS* 88 [1968]: 59–66). However, it is theology, not
practicality, that is driving the division.

6. Stevenson, *Vision of Transformation*, 107–8.

7. Menahem Haran, "The Law-Code of Ezekiel 40–48 and Its Relation to the Priestly
School," *HUCA* 50 (1979): 57.

The primary purpose of this sacred district is to provide a zone of graded holiness outside the temple, exactly analogous to that inside the temple.[3] The entire temple complex is, from the perspective of the land, a "Most Holy Place" (45:3). The area immediately around the sanctuary is therefore reserved for the priests, in which they are to build their homes (45:3–4). The strip parallel to the priestly portion and to its north is reserved for the Levites and their cities (45:5), while the half-size strip to its south is for the city (45:6).[4] To the east and west of the 25,000 cubit sacred square, the remainder of the sacred strip is to be allocated to the prince (*nāśîʾ*) as his personal (or rather familial) inheritance.

The same principles of graded access that applied within the temple complex have thus been extrapolated to the land itself, resulting in an entirely temple-oriented geography. This is evident not simply from the central position of the temple within the land and the restricted access allowed to different groups and individuals, but even from the east-west alignment of the strips into which the land has been divided. In contrast to the rather randomly shaped chunks into which the land was divided in Joshua 12–21, in Ezekiel the entire land is aligned with the east-west orientation of the temple.[5]

Holiness is thus the key principle underlying the division of the land, as is evident from the fact that the word *qōdēš* and its cognates occur no fewer than eleven times in 45:1–6. At the center of this Holy Land is the temple, not the city or the king. The old Zion theology, which found its focus in the twin pillars of the election of Jerusalem and David, is now refocused on the central assertion of Yahweh's kingship and rule in the temple.[6]

Even the future kings of the land, now addressed as "my princes," are subject to the Lord's oversight (45:8). Unlike the tribal "leaders" (same Heb. word) in the first division of the land in the days of Joshua (Num. 34:18), these princes in Ezekiel have no active part to play in distributing the land. The divine king has already allocated it, and their responsibility is limited to allowing the house of Israel to possess their tribal land in peace (Ezek. 45:8). Examples of this abuse in Israel's past are too numerous to require documentation; perhaps the classic case is Jezebel's judicial murder of Naboth in order to procure his vineyard for Ahab (1 Kings 21:1–16). Indeed, we may go so far as to say that this is the significant motivation in assigning a substantial portion of the land to the prince and his descendants. The prophet is not concerned so much to keep them in the manner to which they would like to become accustomed but rather to enable them to meet their own needs and to support the ministry of the temple without burdening and oppressing the people.

---

8. See the discussion of the centrality of these features in Ezekiel 43.

9. Block, *Ezekiel 25–48*, 667.

The primary focus of the prince's duties is temple-centered, as with virtually everything else in Ezekiel 40–48. Thus the prince is responsible to ensure that accurate weights and measures are used in gathering up the offerings and gifts of the people (45:10–12). All are required to participate in the sacred offerings provided by the prince (45:13–16), and it is foreseen that this might be viewed as a possible means for the prince to enrich himself at the cost of the people by using disproportionate measures.[7] Such a possibility is immediately disallowed.

But although the people provide the materials for the regular offerings (45:15–16), it is the prince's responsibility from his own resources to provide the offerings for the special occasions: Sabbaths, New Moons, and annual festivals (45:17). In both the regular and the special offerings, the prince has a central role as the representative of the people in worship, presenting the "sin offerings, grain offerings, burnt offerings and fellowship offerings to make atonement for the house of Israel" (45:17). This is a great privilege, especially given the central significance of purification and atonement in chapters 40–48.[8]

Mention of the sacrifices on these special occasions in the ritual calendar leads into a discussion of the ritual calendar itself. Like the vision of the temple itself, Ezekiel's calendar appears to be a stripped-down, focused edition of what had previously been in force. There is no mention of the Feast of Weeks, the third annual festival, and the remaining two festivals (Passover and Tabernacles) have become virtually symmetrical festivals of purification, celebrated in the first and seventh months of the year respectively (45:18–25). Of the two, the Feast of Passover retains more of its distinctive features: It is explicitly named "the Passover," and the seven-day feast during which only unleavened bread is to be eaten and the application of sacrificial blood to the doorposts clearly recall the original festival (45:19–21). Yet its original character as a festival of the Lord's deliverance from Egypt is now subordinated to a concern for purifying the sanctuary.[9]

The Passover feast proper is now preceded by a dual ceremony of cleansing the temple on the first and seventh days of the first month (45:18–20). During the seven days of the feast, the prince is to provide seven bulls and

10. Zimmerli, *Ezekiel*, 2:486.

11. Here ʿ*am hāʾāreṣ* seems to denote the entire worshiping community. See my *Ezekiel and the Leaders of Israel*, 120–21.

12. Zimmerli, *Ezekiel*, 2:490.

13. Dennis J. McCarthy, *Treaty and Covenant* (AnBib 21a; Rome: Biblical Institute, 1981), 57.

14. Of course, given the permanently closed east gate of the outer court and the absence of any gate on the west, this is the only axis on which a procession through the temple can take place. Elsewhere, however, processions tend to be to or around sacred objects rather than through them (Ps. 26:6; 42:4; 68:24; cf. Neh. 12:37–43), and it seems to me that there is more at stake in this verse than mere "traffic control."

seven rams daily as a burnt offering, along with the daily purification offering of a male goat (45:23). This represents a substantial increase from the sacrifices demanded for the Passover in the Mosaic legislation of Numbers 28. The requirement to offer a bull as a purification offering for the prince himself and the entire community before the feast begins is in line with the requirements of Leviticus 4:14, however (Ezek. 45:22).

If the Passover feast is still named and recognizable, the festival in the seventh month, which takes place at the time of the Feast of Tabernacles, has lost all its original distinctiveness. It lacks any name or description, except for the fact that the prince is to provide the same offerings for it as at the Passover (45:25). There is apparently no comparable purification ceremony before it, nor is any ceremony recorded that might correspond to the Day of Atonement ceremony associated with this festival in Leviticus 16. The primary annual ritual purification of the central sanctuary now takes place at the beginning of the year. But Ezekiel's special interest in purification remains clear in the prominent place given to the sin offerings in the list of 45:25. Both festivals thereby come to share the same interest in atonement for sin, which is the recurrent theme of Ezekiel's cult.[10]

The prince is also required to provide the offerings for the Sabbath and New Moon festivals (46:1–8). On the Sabbath, he is to offer six lambs and a ram as a burnt offering, along with the proportionate grain and oil offerings to accompany them (46:4–5), while on the monthly New Moon festival, he is to offer the same plus a young bull (46:6). Of course, he cannot enter the inner court to offer these sacrifices himself; the priests must offer them on his behalf (46:2). However, he has the unique privilege as a layman of approaching to the threshold of the inner east gate and prostrating himself there before the Lord (46:2). "The people of the land,"[11] however, are only permitted to approach to the entrance of the gate (46:3). With eight steps leading up to the gateway and beyond it a corridor almost ninety feet long, it is clear that their view of the activities of the inner court is decidedly limited.[12] In Ezekiel's program, the laity are being kept at a "safe" distance from the holy things.

At the annual festivals, God's people are required to present themselves and prostrate themselves before the Lord (46:9). The command for the vassal to present himself at the court of the great king was a common require-

---

15. Tryggve N. D. Mettinger, *Solomonic State Officials: A Study of the Civil Government Officials of the Israelite Monarchy* (Lund: Gleerup, 1971), 80–110.

16. From the outside to the center (40:5–41:4); from the center to the outside (41:5–42:20); from the outside to the center (43:1–5); and from the center to the outside (43:13–46:24).

ment of ancient covenant treaties;[13] this is therefore an act of corporate submission on the part of the people before the divine king. The community at large is assigned no other tasks in the cult. Even their annual processions through the temple are in the "profane" north-south or south-north direction (46:9), at right angles to the "holy" east-west orientation of priestly ministrations at the altar of burnt offering (43:17).[14] Though the people are clearly expected to offer sacrifices of their own (cf. 46:24), these are relegated to footnote status, barely perceptible in the peripheral vision of the prophet.

The representative nature of the prince as chief worshiper is clear from the fact that he enters in the midst of the people and goes out with them (46:10). But his privileged position is clear also from his access to the east gate of the inner court, which is opened for him whenever he wishes to offer a freewill sacrifice (46:12).

The section on the sacrifices closes with the requirements for the daily sacrifice, which is now limited to a single morning sacrifice of a year-old lamb, with its associated grain offering (46:13–14). The former practice of offering also an evening sacrifice, attested in Numbers 28:4 and 1 Kings 18:29, 36, goes unmentioned.

After his discussion of the sacrifices, Ezekiel returns to his previous topic, the inheritance of the prince (46:16–18; cf. 45:7–8). The prince holds this land leasehold rather than outright, in trust for future generations. He can therefore only give it permanently to his children; if he should give it as a gift to one of his servants, it will revert to the crown at the year of freedom, the Jubilee year, when all land reverted to its original owners (Lev. 25:13). The purpose of this regulation is straightforward: In an economy where the

---

17. *b. Šabb.* 13b.

18. So Rashi, *Ezekiel*, 2.406.

19. *b. Menaḥ* 45a.

20. *The Scofield Reference Bible*, 908; Feinberg, *Ezekiel*, 234.

21. As is pointed out by fellow dispensationalist Jerry M. Hullinger ("The Problem of Animal Sacrifices in Ezekiel 40–48," *BibSac* 152 [1995]: 280). Hullinger's own proposal is that the sacrifices achieve genuine "atonement" in the sense of purgation, protecting the restored sancta from accumulations of impurity. While this treatment is more sensitive to the significance of the various different sacrifices in the levitical system, it is doubtful that it is an adequate solution to the problem since Hebrews presents Christ's once-for-all sacrifice as the ultimate and definitive purgation (Heb. 9:12–14). If Christ has effectively cleansed the heavenly tabernacle once and for all, it is hard to see how there can be earthly repetitions of that purgation that do not detract from it. It is striking that *The New Scofield Reference Bible* at least allows the possibility that the sacrifices may not be intended "to be taken literally, in view of the putting away of such offerings, but is rather to be regarded as a presentation of the worship of redeemed Israel, in her own land and in a millennial temple, using the terms with which the Jews were familiar in Ezekiel's day" (888). No explanation is advanced of what this "nonliteral" sacrificial worship might look like.

king typically rewarded loyal service by gifts of land, there would have been a perpetual temptation for the king to acquire ever more land with which to reward his followers.[15] Not so in the new Israel, which will be reconstituted as a nation of free peasants with an inalienable claim to their own land.

The fact that this powerful assertion against land stealing brackets the sacrificial regulations emphasizes the fact that the driving force behind the division of the land is not egalitarianism but divine sovereignty: The land is the Lord's and he divides it. For the prince to intrude on that divinely sanctioned division by amassing greater quantities of land for himself is as impermissible as intruding on the central presence of God in the inner sanctuary or offering improper sacrifices to God. The prince is thereby continually reminded that he is a vassal of the great king and must behave as such.

The entire section of 44:1–46:24 is rounded off by a return to the beginning. The heavenly messenger, inactive since 44:4, returns to guide the prophet out of the inner court via the sacred rooms where the priests cook and eat the sacred offerings that are not permitted to leave the sanctity of the inner court (46:19–20). Together they arrive back at the outer court, where the prophet is shown "the kitchens" (L) at its four extremities, where the Levites are to cook the sacrifices of the people (46:21–24). The tour of the temple is thus neatly completed, having gone from the outside to the center (40:5–41:4) and back out again twice.[16]

INTERPRETIVE PROBLEMS and their attempted solutions. The middle section of Ezekiel's temple vision has provided almost insoluble problems for a number of different interpretative approaches. The rabbis, convinced in the unbreakable unity of the Old Testament and able at times to resort to considerable ingenuity in their harmonizations, found it virtually impossible to harmonize the regulations of Ezekiel with those of Moses in the Pentateuch. Indeed, it is recorded that one rabbi, Hananiah ben Hezekiah, hid himself away in his attic and burned three hundred barrels of oil in his

---

22. Stuart, *Ezekiel*, 400; Willem VanGemeren, *Interpreting the Prophetic Word* (Grand Rapids: Zondervan, 1990), 336.

23. Thomas, *God Strengthens*, 287; Feinberg, *Ezekiel*, 257.

24. Greenberg, "Design and Themes," 208; Steven Tuell, "The Temple Vision of Ezekiel 40–48: A Program for Restoration," *Proceedings of the Eastern Great Lakes Biblical Society* 2 (1982): 96.

25. Daniel I. Block, "Bringing Back David," in *The Lord's Anointed: Interpretation of Old Testament Messianic Texts*, ed. P. E. Satterthwaite, R. S. Hess, and G. J. Wenham (Grand Rapids: Baker, 1995), 181.

lamp before being finally able to reconcile the different laws. But for his labors, the book of Ezekiel as a whole was in danger of being excluded from the canon.[17] Unfortunately, the fruits of his efforts were lost to future generations "because of our iniquities."[18] At times, the rabbis gave up altogether and referred their pupils to a higher authority: Elijah would explain it when he came.[19]

From an entirely different perspective, the middle portion of Ezekiel's temple vision has proved problematic to dispensationalists. Their difficulty is not in harmonizing Ezekiel and Moses but in harmonizing a "literal" interpretation of Ezekiel's temple as the millennial temple of the restored Jewish nation with the apparently plain New Testament teaching that the levitical sacrifices have been brought to an end with the death of Christ (Heb. 10). Once again, a number of different solutions have been suggested. The majority of dispensationalists have argued that the sacrifices are memorials to the sacrifice of Christ, with no atoning character.[20] However, the idea that these are memorial sacrifices is nowhere apparent in Ezekiel, and it is specifically claimed by Ezekiel that these offerings *will* make atonement (45:15, 17, 20).[21]

Others have struggled with the identity of "the prince" (*nāśîʾ*) in Ezekiel 40–48. Is he a messianic figure, as the "prince" of Ezekiel 34 and 37 appears to be?[22] How then do we explain the need to warn the Messiah against sin (45:9; 46:18)? Does the Messiah need to offer a sin offering on his own behalf (45:22), and does he have children (46:16)?[23] But if he is not the Messiah, who is he?

These approaches, it seems to me, have run into difficulty because they have fallen into the classic temptation that besets those of us who take the unity of Scripture seriously. They have given priority to the universal over the particular, asking, "How can I make this text fit with what I know from the rest of Scripture?" rather than, "What distinctive truth does this particular passage teach?" As a result, commentaries on this passage tend to be long on harmonization and short on explanation. Actually, the interpretative problems that so stubbornly resist harmonization are significant keys to understanding the meaning of the passage and of the temple vision as a whole, for which this provides the center.

The nature of a vision and its message here. What the approach of rabbis and dispensationalists alike forget is that Ezekiel 40–48 presents a *vision*, not legislation. To be sure, part of the vision is in legislative form, but it is

---

26. Samson H. Levey, *The Messiah: An Aramaic Interpretation: The Messianic Exegesis of the Targum* (Cincinnati: Hebrew Union College, 1974), xix.

27. Duguid, *Ezekiel and the Leaders of Israel*, 55–56.

28. John Taylor is at least interested in asking that question, even if his answer ("It illustrates the fact that in ancient Israel no less than today liturgical experimentation was demanded by new situations") fails to convince (*Ezekiel*, 275).

vision in the form of legislation, not legislation in the form of vision. Legislation is a law program designed to be carried out; it must therefore either be harmonized with existing legislation or supersede it. Legislation is intended to be interpreted literally as meaning exactly what it says. If God's intent through Ezekiel was to impart new legislation to supplement or supersede the law of Moses, then it was a failure. The returning Jews made no apparent effort to implement the changes proposed, even those that would have required no radical expense or earth-moving equipment, such as the two annual festivals.[24] Nor is there any indication within the vision that its implementation is to be postponed to a future millennial temple. Unlike the battle with Gog, which has frequent time indicators fixing it in the distant future, the temple of Ezekiel 40–48 is already extant in visionary form in Ezekiel's own time.[25]

A *vision*, however, does not need to be carried out in its details to achieve its purpose. When Martin Luther King Jr. cried out in his famous speech "I have a dream . . ." and went on to outline a vision of black and white children playing together in harmony, his purpose was to encourage repentance, changed hearts, and hope. Provided that emotions were stirred and minds changed to feel sorrow over past attitudes and to envision the possibility of a new future, the dream would have accomplished its purpose, even had repressive laws and practical difficulties prevented the physical realization of the dream. In the same way, Ezekiel's vision was intended to encourage repentance, faithful endurance, and hope of a future unlike the past.

In what ways, then, does Ezekiel 45–46 contribute to this goal of bringing the exiles to repentance, endurance, and hope? (1) The passage (and the vision) asserts that the Lord alone is King. Instead of asking whether "the prince" is a messianic figure, it would be better to ask why the messianic figure of this vision appears in so muted tones, with such limited powers. He is certainly still a figure of great privilege. He owns a substantial portion of real estate bordering on the sacred district; he approaches closer to the Most Holy Place than any other non-Levite; he offers sacrifices on behalf of the whole people; he is the head of a dynasty. But in power he is still well short of the classic form of the central royal figure of the future golden age.[26]

Even the identification of the prince as a descendant of David is lacking (unlike chs. 34 and 37), although it is hard to imagine that Ezekiel had a dif-

---

29. Similarly the new re-creation in Ezek. 37 results not in the formation of one new man but an entire army!

30. Thus Gen. 1 involves three basic elements: forming the spaces (days 1–3), filling the spaces with occupants (days 4–6), and ordering time itself (the framework of "days"). On the priestly concern with the ordering of time, see Philip P. Jenson, *Graded Holiness: A Key to the Priestly Conception of the World* (JSOTS 106; Sheffield: JSOT, 1992), 182–209.

ferent dynasty in mind. Why is that? Because in Ezekiel's vision there is another central royal figure, the Lord himself reigning in the temple. The past abuses of the monarchy will be done away with, legislated out of existence by a rearrangement of the land and by specific commands to the future monarch; but the monarch himself remains as a representative of the people. He remains in place, but only as the vassal of the Great King, God himself.[27]

(2) The passage (and the vision) teaches that God is doing a new and greater thing that involves time as well as space. Instead of asking how we can square Ezekiel's sacrificial legislation with that of the Pentateuch, it would be better to ask about the distinctive goal of his program.[28] In contrast to the Pentateuchal program, Ezekiel's sacrifices appear to be more numerous and more focused on the concept of purification. This is another way of conveying the same message as the temple building itself, which is larger and more restricted in access than the former temple. God is doing something greater than the former things, a greatness that shows itself in the dimensions of the holy space and the number of the sacrifices.[29] God is also doing something that will prevent any repetition of the contamination of the past that drove him from the land, through erecting high walls and buffer zones and inaugurating more rites of purgation.

But the cosmogonic process of creating a new world involves ordering not merely spaces and inhabitants but time itself.[30] For that reason, the distinct lack of "timelessness" in the vision is significant. Unlike most eschatological visions in the Bible, which are essentially static tableaux, frozen in time, Ezekiel envisages a place with Sabbaths and New Moons and new years, a place where the year of Jubilee rolls around and the prince has children. In Ezekiel's reordering of the festival calendar, time itself is brought under the discipline of the new age.

(3) The passage once again underlines the message that the temple is at the center of time and space in the new age. It dominates the restored land, which is entirely oriented with reference to it. Social status is entirely determined by access and position relative to it. Providing for its worship services is to be the dominant concern of the prince and people alike. In place of the old centers of Zion and the Davidic king, now everything revolves around the temple. The city and the king are still there, but they no longer have personal names, so that nothing may detract from the glory and prominence of the dwelling of Yahweh in the midst of his people. To put it into a

---

31. The first three elements are from Roland de Vaux, *Ancient Israel: Its Life and Institutions* (New York: McGraw-Hill, 1965), 451–54. The fourth expresses the essence of the sin offering (ḥaṭṭā˒t).

paraphrase of Isaiah's distinctly messianic language, Ezekiel would have said, "For unto us a temple is constructed, to us a sanctuary is given" (cf. Isa. 9:6).

The prince's position, tasks, and responsibilities are all subordinated to the central vision of God's dwelling in the midst of his people in the temple. Thus, since Jesus is the new temple, the glory of God dwelling in the midst of men and women, it is the temple that is the primary "messianic" figure in Ezekiel 40–48. It is the temple that points us to Jesus, not the prince.

The nature of sacrifice and its relation to Jesus. This concern with the presence of God in the midst of his people explains why the sacrifices are central to the temple vision. The entire levitical system of sacrifice served to undergird the covenant relationship of Israel and God. Sacrifice functioned primarily in four different ways in ancient Israel, each reflecting an aspect of the covenant relationship. (1) It provided a means of restoring breaches in the covenant relationship between the vassal and the Great King, through the giving of a substitute as a ransom payment for the sinner. (2) It functioned as a tribute payment from the vassal to his overlord. (3) It provided an opportunity for the vassal king to enjoy a covenant meal with his suzerain. (4) It served as a means of ensuring the necessary cleansing of impurity so that the holy suzerain might dwell with the vassal.[31] The various sacrifices of the Old Testament each served one or more of these goals.

For the New Testament, however, all of these sacrifices find their fulfillment in Christ. He is the One who atones for us; he is the One who pays our tribute for us; he is the One in whom we experience the blessings of intimate fellowship with the Father; he is the One who cleansed the heavenly temple once and for all on our behalf.

(1) Jesus is our ransom, the atoning sacrifice paid for our redemption. As Mark 10:45 reminds us, Jesus came in order "to give his life as a ransom for many." The apostle Peter tells us, "it was not with perishable things such as silver or gold that you were redeemed ... but with the precious blood of Christ, a lamb without blemish or defect" (1 Peter 1:18–19). Jesus, like Isaac, is the beloved Son, to be offered by his own Father (Matt. 3:17)—though for him there is no animal substituted. Jesus himself is "the Lamb of God, who takes away the sin of the world" (John 1:29). The wages of sin require the death of the covenant-breaker unless a ransom be paid on his or her behalf. Yet unlike the burnt offering, which was offered daily, Jesus offered his sacrifice once and "for all time" on the cross (Heb. 10:12–14). There is no need for a continued repetition of the death of Christ for it was of infinite value.

(2) In addition, Jesus has offered tribute in our place. He lived the perfect life for us, thus fulfilling all the obligations of the covenant. He humbled

---

32. Block, *Ezekiel 25–48*, 686.

himself and became obedient even to the point of death (Phil. 2:8). That is the importance of what theologians call Christ's "active obedience," the fact that his work was not simply to come and die on the cross to pay for our sins, but first of all to come and live the perfect life for us, which is now credited to our account. Without it, his death would not have been sufficient; it would merely have removed our covenant breaking. What God demands of his people, however, is not only no covenant *breaking* but perfect covenant *keeping*. Jesus kept the demands of the law fully in our place.

(3) But as well as being our atonement and our tribute offering, Jesus is also our fellowship offering. In the Lord's Supper, we remember Jesus' death on the cross, where he became the atoning sacrifice for our sins. Yet the meal aspect of the Lord's Supper belongs to the symbolism of the fellowship offering. Unlike Mesopotamian observances, in which the table was laid primarily for the benefit of the deity, the Lord invites his people to sit down to table in his presence and celebrate our deliverance together.[32] We feed on the body of Christ, just as in Old Testament times the people actually ate the fellowship offering. The cup we share is called by Jesus "the new covenant in my blood" (1 Cor. 11:25), recalling the blood of the old covenant, the blood of the burnt offerings and peace offerings sacrificed at Mount Sinai, which was sprinkled on the people (Ex. 24:8). Like the peace offering, the Lord's Supper is a covenant meal, a celebration of the new covenant family of God's goodness and radical self-giving.

(4) Finally, Jesus is our purification offering. Hence in the book of Hebrews the blood of Jesus is not simply applied to the saints, it is applied to the heavenly sanctuary itself. It is efficacious to purify that heavenly sanctuary once and for all, thus ensuring that God can dwell forever in the midst of his people (Heb. 9:23). Because of this definitive purgation, believers now have confident and direct access to the Most Holy Place itself (10:19)! That purgation no longer needs to be repeated in the shadowy forms of the levitical order because in Christ the fullness of the new order has come!

Contemporary Significance

A PATTERN FOR **Christian worship.** If the goal of the vision of Ezekiel 45—46 is to bring the exiles to repentance, endurance, and hope through a vision of reordered worship, how may this passage have the same effect on us?

In the first place, it reminds us as well as them that the heavenly order is different from the appearances of the mundane world in which we live. In our worship, we are constructing an alternative outlook on the world, an alternative view of reality, which challenges the worldview of the majority. In our liturgy, we come apart from the everyday world in which we live the rest of the week and envision a different world, a place where we exiles can find a home. Ezekiel's temple provides us a four-dimensional map of that sacred space, inviting us to consider well its spiritual geography, topography, and chronology and to repent and leave behind our earthbound focus.

Moreover, in Ezekiel's vision the Lord is enthroned as King, exalted far above any rivals. In our worship too, there should be no doubt about the sovereignty of God. Our songs, prayers, readings, testimonies, and other varied elements should be theocentric and Christocentric, exalting the triune God, Father, Son, and Holy Spirit. In the world, God the Father may be denigrated, disregarded, and ridiculed; his Son's name may be most often heard taken in vain; his Spirit may be regularly grieved and blasphemed against. But the meetings of his people should all the more be filled with his praises and focused on hearing and doing his will.

In Ezekiel's vision, the prophet clearly anticipates God's doing something new, something greater even than the faith once delivered to Moses. What Ezekiel and the other Old Testament saints looked forward to has now come about in Christ. As the writer to the Hebrews put it: "In the past God spoke to our forefathers through the prophets at many times and in various ways, but in these last days he has spoken to us by his Son" (Heb. 1:1–2). This greater privilege that we have gives us reason to worship with greater joy and greater reverence and awe than our spiritual forefathers, who lived ahead of the coming of Christ (12:28).

Specifically, the pattern of the Old Testament sacrifices, as delivered to Moses and writ large by Ezekiel, provides a pattern for Christian worship.

- Over the doorway into worship stands written the need for the forgiveness of sins, and at the heart of worship must be the continual return to God's provided ransom, "the Lamb of God, who takes away the sin of the world." This was the focus of the burnt offering.
- In our worship, we should focus our thoughts and give thanks not simply for the passive obedience of Christ—his death on the cross for us—but also for his active obedience—his perfect life lived for us, by which the obligations of the covenant are fulfilled. This was the focus of the grain or tribute offering.
- The goal of our worship—what Christ has achieved for us through his perfect life and atoning death—is nothing less than fellowship with God and with one another around the Lord's Table. This was the focus of the fellowship offering.
- In order for us to worship in the presence of God, both we and the heavenly tabernacle itself must be purified of all unrighteousness. This

was the focus of the purification offering and of the self-offering of Jesus, whose blood purifies us from all sin (1 John 1:7).

Contemporary worship. Worship informed by this pattern will be different in a number of ways from much of what passes for worship in the contemporary church. To begin with, it will have a God-centered (and not merely Christ-centered) focus. The goal of Jesus' earthly ministry was to bring glory to the Father's name (John 12:27–28); in return, God the Father would glorify him (13:31–32). Yet so often the Father disappears almost completely from our contemporary worship songs, replaced by an exclusive focus on my relationship with Jesus.

True worship should also preserve the law-gospel dynamic, which lies at the heart of the best historic liturgies. In other words, in order to appreciate the good news of the gospel we need to confront ourselves again with the reality of God's perfect law, which condemns our own sin and points us to Jesus as our sinless substitute. We need to remind ourselves of our personal impurity, which must be cleansed away before we can approach the all-holy God. Without a deep appreciation of our sinfulness and impurity, real worship is not a possibility.

In that worship, all God's people now have a central part to play. Here is where our privilege once again far exceeds that envisaged by Ezekiel. Whereas the ordinary people in his vision were to be kept at a distance from God's presence because of their past sins and a concern to protect his holiness, now, covered in the blood of Christ, we may draw near to the Most Holy Place itself (Heb. 10:19). We need no human priests to interpose between us and the holy God, to conduct our worship on our behalf, for we have a great priest, Jesus, who has perfectly met our needs (10:21).

In the light of that incredible privilege, let us indeed count it a great blessing to draw near to God in worship and adoration. Let us hold unswervingly to the hope we profess, and let us stir one another on to love and good deeds and lives of purified holiness, until the approaching day comes when Christ our King will return and we will be exiles no more (Heb. 10:22–25).

Ezekiel 47:1-12

🌿

THE MAN BROUGHT me back to the entrance of the temple, and I saw water coming out from under the threshold of the temple toward the east (for the temple faced east). The water was coming down from under the south side of the temple, south of the altar. ²He then brought me out through the north gate and led me around the outside to the outer gate facing east, and the water was flowing from the south side.

³As the man went eastward with a measuring line in his hand, he measured off a thousand cubits and then led me through water that was ankle-deep. ⁴He measured off another thousand cubits and led me through water that was knee-deep. He measured off another thousand and led me through water that was up to the waist. ⁵He measured off another thousand, but now it was a river that I could not cross, because the water had risen and was deep enough to swim in—a river that no one could cross. ⁶He asked me, "Son of man, do you see this?"

Then he led me back to the bank of the river. ⁷When I arrived there, I saw a great number of trees on each side of the river. ⁸He said to me, "This water flows toward the eastern region and goes down into the Arabah, where it enters the Sea. When it empties into the Sea, the water there becomes fresh. ⁹Swarms of living creatures will live wherever the river flows. There will be large numbers of fish, because this water flows there and makes the salt water fresh; so where the river flows everything will live. ¹⁰Fishermen will stand along the shore; from En Gedi to En Eglaim there will be places for spreading nets. The fish will be of many kinds—like the fish of the Great Sea. ¹¹But the swamps and marshes will not

---

1. Raymond Dillard and Tremper Longman III, *An Introduction to the Old Testament* (Grand Rapids: Zondervan, 1994), 327.

2. Gwilym H. Jones, *1 & 2 Kings* (NCB; Grand Rapids: Eerdmans, 1984), 184.

3. See Day, *God's Conflict With the Dragon and the Sea.*

4. For this as a theme in Ezekiel, see the comments on chapter 1.

5. Wenham, "Sanctuary Symbolism," 402.

become fresh; they will be left for salt. ¹²Fruit trees of all kinds will grow on both banks of the river. Their leaves will not wither, nor will their fruit fail. Every month they will bear, because the water from the sanctuary flows to them. Their fruit will serve for food and their leaves for healing."

EZEKIEL'S TOUR OF the temple is now complete. His vision at this point turns outward to the rest of the land and the influence that the thorough restoration of the temple as the place of God's dwelling will have on it. That influence is nothing short of a total transformation from death to life, a transformation expressed in the visionary form of a life-giving river that flows out from the temple.

The source of the living water is the temple itself, or, more precisely, the south side of the temple, south of the altar (47:1). This was the site of the "Sea" in Solomon's temple,¹ a massive bronze pool whose practical purpose was to provide the water required for cleansing (1 Kings 7:23, 39). Its significance was more than merely practical, however. By calling it "the Sea" (*hayyām*), a rather grandiose title for an object smaller than most aboveground swimming pools today (fifteen feet in diameter), it also appears to have had a symbolic significance, representing the forces of chaos subjugated in the orderly cosmos of the temple.² In ancient Near Eastern mythology, the sea (*hayyām*) was one of the chief enemies of the gods, whose defeat was necessary before the cosmic order could be established.³ This same imagery is present in the Psalms, especially in the enthronement psalms, where the sea's chaos is subjugated by the Lord (Ps. 46:2–3; 93:3–4; 95:5; 96:11; 98:7).

In Ezekiel's vision, the static categories of the old symbolism have been transformed into dynamic motion.⁴ The "Sea" now becomes the source of a life-giving river that flows out from the temple, another idea with extensive roots in the Bible. Thus in Psalm 46, in response to the imagined chaos of the earth giving way and the mountains falling "into the heart of the sea" (!), the psalmist draws strength from the idyllic picture of the river whose streams make glad the city of God, the holy place where the Most High dwells (46:2–4). The archetype of this river is the earth-fructifying stream that

---

6. The fact that the prophet is instructed to measure the river at four different points is probably not coincidental (Zimmerli, *Ezekiel*, 2:512).

7. Ibid., 2:514.

flows out in four branches from the prototypical sanctuary of Eden (Gen. 2:10–14).[5]

The river flowing from Ezekiel's temple follows the sacred route eastward from the inner court, out through the (closed!) east gate of the outer court (Ezek. 47:2). Because Ezekiel cannot follow it through there, he is brought round by the north gate and sees it trickling out of the south side of the gate. In comparison with the abundant streams of the traditional picture, the renewed temple provides at first a minimal flow. Yet the stream that starts out so pitifully small miraculously becomes progressively larger the further he journeys along it. At first, it is a trickle; after a thousand cubits (1,500 feet), it is ankle-deep (47:3); after another thousand cubits, it is knee-deep (47:4), then waist-deep (47:4), and finally an uncrossable torrent (47:5).[6] The guiding angel asks him to pause here and ponder its significance: "Son of man, do you see this?" (47:6).

The miraculous growth of this river from small beginnings is not the only lesson to be observed, however. This river is also a transforming force wherever it flows. It brings fertility to the ground surrounding it, indicated by the presence of a great many trees on both sides of the river (47:7). After flowing eastward and then south through the Arabah, which here seems to indicate simply the region of the Jordan Valley, the river transforms the Dead Sea, healing its waters—that is, turning its salty water, which is undrinkable and hostile to life, into drinkable, life-supporting water (47:8). This Edenic river will induce Paradise-like levels of fertility, teeming with all kinds of swarming creatures (47:9), like the waters of Genesis 1:20, and a great many fish "of many kinds" (Ezek. 47:10 cf. Gen. 1:21). To sum up the pictorial message in straightforward speech: "Where the river flows everything will live" (Ezek. 47:9).

Nor is this abundant fertility merely fertility in the abstract. It is explicitly fertility as a blessing to the restored people of Israel. The abundant fish will support an equally abundant number of fishermen, from En Gedi to En Eglaim. These are two locations span the shores of the Dead Sea; thus, "from En Gedi to En Eglaim" encompasses the scope of the whole Dead Sea.[7] But even while the waters of the Dead Sea will be healed, its one existing use, as the source of valuable salt deposits, will not be eliminated (47:11).

The numerous trees of 47:7 are now more closely defined as "fruit trees" (lit., "food trees," 47:12). They will not suffer from any lack of moisture; rather, as with the depiction of the righteous person in Psalm 1, "their leaves will not wither, nor will their fruit fail." Indeed, they will be so full of life that

---

8. Clifford, *Cosmic Mountain*, 49–51.
9. Zimmerli, *Ezekiel*, 2:515.

they will bear new fruit every month to feed the population, and their leaves will be for healing (47:12). All of this will be brought about because they are fed from the source of life-giving fruitfulness, the stream that flows from the temple.

Bridging Contexts

DISTINCTIVENESS IN EZEKIEL'S **use of the river.** The image of a life-giving stream flowing from the sanctuary is ubiquitous in the Scriptures, from the opening chapters of Genesis (Gen. 2:10–14) to the closing chapter of Revelation. Revelation 22 features a river similar in many respects to that of Ezekiel 47, which flows from the throne of God and the Lamb out to nourish the (single) tree of life, whose fruit appears every month and whose leaves are "for the healing of the nations" (Rev. 22:1–2). The motif is also attested in mythological literature from the ancient Near East.[8] Yet because of the frequent use of this motif, it would be easy to overlook what is distinctive about Ezekiel's use.

(1) The most striking aspect of Ezekiel's river is that, unlike the other rivers of life, it starts out as an insignificant trickle and only ends up as a thunderous torrent after a distance.[9] This is something that no upheaval in the topography of Palestine can accomplish literally. What is more, it is precisely this growth from insignificant beginnings that the prophet is instructed to observe. In the language of his later colleague, the lesson is that he should not despise the day of small things (Zech. 4:10). Though the work of God starts out in tiny, seemingly insignificant ways, it will ultimately accomplish God's goals with unstoppable power. In a similar way the tiny mustard seed, to which Jesus likened the kingdom of God, grows to become a mighty tree (Matt. 13:31).

(2) Another aspect that Ezekiel's river gives prominence to is the theme of transformation. The other rivers of life are eternal, fertility-inducing streams. They bring life to everything they touch, but there is no reflection on any prior state of the land that they impact. In contrast, Ezekiel's river

---

10. D. Ralph Davis, "The Kingdom of God in Transition: Interpreting 2 Kings 2," *WTJ* 46 (1984): 390–91. In this covenant context, the use of salt by Elisha in "healing the waters" perhaps takes on a more transparent significance as a key ingredient in covenant renewal ceremonies.

11. Thus the distinction between "universal" versus "national" restoration, drawn by Darr, is not quite accurate ("Wall Around Paradise," 271–79). Certainly the restoration is not universal in scope, but it is more than simply ethnic-national: It encompasses all who are part of God's renewed people.

---

brings not merely life but life-from-the-dead. It not only provides fresh, living water, but "heals" the dead, salt-contaminated water of the Dead Sea.

The motif of "healing the water" brings with it echoes of Israel's earlier history. At Marah, Israel's first stop in the desert after crossing over the Reed Sea, the water was so bitter that Israel could not drink it. In spite of the people's grumbling, the Lord graciously gave Moses the answer to their need: a piece of wood that, when thrown into the water, turned it sweet. Then the Lord promised that if they walked in faithfulness to the covenant they would experience him as *yahweh rāpā*', "the LORD, who heals you" (Ex. 15:22–26). Similarly, in 2 Kings 2:19, the men of the city of Jericho appealed to Elisha because of the "bad water" of that city. This "bad water" was itself the result of the city's being under a covenant curse (see 1 Kings 16:34), yet God graciously transformed that curse into a blessing through his prophet (2 Kings 2:21–22).

In both cases, then, in spite of their past unfaithfulness, Israel experienced the Lord as their healer by turning to the prophet (Moses and Elisha respectively) and trusting in God's Word.[10] So too in Ezekiel 47, the message is that God's transforming power flows out from the temple into the lives of sinners, healing them and restoring them to their place in the covenant community. In this context, the reference to the continued existence of the salt marshes (47:11) is not merely a footnote driven by the pragmatic necessities of life; such concerns are signally lacking in this vision. Rather, it is necessary that salt should be available as an element of covenant consummation.

(3) The third distinctive to be noted about the river of Ezekiel's vision is the way in which it runs counter to the general trend in this vision to separate off the holy from the profane, to protect the glory of the divine presence from contamination by sinful humankind. The river bridges the gap, demonstrating the fact that the protection of the sphere of the holy is not an end in itself. It is intended to ensure the presence of God in the midst of his people, a presence that will have visible and tangible effects of blessing for the people. Blessing is not a category restricted to those who have access to the inner reaches of the holy space; it flows out as widely as the river of life does. This does not yet mean global transformation and renewal, for the river itself flows

---

12. In his book *Slouching Toward Gomorrah: Modern Liberalism and American Decline* (New York: Regan, 1996), Robert Bork describes the danger presented to society by the trend toward unbridled antinomianism in our era: "Our modern, virtually unqualified, enthusiasm for liberty forgets that liberty can only be 'the space between the walls,' the walls of morality and law based upon morality. It is sensible to argue about how far apart the walls should be set, but it is cultural suicide to demand all space and no walls" (p. 65).

only as far as the Dead Sea. But it means renewal for all who are part of God's covenant people, native-born Israelite and resident alien alike (cf. 47:22).[11]

The river in the New Testament. In the New Testament, apart from Revelation 22 (see above), the Gospel of John develops this vision of Ezekiel most fully. Jesus tells the Samaritan woman that the water he gives will become a spring of water welling up to eternal life (John 4:14).

More explicitly still, Jesus stands up on the last day of the Feast of Tabernacles and calls the thirsty to come and drink from him. He promises that "streams of living water will flow from within him," and John adds the interpretive note, "By this he meant the Spirit" (John 7:38–39). Against the background of Ezekiel 47, the imagery is transparent. The indwelling of the Holy Spirit in the heart of believers, which was accomplished at Pentecost, turns each believer into a miniature temple. As such, he or she becomes not simply a separated sphere of holiness, a walled garden in the midst of a wasteland. Rather, the believer as a temple is to be a source of blessing to all around him or her, by transmitting to them the life-giving message of the gospel. By its transforming power, the gospel heals the spiritually dead, making them alive in Christ and fruitful in their service for God.

THE WALLS OR THE RIVER? Christianity has always struggled against two pale imitations of itself, each of which seizes on one aspect of the truth and absolutizes it. On the one hand is legalism, which emphasizes the need for separation and distinctive living, for absolute obedience to the law. But legalism lacks the freedom and joy and fullness of life that are key marks of the Christian walk. On the other hand is antinomianism, the attitude that celebrates the freedom of being a Christian. But antinomianism tends to throw off any moral imperatives.

Legalism delights in preaching the walls of Ezekiel 40–46, but speaks only under its breath about the river of life in Ezekiel 47. Antinomianism loudly proclaims the wonderful benefits of the river of life, but does its best to conceal the walls of Ezekiel's temple by relegating them to a different time period in God's dealings with humankind.[12] Ezekiel's vision and the New Testament teachings that draw on it for inspiration hold together in creative tension walls and river, law and grace, as an eternal aspect of God's dealings with humankind.

---

13. See Timothy Keller, "Preaching Morality in an Amoral Age: How Can You Blow the Whistle When People Don't Believe There Are Rules?" *Leadership* 17 (1996): 110–15, and "Preaching Hell in a Tolerant Age: Brimstone for the Broadminded," *Leadership* 18 (1997): 42–48.

Now I have never met anyone who admits to being a legalist or an anti-nomian; it is not a title like Calvinist or Arminian, Lutheran or Reformed, which devotees claim joyfully. Yet if we search our hearts honestly, most of us would probably find in our thinking about ourselves and in our presenta-tion of the gospel a struggle over how to keep those biblical truths in balance. By nature, we are each drawn towards an unhealthy emphasis on either the walls or the river. Only Jesus has maintained the perfect balance between the two. On the one hand, he showed the rich young ruler a wall so high he could not cross it, whose gate was so narrow that he could not carry his wealth through with him (Matt. 19:16–24). On the other hand, he extended the gra-cious offer of living water without barriers to a despised Samaritan woman, whose marital history and present sexual involvement left much to be desired (John 4).

The example of Jesus shows us that keeping these truths in balance means that there is more than one way to present the gospel faithfully. Tradition-ally, most evangelistic efforts have presented sin as humanity's basic problem, forgiveness (freedom from the guilt of sin) as humanity's basic need, and the gospel as the means by which we reach the solution, peace with God. His-torically, this presentation of the gospel has worked well in communities with a strong ethical-moral sense, where people generally feel an obligation to live up to a certain standard or code of morality. It is a way of showing those who believe in the existence of walls, like the rich young ruler, that they themselves are on the outside. This is essentially Paul's approach in the let-ter to the Romans: "All have sinned and fall short of the glory of God," "the wages of sin is death," but "there is ... no condemnation for those who are in Christ Jesus" (Rom. 3:23; 6:23, 8:1).

Increasingly, however, we are living in a society that is not merely immoral but amoral, unused to thinking in the categories of right and wrong.[13] In such a postmodern society, where fewer and fewer people feel any sense of guilt over their lifestyle, it is important that we recognize there is another way of presenting the gospel. In this approach, similar to that which Jesus used with the Samaritan woman, the focus is on bondage or emptiness, not guilt, as humanity's basic problem. One's basic need then becomes liberation (free-dom from the slavery and futility of sin), and the gospel is the means whereby we enter the freedom to be what we were created to be—God-centered worshipers. This is Paul's approach to the gospel in Galatians: You were in bondage to a futile, empty lifestyle, but Christ came to set you free.

The gospel as freedom and fullness. Ezekiel 47:1–12 presents the gospel as freedom and fullness. Life in all its fullness is what all God's people will experience through the renewing presence of God in their land. A temple-centered life, which is nothing less than a God-centered life, is the way to true freedom. The river that flows from that center has the power to take a dead life as well as a dead land and fill it with true health. Abandoning that center means nothing less than abandoning the source of all life.

Ironically, many people abandon the temple-centered life because they are in search of total freedom. They want a life without any rules and restrictions, without the kind of boundaries that Ezekiel 40–46 has so laboriously set up. But all they achieve is trading one center for another, the true God for idols. Sin is not just breaking the rules, it is living a life centered around something other than God. The testimony of Ezekiel 47 is that though such a life may seem to impart a kind of freedom, it really leads to bondage and death.

True freedom, the kind that comes from centering your life on the true and living God, is contagiously life-giving. Even the Dead Sea cannot hold out against its life-giving power. Life and fruitfulness are evident everywhere it flows. So also our lives as believers are to have an infectious attractiveness as people see something unique in us. What people taste as they come in contact with our lives should be honey, not gall. New covenant believers are themselves indwelt by the power of the Holy Spirit, so they become themselves miniature temples, centers from which life-giving water will flow out to the nations (John 7:38). The thirsty world should find in the church the only drink that will slake their thirst. Regrettably, all too often we require sinners to get their act together before they are allowed anywhere near our fountains, for fear that they might contaminate them. Too many churches have hung up the spiritual equivalent of signs that say: "No shoes, no shirt, no service."

"Fishers of men." Just as the water is transformed in Jesus' interpretation from a physical to a spiritual flow, so also is the activity of those who stand beside it. In place of literal fishermen surrounding the Dead Sea, Jesus calls his disciples to be "fishers of men" (Mark 1:17). The mark of Jesus' resurrection power in John's Gospel is, not coincidentally, a miraculous catch of a huge number of fish, which closes out the careers of the disciples as ordinary fishermen and inaugurates their ministry as those through whom eternal life will be brought to the nations.

We too are called to be "fishers of men" in God's service, yet what kind of fishermen are we? What kind of fishermen wait for the fish to come to them and give up at the first refusal? On the contrary, effective fishermen take on themselves the task of pursuing the fish where they are and refusing to take no for an answer, studying diligently how best to increase their catch. One way or another, insofar as it lies in their power, they will land that fish.

Yet, lest in our enthusiasm for the gospel we become too triumphalist, Ezekiel 47 reminds us that God's work often starts out from small beginnings and progresses slowly. The mighty river of life, which at the end is too deep to cross, begins with the barest trickle. The temptation is for us to be impressed by large numbers and impressive presentation and to look down on the slow, steady work of the Spirit in building his church individual by individual. We seek reenactments of the Day of Pentecost, when three thousand believers were added to the church, and scorn the slow, steady accretion of Christians to the fold.

But the church of Jesus Christ, for all its impressive final form, when multitudes will flock in "from east and west and north and south, and will take their places at the feast in the kingdom of God" (Luke 13:29), often exists in the present as a trickle, not as a flood. God's work is often done in slow and steady ways that may never catch the headlines but nonetheless achieve his purposes. Our task, whether seeing the work of God progress like a mighty river or a dripping tap, is to seek to be faithful in centering our lives around Jesus Christ, our temple. We are called to taste the goodness of life in all its fullness in him, even in our present exile, and to point others joyfully to him as the source of our life.

Ezekiel 47:13-48:35

❧

THIS IS WHAT THE Sovereign LORD says: "These are the boundaries by which you are to divide the land for an inheritance among the twelve tribes of Israel, with two portions for Joseph. ¹⁴You are to divide it equally among them. Because I swore with uplifted hand to give it to your forefathers, this land will become your inheritance.

¹⁵"This is to be the boundary of the land:

"On the north side it will run from the Great Sea by the Hethlon road past Lebo Hamath to Zedad, ¹⁶Berothah and Sibraim (which lies on the border between Damascus and Hamath), as far as Hazer Hatticon, which is on the border of Hauran. ¹⁷The boundary will extend from the sea to Hazar Enan, along the northern border of Damascus, with the border of Hamath to the north. This will be the north boundary.

¹⁸"On the east side the boundary will run between Hauran and Damascus, along the Jordan between Gilead and the land of Israel, to the eastern sea and as far as Tamar. This will be the east boundary.

¹⁹"On the south side it will run from Tamar as far as the waters of Meribah Kadesh, then along the Wadi of Egypt to the Great Sea. This will be the south boundary.

²⁰"On the west side, the Great Sea will be the boundary to a point opposite Lebo Hamath. This will be the west boundary.

²¹"You are to distribute this land among yourselves according to the tribes of Israel. ²²You are to allot it as an inheritance for yourselves and for the aliens who have settled among you and who have children. You are to consider them as native-born Israelites; along with you they are to be allotted an inheritance among the tribes of Israel. ²³In whatever tribe the alien settles, there you are to give him his inheritance," declares the Sovereign LORD.

⁴⁸:¹"These are the tribes, listed by name: At the northern frontier, Dan will have one portion; it will follow the Hethlon road to Lebo Hamath; Hazar Enan and the northern border of Damascus next to Hamath will be part of its border from the east side to the west side.

²"Asher will have one portion; it will border the territory of Dan from east to west.

³"Naphtali will have one portion; it will border the territory of Asher from east to west.

⁴"Manasseh will have one portion; it will border the territory of Naphtali from east to west.

⁵"Ephraim will have one portion; it will border the territory of Manasseh from east to west.

⁶"Reuben will have one portion; it will border the territory of Ephraim from east to west.

⁷"Judah will have one portion; it will border the territory of Reuben from east to west.

⁸"Bordering the territory of Judah from east to west will be the portion you are to present as a special gift. It will be 25,000 cubits wide, and its length from east to west will equal one of the tribal portions; the sanctuary will be in the center of it.

⁹"The special portion you are to offer to the LORD will be 25,000 cubits long and 10,000 cubits wide. ¹⁰This will be the sacred portion for the priests. It will be 25,000 cubits long on the north side, 10,000 cubits wide on the west side, 10,000 cubits wide on the east side and 25,000 cubits long on the south side. In the center of it will be the sanctuary of the LORD. ¹¹This will be for the consecrated priests, the Zadokites, who were faithful in serving me and did not go astray as the Levites did when the Israelites went astray. ¹²It will be a special gift to them from the sacred portion of the land, a most holy portion, bordering the territory of the Levites.

¹³"Alongside the territory of the priests, the Levites will have an allotment 25,000 cubits long and 10,000 cubits wide. Its total length will be 25,000 cubits and its width 10,000 cubits. ¹⁴They must not sell or exchange any of it. This is the best of the land and must not pass into other hands, because it is holy to the LORD.

¹⁵"The remaining area, 5,000 cubits wide and 25,000 cubits long, will be for the common use of the city, for houses

and for pastureland. The city will be in the center of it [16]and will have these measurements: the north side 4,500 cubits, the south side 4,500 cubits, the east side 4,500 cubits, and the west side 4,500 cubits. [17]The pastureland for the city will be 250 cubits on the north, 250 cubits on the south, 250 cubits on the east, and 250 cubits on the west. [18]What remains of the area, bordering on the sacred portion and running the length of it, will be 10,000 cubits on the east side and 10,000 cubits on the west side. Its produce will supply food for the workers of the city. [19]The workers from the city who farm it will come from all the tribes of Israel. [20]The entire portion will be a square, 25,000 cubits on each side. As a special gift you will set aside the sacred portion, along with the property of the city.

[21]"What remains on both sides of the area formed by the sacred portion and the city property will belong to the prince. It will extend eastward from the 25,000 cubits of the sacred portion to the eastern border, and westward from the 25,000 cubits to the western border. Both these areas running the length of the tribal portions will belong to the prince, and the sacred portion with the temple sanctuary will be in the center of them. [22]So the property of the Levites and the property of the city will lie in the center of the area that belongs to the prince. The area belonging to the prince will lie between the border of Judah and the border of Benjamin.

[23]"As for the rest of the tribes: Benjamin will have one portion; it will extend from the east side to the west side.

[24]"Simeon will have one portion; it will border the territory of Benjamin from east to west.

[25]"Issachar will have one portion; it will border the territory of Simeon from east to west.

---

1. Allen, *Ezekiel 20–48*, 285.

2. Stevenson, *Vision of Transformation*, 151.

3. Numbers 34 names this location Kadesh Barnea. Ezekiel's choice of name recalls the rebellion that took place there during the desert wanderings, when the Lord provided water for his rebellious people from the rock (Num. 20:13). It is not coincidental that Ezekiel has just described the river of life flowing out of the temple to provide for Israel's needs.

4. The order in which the boundaries are listed is different in the two accounts: Ezekiel starts in the north and moves counterclockwise to the eastern, southern, and western boundaries, while Numbers starts in the south and moves counterclockwise from there. In addition,

²⁶"Zebulun will have one portion; it will border the territory of Issachar from east to west.

²⁷"Gad will have one portion; it will border the territory of Zebulun from east to west.

²⁸"The southern boundary of Gad will run south from Tamar to the waters of Meribah Kadesh, then along the Wadi of Egypt to the Great Sea.

²⁹"This is the land you are to allot as an inheritance to the tribes of Israel, and these will be their portions," declares the Sovereign LORD.

³⁰"These will be the exits of the city: Beginning on the north side, which is 4,500 cubits long, ³¹the gates of the city will be named after the tribes of Israel. The three gates on the north side will be the gate of Reuben, the gate of Judah and the gate of Levi.

³²"On the east side, which is 4,500 cubits long, will be three gates: the gate of Joseph, the gate of Benjamin and the gate of Dan.

³³"On the south side, which measures 4,500 cubits, will be three gates: the gate of Simeon, the gate of Issachar and the gate of Zebulun.

³⁴"On the west side, which is 4,500 cubits long, will be three gates: the gate of Gad, the gate of Asher and the gate of Naphtali.

³⁵"The distance all around will be 18,000 cubits.

"And the name of the city from that time on will be:

THE LORD IS THERE."

THE FINAL SECTION of Ezekiel's book records the delineation and distribution of the renewed land, continuing the trend of the vision to move out-

---

Numbers gives most detail to the southern boundary markers while Ezekiel is most precise in the north. Steven Tuell argues that the difference between them is essentially one of perspective: The account in Numbers views the land from an Egyptian perspective, while Ezekiel's description is that of the Persian or Assyrian authorities (*Law of the Temple*, 155—56).

5. Block, *Ezekiel 25—48*, 716.

6. G. Ch. Macholz, "Noch Einmal: Planungen für den Wiederaufbau nach der Katastrophe von 587," *VT* 19 (1969): 350.

7. Diether Kellermann, "גּוּר," *TDOT*, 2:444.

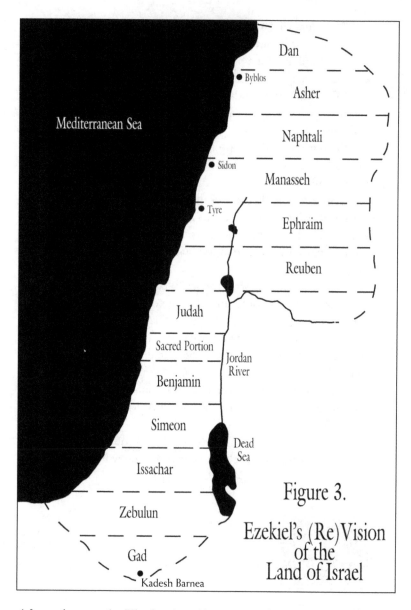

Figure 3.

Ezekiel's (Re)Vision of the Land of Israel

ward from the temple. The land itself is oriented around the temple, however, and so the final section of the book will return to themes that have been central throughout the vision of chapters 40–48. In the same way as chapters 40–42 presented theology in architectural form, this final section renders theological concepts in geographical form.[1] In both formats, the concepts of space, access, and position relative to the temple are crucial.[2]

The passage opens with the description of the boundaries of the new Promised Land (47:13–20). The area circumscribed is broadly similar to the original area allotted to Moses in Numbers 34:1–12, stretching from Lebo Hamath in the north to the Wadi of Egypt and Meribah Kadesh[3] in the south, and from the Mediterranean in the west to the Jordan River in the east.[4] This is a larger area of territory than was ever controlled by Israel, even at the height of the Davidic empire; however, of greater significance than its absolute size is the fact that it is the same land that God promised to Moses. In receiving this land, the people receive the fulfillment of the covenant promise.

Strikingly absent from the land to be divided is the territory in the Transjordan (east of the Jordan River), which *was* occupied by Israel for much of its history. This land, historically the home of Reuben, Gad, and half of the tribe of Manasseh, is no longer considered part of the Promised Land, for the simple reason that it was not part of the original promise.[5] Even in Numbers 34, it is evident that the Transjordanian region is not part of the Promised Land proper. Although the fact of its reception by the two and a half tribes as their inheritance is mentioned (34:14–15), it lies outside the boundaries defined for the land itself.

Similarly, in the book of Joshua there is a clear distinction between the inheritance of the nine and a half tribes in Canaan, which it terms "the LORD's land" (Josh. 22:19), and the territory of the Transjordanian tribes. In Ezekiel 48, in line with this long-standing distinction, the more radical move is made to allot all twelve of the tribes land within the boundaries of the Promised Land proper. For Ezekiel, there can be no inheritance outside the land.

Equally radical is the distribution of the land itself (47:21–23). It is to be distributed "according to the tribes of Israel," which represents a return to the premonarchic state of affairs. In place of the preexilic historic reality of two divided kingdoms, the reunited people receive the land as twelve tribes. Yet it is a return to the beginning that takes into account the intervening history, for the twelve tribes are now united under a single "prince" (48:21).[6]

Further, there is to be an inheritance in the land not merely for the native-born Israelite and his children but also for the resident alien (*gēr*) and his children. In earlier Old Testament legislation, the *gēr* was considered consistently in need of special protection as part of a powerless class, subject to exploitation (Lev. 19:33). Because the *gēr* did not own land, he did not have the rights of full citizenship.[7] But although socially a second-class citizen, the *gēr* was able

---

8. Stevenson, *Vision of Transformation*, 39–40.

9. Levenson, *Theology*, 116–17.

10. Ibid., 118.

to participate fully in religious affairs if he chose to do so. If he and his household were circumcised, he could partake of the Passover meal (Ex. 12:48), and he could present sacrifices to the Lord just like a native-born Israelite (Lev. 22:18). This provision recognized the fact that some resident aliens in Israel were proselytes, who had relocated for religious rather than economic reasons. The status of these proselytes is confirmed by Ezekiel through the allocation to them also of a hereditary portion in the renewed land. Given the significance of the land in Ezekiel 40—48, this is high privilege indeed.

In chapter 48, the prophet moves on to the division of the land itself among the tribes. Each of the twelve tribes is assigned an equal portion (47:14), running in a strip from east to west. This is not merely a fair way of dividing a country whose major topographic features run from north to south. It is far more fundamentally a way of orientating the entire land along the sacred east-west axis of the temple. The tribal strips themselves are left dimensionally undefined, with the borders between the tribes unmarked by geographic indicators. Only the central sacred portion has dimensions that are minutely recorded.

This contrasts dramatically with the division of the land in Joshua 14—21, whose roots are in historical rather than theological geography, where the boundaries between the different tribes are clearly defined. However, it corresponds exactly with the trend within the temple complex itself to define precisely the areas within the most holy zone, while leaving the outer areas less completely defined.[8] Holy space is important, so it must be completely defined. Profane space is less significant and may therefore have blurred edges.

---

11. As Cameron M. Mackay pointed out more than seventy years ago ("Ezekiel's Division of Palestine Among the Tribes," *PTR* 22 [1924]: 29). Most of the maps in commentaries and Bible atlases locate the sacred area further south, because they identify the "city" of the sacred reservation with Jerusalem, in spite of the fact that it is nowhere given that name in Ezekiel's vision. The result is that their diagrams depict significantly larger strips for the northern tribes than the southern tribes, although they never discuss how this can be maintained exegetically. Note, for example, the contradiction between the (correct) observation by Block that the tribal strips were all the same width (*Ezekiel 25—48*, 723) with the map given on p. 711, which shows the strips of the northern tribes as much wider than those of the southern tribes, while the sacred reservation turns out to be on the site of Jerusalem. Incidentally, this relocation of the temple away from Jerusalem provides another knotty problem for the dispensational view that Ezekiel's vision will literally be fulfilled in a future millennial kingdom.

12. So, e.g., Zimmerli, *Ezekiel*, 2:535. This assumes that the description of the sacred portion proceeds from the center out. Others have argued that the description of the sacred portion continues the pattern of the north-south progress of the tribal land division, which would place the levitical portion south of the priestly portion. So, for instance, Macholz, "Planungen," 335.

The arrangement of the tribes within the land is not a random process. The number twelve is maintained, even though the tribe of Levi has no portion of its own, by treating the two half-tribes descended from Joseph (Ephraim and Manasseh) as tribes in their own right, as in the original division of the land (Ezek. 47:13). The four tribes most distant from the sacred zone, and therefore in the position of least honor, are Dan, Asher, Naphtali, and Gad, the sons of Jacob's concubines, Zilpah and Bilhah (48:1–3, 27–28). The eight sons of Jacob's wives, Rachel and Leah, take the four strips immediately to the north and the four to the south of the sacred zone (48:4–7, 23–26).[9] Of these, Benjamin and Judah, historically located immediately to the north and south of Jerusalem, are immediately north and south of the sacred zone (48:7, 23). Their historical order has been reversed, moving Judah to the north of the sacred reservation while Benjamin is on the south. This may be due to a desire to stress the integration of the new nation. No longer are they "north" and "south," "Israel" and "Judah"; now Judah itself, the royal nation, is part of the north.[10]

It should also be noted that the site of the temple itself seems to have migrated north in Ezekiel's vision. Given that the tribal strips are equal (47:14) and that there are seven to the north of the sacred reservation and five to the south, the site of the temple ought in strict geographical terms to be located somewhere close to Shiloh, thirty miles north of its old location.[11] Although the vision (perhaps surprisingly) does not explicitly identify the location of the heart of the sacred portion within the renewed Israel, it would not be surprising to find that Ezekiel envisaged a change in place for the sanctuary. Given his radical assessment of the defilement of the temple's former home in Jerusalem, a location in the heartland of the old traditions, such as Shiloh, may well have proved attractive. Yet the shift in theological geography may also have been driven by a simple desire to locate the temple closer to the center of the land, in the midst of the people, while still (in deference to history) slightly south of center.

The sacred portion is certainly the spiritual center of the land (48:8–22; for the layout, see Fig. 2). Its importance is indicated not only by its physically central location and detailed dimensions but, in literary terms, by the amount of attention devoted to it. Whereas the other tribal portions can be taken up and dismissed in a single verse, the sacred portion receives no fewer than fifteen verses. The sacred strip is 25,000 cubits (almost eight miles)

---

13. In ch. 45, Ezekiel had already indicated that this land will provide the resources for the prince to maintain the cult.

14. Levenson notes that this represents a distinct shift from tribal arrangement when Israel camped in the desert. In that arrangement (see Num. 2), the north was the least favored direction (*Theology*, 121).

wide and extends across the breadth of the land (48:8). At its heart is a 25,000-cubit square, which is itself comprised of three east-west strips, two of 10,000 cubits breadth and one of 5,000 cubits.

The first of these 10,000-cubit strips is assigned to the Zadokite priests (48:10–11). It is (lit.) "a sacred portion within the sacred portion of the land" (48:12), a kind of Holy of Holies for the land. Within it is the sanctuary itself, which the priestly land surrounds as a buffer of holiness. The second 10,000-cubit strip, which most commentators locate to the north of the priestly portion,[12] is allocated to the Levites (48:13). It too is privileged ground, "the best of the land" (48:14), and must not be sold into other hands.

The remaining 5,000-cubit strip along the southern edge of the sacred portion is the location of "the city" (48:15–19). The city, which occupies a 4,500-cubit (1.5 mile) square, is surrounded by a 250-cubit perimeter of pasture land and flanked by two strips of land stretching east and west for food production. In this way, the "holy" square shape is maintained in the middle of an east-west oriented strip. The city functions as a visible symbol and focus of the unity of the tribes, inhabited and maintained by workers from all of the tribes (48:19).

Flanking the square sacred portion on both sides and occupying the remainder of the sacred strip is the land belonging to the prince (*nāśîʾ*, 48:21–22). This is land of an intermediate level of holiness. It is part of the sacred strip but not part of the central square. It is defined in one direction (25,000 cubits broad) but relatively undefined in the other (extending "to the eastern border" and "to the western border"). The purpose of this land is not the focus here.[13] Rather, in this context it serves to indicate the prince's status: He ranks above the ordinary lay members of the tribes of Israel, yet below the priests and Levites. The entire land is assigned to God's people on the basis of a graded hierarchy, in exactly the same way (and with the same gradations) as was the temple itself.

The closing verses of the book (48:30–35) bring us back to contemplate the city and some of the major themes of the vision of chapters 40–48. The prophet notes the exits of the city, recalling 43:11, where the prophet was instructed to bring to the attention of the people the entrances and exits of

---

15. For a similar dual image to convey complementary truths, consider the two sacrificial goats in the Day of Atonement ritual. One goat is slaughtered and its blood applied to the Most Holy Place to purify it, while the other goat has the sins of the people placed on its head and is driven off outside the camp (Lev. 16). This provides a twofold picture of atonement. On the one hand, blood is shed and presented to God, for "without the shedding of blood there is no forgiveness" (Heb. 9:22). On the other hand, a sin-laden goat is driven out of the camp into the realm of death, demonstrating the theme of Ps. 103:12: "As far as the east is from the west, so far has he removed our transgressions from us."

the temple. Like the temple, the city is a precisely measured square. With its twelve gates, named for the twelve tribes of Israel (this time including Levi and counting Ephraim and Manasseh as one tribe, Joseph), the city functions as a visible focus of the unity of the restored people.

Yet the city is not an end in itself: It faces north, toward the temple, the center of the renewed land. For that reason, the north wall and north gates are described first and assigned to the favored tribes of Reuben, Judah, and Levi, the three most significant tribes descended from Leah. The other three tribes descended from Leah (Simeon, Issachar, and Zebulun) are assigned the southern gates. The gates to the east are the tribes descended from Rachel (Joseph and Benjamin) and one from her servant Bilhah (Dan), while the least-favored west gates are assigned to Gad, Asher, and Naphtali, descendants of the concubines, Bilhah and Zilpah (48:34).[14]

Finally, the city is given a new name, reflecting the focus of the entire temple vision: "THE LORD IS THERE" (*yahweh šāmmâ*, 48:35). At first sight, this seems to conflict with the earlier assertion that God is present in his temple, which has been separated from the city by a priestly buffer zone, protecting its holiness. However, the language of God's dual presence is necessary in order to communicate both God's transcendence and his immanence.[15]

Both of these themes have been developed in Ezekiel 40–48: The high walls of the temple underline God's transcendent presence in the midst of God's people but separate from them, while the river of life speaks of God's immanent presence for blessing in the midst of his people. Similarly, God's transcendence is emphasized in the separation of the temple from the city, while at the same time his immanence is asserted by the sacred shape given to the city and its new name, "THE LORD IS THERE."

Temple and city are where Ezekiel 40–48 started out (40:2), and they are where the vision ends. Both are transformed versions of the defiled and destroyed earthly institutions. In place of the earthly temple, contaminated by the sins of the people and abandoned by the presence of God (chs. 8–11), Ezekiel has seen an undefiled temple, refilled by God's glory (chs. 40–43). In place of an adulterous city named Jerusalem, which is put to death on account of her sins, Ezekiel has seen a holy city named "THE LORD IS THERE," the habitat of the twelve renewed tribes of Israel. In place of a devastated land, Ezekiel has seen a land of peace and prosperity, watered by the river of life. In short, Ezekiel's entire temple vision is the unfolding of his earlier prophecy:

---

16. Jürgen H. Ebach, *Kritik und Utopie: Untersuchungen zum Verhältnis vom Volk und Herrscher im Verfassungsentwurf des Ezechiel (Kap. 40–48)* (Ph.D. diss.; Univ. of Hamburg, 1972), 2.

17. Macholz, "Planungen," 349.

18. Duguid, *Ezekiel and the Leaders of Israel*, 140–42.

I will make a covenant of peace with them; it will be an everlasting covenant. I will establish them and increase their numbers, and I will put my sanctuary among them forever. My dwelling place will be with them; I will be their God, and they will be my people. (37:26–27)

THEOLOGY IN THE FORM of geography. The perspective of 47:13–48:35 is a modified utopianism. It is utopian in that it is a document whose message is drawn in broad strokes, setting out a better future in direct contrast to the past and to the existing state of affairs, without addressing the means whereby such change is to be brought about.[16] Only the intervention of the Lord can bring about these changes. Yet it is not pure utopianism, since this Promised Land is not located somewhere over the rainbow, in a land where dreams come true. Redemption for Israel will take place not in an emerald city at the end of the yellow brick road, but rather in the land of Israel, which the Lord swore to give to the patriarchs.[17]

In Ezekiel's vision, the past history of Israel is not abolished or ignored, with a return to some "perfect" earlier point in history. Rather, it is reformed and brought to its intended fulfillment. Thus, even though the land is divided among the twelve tribes, there is still room for a reformed monarchy in the figure of the prince. The historical "accidents" of birth are not abolished but continue to play a role in the location of the twelve tribes. This does not mean that we should therefore anticipate a "literal" future fulfillment of this chapter, any more than of the temple of Ezekiel 40–42. This section is "theology in the form of geography," just as the earlier depiction was theology in the form of architecture.

However, it is the history of promise and fulfillment that provides the background for the future hope. The God who covenanted with Abraham, who brought the twelve tribes out of Egypt, who provided the rebels with life-giving water at Meribah Kadesh, is the same God who will graciously restore the rebels of Ezekiel's day and provide for them life-giving water. The goal of chapters 40–48 is to encourage repentance, faithfulness, and hope: repentance over the sins of the past, faithfulness in the difficult present, and hope for a brighter future through God's grace.[18]

The book of Ezekiel in the light of the book of Revelation. Given this genre, how shall we appropriate the message of Ezekiel 40–48 in our very different situation? The best answer is to look again at how the New Testament appropriates its message. The book of Revelation adopts the central thrust of Ezekiel's vision, yet transforms it in important ways in the light of the fulfillment of the old covenant in Christ. The city that John sees is no longer called "THE LORD IS THERE" but "the new Jerusalem" (Rev. 21:2). That is certainly not because the Lord is not there in the new Jerusalem, but rather because Babylon has taken over from Jerusalem the role of the anti-heavenly city in Revelation. The city still has twelve gates with the names of the twelve tribes on them (21:12), but added to that are twelve foundations for the walls inscribed with the names of the twelve apostles of the Lamb (21:14).

Most strikingly, the city has no temple, not because the temple is sited elsewhere as in Ezekiel's vision, but because the Lord God and the Lamb are its temple (Rev. 21:22). Moreover, John's new Jerusalem is substantially larger than Ezekiel's, comprising a cube with sides 1,400 miles long, rather than a square with sides about eight miles long. In other words, the new Jerusalem is not a literal fulfillment of Ezekiel's vision but a creative appropriation of its central themes for the different situation of the early church.

The fundamental theme of 47:13–48:35 is inheritance. For the landless people to whom Ezekiel's vision is communicated, the commitment is made that God's promise to Abraham and Isaac and to Moses will be fulfilled. God's people will ultimately possess the land as an inheritance for themselves and their descendants and the resident aliens, those whom God calls out from the nations to join them. They will finally enter their rest. The rest that the people of Joshua's day sought in vain in their conquest of the land will one day become a reality.

According to the New Testament it becomes a reality not through the reoccupation of the physical territory of Israel that Ezekiel has described but through a spiritual appropriation of the heavenly reality to which the land of Canaan always pointed. "Entering God's rest" is begun in this present age by faith (Heb. 3:18–19; 4:2–3), specifically faith in Christ, the One who came to bring rest to the "weary and burdened" (Matt. 11:28). Those who inherit the land in New Testament terminology are the meek (5:5), the sheep gathered from all nations (25:32–34). Those who will inherit are those who overcome in Christ, not simply those who may be physically descended from Abraham (Rev. 21:7). The land they seek to inherit does not stretch from Lebo Hamath to the Wadi of Egypt, like that of Ezekiel's vision. Rather, they seek the reality that Abraham sought and that Ezekiel tried to describe—the heavenly "city with foundations, whose architect and builder is God" (Heb. 11:10).

---

19. D. Martyn Lloyd-Jones, *Studies in the Sermon on the Mount* (Grand Rapids: Eerdmans, 1959–1960), 1:69.

20. Wilken, *The Land Called Holy*, 48.

Contemporary
Significance

THE VERTICAL DIMENSION. Does the person who dies with the most toys win? To the Israelites in exile, the temptation to think so was real. What significance could God and his ancient promise of a land of their own have to a people who felt abandoned by him and who had been exiled from his land? Why not just assimilate into the local culture and live to accumulate toys? Ezekiel's answer is to point the exiles up to God's heavenly temple and back to God's promises to Moses that Abraham's descendants would indeed inherit the land of Canaan.

Many people in the world in which we live are similarly driven by the desire to own and possess a significant slice of this world's action. In part, this is a natural response to the loss of a vertical dimension in their lives. Robbed of spiritual significance, what else is there for people to live for than material possessions? If our treasure is not stored up in heaven, where else shall we put it other than on the earth?

In the Beatitudes, Jesus points Christians in a different direction. Instead of envying and imitating the lifestyles of the rich and famous, Christians are to envy and emulate the meek, who act humbly and gently toward others based on a true estimate of their own standing before God (Matt. 5:5).[19] But why are the meek so blessed? Why should we envy their lifestyle so much and seek to imitate them? Because, according to Jesus, it is they who "will inherit the land."

Most English translations today render Jesus' words in the form that has become proverbial, "The meek will inherit the earth," but that translation obscures what it is that Jesus is promising. Jesus is here quoting from Psalm 37:11, which says, "The meek will inherit the land and enjoy great peace." "Land" gets across what he is driving at far better than "earth," because it carries overtones of God's promise to Israel, which spoke of a land that may only be possessed spiritually.[20] As the philosopher Nietzsche and the pop group "Tears for Fears" each expressed in their own way, "Everybody wants to rule the world"; but only those who are spiritual long for God's land. Just as God promised Abraham to give his descendants a spiritual land of their own, Jesus extends that same promise to the meek, those who are the citizens of his new kingdom.

But the meek will not invade the land. They will not overpower the land. They will not overrun the land because of their great might. They will *inherit* the land. It is God's gift to them, not the fruit of their own efforts. So it is with the temple-centered land of Ezekiel's vision. It is not offered to the rich and powerful, on sale for those who can afford its hefty price tag. Nor is it a program to be implemented by God's people to bring about heaven on earth, after their return from exile. The land they are to seek is a heavenly land, which they are to pursue by faith, just as did their ancestor Abraham (Heb. 11:8–10).

We then, as Christians, look upward and onward to our Promised Land, just as Ezekiel did. We look forward to a future city with foundations, a place where God will dwell in our midst and will wipe away all of our tears. We look forward to a place where suffering and sin will be no more, where all of God's children will be arrayed around the throne, inheriting the spiritual blessings that are ours in Christ.

Danger! The danger for Israel throughout the Old Testament was that they would become more attached to the earth than to the land, more interested in settling down and owning property than in seeking after God. That danger applies similarly to us, for we too can become more interested in possessing the earth, or at least a little part of it, than in inheriting the land. We long more for a rich, comfortable, easy life than for a dynamic spiritual walk with the Lord and a powerful witness to his glory and grace. As pastors, we want to build large, successful churches that will free us from the messiness of one-on-one pastoral ministry and enable us to bask in our achievements.

But that is not the way it should be for Christians! "Here we do not have an enduring city" (Heb. 13:14). This world is not our home; we are simply exiles here, resident aliens, whose hearts are elsewhere. This world's judgment on us is not what counts. What counts is God's judgment on us and the glorious inheritance that he in his mercy and grace has stored up for us.

As we wait, we are to live lives completely centered on the new covenant temple, Jesus himself (Heb. 12:22–28). Such lives revolve around the powerful worship of the awe-inspiring God, the living presence in our hearts of Jesus Christ our King, and the life-giving activity of his Spirit in our lives. So nourished, we are empowered to take the gospel out to all the nations of the earth. The inheritance that is ours in Christ is offered not simply to the twelve historic tribes of Israel, nor even to those who are resident aliens in their midst, but to all to whom the Word of God comes. As Peter put it on the day of Pentecost: "The promise is for you and for your children and for all who are far off—for all whom the Lord our God will call" (Acts 2:39).

Thus, the nations will be brought in from the north and south and east and west and will sit down to feast with one another in the heavenly city, and the Lord of hosts and the Lamb will be there in their midst. Then indeed the heavenly city, the new Jerusalem, will fittingly bear the name that Ezekiel ascribed to it, *yahweh šāmmâ,* "THE LORD IS THERE."

Scripture Index

Genesis

1–11	294, 479–80
1	337, 488, 524
1:2	59, 337
1:20–21	531
1:21	355
1:24–28	59
1:28	406, 409
2	427, 480, 488
2:1–4	261
2:7	69
2:10–14	530, 532
2:17	79, 480
3	346, 479
3:1	267–68, 295
3:5	295, 350
3:6	70
3:12–13	123
3:15	480
3:24	278
4:6–7	268
4:11–12	480
4:20–22	294
6	117
6:9	193, 240
6:13	118
7:4	288
7:11	46, 288
8:1	59
8:13	46
9:6	317
9:13–15	37, 59
10:2	453
11:2	426
12	480
12:3	38, 326, 347, 454
12:10	363
13:10	363
15:16	136, 213
16:1–4	363
17:1	505

17:7	196, 422, 480
17:8	388
18:23	194
18:25	319
19:4–9	214
19:29	196
20:7	81
24:40	505
25:22–23	407
25:25–26	153
25:29–34	407
26:5	505
27–28	404
27:23	154
27:41	407
31:38–40	400
32:28	69
33	404
49:9–10	228, 247–48, 250, 277–78

Exodus

1:13–14	394
3:8	150, 209
3:14	418
3:17	209
4:22–23	262
6:6–8	150–51, 347, 359
7:4–5	359
10:21–22	375
12:12	150, 359
12:23	134
12:29	161, 375
12:48	543
14:4, 18	109, 347, 359
15:4	228
15:7	202
15:22–27	253, 532
15:23–24	302
15:26	119
17:7	363
19:6	228, 287, 418

20:5	100, 196
22:26	236
23:21	419
24:1–11	132, 500
24:8	526
25–40	438
28	346
28:38	89
31:16–17	261
32	261, 302, 364
32:7–14	68, 113, 405
32:13	49
33:11	264
33:18–23	56, 492
34:6	49, 100, 137
34:14	100, 114
34:29–30	492
40:34–37	147, 440, 492

Leviticus

1:4	313
2:13	492
3:2	313
4:14	518
8:22–23	492
8:35	501
10:1–3	503
10:6	318
10:10–11	417
10:17	89
11:4	416
11:5	154
11:16	27
13:45–46	417
15	415
15:2–15	417
15:19–24	413
16	518, 547
16:8	314
17–26	286
17	184
17:6	291

17:11	291, 316	18:25–29	504
17:13	291, 314, 317	20:13	541
18–20	286, 289	20:14–21	407
19	286–87	20:14–15	324
19:33	542	24:17	228
20	286–57	25	302
20:4	289	28	518
20:9–21	235	28:4	520
20:10	307	33:4	359
21	318	34:2	405
21:6	417	34:1–12	541
22:2	417	34:14–15	541
22:18	543	34:18	517
25	286, 289		

Deuteronomy

25:8–13	470		
25:13	520	4:34	264, 372
25:36–37	236	6:13, 16	364
25:43, 46	394	7:18	304
26	99–101, 104,	8:3	363
	107–9, 114, 193,	8:7	426
	196, 385, 396	8:14, 19	286
26:19	288	9:25	262
26:40	193	10:16	239
26:44–45	100	11:11	426
27:28	504	11:13–14	186
		12	107

Numbers

		12:5	419
2	546	12:10	57, 437
3:32	448	12:11	99, 152, 419
5:12	193	12:16, 24	314, 317
5:13	183	12:27	317
5:27	193	13:1–5	185
6:27	419	13:9	100, 108
11:1	279	15:15	304
11:5	304, 362	16:3, 12	304
11:16–30	132	17:14–20	228
11:24–25	259	18:9	260
11:29	430	18:15, 18	56
12:6–8	30, 56	18:22	92
13–14	241	22:22	213
13:1–2	261	23:7–8	324, 408
13:26–33	302, 406	23:9–14	503
14:15–16	262, 414	24:16	235, 237
14:33	89	24:18, 22	304
14:34	90	26:5	209
16	302	28	118
16:35	279	29:22–28	414
17:6–10	435	30:15–20	239–40

32:16	131		
32:47	278		
32:48–52	471		
33:20	248		

Joshua

2:12–13	196
5:13	278
6:17	196
6:21	134
7	195
7:1	193
10:6	209
12–21	517, 544
15–19	150
22:19	542

Judges

9:7–20	223

Ruth

3:9	210

1 Samuel

1:27–28	154
2:35	507
4	228
4:22	57
7:2–14	228
8	263
8:5	154
8:20	228
9:7	175
13:14	396
16:7	184
17:46	450

2 Samuel

1:19–27	246
4:11–13	79
5:2	394
7	210
7:1	57, 437
7:12	396
7:16	226
7:25	396
8:14	407
10:4	98
12:1–10	200, 308

21:1–9	196
21:13–14	356

1 Kings

2:3	505
3:2	107
4:2	154
6	438
6:29	476
7:2	224
7:23, 39	530
7:48	477
8:10–11	56, 153, 489, 492
8:25	505
8:27	152
8:28–54	475
8:29	152
8:51	202
9:3	290
9:4	505
10:29	209
11:7–8	211
12:7, 25–36	436
12:28–33	214
13:2	108
14:15	356
16:34	532
17	241
17:17–24	426, 430
18:29, 36	520
20:28	106
20:35–43	92
21:1–16	517
22	185

2 Kings

2:19	532
2:21–22	533
4:18–37	426, 430
6:32	131
8:20	407
11:5	501
11:14–19	501
11:15–16	134
13:15–19	276
13:21	426, 430
16:3	211

16:5–7	303
16:7–8	212
16:10–16	212, 501
17	19, 214, 216
17:9–10	211
17:26	248
18:5	357
18:21	356
19:35	19
20:12–19	212, 303
20:13	19
20:14–18	20
20:19	20
21:6	211
21:13	214
22:3–14	132
23:4–7, 9	107
23:16	108
23:26	239
23:30	240
23:33	110, 247
23:34	20, 247
24:17	21
25	50
25:21	149

1 Chronicles

5:24	154
7:40	448
21:16	278
22:9	57
28:9	505

2 Chronicles

1:17	209
7:1–2	35
7:14	416
12:3	363
20	120
23:1	45
26:19	132
36:13	227

Ezra

1	153
2:62–63	173

Nehemiah

1:1	46

2:1	46
4:3	172
7:63–64	173
12:37–43	519

Job

1:8	193
2:10	317
13:15	340
22:9	371

Psalms

2	405, 455, 461
2:12	462
10:1	149
10:15	371
15	235, 290
16	29
18:4–19	430
18:9–14	58
19	496
22	29
23:1	397
24:3	290, 500
26:6	108, 519
27:5	120
28:1	335
42:4	519
46	455, 530
46:1	462
46:5	291
48	211, 290, 336, 455
48:2	210, 336, 449
49	373
49:14–15	429
51:10–11	423
68:24	519
72:1–4	286
73:3, 25–28	508
76	455
80:8–9	201, 224
88:3	373
88:4	335
93:3–4	337, 530
95:5	530
96:11	530
98:7	530
103:12	547

104:8	426	25:2	416	15:16	70
106:7–39	302	30:1–7	227	17:4	279
106:23	290	30:27	419	17:9	424
118:27	108	31:1–3	227	19:1–13	92
121:1	236	31:8	278	19:5	211
122	290	33:14	396	22:13–17	248
126:1	49	33:15	235	22:23	224
127:1–3	250	34:2–10	407	23:3	288
137:1–48	48	34:5–6	278	24:8–10	253
137:7–8	48	36–37	57	26:8	183
137:7	407	36:6	356	26:11	57
143:7	335	38:3	505	26:24	132

Proverbs

		39:5–8	171	28	131
		40:1–2	49	29:1	259
16:33	36, 242	40:3	30	29:3	132
22:6	303	40:15–24	325	29:5	149
26:9	234	42:6	361	29:11	252
28:15	248	44:6–20	109	29:14	288
		45	278	29:15–23	49

Song of Songs

		48:10	202, 288	29:21–23	253
2:7	304	49:4	75	31:8, 10	288
3:5	304	49:6	361	32:17	250
8:4	304	49:9	82	32:35	107, 211
		51:2–3	385, 415	32:37	288

Isaiah

		51:9	355	32:39	151
1:9–10	214	53:3, 7	86	37:5	371
1:21–31	288	56:7	475	38:25	148
1:25–26	202	56:10	78	39:1	371
2:2–4	448	57:19	109	39:14	132
2:2–3	471	61:1	82	49:5	288
5:1–7	200–201, 224	63	407	49:31	416
5:24	202	65:9	106	51:59–64	325
6	56				

Jeremiah

Lamentations

6:5	36, 493	1	60		
6:6–7	57, 493	2:21	201	2:18	48
6:8	81	2:36	212	3:22–23	60, 252
6:11	57	4–6	449	3:42	49
7:1–2	303	5:1–2	152	3:49	48
7:14	29, 493	6:14	91, 172	4:12	57
7:20	98	6:17	78	4:13	49
8:8	493	6:27–30	288	4:20	228, 373
9:6	524	7:4	57	5:7	235
10:33	226	7:12–15	57	5:15	48
11:1	226, 253	7:31	107, 211	5:18	172
11:2–16	253	8:10–11	37, 91, 172	5:21	49
14	348	12:12	279		
14:13	449	13:16	161	**Ezekiel**	
14:25	106	15:14	279	1–24	22, 38, 382–83
14:28	162				

1:1–3:15	60	7:14	275	14:3	259, 416
1	35, 78, 147, 346	7:20	130, 151	14:4	260
1:1	56, 470	7:23	130	14:9	173
1:2–3	19, 25, 426,	8–11	35, 47, 130,	14:11	170
	470–71		154–55, 160, 199,	14:12–15:8	200
1:4	274		479, 481, 489, 547	14:12–23	201
1:27	17, 131	8–9	146	14:12–20	37
1:28	37, 68, 78,	8	35, 152, 183, 436,	14:13	173, 199
	135, 427		472	14:16	199
2–3	433	8:1	259, 426	15	37, 209, 217, 259
2	79	8:10	303	16	36, 247, 259, 301,
2:2	427	8:12	154, 160		310
2:3	263	8:16	491	16:3	237
2:5–8	313	8:18	414	16:6, 22	249
2:5	171	9	35, 146	16:27	173
2:6	93	9:4	37, 275	16:29	223
2:7	79	9:5	414	16:41–42	170
3	238	9:6	37, 150	16:46	147, 297
3:7	151	9:8	150	16:49–51	36
3:9	313	9:9–11	150	16:54	451
3:14	426	9:9	37, 160	16:59	225
3:17–21	174–75	9:10	414	16:63	170
3:22	426	10–11	35, 130	17	37, 162, 237,
3:23–24	427	10	58, 131, 346		247, 249, 259
3:26–27	37, 313,	10:18	472, 489	17:2	30–31
	316, 384	11	202, 428	17:12	313
4–5	103	11:3	160, 202	17:15	212
4	103, 130	11:4	428	17:19–21	162
4:5	99	11:7–12	202	17:20	193
4:6	357	11:9	314	17:22–24	250, 253, 277
5	37, 107, 109, 117	11:13	427–28	18	37, 259–60, 383
5:2	304	11:15	202	18:6	286
5:3	37, 109	11:16	35, 163, 202	18:9	260
5:5	290, 448	11:17	36, 118, 163, 287	18:11	286
5:11	414	11:19	160, 190, 238	18:13	260
5:16	119	11:21	290	18:15	286
5:17	106	11:24–25	130	18:31–32	383
6	117, 405	11:25	160, 171	19	162, 237, 259, 277
6:3–7	235	12	37	19:8	374
6:8	37	12:2–3, 9	313	19:11	372
6:11	276	12:15	287, 357	20	36, 183, 239
6:12	148	12:22	428	20:1	131, 259
6:14	173, 404	12:25	313	20:3	416
7	37, 130, 275	13	289	20:4–29	237
7:4	130, 414	13:5	290	20:23	287, 357
7:5, 6, 7	275	13:7	277	20:30–42	150
7:9	134	14	199, 259, 345	20:30–32	237
7:12	275	14:1	131, 259	20:32	324

20:35–36	90, 356	33:21–22	22, 38		479–80, 482, 488,
20:37	287	33:24–29	515		517–18, 522, 524,
20:41	288	33:24	286		541, 543, 547–48
21	36–37, 285	34–48	22, 38,	40–43	131, 541, 547–48
21:8–17	36		316, 382–83	40	515
21:12	450	34–37	435, 437,	40:1	334, 426
21:21	36		448, 455, 471	40:2	231, 426, 547
21:27	247	34	38, 404, 436, 454,	40:6–8	26
21:30–32	307		522–23	40:16	26
22	36, 305, 314	34:10	170	42:13–14	503
22:5	148	34:13	288	42:16–20	515
22:7–12	36	34:22	170	43	36, 485
22:15	357	34:28–29	170	43:1–5	38, 153
22:19–22	314–15	35:1–36:15	454	43:7	170
22:25–29	24, 176	36	439, 454	43:8	480
22:25	247	36:11	38	43:10–12	472, 479,
22:26	417, 502	36:12	170		501, 546
22:30	37	36:14–15	170	43:17	519
23	36, 490	36:19	287	44:4	520
23:3	36	36:22–23	263	44:6–16	38
23:24	277	36:24	288	44:6	313
23:27	170	36:26–27	69, 426, 437	44:7	480
24	37–38, 382, 384	36:27–36	428	44:11	134
24:17, 23	503	36:30	170	44:16	477
24:26	382	36:33–38	426	44:19	481
24:27	22, 382	36:35	38	44:23–24	289, 417
25–32	37, 194, 307,	36:38	397	44:28–30	477, 514
	316, 323, 382, 454	37	47, 69, 90, 451,	45	546
25–29	323, 355		454, 470, 472,	45:8	170
25	333, 338		479, 522–24	45:17	39
25:3	90	37:1–14	38, 435	46:16–18	38, 471
25:7	173	37:11	35, 483	46:24	489
25:12–14	173, 404	37:12	79	47	39, 479
25:16	173	37:15–28	38, 405	47:13–48:35	514
26–27	344, 349, 357	37:21	288	47:16	110
26:19–20	345–46	37:22–23	170	48	39, 150, 455, 479
27	346, 348, 373	37:24–28	454, 489, 547	48:1	110
28	194, 333, 373	38–39	38, 435, 437,	48:20	515
28:3	194		470, 479, 483, 493		
28:13–14	373	38:8	288	**Daniel**	
28:19–26	333	38:11	416	2:21–23, 47	345
28:25	288	38:12	290	4:6	345
29	373–74	38:21	106	4:10–12	373
29:12–13	90, 288	38:22	288	4:18	345
30–32	323	39:7	170	5:12	345
31:3, 10, 14	249	39:27	288	7	71–72
33	37, 316, 454	39:28	170	11:34	151
33:1–9	174–75	40–48	30, 47, 264, 426,		
33:2–3	78		435, 437–39, 454,		

Hosea

1:9	68, 215
1:11	436
2:4–14	211
2:23	408
9:8	78
11:8–11	263

Joel

2:2	395
2:3	415
2:28–29	71, 430

Amos

1:1	45
1:2	57
5:4–5	259
5:18–20	118
8:1–2	118
9:11	396

Obadiah

1–15	408
7	359
11–14	324

Jonah

2:7	109
3:4	74

Micah

5:2	29
7:18–19	385

Nahum

1:3	58
2:12–13	248
3:5	213

Habakkuk

1:13	103
2:2–3	171

Zephaniah

1:11	223
1:15	395
3:3–4	24, 176, 289

Haggai

2:6	151
2:12	481

Zechariah

2	462
4:10	250, 532
13:7, 9	279
14:21	223

Malachi

1:4	408
3:2	103, 202, 279, 288

Matthew

1:23	494
2:4–5	29
3:17	525
4:1–11	363
4:8	338
5–7	401
5:5	549
5:17	401
5:39–42	138
5:48	423
6:9	419
7:14	495
7:22–23	179
7:24–27	180
9:11	231
9:12–13	388
9:36	400
10:34	279
10:38	96
11:19	156
11:28	549
13:1–23	84
13:5–6	388
13:31	532
16:26	230, 508
17:2	494
18:20	156, 191, 419
19:16–22	84, 534
19:16	115
20:1–16	506
21:1–13	494
21:5	231
21:9	401
22:32	430
23:37–24:3	153
24:1–2	156
25:21	124, 505, 507

25:32	397, 549
25:34, 41	410
27:39–40	104
27:45	297
27:46	95
28:19	409, 419
28:20	494

Mark

1:17	536
4:30–32	231
8:34–35	459
9:12–13	18
10:38	509
10:45	72, 218, 509, 525

Luke

1:32–33, 52	230
1:68–69	365
3:4	30
4:18	73, 270
6:38	328
9:54	72, 138
12:15	508
12:33	508
12:49	279
13:23–24	167
13:29	537
14:16–24	155
15:4–6	397
17:1–3	361
18:11	219, 360
19:17–19	507
22:12	348
24:25–27	31
24:44–47	31

John

1:5	481
1:11	75
1:12	419
1:14	39, 73, 153, 156, 440, 481, 494
1:29	525
2:11	494
2:19	156, 440, 481
3:3	158
3:5	422
3:16	95

Scripture Index

4:14	533	**Romans**		2:2	33
4:21–24	440	1:18–25	186	2:9	252
4:22	441	1:18	71, 421	3:11–15	506
4:23	153	1:21–23	495	3:13	279
5:39	18	1:25	377	3:15	280
7:38–39	533, 536	1:26–28	186	4:7	217
8:39	197	1:27	122	5:1–5	442
9:3	63, 203, 242	2:4–5	122, 138	6:9–11	96, 309
10:11	39, 397	3:22	506	6:11	96, 421
10:16	397, 441	3:23	123, 164, 197,	7:29–31	319
11:24	429		219, 242, 254,	9:22	74
12:27–29	75, 419, 527		293, 496, 505, 535	10:14	140
12:32	221	5:1	398	10:16	220
13:31–32	527	5:12–20	196	10:21–22	141
15	203	6:4	509	11:19	442
15:6	409	6:8	432	11:25	220, 526
15:9–17	64	6:14	496	12:3	441
15:16, 18	409	6:23	535	13:12	442
16:13	18	8:1	104, 535	14:6, 8	179
16:15	76	8:4, 11, 12	433	15:12	432
16:33	398	8:13	423	15:20–23	433
17:21	442	8:16	432	15:44–49	73, 401
17:23	179, 439	8:17–25	401, 508	15:45–54	351
19:30	190	8:17	509		
		8:28	54, 123	**2 Corinthians**	
Acts		8:30	421	2:15–16	73, 84
1:8	165	8:31–32	462	3:3	96, 165
2	71, 430	8:35–39	446	4:5	71
2:4	71	8:35	123, 401	4:7–10	204
2:23	317	8:37	54	4:7	71
2:38–39	361	9:6	409–10	5:10	124, 328
2:39	388, 422, 551	9:11, 18	408	5:17	39, 158
2:42–47	54	10:9	441	5:20	83
3:18	32	11:1	113	6:4–10	82
3:21, 24	32	11:17–24	361	6:14–7:1	482
10:10–16	96	11:17	409	6:16	156
10:15	418	11:22	113, 410	7:1	96
11:5–10	96	11:26	409	11:14	326
12:22	349	12:17–21	138	12:7	82
15:14	412			12:9	463
17	111, 142	**1 Corinthians**		13:14	102
17:2–3	33	1:10	442		
17:11	179	1:18–23	482	**Galatians**	
17:16, 22	111	1:18	351	1:8	112
17:30–31	111	1:20	350	3:28	441
20:23	82	1:23	95	5:12	112
20:28–29	397	1:24	351	5:22–26	64
26:22–23	33	1:27	157	6:15–16	360, 409, 430

Ephesians

1–3	34
1:3	102, 231, 398
1:7	102
2:1	71, 74, 166, 294, 431
2:3	83, 103, 158, 219, 294, 420, 462
2:5–6	219
2:8–10	187, 421, 433
2:11–12	418, 440, 482
2:12	486
2:13–15	398
2:13	361
2:17–18	71
2:19–22	102, 361
2:20	441
3:20–21	35
4–6	34
4:13	441
4:18	83
5:2	268
5:18	39
5:26	422
6:10–18	138

Philippians

2:7–8	181, 525
2:9	231
2:10–11	164
3:2	112
4:5, 7	398

Colossians

1:15	351
1:27–28	433
2:12–14	431
3:1–2	53

1 Thessalonians

4:13	424
5:9–10	104

2 Thessalonians

2:11–12	186

1 Timothy

1:13	410
1:15	424

2 Timothy

1:12	462
2:9	82
2:19	85
3:5	63
3:16	18, 27
4:1–5	251

Hebrews

1:1–2	54, 527
1:3	494
2:8–10	54
2:17–18	398, 508
3:18–19	549
4:2–3	549
4:15–16	398, 508
4:16	39, 486
7:25	486
8:1	486
9:9	90
9:11–15	39, 521
9:12	494
9:22	547
9:23	494, 526
9:27	121
10:1–11	90
10:10	39
10:11–12	494
10:12–14	525
10:19	39
10:26–31	319, 461
10:31	83
11:1–2	53
11:10	549–50
11:13–16	53
12:11	203, 340
12:21	103
12:22–24	270, 551
13:5–6	462
13:12–13	39
13:14	52, 551

James

1:7	188
1:17	217
2:20–24	389

1 Peter

1:10–12	32
1:11	39
1:18–19	218, 525
2:5	482
3:15–16	142
4:1–7	53
4:4	510
4:17	142
5:2–4	397
5:8	326

2 Peter

2:1	361
2:7	240
3:3–4	318
3:9–10	198, 318, 327, 460
3:11–14	365

1 John

1:7	527
1:8	423
2:4–6	197
2:18	456
3:2–6	423, 510
4:1–2	179

2 John

10–11	442

Jude

8–16	112
14–15	127

Revelation

1	72
1:10–20	61
1:13	71
2–3	338
2:1	62
2:2–5	62–3
2:5–7, 9, 13	62
3:1, 8, 15	62
3:16	188
4	60–61
5:5–6	254
5:10	418
6	109

6:10	327, 459	18	326	21:3	191
7:5–9	39	19:15	73, 255, 280	21:7	549
7:14	181	20:8	454	21:12, 14	548
7:17	401	20:10	327	21:22	39, 549
10	73	20:14–15	280	22	30, 294,
12:17	456	21–22	294		482–83, 532
14:1	138	21	454, 482–83, 506	22:7	102
16:12	452	21:1–3	409	22:15	112
17–18	339	21:1	337	22:19	102
		21:2	548		

Subject Index

Abraham, 196–97, 319, 384–85, 404, 408, 480, 550
Adam, 69, 73, 79, 103, 157, 242, 346, 427
anti-exodus, 149, 151, 162
apocalyptic, 131–32
Asherah, 131–32

baptism, 95–96, 141, 422
blame-shifting, 123
blood, 291, 314, 316–17

cherubim, 58–59, 147–48, 278
church, marks of, 64, 156–57
city, 294, 546–48, 551
civil rights movement, 93
clean and unclean, 416–18
corporate responsibility, 195–97, 239–40
covenant, 99–102, 111, 193, 196, 227, 265–66, 360, 396, 398, 404, 415, 422, 504
creation, 38, 59

Daniel, 193–95, 345
Day of the Lord, 118, 291–92, 364
divine warrior, 58, 65, 78, 88, 278
drama, 94, 163, 166

Edom, 278, 324, 404–8
Egypt, 91, 104, 132, 150, 212, 224, 229, 247, 260, 262, 301–3, 355–79
election, 68, 262–63, 266, 269, 408–10
evangelism, 73–75, 166–67
exile: Assyrian and Babylonian policy, 22; historical background, 18–23; learning to live in, 50–53; stages of, 48–49
exodus, 151, 270
Ezekiel: authorship of book, 23–26; call of, 60, 78; difficulty of reading book, 17; dumbness of, 38, 80, 384; psychological analysis of, 81

God: abandonment of Jerusalem , 35, 152, 155; faithfulness of, 104; glory of, 56, 78, 80, 153, 492–94; justice of, 104, 235, 238, 281–83, 318, 384; name of, 418–19; presence of, 152–53, 155–56, 485–86; sovereignty of, 35–36, 68, 235, 489–90, 496–97, 551; wrath of, 103–4, 137–38, 197–98, 293–94, 309, 320

harvest, 73
heaven and hell, 124, 379
hell, 269, 281–82, 309
Hezekiah, 20, 107, 171, 212, 303, 356
high places, 107, 269
holiness, 157, 438–39, 503–4
hope, 157

idolatry, 111–14, 131–34, 138–39, 142, 184, 188–90, 211, 268
interpretation: allegorical, 26–28, 60; Christ-centered, 30–33; literal, 29

Jesus: good shepherd, 400–401; new king, 231, 441–42; new temple, 156, 439–41, 481–82, 551; second Adam, 73, 351, 401
Jonah, 60, 74
Josiah, 107, 132
judgment, 37, 58–62, 78, 98–100, 103–4, 115, 117–22, 136–38, 150, 269, 278, 285–90, 319–20, 327–28

lament, 246–47, 253–54
law and grace, 295–96
life and death, 78–79, 240
Lincoln, Abraham , 61, 65
Lord's Supper, 95–96, 220
Lucifer, 348

martyrdom, 459–61
missions, 74, 320

Subject Index

monarchy, 228–29, 231
mourning, 315–16, 318
names, 153

Nebuchadnezzar, 21, 147, 149, 162, 224–27, 276–78, 313, 357–58, 371, 376
Noah, 193–95

oracles against nations, 325–26, 359–60
optimism and pessimism, 249

perseverance, 85
pictorial speech, 226, 234–35, 274, 305–8
pluralism, 110, 139–40
political miscalculation, 229–30
postmodernism, 266–67, 386–87
preaching, 26–33, 280, 389–90
preservation, 85, 462
priestly case law, 235, 240, 286
problem of evil, 95, 241–42

recognition formula, 108
remembering, 219
resurrection, 429, 431–33
rewards, 505–10, 549–51

Sabbath, 261, 518

sacraments, 95–96
sacrifices, 518–20, 524–27
sanctification, 421–23
Satan, 348
Satan's strategies, 326, 338–39, 349–51, 362–64
sea, 337
seeker services, 62, 94
Sheol, 373–74, 376, 429
shame, 423–24, 451
shepherds, 394–401
sign-acts, 88–94, 98–100, 161–62, 275
sin: communicating reality of, 293, 308–9, 387–88; ugliness of, 36, 217–18
Sodom, 147, 213–14, 240, 97, 319, 414
son of man, 71–73, 75, 86, 340
suffering, 202–4, 390–91, 460
Sunday, 53

Tammuz, 132–3
temple, 107, 120, 131–36, 152–53, 437–41, 470–528, 544–45
Tyre, 333–51, 357

vine, 199–204, 223

watchman, 78, 82, 84, 383

Author Index

Alexander, R. H. 452
Allen, L. C. 46, 58, 89–90, 93, 106–7,
    109, 147, 149–51, 162, 172, 195,
    200, 213, 223, 238, 246, 248, 262,
    274–76, 287–88, 301, 304–5, 314,
    324, 334, 344, 355, 358–59, 372,
    382, 385, 395, 406, 414, 435, 447,
    449, 474, 476, 541
Alstyne, F. van 220
Ambrose 452
Anbar, M. 288
Anderson, L. 399
Andrew, M. E. 85
Augustine 452

Belleville, L. L. 422
Bloch-Smith, E. 490
Block, D. I. 21, 25, 47, 80, 98, 100, 107,
    110, 119–20, 132–34, 147, 162,
    173, 195, 246–68, 260, 264, 276,
    313–16, 323, 345, 347, 355, 358–
    59, 376, 395, 405, 408, 414, 423,
    426, 446–47, 449, 456, 472, 503,
    518, 522, 526, 542, 545
Bloesch, D. 177
Bly, R. W 483
Boadt, L. 106, 199, 372, 374
Bock, D. L. 508
Bodi, D. 110
Bork, R. 534
Boston, T. 125, 340, 387
Braun, R. L. 57
Brenner, A. 306
Bright, J. 21, 23
Bruce, F. F. 178
Bruggemann, W. 226
Burrelli, R. 108

Calvin, J. 46, 74, 89, 115, 122, 141, 156,
    158, 189, 219
Campbell, A. V. 397
Candlish, R. S. 137

Carley, K. 430
Cassidy, A. 349
Chapell, B. 72
Clapp, R. 265
Clements, R. E. 57, 99, 306, 382, 404
Clifford, R. J. 290, 449, 532
Clowney, E. P. 31–32, 361, 481, 483
Cogan, M. 212, 227
Colson, C. C. 350
Conforti, J. 507, 509
Conn, H. M. 166
Cook, S. L. 455
Cooke, G. A. 46, 110, 149, 161–62,
    277, 334
Corrie, J. 267
Coupland, D. 386
Covey, S. 114
Cowper, W. 310
Craigie, P. C. 478

Dallimore, A. 94
Darr, K. P. 479, 533
Davis, D. R. 533
Davis, E. F. 80
Day, J. 193, 345, 355, 530
Dever, W. G. 107
DeVries, S. J. 304
Dillard, R. B. 530
Donne, J. 496
Drijvers, H. J. W. 107
Duguid, I. M. 24, 57, 121, 133, 136,
    148, 174, 183, 247, 259, 279, 286,
    363, 395–96, 428, 448, 475, 490,
    500–503, 519, 523, 548
Duke, R. K. 134, 502
Dumbrell, W. J. 71
Dürr, L. 394

Ebach, J. H. 490, 548
Edwards, J. 93
Egner, D. 452
Eichrodt, W. 69, 149, 305

Author Index

Elliot, J. 28, 86
Ellison, H. L. 172, 454
Eph'al, I. 173
Eskenazi, T. C. 48
Exum, J. C. 306

Fairbairn, P. 89, 149, 414
Feinberg, C. L. 452, 479, 521–22
Flavel, J. 340
Frame, J. 439
Freedy, K. S. 372
Friebel, K. G. 89

Gaebelein, A. C. 452
Galambush, J. 209, 211, 301–2, 307
Galli, M. 327
Garscha, J. 24
Gerstner, J. 282
Gesenius, W. 452
Geyer, J. B. 194
Gorman, F. H. Jr. 489
Gosse, B. 404
Gowan, D. E. 358
Greenberg, M. 24–25, 59, 68, 79–80,
    89–90, 118–19, 121, 130, 136, 147,
    149, 151, 161–62, 171, 173, 175,
    183–85, 194, 199, 201, 210, 213–
    15, 225, 236–37, 248–49, 260, 263,
    275, 289, 304, 313, 315, 324, 345–
    46, 357–59, 385, 396, 416, 429,
    435, 476–77, 500, 517, 522
Greenhill, W. 26, 46, 59, 75, 452
Gregory the Great 26, 60
Greidanus, S. 32
Grenz, S. 387
Guinness, O. 349
Gutiérrez, G. 270
Gwaltney, W. C. 19

Halperin, D. 81, 131, 267
Hals, R. M. 247
Haran, M. 475, 517
Harrelson, W. 261
Heider, G. C. 262
Heine, H. 122
Held, M. 247
Hengstenberg, E. W. 70, 397
Herodotus 447
Herrmann, J. 170

Heschel, A. 242
Hillers, D. R. 101
Himmelfarb, G. 293
Hoekema, A. 506
Hoffmeier, J. K. 371
Hölscher, G. 11
Horbury, W. 184
Hullinger, J. M. 521
Hunter, K. R. 400

Ironside, H. A. 452, 479

Jacobsen, T. 133
Jenson, P. P. 524
Jerome 17, 141
Johnston, P. S. 373
Jones, G. H. 530
Jones, P. R. 495
Josephus 358
Joyce, P. M. 184, 237–38

Kaiser, O. 226
Keil, C. F. 151, 453
Keller, T. J. 535
Kellermann, D. 542
King, E. G. 515
Klein, R. W. 395
Kline, M. G. 102–3
Körtner, U. 458
Kramp, J. 461
Krüger, T. 162
Kuiper, R. B. 295
Kushner, H. 164, 241

Laato, A. 237
Lampe, G. W. H. 166
Lang, B. 92–93
Lasch, C. 250
Lemke, W. E. 394
Levenson, J. D. 226, 290, 395, 426,
    471, 544, 546
Levey, S. H. 523
Levine, B. A. 492
Lewis, C. S. 115, 198, 267, 282, 379,
    433, 508
Lewis, T. J. 490
Lind, M. 292, 356, 404, 414, 435, 448,
    451
Lindsey, H. 452

Lloyd-Jones, D. M. 294, 550
Long, B. O. 132
Longman, T. III 530
Lovelace, R. F. 34, 142
Luther, M. 320

Macholz, G. Ch. 542, 545, 548
Malul, M. 210
Margalit, B. 194
Marshall, I. H. 96
Mason, C. E. Jr. 452
Mathewes-Green, F. 269
Matties, G. H. 235, 239
Maudlin, M. G. 176
McCarthy, D. J. 519
McCartney, D. G. 95, 241
McConville, J. G. 153, 239, 491
McGinn, B. 452
McGregor, J. 387
McKane, W. 222
Mackay, C. M. 517, 545
McMahon, G. 209
Mettinger, T. N. D. 520
Meyers, C. 437
Milgrom, J. 290, 414, 417, 477, 491–92, 500–501, 503
Millard, A. R. 303
Miller, C. J. 34
Miller, J. E. 46
Moberly, R. W. L. 418
Moran, W. 277
Moynihan, D. P. 293
Murray, J. 26, 421

Neiman, D. 490
Newbigin, L. 113
Newton, J. 34, 338, 510
Niditch, S. 479
Niebuhr, H. R. 137

O'Connor, F. 218
Oded, B. 22
Odell, M. S. 46, 70, 78, 82
Oden, T. C. 399
Oesterly, W. O. E. 108
Old, H. O. 34
Orelli, C. von 46
Ortiz, G. 457
Overholt, T. 148

Owen, R. 139, 484

Perkins, W. 295
Peterson, E. 72, 340, 399–400
Pfafflin, U. 51
Phillips, A. 184
Piper, J. 75, 419
Pleins, J. D. 396
Ploeg, J. P. M. vander 148
Postman, N. 94
Powlison, D. 188
Poythress, V. 307, 398
Price, J. D. 448

Rad, G. von 78, 92
Redford, D. 372
Reid, J. K. S. 441
Renz, T. 106, 426
Reventlow, H. G. 99, 277, 286
Richardson, D. 306
Ricoeur, P. 301
Robertson, O. P. 102
Roof, W. C. 176, 265
Rosenberg, A. J. 471
Roux, M. 457
Ruiz, J-P. 51
Ryken, L. 111
Ryrie, C. C. 29

Saint, S. 410
Saggs, H. W. F. 174
Sasson, J. M. 375
Schaeffer, F. 108, 495
Schmidt, M. 132
Scholl, D. G. 201
Schottroff, W. 287
Schuller, R. 423
Schult, H. 99
Schuringa, H. D. 94
Scofield, C. I. 452, 521
Sedlmeier, F. 260
Skinner, J. 69, 89, 325, 504
Smith, D. L. 183, 506
Snodgrass, K. 440
Spafford, H. 390
Speiser, E. A. 453
Sproul, R. C. 265
Spurgeon, C. H. 27, 215, 244, 295
Stacey, W. D. 92

Author Index

Stevenson, K. R. 472, 474–76, 489–90, 501, 503, 515, 517, 541, 544
Strom, M. R. 349
Stuart, D. 46, 91, 215, 323, 382, 406, 474, 522

Tada, J. E. 461
Talmon, S. 121, 163, 289
Tapia, A. 267
Taylor, J. B. 69, 89, 130, 383, 523
Tertullian 137, 141, 189
Thomas, D. 80, 478, 522
Tromp, N. 80
Tsevat, M. 261
Tuell, S. 474, 522, 542
Turner, H. 438

Ussishkin, D. 173

VanGemeren, W. 522
Vaughn, P. H. 107
Vaux, R. de 525
Vawter, B. 136, 162, 171
Volf, M. 52
Vos, G. 493

Wagner, C. P. 251
Wahl, H-M. 194
Weinfeld, M. 235, 261, 505
Welch, E. T. 188, 423
Wellhausen, J. 501

Wenham, G. J. 111, 215, 313, 346, 530
Wesley, C. 187, 411, 433
Wevers, J. 58, 148–49, 274
Whitefield, G. 190
Wilken, R. L. 452, 550
Williamson, H. G. M. 153, 270
Willimon, W. H. 141
Willmes, B. 395
Wilson, R. R. 58, 80
Winston, D. 140
Wiseman, D. J. 277
Woiwode, L. 218
Wright, C. J. H. 398

Yadin, Y. 474
Yamauchi, E. 453
Yancey, P. 460
Yarbrough, R. 178
York, A. D. 46
Young, E. J. 31
Younger, K. L. Jr. 22

Zevit, Z. 107
Zimmerli, W. 79–80, 89, 92–93, 106, 108–9, 118, 131, 148–49, 175, 210–11, 235, 240, 247, 261, 263, 276–77, 286–88, 305, 335, 372, 382, 394–95, 414, 416, 429, 435, 436, 447, 449, 451, 471, 474–76, 492, 503, 519, 531–32, 545

Bring ancient truth to modern life with the
NIV Application Commentary *series*

Covering both the Old and New Testaments, the **NIV Application Commentary** series is a staple reference for pastors seeking to bring the Bible's timeless message into a modern context. It explains not only what the Bible means but also how that meaning impacts the lives of believers today.

Genesis
This commentary demonstrates how the text charts a course of theological affirmation that results in a simple but majestic account of an ordered, purposeful cosmos with God at the helm, masterfully guiding it, and what this means to us today.

John H. Walton   ISBN: 0-310-206170

Exodus
The truth of Christ's resurrection and its resulting impact on our lives mean that to Christians, the application of Exodus is less about how to act than it is about what God has done and what it means to be his children.

Peter Enns   ISBN: 0-310-20607-3

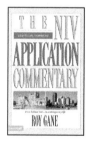

Leviticus, Numbers
Roy Gane's commentary on Leviticus and Numbers helps readers understand how the message of these two books, which are replete with what seem to be archaic laws, can have a powerful impact on Christians today.

Roy Gane   ISBN: 0-310-21088-7

Judges, Ruth
This commentary helps readers learn how the messages of Judges and Ruth can have the same powerful impact today that they did when they were first written. Judges reveals a God who employs very human deliverers but refuses to gloss over their sins and the consequences of those sins. Ruth demonstrates the far-reaching impact of a righteous character.

K. Lawson Younger Jr.   ISBN: 0-310-20636-7

1&2 Samuel

In Samuel, we meet Saul, David, Goliath, Jonathan, Bathsheba, the witch of Endor, and other unforgettable characters. And we encounter ourselves. For while the culture and conditions of Israel under its first kings are vastly different from our own, the basic issues of humans in relation to God, the Great King, have not changed. Sin, repentance, forgiveness, adversity, prayer, faith, and the promises of God — these continue to play out in our lives today.

Bill T. Arnold   ISBN: 0-310-21086-0

1&2 Chronicles

First and Second Chronicles are a narrative steeped in the best and worst of the human heart — but they are also a revelation of Yahweh at work, forwarding his purposes in the midst of fallible people, but a people who trust in the Lord and his word through the prophets. God has a plan to which he is committed.

Andrew E. Hill   ISBN: 0-310-20610-3

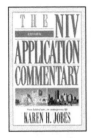

Esther

Karen H. Jobes shows what a biblical narrative that never mentions God tells Christians about him today.

Karen H. Jobes   ISBN: 0-310-20672-3

Psalms Volume 1

Gerald Wilson examines Books 1 and 2 of the Psalter. His seminal work on the shaping of the Hebrew Psalter has opened a new avenue of psalms research by shifting focus from exclusive attention to individual psalms to the arrangement of the psalms into groups.

Gerald H. Wilson   ISBN: 0-310-20635-9

Proverbs

Few people can remember when they last heard a sermon from Proverbs or looked together at its chapters. In this NIV Application Commentary on Proverbs, Paul Koptak gives numerous aids to pastors and church leaders on how to study, reflect on, and apply this book on biblical wisdom as part of the educational ministry of their churches.

Paul Koptak   ISBN: 0-310-21852-7

Ecclesiastes, Song of Songs

Ecclesiastes and Songs of Songs have always presented particular challenges to their readers, especially if those readers are seeking to understand them as part of Christian Scripture. Revealing the links between the Scriptures and our own times, Iain Provan shows how these wisdom books speak to us today with relevance and conviction.

Iain Provan   ISBN: 0-310-21372-X

Isaiah

Isaiah wrestles with the realities of people who are not convicted by the truth but actually hardened by it, and with a God who sometimes seems unintelligible, or even worse, appears to be absent. Yet Isaiah penetrates beyond these experiences to an even greater reality, seeing God's rule over history and his capacity to use the worst human actions for good. He declares that even in the darkest hours, the Holy One of Israel is infinitely trustworthy.

John N. Oswalt   ISBN: 0-310-20613-8

Jeremiah/Lamentations

These two books cannot be separated from the political conditions of ancient Judah. Beginning with the time of King Josiah, who introduced religious reform, Jeremiah reflects the close link between spiritual and political prosperity or disaster for the nation as a whole.

J. Andrew Dearman   ISBN: 0-310-20616-2

Ezekiel

Discover how, properly understood, this mysterious book with its obscure images offers profound comfort to us today.

Iain M. Duguid   ISBN: 0-310-21047-X

Daniel

Tremper Longman III reveals how the practical stories and spellbinding apocalyptic imagery of Daniel contain principles that are as relevant now as they were in the days of the Babylonian Captivity.

Tremper Longman III   ISBN: 0-310-20608-1

Hosea, Amos, Micah

Scratch beneath the surface of today's culture and you'll find we're not so different from ancient Israel. Revealing the links between Israel eight centuries B.C. and our own times, Gary V. Smith shows how the prophetic writings of Hosea, Amos, and Micah speak to us today with relevance and conviction.

Gary V. Smith   ISBN: 0-310-20614-6

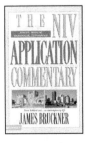

Jonah, Nahum, Habakkuk, Zephaniah

James Bruckner shows how the messages of these four Old Testament prophets, who lived during some of Israel and Judah's most turbulent times, are as powerful in today's turbulent times as when first written.

James Bruckner   ISBN: 0-310-20637-5

Joel, Obadiah, Malachi

David Baker shows how these three short prophetic books contain both a message of impending judgment (for Israel's enemies and for Israel herself) and a message of great hope — of the outpouring of God's Spirit, of restoration and renewal, and of a coming Messiah. We need to hear that same message today.

David W. Baker   ISBN: 0-310-20723-1

Haggai, Zechariah

This commentary on Haggai and Zechariah helps readers learn how the message of these two prophets who challenged and encouraged the people of God after the return from Babylon can have the same powerful impact on the community of faith today.

Mark J. Boda   ISBN: 0-310-20615-4

Matthew

Matthew helps readers learn how the message of Matthew's gospel can have the same powerful impact today that it did when the author first wrote it.

Michael J. Wilkins

ISBN: 0-310-49310-2

Mark

Learn how the challenging gospel of Mark can leave recipients with the same powerful questions and answers it did when it was written.

David E. Garland

ISBN: 0-310-49350-1

Luke

Focus on the most important application of all: "the person of Jesus and the nature of God's work through him to deliver humanity."

Darrell L. Bock

ISBN: 0-310-49330-7

John

Learn both halves of the interpretive task. Gary M. Burge shows readers how to bring the ancient message of John into a modern context. He also explains not only what the book of John meant to its original readers but also how it can speak powerfully today.

Gary M. Burge

ISBN: 0-310-49750-7

Acts

Study the first portraits of the church in action around the world with someone whose ministry mirrors many of the events in Acts. Biblical scholar and worldwide evangelist Ajith Fernando applies the story of the church's early development to the global mission of believers today.

Ajith Fernando

ISBN: 0-310-49410-9

Romans
Paul's letter to the Romans remains one of the most important expressions of Christian truth ever written. Douglas Moo comments on the text and then explores issues in Paul's culture and in ours that help us understand the ultimate meaning of each paragraph.

Douglas J. Moo   ISBN: 0-310-49400-1

1 Corinthians
Is your church struggling with the problem of divisiveness and fragmentation? See the solution Paul gave the Corinthian Christians over 2,000 years ago. It still works today!

Craig Blomberg   ISBN: 0-310-48490-1

2 Corinthians
Often recognized as the most difficult of Paul's letters to understand, 2 Corinthians can have the same powerful impact today that it did when it was first written.

Scott J. Hafemann   ISBN: 0-310-49420-6

Galatians
A pastor's message is true not because of his preaching or people-management skills, but because of Christ. Learn how to apply Paul's example of visionary church leadership to your own congregation.

Scot McKnight   ISBN: 0-310-48470-7

Ephesians
Explore what the author calls "a surprisingly comprehensive statement about God and his work, about Christ and the gospel, about life with God's Spirit, and about the right way to live."

Klyne Snodgrass   ISBN: 0-310-49340-4

Philippians

The best lesson Philippians provides is how to encourage people who actually are doing quite well. Learn why not all the New Testament letters are reactions to theological crises.

Frank Thielman

ISBN: 0-310-49300-5

Colossians/Philemon

The temptation to trust in the wrong things has always been strong. Use this commentary to learn the importance of trusting only in Jesus, God's Son, in whom all the fullness of God lives. No message is more important for our post-modern culture.

David E. Garland

ISBN: 0-310-48480-4

1&2 Thessalonians

Paul's letters to the Thessalonians say as much to us today about Christ's return and our resurrection as they did in the early church. This volume skillfully reveals Paul's answers to these questions and how they address the needs of contemporary Christians.

Michael W. Holmes

ISBN: 0-310-49380-3

1&2 Timothy, Titus

Reveals the context and meanings of Paul's letters to two leaders in the early Christian Church and explores their present-day implications to help you to accurately apply the principles they contain to contemporary issues.

Walter L. Liefeld

ISBN: 0-310-50110-5

Hebrews

The message of Hebrews can be summed up in a single phrase: "God speaks effectively to us through Jesus." Unpack the theological meaning of those seven words and learn why the gospel still demands a hearing today.

George H. Guthrie

ISBN: 0-310-49390-0

James

Give your church the best antidote for a culture of people who say they believe one thing but act in ways that either ignore or contradict their belief. More than just saying, "Practice what you preach," James gives solid reasons why faith and action must coexist.

David P. Nystrom   ISBN: 0-310-49360-9

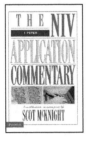

1 Peter

The issue of the church's relationship to the state hits the news media in some form nearly every day. Learn how Peter answered the question for Christians surviving under Roman rule and how it applies similarly to believers living amid the secular institutions of the modern world.

Scot McKnight   ISBN: 0-310-49290-4

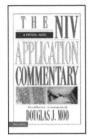

2 Peter, Jude

Introduce your modern audience to letters they may not be familiar with and show why they'll want to get to know them.

Douglas J. Moo   ISBN: 0-310-20104-7

Letters of John

Like the community in John's time, which faced disputes over erroneous "secret knowledge," today's church needs discernment in affirming new ideas supported by Scripture and weeding out harmful notions. This volume will help you show today's Christians how to use John's example.

Gary M. Burge   ISBN: 0-310-48620-3

Revelation

Craig Keener offers a "new" approach to the book of Revelation by focusing on the "old." He stresses the need for believers to prepare for the possibility of suffering for the sake of Jesus.

Craig S. Keener   ISBN: 0-310-23192-2

CPSIA information can be obtained
at www.ICGtesting.com
Printed in the USA
BVHW041347070619
550419BV00002B/2/P